History of the African Continent

Editor
Janelle Pounds

Scribbles

Year of Publication 2018

ISBN : 9789352979660

Book Published by

Scribbles

(An Imprint of Alpha Editions)

email - alphaedis@gmail.com

Produced by: PediaPress GmbH
Limburg an der Lahn
Germany
http://pediapress.com/

The content within this book was generated collaboratively by volunteers. Please be advised that nothing found here has necessarily been reviewed by people with the expertise required to provide you with complete, accurate or reliable information. Some information in this book may be misleading or simply wrong. Alpha Editions and PediaPress does not guarantee the validity of the information found here. If you need specific advice (for example, medical, legal, financial, or risk management) please seek a professional who is licensed or knowledgeable in that area.

Sources, licenses and contributors of the articles and images are listed in the section entitled "References". Parts of the books may be licensed under the GNU Free Documentation License. A copy of this license is included in the section entitled "GNU Free Documentation License"

The views and characters expressed in the book are those of the contributors and his/her imagination and do not represent the views of the Publisher.

Contents

Articles   **1**
    Introduction 1

History   **3**
    Recent African origin of modern humans 3
    History of Africa 18

Height of slave trade   **101**
    Arab slave trade 101
    Atlantic slave trade 123

Colonialism   **167**
    Colonisation of Africa 167
    Scramble for Africa 179

Geography of Africa   **215**
    Geography of Africa 215
    African Plate 230
    Climate of Africa 233
    Fauna of Africa 239

Politics   **251**
    List of political parties in Africa by country 251
    African Union 255

Economy — 289

- Economy of Africa 289
- Economy of the African Union 321

Demographics — 323

- Demographics of Africa 323

Languages — 339

- Languages of Africa 339

Culture — 357

- Culture of Africa 357

Music of Africa — 373

- Music of Africa 373

Religion — 385

- Religion in Africa 385

Territories and regions — 401

- List of regions of Africa 401

Appendix — 413

- References 413
- Article Sources and Contributors 439
- Image Sources, Licenses and Contributors 442

Article Licenses — 449

Index — 451

Introduction

Africa is the world's second largest and second most-populous continent (behind Asia in both categories). At about 30.3 million km2 (11.7 million square miles) including adjacent islands, it covers 6% of Earth's total surface area and 20% of its land area. With 1.2 billion people as of 2016, it accounts for about 16% of the world's human population. The continent is surrounded by the Mediterranean Sea to the north, the Isthmus of Suez and the Red Sea to the northeast, the Indian Ocean to the southeast and the Atlantic Ocean to the west. The continent includes Madagascar and various archipelagos. It contains 54 fully recognised sovereign states (countries), nine territories and two de facto independent states with limited or no recognition. The majority of the continent and its countries are in the Northern Hemisphere, with a substantial portion and number of countries in the Southern Hemisphere. Africa's average population is the youngest amongst all the continents; the median age in 2012 was 19.7, when the worldwide median age was 30. Algeria is Africa's largest country by area, and Nigeria is its largest by population. Africa, particularly central Eastern Africa, is widely accepted as the place of origin of humans and the Hominidae clade (great apes), as evidenced by the discovery of the earliest hominids and their ancestors as well as later ones that have been dated to around 7 million years ago, including Sahelanthropus tchadensis, Australopithecus africanus, A. afarensis, Homo erectus, H. habilis and H. ergaster—the earliest Homo sapiens (modern human), found in Ethiopia, date to circa 200,000 years ago. Africa straddles the equator and encompasses numerous climate areas; it is the only continent to stretch from the northern temperate to southern temperate zones. Africa hosts a large diversity of ethnicities, cultures and languages. In the late 19th century, European countries colonised almost all of Africa; most present states in Africa originated from a process of decolonisation in the 20th century. African nations cooperate through the establishment of the African Union, which is headquartered in Addis Ababa.

History

Recent African origin of modern humans

In paleoanthropology, the **recent African origin of modern humans**, also called the "**Out of Africa**" **theory (OOA)**, **recent single-origin hypothesis (RSOH)**, **replacement hypothesis**, or **recent African origin model (RAO)**, is the dominant model of the geographic origin and early migration of anatomically modern humans (*Homo sapiens*).

The model proposes a "single origin" of *Homo sapiens* in the taxonomic sense, precluding parallel evolution of traits considered anatomically modern in other regions, but not precluding limited admixture between *H. sapiens* and archaic humans in Europe and Asia.[1] *H. sapiens* most likely developed in the Horn of Africa between 300,000 and 200,000 years ago. The "recent African origin" model proposes that all modern non-African populations are substantially descended from populations of *H. sapiens* that left Africa after that time.

There were at least several "out-of-Africa" dispersals of modern humans, possibly beginning as early as 270,000 years ago, and certainly during 130,000 to 115,000 ago via northern Africa. These early waves appear to have mostly died out or retreated by 80,000 years ago.[2]

The most significant "recent" wave took place about 70,000 years ago, via the so-called "Southern Route", spreading rapidly along the coast of Asia and reaching Australia by around 65,000–50,000 years ago,[3] while Europe was populated by an early offshoot which settled the Near East and Europe less than 55,000 years ago.[4,5]

In the 2010s, studies in population genetics have uncovered evidence of interbreeding of *H. sapiens* with archaic humans both in Africa and in Eurasia, which means that all modern population groups, both African and non-African, while mostly derived from early *H. sapiens*, to a lesser extent are also descended from regional variants of archaic humans.

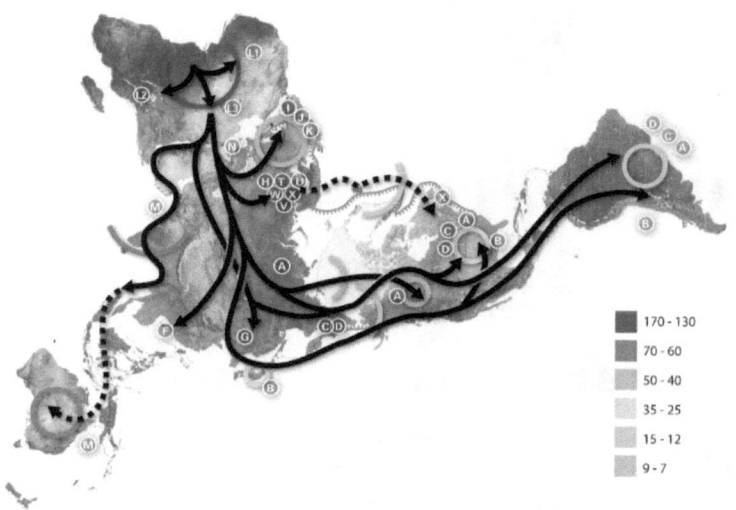

Figure 1: *Map of the migration of modern humans out of Africa, based on mitochondrial DNA. Colored rings indicate thousand years before present.*

Proposed waves

*See Early hominin expansions out of Africa for archaic humans (*H. erectus, H. heidelbergensis, Neanderthals, Denisovans*).*

"Recent African origin," or *Out of Africa II*, refers to the migration of anatomically modern humans (*Homo sapiens*) out of Africa after their emergence at c. 300,000 to 200,000 years ago, in contrast to "Out of Africa I", the migration of archaic humans from Africa to Eurasia between roughly 1.8 to 0.5 million years ago.

Since the early 21st century, the picture of "recent single-origin" migrations has become significantly more complex, not just due to the discovery of modern-archaic admixture but also due to the increasing evidence that the "recent out-of-Africa" migration took place in a number of waves spread over a long time period. As of 2010, there were two main accepted dispersal routes for the out-of-Africa migration of early anatomically modern humans: via the "Northern Route" (via Nile Valley and Sinai) and the "Southern Route" via the Bab al Mandab strait.[6]

- Posth et al. (2017) suggest that early *Homo sapiens*, or "another species in Africa closely related to us," might have first migrated out of Africa around 270,000 years ago.[7]

- Finds at Misliya cave, which include a partial jawbone with eight teeth have been dated to around 185,000 years ago. Layers dating from between 250,000 and 140,000 years ago in the same cave contained tools of the Levallois type which could put the date of the first migration even earlier if the tools can be associated with the modern human jawbone finds.
- An Eastward Dispersal from Northeast Africa to Arabia during 150–130 kya based on the finds at Jebel Faya dated to 127 kya (discovered in 2011). Possibly related to this wave are the finds from Zhirendong cave, Southern China, dated to more than 100 kya.[6] Other evidence of modern human presence in China has been dated to 80,000 years ago.
- The most significant dispersal took place around 70,000 years ago via the so-called Southern Route, either before[8] or after the Toba event, which happened between 69,000 and 77,000 years ago.[8] This dispersal followed the southern coastline of Asia, and reached Australia around 65,000-50,000 years ago. Western Asia was "re-occupied" by a different derivation from this wave around 50,000 years ago, and Europe was populated from Western Asia beginning around 43,000 years ago.[6]
- Wells (2003) describes an additional wave of migration after the southern coastal route, namely a northern migration into Europe at circa 45,000 years ago.[9]</ref> This possibility is ruled out by Macaulay et al. (2005) and Posth et al. (2016), arguing for a single coastal dispersal, with an early offshoot into Europe.

Northern Route dispersal

Beginning 135,000 years ago, tropical Africa experienced megadroughts which drove the humans from the land and towards the sea shores, and forced them to cross over to other continents.[10]</ref>

Modern humans crossed the Straits of Bab el Mandab in the southern Red Sea, and moved along the green coastlines around Arabia, and thence to the rest of Eurasia. Fossils of early *Homo sapiens* were found in Qafzeh cave in Israel and have been dated 80,000 to 100,000 years ago. These humans seem to have either become extinct or retreated back to Africa 70,000 to 80,000 years ago, possibly replaced by southbound Neanderthals escaping the colder regions of ice-age Europe.[11] Hua Liu *et al.* analyzed autosomal microsatellite markers dating to about 56,000 years ago. They interpret the paleontological fossil as an isolated early offshoot that retracted back to Africa.[12]

The discovery of stone tools in the United Arab Emirates in 2011 at the Faya-1 site in Mleiha, Sharjah, indicated the presence of modern humans at least

125,000 years ago, leading to a resurgence of the "long-neglected" North African route.

In Oman, a site was discovered by Bien Joven in 2011 containing more than 100 surface scatters of stone tools belonging to the late Nubian Complex, known previously only from archaeological excavations in the Sudan. Two optically stimulated luminescence age estimates place the Arabian Nubian Complex at approximately 106,000 years old. This provides evidence for a distinct stone age technocomplex in southern Arabia, around the earlier part of the Marine Isotope Stage 5.

According to Kuhlwilm and his co-authors, Neanderthals contributed to modern humans genetically around 100,000 years ago, from humans which split off from other modern humans around 200,000 years ago.[13] They found that "the ancestors of Neanderthals from the Altai Mountains and early modern humans met and interbred, possibly in the Near East, many thousands of years earlier than previously thought". According to co-author Ilan Gronau, "This actually complements archaeological evidence of the presence of early modern humans out of Africa around and before 100 ka by providing the first genetic evidence of such populations." Similar genetic admixture events have been noted in other regions as well.

In China, the Liujiang man (Chinese: 柳江人) is among the earliest modern humans found in East Asia. The date most commonly attributed to the remains is 67,000 years ago. High rates of variability yielded by various dating techniques carried out by different researchers place the most widely accepted range of dates with 67,000 BP as a minimum, but does not rule out dates as old as 159,000 BP. Liu, Martinón-Torres et al. (2015) claim that modern human teeth have been found in China dating to at least 80,000 years ago.

Southern Route dispersal

Coastal route

By some 70,000 years ago, a part of the bearers of mitochondrial haplogroup L3 migrated from East Africa into the Near East. It has been estimated that from a population of 2,000 to 5,000 individuals in Africa, only a small group, possibly as few as 150 to 1,000 people, crossed the Red Sea. The group that crossed the Red Sea travelled along the coastal route around Arabia and Persia to India, which appears to be the first major settling point. Wells (2003) argued for the route along the southern coastline of Asia, across about 250 kilometres (155 mi)Wikipedia:Accuracy dispute#Disputed statement, reaching Australia by around 50,000 years ago.

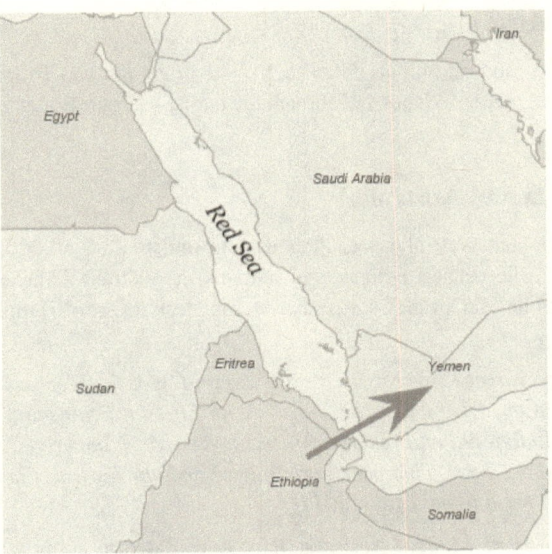

Figure 2: *Red Sea crossing*

Today at the Bab-el-Mandeb straits, the Red Sea is about 20 kilometres (12 mi) wide but 50,000 years ago sea levels were 70 m (230 ft) lower (owing to glaciation) and the water was much narrower. Though the straits were never completely closed, they were narrow enough and there may have been islands in between to have enabled crossing using simple rafts.[6] Shell middens 125,000 years old have been found in Eritrea, indicating the diet of early humans included seafood obtained by beachcombing.

The dating of the Southern Dispersal is a matter of dispute.[8] It may have happened either pre- or post-Toba, a catastrophic volcanic eruption that took place between 69,000 and 77,000 years ago at the site of present-day Lake Toba. Stone tools discovered below the layers of ash disposed in India may point to a pre-Toba dispersal but the source of the tools is disputed.[8] An indication for post-Toba is haplo-group L3, that originated before the dispersal of humans out of Africa and can be dated to 60,000–70,000 years ago, "suggesting that humanity left Africa a few thousand years after Toba".[8] New research showing slower than expected genetic mutations in human DNA was published in 2012, indicating a revised dating for the migration to between 90,000 and 130,000 years ago.

Western Asia

A fossil of a modern human dated to 54,700 years ago was found in Manot Cave in Israel, named Manot 1,[14] though the dating was questioned by Groucutt et al. (2015).

South-Asia and Australia

It is thought that Australia was inhabited around 65,000-50,000 years ago. As of 2017, the earliest evidence of humans in Australia is at least 65,000 years old, while McChesney stated that <templatestyles src="Template:Quote/styles.css"/>

> ...*genetic evidence suggests that a small band with the marker M168 migrated out of Africa along the coasts of the Arabian Peninsula and India, through Indonesia, and reached Australia very early, between 60,000 and 50,000 years ago. This very early migration into Australia is also supported by Rasmussen et al. (2011).*[4]

Fossils from Lake Mungo, Australia, have been dated to about 42,000 years ago. Other fossils from a site called Madjedbebe have been dated to at least 65,000 years ago.

East Asia

Tianyuan man from China has a probable date range between 38,000 and 42,000 years ago, while Liujiang man from the same region has a probable date range between 67,000 and 159,000 years ago. According to 2013 DNA tests, Tianyuan man is related "to many present-day Asians and Native Americans". Tianyuan is similar in morphology to Minatogawa Man, modern humans dated between 17,000 and 19,000 years ago and found on Okinawa Island, Japan.

Europe

According to Macaulay et al. (2005), an early offshoot from the southern dispersal with haplogroup N followed the Nile from East Africa, heading northwards and crossing into Asia through the Sinai. This group then branched, some moving into Europe and others heading east into Asia. This hypothesis is supported by the relatively late date of the arrival of modern humans in Europe as well as by archaeological and DNA evidence. Based on an analysis of 55 human mitochondrial genomes (mtDNAs) of hunter-gatherers, Posth et al. (2016) argue for a "rapid single dispersal of all non-Africans less than 55,000 years ago."

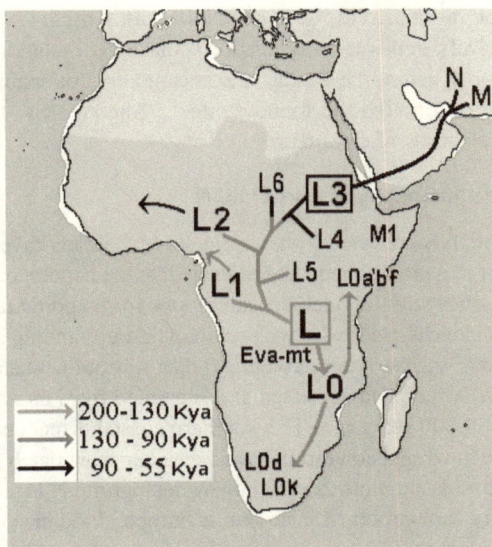

Figure 3: *Map of early diversification of modern humans according to mitochondrial population genetics (see: Haplogroup L).*

Genetic reconstruction

Mitochondrial haplogroups

Within Africa

The first lineage to branch off from Mitochondrial Eve is L0. This haplogroup is found in high proportions among the San of Southern Africa and the Sandawe of East Africa. It is also found among the Mbuti people. These groups branched off early in human history and have remained relatively genetically isolated since then. Haplogroups L1, L2 and L3 are descendants of L1-6 and are largely confined to Africa. The macro haplogroups M and N, which are the lineages of the rest of the world outside Africa, descend from L3. L3 is about 84,000 years old and haplogroup M and N are about 63,000 years old. The relationship between such gene trees and demographic history is still debated when applied to dispersals.[15]

Of all the lineages present in Africa, only the female descendants of one lineage, mtDNA haplogroup L3, are found outside Africa. If there had been several migrations, one would expect descendants of more than one lineage to be found. L3's female descendants, the M and N haplogroup lineages, are found in very low frequencies in Africa (although haplogroup M1 populations are very ancient and diversified in North and North-east Africa) and appear to be more recent arrivals. A possible explanation is that these mutations occurred in East Africa shortly before the exodus and became the dominant haplogroups after the departure through the founder effect. Alternatively, the mutations may have arisen shortly afterwards.

Southern Route and haplogroups M and N

Results from mtDNA collected from aboriginal Malaysians called Orang Asli and the creation of a phylogenetic tree indicate that the hapologroups M and N share characteristics with original African groups from approximately 85,000 years ago and share characteristics with sub-haplogroups among coastal southeast Asian regions, such as Australasia, the Indian subcontinent and throughout continental Asia, which had dispersed and separated from its African origins approximately 65,000 years ago. This southern coastal dispersion would have occurred before the dispersion through the Levant approximately 45,000 years ago. This hypothesis attempts to explain why haplogroup N is predominant in Europe and why haplogroup M is absent in Europe. Evidence of the coastal migration is thought to have been destroyed by the rise in sea levels during the Holocene epoch. Alternatively, a small European founder population that had expressed haplogroup M and N at first, could have lost haplogroup M through random genetic drift resulting from a bottleneck (i.e. a founder effect).

The group that crossed the Red Sea travelled along the coastal route around Arabia and Persia until reaching India. Haplogroup M is found in high frequencies along the southern coastal regions of Pakistan and India and it has the greatest diversity in India, indicating that it is here where the mutation may have occurred. Sixty percent of the Indian population belong to Haplogroup M. The indigenous people of the Andaman Islands also belong to the M lineage. The Andamanese are thought to be offshoots of some of the earliest inhabitants in Asia because of their long isolation from the mainland. They are evidence of the coastal route of early settlers that extends from India to Thailand and Indonesia all the way to Papua New Guinea. Since M is found in high frequencies in highlanders from New Guinea and the Andamanese and New Guineans have dark skin and Afro-textured hair, some scientists think they are all part of the same wave of migrants who departed across the Red Sea ~60,000 years ago in the Great Coastal Migration. The proportion of haplogroup M increases eastwards from Arabia to India; in eastern India, M outnumbers N by a ratio of 3:1. Crossing into Southeast Asia, haplogroup N (mostly in the form of derivatives of its R subclade) reappears as the predominant lineage.Wikipedia:Citation needed M is predominant in East Asia, but amongst Indigenous Australians, N is the more common lineage.Wikipedia:Citation needed This haphazard distribution of Haplogroup N from Europe to Australia can be explained by founder effects and population bottlenecks.

Autosomal DNA

A 2002 study of African, European and Asian populations, found greater genetic diversity among Africans than among Eurasians, and that genetic diversity among Eurasians is largely a subset of that among Africans, supporting the out of Africa model. A large study by Coop *et al*. (2009) found evidence for natural selection in autosomal DNA outside of Africa. The study distinguishes non-African sweeps (notably KITLG variants associated with skin color), West-Eurasian sweeps (SLC24A5) and East-Asian sweeps (MC1R, relevant to skin color). Based on this evidence, the study concluded that human populations encountered novel selective pressures as they expanded out of Africa.[16] MC1R and its relation to skin color had already been discussed by Liu, Harding et al. (2000), p. 135. According to this study, Papua New Guineans continued to be exposed to selection for dark skin color so that, although these groups are distinct from Africans in other places, the allele for dark skin color shared by contemporary Africans, Andamanese and New Guineans is an archaism. Endicott et al. (2003) suggest convergent evolution. A 2014 study by Gurdasani et al. indicate that higher genetic diversity in Africa was caused by relatively recent Eurasian migrations *into* Africa.

Pathogen DNA

Another promising route towards reconstructing human genetic genealogy is via the JC virus (JCV), a type of human polyomavirus which is carried by 70–90 percent of humans and which is usually transmitted vertically, from parents to offspring, suggesting codivergence with human populations. For this reason, JCV has been used as a genetic marker for human evolution and migration.[17] This method does not appear to be reliable for the migration out of Africa, in contrast to human genetics, JCV strains associated with African populations are not basal. From this Shackelton et al. (2006) conclude that either a basal African strain of JCV has become extinct or that the original infection with JCV post-dates the migration from Africa.

Admixture of archaic and modern humans

Evidence for archaic human species (descended from *Homo heidelbergensis*) having interbred with modern humans outside of Africa, was discovered in the 2010s. This concerns primarily Neanderthal admixture in all modern populations except for Sub-Saharan Africans but evidence has also been presented for Denisova hominin admixture in Australasia (i.e. in Melanesians, Aboriginal Australians and some Negritos).

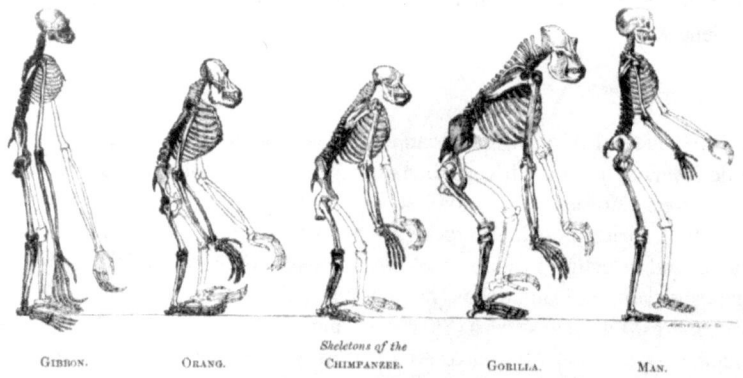

Figure 4: *The frontispiece to Huxley's Evidence as to Man's Place in Nature (1863): the image compares the skeleton of a human to other apes.*

The rate of admixture of Neanderthal admixture to European and Asian populations as of 2017 has been estimated at between about 2%–3%.[18]

Archaic admixture in some Sub-Saharan African populations hunter-gatherer groups (Biaka Pygmies and San), derived from archaic hominins that broke away from the modern human lineage around 700,000 years, was discovered in 2011. The rate of admixture was estimated at around 2%. Admixture from archaic hominins of still earlier divergence times, estimated at 1.2 to 1.3 million years ago, was found in Pygmies, Hadza and five Sandawe in 2012. Archaic admixture in West African agricultural populations (Mende and Yoruba) was found in 2017.

Stone tools

In addition to genetic analysis, Petraglia *et al.* also examines the small stone tools (microlithic materials) from Indian subcontinent and explains the expansion of population based on the reconstruction of paleoenvironment. He proposed that the stone tools could be dated to 35 ka in South Asia, and the new technology might be influenced by environmental change and population pressure.

History of the theory

Classical paleoanthropology

The cladistic relationship of humans with the African apes was suggested by Charles Darwin after studying the behaviour of African apes, one of which was displayed at the London Zoo. The anatomist Thomas Huxley had also supported the hypothesis and suggested that African apes have a close evolutionary relationship with humans. These views were opposed by the German biologist Ernst Haeckel, who was a proponent of the Out of Asia theory. Haeckel argued that humans were more closely related to the primates of South-east Asia and rejected Darwin's African hypothesis.

In the *Descent of Man*, Darwin speculated that humans had descended from apes, which still had small brains but walked upright, freeing their hands for uses which favoured intelligence; he thought such apes were African:

<templatestyles src="Template:Quote/styles.css"/>

> *In each great region of the world the living mammals are closely related to the extinct species of the same region. It is, therefore, probable that Africa was formerly inhabited by extinct apes closely allied to the gorilla and chimpanzee; and as these two species are now man's nearest allies, it is somewhat more probable that our early progenitors lived on the African continent than elsewhere. But it is useless to speculate on this subject, for an ape nearly as large as a man, namely the Dryopithecus of Lartet, which was closely allied to the anthropomorphous Hylobates, existed in Europe during the Upper Miocene period; and since so remote a period the earth has certainly undergone many great revolutions, and there has been ample time for migration on the largest scale.*
>
> —Charles Darwin, Descent of Man

In 1871 there were hardly any human fossils of ancient hominins available. Almost fifty years later, Darwin's speculation was supported when anthropologists began finding fossils of ancient small-brained hominins in several areas of Africa (list of hominina fossils). The hypothesis of *recent* (as opposed to archaic) African origin developed in the 20th century. The "Recent African origin" of modern humans means "single origin" (monogenism) and has been used in various contexts as an antonym to polygenism. The debate in anthropology had swung in favour of monogenism by the mid-20th century. Isolated proponents of polygenism held forth in the mid-20th century, such as Carleton Coon, who thought as late as 1962 that *H. sapiens* arose five times from *H. erectus* in five places.

Multiregional origin hypothesis

The historical alternative to the recent origin model is the multiregional origin of modern humans, initially proposed by Milford Wolpoff in the 1980s. This view proposes that the derivation of anatomically modern human populations from *H. erectus* at the beginning of the Pleistocene 1.8 million years BP, has taken place within a continuous world population. The hypothesis necessarily rejects the assumption of an infertility barrier between ancient Eurasian and African populations of *Homo*. The hypothesis was controversially debated during the late 1980s and the 1990s.[19] The now-current terminology of "recent-origin" and "Out of Africa" became current in the context of this debate in the 1990s.[20] Originally seen as an antithetical alternative to the recent origin model, the multiregional hypothesis in its original "strong" form is obsolete, while its various modified weaker variants have become variants of a view of "recent origin" combined with archaic admixture. Stringer (2014) distinguishes the original or "classic" Multiregional model as having existed from 1984 (its formulation) until 2003, to a "weak" post-2003 variant that has "shifted close to that of the Assimilation Model".

Genetics

In the 1980s, Allan Wilson together with Rebecca L. Cann and Mark Stoneking worked on genetic dating of the matrilineal most recent common ancestor of modern human populations (dubbed "Mitochondrial Eve"). To identify informative genetic markers for tracking human evolutionary history, Wilson concentrated on mitochondrial DNA (mtDNA), passed from mother to child. This DNA material mutates quickly, making it easy to plot changes over relatively short times. With his discovery that human mtDNA is genetically much less diverse than chimpanzee mtDNA, Wilson concluded that modern human populations had diverged recently from a single population while older human species such as Neanderthals and *Homo erectus* had become extinct. With the advent of archaeogenetics in the 1990s, the dating of mitochondrial and Y-chromosomal haplogroups became possible with some confidence. By 1999, estimates ranged around 150,000 years for the mt-MRCA and 60,000 to 70,000 years for the migration out of Africa.[21]

From 2000–2003, there was controversy about the mitochondrial DNA of "Mungo Man 3" (LM3) and its possible bearing on the multiregional hypothesis. LM3 was found to have more than the expected number of sequence differences when compared to modern human DNA (CRS). Comparison of the mitochondrial DNA with that of ancient and modern aborigines, led to the conclusion that Mungo Man fell outside the range of genetic variation seen in Aboriginal Australians and was used to support the multiregional origin hypothesis. A reanalysis on LM3 and other ancient specimens from the area published in 2016, showed it to be akin to modern Aboriginal Australian sequences, inconsistent with the results of the earlier study.

Sources

<templatestyles src="Template:Refbegin/styles.css" />

- Appenzeller, Tim (2012). "Human migrations: Eastern odyssey. Humans had spread across Asia by 50,000 years ago. Everything else about our original exodus from Africa is up for debate"[22]. *Nature*. **485** (7396).<templatestyles src="Module:Citation/CS1/styles.css"></templatestyles>
- Beyin, Amanuel (2011). "Upper Pleistocene Human Dispersals out of Africa: A Review of the Current State of the Debate". *International Journal of Evolutionary Biology*. **2011** (615094): 1–17. doi: 10.4061/2011/615094[23].<templatestyles src="Module:Citation/CS1/styles.css"></templatestyles>
- Endicott, Phillip; Gilbert, M. Thomas P.; Stringer, Chris; Lalueza-Fox, Carles; Willerslev, Eske; Hansen, Anders J.; Cooper, Alan (January 2003). "The genetic origins of the Andaman Islanders"[24]. *AJHG*. **72** (1): 178–84. doi: 10.1086/345487[25]. PMC 378623[24]. PMID 12478481[26].<templatestyles src="Module:Citation/CS1/styles.css"></templatestyles>
- Finlayson, Clive (2009). *The humans who went extinct: why Neanderthals died out and we survived*[27]. Oxford University Press US. ISBN 978-0-19-923918-4.<templatestyles src="Module:Citation/CS1/styles.css"></templatestyles>
- Groucutt, Huw S.; et al. (2015). "Rethinking the dispersal of *Homo sapiens* out of Africa". *Evolutionary Anthropology*. **24** (4 - July/August): 149–164. doi: 10.1002/evan.21455[28].<templatestyles src="Module:Citation/CS1/styles.css"></templatestyles>
- Harding, Rosalind M.; Healy, Eugene; Ray, Amanda J.; Ellis, Nichola S.; Flanagan, Niamh; Todd, Carol; Dixon, Craig; Sajantila, Antti; Jackson, Ian J.; Birch-Machin, Mark A.; Rees, Jonathan L. (April 2000). "Evidence for variable selective pressures at MC1R"[29]. *AJHG*. **66** (4): 1351–61. doi: 10.1086/302863[30]. PMC 1288200[29]. PMID 10733465[31].<templatestyles src="Module:Citation/CS1/styles.css"></templatestyles>
- Hershkovitz, Israel; Marder, Ofer; Ayalon, Avner; Bar-Matthews, Miryam; Yasur, Gal; Boaretto, Elisabetta; Caracuta, Valentina; Alex, Bridget; et al. (2015). "Levantine cranium from Manot Cave (Israel) foreshadows the first European modern humans". *Nature*. **520**: 216–9. Bibcode: 2015Natur.520..216H[32]. doi: 10.1038/nature14134[33]. PMID

25629628³⁴.<templatestyles src="Module:Citation/CS1/styles.css"></templatestyles>
- Kuhlwilm, Martin; et al. (2016). "Ancient gene flow from early modern humans into Eastern Neanderthals"³⁵. *Nature.* **530**: 429–33. Bibcode: 2016Natur.530..429K³⁶. doi: 10.1038/nature16544³⁷. PMC 4933530³⁵. PMID 26886800³⁸.<templatestyles src="Module:Citation/CS1/styles.css"></templatestyles>
- Liu, Hua; Prugnolle, Franck; Manica, Andrea; Balloux, François (August 2006). "A geographically explicit genetic model of worldwide human-settlement history"³⁹. *AJHG.* **79** (2): 230–7. doi: 10.1086/505436⁴⁰. PMC 1559480³⁹. PMID 16826514⁴¹.<templatestyles src="Module:Citation/CS1/styles.css"></templatestyles>
- Liu, Wu; Martinón-Torres, María; Cai, Yan-jun; Xing, Song; Tong, Hao-wen; Pei, Shu-wen; Sier, Mark Jan; Wu, Xiao-hong; Edwards, R. Lawrence (2015). "The earliest unequivocally modern humans in southern China"⁴². *Nature.* **526**: 696–9. Bibcode: 2015Natur.526..696L⁴³. doi: 10.1038/nature15696⁴⁴. PMID 26466566⁴⁵.<templatestyles src="Module:Citation/CS1/styles.css"></templatestyles>
- Macaulay, Vincent; Hill, Catherine; Achilli, Alessandro; Rengo, Chiara; Clarke, Douglas; Meehan, William; Blackburn, James; Semino, Ornella; Scozzari, Rosaria; Cruciani, Fulvio; Taha, Adi; Shaari, Norazila Kassim; Raja, Joseph Maripa; Ismail, Patimah; Zainuddin, Zafarina; Goodwin, William; Bulbeck, David; Bandelt, Hans-Jürgen; Oppenheimer, Stephen; Torroni, Antonio; Richards, Martin (13 May 2005). "Single, Rapid Coastal Settlement of Asia Revealed by Analysis of Complete Mitochondrial Genomes". *Science.* **308** (5724): 1034–6. Bibcode: 2005Sci...308.1034M⁴⁶. doi: 10.1126/science.1109792⁴⁷. PMID 15890885⁴⁸.<templatestyles src="Module:Citation/CS1/styles.css"></templatestyles>
- Meredith, Martin (2011). *Born in Africa: The Quest for the Origins of Human Life*⁴⁹. New York City: PublicAffairs. ISBN 1-58648-663-2.<templatestyles src="Module:Citation/CS1/styles.css"></templatestyles>
- Posth, Cosimo; Renaud, Gabriel; Mittnik, Alissa; Drucker, Dorothée G.; et al. (2016). "Pleistocene Mitochondrial Genomes Suggest a Single Major Dispersal of Non-Africans and a Late Glacial Population Turnover in Europe"⁵⁰. *Current Biology.* **26**: 827–833. doi: 10.1016/j.cub.2016.01.037⁵¹. PMID 26853362⁵².<templatestyles src="Module:Citation/CS1/styles.css"></templatestyles>
- Shackelton, Laura A.; Rambaut, Andrew; Pybus, Oliver G.; Holmes, Edward C. (2006). "JC Virus Evolution and Its Association with Human Populations"⁵³. *Journal of Virology.* **80**: 9928–33. doi: 10.1128/

JVI.00441-06[54]. PMC 1617318[53]. PMID 17005670[55].<templatestyles src="Module:Citation/CS1/styles.css"></templatestyles>
- Shen, Guanjun; Wang, Wei; Wang, Qian; Zhao, Jianxin; Collerson, Kenneth; Zhou, Chunlin; Tobias, Phillip V. (2002). "U-Series dating of Liujiang hominid site in Guangxi, Southern China". *J. Hum. Evol.* **43** (6): 817–29. doi: 10.1006/jhev.2002.0601[56]. PMID 12473485[57].<templatestyles src="Module:Citation/CS1/styles.css"></templatestyles>
- Young McChesney, Kai (2015), "Teaching Diversity. The Science You Need to Know to Explain Why Race Is Not Biological"[58], *SAGE open*, **5**: 2158244015611712, doi: 10.1177/2158244015611712[59]<templatestyles src="Module:Citation/CS1/styles.css"></templatestyles>
- Wells, Spencer (2003) [2002]. *The Journey of Man: A Genetic Odyssey*. New York: Random House Trade Paperbacks. ISBN 0-8129-7146-9.<templatestyles src="Module:Citation/CS1/styles.css"></templatestyles>

Further reading <templatestyles src="Template:Refbegin/styles.css" />

- Stringer, Chris (2011). *The Origin of Our Species*. London: Allen Lane. ISBN 978-1-84614-140-9.<templatestyles src="Module:Citation/CS1/styles.css"></templatestyles>
- Wells, Spencer (2006). *Deep ancestry: inside the Genographic Project*. Washington, D.C: National Geographic. ISBN 0-7922-6215-8.<templatestyles src="Module:Citation/CS1/styles.css"></templatestyles>
- Wade, N. (2006). *Before the Dawn : Recovering the Lost History of Our Ancestors*. Penguin Press HC, The. ISBN 1-59420-079-3.<templatestyles src="Module:Citation/CS1/styles.css"></templatestyles>
- Sykes, Bryan (2004). *The Seven Daughters of Eve: The Science That Reveals Our Genetic Ancestry*. Corgi Adult. ISBN 0-552-15218-8.<templatestyles src="Module:Citation/CS1/styles.css"></templatestyles>

External links

- Encyclopædia Britannica, *Human Evolution*[60]
- Human Timeline (Interactive)[61] – Smithsonian, National Museum of Natural History (August 2016).

History of Africa

The **history of Africa** begins with the emergence of hominids, archaic humans and – at least 200,000 years ago – anatomically modern humans (*Homo sapiens*), in East Africa, and continues unbroken into the present as a patchwork of diverse and politically developing nation states. The earliest known recorded history arose in the Kingdom of Kush, and later in Ancient Egypt, the Sahel, the Maghreb and the Horn of Africa.

Following the desertification of the Sahara, North African history became entwined with the Middle East and Southern Europe while the Bantu expansion swept from modern day Cameroon (West Africa) across much of the sub-Saharan continent in waves between around 1000 BC and 0 AD, creating a linguistic commonality across much of the central and Southern continent.

During the Middle Ages, Islam spread west from Arabia to Egypt, crossing the Maghreb and the Sahel. Some notable pre-colonial states and societies in Africa include the Ajuran Empire, D'mt, Adal Sultanate, Warsangali Sultanate, Kingdom of Nri, Nok culture, Mali Empire, Songhai Empire, Benin Empire, Oyo Empire, Ashanti Empire, Ghana Empire, Mossi Kingdoms, Mutapa Empire, Kingdom of Mapungubwe, Kingdom of Sine, Kingdom of Sennar, Kingdom of Saloum, Kingdom of Baol, Kingdom of Cayor, Kingdom of Zimbabwe, Kingdom of Kongo, Empire of Kaabu, Kingdom of Ile Ife, Ancient Carthage, Numidia, Mauretania, and the Aksumite Empire. At its peak, prior to European colonialism, it is estimated that Africa had up to 10,000 different states and autonomous groups with distinct languages and customs.[62]

From the mid-7th century, the Arab slave trade saw Muslim Arabs enslave Africans Following an armistice between the Rashidun Caliphate and the Kingdom of Makuria after the Second Battle of Dongola in 652 AD, they were transported, along with Asians and Europeans, across the Red Sea, Indian Ocean, and Sahara Desert.

From the late 15th century, Europeans joined the slave trade (some 850 years later). One could say the Portuguese was part of it all in partnership with the European. That includes the triangular trade, with the Portuguese initially acquiring slaves through trade and later by force as part of the Atlantic slave trade. They transported enslaved West, Central, and Southern Africans overseas.[63] Subsequently, European colonization of Africa developed rapidly from around 10% (1870) to over 90% (1914) in the Scramble for Africa (1881-1914). However following struggles for independence in many parts of the continent, as well as a weakened Europe after the Second World War (1939 - 1945), decolonization took place across the continent, culminating in the 1960 Year of Africa.

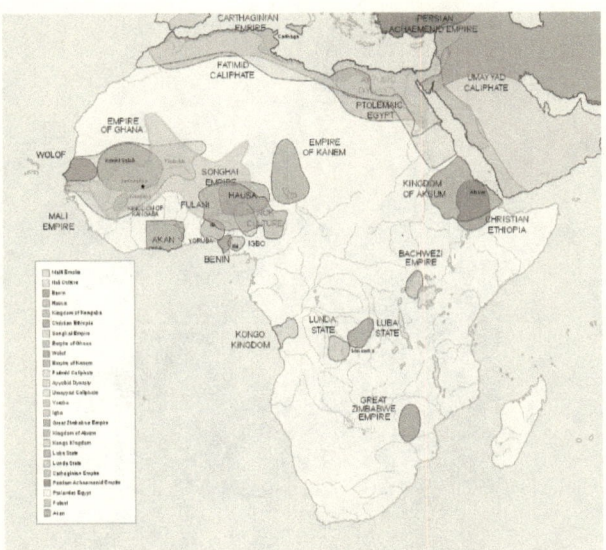

Figure 5: *Pre-colonial African states from different time periods*

Figure 6: *Obelisk at temple of Luxor, Egypt. c. 1200 BC*

Figure 7: *Baguirmi knight in full padded armour suit*

Africa's pre-colonial history has been challenging to research, mostly due to the almost extreme lack of documentation and architecture that the continents of Europe and Asia are so richly dense in. Disciplines such as the recording of oral history, historical linguistics, archaeology and genetics have been crucial.

Human history
↑ Prehistory
Recorded history
Ancient
• Earliest records • Africa • Americas • Oceania • East Asia • South Asia • Southeast Asia • Middle East • Europe
Postclassical

- Africa
- Americas
- Oceania
- East Asia
- South Asia
- Southeast Asia
- Middle East
- Europe

	Modern	
	• Early modern • Late modern	
	See also	
	• Contemporary • Modernity • Futurology	

↓ Future

- v
- t
- e[64]

Prehistory

Paleolithic

The first known hominids evolved in Africa. According to paleontology, the early hominids' skull anatomy was similar to that of the gorilla and the chimpanzee, great apes that also evolved in Africa, but the hominids had adopted a bipedal locomotion which freed their hands. This gave them a crucial advantage, enabling them to live in both forested areas and on the open savanna at a time when Africa was drying up and the savanna was encroaching on forested areas. This would have occurred 10 to 5 million years ago, but these claims are controversial because biologists and genetics have humans appearing around the last 70 thousand to 200 thousand years.[65] https://web.archive.org/web/20150907140051/http://genome.wellcome.ac.uk/doc_WTD020876.html

By 4 million years ago, several australopithecine hominid species had developed throughout Southern, Eastern and Central Africa. They were tool users, and makers of tools. They scavenged for meat and were omnivores.[66]

By approximately 3.3 million years ago, primitive stone tools were first used to scavenge kills made by other predators and to harvest carrion and marrow from their bones. In hunting, *Homo habilis* was probably not capable of competing with large predators and was still more prey than hunter. *H. habilis* probably did steal eggs from nests and may have been able to catch small game and weakened larger prey (cubs and older animals). The tools were classed as Oldowan.[67]

Figure 8: *African biface artifact (spear point) dated in Late Stone Age period*

Around 1.8 million years ago, *Homo ergaster* first appeared in the fossil record in Africa. From *Homo ergaster*, *Homo erectus* evolved 1.5 million years ago. Some of the earlier representatives of this species were still fairly small-brained and used primitive stone tools, much like *H. habilis*. The brain later grew in size, and *H. erectus* eventually developed a more complex stone tool technology called the Acheulean. Possibly the first hunters, *H. erectus* mastered the art of making fire and was the first hominid to leave Africa, colonizing most of Afro-Eurasia and perhaps later giving rise to *Homo floresiensis*. Although some recent writers have suggested that *Homo georgicus* was the first and primary hominid ever to live outside Africa, many scientists consider *H. georgicus* to be an early and primitive member of the *H. erectus* species.[68,69]

The fossil record shows *Homo sapiens* living in Southern and Eastern Africa at least 200,000 to 150,000 years ago. Around 40,000 years ago, the species' expansion out of Africa launched the colonization of the planet by modern human beings. By 10,000 BC, *Homo sapiens* had spread to most corners of Afro-Eurasia. Their disperals are traced by linguistic, cultural and genetic evidence.[70,71] The earliest physical evidence of astronomical activity appears to be a lunar calendar found on the Ishango bone dated to between 23,000 and 18,000 BC.

Scholars have argued that warfare was absent throughout much of humanity's prehistoric past, and that it emerged from more complex political systems as a result of sedentism, agricultural farming, etc. However, the findings at the site of Nataruk in Turkana County, Kenya, where the remains of 27 individuals who died as the result of an intentional attack by another group 10,000 years ago, suggest that inter-human conflict has a much longer history.

Emergence of agriculture and desertification of the Sahara

Around 16,000 BC, from the Red Sea hills to the northern Ethiopian Highlands, nuts, grasses and tubers were being collected for food. By 13,000 to 11,000 BC, people began collecting wild grains. This spread to Western Asia, which domesticated its wild grains, wheat and barley. Between 10,000 and 8000 BC, Northeast Africa was cultivating wheat and barley and raising sheep and cattle from Southwest Asia. A wet climatic phase in Africa turned the Ethiopian Highlands into a mountain forest. Omotic speakers domesticated enset around 6500–5500 BC. Around 7000 BC, the settlers of the Ethiopian highlands domesticated donkeys, and by 4000 BC domesticated donkeys had spread to Southwest Asia. Cushitic speakers, partially turning away from cattle herding, domesticated teff and finger millet between 5500 and 3500 BC.[72,73]

In the steppes and savannahs of the Sahara and Sahel in Northern West Africa, the Nilo-Saharan speakers and Mandé peoples started to collect and domesticate wild millet, African rice and sorghum between 8000 and 6000 BC. Later, gourds, watermelons, castor beans, and cotton were also collected and domesticated. The people started capturing wild cattle and holding them in circular thorn hedges, resulting in domestication.[74] They also started making pottery and built stone settlements (see Tichitt and Oualata). Fishing, using bone-tipped harpoons, became a major activity in the numerous streams and lakes formed from the increased rains.Wikipedia:Citation needed Mande peoples have been credited with the independent development of agriculture about 3000–4000 BC.[75]

In West Africa, the wet phase ushered in an expanding rainforest and wooded savanna from Senegal to Cameroon. Between 9000 and 5000 BC, Niger–Congo speakers domesticated the oil palm and raffia palm. Two seed plants, black-eyed peas and voandzeia (African groundnuts), were domesticated, followed by okra and kola nuts. Since most of the plants grew in the forest, the Niger–Congo speakers invented polished stone axes for clearing forest.[76]

Most of Southern Africa was occupied by pygmy peoples and Khoisan who engaged in hunting and gathering. Some of the oldest rock art was produced by them.[77]

For several hundred thousand years the Sahara has alternated between desert and savanna grassland in a 41,000 year cycle caused by changes ("precession") in the Earth's axis as it rotates around the sun which change the location of the North African Monsoon.[78] When the North African monsoon is at its strongest annual precipitation and subsequent vegetation in the Sahara region increase, resulting in conditions commonly referred to as the "green Sahara". For a relatively weak North African monsoon, the opposite is true, with decreased annual precipitation and less vegetation resulting in a phase of the Sahara climate cycle known as the "desert Sahara". The Sahara has been a desert for several thousand years, and is expected to become green again in about 15,000 years time (17,000 AD).

Just prior to Saharan desertification, the communities that developed south of Egypt, in what is now Sudan, were full participants in the Neolithic revolution and lived a settled to semi-nomadic lifestyle, with domesticated plants and animals.[79] It has been suggested that megaliths found at Nabta Playa are examples of the world's first known archaeoastronomical devices, predating Stonehenge by some 1,000 years.[80] The sociocultural complexity observed at Nabta Playa and expressed by different levels of authority within the society there has been suggested as forming the basis for the structure of both the Neolithic society at Nabta and the Old Kingdom of Egypt.[81] By 5000 BC, Africa entered a dry phase, and the climate of the Sahara region gradually became drier. The population trekked out of the Sahara region in all directions, including towards the Nile Valley below the Second Cataract, where they made permanent or semipermanent settlements. A major climatic recession occurred, lessening the heavy and persistent rains in Central and Eastern Africa. Since then, dry conditions have prevailed in Eastern Africa.Wikipedia:Citation needed

Central Africa

Archaeological finds in Central Africa have been discovered dating back to over 100,000 years. Extensive walled sites and settlements have recently been found in Zilum, Chad approximately 60 km (37 mi) southwest of Lake Chad dating to the first millennium BC.[82]

Trade and improved agricultural techniques supported more sophisticated societies, leading to the early civilizations of Sao, Kanem, Bornu, Shilluk, Baguirmi, and Wadai.[83]

Around 1,000 BC, Bantu migrants had reached the Great Lakes Region in Central Africa. Halfway through the first millennium BC, the Bantu had also settled as far south as what is now Angola.

Figure 9: *9th-century bronze staff head in form of a coiled snake, Igbo-Ukwu, Nigeria*

Metallurgy

The first metals to be smelted in Africa were lead, copper, and bronze in the fourth millennium BC.[84]

Copper was smelted in Egypt during the predynastic period, and bronze came into use after 3,000 BC at the latest[85] in Egypt and Nubia. Nubia was a major source of copper as well as gold.[86] The use of gold and silver in Egypt dates back to the predynastic period.[87,88]

In the Aïr Mountains, present-day Niger, copper was smelted independently of developments in the Nile valley between 3,000 and 2,500 BC. The process used was unique to the region, indicating that it was not brought from outside the region; it became more mature by about 1,500 BC.

By the 1st millennium BC, iron working had been introduced in Northwestern Africa, Egypt, and Nubia.[89] According to Zangato an Holl, there is evidence of iron-smelting in the Central African Republic and Cameroon that may date back to 3,000 to 2,500 BC.[90] In 670 BC, Nubians were pushed out of Egypt by Assyrians using iron weapons, after which the use of iron in the Nile valley became widespread.

The theory of iron spreading to Sub-Saharan Africa via the Nubian city of Meroe is no longer widely accepted. Metalworking in West Africa has been dated as early as 2,500 BC at Egaro west of the Termit in Niger, and iron working was practiced there by 1,500 BC.[91] In Central Africa, there is evidence that iron working may have been practiced as early as the 3rd millennium BC. Iron smelting was developed in the area between Lake Chad and the African Great Lakes between 1,000 and 600 BC, long before it reached Egypt. Before 500 BC, the Nok culture in the Jos Plateau was already smelting iron.[92,93]

Antiquity

The ancient history of North Africa is inextricably linked to that of the Ancient Near East. This is particularly true of Ancient Egypt and Nubia. In the Horn of Africa the Kingdom of Aksum ruled modern-day Eritrea, northern Ethiopia and the coastal area of the western part of the Arabian Peninsula. The Ancient Egyptians established ties with the Land of Punt in 2,350 BC. Punt was a trade partner of Ancient Egypt and it is believed that it was located in modern-day Somalia, Djibouti or Eritrea.[94] Phoenician cities such as Carthage were part of the Mediterranean Iron Age and classical antiquity. Sub-Saharan Africa developed more or less independently in those times. Wikipedia:Citation needed

Ancient Egypt

After the desertification of the Sahara, settlement became concentrated in the Nile Valley, where numerous sacral chiefdoms appeared. The regions with the largest population pressure were in the Nile Delta region of Lower Egypt, in Upper Egypt, and also along the second and third cataracts of the Dongola reach of the Nile in Nubia. This population pressure and growth was brought about by the cultivation of southwest Asian crops, including wheat and barley, and the raising of sheep, goats, and cattle. Population growth led to competition for farm land and the need to regulate farming. Regulation was established by the formation of bureaucracies among sacral chiefdoms. The first and most powerful of the chiefdoms was Ta-Seti, founded around 3,500 BC. The idea of sacral chiefdom spread throughout Upper and Lower Egypt.[95]

Later consolidation of the chiefdoms into broader political entities began to occur in Upper and Lower Egypt, culminating into the unification of Egypt into one political entity by Narmer (Menes) in 3,100 BC. Instead of being viewed as a sacral chief, he became a divine king. The henotheism, or worship of a single god within a polytheistic system, practiced in the sacral chiefdoms along Upper and Lower Egypt, became the polytheistic Ancient Egyptian religion. Bureaucracies became more centralized under the pharaohs, run by viziers, governors, tax collectors, generals, artists, and technicians. They engaged in

Figure 10: *Map of Ancient Egypt and nomes*

Figure 11: *The pyramids of Giza, symbols of the civilization of ancient Egypt*

tax collecting, organizing of labor for major public works, and building irrigation systems, pyramids, temples, and canals. During the Fourth Dynasty (2,620–2,480 BC), long distance trade was developed, with the Levant for timber, with Nubia for gold and skins, with Punt for frankincense, and also with the western Libyan territories. For most of the Old Kingdom, Egypt developed her fundamental systems, institutions and culture, always through the central bureaucracy and by the divinity of the Pharaoh.[96]

After the fourth millennium BC, Egypt started to extend direct military and political control over her southern and western neighbors. By 2,200 BC, the Old Kingdom's stability was undermined by rivalry among the governors of the nomes who challenged the power of pharaohs and by invasions of Asiatics into the Nile Delta. The First Intermediate Period had begun, a time of political division and uncertainty.[97]

Middle Kingdom of Egypt arose when Mentuhotep II of Eleventh Dynasty unified Egypt once again between 2041 and 2016 BC beginning with his conquering of Tenth Dynasty in 2041 BC.[98,99,100] Pyramid building resumed, long-distance trade re-emerged, and the center of power moved from Memphis to Thebes. Connections with the southern regions of Kush, Wawat and Irthet at the second cataract were made stronger. Then came the Second Intermediate Period, with the invasion of the Hyksos on horse-drawn chariots and utilizing bronze weapons, a technology heretofore unseen in Egypt. Horse-drawn chariots soon spread to the west in the inhabitable Sahara and North Africa. The Hyksos failed to hold on to their Egyptian territories and were absorbed by Egyptian society. This eventually led to one of Egypt's most powerful phases, the New Kingdom (1,580–1,080 BC), with the Eighteenth Dynasty. Egypt became a superpower controlling Nubia and Judea while exerting political influence on the Libyans to the West and on the Mediterranean.

As before, the New Kingdom ended with invasion from the west by Libyan princes, leading to the Third Intermediate Period. Beginning with Shoshenq I, the Twenty-second Dynasty was established. It ruled for two centuries.

To the south, Nubian independence and strength was being reasserted. This reassertion led to the conquest of Egypt by Nubia, begun by Kashta and completed by Piye (Pianhky, 751–730 BC) and Shabaka (716–695 BC). This was the birth of the Twenty-fifth Dynasty of Egypt. The Nubians tried to reestablish Egyptian traditions and customs. They ruled Egypt for a hundred years. This was ended by an Assyrian invasion, with Taharqa experiencing the full might of Assyrian iron weapons. The Nubian pharaoh Tantamani was the last of the Twenty-fifth dynasty.

When the Assyrians and Nubians left, a new Twenty-sixth Dynasty emerged from Sais. It lasted until 525 BC, when Egypt was invaded by the Persians.

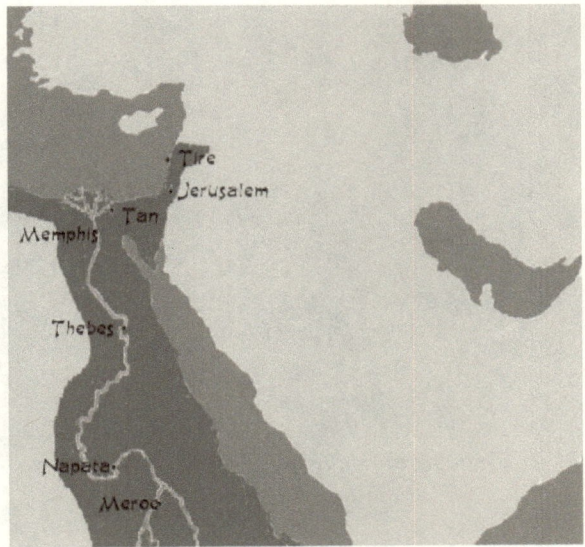

Figure 12: *Nubian Empire at its greatest extent*

Unlike the Assyrians, the Persians stayed. In 332, Egypt was conquered by Alexander the Great. This was the beginning of the Ptolemaic dynasty, which ended with Roman conquest in 30 BC. Pharaonic Egypt had come to an end.

Nubia

Around 3,500 BC, one of the first sacral kingdoms to arise in the Nile was Ta-Seti, located in northern Nubia. Ta-Seti was a powerful sacral kingdom in the Nile Valley at the 1st and 2nd cataracts that exerted an influence over nearby chiefdoms based on pictorial representation ruling over Upper Egypt. Ta-Seti traded as far as Syro-Palestine, as well as with Egypt. Ta-Seti exported gold, copper, ostrich feathers, ebony and ivory to the Old Kingdom. By the 32nd century BC, Ta-Seti was in decline. After the unification of Egypt by Narmer in 3,100 BC, Ta-Seti was invaded by the Pharaoh Hor-Aha of the First Dynasty, destroying the final remnants of the kingdom. Ta-Seti is affiliated with the A-Group Culture known to archaeology.[101]

Small sacral kingdoms continued to dot the Nubian portion of the Nile for centuries after 3,000 BC. Around the latter part of the third millennium, there was further consolidation of the sacral kingdoms. Two kingdoms in particular emerged: the Sai kingdom, immediately south of Egypt, and the Kingdom of Kerma at the third cataract. Sometime around the 18th century BC, the

Figure 13: *Nubian Temple of Apedemak, Naqa*

Kingdom of Kerma conquered the Kingdom of Sai, becoming a serious rival to Egypt. Kerma occupied a territory from the first cataract to the confluence of the Blue Nile, White Nile, and Atbarah River. About 1,575 to 1,550 BC, during the latter part of the Seventeenth Dynasty, the Kingdom of Kerma invaded Egypt.[102] The Kingdom of Kerma allied itself with the Hyksos invasion of Egypt.[103]

Egypt eventually re-energized under the Eighteenth Dynasty and conquered the Kingdom of Kerma or Kush, ruling it for almost 500 years. The Kushites were Egyptianized during this period. By 1100 BC, the Egyptians had withdrawn from Kush. The region regained independence and reasserted its culture. Kush built a new religion around Amun and made Napata its spiritual center. In 730 BC, the Kingdom of Kush invaded Egypt, taking over Thebes and beginning the Nubian Empire. The empire extended from Palestine to the confluence of the Blue Nile, the White Nile, and River Atbara.[104]

In 760 BC, the Kushites were expelled from Egypt by iron-wielding Assyrians. Later, the administrative capital was moved from Napata to Meröe, developing a new Nubian culture. Initially, Meroites were highly Egyptianized, but they subsequently began to take on distinctive features. Nubia became a center of iron-making and cotton cloth manufacturing. Egyptian writing was replaced by the Meroitic alphabet. The lion god Apedemak was added to the Egyptian pantheon of gods. Trade links to the Red Sea increased, linking Nubia with Mediterranean Greece. Its architecture and art diversified, with pictures of lions, ostriches, giraffes, and elephants. Eventually, with the rise of Aksum, Nubia's trade links were broken and it suffered environmental degradation from

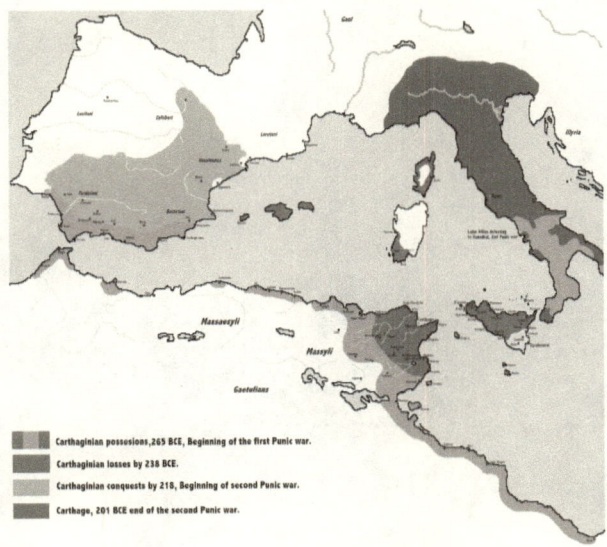

Figure 14: *Carthaginian Empire*

the tree cutting required for iron production. In 350 AD, the Aksumite king Ezana brought Meröe to an end.[105]

Carthage

The Egyptians referred to the people west of the Nile, ancestral to the Berbers, as Libyans. The Libyans were agriculturalists like the Mauri of Morocco and the Numidians of central and eastern Algeria and Tunis. They were also nomadic, having the horse, and occupied the arid pastures and desert, like the Gaetuli. Berber desert nomads were typically in conflict with Berber coastal agriculturalists.[106]

The Phoenicians were Mediterranean seamen in constant search for valuable metals such as copper, gold, tin, and lead. They began to populate the North African coast with settlements—trading and mixing with the native Berber population. In 814 BC, Phoenicians from Tyre established the city of Carthage. By 600 BC, Carthage had become a major trading entity and power in the Mediterranean, largely through trade with tropical Africa. Carthage's prosperity fostered the growth of the Berber kingdoms, Numidia and Mauretania. Around 500 BC, Carthage provided a strong impetus for trade with Sub-Saharan Africa. Berber middlemen, who had maintained contacts with Sub-Saharan Africa since the desert had desiccated, utilized pack animals to

Figure 15: *Ruins of Carthage*

transfer products from oasis to oasis. Danger lurked from the Garamantes of Fez, who raided caravans. Salt and metal goods were traded for gold, slaves, beads, and ivory.[107]

The Carthaginians were rivals to the Greeks and Romans. Carthage fought the Punic Wars, three wars with Rome: the First Punic War (264 to 241 BC), over Sicily; the Second Punic War (218 to 201 BC), in which Hannibal invaded Europe; and the Third Punic War (149 to 146 BC). Carthage lost the first two wars, and in the third it was destroyed, becoming the Roman province of Africa, with the Berber Kingdom of Numidia assisting Rome. The Roman province of Africa became a major agricultural supplier of wheat, olives, and olive oil to imperial Rome via exorbitant taxation. Two centuries later, Rome brought the Berber kingdoms of Numidia and Mauretania under its authority. In the 420's AD, Vandals invaded North Africa and Rome lost her territories. The Berber kingdoms subsequently regained their independence.[108]

Christianity gained a foothold in Africa at Alexandria in the 1st century AD and spread to Northwest Africa. By 313 AD, with the Edict of Milan, all of Roman North Africa was Christian. Egyptians adopted Monophysite Christianity and formed the independent Coptic Church. Berbers adopted Donatist Christianity. Both groups refused to accept the authority of the Roman Catholic Church. Wikipedia:Citation needed

Role of the Berbers

As Carthaginian power grew, its impact on the indigenous population increased dramatically. Berber civilization was already at a stage in which agriculture, manufacturing, trade, and political organization supported several states. Trade links between Carthage and the Berbers in the interior grew, but territorial expansion also resulted in the enslavement or military recruitment of some Berbers and in the extraction of tribute from others. By the early 4th century BC, Berbers formed one of the largest element, with Gauls, of the Carthaginian army. In the Revolt of the Mercenaries, Berber soldiers participated from 241 to 238 BC after being unpaid following the defeat of Carthage in the First Punic War. Berbers succeeded in obtaining control of much of Carthage's North African territory, and they minted coins bearing the name Libyan, used in Greek to describe natives of North Africa. The Carthaginian state declined because of successive defeats by the Romans in the Punic Wars; in 146 BC the city of Carthage was destroyed. As Carthaginian power waned, the influence of Berber leaders in the hinterland grew. By the 2nd century BC, several large but loosely administered Berber kingdoms had emerged. Two of them were established in Numidia, behind the coastal areas controlled by Carthage. West of Numidia lay Mauretania, which extended across the Moulouya River in Morocco to the Atlantic Ocean. The high point of Berber civilization, unequaled until the coming of the Almohads and Almoravid dynasty more than a millennium later, was reached during the reign of Masinissa in the 2nd century BC. After Masinissa's death in 148 BC, the Berber kingdoms were divided and reunited several times. Masinissa's line survived until 24 AD, when the remaining Berber territory was annexed to the Roman Empire.

Somalia

The ancestors of the Somali people were an important link in the Horn of Africa connecting the region's commerce with the rest of the ancient world. Somali sailors and merchants were the main suppliers of frankincense, myrrh and spices, all of which were valuable luxuries to the Ancient Egyptians, Phoenicians, Mycenaeans and Babylonians.[109,110]

In the classical era, several flourishing Somali city-states such as Opone, Mosylon, Cape Guardafui, and Malao competed with the Sabaeans, Parthians and Axumites for the rich Indo–Greco-Roman trade.[111]

Figure 16: *Ruins of Qa'ableh, an early center of Somali civilization*

Roman North Africa

<templatestyles src="Multiple_image/styles.css" />

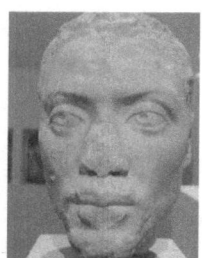

Left: Memnon, foster child of Herodes Atticus; marble bust (showing sub-Saharan facial features), ca. 170 AD, from the villa of Herodes Atticus at Eva,

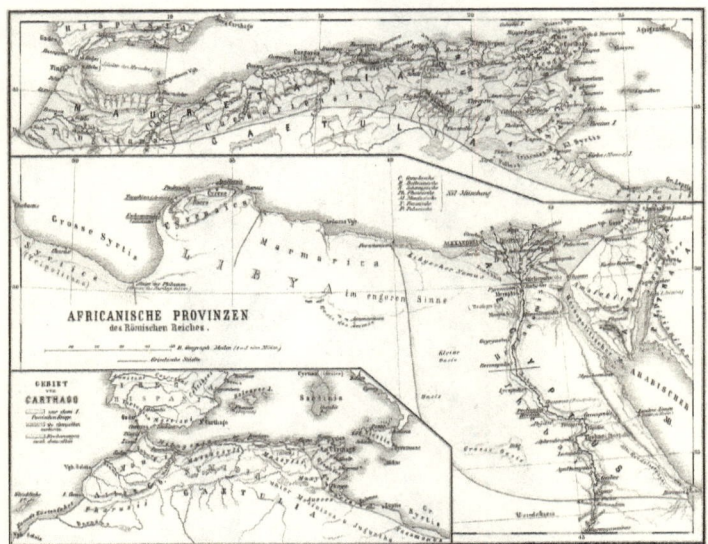

Figure 17: *Northern Africa under Roman rule*

Arcadia.
Right: an ancient Roman mosaic from Antioch depicting a black sub-Saharan African man carrying goods over his shoulder

Increases in urbanization and in the area under cultivation during Roman rule caused wholesale dislocations of the Berber society, forcing nomad tribes to settle or to move from their traditional rangelands. Sedentary tribes lost their autonomy and connection with the land. Berber opposition to the Roman presence was nearly constant. The Roman emperor Trajan established a frontier in the south by encircling the Aurès and Nemencha mountains and building a line of forts from Vescera (modern Biskra) to Ad Majores (Hennchir Besseriani, southeast of Biskra). The defensive line extended at least as far as Castellum Dimmidi (modern Messaâd, southwest of Biskra), Roman Algeria's southernmost fort. Romans settled and developed the area around Sitifis (modern Sétif) in the 2nd century, but farther west the influence of Rome did not extend beyond the coast and principal military roads until much later. Wikipedia:Citation needed

The Roman military presence of North Africa remained relatively small, consisting of about 28,000 troops and auxiliaries in Numidia and the two Mauretanian provinces. Starting in the 2nd century AD, these garrisons were manned mostly by local inhabitants.Wikipedia:Citation needed

Figure 18: *Roman portrait of Demetrios, a citizen of Roman Egypt, Fayum mummy portraits, c. 100 AD, Brooklyn Museum*

Aside from Carthage, urbanization in North Africa came in part with the establishment of settlements of veterans under the Roman emperors Claudius (reigned 41–54), Nerva (96–98), and Trajan (98–117). In Algeria such settlements included Tipasa, Cuicul or Curculum (modern Djemila, northeast of Sétif), Thamugadi (modern Timgad, southeast of Sétif), and Sitifis (modern Sétif). The prosperity of most towns depended on agriculture. Called the "granary of the empire", North Africa became one of the largest exporters of grain in the empire, shipping to the provinces which did not produce cereals, like Italy and Greece. Other crops included fruit, figs, grapes, and beans. By the 2nd century AD, olive oil rivaled cereals as an export item.Wikipedia:Citation needed

The beginnings of the Roman imperial decline seemed less serious in North Africa than elsewhere. However, uprisings did take place. In 238 AD, landowners rebelled unsuccessfully against imperial fiscal policies. Sporadic tribal revolts in the Mauretanian mountains followed from 253 to 288, during the Crisis of the Third Century. The towns also suffered economic difficulties, and building activity almost ceased.Wikipedia:Citation needed

The towns of Roman North Africa had a substantial Jewish population. Some Jews had been deported from Judea or Palestine in the 1st and 2nd centuries AD for rebelling against Roman rule; others had come earlier with

Punic settlers. In addition, a number of Berber tribes had converted to Judaism.Wikipedia:Citation needed

Christianity arrived in the 2nd century and soon gained converts in the towns and among slaves. More than eighty bishops, some from distant frontier regions of Numidia, attended the Council of Carthage (256) in 256. By the end of the 4th century, the settled areas had become Christianized, and some Berber tribes had converted *en masse*.Wikipedia:Citation needed

A division in the church that came to be known as the Donatist heresy began in 313 among Christians in North Africa. The Donatists stressed the holiness of the church and refused to accept the authority to administer the sacraments of those who had surrendered the scriptures when they were forbidden under the Emperor Diocletian (reigned 284–305). The Donatists also opposed the involvement of Constantine the Great (reigned 306–337) in church affairs in contrast to the majority of Christians who welcomed official imperial recognition.Wikipedia:Citation needed

The occasionally violent Donatist controversy has been characterized-Wikipedia:Manual of Style/Words to watch#Unsupported attributions as a struggle between opponents and supporters of the Roman system. The most articulate North African critic of the Donatist position, which came to be called a heresy, was Augustine, bishop of Hippo Regius. Augustine maintained that the unworthiness of a minister did not affect the validity of the sacraments because their true minister was Jesus Christ. In his sermons and books Augustine, who is considered a leading exponent of Christian dogma, evolved a theory of the right of orthodox Christian rulers to use force against schismatics and heretics. Although the dispute was resolved by a decision of an imperial commission in Carthage in 411, Donatist communities continued to exist as late as the 6th century.Wikipedia:Citation needed

A decline in trade weakened Roman control. Independent kingdoms emerged in mountainous and desert areas, towns were overrun, and Berbers, who had previously been pushed to the edges of the Roman Empire, returned.

During the Vandalic War, Belisarius, general of the Byzantine emperor Justinian I based in Constantinople, landed in North Africa in 533 with 16,000 men and within a year destroyed the Vandal Kingdom. Local opposition delayed full Byzantine control of the region for twelve years, however, and when imperial control came, it was but a shadow of the control exercised by Rome. Although an impressive series of fortifications were built, Byzantine rule was compromised by official corruption, incompetence, military weakness, and lack of concern in Constantinople for African affairs, which made it an easy target for the Arabs during the Early Muslim conquests . As a result, many rural areas reverted to Berber rule. Wikipedia:Citation needed

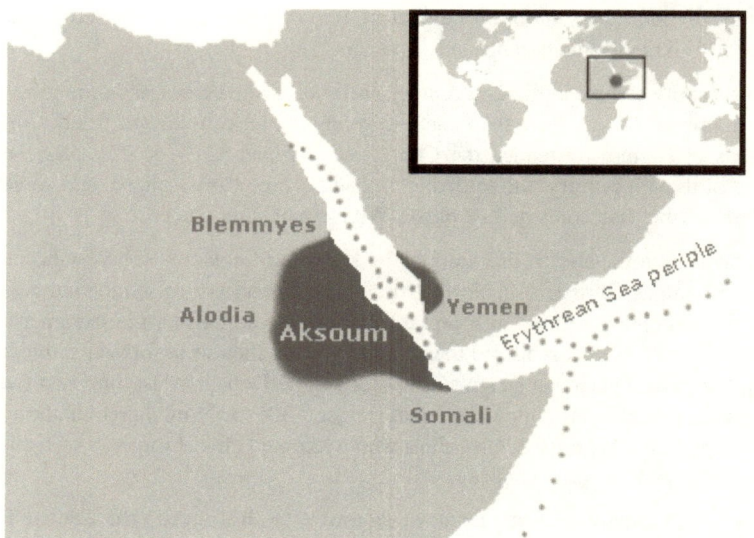

Figure 19: *Aksumite Empire*

Aksum

The earliest state in Eritrea and northern Ethiopia, D'mt, dates from around the 8th and 7th centuries BC. D'mt traded through the Red Sea with Egypt and the Mediterranean, providing frankincense. By the 5th and 3rd centuries, D'mt had declined, and several successor states took its place. Later there was greater trade with South Arabia, mainly with the port of Saba. Adulis became an important commercial center in the Ethiopian Highlands. The interaction of the peoples in the two regions, the southern Arabia Sabaeans and the northern Ethiopians, resulted in the Ge'ez culture and language and eventual development of the Ge'ez script. Trade links increased and expanded from the Red Sea to the Mediterranean, with Egypt, Greece, and Rome, to the Black Sea, and to Persia, India, and China. Aksum was known throughout those lands. By the 5th century BC, the region was very prosperous, exporting ivory, hippopotamus hides, gold dust, spices, and live elephants. It imported silver, gold, olive oil, and wine. Aksum manufactured glass crystal, brass, and copper for export. A powerful Aksum emerged, unifying parts of eastern Sudan, northern Ethiopia (Tigre), and Eritrea. Its kings built stone palatial buildings and were buried under megalithic monuments. By 300 AD, Aksum was minting its own coins in silver and gold.[112]

Figure 20: *Aksum Obelisk, symbol of the Aksumite civilization*

In 331 AD, King Ezana (320–350 AD) was converted to Miaphysite Christianity which believes one unite divine-human nature of Christ], supposedly by Frumentius and Aedesius, who became stranded on the Red Sea coast. Some scholars believed the process was more complex and gradual than a simple conversion. Around 350, the time Ezana sacked Meroe, the Syrian monastic tradition took root within the Ethiopian church.[113]

In the 6th century Aksum was powerful enough to add Saba on the Arabian peninsula to her empire. At the end of the 6th century, the Sasanian Empire pushed Aksum out of the peninsula. With the spread of Islam through Western Asia and Northern Africa, Aksum's trading networks in the Mediterranean faltered. The Red Sea trade diminished as it was diverted to the Persian Gulf and dominated by Arabs, causing Aksum to decline. By 800 AD, the capital was moved south into the interior highlands, and Aksum was much diminished.[114]

West Africa

In the western Sahel the rise of settled communities occurred largely as a result of the domestication of millet and of sorghum. Archaeology points to sizable urban populations in West Africa beginning in the 2nd millennium BC. Symbiotic trade relations developed before the trans-Saharan trade, in response to the opportunities afforded by north-south diversity in ecosystems

Figure 21: *Nok sculpture, terracotta, Louvre*

across deserts, grasslands, and forests. The agriculturists received salt from the desert nomads. The desert nomads acquired meat and other foods from pastoralists and farmers of the grasslands and from fishermen on the Niger River. The forest-dwellers provided furs and meat.[115]

Dhar Tichitt and Oualata in present-day Mauritania figure prominently among the early urban centers, dated to 2,000 BC. About 500 stone settlements litter the region in the former savannah of the Sahara. Its inhabitants fished and grew millet. It has been foundWikipedia:Manual of Style/Words to watch#Unsupported attributions that the Soninke of the Mandé peoples were responsible for constructing such settlements. Around 300 BC the region became more desiccated and the settlements began to decline, most likely relocating to Koumbi Saleh. Architectural evidence and the comparison of pottery styles suggest that Dhar Tichitt was related to the subsequent Ghana Empire. Djenné-Djenno (in present-day Mali) was settled around 300 BC, and the town grew to house a sizable Iron Age population, as evidenced by crowded cemeteries. Living structures were made of sun-dried mud. By 250 BC Djenné-Djenno had become a large, thriving market town.[116,117]

Farther south, in central Nigeria, around 1,000 BC, the Nok culture developed on the Jos Plateau. It was a highly centralized community. The Nok people produced lifelike representations in terracotta, including human heads,

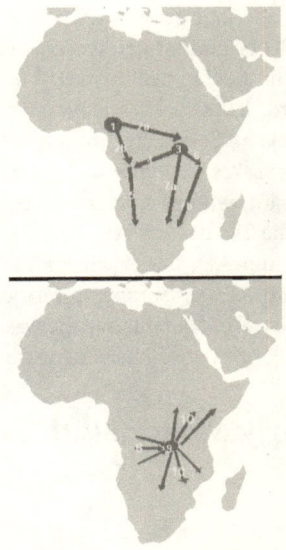

Figure 22: *1 = 3000 – 1500 BC origin*
2 = c. 1500 BC first migrations
2.a = Eastern Bantu, 2.b = Western Bantu
3 = 1000 – 500 BC Urewe nucleus of Eastern Bantu
4 – 7 = southward advance
9 = 500 BC – 0 Congo nucleus
10 = 0 – 1000 CE last phase[119]

elephants, and other animals. By 500 BC they were smelting iron. By 200 AD the Nok culture had vanished. Based on stylistic similarities with the Nok terracottas, the bronze figurines of the Yoruba kingdom of Ife and those of the Bini kingdom of Benin are nowWikipedia:Manual of Style/Dates and numbers#Chronological items believedWikipedia:Manual of Style/Words to watch#Unsupported attributions to be continuations of the traditions of the earlier Nokite culture.[118]

Bantu expansion

The Bantu expansion involved a significant movement of people in African history and in the settling of the continent.Wikipedia:Citation needed People speaking Bantu languages (a branch of the Niger–Congo family) began in the second millennium BC to spread from Cameroon eastward to the Great Lakes region. In the first millennium BC, Bantu languages spread from the Great Lakes to southern and east Africa. One early movement headed south to the upper Zambezi valley in the 2nd century BC. Then Bantu-speakers pushed westward to the savannahs of present-day Angola and eastward into Malawi, Zambia, and Zimbabwe in the 1st century AD. The second thrust from the Great Lakes was eastward, 2,000 years ago, expanding to the Indian Ocean coast, Kenya and Tanzania. The eastern group eventually met the southern migrants from the Great Lakes in Malawi, Zambia, and Zimbabwe. Both groups continued southward, with eastern groups continuing to Mozambique and reaching Maputo in the 2nd century AD, and expanding as far as Durban. By the later first millennium AD, the expansion had reached the Great Kei River in present-day South Africa. Sorghum, a major Bantu crop, could not thrive under the winter rainfall of Namibia and the western Cape. Khoisan people inhabited the remaining parts of southern Africa.[120]Wikipedia:Verifiability

Medieval and Early Modern (6th to 18th centuries)

Sao civilization

The Sao civilization flourished from ca. the sixth century BC to as late as the 16th century AD in Central Africa. The Sao lived by the Chari River south of Lake Chad in territory that later became part of Cameroon and Chad. They are the earliest people to have left clear traces of their presence in the territory of modern Cameroon. Today, several ethnic groups of northern Cameroon and southern Chad but particularly the Sara people claim descent from the civilization of the Sao. Sao artifacts show that they were skilled workers in bronze, copper, and iron.[121] Finds include bronze sculptures and terra cotta statues of human and animal figures, coins, funerary urns, household utensils, jewelry, highly decorated pottery, and spears.[122] The largest Sao archaeological finds have been made south of Lake Chad. Wikipedia:Citation needed

Kanem Empire

The Kanem Empire was centered in the Chad Basin. It was known as the Kanem Empire from the 9th century AD onward and lasted as the independent kingdom of Bornu until 1893. At its height it encompassed an area covering not only much of Chad, but also parts of modern southern Libya, eastern Niger, northeastern Nigeria, northern Cameroon, parts of South Sudan and the Central African Republic. The history of the Empire is mainly known from the Royal Chronicle or *Girgam* discovered in 1851 by the German traveller Heinrich Barth.[123] Kanem rose in the 8th century in the region to the north and east of Lake Chad. The Kanem empire went into decline, shrank, and in the 14th century was defeated by Bilala invaders from the Lake Fitri region.[124]

Around the 9th century AD, the central Sudanic Empire of Kanem, with its capital at Njimi, was founded by the Kanuri-speaking nomads. Kanem arose

History of Africa

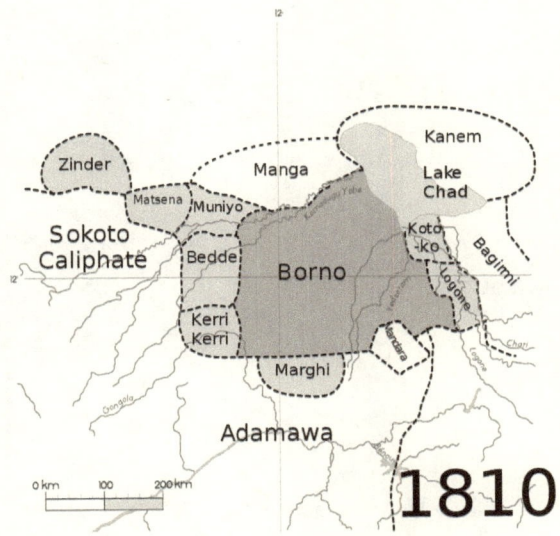

Figure 23: *The Kanem and Bornu Empires in 1810*

by engaging in the trans-Saharan trade. It exchanged slaves captured by raiding the south for horses from North Africa, which in turn aided in the acquisition of slaves. By the late 11th century, the Islamic Sayfawa (Saifawa) dynasty was founded by Humai (Hummay) ibn Salamna. The Sayfawa Dynasty ruled for 771 years, making it one of the longest-lasting dynasties in human history. In addition to trade, taxation of local farms around Kanem became a source of state income. Kanem reached its peak under *Mai* (king) Dunama Dibalemi ibn Salma (1210–1248). The empire reportedly was able to field 40,000 cavalry, and it extended from Fezzan in the north to the Sao state in the south. Islam became firmly entrenched in the empire. Pilgrimages to Mecca were common; Cairo had hostels set aside specifically for pilgrims from Kanem.[125,126]

Bornu Empire

The Kanuri people led by the Sayfuwa migrated to the west and south of the lake, where they established the Bornu Empire. By the late 16th century the Bornu empire had expanded and recaptured the parts of Kanem that had been conquered by the Bulala.[127] Satellite states of Bornu included the Damagaram in the west and Baguirmi to the southeast of Lake Chad. Around 1400, the Sayfawa Dynasty moved its capital to Bornu, a tributary state southwest of Lake Chad with a new capital Birni Ngarzagamu. Overgrazing had caused the pastures of Kanem to become too dry. In addition, political rivalry from the

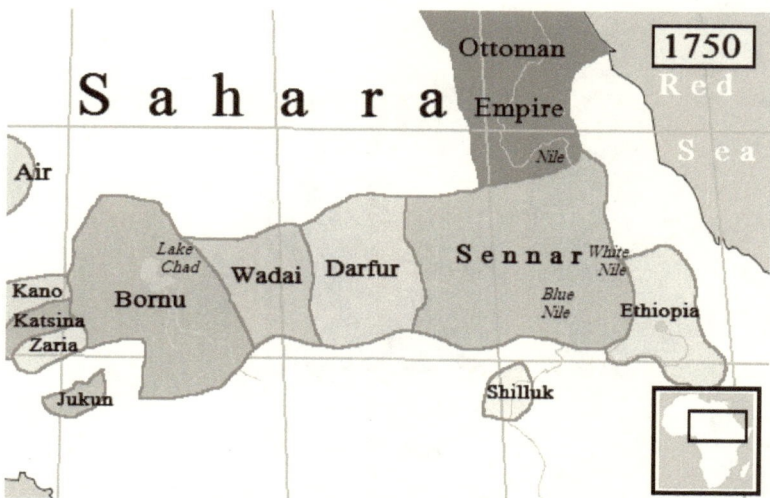

Figure 24: *Major states of Middle Africa in 1750*

Bilala clan was becoming intense. Moving to Bornu better situated the empire to exploit the trans-Saharan trade and to widen its network in that trade. Links to the Hausa states were also established, providing horses and salt from Bilma for Akan gold.[128] Mai Ali Gazi ibn Dunama (c. 1475–1503) defeated the Bilala, reestablishing complete control of Kanem.[129] During the early 16th century, the Sayfawa Dynasty solidified its hold on the Bornu population after much rebellion. In the latter half of the 16th century, *Mai* Idris Alooma modernized its military, in contrast to the Songhai Empire. Turkish mercenaries were used to train the military. The Sayfawa Dynasty were the first monarchs south of the Sahara to import firearms. The empire controlled all of the Sahel from the borders of Darfur in the east to Hausaland to the west. Friendly relationship was established with the Ottoman Empire via Tripoli. The *Mai* exchanged gifts with the Ottoman sultan.[130]

During the 17th and 18th centuries, not much is known about Bornu. During the 18th century, it became a center of Islamic learning. However, Bornu's army became outdated by not importing new arms, and Kamembu had also begun its decline. The power of the *mai* was undermined by droughts and famine that were becoming more intense, internal rebellion in the pastoralist north, growing Hausa power, and the importation of firearms which made warfare more bloody. By 1841, the last *mai* was deposed, bringing to an end the long-lived Sayfawa Dynasty. In its place, the al-Kanemi dynasty of the *shehu* rose to power.

Figure 25: *Abéché, capital of Wadai, in 1918 after the French had taken over*

Shilluk Kingdom

The Shilluk Kingdom was centered in South Sudan from the 15th century from along a strip of land along the western bank of the White Nile, from Lake No to about 12° north latitude. The capital and royal residence was in the town of Fashoda. The kingdom was founded during the mid-15th century AD by its first ruler, Nyikang. During the 19th century, the Shilluk Kingdom faced decline following military assaults from the Ottoman Empire and later British and Sudanese colonization in Anglo-Egyptian Sudan.Wikipedia:Citation needed

Baguirmi Kingdom

The Kingdom of Baguirmi existed as an independent state during the 16th and 17th centuries southeast of Lake Chad in what is now the country of Chad. Baguirmi emerged to the southeast of the Kanem-Bornu Empire. The kingdom's first ruler was Mbang Birni Besse. Later in his reign, the Bornu Empire conquered and made the state a tributary.Wikipedia:Citation needed

Wadai Empire

The Wadai Empire was centered on Chad and the Central African Republic from the 17th century. The Tunjur people founded the Wadai Kingdom to the

Figure 26: *Luba pottery*

east of Bornu in the 16th century. In the 17th century there was a revolt of the Maba people who established a Muslim dynasty.

At first Wadai paid tribute to Bornu and Durfur, but by the 18th century Wadai was fully independent and had become an aggressor against its neighbors.[83] To the west of Bornu, by the 15th century the Kingdom of Kano had become the most powerful of the Hausa Kingdoms, in an unstable truce with the Kingdom of Katsina to the north.[131] Both were absorbed into the Sokoto Caliphate during the Fulani Jihad of 1805, which threatened Bornu itself.[132]

Luba Empire

Sometime between 1300 and 1400 AD, Kongolo Mwamba (Nkongolo) from the Balopwe clan unified the various Luba peoples, near Lake Kisale. He founded the Kongolo Dynasty, which was later ousted by Kalala Ilunga. Kalala expanded the kingdom west of Lake Kisale. A new centralized political system of spiritual kings (*balopwe*) with a court council of head governors and sub-heads all the way to village heads. The *balopwe* was the direct communicator with the ancestral spirits and chosen by them. Conquered states were integrated into the system and represented in the court, with their titles. The authority of the *balopwe* resided in his spiritual power rather than his military

Figure 27: *Lunda town and dwelling*

authority. The army was relatively small. The Luba was able to control regional trade and collect tribute for redistribution. Numerous offshoot states were formed with founders claiming descent from the Luba. The Luba political system spread throughout Central Africa, southern Uganda, Rwanda, Burundi, Malawi, Zambia, Zimbabwe, and the western Congo. Two major empires claiming Luba descent were the Lunda Empire and Maravi Empire. The Bemba people and Basimba people of northern Zambia were descended from Luba migrants who arrived in Zambia during the 17th century.[133,134]

Lunda Empire

In the 1450s, a Luba from the royal family Ilunga Tshibinda married Lunda queen Rweej and united all Lunda peoples. Their son *mulopwe* Luseeng expanded the kingdom. His son Naweej expanded the empire further and is known as the first Lunda emperor, with the title *mwato yamvo* (*mwaant yaav*, *mwant yav*), the Lord of Vipers. The Luba political system was retained, and conquered peoples were integrated into the system. The *mwato yamvo* assigned a *ciloo1* or *kilolo* (royal adviser) and tax collector to each state conquered.[135,136]

Numerous states claimed descent from the Lunda. The Imbangala of inland Angola claimed descent from a founder, Kinguri, brother of Queen Rweej, who could not tolerate the rule of *mulopwe* Tshibunda. *Kinguri* became the title of kings of states founded by Queen Rweej's brother. The Luena (Lwena) and Lozi (Luyani) in Zambia also claim descent from Kinguri. During the 17th century, a Lunda chief and warrior called Mwata Kazembe set up an Eastern Lunda kingdom in the valley of the Luapula River. The Lunda's western expansion also saw claims of descent by the Yaka and the Pende. The Lunda linked Central Africa with the western coast trade. The kingdom of Lunda came to an end in the 19th century when it was invaded by the Chokwe, who were armed with guns.[137]

Kingdom of Kongo

By the 15th century AD, the farming Bakongo people (*ba* being the plural prefix) were unified as the Kingdom of Kongo under a ruler called the *manikongo*, residing in the fertile Pool Malebo area on the lower Congo River. The capital was M'banza-Kongo. With superior organization, they were able to conquer their neighbors and extract tribute. They were experts in metalwork, pottery, and weaving raffia cloth. They stimulated interregional trade via a tribute system controlled by the *manikongo*. Later, maize (corn) and cassava (manioc) would be introduced to the region via trade with the Portuguese at their ports at Luanda and Benguela. The maize and cassava would result in population growth in the region and other parts of Africa, replacing millet as a main staple.Wikipedia:Citation needed

By the 16th century, the *manikongo* held authority from the Atlantic in the west to the Kwango River in the east. Each territory was assigned a *mani-mpembe* (provincial governor) by the *manikongo*. In 1506, Afonso I (1506–1542), a Christian, took over the throne. Slave trading increased with Afonso's wars of conquest. About 1568 to 1569, the Jaga invaded Kongo, laying waste to the kingdom and forcing the *manikongo* into exile. In 1574, Manikongo Álvaro I was reinstated with the help of Portuguese mercenaries. During the latter part of the 1660s, the Portuguese tried to gain control of Kongo. Manikongo António I (1661–1665), with a Kongolese army of 5,000, was destroyed by an army of Afro-Portuguese at the Battle of Mbwila. The empire dissolved into petty polities, fighting among each other for war captives to sell into slavery.[138,139,140]

Kongo gained captives from the Kingdom of Ndongo in wars of conquest. Ndongo was ruled by the *ngola*. Ndongo would also engage in slave trading with the Portuguese, with São Tomé being a transit point to Brazil. The kingdom was not as welcoming as Kongo; it viewed the Portuguese with great suspicion and as an enemy. The Portuguese in the latter part of the 16th century tried to gain control of Ndongo but were defeated by the Mbundu. Ndongo experienced depopulation from slave raiding. The leaders established another

Figure 28: *Kongo in 1711*

state at Matamba, affiliated with Queen Nzinga, who put up a strong resistance to the Portuguese until coming to terms with them. The Portuguese settled along the coast as trade dealers, not venturing on conquest of the interior. Slavery wreaked havoc in the interior, with states initiating wars of conquest for captives. The Imbangala formed the slave-raiding state of Kasanje, a major source of slaves during the 17th and 18th centuries.[141,142]

Horn of Africa

Somalia

The birth of Islam opposite Somalia's Red Sea coast meant that Somali merchants and sailors living on the Arabian Peninsula gradually came under the influence of the new religion through their converted Arab Muslim trading partners. With the migration of Muslim families from the Islamic world to Somalia in the early centuries of Islam, and the peaceful conversion of the Somali population by Somali Muslim scholars in the following centuries, the ancient city-states eventually transformed into Islamic Mogadishu, Berbera, Zeila, Barawa and Merka, which were part of the *Berber* (the medieval Arab term for the ancestors of the modern Somalis) civilization.[143,144] The city of Mogadishu came to be known as the *City of Islam*[145] and controlled the East African gold trade for several centuries.[146]

Figure 29: *The Citadel of Gondershe, Somalia was an important city in the medieval Somali Ajuran Empire*

Figure 30: *Almnara Tower, Mogadishu.*

During this period, sultanates such as the Ajuran Empire and the Sultanate of Mogadishu, and republics like Barawa, Merca and Hobyo and their respective ports flourished and had a lucrative foreign commerce with ships sailing to and coming from Arabia, India, Venice,[147] Persia, Egypt, Portugal and as far away as China. Vasco da Gama, who passed by Mogadishu in the 15th century, noted that it was a large city with houses four or five stories high and big palaces in its centre, in addition to many mosques with cylindrical minarets.[148]

In the 16th century, Duarte Barbosa noted that many ships from the Kingdom of Cambaya in modern-day India sailed to Mogadishu with cloth and spices, for which they in return received gold, wax, and ivory. Barbosa also highlighted the abundance of meat, wheat, barley, horses, and fruit in the coastal markets, which generated enormous wealth for the merchants.[149] Mogadishu, the center of a thriving weaving industry known as *toob benadir* (specialized for the markets in Egypt and Syria),[150] together with Merca and Barawa, served as a transit stop for Swahili merchants from Mombasa and Malindi and for the gold trade from Kilwa.[151] Jewish merchants from the Strait of Hormuz brought their Indian textiles and fruit to the Somali coast to exchange for grain and wood.[152]

Trading relations were established with Malacca in the 15th century,[153] with cloth, ambergris, and porcelain being the main commodities of the trade.[154] Giraffes, zebras, and incense were exported to the Ming Empire of China, which established Somali merchants as leaders in the commerce between the Asia and Africa[155] and influenced the Chinese language with borrowings from the Somali language in the process. Hindu merchants from Surat and southeast African merchants from Pate, seeking to bypass both the Portuguese blockade and Omani meddling, used the Somali ports of Merca and Barawa (which were out of the two powers' jurisdiction) to conduct their trade in safety and without any problems.[156]

Ethiopia

The Zagwe dynasty ruled many parts of modern Ethiopia and Eritrea from approximately 1137 to 1270. The name of the dynasty comes from the Cushitic speaking Agaw of northern Ethiopia. From 1270 AD and on for many centuries, the Solomonic dynasty ruled the Ethiopian Empire. Wikipedia:Citation needed

In the early 15th century Ethiopia sought to make diplomatic contact with European kingdoms for the first time since Aksumite times. A letter from King Henry IV of England to the Emperor of Abyssinia survives.[157] In 1428, the Emperor Yeshaq I sent two emissaries to Alfonso V of Aragon, who sent return emissaries who failed to complete the return trip.[158]

Figure 31: *King Fasilides's Castle*

The first continuous relations with a European country began in 1508 with the Kingdom of Portugal under Emperor Lebna Dengel, who had just inherited the throne from his father.[159] This proved to be an important development, for when the empire was subjected to the attacks of the Adal general and imam, Ahmad ibn Ibrahim al-Ghazi (called *"Grañ"*, or "the Left-handed"), Portugal assisted the Ethiopian emperor by sending weapons and four hundred men, who helped his son Gelawdewos defeat Ahmad and re-establish his rule.[160] This Abyssinian–Adal War was also one of the first proxy wars in the region as the Ottoman Empire, and Portugal took sides in the conflict.Wikipedia:Citation needed

When Emperor Susenyos converted to Roman Catholicism in 1624, years of revolt and civil unrest followed resulting in thousands of deaths.[161] The Jesuit missionaries had offended the Orthodox faith of the local Ethiopians, and on June 25, 1632, Susenyos's son, Emperor Fasilides, declared the state religion to again be Ethiopian Orthodox Christianity and expelled the Jesuit missionaries and other Europeans.[162,163]

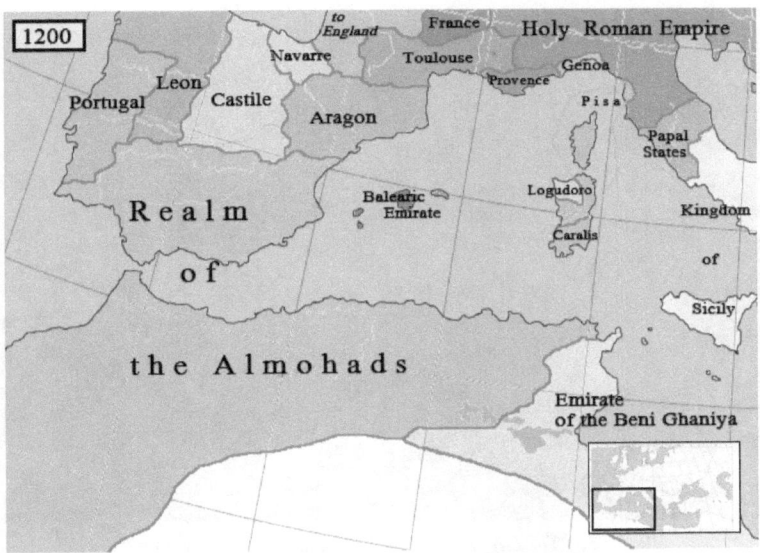

Figure 32: *Almohad Empire, c. 1200*

North Africa

Maghreb

By 711 AD, the Umayyad Caliphate had conquered all of North Africa. By the 10th century, the majority of the population of North Africa was Muslim.[164]

By the 9th century AD, the unity brought about by the Islamic conquest of North Africa and the expansion of Islamic culture came to an end. Conflict arose as to who should be the successor of the prophet. The Umayyads had initially taken control of the Caliphate, with their capital at Damascus. Later, the Abbasids had taken control, moving the capital to Baghdad. The Berber people, being independent in spirit and hostile to outside interference in their affairs and to Arab exclusivity in orthodox Islam, adopted Shi'ite and Kharijite Islam, both considered unorthodox and hostile to the authority of the Abbasid Caliphate. Numerous Kharijite kingdoms came and fell during the 8th and 9th centuries, asserting their independence from Baghdad. In the early 10th century, Shi'ite groups from Syria, claiming descent from Muhammad's daughter Fatimah, founded the Fatimid Dynasty in the Maghreb. By 950, they had conquered all of the Maghreb and by 969 all of Egypt. They had immediately broken away from Baghdad.[165]

Figure 33: *The Great Mosque of Kairouan (also known as the Mosque of Uqba), first built in 670 by the Umayyad general Uqba Ibn Nafi, is the oldest and most prestigious mosque in the Maghreb and North Africa, located in the city of Kairouan, Tunisia*

In an attempt to bring about a purer form of Islam among the Sanhaja Berbers, Abdallah ibn Yasin founded the Almoravid movement in present-day Mauritania and Western Sahara. The Sanhaja Berbers, like the Soninke, practiced an indigenous religion alongside Islam. Abdallah ibn Yasin found ready converts in the Lamtuna Sanhaja, who were dominated by the Soninke in the south and the Zenata Berbers in the north. By the 1040s, all of the Lamtuna was converted to the Almoravid movement. With the help of Yahya ibn Umar and his brother Abu Bakr ibn Umar, the sons of the Lamtuna chief, the Almoravids created an empire extending from the Sahel to the Mediterranean. After the death of Abdallah ibn Yassin and Yahya ibn Umar, Abu Bakr split the empire in half, between himself and Yusuf ibn Tashfin, because it was too big to be ruled by one individual. Abu Bakr took the south to continue fighting the Soninke, and Yusuf ibn Tashfin took the north, expanding it to southern Spain. The death of Abu Bakr in 1087 saw a breakdown of unity and increase military dissension in the south. This caused a re-expansion of the Soninke. The Almoravids were once held responsible for bringing down the Ghana Empire in 1076, but this view is no longer credited.[166]

During the 10th through 13th centuries, there was a large-scale movement of bedouins out of the Arabian Peninsula. About 1050, a quarter of a million Arab

Figure 34: *The Almohad minaret in Safi*

nomads from Egypt moved into the Maghreb. Those following the northern coast were referred to as Banu Hilal. Those going south of the Atlas Mountains were the Banu Sulaym. This movement spread the use of the Arabic language and hastened the decline of the Berber language and the Arabisation of North Africa. Later an Arabised Berber group, the Hawwara, went south to Nubia via Egypt.[167]

In the 1140s, Abd al-Mu'min declared jihad on the Almoravids, charging them with decadence and corruption. He united the northern Berbers against the Almoravids, overthrowing them and forming the Almohad Empire. During this period, the Maghreb became thoroughly Islamised and saw the spread of literacy, the development of algebra, and the use of the number zero and decimals. By the 13th century, the Almohad states had split into three rival states. Muslim states were largely extinguished in the Iberian Peninsula by the Christian kingdoms of Castile, Aragon, and Portugal. Around 1415, Portugal engaged in a *reconquista* of North Africa by capturing Ceuta, and in later centuries Spain and Portugal acquired other ports on the North African coast. In 1492, at the end of the Granada War, Spain defeated Muslims in the Emirate of Granada, effectively ending eight centuries of Muslim domination in southern Iberia.[168]

Portugal and Spain took the ports of Tangiers, Algiers, Tripoli, and Tunis. This put them in direct competition with the Ottoman Empire, which re-took the ports using Turkish corsairs (pirates and privateers). The Turkish corsairs would use the ports for raiding Christian ships, a major source of booty for the towns. Technically, North Africa was under the control of the Ottoman Empire, but only the coastal towns were fully under Istanbul's control. Tripoli benefited from trade with Borno. The pashas of Tripoli traded horses, firearms, and armor via Fez with the sultans of the Bornu Empire for slaves.[169]

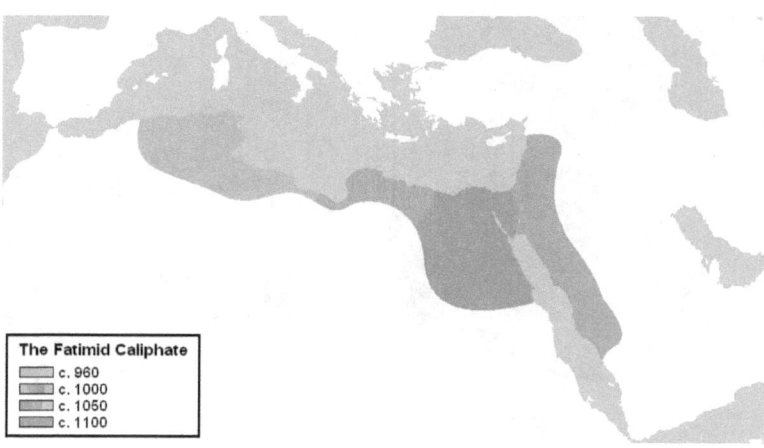

Figure 35: *Fatimid Caliphate*

In the 16th century, an Arab nomad tribe that claimed descent from Muhammad's daughter, the Saadis, conquered and united Morocco. They prevented the Ottoman Empire from reaching to the Atlantic and expelled Portugal from Morocco's western coast. Ahmad al-Mansur brought the state to the height of its power. He invaded Songhay in 1591, to control the gold trade, which had been diverted to the western coast of Africa for European ships and to the east, to Tunis. Morocco's hold on Songhay diminished in the 17th century. In 1603, after Ahmad's death, the kingdom split into the two sultanates of Fes and Marrakesh. Later it was reunited by Moulay al-Rashid, founder of the Alaouite Dynasty (1672–1727). His brother and successor, Ismail ibn Sharif(1672–1727), strengthened the unity of the country by importing slaves from the Sudan to build up the military.[170]

Nile Valley

Egypt

In 642 AD, the Rashidun Caliphate conquered Byzantine Egypt.

Egypt under the Fatimid Caliphate was prosperous. Dams and canals were repaired, and wheat, barley, flax, and cotton production increased. Egypt became a major producer of linen and cotton cloth. Its Mediterranean and Red Sea trade increased. Egypt also minted a gold currency called the Fatimid dinar, which was used for international trade. The bulk of revenues came from taxing the fellahin (peasant farmers), and taxes were high. Tax collecting was leased to Berber overlords, who were soldiers who had taken part in the Fatimid conquest in 969 AD. The overlords paid a share to the caliphs and retained what was left. Eventually, they became landlords and constituted a settled land aristocracy.[171]

To fill the military ranks, Mamluk Turkish slave cavalry and Sudanese slave infantry were used. Berber freemen were also recruited. In the 1150s, tax revenues from farms diminished. The soldiers revolted and wreaked havoc in the countryside, slowed trade, and diminished the power and authority of the Fatimid caliphs.[172]

During the 1160s, Fatimid Egypt came under threat from European crusaders. Out of this threat, a Kurdish general named Ṣalāḥ ad-Dīn Yūsuf ibn Ayyūb (Saladin), with a small band of professional soldiers, emerged as an outstanding Muslim defender. Saladin defeated the Christian crusaders at Egypt's borders and recaptured Jerusalem in 1187. On the death of Al-Adid, the last Fatimid caliph, in 1171, Saladin became the ruler of Egypt, ushering in the Ayyubid Dynasty. Under his rule, Egypt returned to Sunni Islam, Cairo became an important center of Arab Islamic learning, and Mamluk slaves were increasingly recruited from Turkey and southern Russia for military service. Support for the military was tied to the *iqta*, a form of land taxation in which soldiers were given ownership in return for military service.[173]

Over time, Mamluk slave soldiers became a very powerful landed aristocracy, to the point of getting rid of the Ayyubid dynasty in 1250 and establishing a Mamluk dynasty. The more powerful Mamluks were referred to as *amirs*. For 250 years, Mamluks controlled all of Egypt under a military dictatorship. Egypt extended her territories to Syria and Palestine, thwarted the crusaders, and halted a Mongol invasion in 1260 at the Battle of Ain Jalut. Mamluk Egypt came to be viewed as a protector of Islam, and of Medina and Mecca. Eventually the *iqta* system declined and proved unreliable for providing an adequate military. The Mamluks started viewing their *iqta* as hereditary and became attuned to urban living. Farm production declined, and dams and canals lapsed into disrepair. Mamluk military skill and technology did not keep pace with new technology of handguns and cannons.[174]

With the rise of the Ottoman Empire, Egypt was easily defeated. In 1517, at the end of an Ottoman–Mamluk War, Egypt became part of the Ottoman Empire. The Istanbul government revived the *iqta* system. Trade was reestablished in the Red Sea, but it could not completely connect with the Indian Ocean trade because of growing Portuguese presence. During the 17th and 18th centuries, hereditary Mamluks regained power. The leading Mamluks were referred to as *beys*. Pashas, or viceroys, represented the Istanbul government in name only, operating independently. During the 18th century, dynasties of pashas became established. The government was weak and corrupt.[175]

In 1798, Napoleon invaded Egypt. The local forces had little ability to resist the French conquest. However, the British Empire and the Ottoman Empire

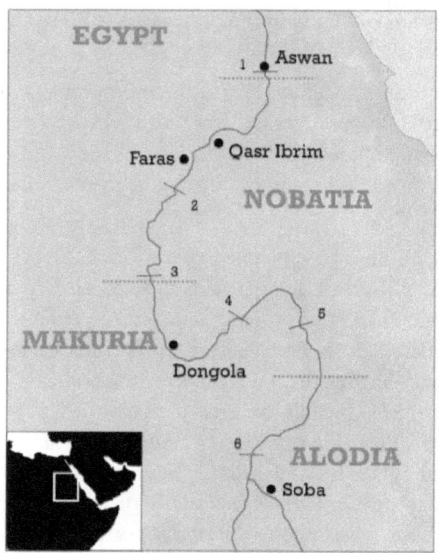

Figure 36: *Christian Nubia and the Nile cataracts*

were able to remove French occupation in 1801. These events marked the beginning of a 19th-century Anglo-Franco rivalry over Egypt.[176]

Christian and Islamic Nubia

After Ezana of Aksum sacked Meroe, people associated with the site of Ballana moved into Nubia from the southwest and founded three kingdoms: Makuria, Nobatia, and Alodia. They would rule for 200 years. Makuria was above the third cataract, along the Dongola Reach with its capital at Dongola. Nobadia was to the north with its capital at Faras, and Alodia was to the south with its capital at Soba. Makuria eventually absorbed Nobadia. The people of the region converted to Monophysite Christianity around 500 to 600 CE. The church initially started writing in Coptic, then in Greek, and finally in Old Nubian, a Nilo-Saharan language. The church was aligned with the Egyptian Coptic Church.[177,178]

By 641, Egypt was conquered by the Rashidun Caliphate. This effectively blocked Christian Nubia and Aksum from Mediterranean Christendom. In 651–652, Arabs from Egypt invaded Christian Nubia. Nubian archers soundly defeated the invaders. The Baqt (or Bakt) Treaty was drawn, recognizing Christian Nubia and regulating trade. The treaty controlled relations between Christian Nubia and Islamic Egypt for almost six hundred years.[179]

By the 13th century, Christian Nubia began its decline. The authority of the monarchy was diminished by the church and nobility. Arab bedouin tribes began to infiltrate Nubia, causing further havoc. *Fakirs* (holy men) practicing Sufism introduced Islam into Nubia. By 1366, Nubia had become divided into petty fiefdoms when it was invaded by Mamluks. During the 15th century, Nubia was open to Arab immigration. Arab nomads intermingled with the population and introduced the Arab culture and the Arabic language. By the 16th century, Makuria and Nobadia had been Islamized. During the 16th century, Abdallah Jamma headed an Arab confederation that destroyed Soba, capital of Alodia, the last holdout of Christian Nubia. Later Alodia would fall under the Funj Sultanate.[180]

During the 15th century, Funj herders migrated north to Alodia and occupied it. Between 1504 and 1505, the kingdom expanded, reaching its peak and establishing its capital at Sennar under Badi II Abu Daqn (c. 1644–1680). By the end of the 16th century, the Funj had converted to Islam. They pushed their empire westward to Kordofan. They expanded eastward, but were halted by Ethiopia. They controlled Nubia down to the 3rd Cataract. The economy depended on captured enemies to fill the army and on merchants travelling through Sennar. Under Badi IV (1724–1762), the army turned on the king, making him nothing but a figurehead. In 1821, the Funj were conquered by Muhammad Ali (1805–1849), Pasha of Egypt.[181]

Southern Africa

Settlements of Bantu-speaking peoples who were iron-using agriculturists and herdsmen were present south of the Limpopo River by the 4th or 5th century CE, displacing and absorbing the original Khoisan speakers. They slowly moved south, and the earliest ironworks in modern-day KwaZulu-Natal Province are believed to date from around 1050. The southernmost group was the Xhosa people, whose language incorporates certain linguistic traits from the earlier Khoi-San people, reaching the Great Fish River in today's Eastern Cape Province. Wikipedia:Citation needed

Great Zimbabwe and Mapungubwe

The Kingdom of Mapungubwe was the first state in Southern Africa, with its capital at Mapungubwe. The state arose in the 12th century CE. Its wealth came from controlling the trade in ivory from the Limpopo Valley, copper from the mountains of northern Transvaal, and gold from the Zimbabwe Plateau between the Limpopo and Zambezi rivers, with the Swahili merchants at Chibuene. By the mid-13th century, Mapungubwe was abandoned.[182]

After the decline of Mapungubwe, Great Zimbabwe rose on the Zimbabwe Plateau. *Zimbabwe* means stone building. Great Zimbabwe was the first city

Figure 37: *Towers of Great Zimbabwe.*

in Southern Africa and was the center of an empire, consolidating lesser Shona polities. Stone building was inherited from Mapungubwe. These building techniques were enhanced and came into maturity at Great Zimbabwe, represented by the wall of the Great Enclosure. The dry-stack stone masonry technology was also used to build smaller compounds in the area. Great Zimbabwe flourished by trading with Swahili Kilwa and Sofala. The rise of Great Zimbabwe parallels the rise of Kilwa. Great Zimbabwe was a major source of gold. Its royal court lived in luxury, wore Indian cotton, surrounded themselves with copper and gold ornaments, and ate on plates from as far away as Persia and China. Around the 1420s and 1430s, Great Zimbabwe was on decline. The city was abandoned by 1450. Some have attributed the decline to the rise of the trading town Ingombe Ilede.[183,184]

A new chapter of Shona history ensued. Nyatsimba Mutota, a northern Shona king of the Karanga, engaged in conquest. He and his son Mutope conquered the Zimbabwe Plateau, going through Mozambique to the east coast, linking the empire to the coastal trade. They called their empire *Wilayatu 'l Mu'anamutapah* or *mwanamutapa* (Lord of the Plundered Lands), or the Kingdom of Mutapa. *Monomotapa* was the Portuguese corruption. They did not build stone structures; the northern Shonas had no traditions of building in stone. After the death of Matope in 1480, the empire split into two small empires: Torwa in the south and Mutapa in the north. The split occurred over

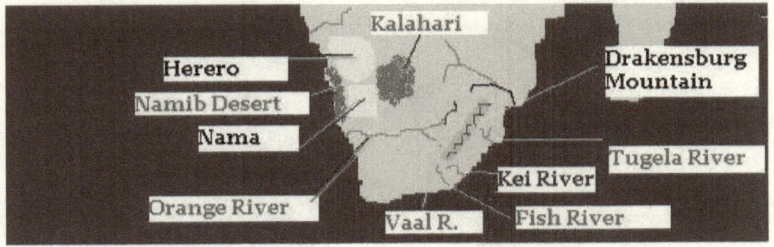

Figure 38: *Herero and Nama territories*

rivalry from two Shona lords, Changa and Togwa, with the *mwanamutapa* line. Changa was able to acquire the south, forming the Kingdom of Butua with its capital at Khami.[185]

The Mutapa Empire continued in the north under the *mwenemutapa* line. During the 16th century the Portuguese were able to establish permanent markets up the Zambezi River in an attempt to gain political and military control of Mutapa. They were partially successful. In 1628, a decisive battle allowed them to put a puppet *mwanamutapa* named Mavura, who signed treaties that gave favorable mineral export rights to the Portuguese. The Portuguese were successful in destroying the *mwanamutapa* system of government and undermining trade. By 1667, Mutapa was in decay. Chiefs would not allow digging for gold because of fear of Portuguese theft, and the population declined.[186]

The Kingdom of Butua was ruled by a *changamire*, a title derived from the founder, Changa. Later it became the Rozwi Empire. The Portuguese tried to gain a foothold but were thrown out of the region in 1693, by Changamire Dombo. The 17th century was a period of peace and prosperity. The Rozwi Empire fell into ruins in the 1830s from invading Nguni from Natal.

Namibia

By 1500 AD, most of southern Africa had established states. In northwestern Namibia, the Ovambo engaged in farming and the Herero engaged in herding. As cattle numbers increased, the Herero moved southward to central Namibia for grazing land. A related group, the Ovambanderu, expanded to Ghanzi in northwestern Botswana. The Nama, a Khoi-speaking, sheep-raising group, moved northward and came into contact with the Herero; this would set the stage for much conflict between the two groups. The expanding Lozi states pushed the Mbukushu, Subiya, and Yei to Botei, Okavango, and Chobe in northern Botswana.[187]

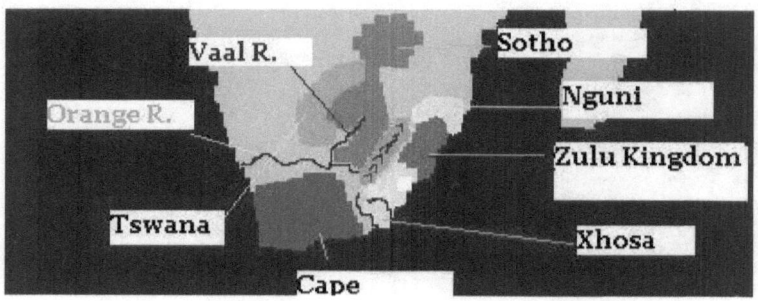

Figure 39: *South African ethnic groups*

South Africa and Botswana

Sotho–Tswana

The development of Sotho–Tswana states based on the highveld, south of the Limpopo River, began around 1000 CE. The chief's power rested on cattle and his connection to the ancestor. This can be seen in the Toutswemogala Hill settlements with stone foundations and stone walls, north of the highveld and south of the Vaal River. Northwest of the Vaal River developed early Tswana states centered on towns of thousands of people. When disagreements or rivalry arose, different groups moved to form their own states.[188]

Nguni peoples

Southeast of the Drakensberg mountains lived Nguni-speaking peoples (Zulu, Xhosa, Swazi, and Ndebele). They too engaged in state building, with new states developing from rivalry, disagreements, and population pressure causing movement into new regions. This 19th-century process of warfare, state building and migration later became known as the Mfecane (Nguni) or Difaqane (Sotho). Its major catalyst was the consolidation of the Zulu Kingdom.[189] They were metalworkers, cultivators of millet, and cattle herders.

Khoisan and Afrikaaner

The Khoisan lived in the southwestern Cape Province, where winter rainfall is plentiful. Earlier Khoisan populations were absorbed by Bantu peoples, such as the Sotho and Nguni, but the Bantu expansion stopped at the region with winter rainfall. Some Bantu languages have incorporated the click consonant of the Khoisan languages. The Khoisan traded with their Bantu neighbors,

Figure 40: *Political map of Southern Africa in 1885*

providing cattle, sheep, and hunted items. In return, their Bantu speaking neighbors traded copper, iron, and tobacco.

By the 16th century, the Dutch East India Company established a replenishing station at Table Bay for restocking water and purchasing meat from the Khoikhoi. The Khoikhoi received copper, iron, tobacco, and beads in exchange. In order to control the price of meat and stock and make service more consistent, the Dutch established a permanent settlement at Table Bay in 1652. They grew fresh fruit and vegetables and established a hospital for sick sailors. To increase produce, the Dutch decided to increase the number of farms at Table Bay by encouraging freeburgher *boers* (farmers) on lands worked initially by slaves from West Africa. The land was taken from Khoikhoi grazing land, triggering the first Khoikhoi-Dutch war in 1659. No victors emerged, but the Dutch assumed a "right of conquest" by which they claimed all of the cape. In a series of wars pitting the Khoikhoi against each other, the Boers assumed all Khoikhoi land and claimed all their cattle. The second Khoikoi-Dutch war (1673–1677) was a cattle raid. The Khoikhoi also died in thousands from European diseases.[190]

By the 18th century, the cape colony had grown, with slaves coming from Madagascar, Mozambique, and Indonesia. The settlement also started to expand northward, but Khoikhoi resistance, raids, and guerrilla warfare slowed

Figure 41: *A traditional Zanzibari-style Swahili coast door in Zanzibar.*

the expansion during the 18th century. Boers who started to practice pastoralism were known as *trekboers*. A common source of *trekboer* labor was orphan children who were captured during raids and whose parents had been killed.[191]

Southeast Africa

Prehistory

According to the theory of recent African origin of modern humans, the mainstream position held within the scientific community, all humans originate from either Southeast Africa or the Horn of Africa. During the first millennium CE, Nilotic and Bantu-speaking peoples moved into the region.Wikipedia:Citation needed

Swahili coast

Following the Bantu Migration, on the coastal section of Southeast Africa, a mixed Bantu community developed through contact with Muslim Arab and Persian traders, leading to the development of the mixed Arab, Persian and African Swahili City States. The Swahili culture that emerged from these exchanges evinces many Arab and Islamic influences not seen in traditional Bantu culture, as do the many Afro-Arab members of the Bantu Swahili people. With

Figure 42: *Arab slave traders and their captives along the Ruvuma River in Mozambique along the Swahili coast.*

its original speech community centered on the coastal parts of Tanzania (particularly Zanzibar) and Kenya—a seaboard referred to as the Swahili Coast—the Bantu Swahili language contains many Arabic language loan-words as a consequence of these interactions.[192]

The earliest Bantu inhabitants of the Southeast coast of Kenya and Tanzania encountered by these later Arab and Persian settlers have been variously identified with the trading settlements of Rhapta, Azania and Menouthias[193] referenced in early Greek and Chinese writings from 50 AD to 500 AD,[194,195,196,197,198,199] ultimately giving rise to the name for Tanzania.[200,201] These early writings perhaps document the first wave of Bantu settlers to reach Southeast Africa during their migration.[202]

Historically, the Swahili people could be found as far north as northern Kenya and as far south as the Ruvuma River in Mozambique. Arab geographers referred to the Swahili coast as the land of the *zanj* (blacks).[203]

Although once believed to be the descendants of Persian colonists, the ancient Swahili are now recognized by most historians, historical linguists, and archaeologists as a Bantu people who had sustained important interactions with Muslim merchants, beginning in the late 7th and early 8th centuries AD.

Medieval Swahili kingdoms are known to have had island trade ports, described by Greek historians as "metropolises", and to have established regular trade routes[204] with the Islamic world and Asia.[205] Ports such as Mombasa,

Zanzibar, and Kilwa were known to Chinese sailors under Zheng He and medieval Islamic geographers such as the Berber traveller Abu Abdullah ibn Battuta.[206] The main Swahili exports were ivory, slaves, and gold. They traded with Arabia, India, Persia, and China.

The Portuguese arrived in 1498. On a mission to economically control and Christianize the Swahili coast, the Portuguese attacked Kilwa first in 1505 and other cities later. Because of Swahili resistance, the Portuguese attempt at establishing commercial control was never successful. By the late 17th century, Portuguese authority on the Swahili coast began to diminish. With the help of Omani Arabs, by 1729 the Portuguese presence had been removed. The Swahili coast eventually became part of the Sultanate of Oman. Trade recovered, but it did not regain the levels of the past.[207]

Urewe

The **Urewe** culture developed and spread in and around the Lake Victoria region of Africa during the African Iron Age. The culture's earliest dated artifacts are located in the Kagera Region of Tanzania, and it extended as far west as the Kivu region of the Democratic Republic of the Congo, as far east as the Nyanza and Western provinces of Kenya, and north into Uganda, Rwanda and Burundi. Sites from the Urewe culture date from the Early Iron Age, from the 5th century BC to the 6th century AD.

The origins of the Urewe culture are ultimately in the Bantu expansion originating in Cameroon. Research into early Iron Age civilizations in Sub-Saharan Africa has been undertaken concurrently with studies on African linguistics on Bantu expansion. The Urewe culture may correspond to the Eastern subfamily of Bantu languages, spoken by the descendants of the first wave of Bantu peoples to settle East Africa. At first sight, Urewe seems to be a fully developed civilization recognizable through its distinctive, stylish earthenware and highly technical and sophisticated iron working techniques. Given our current level of knowledge, neither seems to have developed or altered for nearly 2,000 years. However, minor local variations in the ceramic ware can be observed.Wikipedia:Citation needed

Urewe is the name of the site in Kenya brought to prominence through the publication in 1948 of Mary Leakey's archaeological findings. She described the early Iron Age period in the Great Lakes region in Central East Africa around Lake Victoria.

Madagascar and Merina

Madagascar was apparently first settled by Austronesian speakers from Southeast Asia before the 6th century AD and subsequently by Bantu speakers from the east African mainland in the 6th or 7th century, according to archaeological and linguistic data. The Austronesians introduced banana and rice cultivation, and the Bantu speakers introduced cattle and other farming practices. About the year 1000, Arab and Indian trade settlement were started in northern Madagascar to exploit the Indian Ocean trade.[208] By the 14th century, Islam was introduced on the island by traders. Madagascar functioned in the East African medieval period as a contact port for the other Swahili seaport city-states such as Sofala, Kilwa, Mombasa, and Zanzibar.Wikipedia:Citation needed

Several kingdoms emerged after the 15th century: the Sakalava Kingdom (16th century) on the west coast, Tsitambala Kingdom (17th century) on the east coast, and Merina (15th century) in the central highlands. By the 19th century, Merina controlled the whole island. In 1500, the Portuguese were the first Europeans on the island, raiding the trading settlements.[209]

The British and later the French arrived. During the latter part of the 17th century, Madagascar was a popular transit point for pirates. Radama I (1810–1828) invited Christian missionaries in the early 19th century. Queen Ranavalona I "the Cruel" (1828–61) banned the practice of Christianity in the kingdom, and an estimated 150,000 Christians perished. Under Radama II (1861–1863), Madagascar took a French orientation, with great commercial concession given to the French. In 1895, in the second Franco-Hova War, the French invaded Madagascar, taking over Antsiranana (Diego Suarez) and declaring Madagascar a protectorate.

Lake Plateau states and empires

Between the 14th and 15th centuries, large Southeast African kingdoms and states emerged, such as the Buganda[210] and Karagwe Kingdoms of Uganda and Tanzania.Wikipedia:Citation needed

Kitara and Bunyoro

By 1000 AD, numerous states had arisen on the Lake Plateau among the Great Lakes of East Africa. Cattle herding, cereal growing, and banana cultivation were the economic mainstays of these states. The Ntusi and Bigo earthworks are representative of one of the first states, the Bunyoro kingdom, which oral tradition stipulates was part of the Empire of Kitara that dominated the whole Lakes region. A Luo ethnic elite, from the Bito clan, ruled over the Bantu-speaking Nyoro people. The society was essentially Nyoro in its culture, based on the evidence from pottery, settlement patterns, and economic specialization.[211]

The Bito clan claimed legitimacy by being descended from the Bachwezi clan, who were said to have ruled the Empire of Kitara. However, very little is known about Kitara; some scholars even question its historical existence. Most founding leaders of the various polities in the lake region seem to have claimed descent from the Bachwezi. There are now 13 million Tara who are part of the second African loss,(Nafi and Uma are two losses).Wikipedia:Citation needed

Buganda

The Buganda kingdom was founded by Kato Kintu around the 14th century AD. Kato Kintu may have migrated to the northwest of Lake Victoria as early as 1000 BC. Buganda was ruled by the *kabaka* with a *bataka* composed of the clan heads. Over time, the *kabakas* diluted the authority of the *bataka*, with Buganda becoming a centralized monarchy. By the 16th century, Buganda was engaged in expansion but had a serious rival in Bunyoro. By the 1870s, Buganda was a wealthy nation-state. The *kabaka* ruled with his *Lukiko* (council of ministers). Buganda had a naval fleet of a hundred vessels, each manned by thirty men. Buganda supplanted Bunyoro as the most important state in the region. However, by the early 20th century, Buganda became a province of the British Uganda Protectorate.[212]

Rwanda

Southeast of Bunyoro, near Lake Kivu at the bottom of the western rift, the Kingdom of Rwanda was founded, perhaps during the 17th century. Tutsi (BaTutsi) pastoralists formed the elite, with a king called the *mwami*. The Hutu (BaHutu) were farmers. Both groups spoke the same language, but there were strict social norms against marrying each other and interaction. According to oral tradition, the Kingdom of Rwanda was founded by Mwami Ruganzu II (Ruganzu Ndori) (c. 1600–1624), with his capital near Kigali. It took 200 years to attain a truly centralized kingdom under Mwami Kigeli IV (Kigeri Rwabugiri) (1840–1895). Subjugation of the Hutu proved more difficult than subduing the Tutsi. The last Tutsi chief gave up to Mwami Mutara II (Mutara Rwogera) (1802–1853) in 1852, but the last Hutu holdout was conquered in the 1920s by Mwami Yuhi V (Yuli Musinga) (1896–1931).[213]

Burundi

South of the Kingdom of Rwanda was the Kingdom of Burundi. It was founded by the Tutsi chief Ntare Rushatsi (c. 1657–1705). Like Rwanda, Burundi was built on cattle raised by Tutsi pastoralists, crops from Hutu farmers, conquest, and political innovations. Under Mwami Ntari Rugaamba (c.

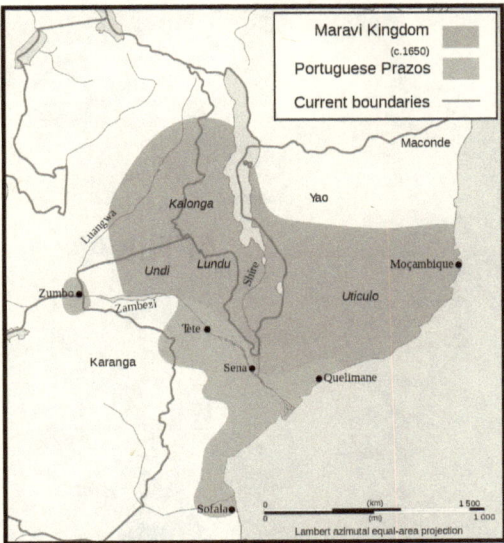

Figure 43: *Maravi Kingdom*

1795–1852), Burundi pursued an aggressive expansionist policy, one based more on diplomacy than force.[214]

Maravi (Malawi)

The Maravi claimed descent from Karonga (*kalonga*), who took that title as king. The Maravi connected Central Africa to the east coastal trade, with Swahili Kilwa. By the 17th century, the Maravi Empire encompassed all the area between Lake Malawi and the mouth of the Zambezi River. The *karonga* was Mzura, who did much to extend the empire. Mzura made a pact with the Portuguese to establish a 4,000-man army to attack the Shona in return for aid in defeating his rival Lundi, a chief of the Zimba. In 1623, he turned on the Portuguese and assisted the Shona. In 1640, he welcomed back the Portuguese for trade. The Maravi Empire did not long survive the death of Mzura. By the 18th century, it had broken into its previous polities.[215]

Figure 44: *Ghana at its greatest extent*

West Africa

Sahelian empires & states

Ghana

The Ghana Empire may have been an established kingdom as early as the 8th century AD, founded among the Soninke by Dinge Cisse. Ghana was first mentioned by Arab geographer Al-Farazi in the late 8th century. Ghana was inhabited by urban dwellers and rural farmers. The urban dwellers were the administrators of the empire, who were Muslims, and the *Ghana* (king), who practiced traditional religion. Two towns existed, one where the Muslim administrators and Berber-Arabs lived, which was connected by a stone-paved road to the king's residence. The rural dwellers lived in villages, which joined together into broader polities that pledged loyalty to the *Ghana*. The *Ghana* was viewed as divine, and his physical well-being reflected on the whole society. Ghana converted to Islam around 1050, after conquering Aoudaghost.[216]

The Ghana Empire grew wealthy by taxing the trans-Saharan trade that linked Tiaret and Sijilmasa to Aoudaghost. Ghana controlled access to the goldfields of Bambouk, southeast of Koumbi Saleh. A percentage of salt and gold going through its territory was taken. The empire was not involved in production.[217]

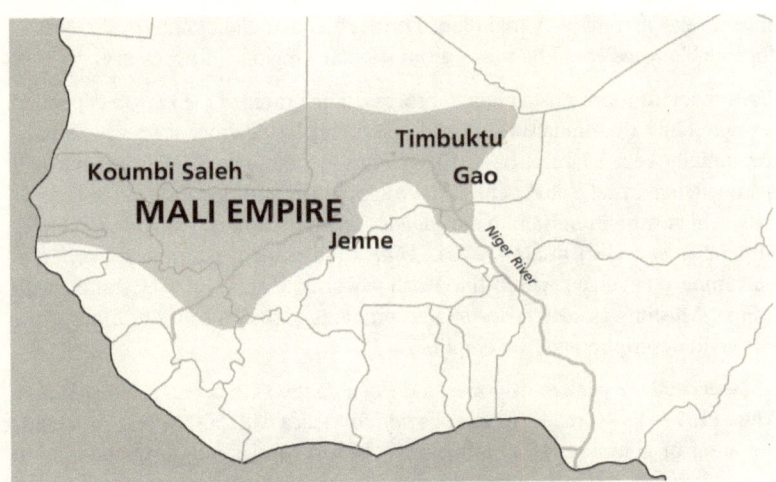

Figure 45: *Mali Empire at its greatest extent*

By the 11th century, Ghana was in decline. It was once thought that the sacking of Koumbi Saleh by Berbers under the Almoravid dynasty in 1076 was the cause. This is no longer accepted. Several alternative explanations are cited. One important reason is the transfer of the gold trade east to the Niger River and the Taghaza Trail, and Ghana's consequent economic decline. Another reason cited is political instability through rivalry among the different hereditary polities.[218] The empire came to an end in 1230, when Takrur in northern Senegal took over the capital.[219,220]

Mali

The Mali Empire began in the 13th century AD, when a Mande (Mandingo) leader, Sundiata (Lord Lion) of the Keita clan, defeated Soumaoro Kanté, king of the Sosso or southern Soninke, at the Battle of Kirina in c. 1235. Sundiata continued his conquest from the fertile forests and Niger Valley, east to the Niger Bend, north into the Sahara, and west to the Atlantic Ocean, absorbing the remains of the Ghana Empire. Sundiata took on the title of *mansa*. He established the capital of his empire at Niani.[221]

Although the salt and gold trade continued to be important to the Mali Empire, agriculture and pastoralism was also critical. The growing of sorghum, millet, and rice was a vital function. On the northern borders of the Sahel, grazing cattle, sheep, goats, and camels were major activities. Mande society was organize around the village and land. A cluster of villages was called a *kafu*, ruled by a *farma*. The *farma* paid tribute to the *mansa*. A dedicated army of elite cavalry and infantry maintained order, commanded by the royal court. A formidable force could be raised from tributary regions, if necessary.[222]

Conversion to Islam was a gradual process. The power of the *mansa* depended on upholding traditional beliefs and a spiritual foundation of power. Sundiata initially kept Islam at bay. Later *mansas* were devout Muslims but still acknowledged traditional deities and took part in traditional rituals and festivals, which were important to the Mande. Islam became a court religion under Sundiata's son Uli I (1225–1270). *Mansa* Uli made a pilgrimage to Mecca, becoming recognized within the Muslim world. The court was staffed with literate Muslims as secretaries and accountants. Muslim traveller Ibn Battuta left vivid descriptions of the empire.

Mali reached the peak of its power and extent in the 14th century, when *Mansa* Musa (1312–1337) made his famous *hajj* to Mecca with 500 slaves, each holding a bar of gold worth 500 mitqals.[223] *Mansa* Musa's *hajj* devalued gold in Mamluk Egypt for a decade. He made a great impression on the minds of the Muslim and European world. He invited scholars and architects like Ishal al-Tuedjin (al-Sahili) to further integrate Mali into the Islamic world.

The Mali Empire saw an expansion of learning and literacy. In 1285, Sakura, a freed slave, usurped the throne. This *mansa* drove the Tuareg out of Timbuktu and established it as a center of learning and commerce. The book trade increased, and book copying became a very respectable and profitable profession. Timbuktu and Djenné became important centers of learning within the Islamic world.[224]

After the reign of Mansa Suleyman (1341–1360), Mali began its spiral downward. Mossi cavalry raided the exposed southern border. Tuareg harassed the northern border in order to retake Timbuktu. Fulani (Fulbe) eroded Mali's authority in the west by establishing the independent Imamate of Futa Toro, a successor to the kingdom of Takrur. Serer and Wolof alliances were broken. In 1545 to 1546, the Songhai Empire took Niani. After 1599, the empire lost the Bambouk goldfields and disintegrated into petty polities.

Songhai

The Songhai people are descended from fishermen on the Middle Niger River. They established their capital at Kukiya in the 9th century AD and at Gao in the 12th century. The Songhai speak a Nilo-Saharan language.[225]

Sonni Ali, a Songhai, began his conquest by capturing Timbuktu in 1468 from the Tuareg. He extended the empire to the north, deep into the desert, pushed the Mossi further south of the Niger, and expanded southwest to Djenne. His army consisted of cavalry and a fleet of canoes. Sonni Ali was not a Muslim,

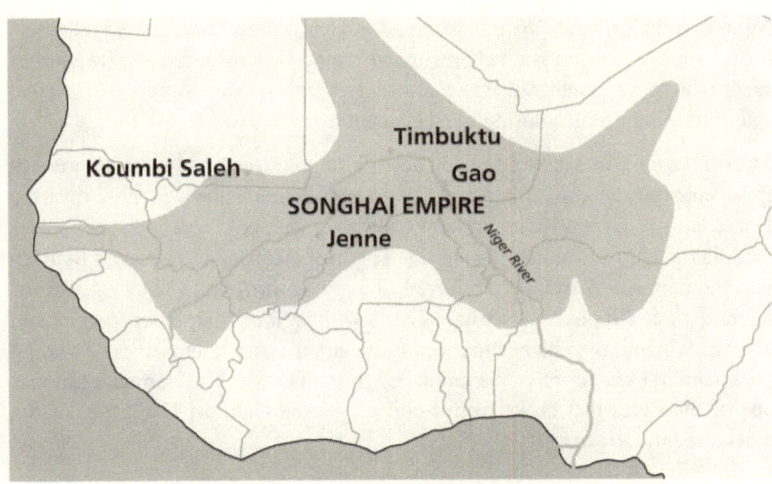

Figure 46: *The Songhai Empire, c. 1500*

and he was portrayed negatively by Berber-Arab scholars, especially for attacking Muslim Timbuktu. After his death in 1492, his heirs were deposed by General Muhammad Ture, a Muslim of Soninke origins[226]

Muhammad Ture (1493–1528) founded the Askiya Dynasty, *askiya* being the title of the king. He consolidated the conquests of Sonni Ali. Islam was used to extend his authority by declaring jihad on the Mossi, reviving the trans-Saharan trade, and having the Abbasid "shadow" caliph in Cairo declare him as caliph of Sudan. He established Timbuktu as a great center of Islamic learning. Muhammad Ture expanded the empire by pushing the Tuareg north, capturing Aïr in the east, and capturing salt-producing Taghaza. He brought the Hausa states into the Songhay trading network. He further centralized the administration of the empire by selecting administrators from loyal servants and families and assigning them to conquered territories. They were responsible for raising local militias. Centralization made Songhay very stable, even during dynastic disputes. Leo Africanus left vivid descriptions of the empire under Askiya Muhammad. Askiya Muhammad was deposed by his son in 1528. After much rivalry, Muhammad Ture's last son Askiya Daoud (1529–1582) assumed the throne.[227]

In 1591, Morocco invaded the Songhai Empire under Ahmad al-Mansur of the Saadi Dynasty in order to secure the goldfields of the Sahel. At the Battle of Tondibi, the Songhai army was defeated. The Moroccans captured Djenne, Gao, and Timbuktu, but they were unable to secure the whole region. Askiya

Nuhu and the Songhay army regrouped at Dendi in the heart of Songhai territory where a spirited guerrilla resistance sapped the resources of the Moroccans, who were dependent upon constant resupply from Morocco. Songhai split into several states during the 17th century.

Morocco found its venture unprofitable. The gold trade had been diverted to Europeans on the coast. Most of the trans-Saharan trade was now diverted east to Bornu. Expensive equipment purchased with gold had to be sent across the Sahara, an unsustainable scenario. The Moroccans who remained married into the population and were referred to as *Arma* or *Ruma*. They established themselves at Timbuktu as a military caste with various fiefs, independent from Morocco. Amid the chaos, other groups began to assert themselves, including the Fulani of Futa Tooro who encroached from the west. The Bambara Empire, one of the states that broke from Songhai, sacked Gao. In 1737, the Tuareg massacred the *Arma*.[228,229]

Sokoto Caliphate

The Fulani were migratory people. They moved from Mauritania and settled in Futa Tooro, Futa Djallon, and subsequently throughout the rest of West Africa. By the 14th century CE, they had converted to Islam. During the 16th century, they established themselves at Macina in southern Mali. During the 1670s, they declared jihads on non-Muslims. Several states were formed from these jihadist wars, at Futa Toro, Futa Djallon, Macina, Oualia, and Bundu. The most important of these states was the Sokoto Caliphate or Fulani Empire.Wikipedia:Citation needed

In the city of Gobir, Usman dan Fodio (1754–1817) accused the Hausa leadership of practicing an impure version of Islam and of being morally corrupt. In 1804, he launched the Fulani War as a jihad among a population that was restless about high taxes and discontented with its leaders. Jihad fever swept northern Nigeria, with strong support among both the Fulani and the Hausa. Usman created an empire that included parts of northern Nigeria, Benin, and Cameroon, with Sokoto as its capital. He retired to teach and write and handed the empire to his son Muhammed Bello. The Sokoto Caliphate lasted until 1903 when the British conquered northern Nigeria.[230]

Figure 47: *Ashanti Kente cloth patterns*

Forest empires and states

Akan kingdoms and emergence of Asante Empire

The Akan speak a Kwa language. The speakers of Kwa languages are believed to have come from East/Central Africa, before settling in the Sahel. By the 12th century, the Akan Kingdom of Bonoman (Bono State) was established. During the 13th century, when the gold mines in modern-day Mali started to dry up, Bonoman and later other Akan states began to rise to prominence as the major players in the Gold trade. It was Bonoman and other Akan kingdoms like Denkyira, Akyem, Akwamu which were the predecessors to what became the all-powerful Empire of Ashanti. When and how the Ashante got to their present location is debatable. What is known is that by the 17th century an Akan people were identified as living in a state called Kwaaman. The location of the state was north of Lake Bosomtwe. The state's revenue was mainly derived from trading in gold and kola nuts and clearing forest to plant yams. They built towns between the Pra and Ofin rivers. They formed alliances for defense and paid tribute to Denkyira one of the more powerful Akan states at that time along with Adansi and Akwamu. During the 16th century, Ashante society experienced sudden changes, including population growth because of cultivation of New World plants such as cassava and maize and an increase in the gold trade between the coast and the north.[231]

By the 17th century, Osei Kofi Tutu I (c. 1695–1717), with help of Okomfo Anokye, unified what became the Ashante into a confederation with the Golden Stool as a symbol of their unity and spirit. Osei Tutu engaged in a massive territorial expansion. He built up the Ashante army based on the Akan state of Akwamu, introducing new organization and turning a disciplined militia into an effective fighting machine. In 1701, the Ashante conquered Denkyira, giving them access to the coastal trade with Europeans, especially the Dutch. Opoku Ware I (1720–1745) engaged in further expansion, adding other southern Akan states to the growing empire. He turned north adding Techiman, Banda, Gyaaman, and Gonja, states on the Black Volta. Between 1744 and 1745, *Asantehene* Opoku attacked the powerful northern state of Dagomba, gaining control of the important middle Niger trade routes. Kusi Obodom (1750–1764) succeeded Opoku. He solidified all the newly won territories. Osei Kwadwo (1777–1803) imposed administrative reforms that allowed the empire to be governed effectively and to continue its military expansion. Osei Kwame Panyin (1777–1803), Osei Tutu Kwame (1804–1807), and Osei Bonsu (1807–1824) continued territorial consolidation and expansion. The Ashante Empire included all of present-day Ghana and large parts of the Ivory Coast.[232]

The *ashantehene* inherited his position from his mother. He was assisted at the capital, Kumasi, by a civil service of men talented in trade, diplomacy, and the military, with a head called the *Gyaasehene*. Men from Arabia, Sudan, and Europe were employed in the civil service, all of them appointed by the *ashantehene*. At the capital and in other towns, the *ankobia* or special police were used as bodyguards to the *ashantehene*, as sources of intelligence, and to suppress rebellion. Communication throughout the empire was maintained via a network of well-kept roads from the coast to the middle Niger and linking together other trade cities.[233,234]

For most of the 19th century, the Ashante Empire remained powerful. It was later destroyed in 1900 by British superior weaponry and organization following the four Anglo-Ashanti wars.[235]

Dahomey

The Dahomey Kingdom was founded in the early 17th century when the Aja people of the Allada kingdom moved northward and settled among the Fon. They began to assert their power a few years later. In so doing they established the Kingdom of Dahomey, with its capital at Agbome. King Houegbadja (c. 1645–1685) organized Dahomey into a powerful centralized state. He declared all lands to be owned of the king and subject to taxation. Primogeniture in the kingship was established, neutralizing all input from village chiefs. A

Figure 48: *Dahomey Amazons, an all-women fighting unit*

"cult of kingship" was established. A captive slave would be sacrificed annually to honor the royal ancestors. During the 1720s, the slave-trading states of Whydah and Allada were taken, giving Dahomey direct access to the slave coast and trade with Europeans. King Agadja (1708–1740) attempted to end the slave trade by keeping the slaves on plantations producing palm oil, but the European profits on slaves and Dahomey's dependency on firearms were too great. In 1730, under king Agaja, Dahomey was conquered by the Oyo Empire, and Dahomey had to pay tribute. Taxes on slaves were mostly paid in cowrie shells. During the 19th century, palm oil was the main trading commodity.[236] France conquered Dahomey during the Second Franco-Dahomean War (1892–1894) and established a colonial government there. Most of the troops who fought against Dahomey were native Africans. Wikipedia:Citation needed

Yoruba

Traditionally, the Yoruba people viewed themselves as the inhabitants of a united empire, in contrast to the situation today, in which "Yoruba" is the cultural-linguistic designation for speakers of a language in the Niger–Congo family. The name comes from a Hausa word to refer to the Oyo Empire. The first Yoruba state was Ile-Ife, said to have been founded around 1000 AD by a supernatural figure, the first *oni* Oduduwa. Oduduwa's sons would be the founders of the different city-states of the Yoruba, and his daughters would become the mothers of the various Yoruba *obas*, or kings. Yoruba city-states were usually governed by an *oba* and an *iwarefa*, a council of chiefs

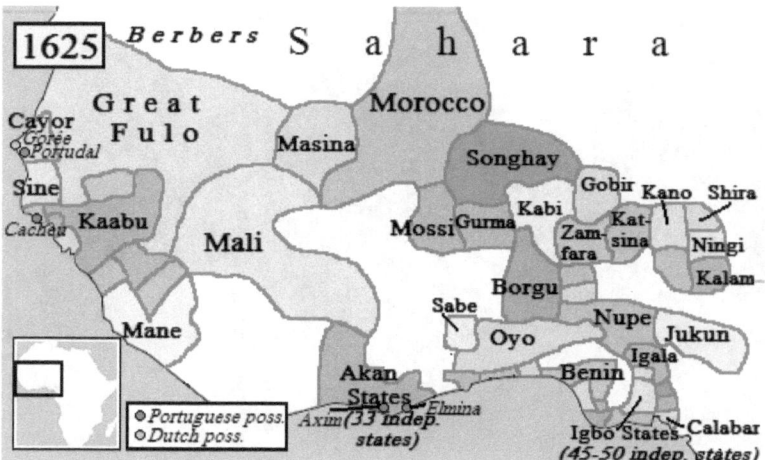

Figure 49: *Oyo Empire and surrounding states, c. 1625*

who advised the *oba*. by the 18th century, the Yoruba city-states formed a loose confederation, with the *Oni* of Ife as the head and Ife as the capital. As time went on, the individual city-states became more powerful with their *obas* assuming more powerful spiritual positions and diluting the authority of the *Oni* of Ife. Rivalry became intense among the city-states.[237]

The Oyo Empire rose in the 16th century. The Oyo state had been conquered in 1550 by the kingdom of Nupe, which was in possession of cavalry, an important tactical advantage. The *alafin* (king) of Oyo was sent into exile. After returning, *Alafin* Orompoto (c. 1560–1580) built up an army based on heavily armed cavalry and long-service troops. This made them invincible in combat on the northern grasslands and in the thinly wooded forests. By the end of the 16th century, Oyo had added the western region of the Niger to the hills of Togo, the Yoruba of Ketu, Dahomey, and the Fon nation.Wikipedia:Citation needed

A governing council served the empire, with clear executive divisions. Each acquired region was assigned a local administrator. Families served in king-making capacities. Oyo, as a northern Yoruba kingdom, served as middle-man in the north-south trade and connecting the eastern forest of Guinea with the western and central Sudan, the Sahara, and North Africa. The Yoruba manufactured cloth, ironware, and pottery, which were exchanged for salt, leather, and most importantly horses from the Sudan to maintain the cavalry. Oyo remained strong for two hundred years.[238,239] It became a protectorate of Great

Figure 50: *"Benin Bronze" (brass)*

Britain in 1888, before further fragmenting into warring factions. The Oyo state ceased to exist as any sort of power in 1896.[240]

Benin

The Kwa Niger–Congo speaking Edo people had established the Benin Empire by the middle of the 15th century. It was engaged in political expansion and consolidation from its very beginning. Under *Oba* (king) Ewuare (c. 1450–1480 AD), the state was organized for conquest. He solidified central authority and initiated 30 years of war with his neighbors. At his death, the Benin Empire extended to Dahomey in the west, to the Niger Delta in the east, along the west African coast, and to the Yoruba towns in the north.Wikipedia:Citation needed

Ewuare's grandson *Oba* Esigie (1504–1550) eroded the power of the *uzama* (state council) and increased contact and trade with Europeans, especially with the Portuguese who provided a new source of copper for court art. The *oba* ruled with the advice of the *uzama*, a council consisting of chiefs of powerful families and town chiefs of different guilds. Later its authority was diminished by the establishment of administrative dignitaries. Women wielded power. The queen mother who produced the future *oba* wielded immense influence.[241]

Benin was never a significant exporter of slaves, as Alan Ryder's book Benin and the Europeans showed. By the early 18th century, it was wrecked with dynastic disputes and civil wars. However, it regained much of its former power in the reigns of Oba Eresoyen and Oba Akengbuda. After the 16th century, Benin mainly exported pepper, ivory, gum, and cotton cloth to the Portuguese and Dutch who resold it to other African societies on the coast. In 1897, the British sacked the city.[242]

Niger Delta and Igbo

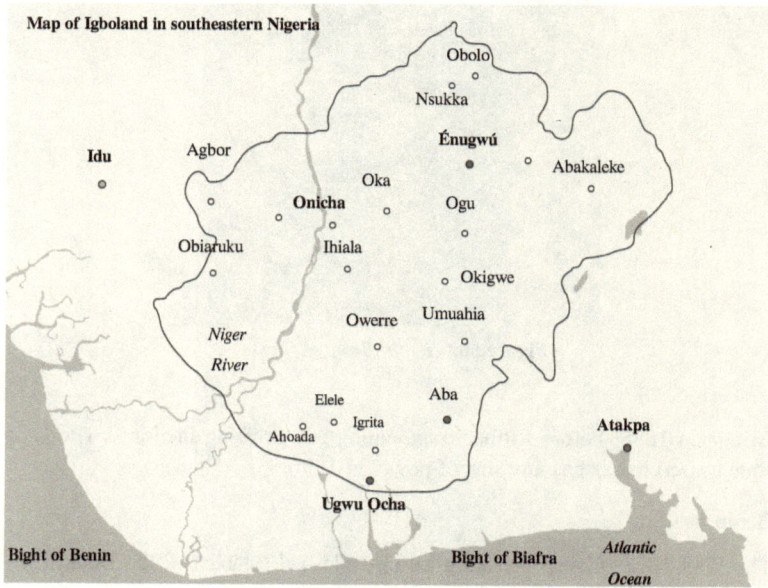

The Niger Delta comprised numerous city-states with numerous forms of government. These city-states were protected by the waterways and thick vegetation of the delta. The region was transformed by trade in the 17th century. The delta's city-states were comparable to those of the Swahili people in East Africa. Some, like Bonny, Kalabari, and Warri, had kings. Others, like Brass, were republics with small senates, and those at Cross River and Old Calabar were ruled by merchants of the *ekpe* society. The *ekpe* society regulated trade and made rules for members known as house systems. Some of these houses, like the Pepples of Bonny, were well known in the Americas and Europe.[243]

The Igbo lived east of the delta (but with the Anioma on the west of the Niger River). The Kingdom of Nri rose in the 9th century, with the *Eze* Nri being its leader. It was a political entity composed of villages, and each village was autonomous and independent with its own territory and name, each recognized by its neighbors. Villages were democratic with all males and sometimes females a part of the decision-making process. Graves at Igbo-Ukwu (800 AD) contained brass artifacts of local manufacture and glass beads from Egypt or India, indicative of extraregional trade.[244,245]

19th century

Southern Africa

By the 1850s, British and German missionaries and traders had penetrated present-day Namibia. Herero and Nama competed for guns and ammunition, providing cattle, ivory, and ostrich feathers. The Germans were more firmly established than the British in the region. By 1884, the Germans declared the coastal region from the Orange River to the Kunene River a German protectorate, part of German South West Africa. They pursued an aggressive policy of land expansion for white settlements. They exploited rivalry between the Nama and Herero.[246]

The Herero entered into an alliance with the Germans, thinking they could get an upper hand on the Nama. The Germans set up a garrison at the Herero capital and started allocating Herero land for white settlements, including the best grazing land in the central plateau, and made tax and labor demands. The Herero and Ovambanderu rebelled, but the rebellion was crushed and leaders were executed. Between 1896 and 1897, rinderpest crippled the economic backbone of the Herero and Nama economy and slowed white expansion. The Germans continued the policy of making Namibia a white settlement by seizing land and cattle, and even trying to export Herero labor to South Africa.[247]

In 1904, the Herero rebelled. German General Lothar von Trotha implemented an extermination policy at the Battle of Waterberg, which drove the Herero west of the Kalahari Desert. At the end of 1905, only 16,000 Herero were alive, out of a previous population of 80,000. Nama resistance was crushed in 1907. All Nama and Herero cattle and land were confiscated from the very diminished population, with remaining Nama and Herero assuming a subordinate position. Labor had to be imported from among the Ovambo.[248]

Nguniland

A moment of great disorder in southern Africa was the *Mfecane*, "the crushing." It was started by the northern Nguni kingdoms of Mthethwa, Ndwandwe, and Swaziland over scarce resource and famine. When Dingiswayo of Mthethwa died, Shaka of the Zulu people took over. He established the Zulu Kingdom, asserting authority over the Ndwandwe and pushing the Swazi north. The scattering Ndwandwe and Swazi caused the Mfecane to spread. During the 1820s, Shaka expanded the empire all along the Drakensberg foothills, with tribute being paid as far south as the Tugela and Umzimkulu rivers. He replaced the chiefs of conquered polities with *indunas*, responsible to him. He introduced a centralized, dedicated, and disciplined military force not seen in the region, with a new weapon in the short stabbing-spear.[249]

In 1828, Shaka was assassinated by his half brother Dingane, who lacked the military genius and leadership skills of Shaka. Voortrekkers tried to occupy Zulu land in 1838. In the early months they were defeated, but the survivors regrouped at the Ncome River and soundly defeated the Zulu. However, the Voortrekkers dared not settle Zulu land. Dingane was killed in 1840 during a civil war. His brother Mpande took over and strengthened Zulu territories to the north. In 1879 the Zulu Kingdom was invaded by Britain in a quest to control all of South Africa. The Zulu Kingdom was victorious at the Battle of Isandlwana but was defeated at the Battle of Ulundi.[250,251]

One of the major states to emerge from the Mfecane was the Sotho Kingdom founded at Thaba Bosiu by Moshoeshoe I around 1821 to 1822. It was a confederation of different polities that accepted the absolute authority of Moshoeshoe. During the 1830s, the kingdom invited missionaries as a strategic means of acquiring guns and horses from the Cape. The Orange Free State slowly diminished the kingdom but never completely defeated it. In 1868, Moshoeshoe asked that the Sotho Kingdom be annexed by Britain, to save the remnant. It became the British protectorate of Basutoland.[252]

Voortrekkers

By the 19th century, most Khoikhoi territory was under Boer control. The Khoikhoi had lost economic and political independence and had been absorbed into Boer society. The Boers spoke Afrikaans, a language or dialect derived from Dutch, and no longer called themselves Boers but Afrikaners. Some Khoikhoi were used as commandos in raids against other Khoikhoi and later Xhosa. A mixed Khoi, slave, and European population called the Cape Coloureds, who were outcasts within colonial society, also arose. Khoikhoi who lived far on the frontier included the Kora, Oorlams, and Griqua. In 1795, the British took over the cape colony from the Dutch.[253]

In the 1830s, Boers embarked on a journey of expansion, east of the Great Fish River into the Zuurveld. They were referred to as *Voortrekkers*. They founded republics of the Transvaal and Orange Free State, mostly in areas of sparse population that had been diminished by the *Mfecane/Difaqane*. Unlike the Khoisan, the Bantu states were not conquered by the Afrikaners, because of population density and greater unity. Additionally, they began to arm themselves with guns acquired through trade at the cape. In some cases, as in the Xhosa/Boer Wars, Boers were removed from Xhosa lands. It required a dedicated imperial military force to subdue the Bantu-speaking states. In 1901,

Figure 51: *1895 .303 tripod mounted Maxim machine gun*

the Boer republics were defeated by Britain in the Second Boer War. The defeat however consummated many Afrikaners' ambition: South Africa would be under white rule. The British placed all power—legislative, executive, administrative—in English and Afrikaner hands.[254]

European trade, exploration and conquest

Between 1878 and 1898, European states partitioned and conquered most of Africa. For 400 years, European nations had mainly limited their involvement to trading stations on the African coast. Few dared venture inland from the coast; those that did, like the Portuguese, often met defeats and had to retreat to the coast. Several technological innovations helped to overcome this 400-year pattern. One was the development of repeating rifles, which were easier and quicker to load than muskets. Artillery was being used increasingly. In 1885, Hiram S. Maxim developed the maxim gun, the model of the modern-day machine gun. European states kept these weapons largely among themselves by refusing to sell these weapons to African leaders.[255]

African germs took numerous European lives and deterred permanent settlements. Diseases such as yellow fever, sleeping sickness, yaws, and leprosy made Africa a very inhospitable place for Europeans. The deadliest disease was malaria, endemic throughout Tropical Africa. In 1854, the discovery of

Figure 52: *David Livingstone, early European explorer of the interior of Africa*

quinine and other medical innovations helped to make conquest and colonization in Africa possible.[256]

Strong motives for conquest of Africa were at play. Raw materials were needed for European factories. Europe in the early part of the 19th century was undergoing its Industrial Revolution. Nationalist rivalries and prestige were at play. Acquiring African colonies would show rivals that a nation was powerful and significant. These factors culminated in the Scramble for Africa.[257]

Knowledge of Africa increased. Numerous European explorers began to explore the continent. Mungo Park traversed the Niger River. James Bruce travelled through Ethiopia and located the source of the Blue Nile. Richard Francis Burton was the first European at Lake Tanganyika. Samuel White Baker explored the Upper Nile. John Hanning Speke located a source of the Nile at Lake Victoria. Other significant European explorers included Heinrich Barth, Henry Morton Stanley (coiner of the term "Dark Continent" for Africa in an 1878 book), Silva Porto, Alexandre de Serpa Pinto, Rene Caille, Friedrich Gerhard Rohlfs, Gustav Nachtigal, George Schweinfurth, and Joseph Thomson. The most famous of the explorers was David Livingstone, who explored southern Africa and traversed the continent from the Atlantic at Luanda to the Indian Ocean at Quelimane. European explorers made use of African guides and servants, and established long-distance trading routes were used.[258,259]

Missionaries attempting to spread Christianity also increased European knowledge of Africa. Between 1884 and 1885, European nations met at the Berlin West Africa Conference to discuss the partitioning of Africa. It was agreed that European claims to parts of Africa would only be recognised if Europeans provided effective occupation. In a series of treaties in 1890–1891, colonial boundaries were completely drawn. All of Sub-Saharan Africa was claimed by European powers, except for Ethiopia (Abyssinia) and Liberia.Wikipedia:Citation needed

The European powers set up a variety of different administrations in Africa, reflecting different ambitions and degrees of power. In some areas, such as parts of British West Africa, colonial control was tenuous and intended for simple economic extraction, strategic power, or as part of a long term development plan. In other areas, Europeans were encouraged to settle, creating settler states in which a European minority dominated. Settlers only came to a few colonies in sufficient numbers to have a strong impact. British settler colonies included British East Africa (now Kenya), Northern and Southern Rhodesia, (Zambia and Zimbabwe, respectively), and South Africa, which already had a significant population of European settlers, the Boers. France planned to settle Algeria and eventually incorporate it into the French state on an equal basis with the European provinces. Algeria's proximity across the Mediterranean allowed plans of this scale.Wikipedia:Citation needed

In most areas colonial administrations did not have the manpower or resources to fully administer the territory and had to rely on local power structures to help them. Various factions and groups within the societies exploited this European requirement for their own purposes, attempting to gain positions of power within their own communities by cooperating with Europeans. One aspect of this struggle included what Terence Ranger has termed the "invention of tradition." In order to legitimize their own claims to power in the eyes of both the colonial administrators and their own people, native elites would essentially manufacture "traditional" claims to power, or ceremonies. As a result, many societies were thrown into disarray by the new order.Wikipedia:Citation needed

Following the Scramble for Africa, an early but secondary focus for most colonial regimes was the suppression of slavery and the slave trade. By the end of the colonial period they were mostly successful in this aim, though slavery is still very active in Africa.[260]

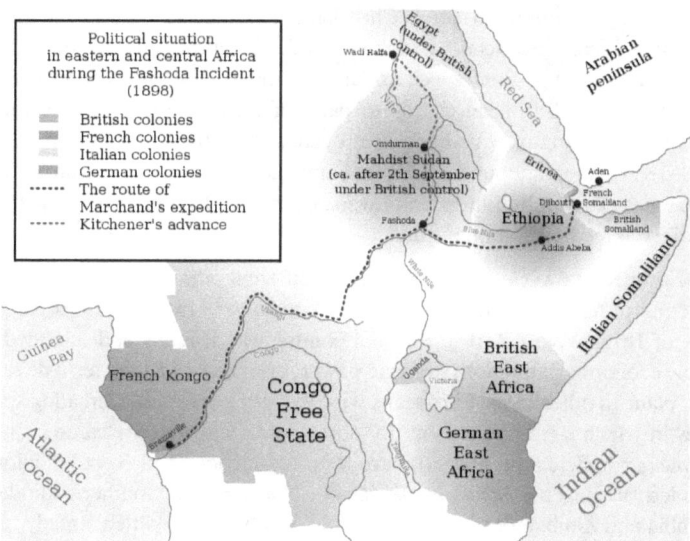

Figure 53: *Central and east Africa, 1898, during the Fashoda Incident.*

France versus Britain: the Fashoda crisis of 1898

As a part of the Scramble for Africa, France had the establishment of a continuous west-east axis of the continent as an objective, in contrast with the British north-south axis. Tensions between Britain and France reached tinder stage in Africa. At several points war was possible, but never happened. The most serious episode was the Fashoda Incident of 1898. French troops tried to claim an area in the Southern Sudan, and a much more powerful British force purporting to be acting in the interests of the Khedive of Egypt arrived to confront them. Under heavy pressure the French withdrew securing British control over the area. The status quo was recognised by an agreement between the two states acknowledging British control over Egypt, while France became the dominant power in Morocco, but France suffered a humiliating defeat overall.[261,262]

European colonial territories

Belgium

- Congo Free State and Belgian Congo (today's Democratic Republic of the Congo)
- Ruanda-Urundi (comprising modern Rwanda and Burundi, between 1916 and 1960)

History of Africa

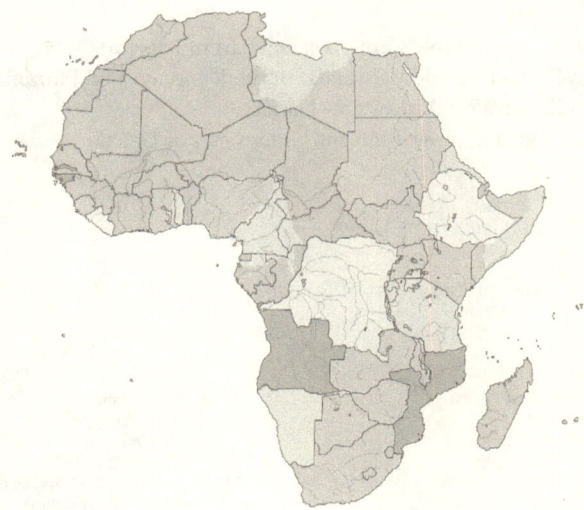

Figure 54: *Areas controlled by European colonial powers on the African continent in 1914; modern-day borders are shown*

France

- French West Africa:
  - Mauritania
  - Senegal
  - French Sudan (now Mali)
  - French Guinea (now Guinea)
  - Ivory Coast
  - Niger
  - French Upper Volta (now Burkina Faso)
  - French Dahomey (now Benin)
- French Equatorial Africa:
  - Gabon
  - Middle Congo (now the Republic of the Congo)
  - Oubangi-Chari (now the Central African Republic)
  - Chad
- French Algeria (now Algeria)
- Tunisia
- French Morocco
- French Somaliland (now Djibouti)
- Madagascar
- Comoros

Germany

- German Kamerun (now Cameroon and part of Nigeria)
- German East Africa (now Rwanda, Burundi and most of Tanzania)
- German South West Africa (now Namibia)
- German Togoland (now Togo and eastern part of Ghana)

Italy

- Italian North Africa (now Libya)
- Eritrea
- Italian Somaliland (now part of Somalia)

Portugal

- Portuguese West Africa (now Angola)
  - Mainland Angola
  - Portuguese Congo (now Cabinda Province of Angola)
- Portuguese East Africa (now Mozambique)
- Portuguese Guinea (now Guinea-Bissau)
- Cape Verde Islands
- São Tomé e Príncipe
  - São Tomé Island
  - Príncipe Island
  - Fort of São João Baptista de Ajudá (now Ouidah, in Benin)

Spain

- Spanish Sahara (now Western Sahara)
  - Río de Oro
  - Saguia el-Hamra
- Spanish Morocco
  - Tarfaya Strip
  - Ifni
- Spanish Guinea (now Equatorial Guinea)
  - Fernando Po
  - Río Muni
  - Annobon

United Kingdom

- Egypt
- Anglo-Egyptian Sudan (now Sudan)
- British Somaliland (now part of Somalia)
- British East Africa:
  - Kenya
  - Uganda Protectorate (now Uganda)
  - Tanganyika (1919–1961, now part of Tanzania)
- Zanzibar (now part of Tanzania)
- Bechuanaland (now Botswana)
- Southern Rhodesia (now Zimbabwe)
- Northern Rhodesia (now Zambia)
- British South Africa (now South Africa)
  - Transvaal (now part of South Africa)
  - Cape Colony (now part of South Africa)
  - Colony of Natal (now part of South Africa)
  - Orange Free State (now part of South Africa)
- The Gambia
- Sierra Leone
- Nigeria
- Cameroons (now parts of Cameroon and Nigeria)
- British Gold Coast (now Ghana)

- Nyasaland (now Malawi)
- Basutoland (now Lesotho)
- Swaziland

Independent states

- Liberia, founded by the American Colonization Society of the United States in 1821; declared independence in 1847
- Ethiopian Empire (Abyssinia) had its borders re-drawn with Italian Eritrea and French Somaliland (modern Djibouti), briefly occupied by Italy from 1936 to 1941 during the Abyssinia Crisis;
- Sudan, independent under Mahdi rule between 1885 and 1899. It was then under British rule from 1899 to 1956.[263]

20th century

In the 1880s the European powers had divided up almost all of Africa (only Ethiopia and Liberia were independent). They ruled until after World War II when forces of nationalism grew much stronger. In the 1950s and 1960s the colonial holdings became independent states. The process was usually peaceful but there were several long bitter bloody civil wars, as in Algeria,[264] Kenya[265] and elsewhere. Across Africa the powerful new force of nationalism drew upon the organizational skills that natives learned in the British and French and other armies in the world wars. It led to organizations that were not controlled by or endorsed by either the colonial powers not the traditional local power structures that were collaborating with the colonial powers. Nationalistic organizations began to challenge both the traditional and the new colonial structures and finally displaced them. Leaders of nationalist movements took control when the European authorities exited; many ruled for decades or until they died off. These structures included political, educational, religious, and other social organizations. In recent decades, many African countries have undergone the triumph and defeat of nationalistic fervor, changing in the process the loci of the centralizing state power and patrimonial state.[266,267,268]

World War I

With the vast majority of the continent under the colonial control of European governments, the World Wars were significant events in the geopolitical history of Africa. Africa was a theater of war and saw fighting in both wars. More important in most regions, the total war footing of colonial powers impacted the governance of African colonies, through resource allocation, conscription, and taxation. In World War I there were several campaigns in Africa, including the Togoland Campaign, the Kamerun Campaign, the South West Africa campaign, and the East African campaign. In each, Allied forces, primarily British, but also French, Belgian, South African, and Portuguese, sought to force the Germans out of their African colonies. In each, German forces were badly outnumbered and, due to Allied naval superiority, were cut off from reinforcement or resupply. The Allies eventually conquered all German colonies; German forces in East Africa managed to avoid surrender thorughout the war, though they could not hold any territory after 1917. After World War I, former German colonies in Africa were taken over by France, Belgium, and the British Empire.

After World War I, colonial powers continued to consolidate their control over their African territories. In some areas, particularly in Southern and East Africa, large settler populations were successful in pressing for additional devolution of administration, so-called "home rule" by the white settlers. In many cases, settler regimes were harsher on African populations, tending to see them more as a threat to political power, as opposed to colonial regimes which had generally endeavored to coopt local populations into economic production. The Great Depression strongly affected Africa's non-subsistence economy, much of which was based on commodity production for Western markets. As demand increased in the late 1930s, Africa's economy rebounded as well.

Africa was the site of one of the first instances of fascist territorial expansions in the 1930s. Italy had attempted to conquer Ethiopia in the 1890s but had been rebuffed in the First Italo-Ethiopian War. Ethiopia lay between two Italian colonies, Italian Somaliland and Eritrea and was invaded in October 1935. With an overwhelming advantage in armor and aircraft, by May 1936, Italian forces had occupied the capital of Addis Ababa and effectively declared victory. Ethiopia and their other colonies were consolidated into Italian East Africa.

World War II: Political

Africa was a large continent whose geography gave it strategic importance during the war. North Africa was the scene of major British and American campaigns against Italy and Germany; East Africa was the scene of a major British campaign against Italy. The vast geography provided major transportation routes linking the United States to the Middle East and Mediterranean regions. The sea route around South Africa was heavily used even though it added 40 days to voyages that had to avoid the dangerous Suez region. Lend Lease supplies to Russia often came this way. Internally, long-distance road and railroad connections facilitated the British war effort. The Union of Africa

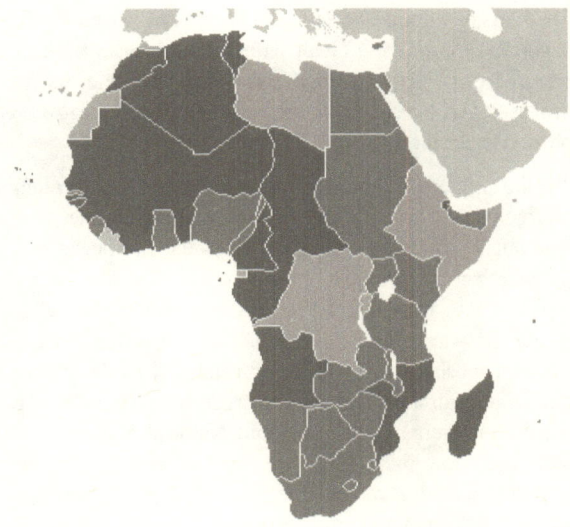

Figure 55: *Areas controlled by European powers in 1939. British (red) and Belgian (Orange) colonies fought with the Allies. Italian (green) with the Axis. French colonies (dark blue) fought alongside the Allies until the Fall of France in June 1940. Vichy was in control until the Free French prevailed in late 1942. Portuguese (brown) and Spanish (teal) colonies remained neutral.*

had dominion status and was largely self-governing, the other British possessions were ruled by the colonial office, usually with close ties to local chiefs and kings. Italian holdings were the target of successful British military campaigns. The Belgian Congo, and two other Belgian colonies, were major exporters. In terms of numbers and wealth, the British -controlled the richest portions of Africa, and made extensive use not only of the geography, but the manpower, and the natural resources. Civilian colonial officials made a special effort to upgrade the African infrastructure, promote agriculture, integrate colonial Africa with the world economy, and recruit over a half million soldiers.[269,270]

Before the war, Britain had made few plans for the utilization of Africa, but it quickly set up command structures. The Army set up the West Africa Command, which recruited 200,000 soldiers. The East Africa Command was created in September 1941 to support the overstretched Middle East Command. It provided the largest number of men, over 320,000, chiefly from Kenya, Tanganyika, and Uganda. The Southern Command was the domain of South Africa. The Royal Navy set up the South Atlantic Command based in Sierra Leone, that became one of the main convoy assembly points. The RAF Coastal

Command had major submarine-hunting operations based in West Africa, while a smaller RAF command Dealt with submarines in the Indian Ocean. Ferrying aircraft from North America and Britain was the major mission of the Western Desert Air Force. In addition smaller more localized commands were set up throughout the war.[271]

Before 1939, the military establishments were very small throughout British Africa, and largely consisted of whites, who comprised under two percent of the population outside South Africa. As soon as the war began, newly created African units were set up, primarily by the Army. The new recruits were almost always volunteers, usually provided in close cooperation with local tribal leaders. During the war, military pay scales far exceeded what civilians natives could earn, especially when food, housing and clothing allowances are included. The largest numbers were in construction units, called Pioneer units, with over 82,000 soldiers.. The RAF and Navy also did some recruiting. The volunteers did some fighting, a great deal of guard duty, and construction work. 80,000 served in the Middle East. A special effort was made not to challenge white supremacy, certainly before the war, and to a large extent during the war itself. Nevertheless, the soldiers were drilled and train to European standards, given strong doses of propaganda, and learn leadership and organizational skills that proved essential to the formation of nationalistic and independence movements after 1945. There were minor episodes of discontent, but nothing serious, among the natives.[272] Afrikaner nationalism was a factor in South Africa, But the proto-German Afrikaner prime minister was replaced in 1939 by Jan Smuts, an Afrikaner who was an enthusiastic supporter of the British Empire. His government closely cooperated with London and raised 340,000 volunteers (190,000 were white, or about one-third of the eligible white men).[273]

French Africa

As early as 1857, the French established volunteer units of black soldiers in sub- Sahara Africa, termed the *tirailleurs senegalais*. They served in military operations throughout the Empire, including 171,000 soldiers in World War I and 160,000 in World War II.[274] About 90,000 became POWs in Germany. The veterans played a central role in the postwar independence movement in French Africa.[275,276]

authorities in West Africa declared allegiance to the Vichy regime, as did the colony of French Gabon Vichy forces defeated an Free French Forces invasion of French West Africa in the two battles of Dakar in July and September 1940. Gabon fell to Free France after the Battle of Gabon in November 1940, but West Africa remained under Vichy control until November 1942. Vichy forces tried to resist the overwhelming Allied landings in North Africa (operation *Torch*) in November 1942. Vichy Admiral François Darlan suddenly switched sides and the fighting ended.[277] The Allies gave Darlan control of North African French forces in exchange for support from both French North Africa as well as French West Africa. Vichy was now eliminated as a factor in Africa. Darlan was assassinated in December, and the two factions of Free French, led by Charles de Gaulle and Henri Giraud, jockeyed for power. De Gaulle finally won out.[278]

World War II: Military

Since Germany had lost its African colonies following World War I, World War II did not reach Africa until Italy joined the war on June 10, 1940, controlling Libya and Italian East Africa. With the fall of France on June 25, most of France's colonies in North and West Africa were controlled by the Vichy government, though much of Central Africa fell under Free French control after some fighting between Vichy and Free French forces at the Battle of Dakar and the Battle of Gabon. After the fall of France, Africa was the only active theater for ground combat until the Italian invasion of Greece in October. In the Western Desert campaign Italian forces from Libya sought to overrun Egypt, controlled by the British. Simultaneously, in the East African campaign, Italian East African forces overran British Somaliland and some British outposts in Kenya and Anglo-Egyptian Sudan. When Italy's efforts to conquer Egypt (including the crucial Suez Canal) and Sudan fell short, they were unable to reestablish supply to Italian East Africa. Without the ability to reinforce or resupply and surrounded by Allied possessions, Italian East Africa was conquered by mainly British and South African forces in 1941. In North Africa, the Italians soon requested help from the Germans who sent a substantial force under General Rommel. With German help, the Axis forces regained the upper hand but were unable to break through British defenses in two tries at El Alamein. In late 1942, Allied forces, mainly Americans and Canadians, invaded French North Africa in Operation Torch, where Vichy French forces initially surprised them with their resistance but were convinced to stop fighting after three days. The second front relieved pressure on the British in Egypt who began pushing west to meet up with the Torch forces, eventually pinning German and Italian forces in Tunisia, which was conquered by May 1943 in the Tunisia campaign, ending the war in Africa. The only other significant operations occurred in the French colony of Madagascar, which was invaded by the British in May 1942 to deny its ports to the Axis (potentially the Japanese who had reached the eastern Indian Ocean). The French garrisons in Madagascar surrendered in November 1942.

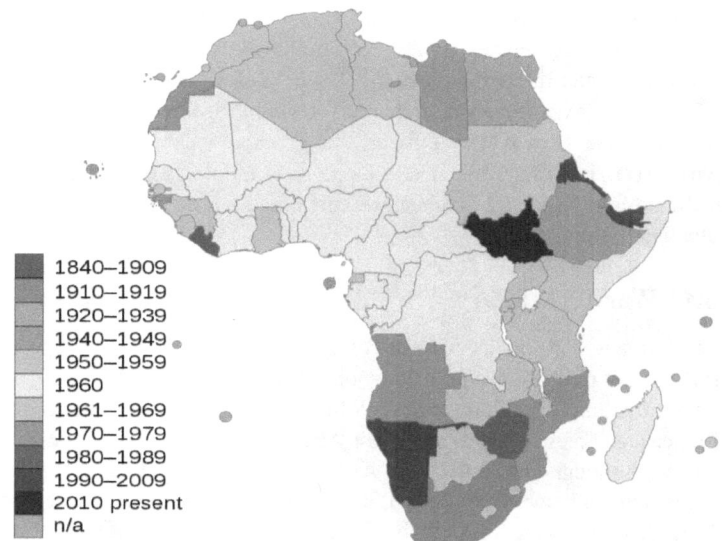

Figure 56: *Dates of independence of African countries*

Post-war Africa: decolonization

The decolonization of Africa started with Libya in 1951, although Liberia, South Africa, Egypt and Ethiopia were already independent. Many countries followed in the 1950s and 1960s, with a peak in 1960 with the Year of Africa, which saw 17 African nations declare independence, including a large part of French West Africa. Most of the remaining countries gained independence throughout the 1960s, although some colonizers (Portugal in particular) were reluctant to relinquish sovereignty, resulting in bitter wars of independence which lasted for a decade or more. The last African countries to gain formal independence were Guinea-Bissau (1974), Mozambique (1975) and Angola (1975) from Portugal; Djibouti from France in 1977; Zimbabwe from the United Kingdom in 1980; and Namibia from South Africa in 1990. Eritrea later split off from Ethiopia in 1993.[279]

East Africa

The Mau Mau Uprising took place in Kenya from 1952 until 1956 but was put down by British and local forces. A state of emergency remained in place until 1960. Kenya became independent in 1963, and Jomo Kenyatta served as its first president.[280]

The early 1960s also signaled the start of major clashes between the Hutus and the Tutsis in Rwanda and Burundi. In 1994 this culminated in the Rwandan Genocide, a conflict in which over 800,000 people were murdered.[281]

North Africa

Moroccan nationalism developed during the 1930s; the Istiqlal Party was formed, pushing for independence. In 1953 sultan Mohammed V of Morocco called for independence. On March 2, 1956, Morocco became independent of France. Mohammed V became ruler of independent Morocco.[282]

In 1954, Algeria formed the National Liberation Front (FLN) as it split from France. This resulted in the Algerian War, which lasted until independence negotiations in 1962. Muhammad Ahmed Ben Bella was elected President of Algeria. Over a million French nationals, predominantly Pied-Noirs, left the country, crippling the economy.[283]

In 1934, the "Neo Destour" (New Constitution) party was founded by Habib Bourguiba pushing for independence in Tunisia. Tunisia became independent in 1955. Its *bey* was deposed and Habib Bourguiba elected as President of Tunisia.[284]

In 1954, Gamal Abdel Nasser deposed the monarchy of Egypt in the Egyptian Revolution of 1952 and came to power as Prime Minister of Egypt. Muammar Gaddafi led the 1969 Libyan coup d'état which deposed Idris of Libya. Gaddafi remained in power until his death in the Libyan Civil War of 2011.

Egypt was involved in several wars against Israel and was allied with other Arab countries. The first was the 1948 Arab–Israeli War, right after the state of Israel was founded. Egypt went to war again in the Six-Day War of 1967 and lost the Sinai Peninsula to Israel. They went to war yet again in the Yom Kippur War of 1973. In 1979, President of Egypt Anwar Sadat and Prime Minister of Israel Menachem Begin signed the Camp David Accords, which gave back the Sinai Peninsula to Egypt in exchange for the recognition of Israel. The accords are still in effect today. In 1981, Sadat was assassinated by members of the Egyptian Islamic Jihad under Khalid Islambouli. The assassins were Islamists who targeted Sadat for his signing of the Accords.[285]

Southern Africa

In 1948 the apartheid laws were started in South Africa by the dominant National Party. These were largely a continuation of existing policies; the difference was the policy of "separate development" (Apartheid). Where previous policies had only been disparate efforts to economically exploit the African majority, Apartheid represented an entire philosophy of separate racial goals, leading to both the divisive laws of 'petty apartheid,' and the grander scheme of African homelands.[286]

In 1994, the South African government abolished Apartheid. South Africans elected Nelson Mandela of the African National Congress in the South African general election, 1994, the country's first multiracial presidential election.[287]

West Africa

Following World War II, nationalist movements arose across West Africa, most notably in Ghana under Kwame Nkrumah.[288] In 1957, Ghana became the first sub-Saharan colony to achieve its independence, followed the next year by France's colonies; by 1974, West Africa's nations were entirely autonomous. Since independence, many West African nations have been plagued by corruption and instability, with notable civil wars in Nigeria, Sierra Leone, Liberia, and Ivory Coast, and a succession of military coups in Ghana and Burkina Faso. Many states have failed to develop their economies despite enviable natural resources, and political instability is often accompanied by undemocratic government.[289,290]

See also 2014 Ebola virus epidemic in Sierra Leone, 2014 Ebola virus epidemic in Guinea, and 2014 Ebola virus epidemic in LiberiaWikipedia:Citation needed

Historiography of British Africa

The first historical studies in English appeared in the 1890s, and followed one of four approaches. 1) The territorial narrative was typically written by a veteran soldier or civil servant who gave heavy emphasis to what he had seen. 2) The "apologia" were essays designed to justify British policies. 3) Popularizers tried to reach a large audience. 4) Compendia appeared designed to combine academic and official credentials. Professional scholarship appeared around 1900, and began with the study of business operations, typically using government documents and unpublished archives.Wikipedia:Citation needed

The economic approach was widely practiced in the 1930s, primarily to provide descriptions of the changes underway in the previous half-century. In 1935, American historian William L. Langer published *The Diplomacy of Imperialism: 1890–1902*, a book that is still widely cited. In 1939, Oxford professor Reginald Copeland published *The Exploitation of East Africa, 1856–1890: The Slave Trade and the Scramble*, another popular treatment.Wikipedia:Citation needed

World War II diverted most scholars to wartime projects and accounted for a pause in scholarship during the 1940s.

By the 1950s many African students were studying in British universities, and they produced a demand for new scholarship, and started themselves to supply it as well. Oxford University became the main center for African studies, with activity as well at Cambridge University and the London School of Economics. The perspective of British government policymakers or international business operations slowly gave way to a new interest in the activities of the natives, especially nationalistic movements and the growing demand for independence.[291] The major breakthrough came from Ronald Robinson and John Andrew Gallagher, especially with their studies of the impact of free trade on Africa.[292] In 1985 *The Oxford History of South Africa* (2 vols.) was published,[293] attempting to synthesize the available materials. In 2013, *The Oxford Handbook of Modern African History* was published,[294] bringing the scholarship up to date. Wikipedia:Citation needed

References

- Akyeampong. Emmanuel and Robert H. Bates, eds. *Africa's Development in Historical Perspective* (2014)
- Collins, Robert O.; Burns, James M. (2007). *A History of Sub-Saharan Africa*. NY: Cambridge UP, <templatestyles src="Module:Citation/CS1/styles.css" />ISBN 978-0-521-68708-9.
- Davidson, Basil (1991). *Africa In History, Themes and Outlines*. Revised and expanded ed. New York City: Simon & Schuster, <templatestyles src="Module:Citation/CS1/styles.css" />ISBN 0-684-82667-4
- Ehret, Christopher (2002). *The Civilizations of Africa*. Charlottesville, Virginia: University of Virginia, <templatestyles src="Module:Citation/CS1/styles.css" />ISBN 0-8139-2085-X.
- Iliffe, John (2007). *Africans: The History of a Continent*. 2nd ed. NY : Cambridge University Press, <templatestyles src="Module:Citation/CS1/styles.css" />ISBN 978-0-521-68297-8.
- Lye, Keith (2002). *Encyclopedia of African Nations and Civilization*. NY: The Diagram Group, <templatestyles src="Module:Citation/CS1/styles.css" />ISBN 0-8160-4568-2.
- Manning, Patrick. (2014) "The African Diaspora: Slavery, Modernity, and Globalization."[295] *The International Journal of African Historical Studies* 47.1 (2014): 147+.
- Manning, Patrick. (2009) *The African Diaspora: A History Through Culture* (NY: Columbia UP); looks at the slave trade, the adaptation of Africans to new conditions, their struggle for freedom and equality, and the establishment of a "black" diaspora and its local influence around the world; covers 1430 to 2001.

- Martin, Phyllis M., and O'Meara, Patrick (1995). *Africa*. 3rd ed. Bloomington: Indiana University Press, <templatestyles src="Module:Citation/CS1/styles.css" />ISBN 0-253-20984-6.
- Page, Willie F. (2001). *Encyclopedia of African History and Culture: From Conquest to Colonization (1500–1850)*. New York City: Learning Source Books, <templatestyles src="Module:Citation/CS1/styles.css" />ISBN 0-8160-4472-4.
- Shillington, Kevin (2005). *History of Africa*. Revised 2nd ed. New York City: Palgrave Macmillan, <templatestyles src="Module:Citation/CS1/styles.css" />ISBN 0-333-59957-8.
- Diamond, Jared M. (1999). *Guns, Germs, and Steel: The Fates of Human Societies*. New York City: W. W. Norton. ISBN 0-393-31755-2.<templatestyles src="Module:Citation/CS1/styles.css"></templatestyles>
- Stearns, Peter, ed. (2001). *The Encyclopedia of World History: Ancient, Medieval, and Modern, Chronologically Arranged*. Boston: Houghton Mifflin. OCLC 644651969[296].<templatestyles src="Module:Citation/CS1/styles.css"></templatestyles>
- Chisholm, Hugh, ed. (1911). "Africa". *Encyclopædia Britannica*. 1 (11th ed.). Cambridge University Press. pp. 320–358.<templatestyles src="Module:Citation/CS1/styles.css"></templatestyles>
- Grimal, Nicolas (1988). *A History of Ancient Egypt*. Librairie Arthéme Fayard.<templatestyles src="Module:Citation/CS1/styles.css"></templatestyles>
- Habachi, Labib (1963). "King Nebhepetre Menthuhotep: his monuments, place in history, deification and unusual representations in form of gods". *Annales du Service des Antiquités de l'Égypte*. **19**: 16–52.<templatestyles src="Module:Citation/CS1/styles.css"></templatestyles>

Further reading

- Cheikh Anta Diop (1987). *Precolonial Black Africa*. Chicago Review Press.
- Clark, J. Desmond (1970). *The Prehistory of Africa*. Thames and Hudson
- Davidson, Basil (1964). *The African Past*. Penguin, Harmondsworth
- Fage, J.D. and Roland Oliver, eds. *The Cambridge History of Africa (8 vol 1975–1986)*
- Falola, Toyin. Africa, Volume 1–5.
- Freund, Bill (1998). *The Making of Contemporary Africa*, Lynne Rienner, Boulder (including a substantial "Annotated Bibliography" pp. 269–316).

- July, Robert (1998). *A History of the African People*, Longrove, Il.: Waveland Press, 1998.
- Killingray, David, and Richard Rathbone, eds. *Africa and the Second World War* (Springer, 1986).
- Reader, John (1997). *Africa: A Biography of the Continent*. Hamish Hamilton. <templatestyles src="Module:Citation/CS1/styles.css" />ISBN 0-241-13047-6
- Roberts, Stephen H. *History of French Colonial Policy (1870-1925)* (2 vol 1929) vol 1 online[297] also vol 2 online[298]; comprehensive scholarly history
- Shillington, Kevin (1989). *History of Africa*, New York: St. Martin's.
- UNESCO (1980–1994). *General History of Africa*. 8 volumes.
- Théophile Obenga (1980). *Pour une Nouvelle Histoire* Présence Africaine, Paris
- Worden, Nigel (1995). *The Making of Modern South Africa*, Oxford UK, Cambridge USA: Blackwell.

Atlases

- Ajayi, A. J. F. and Michael Crowder. *Historical Atlas of Africa* (1985); 300 color maps.
- Fage, J.D. *Atlas of African History* (1978)
- Freeman-Grenville, G. S. P. *The New Atlas of African History* (1991).
- Kwamena-Poh, Michael, et al. *African history in maps* (Longman, 1982).
- McEvedy, Colin. *The Penguin Atlas of African History* (2nd ed. 1996). excerpt[299]

Historiography

- Boyd, Kelly, ed. *Encyclopedia of Historians and Historical Writers* (Rutledge, 1999) 1:4–14.
- Manning, Patrick (2013), "African and World Historiography"[300] (PDF), *The Journal of African History*, **54** (3): 319, doi: 10.1017/S0021853713000753[301]<templatestyles src="Module:Citation/CS1/styles.css"></templatestyles>
- Manning, Patrick (2016). "Locating Africans on the World Stage: A Problem in World History". *Journal of World History*. **27** (3): 605–637.<templatestyles src="Module:Citation/CS1/styles.css"></templatestyles>

External links

- Worldtimelines.org.uk -Africa[302] The British Museum. 2005
- The Historyscoper[303]
- About.com:African History[304]
- The Story of Africa[305] BBC World Service
- Wonders of the African World[306], PBS
- Civilization of Africa by Richard Hooker[307], Washington State University.
- African Art[308] (chunk of historical data) Metropolitan Museum of Art.
- African Kingdoms, by Khaleel Muhammad[309]
- Mapungubwe Museum[310] at the University of Pretoria
- http://www.omarviktor.com/project-diaspora

Height of slave trade

Arab slave trade

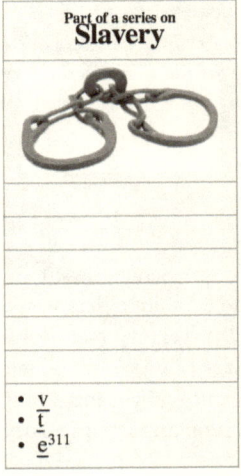

Part of a series on
Slavery

- v
- t
- e³¹¹

The **Arab slave trade** was the intersection of slavery and trade in the Arab world, mainly in Western Asia, North Africa, the Horn of Africa, Southeast Africa and Europe. This barter occurred chiefly between the medieval era and the early 20th century. The trade was conducted through slave markets in these areas, with the slaves captured mostly from Africa's interior and Southern Europe.³¹²

Walter Rodney argues that the term *Arab Slave Trade* is a historical misnomer since bilateral trade agreements between myriad ethnic groups across the proposed 'Zanj trade network' characterized much of the acquisition process of chattel, and more often than not indentured servants.

Figure 57: *Arab slave traders and their captives along the Ruvuma River in Mozambique.*

Scope of the trade

African Zanj slaves

The Arab slave trade, across the Sahara desert and across the Indian Ocean, began after Muslim Arab and Swahili traders won control of the Swahili Coast and sea routes during the 9th century (see Sultanate of Zanzibar). These traders captured Bantu peoples (Zanj) from the interior in present-day Kenya, Mozambique and Tanzania and brought them to the coast. There, the slaves gradually assimilated in the rural areas, particularly on the Unguja and Pemba islands.

Some historians assert that as many as 17 million people were sold into slavery on the coast of the Indian Ocean, the Middle East, and North Africa, and approximately 5 million African slaves were bought by Muslim slave traders and taken from Africa across the Red Sea, Indian Ocean, and Sahara desert between 1500 and 1900.

The captives were sold throughout the Middle East. This trade accelerated as superior ships led to more trade and greater demand for labour on plantations in the region. Eventually, tens of thousands of captives were being taken every year.

The Indian Ocean slave trade was multi-directional and changed over time. To meet the demand for menial labor, Bantu slaves bought by Arab slave traders from southeastern Africa were sold in cumulatively large numbers over the

Figure 58: *A 19th-century European engraving of Arab slave-trading caravan transporting African slaves across the Sahara.*

centuries to customers in Egypt, Arabia, the Persian Gulf, India, European colonies in the Far East, the Indian Ocean islands, Ethiopia and Somalia.[313]

Slave labor in East Africa was drawn from the *Zanj*, Bantu peoples that lived along the East African coast. The Zanj were for centuries shipped as slaves by Arab traders to all the countries bordering the Indian Ocean. The Umayyad and Abbasid caliphs recruited many Zanj slaves as soldiers and, as early as 696, there were revolts of Zanj slave soldiers in Iraq. A 7th-century Chinese text mentions ambassadors from Java presenting the Chinese emperor with two *Seng Chi* (Zanj) slaves as gifts in 614, and 8th- and 9th-century chronicles mention Seng Chi slaves reaching China from the Hindu kingdom of Sri Vijaya in Java.

The Zanj Rebellion, a series of uprisings that took place between 869 and 883 AD near the city of Basra (also known as Basara), situated in present-day Iraq, is believed to have involved enslaved Zanj that had originally been captured from the African Great Lakes region and areas further south in East Africa. It grew to involve over 500,000 slaves and free men who were imported from across the Muslim empire and claimed over "tens of thousands of lives in lower Iraq". The Zanj who were taken as slaves to the Middle East were often used in strenuous agricultural work. As the plantation economy boomed and the Arabs became richer, agriculture and other manual labor work was thought to be demeaning. The resulting labor shortage led to an increased slave market.

> It is certain that large numbers of slaves were exported from eastern Africa; the best evidence for this is the magnitude of the Zanj revolt in Iraq in the 9th century, though not all of the slaves involved were Zanj. There is little evidence of what part of eastern Africa the Zanj came from, for the name is here evidently used in its general sense, rather than to designate the particular stretch of the coast, from about 3°N. to 5°S., to which the name was also applied.

The Zanj were needed to take care of:

> the Tigris-Euphrates delta, which had become abandoned marshland as a result of peasant migration and repeated flooding, could be reclaimed through intensive labor. Wealthy proprietors "had received extensive grants of tidal land on the condition that they would make it arable." Sugar cane was prominent among the products of their plantations, particularly in Khūzestān Province. Zanj also worked the salt mines of Mesopotamia, especially around Basra.

Their jobs were to clear away the nitrous topsoil that made the land arable. The working conditions were also considered to be extremely harsh and miserable. Many other people were imported into the region, besides Zanj.

Historian M. A. Shaban has argued that rebellion was not a slave revolt, but a revolt of blacks (*zanj*). In his opinion, although a few runaway slaves did join the revolt, the majority of the participants were Arabs and free Zanj. If the revolt had been led by slaves, they would have lacked the necessary resources to combat the Abbasid government for as long as they did.[314]

Ibn Battuta who visited the ancient African kingdom of Mali in the mid-14th century recounts that the local inhabitants vie with each other in the number of slaves and servants they have, and was himself given a slave boy as a "hospitality gift."[315]

European slaves

Muslims also enslaved Europeans. According to Robert Davis, between 1 million and 1.25 million Europeans were captured between the 16th and 19th centuries by Barbary corsairs, who were vassals of the Ottoman Empire, and sold as slaves.[316] These slaves were captured mainly from seaside villages from Italy, Spain, Portugal, Ireland, and also from more distant places like France or England, the Netherlands, and even Iceland. They were also taken from ships stopped by the pirates.

The effects of these attacks were devastating: France, England, and Spain each lost thousands of ships. Long stretches of the Spanish and Italian coasts were almost completely abandoned by their inhabitants, because of frequent pirate attacks. Pirate raids discouraged settlement along the coast until the 19th century.

Periodic Muslim raiding expeditions were sent from Islamic Iberia to ravage the Christian Iberian kingdoms, bringing back slaves. In a raid against Lisbon in 1189, for example, the Almohad Berber Muslim caliph, Abu Yusuf Yaqub al-Mansur, took 3,000 female and child captives, while his governor of Córdoba, in a subsequent attack upon Silves in 1191, took 3,000 Christian slaves.

Arab slaves

Arabs were sometimes made into slaves in the Muslim world.[317] Sometimes castration was done on Arab slaves. In Mecca, Arab women were sold as slaves according to Ibn Butlan, and certain rulers in West Africa had slave girls of Arab origin. According to al-Maqrizi, slave girls with lighter skin were sold to West Africans on hajj. Ibn Battuta met an Arab slave girl near Timbuktu in Mali in 1353. Battuta wrote that the slave girl was fluent in Arabic, from Damascus, and her master's name was Farbá Sulaymán. Besides his Damascus slave girl and a secretary fluent in Arabic, Arabic was also comprehended by Farbá himself.

Islamic and Oriental aspect

Patrick Manning writes that although the "Oriental" or "Arab" slave trade is sometimes called the "Islamic" slave trade, a religious imperative was not the driver of the slavery. He further argues such use of the terms "Islamic trade" or "Islamic world" erroneously treats Africa as being outside Islam, or a negligible portion of the Islamic world.[318] According to European historians, propagators of Islam in Africa often revealed a cautious attitude towards proselytizing because of its effect in reducing the potential reservoir of slaves.[319]

The subject merges with the Oriental slave trade, which followed two main routes in the Middle Ages:

- Overland routes across the Maghreb and Mashriq deserts (Trans-Saharan route)
- Sea routes to the east of Africa through the Red Sea and Indian Ocean (Oriental route)

The Arab slave trade originated before Islam and lasted more than a millennium.[320,321] To meet the demand for plantation labor, these captured Zanj slaves were shipped to the Arabian peninsula and the Near East, among other areas.

History of the Arab slave trade

African Zanj slaves

The Arab trade of Zanj (Bantu) slaves in Southeast Africa is one of the oldest slave trades, predating the European transatlantic slave trade by 700 years.[322,323] Male slaves were often forced to work as servants, soldiers, or laborers by their owners, while female slaves, including those from Africa, were long traded to the Middle Eastern countries and kingdoms by Arab and Oriental traders as concubines and servants. Arab, African and Oriental-Wikipedia:Accuracy dispute#Disputed statement traders were involved in the capture and transport of slaves northward across the Sahara desert and the Indian Ocean region into the Middle East, Persia and the Far East.

From the 7th century until around the 1960s, the Arab slave trade continued in one form or another. Historical accounts and references to slave-owning nobility in Arabia, Yemen and elsewhere are frequent into the early 1920s.

In 641 during the Baqt, a treaty between the Nubian Christian state of Makuria and the new Muslim rulers of Egypt, the Nubians agreed to give Arab traders more privileges of trade in addition to a share in their slave trading.[324]

In Somalia, the Bantu minorities are descended from Bantu groups that had settled in Southeast Africa after the initial expansion from Nigeria/Cameroon. To meet the demand for menial labor, Bantus from southeastern Africa captured by Somali slave traders were sold in cumulatively large numbers over the centuries to customers in Somalia and other areas in Northeast Africa and Asia.[325] People captured locally during wars and raids were also sometimes enslaved by Somalis.[326] However, the perception, capture, treatment and duties of both groups of slaves differed markedly.[327] From 1800 to 1890, between 25,000–50,000 Bantu slaves are thought to have been sold from the slave market of Zanzibar to the Somali coast. Most of the slaves were from the Majindo, Makua, Nyasa, Yao, Zalama, Zaramo and Zigua ethnic groups of Tanzania, Mozambique and Malawi. Collectively, these Bantu groups are known as *Mushunguli*, which is a term taken from *Mzigula*, the Zigua tribe's word for "people" (the word holds multiple implied meanings including "worker", "foreigner", and "slave").[328]

In Ethiopia, during the second half of the 19th century and early 20th century, slaves shipped from there had a high demand in the markets of the Arabian peninsula and elsewhere in the Middle East. They were mostly domestic servants, though some served as agricultural labourers, or as water carriers, herdsmen, seamen, camel drivers, porters, washerwomen, masons, shop assistants and cooks. The most fortunate of the men worked as the officials or bodyguards of the ruler and emirs, or as business managers for rich merchants. They

Figure 59: *The purchase of Christian captives by Catholic monks in the Barbary states.*

enjoyed significant personal freedom and occasionally held slaves of their own. Besides Javanese and Chinese girls brought in from the Far East, "red" (non-black) Ethiopian young females were among the most valued concubines. The most beautiful ones often enjoyed a wealthy lifestyle, and became mistresses of the elite or even mothers to rulers. The principal sources of these slaves, all of whom passed through Matamma, Massawa and Tadjoura on the Red Sea, were the southwestern parts of Ethiopia, in the Oromo and Sidama country.

In the Central African Republic, during the 16th and 17th centuries Muslim slave traders began to raid the region as part of the expansion of the Saharan and Nile River slave routes. Their captives were enslaved and shipped to the Mediterranean coast, Europe, Arabia, the Western Hemisphere, or to the slave ports and factories along the West and North Africa or South the Ubanqui and Congo rivers.[329]

The Arab slave trade in the Indian Ocean, Red Sea, and Mediterranean Sea long predated the arrival of any significant number of Europeans on the African continent south of the Sahara.[330]

Some descendants of African slaves brought to the Middle East during the slave-trade still live there today, and are aware of their African origins.

European slaves

The North African slave markets traded also in European slaves. The European slaves were acquired by Barbary pirates in slave raids on ships and by raids on coastal towns from Italy to Spain, Portugal, France, England, the Netherlands, and as far afield as Iceland. Men, women, and children were captured to such a devastating extent that vast numbers of sea coast towns were abandoned. Ohio State University history Professor Robert Davis describes the white slave trade as minimized by most modern historians in his book *Christian Slaves, Muslim Masters: White Slavery in the Mediterranean, the Barbary Coast and Italy, 1500-1800* (Palgrave Macmillan).[331]

Davis estimates that 1 million to 1.25 million White Christian Europeans were enslaved in North Africa, from the beginning of the 16th century to the middle of the 18th by slave traders from Tunis, Algiers, and Tripoli alone (these numbers do not include the European people which were enslaved by Morocco and by other raiders and traders of the Mediterranean Sea coast), and roughly 700 Americans were held captive in this region as slaves between 1785 and 1815.

16th- and 17th-century customs statistics suggest that Istanbul's additional slave import from the Black Sea may have totaled around 2.5 million from 1450 to 1700.[332]

19th century

In the 1800s, the slave trade from Africa to the Islamic countries picked up significantly. When the European slave trade ended around the 1850s, the slave trade to the east picked up significantlyWikipedia:Accuracy dispute#Disputed statement only to be ended with European colonisation of Africa around 1900.Wikipedia:Citing sources#What information to include

In 1814, Swiss explorer Johann Burckhardt wrote of his travels in Egypt and Nubia, where he saw the practice of slave trading: "I frequently witnessed scenes of the most shameless indecency, which the traders, who were the principal actors, only laughed at. I may venture to state, that very few female slaves who have passed their tenth year, reach Egypt or Arabia in a state of virginity."

David Livingstone wrote of the slave trade in the African Great Lakes region, which he visited in the mid-nineteenth century: <templatestyles src="Template:Quote/styles.css"/>

> To overdraw its evils is a simple impossibility ... We passed a slave woman shot or stabbed through the body and lying on the path. [Onlookers] said an Arab who passed early that morning had done it in anger at losing the price he had given for her, because she was unable to walk any longer. We passed a woman tied by the neck to a tree and dead ... We came

Figure 60: *A photograph of a slave boy in Zanzibar. 'An Arab master's punishment for a slight offence.' c. 1890.*

upon a man dead from starvation ... The strangest disease I have seen in this country seems real to be broken heartedness, and it attacks free men who have been captured and made slaves.[333] Livingstone estimated that 80,000 Africans died each year before ever reaching the slave markets of Zanzibar.

Zanzibar was once East Africa's main slave-trading port, and under Omani Arabs in the 19th century as many as 50,000 slaves were passing through the city each year.

Livingstone wrote in a letter to the editor of the *New York Herald*: <templatestyles src="Template:Quote/styles.css"/>

And if my disclosures regarding the terrible Ujijian slavery should lead to the suppression of the East Coast slave trade, I shall regard that as a greater matter by far than the discovery of all the Nile sources together.[334]

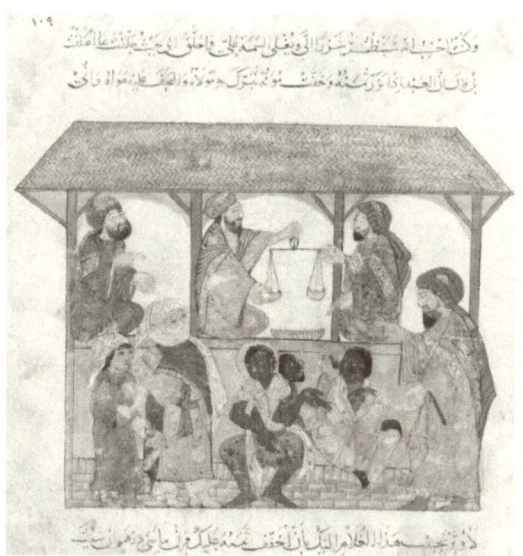

Figure 61: *A 13th-century slave market in Yemen.*

20th century

During the Second Sudanese Civil War (1983-2005) people were taken into slavery; estimates of abductions range from 14,000 to 200,000.

Slavery in Mauritania was legally abolished by laws passed in 1905, 1961, and 1981. It was finally criminalized in August 2007. It is estimated that up to 600,000 Mauritanians, or 20% of Mauritania's population, are currently in conditions which some consider to be "slavery", namely, many of them used as bonded labour due to poverty.[335]

Slavery was comparatively recently outlawed in Oman (1970), Qatar (1952), Saudi Arabia, and Yemen (both in 1962).

Historical and geographical context

Islamic world

Islamic sharia law allowed slavery but prohibited slavery involving other pre-existing Muslims; as a result, the main target for slavery were the people who lived in the frontier areas of the Muslim world. Slaves initially came from various regions, including Central Asia (such as mamluks) and Europe (such as saqaliba), but by the modern period, slaves came mostly from Africa.

According to the sharia law, slaves were allowed to earn their living if they opted for that, otherwise it is the owner's (master) duty to provide for that. They also could not be forced to earn money for their masters unless with an agreement between the slave and the master.

This concept is called مخارجة (mukhārajah) (Lane: "And خَارَجَهُ He made an agreement with him, namely, his slave that he (the latter) should pay him a certain impost at the expiration of every month; the slave being left at liberty to work: in which case the slave is termed "عَبْدٌ مُخَارِجٌ") in Islamic law. If slaves agree to that and they would like the money they earn to be counted toward their emancipation, then this has to be written in the form of a contract between the slave and the master. This is called مكاتبة (mukātaba) in Islamic jurisprudence which is only, by consensus, a recommendation, and accepting a request for a *mukātaba* from slaves is thus not obligatory for masters. Although the owner did not have to comply with it, was considered praiseworthy to do so

The framework of Islamic civilization was a well-developed network of towns and oasis trading centers with the market (*souq, bazaar*) at its heart. These towns were inter-connected by a system of roads crossing semi-arid regions or deserts. The routes were traveled by convoys, and slaves formed part of this caravan traffic.

In contrast to the Atlantic slave trade, where the male-female ratio was 2:1 or 3:1, the Arab slave trade instead usually had a higher female-to-male ratio. This suggests a general preference for female slaves. Concubinage and reproduction served as incentives for importing female slaves (often Caucasian), though many were also imported mainly for performing household tasks.

Arab views on African peoples

Abdelmajid Hannoum a professor at Wesleyan University, states that racist attitudes were not prevalent until the 18th and 19th century. According to Arnold J. Toynbee: "The extinction of race consciousness as between Muslims is one of the outstanding achievements of Islam and in the contemporary world there is, as it happens, a crying need for the propagation of this Islamic virtue."[336]

Ibn Battuta who visited the ancient African kingdom of Mali in the mid-14th century recounts that the local inhabitants vie with each other in the number of slaves and servants they have, and was himself given a slave boy as a "hospitality gift."[337]

Africa: 8th through 19th centuries

In April 1998, Elikia M'bokolo, wrote in *Le Monde diplomatique*. "The African continent was bled of its human resources via all possible routes. Across the Sahara, through the Red Sea, from the Indian Ocean ports and across the Atlantic. At least ten centuries of slavery for the benefit of the Muslim countries (from the ninth to the nineteenth)." He continues: "Four million slaves exported via the Red Sea, another four million through the Swahili ports of the Indian Ocean, perhaps as many as nine million along the trans-Saharan caravan route, and eleven to twenty million (depending on the author) across the Atlantic Ocean"[338]

In the 8th century, Africa was dominated by Arab-Berbers in the north: Islam moved southwards along the Nile and along the desert trails.

- The Sahara was thinly populated. Nevertheless, since antiquity there had been cities living on a trade in salt, gold, slaves, cloth, and on agriculture enabled by irrigation: Tiaret, Oualata, Sijilmasa, Zaouila, and others.Wikipedia:Citation needed
- In the Middle Ages, the general Arabic term *bilâd as-sûdân* ("Land of the Blacks") was used for the vast Sudan region (an expression denoting West and Central Africa), or sometimes extending from the coast of West Africa to Western Sudan.[339]. It provided a pool of manual labour for North and Saharan Africa. This region was dominated by certain states and people: the Ghana Empire, the Empire of Mali, the Kanem-Bornu Empire, the Fulani and Hausa.
- In the Horn of Africa, the coasts of the Red Sea and Indian Ocean were controlled by local Somali and other Muslims, and Yemenis and Omanis had merchant posts along the coasts. The Ethiopian coast, particularly the port of Massawa and Dahlak Archipelago, had long been a hub for the exportation of slaves from the interior by the Kingdom of Aksum and earlier polities. The port and most coastal areas were largely Muslim, and the port itself was home to a number of Arab and Indian merchants.[340] The Solomonic dynasty of Ethiopia often exported Nilotic slaves from their western borderland provinces, or from newly conquered southern provinces.[341] The Somali and Afar Muslim sultanates, such as the Adal Sultanate, also exported Nilotic slaves that they captured from the interior, as well as some vanquished foes.[342]

- In the African Great Lakes region, Omani and Yemeni traders set up slave-trading posts along the southeastern coast of the Indian Ocean; most notably in the archipelago of Zanzibar, along the coast of present-day Tanzania. The Zanj region or Swahili Coast flanking the Indian Ocean continued to be an important area for the Oriental slave trade up until

Figure 62: *A Zanj slave gang in Zanzibar (1889)*

the 19th century. Livingstone and Stanley were then the first Europeans to penetrate to the interior of the Congo Basin and to discover the scale of slavery there. The Arab Tippu Tip extended his influence there and captured many people as slaves. After Europeans had settled in the Gulf of Guinea, the trans-Saharan slave trade became less important. In Zanzibar, slavery was abolished late, in 1897, under Sultan Hamoud bin Mohammed.Wikipedia:Citation needed

Geography of the slave trade

"Supply" zones

There is historical evidence of North African Muslim slave raids all along the Mediterranean coasts across Christian Europe. The majority of slaves traded across the Mediterranean region were predominantly of European origin from the 7th to 15th centuries.

Slaves were also brought into the Arab world via Central Asia, mainly of Turkic or Tartar origin. Many of these slaves later went on to serve in the armies forming an elite rank.

- Nubia and Ethiopia were also "exporting" regions: in the 15th century, Ethiopians sold slaves from western borderland areas (usually just outside

Figure 63: *A slave market in Cairo. Drawing by David Roberts, circa 1848.*

the realm of the Emperor of Ethiopia) or Ennarea,[343] which often ended up in India, where they worked on ships or as soldiers. They eventually rebelled and took power (dynasty of the Habshi Kings).
- The Sudan region and Saharan Africa formed another "export" area, but it is impossible to estimate the scale, since there is a lack of sources with figures.
- Finally, the slave traffic affected eastern Africa, but the distance and local hostility slowed down this section of the Oriental trade.

Routes

According to professor Ibrahima Baba Kaké there were four main slavery routes to the Arab world, from east to west of Africa, from the Maghreb to the Sudan, from Tripolitania to central Sudan and from Egypt to the Middle East. Caravan trails, set up in the 9th century, went past the oasis of the Sahara; travel was difficult and uncomfortable for reasons of climate and distance. Since Roman times, long convoys had transported slaves as well as all sorts of products to be used for barter. To protect against attacks from desert nomads, slaves were used as an escort. Any who slowed down the progress of the caravan were killed.

Historians know less about the sea routes. From the evidence of illustrated documents, and travellers' tales, it seems that people travelled on dhows or

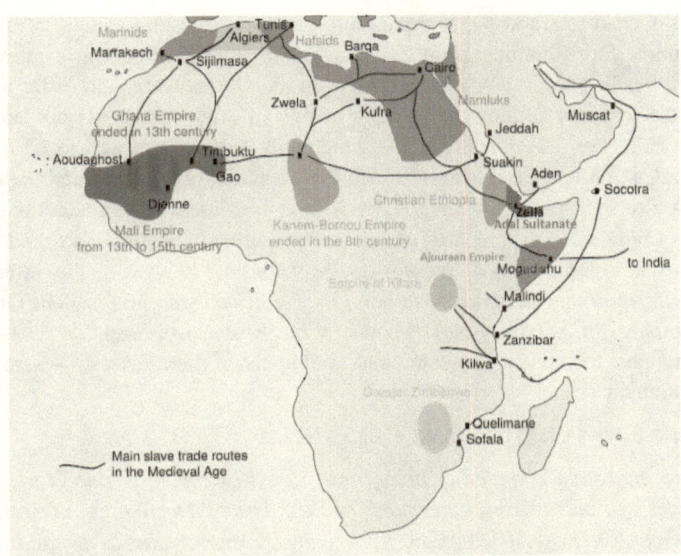

Figure 64: *The main slave routes in Africa during the Middle Ages.*

Figure 65: *Dhows were used to transport goods to Oman.*

jalbas, Arab ships which were used as transport in the Red Sea. Crossing the Indian Ocean required better organisation and more resources than overland transport. Ships coming from Zanzibar made stops on Socotra or at Aden before heading to the Persian Gulf or to India. Slaves were sold as far away as India, or even China: there was a colony of Arab merchants in Canton. Serge Bilé cites a 12th-century text which tells us that most well-to-do families in Canton had black slaves whom they regarded as savages and demons because of their physical appearance. Although Chinese slave traders bought slaves (*Seng Chi* i.e. the *Zanj*) from Arab intermediaries and "stocked up" directly in coastal areas of present-day Somalia, the local Somalis—referred to as *Baribah* and *Barbaroi* (Berbers) by medieval Arab and ancient Greek geographers, respectively (see *Periplus of the Erythraean Sea*),[344,345,348] and no strangers to capturing, owning and trading slaves themselves[347]—were not among them:[348]

<templatestyles src="Template:Quote/styles.css"/>

> *One important commodity being transported by the Arab dhows to Somalia was slaves from other parts of East Africa. During the nineteenth century, the East African slave trade grew enormously due to demands by Arabs, Portuguese, and French. Slave traders and raiders moved throughout eastern and central Africa to meet the rising demand for enslaved men, women, and children. Somalia did not supply slaves – as part of the Islamic world Somalis were at least nominally protected by the religious tenet that free Muslims cannot be enslaved – but Arab dhows loaded with human cargo continually visited Somali ports.*[349]

Barter

Slaves were often bartered for objects of various kinds: in the Sudan, they were exchanged for cloth, trinkets and so on. In the Maghreb, slaves were swapped for horses. In the desert cities, lengths of cloth, pottery, Venetian glass slave beads, dyestuffs and jewels were used as payment. The trade in black slaves was part of a diverse commercial network. Alongside gold coins, cowrie shells from the Indian Ocean or the Atlantic (Canaries, Luanda) were used as money throughout sub-saharan Africa (merchandise was paid for with sacks of cowries).

Slave markets and fairs

Enslaved Africans were sold in the towns of the Arab World. In 1416, al-Maqrizi told how pilgrims coming from Takrur (near the Senegal River) had brought 1,700 slaves with them to Mecca. In North Africa, the main slave

Figure 66: *Cowry shells were used as money in the slave trade.*

Figure 67: *A slave market in Khartoum, Sudan, c. 1876.*

markets were in Morocco, Algiers, Tripoli and Cairo. Sales were held in public places or in souks.

Potential buyers made a careful examination of the "merchandise": they checked the state of health of a person who was often standing naked with wrists bound together. In Cairo, transactions involving eunuchs and concubines happened in private houses. Prices varied according to the slave's quality. Thomas Smee, the commander of the British research ship *Ternate*, visited such a market in Zanzibar in 1811 and gave a detailed description:

> *'The show' commences about four o'clock in the afternoon. The slaves, set off to the best advantage by having their skins cleaned and burnished with cocoa-nut oil, their faces painted with red and white stripes and the hands, noses, ears and feet ornamented with a profusion of bracelets of gold and silver and jewels, are ranged in a line, commencing with the youngest, and increasing to the rear according to their size and age. At the head of this file, which is composed of all sexes and ages from 6 to 60, walks the person who owns them; behind and at each side, two or three of his domestic slaves, armed with swords and spears, serve as guard.*
>
> *Thus ordered the procession begins, and passes through the market-place and the principle streets... when any of them strikes a spectator's fancy the line immediately stops, and a process of examination ensues, which, for minuteness, is unequalled in any cattle market in Europe. The intending purchaser having ascertained there is no defect in the faculties of speech, hearing, etc., that there is no disease present, next proceeds to examine the person; the mouth and the teeth are first inspected and afterwards every part of the body in succession, not even excepting the breasts, etc., of the girls, many of whom I have seen handled in the most indecent manner in the public market by their purchasers; indeed there is every reasons to believe that the slave-dealers almost universally force the young girls to submit to their lust previous to their being disposed of. From such scenes one turns away with pity and indignation.*

Towns and ports involved in the slave trade

- North Africa:
  - Tangier (Morocco)
  - Marrakesh (Morocco)
  - Algiers (Algeria)
  - Tripoli (Libya)
  - Cairo (Egypt)
  - Aswan (Egypt)
- West Africa:
  - Aoudaghost (Mauritania)
  - Timbuktu (Mali)
  - Gao (Mali)
  - Bilma (Niger)
  - Kano (Nigeria)
- Swahili Coast:
  - Bagamoyo (Tanzania)
  - Zanzibar (Tanzania)
  - Kilwa (Tanzania)
  - Sofala (Beira, Mozambique)
  - Mombasa (Kenya)
- Horn of Africa:
  - Assab (Eritrea)
  - Massawa (Eritrea)
  - Nefasit (Eritrea)
  - Tadjoura (Djibouti)
  - Zeila (Somalia)
  - Mogadishu (Somalia)
  - Kismayo (Somalia)
- Arabian Peninsula:
  - Jeddah (Saudi Arabia)
  - Zabīd (Yemen)
  - Muscat (Oman)
  - Aden (Yemen)
  - Socotra (Indian Ocean)
- Indian Ocean:
  - Debal (Sindh, Pakistan)
  - Karachi (Sindh, Pakistan)
  - Janjira (India)
  - Surat (India)
  - Mandvi, Kutch (India)

Legacy

The history of the slave trade has given rise to numerous debates amongst historians. For one thing, specialists are undecided on the number of Africans taken from their homes; this is difficult to resolve because of a lack of reliable statistics: there was no census system in medieval Africa. Archival material for the transatlantic trade in the 16th to 18th centuries may seem useful as a source, yet these record books were often falsified. Historians have to use imprecise narrative documents to make estimates which must be treated with caution: Luiz Felipe de Alencastro states that there were 8 million slaves taken from Africa between the 8th and 19th centuries along the Oriental and the Trans-Saharan routes.[350]

Olivier Pétré-Grenouilleau has put forward a figure of 17 million African people enslaved (in the same period and from the same area) on the basis of Ralph Austen's work.[351] Wikipedia:Citing sources Ronald Segal estimates between 11.5 and 14 million were enslaved by the Arab slave trade.[352] Wikipedia:Citing sources Other estimates place it around 11.2 million.[353]

There has also been a considerable genetic impact on Arabs throughout the Arab world from pre-modern African and European slaves.[354]

Figure 68: *A 1816 illustration of Christian slaves in Algiers.*

Primary sources

Medieval Arabic sources

These are given in chronological order. Scholars and geographers from the Arab world had been travelling to Africa since the time of Muhammad in the 7th century.

- Al-Masudi (died 957), *Muruj adh-dhahab* or *The Meadows of Gold*, the reference manual for geographers and historians of the Muslim world. The author had travelled widely across the Arab world as well as the Far East.
- Ya'qubi (9th century), *Kitab al-Buldan* or *Book of Countries*
- Abraham ben Jacob (Ibrahim ibn Jakub) (10th century), Jewish merchant from Córdoba
- Al-Bakri, author of *Kitāb al-Masālik wa'l-Mamālik* or *Book of Roads and Kingdoms*, published in Córdoba around 1068, gives us information about the Berbers and their activities; he collected eye-witness accounts on Saharan caravan routes.
- Muhammad al-Idrisi (died circa 1165), *Description of Africa and Spain*
- Ibn Battuta (died circa 1377), Moroccan geographer who travelled to sub-Saharan Africa, to Gao and to Timbuktu. His principal work is called

A Gift to Those Who Contemplate the Wonders of Cities and the Marvels of Travelling.
- Ibn Khaldun (died in 1406), historian and philosopher from North Africa. Sometimes considered as the historian of Arab, Berber and Persian societies. He is the author of *Muqaddimah* or*Historical Prolegomena* and *History of the Berbers*.
- Al-Maqrizi (died in 1442), Egyptian historian. His main contribution is his description of Cairo markets.
- Leo Africanus (died circa 1548), author of *Descrittione dell' Africa* or *Description of Africa, a rare description of Africa*.
- Rifa'a al-Tahtawi (1801–1873), who translated medieval works on geography and history. His work is mostly about Muslim Egypt.
- Joseph Cuoq, *Collection of Arabic sources concerning Western Africa between the 8th and 16th centuries (Paris 1975)*

European texts (16th–19th centuries)

- João de Castro, *Roteiro de Lisboa a Goa* (1538)
- James Bruce, (1730–1794), *Travels to Discover the Source of the Nile* (1790)
- René Caillié, (1799–1838), *Journal d'un voyage à Tombouctou*
- Robert Adams, *The Narrative of Robert Adams* (1816)
- Mungo Park, (1771–1806), *Travels in the Interior of Africa* (1816)
- Johann Ludwig Burckhardt, (1784–1817), *Travels in Nubia* (1819)
- Heinrich Barth, (1821–1865), *Travels and Discoveries in North and Central Africa* (1857)
- Richard Francis Burton, (1821–1890), *The Lake Regions of Central Africa* (1860)
- David Livingstone, (1813–1873), *Travel diaries* (1866–1873)
- Henry Morton Stanley, (1841–1904), *Through the Dark Continent* (1878)

Other sources

- Historical manuscripts such as the *Tarikh al-Sudan*, the Adalite *Futuh al-Habash*, the Abyssinian *Kebra Nagast*, and various Arabic and Ajam documents
- African oral tradition
- Kilwa Chronicle (16th century fragments)
- Numismatics: analysis of coins and of their diffusion
- Archaeology: architecture of trading posts and of towns associated with the slave trade
- Iconography: Arab and Persian miniatures in major libraries

- European engravings, contemporary with the slave trade, and some more modern
- Photographs from the 19th century onward

References

This article was initially translated from the featured French wiki article "Traite musulmane" on 19 May 2006.

- Shaban, M.A. (1976). *Islamic History: A New Interpretation, Vol 2: A.D. 750-1055 (A.H. 132-448)*[355]. Cambridge: Cambridge University Press. pp. 100 ff. ISBN 978-0-521-21198-7.<templatestyles src="Module:Citation/CS1/styles.css"></templatestyles>

Further reading

- Edward A. Alpers, *The East African Slave Trade* (Berkeley 1967)
- Ibn Khaldun, *The Muqaddimah*, trans. F. Rosenthal, ed. N. J. Dawood (Princeton 1967)
- Murray Gordon, *Slavery in the Arab World* (New York 1989)
- Habeeb Akande, *Illuminating the Darkness: Blacks and North Africans in Islam* (Ta Ha 2012)
- Bernard Lewis, *Race and Slavery in the Middle East* (OUP 1990)
- Lal, K. S. (1994). Muslim slave system in medieval India. New Delhi: Aditya Prakashan.
- Patrick Manning, *Slavery and African Life: Occidental, Oriental, and African Slave Trades* (Cambridge 1990)
- Paul E. Lovejoy, *Transformations in Slavery: A History of Slavery in Africa* (Cambridge 2000)
- Allan G. B. Fisher, *Slavery and Muslim Society in Africa*, ed. C. Hurst (London 1970, 2nd edition 2001)
- *The African Diaspora in the Mediterranean Lands of Islam* (Princeton Series on the Middle East) Eve Troutt Powell (Editor), John O. Hunwick (Editor) (Princeton 2001)
- Ronald Segal, *Islam's Black Slaves* (Atlantic Books, London 2002)
- Robert C. Davis, *Christian Slaves, Muslim Masters: White Slavery in the Mediterranean, the Barbary Coast, and Italy, 1500-1800* (Palgrave Macmillan, London 2003) <templatestyles src="Module:Citation/CS1/styles.css" />ISBN 978-1-4039-4551-8
- Doudou Diène (2001). *From Chains to Bonds: The Slave Trade Revisited*[356]. Berghahn Books. ISBN 978-1571812650. Retrieved 26 May 2015.<templatestyles src="Module:Citation/CS1/styles.css"></templatestyles>

External links

- Robert Davis. "British Slaves on the Barbary Coast"[357]. BBC. Retrieved 29 April 2015.<templatestyles src="Module:Citation/CS1/styles.css"></templatestyles>
- "Slavery in Islam"[358]. BBC. Retrieved 29 April 2015.<templatestyles src="Module:Citation/CS1/styles.css"></templatestyles>
- "Encyclopædia Britannica's Guide to Black History"[359]. *www.britannica.com*. Encyclopædia Britannica. Archived from the original[360] on October 6, 2014. Retrieved 29 April 2015.<templatestyles src="Module:Citation/CS1/styles.css"></templatestyles>
- iAbolish.ORG! American Anti-Slavery Group (AASG) - particular focus on North African slaves[361]

Atlantic slave trade

<indicator name="pp-default"> 🔒 </indicator>

- v
- t
- e[362]

The **Atlantic slave trade** or **transatlantic slave trade** involved the transportation by slave traders of enslaved African people, mainly to the Americas. The slave trade regularly used the triangular trade route and its Middle Passage, and existed from the 16th to the 19th centuries. The vast majority of those who were enslaved and transported in the transatlantic slave trade were Africans from central and western Africa, who had been sold by other West Africans to Western European slave traders (with a small number being captured directly by the slave traders in coastal raids), who brought them to the Americas. The

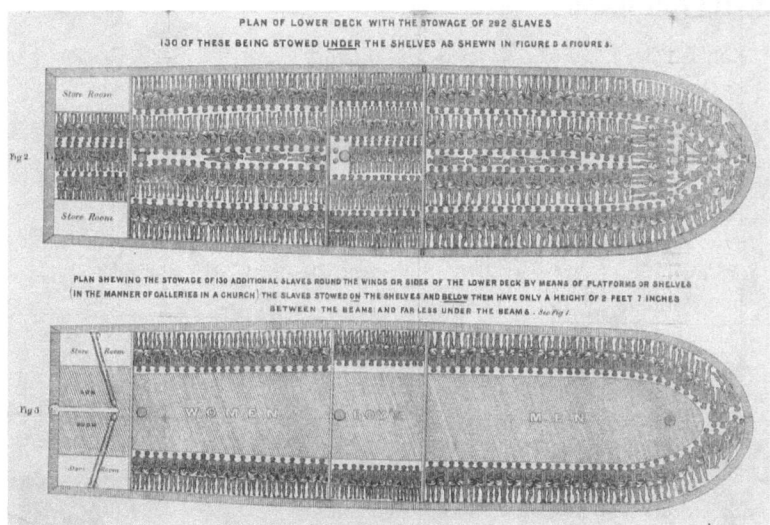

Figure 69: *Stowage of a British slave ship (1788)*

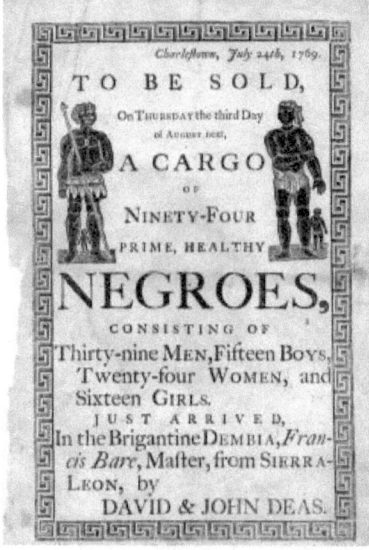

Figure 70: *Reproduction of a handbill advertising a slave auction in Charleston, South Carolina, in 1769.*

South Atlantic and Caribbean economies especially were dependent on the supply of secure labour for the production of commodity crops, making goods and clothing to sell in Europe. This was crucial to those western European countries which, in the late 17th and 18th centuries, were vying with each other to create overseas empires.

The Portuguese were the first to engage in the Atlantic slave trade in the 16th century. In 1526, they completed the first transatlantic slave voyage to Brazil, and other European countries soon followed. Shipowners regarded the slaves as cargo to be transported to the Americas as quickly and cheaply as possible, there to be sold to work on coffee, tobacco, cocoa, sugar and cotton plantations, gold and silver mines, rice fields, construction industry, cutting timber for ships, in skilled labour, and as domestic servants. The first Africans imported to the English colonies were classified as "indentured servants", like workers coming from England, and also as "apprentices for life". By the middle of the 17th century, slavery had hardened as a racial caste, with the slaves and their offspring being legally the property of their owners, and children born to slave mothers were also slaves. As property, the people were considered merchandise or units of labour, and were sold at markets with other goods and services.

The major Atlantic slave trading nations, ordered by trade volume, were: the Portuguese, the British, the French, the Spanish, and the Dutch Empires. Several had established outposts on the African coast where they purchased slaves from local African leaders.[363] These slaves were managed by a factor who was established on or near the coast to expedite the shipping of slaves to the New World. Slaves were kept in a factory while awaiting shipment. Current estimates are that about 12 million Africans were shipped across the Atlantic,[364] although the number purchased by the traders was considerably higher, as the passage had a high death rate.[365,366] Near the beginning of the 19th century, various governments acted to ban the trade, although illegal smuggling still occurred. In the early 21st century, several governments issued apologies for the transatlantic slave trade.

Background

Atlantic travel

The Atlantic slave trade developed after trade contacts were established between the "Old World" (Afro-Eurasia) and the "New World" (the Americas). For centuries, tidal currents had made ocean travel particularly difficult and risky for the ships that were then available, and as such there had been very little, if any, maritime contact between the peoples living in these continents.[367] In the 15th century, however, new European developments in seafaring technologies resulted in ships being better equipped to deal with the tidal currents, and could begin traversing the Atlantic Ocean. Between 1600 and 1800, approximately 300,000 sailors engaged in the slave trade visited West Africa.[368] In doing so, they came into contact with societies living along the west African coast and in the Americas which they had never previously encountered.[369] Historian Pierre Chaunu termed the consequences of European navigation "disenclavement", with it marking an end of isolation for some societies and an increase in inter-societal contact for most others.[370]

Historian John Thornton noted, "A number of technical and geographical factors combined to make Europeans the most likely people to explore the Atlantic and develop its commerce".[371] He identified these as being the drive to find new and profitable commercial opportunities outside Europe as well as the desire to create an alternative trade network to that controlled by the Muslim Empire of the Middle East, which was viewed as a commercial, political and religious threat to European Christendom. In particular, European traders wanted to trade for gold, which could be found in western Africa, and also to find a maritime route to "the Indies" (India), where they could trade for luxury goods such as spices without having to obtain these items from Middle Eastern Islamic traders.[372]

Although many of the initial Atlantic naval explorations were led by Iberians, members of many European nationalities were involved, including sailors from Portugal, Spain, the Italian kingdoms, England, France and the Netherlands. This diversity led Thornton to describe the initial "exploration of the Atlantic" as "a truly international exercise, even if many of the dramatic discoveries were made under the sponsorship of the Iberian monarchs". That leadership later gave rise to the myth that "the Iberians were the sole leaders of the exploration".[373]

African slavery

Slavery was prevalent in many parts of Africa for many centuries before the beginning of the Atlantic slave trade. There is evidence that enslaved people from some parts of Africa were exported to states in Africa, Europe, and Asia prior to the European colonization of the Americas.[374]

The Atlantic slave trade was not the only slave trade from Africa, although it was the largest in volume and intensity. As Elikia M'bokolo wrote in *Le Monde diplomatique*:

<templatestyles src="Template:Quote/styles.css"/>

Figure 71: *Group of men, children, and women being taken to a slave market*

The African continent was bled of its human resources via all possible routes. Across the Sahara, through the Red Sea, from the Indian Ocean ports and across the Atlantic. At least ten centuries of slavery for the benefit of the Muslim countries (from the ninth to the nineteenth) ... Four million enslaved people exported via the Red Sea, another four million through the Swahili ports of the Indian Ocean, perhaps as many as nine million along the trans-Saharan caravan route, and eleven to twenty million (depending on the author) across the Atlantic Ocean.[375]

According to John K. Thornton, Europeans usually bought enslaved people who were captured in endemic warfare between African states.[376] Some Africans had made a business out of capturing Africans from neighboring ethnic groups or war captives and selling them.[377] A reminder of this practice is documented in the Slave Trade Debates of England in the early 19th century: "All the old writers ... concur in stating not only that wars are entered into for the sole purpose of making slaves, but that they are fomented by Europeans, with a view to that object."[378] People living around the Niger River were transported from these markets to the coast and sold at European trading ports in exchange for muskets and manufactured goods such as cloth or alcohol.[379] However, the European demand for slaves provided a large new market for the already existing trade.[380] While those held in slavery in their own region of

Figure 72: *The Portuguese presenting themselves before the Manikongo. The Portuguese initially fostered a good relationship with the Kingdom of Kongo. Civil War within Kongo would lead to many of its subjects ending up as enslaved people in Portuguese and other European vessels.*

Africa might hope to escape, those shipped away had little chance of returning to Africa.

European colonization and slavery in West Africa

Upon discovering new lands through their naval explorations, European colonisers soon began to migrate to and settle in lands outside their native continent. Off the coast of Africa, European migrants, under the directions of the Kingdom of Castile, invaded and colonised the Canary Islands during the 15th century, where they converted much of the land to the production of wine and sugar. Along with this, they also captured native Canary Islanders, the Guanches, to use as slaves both on the Islands and across the Christian Mediterranean.[381]

As historian John Thornton remarked, "the actual motivation for European expansion and for navigational breakthroughs was little more than to exploit the opportunity for immediate profits made by raiding and the seizure or purchase of trade commodities".[382] Using the Canary Islands as a naval base,

Europeans, at the time primarily Portuguese traders, began to move their activities down the western coast of Africa, performing raids in which slaves would be captured to be later sold in the Mediterranean.[383] Although initially successful in this venture, "it was not long before African naval forces were alerted to the new dangers, and the Portuguese [raiding] ships began to meet strong and effective resistance", with the crews of several of them being killed by African sailors, whose boats were better equipped at traversing the west African coasts and river systems.[384]

By 1494, the Portuguese king had entered agreements with the rulers of several West African states that would allow trade between their respective peoples, enabling the Portuguese to "tap into" the "well-developed commercial economy in Africa ... without engaging in hostilities".[385] "Peaceful trade became the rule all along the African coast", although there were some rare exceptions when acts of aggression led to violence. For instance, Portuguese traders attempted to conquer the Bissagos Islands in 1535.[386] In 1571 Portugal, supported by the Kingdom of Kongo, took control of the south-western region of Angola in order to secure its threatened economic interest in the area. Although Kongo later joined a coalition in 1591 to force the Portuguese out, Portugal had secured a foothold on the continent that it continued to occupy until the 20th century.[387] Despite these incidences of occasional violence between African and European forces, many African states ensured that any trade went on in their own terms, for instance, imposing custom duties on foreign ships. In 1525, the Kongolese king, Afonso I, seized a French vessel and its crew for illegally trading on his coast.

Historians have widely debated the nature of the relationship between these African kingdoms and the European traders. The Guyanese historian Walter Rodney (1972) has argued that it was an unequal relationship, with Africans being forced into a "colonial" trade with the more economically developed Europeans, exchanging raw materials and human resources (i.e. slaves) for manufactured goods. He argued that it was this economic trade agreement dating back to the 16th century that led to Africa being underdeveloped in his own time.[388] These ideas were supported by other historians, including Ralph Austen (1987).[389] This idea of an unequal relationship was contested by John Thornton (1998), who argued that "the Atlantic slave trade was not nearly as critical to the African economy as these scholars believed" and that "African manufacturing [at this period] was more than capable of handling competition from preindustrial Europe".[390] However, Anne Bailey, commenting on Thornton's suggestion that Africans and Europeans were equal partners in the Atlantic slave trade, wrote:

<templatestyles src="Template:Quote/styles.css"/>

Figure 73: *Portrait of an African Slave Woman, probably painted by Annibale Carracci in the 1580s*

[*T*]*o see Africans as partners implies equal terms and equal influence on the global and intercontinental processes of the trade. Africans had great influence on the continent itself, but they had no direct influence on the engines behind the trade in the capital firms, the shipping and insurance companies of Europe and America, or the plantation systems in Americas. They did not wield any influence on the building manufacturing centers of the West.*[391]

16th, 17th and 18th centuries

The Atlantic slave trade is customarily divided into two eras, known as the First and Second Atlantic Systems.

The First Atlantic system was the trade of enslaved Africans to, primarily, South American colonies of the Portuguese and Spanish empires; it accounted for slightly more than 3% of all Atlantic slave trade. It started (on a significant scale) in about 1502[392] and lasted until 1580 when Portugal was temporarily united with Spain. While the Portuguese were directly involved in trading enslaved peoples, the Spanish empire relied on the asiento system, awarding merchants (mostly from other countries) the license to trade enslaved people to their colonies. During the first Atlantic system, most of these traders were Portuguese, giving them a near-monopoly during the era. Some Dutch, English, and French traders also participated in the slave trade.[393] After the union, Portugal came under Spanish legislation that prohibited it from directly engaging in the slave trade as a carrier. It became a target for the traditional enemies of Spain, losing a large share of the trade to the Dutch, English, and French.

The Second Atlantic system was the trade of enslaved Africans by mostly English, Portuguese, French and Dutch traders. The main destinations of this phase were the Caribbean colonies and Brazil, as European nations built up economically slave-dependent colonies in the New World.[394] Slightly more than 3% of the enslaved people exported from Africa were traded between 1450 and 1600, and 16% in the 17th century.

It is estimated that more than half of the entire slave trade took place during the 18th century, with the British, Portuguese and French being the main carriers of nine out of ten slaves abducted in Africa. By the 1690s, the English were shipping the most slaves from West Africa. They maintained this position during the 18th century, becoming the biggest shippers of slaves across the Atlantic. By the 18th century, Angola had become one of the principal sources of the Atlantic slave trade.

Following the British and United States' bans on the African slave trade in 1808, it declined, but the period after still accounted for 28.5% of the total volume of the Atlantic slave trade.[395]

A burial ground in Campeche, Mexico, suggests slaves had been brought there not long after Hernán Cortés completed the subjugation of Aztec and Mayan Mexico in the 16th century. The graveyard had been in use from approximately 1550 to the late 17th century.[396]

Triangular trade

The first side of the triangle was the export of goods from Europe to Africa. A number of African kings and merchants took part in the trading of enslaved people from 1440 to about 1833. For each captive, the African rulers would receive a variety of goods from Europe. These included guns, ammunition, and other factory-made goods. The second leg of the triangle exported enslaved Africans across the Atlantic Ocean to the Americas and the Caribbean Islands. The third and final part of the triangle was the return of goods to Europe from the Americas. The goods were the products of slave-labour plantations and included cotton, sugar, tobacco, molasses and rum. Sir John Hawkins, considered the pioneer of the British slave trade, was the first to run the Triangular trade, making a profit at every stop.

Figure 74: *"The Slave Trade" by Auguste François Biard, 1840*

Labour and slavery

The Atlantic Slave Trade was the result of, among other things, labour shortage, itself in turn created by the desire of European colonists to exploit New World land and resources for capital profits. Native peoples were at first utilized as slave labour by Europeans until a large number died from overwork and Old World diseases. Alternative sources of labour, such as indentured servitude, failed to provide a sufficient workforce. Many crops could not be sold for profit, or even grown, in Europe. Exporting crops and goods from the New World to Europe often proved to be more profitable than producing them on the European mainland. A vast amount of labour was needed to create and sustain plantations that required intensive labour to grow, harvest, and process prized tropical crops. Western Africa (part of which became known as "the Slave Coast"), Angola and nearby Kingdoms and later Central Africa, became the source for enslaved people to meet the demand for labour.

The basic reason for the constant shortage of labour was that, with large amounts of cheap land available and lots of landowners searching for workers, free European immigrants were able to become landowners themselves after a relatively short time, thus increasing the need for workers.[397]

Thomas Jefferson attributed the use of slave labour in part to the climate, and the consequent idle leisure afforded by slave labour: "For in a warm climate,

Figure 75: *"Am I Not a Man and a Brother?" 1787 medallion designed by Josiah Wedgwood for the British anti-slavery campaign*

no man will labour for himself who can make another labour for him. This is so true, that of the proprietors of slaves a very small proportion indeed are ever seen to labour."

African participation in the slave trade

Africans played a direct role in the slave trade, selling their captives or prisoners of war to European buyers.[398] The prisoners and captives who were sold were usually from neighbouring or enemy ethnic groups.Wikipedia:Citation needed These captive slaves were considered "other", not part of the people of the ethnic group or "tribe"; African kings held no particular loyalty to them. Sometimes criminals would be sold so that they could no longer commit crimes in that area. Most other slaves were obtained from kidnappings, or through raids that occurred at gunpoint through joint ventures with the Europeans. But some African kings refused to sell any of their captives or criminals. King Jaja of Opobo, a former slave, refused to do business with the slavers completely. Wikipedia:Citation needed

Africans also participated in the slave trade through intermarriage, or cassare, meaning "to set up house". It is derived from the Portuguese word "casar", meaning "to marry". Cassare created political and economic bonds between

Figure 76: *Slave traders in Gorée, Senegal, 18th century*

European and African slave traders. Cassare was a pre-European practice used to integrate the "other" from a differing African tribe. Powerful West African groups used these marriages as an alliance used to strengthen their trade networks with European men by marrying off African women from families with ties to the slave trade. Early on in the Atlantic Slave trade, these marriages were common. The marriages were even performed using African customs, which Europeans did not object to, seeing how important the connections were.

European participation in the slave trade

Although Europeans were the market for slaves, Europeans rarely entered the interior of Africa, due to fear of disease and fierce African resistance. In Africa, convicted criminals could be punished by enslavement, a punishment which became more prevalent as slavery became more lucrative. Since most of these nations did not have a prison system, convicts were often sold or used in the scattered local domestic slave market.Wikipedia:Citation needed

As of 1778, Thomas Kitchin estimated that Europeans were bringing an estimated 52,000 slaves to the Caribbean yearly, with the French bringing the most Africans to the French West Indies (13,000 out of the yearly estimate). The Atlantic slave trade peaked in the last two decades of the 18th century,[399] during and following the Kongo Civil War.[400] Wars among tiny states along

Figure 77: *A slave being inspected*

the Niger River's Igbo-inhabited region and the accompanying banditry also spiked in this period. Another reason for surplus supply of enslaved people was major warfare conducted by expanding states, such as the kingdom of Dahomey,[401] the Oyo Empire, and the Asante Empire.[402]

Slavery in Africa and the New World contrasted

Forms of slavery varied both in Africa and in the New World. In general, slavery in Africa was not heritable – that is, the children of slaves were free – while in the Americas, children of slave mothers were considered born into slavery. This was connected to another distinction: slavery in West Africa was not reserved for racial or religious minorities, as it was in European colonies, although the case was otherwise in places such as Somalia, where Bantus were taken as slaves for the ethnic Somalis.[403,404]

The treatment of slaves in Africa was more variable than in the Americas. At one extreme, the kings of Dahomey routinely slaughtered slaves in hundreds or thousands in sacrificial rituals, and slaves as human sacrifices were also known in Cameroon.[405] On the other hand, slaves in other places were often treated as part of the family, "adopted children", with significant rights including the right to marry without their masters' permission.[406] Scottish explorer Mungo Park wrote:

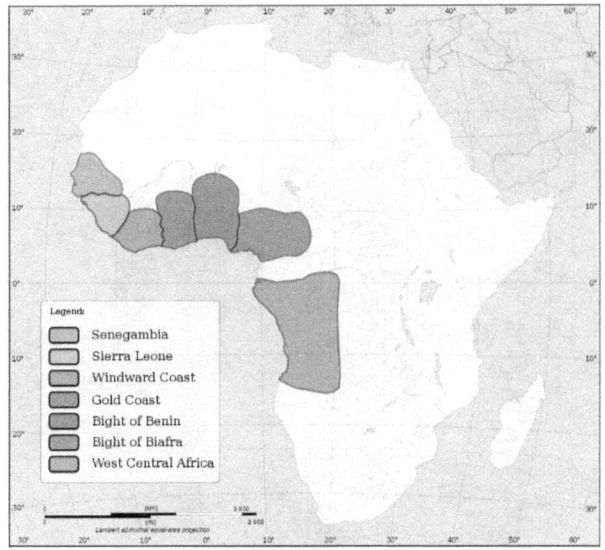

Figure 78: *Major slave trading regions of Africa, 15th–19th centuries*

> The slaves in Africa, I suppose, are nearly in the proportion of three to one to the freemen. They claim no reward for their services except food and clothing, and are treated with kindness or severity, according to the good or bad disposition of their masters ... The slaves which are thus brought from the interior may be divided into two distinct classes – first, such as were slaves from their birth, having been born of enslaved mothers; secondly, such as were born free, but who afterwards, by whatever means, became slaves. Those of the first description are by far the most numerous ...[407]

In the Americas, slaves were denied the right to marry freely and masters did not generally accept them as equal members of the family. New World slaves were considered the property of their owners, and slaves convicted of revolt or murder were executed.[408]

Slave market regions and participation

There were eight principal areas used by Europeans to buy and ship slaves to the Western Hemisphere. The number of enslaved people sold to the New World varied throughout the slave trade. As for the distribution of slaves from

Figure 79: *Ghezo, King of Dahomey, was under pressure from the British to end the slave trade*

regions of activity, certain areas produced far more enslaved people than others. Between 1650 and 1900, 10.24 million enslaved Africans arrived in the Americas from the following regions in the following proportions:[409]

- Senegambia (Senegal and the Gambia): 4.8%
- Upper Guinea (Guinea-Bissau, Guinea and Sierra Leone): 4.1%
- Windward Coast (Liberia and Ivory Coast): 1.8%
- Gold Coast (Ghana and east of Ivory Coast): 10.4%
- Bight of Benin (Togo, Benin and Nigeria west of the Niger Delta): 20.2%
- Bight of Biafra (Nigeria east of the Niger Delta, Cameroon, Equatorial Guinea and Gabon): 14.6%
- West Central Africa (Republic of Congo, Democratic Republic of Congo and Angola): 39.4%
- Southeastern Africa (Mozambique and Madagascar): 4.7%

Although the slave trade was largely global, there was considerable intracontinental slave trade in which 8 million people were enslaved within the African continent. Of those who did move out of Africa, 8 million were forced out of Eastern Africa to be sent to Asia.

African kingdoms of the era

There were over 173 city-states and kingdoms in the African regions affected by the slave trade between 1502 and 1853 when Brazil became the last Atlantic import nation to outlaw the slave trade. Of those 173, no fewer than 68 could be deemed nation states with political and military infrastructures that enabled them to dominate their neighbours. Nearly every present-day nation had a pre-colonial predecessor, sometimes an African Empire with which European traders had to barter.

Ethnic groups

The different ethnic groups brought to the Americas closely corresponds to the regions of heaviest activity in the slave trade. Over 45 distinct ethnic groups were taken to the Americas during the trade. Of the 45, the ten most prominent, according to slave documentation of the era are listed below.

1. The BaKongo of the Democratic Republic of Congo and Angola
2. The Mandé of Upper Guinea
3. The Gbe speakers of Togo, Ghana, and Benin (Adja, Mina, Ewe, Fon)
4. The Akan of Ghana and Ivory Coast
5. The Wolof of Senegal and the Gambia
6. The Igbo of southeastern Nigeria
7. The Mbundu of Angola (includes both Ambundu and Ovimbundu)
8. The Yoruba of southwestern Nigeria
9. The Chamba of Cameroon
10. The Makua of Mozambique

Human toll

The transatlantic slave trade resulted in a vast and as yet still unknown loss of life for African captives both in and outside America. Approximately 1.2 – 2.4 million Africans died during their transport to the New World.[410] More died soon upon their arrival. The number of lives lost in the procurement of slaves remains a mystery but may equal or exceed the number who survived to be enslaved.[411]

The savage nature of the trade led to the destruction of individuals and cultures. The following figures do not include deaths of enslaved Africans as a result of their labour, slave revolts, or diseases suffered while living among New World populations.

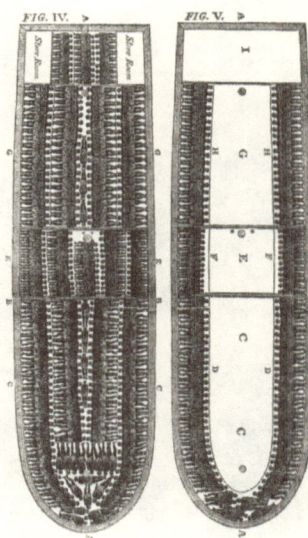

Figure 80: *Diagram of a slave ship from the Atlantic slave trade. From an Abstract of Evidence delivered before a select committee of the House of Commons in 1790 and 1791.*

Historian Ana Lucia Araujo has noted that the process of enslavement did not end with arrival on the American shores; the different paths taken by the individuals and groups who were victims of the Atlantic slave trade were influenced by different factors—including the disembarking region, the kind of work performed, gender, age, religion, and language.[412]

Estimates by Patrick Manning are that about 12 million slaves entered the Atlantic trade between the 16th and 19th century, but about 1.5 million died on board ship. About 10.5 million slaves arrived in the Americas. Besides the slaves who died on the Middle Passage, more Africans likely died during the slave raids in Africa and forced marches to ports. Manning estimates that 4 million died inside Africa after capture, and many more died young. Manning's estimate covers the 12 million who were originally destined for the Atlantic, as well as the 6 million destined for Asian slave markets and the 8 million destined for African markets.[413] Of the slaves shipped to The Americas, the largest share went to Brazil and the Caribbean.[414]

African conflicts

According to Kimani Nehusi, the presence of European slavers affected the way in which the legal code in African societies responded to offenders.

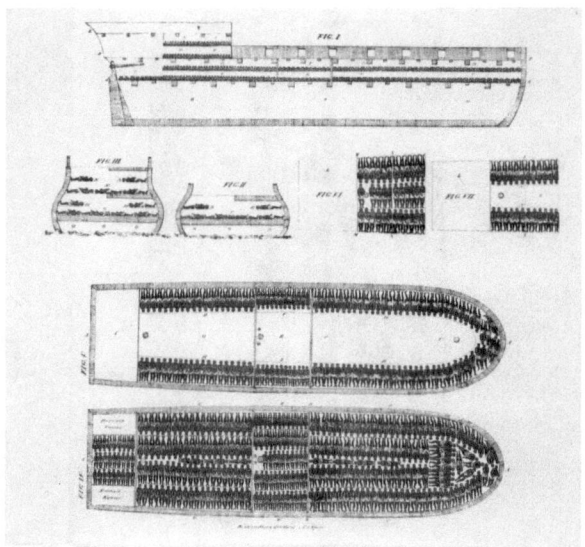

Figure 81: *Diagram of a large slave ship. Thomas Clarkson: The cries of Africa to the inhabitants of Europe, 1822?*

Crimes traditionally punishable by some other form of punishment became punishable by enslavement and sale to slave traders.Wikipedia:Citation needed According to David Stannard's *American Holocaust*, 50% of African deaths occurred in Africa as a result of wars between native kingdoms, which produced the majority of slaves. This includes not only those who died in battles but also those who died as a result of forced marches from inland areas to slave ports on the various coasts.[415] The practice of enslaving enemy combatants and their villages was widespread throughout Western and West Central Africa, although wars were rarely started to procure slaves. The slave trade was largely a by-product of tribal and state warfare as a way of removing potential dissidents after victory or financing future wars.[416] However, some African groups proved particularly adept and brutal at the practice of enslaving, such as Oyo, Benin, Igala, Kaabu, Asanteman, Dahomey, the Aro Confederacy and the Imbangala war bands.[417]

In letters written by the Manikongo, Nzinga Mbemba Afonso, to the King João III of Portugal, he writes that Portuguese merchandise flowing in is what is fueling the trade in Africans. He requests the King of Portugal to stop sending merchandise but should only send missionaries. In one of his letters he writes:

<templatestyles src="Template:Quote/styles.css"/>

> *Each day the traders are kidnapping our people—children of this country, sons of our nobles and vassals, even people of our own family. This corruption and depravity are so widespread that our land is entirely depopulated. We need in this kingdom only priests and schoolteachers, and no merchandise, unless it is wine and flour for Mass. It is our wish that this Kingdom not be a place for the trade or transport of slaves ...*
>
> *Many of our subjects eagerly lust after Portuguese merchandise that your subjects have brought into our domains. To satisfy this inordinate appetite, they seize many of our black free subjects ... They sell them. After having taken these prisoners [to the coast] secretly or at night ... As soon as the captives are in the hands of white men they are branded with a red-hot iron.*

Before the arrival of the Portuguese, slavery had already existed in Kongo. Afonso believed that the slave trade should be subject to Kongo law. When he suspected the Portuguese of receiving illegally enslaved persons to sell, he wrote to King João III in 1526 imploring him to put a stop to the practice.[418]

The kings of Dahomey sold war captives into transatlantic slavery; they would otherwise have been killed in a ceremony known as the Annual Customs. As one of West Africa's principal slave states, Dahomey became extremely unpopular with neighbouring peoples.[419,420,421] Like the Bambara Empire to the east, the Khasso kingdoms depended heavily on the slave trade for their economy. A family's status was indicated by the number of slaves it owned, leading to wars for the sole purpose of taking more captives. This trade led the Khasso into increasing contact with the European settlements of Africa's west coast, particularly the French.[422] Benin grew increasingly rich during the 16th and 17th centuries on the slave trade with Europe; slaves from enemy states of the interior were sold and carried to the Americas in Dutch and Portuguese ships. The Bight of Benin's shore soon came to be known as the "Slave Coast".[423]

King Gezo of Dahomey said in the 1840s:

<templatestyles src="Template:Quote/styles.css"/>

> *The slave trade is the ruling principle of my people. It is the source and the glory of their wealth ... the mother lulls the child to sleep with notes of triumph over an enemy reduced to slavery ...*

In 1807, the UK Parliament passed the Bill that abolished the trading of slaves. The King of Bonny (now in Nigeria) was horrified at the conclusion of the practice:

<templatestyles src="Template:Quote/styles.css"/>

> *We think this trade must go on. That is the verdict of our oracle and the priests. They say that your country, however great, can never stop a trade ordained by God himself.*[424]

Figure 82: *A Liverpool Slave Ship by William Jackson. Merseyside Maritime Museum*

Port factories

After being marched to the coast for sale, enslaved people were held in large forts called factories. The amount of time in factories varied, but Milton Meltzer states in *Slavery: A World History* that around 4.5% of deaths attributed to the transatlantic slave trade occurred during this phase. In other words, over 820,000 people are believed to have died in African ports such as Benguela, Elmina, and Bonny, reducing the number of those shipped to 17.5 million.[425]

Atlantic shipment

After being captured and held in the factories, slaves entered the infamous Middle Passage. Meltzer's research puts this phase of the slave trade's overall mortality at 12.5%. Their deaths were the result of brutal treatment and poor care from the time of their capture and throughout their voyage. Around 2.2 million Africans died during these voyages where they were packed into tight, unsanitary spaces on ships for months at a time. Measures were taken to stem the onboard mortality rate, such as enforced "dancing" (as exercise) above deck and the practice of force-feeding enslaved persons who tried to starve themselves. The conditions on board also resulted in the spread of fatal diseases. Other fatalities were suicides, slaves who escaped by jumping overboard. The slave traders would try to fit anywhere from 350 to 600 slaves on one ship. Before the African slave trade was completely banned by participating nations in 1853, 15.3 million enslaved people had arrived in the Americas.

Raymond L. Cohn, an economics professor whose research has focused on economic history and international migration, has researched the mortality rates among Africans during the voyages of the Atlantic slave trade. He found that mortality rates decreased over the history of the slave trade, primarily because the length of time necessary for the voyage was declining. "In the eighteenth century many slave voyages took at least 2½ months. In the nineteenth century, 2 months appears to have been the maximum length of the voyage, and many voyages were far shorter. Fewer slaves died in the Middle Passage over time mainly because the passage was shorter."[426]

Despite the vast profits of slavery, the ordinary sailors on slave ships were badly paid and subject to harsh discipline. Mortality of around 20% was expected in a ship's crew during the course of a voyage; this was due to disease, flogging, overwork or slave uprisings. Disease (malaria or yellow fever) was the most common cause of death among sailors. A high crew mortality rate on the return voyage was in the captain's interests as it reduced the number of sailors who had to be paid on reaching the home port.

The slave trade was hated by many sailors and those who joined the crews of slave ships often did so through coercion or because they could find no other employment.

Seasoning camps

Meltzer also states that 33% of Africans would have died in the first year at the seasoning camps found throughout the Caribbean. Jamaica held one of the most notorious of these camps. Dysentery was the leading cause of death. Around 5 million Africans died in these camps, reducing the number of survivors to about 10 million.

European competition

The trade of enslaved Africans in the Atlantic has its origins in the explorations of Portuguese mariners down the coast of West Africa in the 15th century. Before that, contact with African slave markets was made to ransom Portuguese who had been captured by the intense North African Barbary pirate attacks on Portuguese ships and coastal villages, frequently leaving them depopulated. The first Europeans to use enslaved Africans in the New World were the Spaniards, who sought auxiliaries for their conquest expeditions and

Figure 83: *Punishing slaves at Calabouco, in Rio de Janeiro, c. 1822*

labourers on islands such as Cuba and Hispaniola. The alarming decline in the native population had spurred the first royal laws protecting them (Laws of Burgos, 1512–13). The first enslaved Africans arrived in Hispaniola in 1501.[427] After Portugal had succeeded in establishing sugar plantations (*engenhos*) in northern Brazil ca. 1545, Portuguese merchants on the West African coast began to supply enslaved Africans to the sugar planters. While at first these planters had relied almost exclusively on the native Tupani for slave labour, after 1570 they began importing Africans, as a series of epidemics had decimated the already destabilized Tupani communities. By 1630, Africans had replaced the Tupani as the largest contingent of labour on Brazilian sugar plantations. This ended the European medieval household tradition of slavery, resulted in Brazil's receiving the most enslaved Africans, and revealed sugar cultivation and processing as the reason that roughly 84% of these Africans were shipped to the New World.

As Britain rose in naval power and settled continental North America and some islands of the West Indies, they became the leading slave traders. At one stage the trade was the monopoly of the Royal Africa Company, operating out of London. But, following the loss of the company's monopoly in 1689,[428] Bristol and Liverpool merchants became increasingly involved in the trade.[429] By the late 17th century, one out of every four ships that left Liverpool harbour was a slave trading ship.[430] Much of the wealth on which the city of Manchester, and

Figure 84: *Recently bought slaves in Brazil on their way to the farms of the landowners who bought them c. 1830.*

surrounding towns, was built in the late 18th century, and for much of the 19th century, was based on the processing of slave-picked cotton and manufacture of cloth.[431] Other British cities also profited from the slave trade. Birmingham, the largest gun-producing town in Britain at the time, supplied guns to be traded for slaves. 75% of all sugar produced in the plantations was sent to London, and much of it was consumed in the highly lucrative coffee houses there.

New World destinations

The first slaves to arrive as part of a labour force in the New World reached the island of Hispaniola (now Haiti and the Dominican Republic) in 1502. Cuba received its first four slaves in 1513. Jamaica received its first shipment of 4000 slaves in 1518. Slave exports to Honduras and Guatemala started in 1526.

The first enslaved Africans to reach what would become the United States arrived in JulyWikipedia:Citation needed 1526 as part of a Spanish attempt to colonize San Miguel de Gualdape. By November the 300 Spanish colonists were reduced to 100, and their slaves from 100 to 70Wikipedia:Please clarify. The enslaved people revolted in 1526 and joined a nearby Native American tribe, while the Spanish abandoned the colony altogether (1527). The area of the future Colombia received its first enslaved people in 1533. El Salvador, Costa Rica and Florida began their stints in the slave trade in 1541, 1563 and 1581, respectively.

Figure 85: *A 19th-century lithograph showing a sugarcane plantation in Suriname.*

The 17th century saw an increase in shipments. Africans arrived in the English colony of Jamestown, Virginia in 1619. The first kidnapped Africans in English North America were classed as indentured servants and freed after seven years. Virginia law codified chattel slavery in 1656, and in 1662 the colony adopted the principle of *partus sequitur ventrem*, which classified children of slave mothers as slaves, regardless of paternity. Irish immigrants took slaves to Montserrat in 1651, and in 1655 slaves were shippedWikipedia:Manual of Style/Words to watch#Unsupported attributions to Belize.

By 1802, Russian colonists noted that "Boston" (U.S.-based) skippers were trading African slaves for otter pelts with the Tlingit people in Southeast Alaska.

Distribution of slaves (1519–1867)[432]

Destination	Percentage
Portuguese America	38.5%
British America (minus North America)	18.4%
Spanish Empire	17.5%
French Americas	13.6%
British North America	6.45%

English Americas	3.25%
Dutch West Indies	2.0%
Danish West Indies	0.3%

The number of the Africans who arrived in each region is calculated from the total number of slaves imported, about 10,000,000.[433]

Economics of slavery

In France in the 18th century, returns for investors in plantations averaged around 6%; as compared to 5% for most domestic alternatives, this represented a 20% profit advantage. Risks—maritime and commercial—were important for individual voyages. Investors mitigated it by buying small shares of many ships at the same time. In that way, they were able to diversify a large part of the risk away. Between voyages, ship shares could be freely sold and bought.[434]

By far the most financially profitable West Indian colonies in 1800 belonged to the United Kingdom. After entering the sugar colony business late, British naval supremacy and control over key islands such as Jamaica, Trinidad, the Leeward Islands and Barbados and the territory of British Guiana gave it an important edge over all competitors; while many British did not make gains, a handful of individuals made small fortunes. This advantage was reinforced when France lost its most important colony, St. Domingue (western Hispaniola, now Haiti), to a slave revolt in 1791 and supported revolts against its rival Britain, after the 1793 French revolution in the name of liberty. Before 1791, British sugar had to be protected to compete against cheaper French sugar.

After 1791, the British islands produced the most sugar, and the British people quickly became the largest consumers. West Indian sugar became ubiquitous as an additive to Indian tea. It has been estimated that the profits of the slave trade and of West Indian plantations created up to one-in-twenty of every pound circulating in the British economy at the time of the Industrial Revolution in the latter half of the 18th century.[435]

Effects

World population (in millions)[436]

Year	1750	1800	1850	1900	1950	1999
World	791	978	1,262	1,650	2,521	5,978
Africa	106	107	111	133	221	767

Asia	502	635	809	947	1,402	3,634
Europe	163	203	276	408	547	729
Latin America and the Caribbean	16	24	38	74	167	511
Northern America	2	7	26	82	172	307
Oceania	2	2	2	6	13	30

World population (by percentage distribution)

Year	1750	1800	1850	1900	1950	1999
World	100	100	100	100	100	100
Africa	13.4	10.9	8.8	8.1	8.8	12.8
Asia	63.5	64.9	64.1	57.4	55.6	60.8
Europe	20.6	20.8	21.9	24.7	21.7	12.2
Latin America and the Caribbean	2.0	2.5	3.0	4.5	6.6	8.5
Northern America	0.3	0.7	2.1	5.0	6.8	5.1
Oceania	0.3	0.2	0.2	0.4	0.5	0.5

Historian Walter Rodney has argued that at the start of the slave trade in the 16th century, although there was a technological gap between Europe and Africa, it was not very substantial. Both continents were using Iron Age technology. The major advantage that Europe had was in ship building. During the period of slavery, the populations of Europe and the Americas grew exponentially, while the population of Africa remained stagnant. Rodney contended that the profits from slavery were used to fund economic growth and technological advancement in Europe and the Americas. Based on earlier theories by Eric Williams, he asserted that the industrial revolution was at least in part funded by agricultural profits from the Americas. He cited examples such as the invention of the steam engine by James Watt, which was funded by plantation owners from the Caribbean.[437]

Other historians have attacked both Rodney's methodology and accuracy. Joseph C. Miller has argued that the social change and demographic stagnation (which he researched on the example of West Central Africa) was caused primarily by domestic factors. Joseph Inikori provided a new line of argument, estimating counterfactual demographic developments in case the Atlantic slave trade had not existed. Patrick Manning has shown that the slave trade did have a profound impact on African demographics and social institutions, but criticized Inikori's approach for not taking other factors (such as famine and drought) into account, and thus being highly speculative.[438]

Figure 86: *Slaves processing tobacco in 17th-century Virginia*

Figure 87: *Cowrie shells were used as money in the slave trade*

Effect on the economy of West Africa

No scholars dispute the harm done to the enslaved people but the effect of the trade on African societies is much debated, due to the apparent influx of goods to Africans. Proponents of the slave trade, such as Archibald Dalzel, argued that African societies were robust and not much affected by the trade. In the

19th century, European abolitionists, most prominently Dr. David Livingstone, took the opposite view, arguing that the fragile local economy and societies were being severely harmed by the trade.

Because the negative effects of slavery on the economies of Africa have been well documented, namely the significant decline in population, some African rulers likely saw an economic benefit from trading their subjects with European slave traders. With the exception of Portuguese controlled Angola, coastal African leaders "generally controlled access to their coasts, and were able to prevent direct enslavement of their subjects and citizens".[439] Thus, as African scholar John Thornton argues, African leaders who allowed the continuation of the slave trade likely derived an economic benefit from selling their subjects to Europeans. The Kingdom of Benin, for instance, participated in the African slave trade, at will, from 1715 to 1735, surprising Dutch traders, who had not expected to buy slaves in Benin. The benefit derived from trading slaves for European goods was enough to make the Kingdom of Benin rejoin the trans-Atlantic slave trade after centuries of non-participation. Such benefits included military technology (specifically guns and gunpowder), gold, or simply maintaining amicable trade relationships with European nations. The slave trade was, therefore, a means for some African elites to gain economic advantages.[440] Historian Walter Rodney estimates that by c.1770, the King of Dahomey was earning an estimated £250,000 per year by selling captive African soldiers and enslaved people to the European slave-traders. Many West African countries also already had a tradition of holding slaves, which was expanded into trade with Europeans.

The Atlantic trade brought new crops to Africa and also more efficient currencies which were adopted by the West African merchants. This can be interpreted as an institutional reform which reduced the cost of doing business. But the developmental benefits were limited as long as the business including slaving.

Both Thornton and Fage contend that while African political elite may have ultimately benefited from the slave trade, their decision to participate may have been influenced more by what they could lose by not participating. In Fage's article "Slavery and the Slave Trade in the Context of West African History", he notes that for West Africans "... there were really few effective means of mobilizing labour for the economic and political needs of the state" without the slave trade.

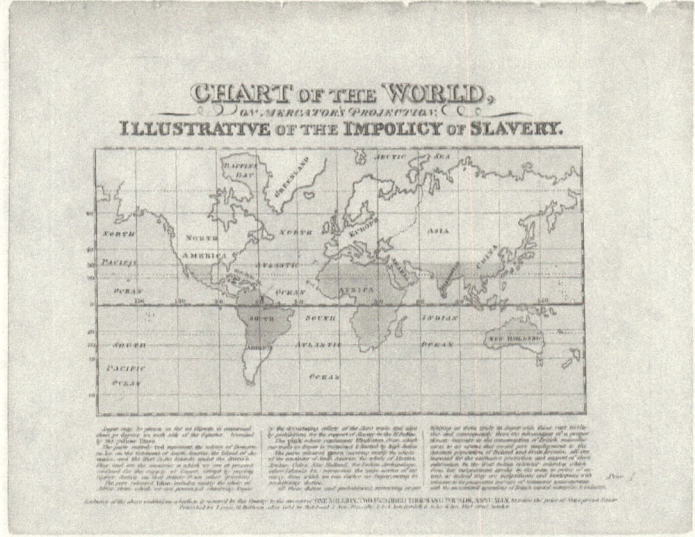

Figure 88: *This map argues that import prohibitions and high duties on sugar were artificially inflating prices and inhibiting manufacturing in England. 1823*

Effects on the British economy

Historian Eric Williams in 1944 argued that the profits that Britain received from its sugar colonies, or from the slave trade between Africa and the Caribbean, was a major factor in financing Britain's industrial revolution. However, he says that by the time of its abolition in 1833 it had lost its profitability and it was in Britain's economic interest to ban it.[441]

Other researchers and historians have strongly contested what has come to be referred to as the "Williams thesis" in academia. David Richardson has concluded that the profits from the slave trade amounted to less than 1% of domestic investment in Britain.[442] Economic historian Stanley Engerman finds that even without subtracting the associated costs of the slave trade (e.g., shipping costs, slave mortality, mortality of British people in Africa, defense costs) or reinvestment of profits back into the slave trade, the total profits from the slave trade and of West Indian plantations amounted to less than 5% of the British economy during any year of the Industrial Revolution. Engerman's 5% figure gives as much as possible in terms of benefit of the doubt to the Williams argument, not solely because it does not take into account the associated costs of the slave trade to Britain, but also because it carries the full-employment assumption from economics and holds the gross value of slave trade profits

Figure 89: *A Linen Market with enslaved Africans. West Indies, circa 1780*

as a direct contribution to Britain's national income. Historian Richard Pares, in an article written before Williams' book, dismisses the influence of wealth generated from the West Indian plantations upon the financing of the Industrial Revolution, stating that whatever substantial flow of investment from West Indian profits into industry there occurred after emancipation, not before.

Seymour Drescher and Robert Anstey argue the slave trade remained profitable until the end, and that moralistic reform, not economic incentive, was primarily responsible for abolition. They say slavery remained profitable in the 1830s because of innovations in agriculture.[443]

Karl Marx in his influential economic history of capitalism *Das Kapital* wrote that "... the turning of Africa into a warren for the commercial hunting of black-skins, signaled the rosy dawn of the era of capitalist production". He argued that the slave trade was part of what he termed the "primitive accumulation" of capital, the 'non-capitalist' accumulation of wealth that preceded and created the financial conditions for Britain's industrialisation.

Demographics

The demographic effects of the slave trade is a controversial and highly debated issue. Although scholars such as Paul Adams and Erick D. Langer have estimated that sub-Saharan Africa represented about 18 percent of the world's population in 1600 and only 6 percent in 1900, the reasons for this demographic shift have been the subject of much debate. In addition to the depopulation Africa experienced because of the slave trade, African nations were left with severely imbalanced gender ratios, with females comprising up to 65 percent of the population in hard-hit areas such as Angola. Moreover, many scholars (such as Barbara N. Ramusack) have suggested a link between the prevalence of prostitution in Africa today with the temporary marriages that were enforced during the course of the slave trade.

Walter Rodney argued that the export of so many people had been a demographic disaster which left Africa permanently disadvantaged when compared to other parts of the world, and it largely explains the continent's continued poverty. He presented numbers showing that Africa's population stagnated during this period, while those of Europe and Asia grew dramatically. According to Rodney, all other areas of the economy were disrupted by the slave trade as the top merchants abandoned traditional industries in order to pursue slaving, and the lower levels of the population were disrupted by the slaving itself.

Others have challenged this view. J. D. Fage compared the demographic effect on the continent as a whole. David Eltis has compared the numbers to the rate of emigration from Europe during this period. In the 19th century alone over 50 million people left Europe for the Americas, a far higher rate than were ever taken from Africa.[444]

Other scholars accused Walter Rodney of mischaracterizing the trade between Africans and Europeans. They argue that Africans, or more accurately African elites, deliberately let European traders join in an already large trade in enslaved people and that they were not patronized.[445]

As Joseph E. Inikori argues, the history of the region shows that the effects were still quite deleterious. He argues that the African economic model of the period was very different from the European model, and could not sustain such population losses. Population reductions in certain areas also led to widespread problems. Inikori also notes that after the suppression of the slave trade Africa's population almost immediately began to rapidly increase, even prior to the introduction of modern medicines.[446]

Legacy of racism

Walter Rodney states,

> *The role of slavery in promoting racist prejudice and ideology has been carefully studied in certain situations, especially in the USA. The simple fact is that no people can enslave another for four centuries without coming out with a notion of superiority, and when the colour and other*

Figure 90: *West Indian Creole woman, with her black servant, circa 1780*

physical traits of those peoples were quite different it was inevitable that the prejudice should take a racist form.

Eric Williams argued that "A racial twist [was] given to what is basically an economic phenomenon. Slavery was not born of racism: rather, racism was the consequence of slavery."

End of the Atlantic slave trade

In Britain, America, Portugal and in parts of Europe, opposition developed against the slave trade. Davis says that abolitionists assumed "that an end to slave imports would lead automatically to the amelioration and gradual abolition of slavery".[447] In Britain and America, opposition to the trade was led by the Religious Society of Friends (Quakers) and establishment Evangelicals such as William Wilberforce. Many people joined the movement and they began to protest against the trade, but they were opposed by the owners of the colonial holdings.[448] Following Lord Mansfield's decision in 1772, slaves became free upon entering the British isles.[449] Under the leadership of Thomas Jefferson, the new state of Virginia in 1778 became the first state and one of the first jurisdictions anywhere to stop the importation of slaves for sale; it made it a crime for traders to bring in slaves from out of state or from overseas for sale; migrants from other states were allowed to bring their own slaves.

Figure 91: *William Wilberforce (1759–1833), politician and philanthropist who was a leader of the movement to abolish the slave trade.*

The new law freed all slaves brought in illegally after its passage and imposed heavy fines on violators.[450,451] Denmark, which had been active in the slave trade, was the first country to ban the trade through legislation in 1792, which took effect in 1803. Britain banned the slave trade in 1807, imposing stiff fines for any slave found aboard a British ship (*see Slave Trade Act 1807*). The Royal Navy moved to stop other nations from continuing the slave trade and declared that slaving was equal to piracy and was punishable by death. The United States Congress passed the Slave Trade Act of 1794, which prohibited the building or outfitting of ships in the U.S. for use in the slave trade. In 1807 Congress outlawed the importation of slaves beginning on 1 January 1808, the earliest date permitted by the United States Constitution for such a ban.

William Wilberforce was a driving force in the British Parliament in the fight against the slave trade in the British Empire. On 22 February 1807, the House of Commons passed a motion 283 votes to 16 to abolish the Atlantic slave trade. The United States abolished the slave trade the same year, but not its internal slave trade which became the dominant character in American slavery until the 1860s.[452] In 1805 the British Order-in-Council had restricted the importation of slaves into colonies that had been captured from France and the Netherlands. Britain continued to press other nations to end its trade; in

Figure 92: *"Am I not a woman and a sister?"
An antislavery medallion from the late 18th century*

1810 an Anglo-Portuguese treaty was signed whereby Portugal agreed to restrict its trade into its colonies; an 1813 Anglo-Swedish treaty whereby Sweden outlawed its slave trade; the Treaty of Paris 1814 where France agreed with Britain that the trade is "repugnant to the principles of natural justice" and agreed to abolish the slave trade in five years; the 1814 Anglo-Netherlands treaty where the Dutch outlawed its slave trade.

The Royal Navy's West Africa Squadron, established in 1808, grew by 1850 to a force of some 25 vessels, which were tasked with combating slavery along the African coast.[453] Between 1807 and 1860, the Royal Navy's Squadron seized approximately 1,600 ships involved in the slave trade and freed 150,000 Africans who were aboard these vessels.[454] Several hundred slaves a year were transported by the navy to the British colony of Sierra Leone, where they were made to serve as "apprentices" in the colonial economy until the Slavery Abolition Act 1833.[455]

The last recorded slave ship to land on U.S. soil was the *Clotilde*, which in 1859 illegally smuggled a number of Africans into the town of Mobile, Alabama. The Africans on board were sold as slaves; however, slavery in the U.S. was abolished five years later following the end of the American Civil War in 1865. The last survivor of the voyage was Cudjoe Lewis, who died in 1935. The last

Figure 93: *Capture of slave ship El Almirante by the British Royal Navy in the 1800s. HMS Black Joke freed 466 slaves.*

country to ban the Atlantic slave trade was Brazil in 1831. However, a vibrant illegal trade continued to ship large numbers of enslaved people to Brazil and also to Cuba until the 1860s, when British enforcement and further diplomacy finally ended the Atlantic slave trade. In 1870 Portugal ended the last trade route with the Americas where the last country to import slaves was Brazil. In Brazil, however, slavery itself was not ended until 1888, making it the last country in the Americas to end involuntary servitude.

The historian Walter Rodney contends that it was a decline in the profitability of the triangular trades that made it possible for certain basic human sentiments to be asserted at the decision-making level in a number of European countries- Britain being the most crucial because it was the greatest carrier of African captives across the Atlantic. Rodney states that changes in productivity, technology, and patterns of exchange in Europe and the Americas informed the decision by the British to end their participation in the trade in 1807. In 1809 President James Madison outlawed the slave trade with the United States.

Nevertheless, Michael Hardt and Antonio Negri[456] argue that it was neither a strictly economic nor moral matter. First, because slavery was (in practice) still beneficial to capitalism, providing not only an influx of capital but also

Figure 94: *House slaves in Brazil c. 1820, by Jean-Baptiste Debret*

disciplining hardship into workers (a form of "apprenticeship" to the capitalist industrial plant). The more "recent" argument of a "moral shift" (the basis of the previous lines of this article) is described by Hardt and Negri as an "ideological" apparatus in order to eliminate the sentiment of guilt in western society. Although moral arguments did play a secondary role, they usually had major resonance when used as a strategy to undercut competitors' profits. This argument holds that Eurocentric history has been blind to the most important element in this fight for emancipation, precisely, the constant revolt and the antagonism of slaves' revolts. The most important of those being the Haitian Revolution. The shock of this revolution in 1804, certainly introduces an essential political argument into the end of the slave trade, which happened only three years later.

Legacy

African diaspora

The African diaspora which was created via slavery has been a complex interwoven part of American history and culture. In the United States, the success of Alex Haley's book *Roots: The Saga of an American Family*, published in 1976, and the subsequent television miniseries based upon it *Roots*, broadcast on the ABC network in January 1977, led to an increased interest and appreciation of African heritage amongst the African-American community.[457] The influence of these led many African Americans to begin researching their family histories and making visits to West Africa. In turn, a tourist industry grew up to supply them. One notable example of this is through the Roots Homecoming Festival held annually in the Gambia, in which rituals are held through which African Americans can symbolically "come home" to Africa.[458] Issues of dispute have however developed between African Americans and African authorities over how to display historic sites that were involved in the Atlantic slave trade, with prominent voices in the former criticising the latter for not displaying such sites sensitively, but instead treating them as a commercial enterprise.[459]

"Back to Africa"

In 1816, a group of wealthy European-Americans, some of whom were abolitionists and others who were racial segregationists, founded the American Colonization Society with the express desire of returning African Americans who were in the United States to West Africa. In 1820, they sent their first ship to Liberia, and within a decade around two thousand African Americans had been settled in the west African country. Such re-settlement continued throughout the 19th century, increasing following the deterioration of race relations in the southern states of the US following Reconstruction in 1877.[460]

Rastafari movement

The Rastafari movement, which originated in Jamaica, where 98% of the population are descended from victims of the Atlantic slave trade, has made great efforts to publicize the slavery and to ensure it is not forgotten, especially through reggae music.[461]

Apologies

Worldwide

In 1998, UNESCO designated 23 August as International Day for the Remembrance of the Slave Trade and its Abolition. Since then there have been a number of events recognizing the effects of slavery.

At the 2001 World Conference Against Racism in Durban, South Africa, African nations demanded a clear apology for slavery from the former slave-trading countries. Some nations were ready to express an apology, but the opposition, mainly from the United Kingdom, Portugal, Spain, the Netherlands, and the United States blocked attempts to do so. A fear of monetary compensation might have been one of the reasons for the opposition. As of 2009, efforts are underway to create a UN Slavery Memorial as a permanent remembrance of the victims of the Atlantic slave trade.

Benin

In 1999, President Mathieu Kerekou of Benin (formerly the Kingdom of Dahomey) issued a national apology for the role Africans played in the Atlantic slave trade.[462] Luc Gnacadja, minister of environment and housing for Benin, later said: "The slave trade is a shame, and we do repent for it."[463] Researchers estimate that 3 million slaves were exported out of the Slave Coast bordering the Bight of Benin.

France

On 30 January 2006, Jacques Chirac (the then French President) said that 10 May would henceforth be a national day of remembrance for the victims of slavery in France, marking the day in 2001 when France passed a law recognising slavery as a crime against humanity.[464]

Ghana

President Jerry Rawlings of Ghana also apologized for his country's involvement in the slave trade.

Netherlands

At a UN conference on the Atlantic slave trade in 2001, the Dutch Minister for Urban Policy and Integration of Ethnic Minorities Roger van Boxtel said that the Netherlands "recognizes the grave injustices of the past." On 1 July 2013, at the 150th anniversary of the abolition of slavery in the Dutch West Indies, the Dutch government expressed "deep regret and remorse" for the involvement of the Netherlands in the Atlantic slave trade. The Dutch government has remained short of a formal apology for its involvement in the Atlantic slave trade, as an apology implies that it considers its own actions of the past as unlawful, and could lead to litigation for monetary compensation by descendants of the enslaved.

Nigeria

In 2009, the Civil Rights Congress of Nigeria has written an open letter to all African chieftains who participated in trade calling for an apology for their role in the Atlantic slave trade: "We cannot continue to blame the white men, as Africans, particularly the traditional rulers, are not blameless. In view of the fact that the Americans and Europe have accepted the cruelty of their roles and have forcefully apologized, it would be logical, reasonable and humbling if African traditional rulers ... [can] accept blame and formally apologize to the descendants of the victims of their collaborative and exploitative slave trade."

Uganda

In 1998, President Yoweri Museveni of Uganda called tribal chieftains to apologize for their involvement in the slave trade: "African chiefs were the ones waging war on each other and capturing their own people and selling them. If anyone should apologise it should be the African chiefs. We still have those traitors here even today."

United Kingdom

On 9 December 1999, Liverpool City Council passed a formal motion apologizing for the City's part in the slave trade. It was unanimously agreed that Liverpool acknowledges its responsibility for its involvement in three centuries of the slave trade. The City Council has made an unreserved apology for Liverpool's involvement and the continual effect of slavery on Liverpool's black communities.[465]

On 27 November 2006, British Prime Minister Tony Blair made a partial apology for Britain's role in the African slavery trade. However African rights activists denounced it as "empty rhetoric" that failed to address the issue properly. They feel his apology stopped shy to prevent any legal retort.[466] Blair again apologized on March 14, 2007.[467]

On 24 August 2007, Ken Livingstone (Mayor of London) apologized publicly for London's role in the slave trade. "You can look across there to see the institutions that still have the benefit of the wealth they created from slavery", he said pointing towards the financial district, before breaking down in tears. He claimed that London was still tainted by the horrors of slavery. Jesse Jackson praised Mayor Livingstone and added that reparations should be made.[468]

United States

On 24 February 2007, the Virginia General Assembly passed House Joint Resolution Number 728[469] acknowledging "with profound regret the involuntary servitude of Africans and the exploitation of Native Americans, and call for reconciliation among all Virginians". With the passing of that resolution, Virginia became the first of the 50 United States to acknowledge through the state's governing body their state's involvement in slavery. The passing of this resolution came on the heels of the 400th-anniversary celebration of the city of Jamestown, Virginia, which was the first permanent English colony to survive in what would become the United States. Jamestown is also recognized as one of the first slave ports of the American colonies. On 31 May 2007, the Governor of Alabama, Bob Riley, signed a resolution expressing "profound regret" for Alabama's role in slavery and apologizing for slavery's wrongs and lingering effects. Alabama is the fourth state to pass a slavery apology, following votes by the legislatures in Maryland, Virginia, and North Carolina.[470]

On 30 July 2008, the United States House of Representatives passed a resolution apologizing for American slavery and subsequent discriminatory laws. The language included a reference to the "fundamental injustice, cruelty, brutality and inhumanity of slavery and Jim Crow" segregation.[471] On 18 June 2009, the United States Senate issued an apologetic statement decrying the "fundamental injustice, cruelty, brutality, and inhumanity of slavery". The news was welcomed by President Barack Obama.[472]

References

Bibliography

Academic books

<templatestyles src="Template:Refbegin/styles.css" />

- Austen, Ralph (1987). *African Economic History: Internal Development and External Dependency*. London: James Currey. ISBN 978-0-85255-009-0.<templatestyles src="Module:Citation/CS1/styles.css"></templatestyles>
- Christopher, Emma (2006). *Slave Ship Sailors and Their Captive Cargoes, 1730–1807*. Cambridge: Cambridge University Press. ISBN 0-521-67966-4.<templatestyles src="Module:Citation/CS1/styles.css"></templatestyles>
- Rodney, Walter (1972). *How Europe Underdeveloped Africa*. London: Bogle L'Ouverture. ISBN 978-0-9501546-4-0.<templatestyles src="Module:Citation/CS1/styles.css"></templatestyles>
- Thornton, John (1998). *Africa and Africans in the Making of the Atlantic World, 1400–1800* (2nd ed.). New York: Cambridge University Press. ISBN 978-0-521-62217-2.<templatestyles src="Module:Citation/CS1/styles.css"></templatestyles>

Academic articles

<templatestyles src="Template:Refbegin/styles.css" />

- Handley, Fiona J. L. (2006). "Back to Africa: Issues of hosting "Roots" tourism in West Africa". *African Re-Genesis: Confronting Social Issues in the Diaspora*. London: UCL Press: 20–31.<templatestyles src="Module:Citation/CS1/styles.css"></templatestyles>
- Osei-Tutu, Brempong (2006). "Contested Monuments: African-Americans and the commoditization of Ghana's slave castles". *African Re-Genesis: Confronting Social Issues in the Diaspora*. London: UCL Press: 09–19.<templatestyles src="Module:Citation/CS1/styles.css"></templatestyles>
- Revealing Histories, Remembering Slavery.[473]

Non-academic sources

Further reading

- Anstey, Roger: *The Atlantic Slave Trade and British Abolition, 1760–1810*. London: Macmillan, 1975. <templatestyles src="Module:Citation/CS1/styles.css" />ISBN 0-333-14846-0.
- Blackburn, Robin (2011). *The American Crucible: Slavery, Emancipation and Human Rights*. London & New York: Verso. ISBN 978-1-84467-569-2.<templatestyles src="Module:Citation/CS1/styles.css"></templatestyles>
- Clarke, Dr. John Henrik: *Christopher Columbus and the Afrikan Holocaust: Slavery and the Rise of European Capitalism*. Brooklyn, NY: A & B Books, 1992. <templatestyles src="Module:Citation/CS1/styles.css" />ISBN 1-881316-14-9.
- Curtin, Philip D. (1969). *The Atlantic Slave Trade*[474]. Madison: University of Wisconsin Press. ISBN 9780299054007. OCLC 46413[475].<templatestyles src="Module:Citation/CS1/styles.css"></templatestyles>
- Daudin, Guillaume (2004). "Profitability of Slave and Long-Distance Trading in Context: The Case of Eighteenth-Century France"[476]. *The Journal of Economic History*. **64** (1): 144–171. doi: 10.1017/S0022050704002633[477]. ISSN 1471-6372[478].<templatestyles src="Module:Citation/CS1/styles.css"></templatestyles>
- Drescher, Seymour (1999). *From Slavery to Freedom : Comparative Studies in the Rise and Fall of Atlantic Slavery*[479]. New York: New York University Press. ISBN 0333737482. OCLC 39897280[480].<templatestyles src="Module:Citation/CS1/styles.css"></templatestyles>
- Eltis, David: "The volume and structure of the transatlantic slave trade: a reassessment", *William and Mary Quarterly* (2001): 17-46. in JSTOR[481]
- Emmer, Pieter C.: *The Dutch in the Atlantic Economy, 1580–1880. Trade, Slavery and Emancipation*. Variorum Collected Studies Series CS614. Aldershot [u.a.]: Variorum, 1998. <templatestyles src="Module:Citation/CS1/styles.css" />ISBN 0-86078-697-8.
- Eli Faber (1998). *Jews, Slaves, and the Slave Trade: Setting the Record Straight*[482]. NYU Press. ISBN 9780814728796.<templatestyles src="Module:Citation/CS1/styles.css"></templatestyles>, argues the role was minimal
- Gleeson, David T., and Simon Lewis (eds): *Ambiguous Anniversary: The Bicentennial of the International Slave Trade Bans* (University of South Carolina Press; 2012) 207 pp.

- Gomez, Michael Angelo: *Exchanging Our Country Marks (The Transformation of African Identities in the Colonial and AnteBellum South)*. Chapel Hill, N.C.: The University of North Carolina Press, 1998. <templatestyles src="Module:Citation/CS1/styles.css" />ISBN 0-8078-4694-5.
- Guasco, Michael. *Slaves and Englishmen: Human Bondage in the Early Modern Atlantic*. Philadelphia, PA: University of Pennsylvania Press, 2014.
- Hall, Gwendolyn Midlo: *Slavery and African Ethnicities in the Americas: Restoring the Links*. Chapel Hill, N.C.: The University of North Carolina Press, 2006. <templatestyles src="Module:Citation/CS1/styles.css" />ISBN 0-8078-2973-0.
- Horne, Gerald: *The Deepest South: The United States, Brazil, and the African Slave Trade*. New York, NY: New York University Press, 2007. <templatestyles src="Module:Citation/CS1/styles.css" />ISBN 978-0-8147-3688-3, <templatestyles src="Module:Citation/CS1/styles.css" />ISBN 978-0-8147-3689-0.
- Inikori, Joseph E., and Stanley L. Engerman (eds) (1992). *The Atlantic Slave Trade: Effects on Economies, Societies and Peoples in Africa, the Americas, and Europe*[483]. Duke UP. ISBN 0822382377.<templatestyles src="Module:Citation/CS1/styles.css"></templatestyles>
- Klein, Herbert S.: *The Atlantic Slave Trade* (2nd edn, 2010).
- Lindsay, Lisa A. *Captives as Commodities: The Transatlantic Slave Trade*. Prentice Hall, 2008. <templatestyles src="Module:Citation/CS1/styles.css" />ISBN 978-0-13-194215-8
- McMillin, James A. *The Final Victims: Foreign Slave Trade to North America, 1783–1810*, (Includes database on CD-ROM) <templatestyles src="Module:Citation/CS1/styles.css" />ISBN 978-1-57003-546-3
- Meltzer, Milton: *Slavery: A World History*. New York: Da Capo Press, 1993. <templatestyles src="Module:Citation/CS1/styles.css" />ISBN 0-306-80536-7.
- Northrup, David: *The Atlantic Slave Trade* (3rd edn, 2010)
- Rawley, James A., and Stephen D. Behrendt: *The Transatlantic Slave Trade: A History* (University of Nebraska Press, 2005)
- Rediker, Marcus (2007). *The Slave Ship: A Human History*[484]. New York, NY: Viking Press. ISBN 978-0-670-01823-9. Archived from the original[485] on 2012-03-31.<templatestyles src="Module:Citation/CS1/styles.css"></templatestyles>
- Rodney, Walter: *How Europe Underdeveloped Africa*. Washington, D.C.: Howard University Press; Revised edn, 1981. <templatestyles src="Module:Citation/CS1/styles.css" />ISBN 0-88258-096-5.
- Rodriguez, Junius P. (ed.), *Encyclopedia of Emancipation and Abolition in the Transatlantic World*. Armonk, NY: M.E. Sharpe, 2007.

<templatestyles src="Module:Citation/CS1/styles.css" />ISBN 978-0-7656-1257-1.
- Solow, Barbara (ed.), *Slavery and the Rise of the Atlantic System*. Cambridge: Cambridge University Press, 1991. <templatestyles src="Module:Citation/CS1/styles.css" />ISBN 0-521-40090-2.
- Thomas, Hugh: *The Slave Trade: The History of the Atlantic Slave Trade 1440–1870*. London: Picador, 1997. <templatestyles src="Module:Citation/CS1/styles.css" />ISBN 0-330-35437-X.; comprehensive history
- Thornton, John: *Africa and Africans in the Making of the Atlantic World, 1400–1800*, 2nd edn Cambridge University Press, 1998. <templatestyles src="Module:Citation/CS1/styles.css" />ISBN 0-521-62217-4, <templatestyles src="Module:Citation/CS1/styles.css" />ISBN 0-521-62724-9, <templatestyles src="Module:Citation/CS1/styles.css" />ISBN 0-521-59370-0, <templatestyles src="Module:Citation/CS1/styles.css" />ISBN 0-521-59649-1.
- Williams, Eric (1994) [1944]. *Capitalism & Slavery*. Chapel Hill: University of North Carolina Press. ISBN 0-8078-2175-6.<templatestyles src="Module:Citation/CS1/styles.css"></templatestyles>
- Araujo, Ana Lucia. *Public Memory of Slavery: Victims and Perpetrators in the South Atlantic*[486] Cambria Press, 2010. <templatestyles src="Module:Citation/CS1/styles.css" />ISBN 9781604977141

External links

Wikimedia Commons has media related to *Slavery*.

Wikivoyage has a travel guide for *Atlantic slave trade*.

- Voyages: The Trans-Atlantic Slave Trade Database[487]
- BBC | Africa|Quick guide: The slave trade[488]
- Teaching resources about Slavery and Abolition on blackhistory4schools.com[489]
- British documents on slave holding and the slave trade, 1788–1793[490]

Colonialism

Colonisation of Africa

The history of external colonization of Africa can be divided into two stages: Classical antiquity and European colonialism. In popular parlance, discussions of colonialism in Africa usually focus on the European conquests that resulted in the scramble for Africa after the Berlin Conference in the 19th century. Settlements established by Europeans while incorporated abjection of natives, also brought with it governing and academic institutions as well as agricultural and technological innovations that offset the extractive institutions commonly attributed to colonialism by Western powers.

In nearly all African countries today, the language used in government and media is a relic inherited from one of these waves of colonisation.

History of Africa

- In Ancient times, people from Southern Europe and Western Asia colonised North Africa, while people from Southeast Asia colonised Madagascar.
- In the Middle Ages, North and East Africa was further colonised by people from Western Asia.
- In the Modern Era, Western Europeans colonised all parts of the continent, culminating in the Scramble for Africa in the late 19th century. A wave of decolonisation followed after World War II.
- The main instance of internal colonisation within the African continent was the Bantu migration.

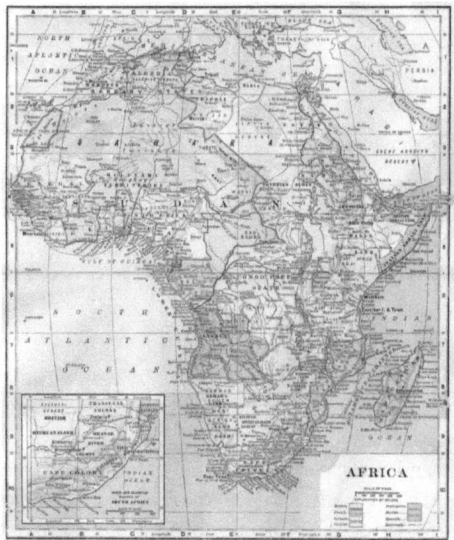

Figure 95: *A map of Africa in 1910*

Ancient and Medieval colonisation

North Africa experienced colonisation from Europe and Western Asia in the early historical period, particularly Greeks and Phoenicians.

Under Egypt's Pharaoh Amasis (570–526 BC) a Greek mercantile colony was established at Naucratis, some 50 miles from the later Alexandria. Greeks also colonised Cyrenaica around the same time. There was also an attempt in 513 BC to establish a Greek colony between Cyrene and Carthage, which resulted in the combined local and Carthaginian expulsion two years later of the Greek colonists.

Alexander the Great (356–323 BC) founded Alexandria during his conquest of Egypt. This became one of the major cities of Hellenistic and Roman times, a trading and cultural centre as well as a military headquarters and communications hub.

Phoenicians established a number of colonies along the coast of North Africa. Some of these were founded relatively early. Utica, for example, was founded c. 1100 BC. Carthage, which means New City, has a traditional foundation date of 814 BC. It was established in what is now Tunisia and became a major power in the Mediterranean by the 4th century BC. The Carthaginians themselves sent out expeditions to explore and establish colonies along Africa's

Colonisation of Africa

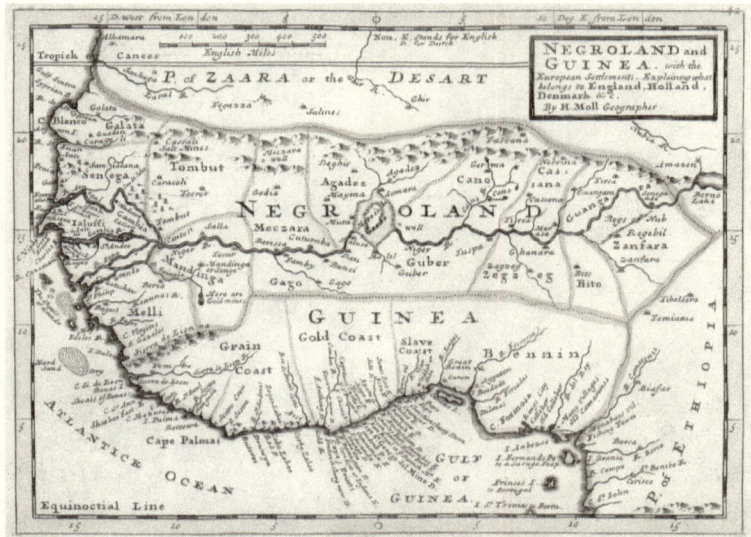

Figure 96: *Map of West Africa, ca. 1736, "explaining what belongs to England, Holland, Denmark, etc."*

Atlantic coast. A surviving account of such is that of Hanno, which Harden who quotes it places at c. 425 BC.

Carthage encountered and struggled with the Romans. After the third and final war between them, the Third Punic War (150–146 BC), Rome completely destroyed Carthage. Scullard mentions plans by such as Gaius Gracchus in the late 2nd century BC, Julius Caesar and Augustus in the mid- and late 1st century BC to establish a new Roman colony near the same site. This was established and under Augustus served as the capital city of African continent Roman province of Africa.

Gothic Vandals briefly established a kingdom there in the 5th century, which shortly thereafter fell to the Romans again, this time the Byzantines. The whole of Roman/Byzantine North Africa eventually fell to the Arabs in the 7th century.

Arabs introduced the Arabic language and Islam in the early Medieval period, while the Malay people introduced varieties of their language to Madagascar even earlier.

Figure 97:
Areas controlled by European colonial powers on the African continent in 1913, shown along with current national boundaries
Belgian
British
French
German
Italian
Portuguese
Spanish
Independent

Early modern period

Early European expeditions by the Portuguese concentrated on colonising previously uninhabited islands such as the Cape Verde Islands and São Tomé Island, or establishing coastal forts as a base for trade.

Scramble for Africa

Established empires, notably Britain, Portugal and France, had already claimed for themselves vast areas of Africa and Asia, and emerging imperial powers like Italy and Germany had done likewise on a smaller scale. With the

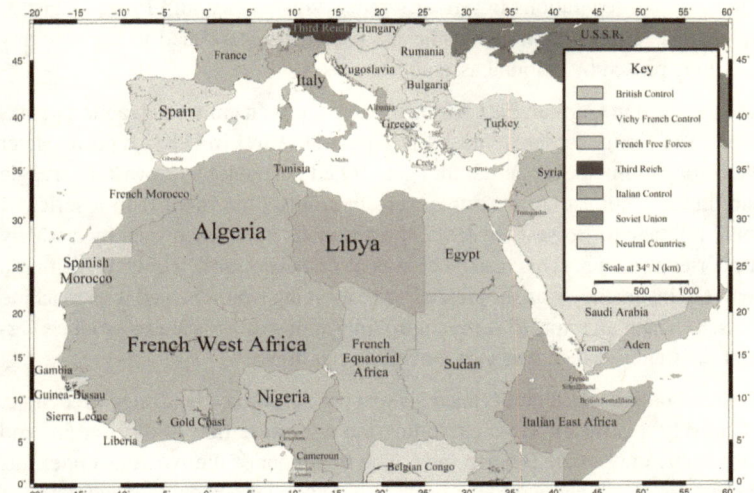

Figure 98: *Southern Europe and Northern Africa between 1936 and 1941*

dismissal of the aging Chancellor Bismarck by Kaiser Wilhelm II, the relatively orderly colonisation became a frantic scramble. The 1885 Berlin Conference, initiated by Bismarck to establish international guidelines for the acquisition of African territory, formalised this "New Imperialism". Between the Franco-Prussian War and the Great War, Europe added almost 9 million square miles (23,000,000 km²)—one-fifth of the land area of the globe—to its overseas colonial possessions.

Vincent Khapoya notes the great self-esteem some European states felt at possessing territory many times larger than themselves. He adds the significant contribution made by Africans to struggle among the Great Powers. He states that one million people of African descent fought for the Allies in World War I and two million in World War II.

Khapoya considers the colonisers' administrative styles. "The French, the Portuguese, the Germans and the Belgians exercised a highly centralised type of administration called 'direct rule.'" The British sought to rule by identifying local power holders and encouraging or forcing these to administer for the British Empire. This was indirect rule.

France ruled from France, appointing chiefs individually without considering traditional criteria, but rather loyalty to France. France established two large colonial federations in Africa, French West Africa and French Equatorial Africa. France appointed officials, passed laws and had to approve any measures passed by colonial assemblies.

Local groups in German East Africa resisted German enforced labour and taxation. The Germans were almost driven out of the area in 1888. A decade later the colony seemed conquered, though, "It had been a long drawn-out struggle and inland administration centres were in reality little more than a series of small military fortresses." In 1905, the Germans were astonished by a widely supported uprising. This resistance was at first successful. However, within a year, the insurgency was suppressed by reinforcing troops armed with machine guns. German attempts to seize control in Southwest Africa also produced ardent resistance, which was very forcefully put down.

King Leopold II of Belgium called his vast private colony the Congo Free State. Effectively this meant those exploiting the area were free of all restraint and answerable only to the Belgian king. The treatment of the Africans under this system was harsh enough to cause the other colonial powers to plead with the Belgian king to exercise some moderating influence. Eventually the Belgian government annexed the territory as a Belgian colony.

Khapoya notes the significant attention colonial powers paid to the economics of colonisation. This included: acquisition of land, often enforced labour, introduction of cash crops, sometimes even to the neglect of food crops, changing inter-African trading patterns of pre-colonial times, introduction of labourers from India, etc. and the continuation of Africa as a source of raw materials for European industry. Colonial powers later focused on abolishing slavery, developing infrastructure, and improving health and education.

Decolonisation

Vincent Khapoya notes the significant resistance of powers faced to their domination in Africa. Technical superiority enabled conquest and control. Pro-independence Africans recognised the value of European education in dealing with Europeans in Africa. Some Africans established their own churches. Africans also noticed the unequal evidence of gratitude they received for their efforts to support Imperialist countries during the world wars.

Vincent Khapoya also notes that while European imposed borders did not correspond to traditional territories, such new territories provided entities to focus efforts by movements for increased political voice up to independence. Among local groups so concerned were professionals such as lawyers and doctors, the petite bourgeoisie (clerks, teachers, small merchants), urban workers, cash crop farmers, peasant farmers, etc. Trade unions and other initially non-political associations evolved into political movements.

Khapoya describes the differences in gaining independence by British and French colonies. Britain sought to follow a process of gradual transfer of power. The French policy of assimilation faced some resentment, especially in North Africa. Shillington describes the granting of independence in March 1956 to Morocco and Tunisia to allow concentration on Algeria where there was a long (1954–62) and bloody armed struggle to achieve independence. Khapoya writes that when President de Gaulle in 1958 held a referendum in its African colonies on the issue, only Guinea voted for outright independence. Nevertheless, in 1959 France amended the constitution to allow other colonies this option.

As Shillington describes farmers in British East Africa were upset by attempts to take their land and to impose agricultural methods against their wishes and experience. In Tanganyika, Julius Nyerere exerted influence not only among Africans, united by the common Swahili language, but also on some white leaders whose disproportionate voice under a racially weighted constitution was significant. He became the leader of an independent Tanganyika in 1961. In Kenya, whites had evicted African tenant farmers in the 1930s; since the '40s there has been conflict, which intensified in 1952. By 1955, Britain had suppressed the revolt, and by 1960 Britain accepted the principle of African majority rule. Kenya became independent three years later.

Shillington vividly portrays Belgium's initial opposition to independence, the demands by some urban Africans, the 1957 & 1958 local elections meant to calm this dissatisfaction, the general unrest that swept the colony, the rapid granting of independence and the civil strife that ensued.

The main period of decolonisation in Africa began after World War II. Growing independence movements, indigenous political parties and trade unions coupled with pressure from within the imperialist powers and from the United States ensured the decolonisation of the majority of the continent by 1980. While some areas, in particular, South Africa, & Namibia retain a large population of European descent, only the Spanish enclaves of Ceuta and Melilla and the islands of Réunion, the Canary Islands, and Madeira remain under European control, the latter two of which were never part of any African polity and have an overwhelmingly European population.

Theoretical frameworks

The theory of colonialism addresses the problems and consequences of the colonisation of a country, and there has been much research conducted exploring these concepts.

Figure 99: *Mahmood Mamdani*

Mahmood Mamdani

Mahmood Mamdani wrote his book *Citizen and Subject* in 1996. The main point of his argument is that the colonial state in Africa took the form of a bifurcated state, "two forms of power under a single hegemonic authority". The colonial state in Africa was divided into two. One state for the colonial European population and one state for the indigenous population. The colonial power was mainly in urban towns and cities and were served by elected governments. The indigenous power was found in rural villages and were ruled by tribal authority, which seemed to be more in keeping with their history and tradition. Mamdani mentions that in urban areas, native institutions were not recognised. The natives, who were portrayed as uncivilised by the Europeans, were excluded from the rights of citizenship. The division of the colonial state created a racial segregation between the European 'citizen' and African 'subject', and a division between institutions of government.

The division Mamdani spoke about in *Citizen and Subject* is still visible in African cities. The segregation he talks about was based on race, but now is also based on wealth and class. Urban areas of African cities are divided between rich areas, and poor areas that do not have services. This is best illustrated by Johnny Miller, who created a project called Unequal Scenes[491] to showcase the inequalities found in some urban African spaces. One city that Miller looks at is Nairobi in Kenya. The photographs he provides highlights the housing inequality. The suburb of Loresho is home to the rich that live in

Figure 100: *Achille Mbembe*

gated communities, and to the poor that live in slum communities. They are only separated by a concrete barrier. This barrier represents a class segregation and the uneven distribution of wealth.

Achille Mbembe

Achille Mbembe is a Cameroonian historian, political theorist, and philosopher who has written and theorized extensively on life in the colony and postcolony. His 2000 book, *On the Postcolony*, critically examines postcolonial life in Africa and is a prolific work within the field of postcolonialism. It is through this examination of the postcolony that Mbembe reveals the modes through which power was exerted in colonial Africa. He reminds the reader that colonial powers demanded use of African bodies in particularly violent ways for the purpose of labor as well as the shaping of subservient colonised identities.

Through a comparison of power in the colony and postcolony, Mbembe demonstrates that violence in the colony was exerted on African bodies largely for the purpose of labor and submission. European colonial powers sought natural resources in African colonies and needed the requisite labor force to extract them and simultaneously build the colonial city around these industries. Because Europeans viewed native bodies as degenerate and in need of taming, violence was necessary to create a submissive laborer.

Colonisers viewed this violence as necessary and good because it shaped the African into a productive worker. They had the simultaneous goals of utilizing the raw labor and shaping the identity and character of the African. By beating into the African a docile nature, colonisers ultimately shaped and enforced the way Africans could move through colonial spaces. The African's day-to-day life then became a show of submission done through exercises like public works projects and military conscription.

Mbembe contrasts colonial violence with that of the postcolony. Mbembe demonstrates that violence in the postcolony is cruder and more generally for the purpose of demonstrating raw power. Expressions of excess and exaggeration characterize this violence.

Mbembe's theorization of violence in the colony illuminates the unequal relationship between the coloniser and colonised and reminds us of the violence inflicted on African bodies throughout the process of colonisation. It cannot be understood nor should be taught without the context of this violence.

Stephanie Terreni Brown

Stephanie Terreni Brown is an academic in the field of Colonialism. In her 2014 paper she examines how sanitation and dirt is used in colonial narratives through the example of Kampala in Uganda. Writing also about Abjection through sanitation planning in the city and how this plays a key role in this narrative of colonisation.

Brown describes Abjection as the process whereby one group others or dehumanizes another. Those who are deemed Abject are often avoided by others, and seen as inferior. Abjectivication is continually used as a mechanism to dominate a group of people, and control them. In the case of colonialism, she argues that it is used by the west to dominate over and control the indigenous population of Africa.

Abjectivication through discourses of dirt and sanitation are used to draw distinctions between the Western governing figures and the local population. Dirt being seen as something out of place, whilst cleanliness being attributed to the "in group", the colonisers, and dirt being paralleled with the indigenous people. The reactions of disgust and displeasure to dirt and uncleanliness are often linked social norms and the wider cultural context, shaping the way in which Africa is still thought of today.

Brown discusses how the colonial authorities were only concerned with constructing a working sewage system to cater for the colonials themselves, and weren't concerned with the Ugandan population. This rhetoric of sanitation is important because it is seen as a key part of modernity and being civilised, which the African population are therefore seen as not being. This lack of sanitation and proper sewage systems add to this discourse of the people of Africa and Africa itself being savages and uncivilised, playing a central role in how the west justified the case of the civilising process. Brown refers to this process of abjectification using discourses of dirt as a physical and material legacy of colonialism that is still very much present in Kampala and other African cities today.

Critique

Critical theory on the colonisation of Africa is largely unified in a condemnation of imperial activities. Postcolonial theory has been derived from this anti-colonial/anti-imperial concept and writers such as Mbembe, Mamdani and Brown, and many more, have used it as a narrative for their work on the colonisation of Africa.

> 'Post colonialism can be described as a powerful interdisciplinary mood in the social sciences and humanities that is refocusing attention on the imperial/colonial past, and critically revising understanding of the place of the west in the world.'

Postcolonial geographers are consistent with the notion that colonialism, although maybe not in such clear-cut forms, is still concurrent today. Both Mbembe, Mamdani and Brown's theories have a consistent theme of the indigenous Africans having been treated as uncivilised, second class citizens and that in many former colonial cities this has continued into the present day with a switch from race to wealth divide.

Mbembe is one of the most prominent writers within the field and this has led to his work being reviewed by numerous academics. On the Postcolony has faced criticism from academics such as Meredith Terreta for focusing too much on specific African nations such as Cameroon. Echoes of this criticism can also be found when looking at the work of Mamdani with his theories questioned for generalising across an Africa that, in reality, was colonised in very different ways, by fundamentally different European imperial ideologies. In contrast to Mbembe and Mamdani, Brown is a less prominent writer and one whose work is yet to be reviewed by other academics meaning it is currently harder to grasp what academic theoretical critiques could be brought against her work.

Notes

Bibliography

<templatestyles src="Template:Refbegin/styles.css" />

- Bensoussan, David (2012). *Il était une fois le Maroc - Témoignages du passé judéo-marocain* (2nd ed.). iUniverse. ISBN 978-1-4759-2609-5.<templatestyles src="Module:Citation/CS1/styles.css"></templatestyles>
- Boardman, John (1973) [1964]. *The Greeks Overseas.* Harmondsworth: Penguin.<templatestyles src="Module:Citation/CS1/styles.css"></templatestyles>
- Crowther, Michael (1978) [1962]. *The Story of Nigeria.* London: Faber and Faber.<templatestyles src="Module:Citation/CS1/styles.css"></templatestyles>
- Davidson, Basil (1966) [1964]. *The African Past.* Harmondsworth: Penguin Books.<templatestyles src="Module:Citation/CS1/styles.css"></templatestyles>
- Ferguson, Niall (2003). *Empire: How Britain Made the Modern World.* London: Allen Lane. ISBN 0-7139-9615-3.<templatestyles src="Module:Citation/CS1/styles.css"></templatestyles>
- Harden, Donald (1971) [1962]. *The Phoenicians.* Harmondsworth: Penguin.<templatestyles src="Module:Citation/CS1/styles.css"></templatestyles>
- Harris, Norman Dwight (1914). *Intervention and Colonization in Africa.* Houghton Mifflin.<templatestyles src="Module:Citation/CS1/styles.css"></templatestyles>
- Khapoya, Vincent B. (1998) [1994]. *The African Experience* (2nd ed.). Upper Saddle River, NJ: Prentice Hall. ISBN 0137458525.<templatestyles src="Module:Citation/CS1/styles.css"></templatestyles>
- Lovejoy, Paul E. (2012). *Transformations of Slavery: a History of Slavery in Africa* (3rd ed.). London: Cambridge University Press. ISBN 9780521176187.<templatestyles src="Module:Citation/CS1/styles.css"></templatestyles>
- Miers, Suzanne; Klein, Martin A. (1998). *Slavery and Colonial Rule in Africa (Slave and Post-Slave Societies and Cultures).* Routledge. ISBN 9780714644363.<templatestyles src="Module:Citation/CS1/styles.css"></templatestyles>
- Rodney, Walter (1972). *How Europe Underdeveloped Africa.* London: Bogle-L'Ouverture. ISBN 0-9501546-4-4.<templatestyles src="Module:Citation/CS1/styles.css"></templatestyles>

- Scullard, H. H. (1976) [1959]. *From the Gracchi to Nero*. London: Methuen and Co.<templatestyles src="Module:Citation/CS1/styles.css"></templatestyles>
- Shillington, Kevin (1995) [1989]. *History of Africa* (2nd ed.). New York: St. Martin's Press. ISBN 9780312125981.<templatestyles src="Module:Citation/CS1/styles.css"></templatestyles>

External links

 Wikimedia Commons has media related to *Colonial Africa*.

- Economic Impact of Colonialism[492]
- Germany Refuses to Apologize for Herero Holocaust[493] – from Africana.com
- Andre Osborn, "Belgium exhumes its colonial demons"[494], *The Guardian*, 12 July 2002

Scramble for Africa

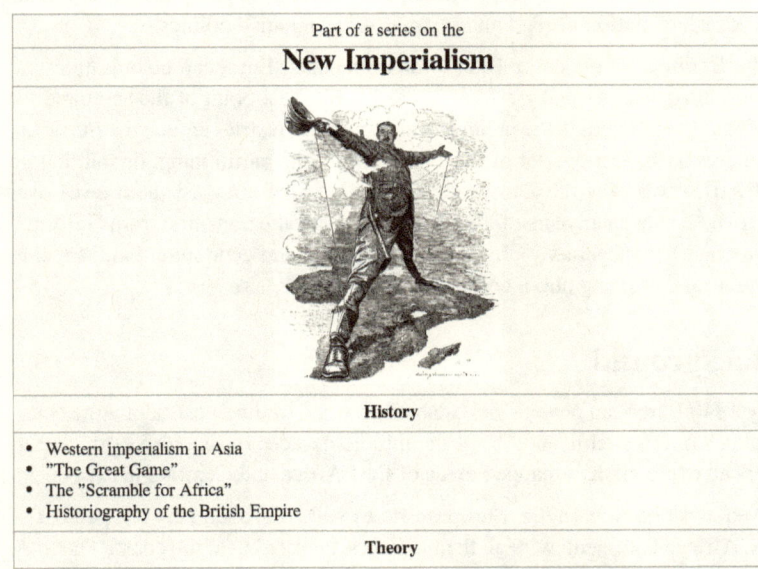

Part of a series on the
New Imperialism
History
• Western imperialism in Asia • "The Great Game" • The "Scramble for Africa" • Historiography of the British Empire
Theory

- *The Expansion of England*
- Gentlemanly capitalism
- *The Imperialism of Free Trade*
- *Imperialism: A Study*
- *Imperialism, the Highest Stage of Capitalism*
- Porter–MacKenzie debate

See also

- Imperialism
- Colonialism
- Decolonization

- v
- t
- e[495]

The **Scramble for Africa** was the occupation, division, and colonization of African territory by European powers during the period of New Imperialism, between 1881 and 1914. It is also called the **Partition of Africa** and by some the **Conquest of Africa**. In 1870, only 10 percent of Africa was under formal European control; by 1914 it had increased to almost 90 percent of the continent, with only Ethiopia (Abyssinia) and Liberia still being independent. There were multiple motivations including the quest for national prestige, tensions between pairs of European powers, religious missionary zeal-Wikipedia:Citation needed and internal African native politics.

The Berlin Conference of 1884, which regulated European colonisation and trade in Africa, is usually referred to as the ultimate point of the scramble for Africa. Consequent to the political and economic rivalries among the European empires in the last quarter of the 19th century, the partitioning, or splitting up of Africa was how the Europeans avoided warring amongst themselves over Africa.[496] The later years of the 19th century saw the transition from "informal imperialism" (hegemony), by military influence and economic dominance, to direct rule, bringing about colonial imperialism.[497]

Background

By 1840 European powers had established small trading posts along the coast, but seldom moved inland.[498] In the middle decades of the 19th century, European explorers had mapped areas of East Africa and Central Africa.

Even as late as the 1870s, European states still controlled only ten percent of the African continent, with all their territories located near the coast. The most important holdings were Angola and Mozambique, held by Portugal; the Cape Colony, held by the United Kingdom; and Algeria, held by France. By 1914, only Ethiopia and Liberia remained independent of European control.[499]

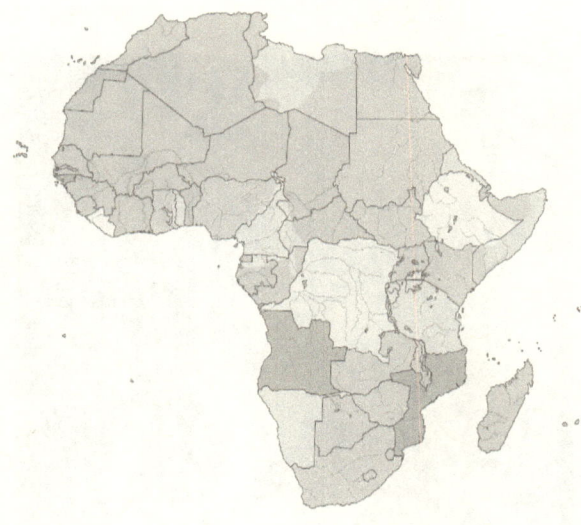

Figure 101:
Areas of Africa controlled by European colonial powers in 1913, shown along with current national boundaries.

Technological advances facilitated European expansion overseas. Industrialisation brought about rapid advancements in transportation and communication, especially in the forms of steamships, railways and telegraphs. Medical advances also played an important role, especially medicines for tropical diseases. The development of quinine, an effective treatment for malaria, made vast expanses of the tropics more accessible for Europeans.

Causes

Africa and global markets

Sub-Saharan Africa, one of the last regions of the world largely untouched by "informal imperialism", was also attractive to Europe's ruling elites for economic, political and social reasons. During a time when Britain's balance of trade showed a growing deficit, with shrinking and increasingly protectionist continental markets due to the Long Depression (1873–96), Africa offered Britain, Germany, France, and other countries an open market that would garner them a trade surplus: a market that bought more from the colonial power than it sold overall.[500]

Figure 102: *David Livingstone, early explorer of the interior of Africa and fighter against the slave trade*

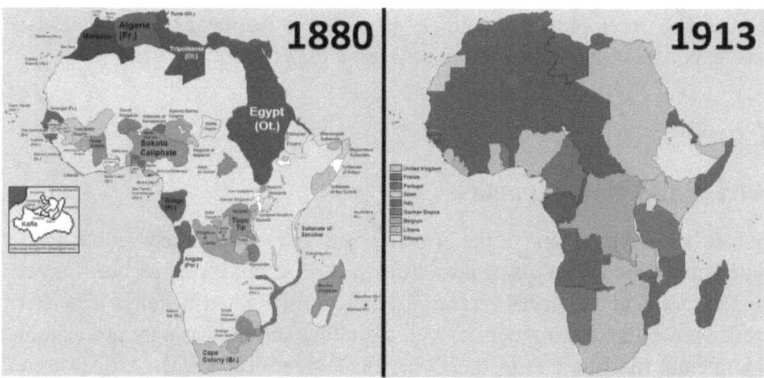

Figure 103: *Comparison of Africa in the years 1880 and 1913*

Surplus capital was often more profitably invested overseas, where cheap materials, limited competition, and abundant raw materials made a greater premium possible. Another inducement for imperialism arose from the demand for raw materials, especially copper, cotton, rubber, palm oil, cocoa, diamonds, tea, and tin, to which European consumers had grown accustomed and upon which European industry had grown dependent. Additionally, Britain wanted the southern and eastern coasts of Africa for stopover ports on the route to Asia and its empire in India.[501] However, in Africa – excluding the area which became the Union of South Africa in 1910 – the amount of capital investment by Europeans was relatively small, compared to other continents. Consequently, the companies involved in tropical African commerce were relatively small, apart from Cecil Rhodes's De Beers Mining Company. Rhodes had carved out Rhodesia for himself; Léopold II of Belgium later, and with considerable brutality, exploited the Congo Free State.

These events might detract from the pro-imperialist arguments of colonial lobbyists such as the *Alldeutscher Verband*, Francesco Crispi and Jules Ferry, who argued that sheltered overseas markets in Africa would solve the problems of low prices and over-production caused by shrinking continental markets. John A. Hobson argued in *Imperialism* that this shrinking of continental markets was a key factor of the global "New Imperialism" period. William Easterly, however, disagrees with the link made between capitalism and imperialism, arguing that colonialism is used mostly to promote state-led development rather than "corporate" development. He has stated that "imperialism is not so clearly linked to capitalism and the free markets... historically there has been a closer link between colonialism/imperialism and state-led approaches to development."

Strategic rivalry

The rivalry between Britain, France, Germany, and the other European powers accounts for a large part of the colonization.

While tropical Africa was not a large zone of investment, other overseas regions were. The vast interior between Egypt and the gold and diamond-rich southern Africa had strategic value in securing the flow of overseas trade. Britain was under political pressure to secure lucrative markets against encroaching rivals in China and its eastern colonies, most notably India, Malaya, Australia and New Zealand. Thus, it was crucial to secure the key waterway between East and West—the Suez Canal. However, a theory that Britain sought to annex East Africa during the 1880 onwards, out of geostrategic concerns connected to Egypt (especially the Suez Canal), has been challenged by historians such as John Darwin (1997) and Jonas F. Gjersø (2015).[502]

Figure 104: *Contemporary illustration of Major Marchand's trek across Africa in 1898*

The scramble for African territory also reflected concern for the acquisition of military and naval bases, for strategic purposes and the exercise of power. The growing navies, and new ships driven by steam power, required coaling stations and ports for maintenance. Defense bases were also needed for the protection of sea routes and communication lines, particularly of expensive and vital international waterways such as the Suez Canal.[503]

Colonies were also seen as assets in "balance of power" negotiations, useful as items of exchange at times of international bargaining. Colonies with large native populations were also a source of military power; Britain and France used large numbers of British Indian and North African soldiers, respectively, in many of their colonial wars (and would do so again in the coming World Wars). In the age of nationalism there was pressure for a nation to acquire an empire as a status symbol; the idea of "greatness" became linked with the sense of duty underlying many nations' strategies.

In the early 1880s, Pierre Savorgnan de Brazza was exploring the Kingdom of Kongo for France, at the same time Henry Morton Stanley explored it on behalf of Léopold II of Belgium, who would have it as his personal Congo Free State (see section below). France occupied Tunisia in May 1881, which may have convinced Italy to join the German-Austrian Dual Alliance in 1882, thus

Figure 105: *The Askari colonial troops in German East Africa, circa 1906*

forming the Triple Alliance. The same year, Britain occupied Egypt (hitherto an autonomous state owing nominal fealty to the Ottoman Empire), which ruled over Sudan and parts of Chad, Eritrea, and Somalia. In 1884, Germany declared Togoland, the Cameroons and South West Africa to be under its protection; and France occupied Guinea. French West Africa (AOF) was founded in 1895, and French Equatorial Africa in 1910.[504,505]

Germany's *Weltpolitik*

Germany was hardly a colonial power before the New Imperialism period, but would eagerly participate in this race. Fragmented in various states, Germany was only unified under Prussia's rule after the 1866 Battle of Königgrätz and the 1870 Franco-Prussian War. A rising industrial power close on the heels of Britain, Germany began its world expansion in the 1880s. After isolating France by the Dual Alliance with Austria-Hungary and then the 1882 Triple Alliance with Italy, Chancellor Otto von Bismarck proposed the 1884–85 Berlin Conference, which set the rules of effective control of a foreign territory. *Weltpolitik* (world policy) was the foreign policy adopted by Kaiser Wilhelm II in 1890, with the aim of transforming Germany into a global power through aggressive diplomacy, the acquisition of overseas colonies, and the development of a large navy.

Some Germans, claiming themselves of Friedrich List's thought, advocated expansion in the Philippines and Timor; others proposed to set themselves up in

Formosa (modern Taiwan), etc. At the end of the 1870s, these isolated voices began to be relayed by a real imperialist policyWikipedia:Citation needed, backed by mercantilist thesis. In 1881, Hübbe-Schleiden, a lawyer, published *Deutsche Kolonisation*, according to which the "development of national consciousness demanded an independent overseas policy".[506] Pan-Germanism was thus linked to the young nation's imperialist drivesWikipedia:Citation needed. In the beginning of the 1880s, the *Deutscher Kolonialverein* was created, and got its own magazine in 1884, the *Kolonialzeitung*. This colonial lobby was also relayed by the nationalist *Alldeutscher Verband*. Generally, Bismarck was opposed to widespread German colonialism,[507] but he had to resign at the insistence of the new German Emperor Wilhelm II on 18 March 1890. Wilhelm II instead adopted a very aggressive policy of colonisation and colonial expansion.

Germany's expansionism would lead to the Tirpitz Plan, implemented by Admiral von Tirpitz, who would also champion the various Fleet Acts starting in 1898, thus engaging in an arms race with Britain. By 1914, they had given Germany the second-largest naval force in the world (roughly three-fifths the size of the Royal Navy). According to von Tirpitz, this aggressive naval policy was supported by the National Liberal Party rather than by the conservatives, implying that imperialism was supported by the rising middle classes.[508]

Germany became the third-largest colonial power in Africa. Nearly all of its overall empire of 2.6 million square kilometres and 14 million colonial subjects in 1914 was found in its African possessions of Southwest Africa, Togoland, the Cameroons, and Tanganyika. Following the 1904 *Entente cordiale* between France and the British Empire, Germany tried to isolate France in 1905 with the First Moroccan Crisis. This led to the 1905 Algeciras Conference, in which France's influence on Morocco was compensated by the exchange of other territories, and then to the Agadir Crisis in 1911. Along with the 1898 Fashoda Incident between France and Britain, this succession of international crises reveals the bitterness of the struggle between the various imperialist nations, which ultimately led to World War I.

Italy's expansion

Italy took possession of parts of Eritrea in 1870[509] and 1882. Following its defeat in the First Italo–Ethiopian War (1895–1896), it acquired Italian Somaliland in 1889–90 and the whole of Eritrea (1899). In 1911, it engaged in a war with the Ottoman Empire, in which it acquired Tripolitania and Cyrenaica (modern Libya). In 1919 Enrico Corradini—who fully supported the war, and later merged his group in the early fascist party (PNF)—developed the concept of *Proletarian Nationalism*, supposed to legitimise Italy's imperialism by a mixture of socialism with nationalism:

Figure 106: *Tapestry depicting the Battle of Adwa between Ethiopian and Italian forces*

<templatestyles src="Template:Quote/styles.css"/>
> *We must start by recognizing the fact that there are proletarian nations as well as proletarian classes; that is to say, there are nations whose living conditions are subject...to the way of life of other nations, just as classes are. Once this is realised, nationalism must insist firmly on this truth: Italy is, materially and morally, a proletarian nation.*[510]

The Second Italo-Abyssinian War (1935–36), ordered by the Fascist Benito Mussolini, would actually be one of the last colonial wars (that is, intended to colonise a foreign country, as opposed to wars of national liberation), occupying Ethiopia—which had remained the last independent African territory, apart from Liberia.

Figure 107: *Henry Morton Stanley*

Crises prior to World War I

Colonisation of the Congo

David Livingstone's explorations, carried on by Henry Morton Stanley, excited imaginations with Stanley's grandiose ideas for colonisation; but these found little support owing to the problems and scale of action required, except from Léopold II of Belgium, who in 1876 had organised the International African Association (the Congo Society). From 1869 to 1874, Stanley was secretly sent by Léopold II to the Congo region, where he made treaties with several African chiefs along the Congo River and by 1882 had sufficient territory to form the basis of the Congo Free State. Léopold II personally owned the colony from 1885 and used it as a source of ivory and rubber.

While Stanley was exploring Congo on behalf of Léopold II of Belgium, the Franco-Italian marine officer Pierre de Brazza travelled into the western Congo basin and raised the French flag over the newly founded Brazzaville in 1881, thus occupying today's Republic of the Congo. Portugal, which also claimed the area due to old treaties with the native Kongo Empire, made a treaty with Britain on 26 February 1884 to block off the Congo Society's access to the Atlantic.

Figure 108: *Pierre Savorgnan de Brazza in his version of "native" dress, photographed by Félix Nadar*

By 1890 the Congo Free State had consolidated its control of its territory between Leopoldville and Stanleyville, and was looking to push south down the Lualaba River from Stanleyville. At the same time, the British South Africa Company of Cecil Rhodes was expanding north from the Limpopo River, sending the Pioneer Column (guided by Frederick Selous) through Matabeleland, and starting a colony in Mashonaland.

To the west, in the land where their expansions would meet, was Katanga, site of the Yeke Kingdom of Msiri. Msiri was the most militarily powerful ruler in the area, and traded large quantities of copper, ivory and slaves — and rumors of gold reached European ears. The scramble for Katanga was a prime example of the period. Rhodes and the BSAC sent two expeditions to Msiri in 1890 led by Alfred Sharpe, who was rebuffed, and Joseph Thomson, who failed to reach Katanga. Leopold sent four CFS expeditions. First, the Le Marinel Expedition could only extract a vaguely worded letter. The Delcommune Expedition was rebuffed. The well-armed Stairs Expedition was given orders to take Katanga with or without Msiri's consent. Msiri refused, was shot, and the expedition cut off his head and stuck it on a pole as a "barbaric lesson" to the people. The Bia Expedition finished the job of establishing an administration of sorts and a "police presence" in Katanga. Thus, the half million square kilometers of Katanga came into Leopold's possession and brought his African realm up

Figure 109: *Native Congo Free State laborers who failed to meet rubber collection quotas were often punished by having their hands cut off.*

to 2,300,000 square kilometres (890,000 sq mi), about 75 times larger than Belgium. The Congo Free State imposed such a terror regime on the colonised people, including mass killings and forced labour, that Belgium, under pressure from the Congo Reform Association, ended Leopold II's rule and annexed it in 1908 as a colony of Belgium, known as the Belgian Congo.

The brutality of King Leopold II of Belgium in his former colony of the Congo Free State, now the Democratic Republic of the Congo, was well documented; up to 8 million of the estimated 16 million native inhabitants died between 1885 and 1908. According to the former Irish diplomat Roger Casement, this depopulation had four main causes: "indiscriminate war", starvation, reduction of births and diseases.[511] Sleeping sickness ravaged the country and must also be taken into account for the dramatic decrease in population; it has been estimated that sleeping sickness and smallpox killed nearly half the population in the areas surrounding the lower Congo River.[512]

Estimates of the total death toll vary considerably. As the first census did not take place until 1924, it is difficult to quantify the population loss of the period. Casement's report set it at three million.[513] William Rubinstein wrote: "More basically, it appears almost certain that the population figures given by Hochschild are inaccurate. There is, of course, no way of ascertaining the

Figure 110: *Port Said entrance to Suez Canal, showing De Lesseps' statue*

population of the Congo before the twentieth century, and estimates like 20 million are purely guesses. Most of the interior of the Congo was literally unexplored if not inaccessible."[514] See Congo Free State for further details including numbers of victims.

A similar situation occurred in the neighbouring French Congo. Most of the resource extraction was run by concession companies, whose brutal methods, along with the introduction of disease, resulted in the loss of up to 50 percent of the indigenous population. The French government appointed a commission, headed by de Brazza, in 1905 to investigate the rumoured abuses in the colony. However, de Brazza died on the return trip, and his "searingly critical" report was neither acted upon nor released to the public.[515] In the 1920s, about 20,000 forced labourers died building a railroad through the French territory.

Suez Canal

French diplomat Ferdinand de Lesseps had obtained many concessions from Isma'il Pasha, the Khedive of Egypt and Sudan, in 1854–56, to build the Suez Canal. Some sources estimate the workforce at 30,000,[516] but others estimate that 120,000 workers died over the ten years of construction due to malnutrition, fatigue and disease, especially cholera.[517] Shortly before its completion in 1869, Khedive Isma'il borrowed enormous sums from British and French

Figure 111: *Otto von Bismarck at the Berlin Conference, 1884*

bankers at high rates of interest. By 1875, he was facing financial difficulties and was forced to sell his block of shares in the Suez Canal. The shares were snapped up by Britain, under its Prime Minister, Benjamin Disraeli, who sought to give his country practical control in the management of this strategic waterway. When Isma'il repudiated Egypt's foreign debt in 1879, Britain and France seized joint financial control over the country, forcing the Egyptian ruler to abdicate, and installing his eldest son Tewfik Pasha in his place. The Egyptian and Sudanese ruling classes did not relish foreign intervention.

During the 1870s, European initiatives against the slave trade caused an economic crisis in northern Sudan, precipitating the rise of Mahdist forces. In 1881, the Mahdist revolt erupted in Sudan under Muhammad Ahmad, severing Tewfik's authority in Sudan. The same year, Tewfik suffered an even more perilous rebellion by his own Egyptian army in the form of the Urabi Revolt. In 1882, Tewfik appealed for direct British military assistance, commencing Britain's administration of Egypt. A joint British-Egyptian military force ultimately defeated the Mahdist forces in Sudan in 1898. Thereafter, Britain (rather than Egypt) seized effective control of Sudan.

Berlin Conference (1884–85)

The occupation of Egypt, and the acquisition of the Congo were the first major moves in what came to be a precipitous scramble for African territory. In

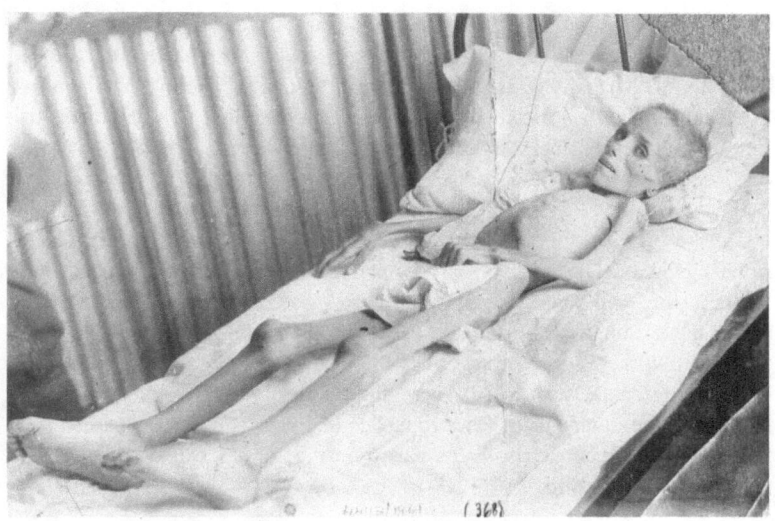

Figure 112: *Boer child in a British concentration camp during the Second Boer War (1899–1902)*

1884, Otto von Bismarck convened the 1884–85 Berlin Conference to discuss the African problem. The diplomats put on a humanitarian façade by condemning the slave trade, prohibiting the sale of alcoholic beverages and firearms in certain regions, and by expressing concern for missionary activities. More importantly, the diplomats in Berlin laid down the rules of competition by which the great powers were to be guided in seeking colonies. They also agreed that the area along the Congo River was to be administered by Léopold II of Belgium as a neutral area, known as the Congo Free State, in which trade and navigation were to be free. No nation was to stake claims in Africa without notifying other powers of its intentions. No territory could be formally claimed prior to being effectively occupied. However, the competitors ignored the rules when convenient and on several occasions war was only narrowly avoided.

Britain's administration of Egypt and South Africa

Britain's administration of Egypt and the Cape Colony contributed to a preoccupation over securing the source of the Nile River. Egypt was overrun by British forces in 1882 (although not formally declared a protectorate until 1914, and never an actual colony); Sudan, Nigeria, Kenya and Uganda were subjugated in the 1890s and early 20th century; and in the south, the Cape

Colony (first acquired in 1795) provided a base for the subjugation of neighboring African states and the Dutch Afrikaner settlers who had left the Cape to avoid the British and then founded their own republics. Theophilus Shepstone annexed the South African Republic (or Transvaal) in 1877 for the British Empire, after it had been independent for twenty years. In 1879, after the Anglo-Zulu War, Britain consolidated its control of most of the territories of South Africa. The Boers protested, and in December 1880 they revolted, leading to the First Boer War (1880–81). British Prime Minister William Gladstone signed a peace treaty on 23 March 1881, giving self-government to the Boers in the Transvaal. The Jameson Raid of 1895 was a failed attempt by the British South Africa Company and the Johannesburg Reform Committee to overthrow the Boer government in the Transvaal. The Second Boer War, fought between 1899 and 1902, was about control of the gold and diamond industries; the independent Boer republics of the Orange Free State and the South African Republic (or Transvaal) were this time defeated and absorbed into the British Empire.

The French thrust into the African interior was mainly from the coasts of West Africa (modern day Senegal) eastward, through the Sahel along the southern border of the Sahara, a huge desert covering most of present-day Senegal, Mali, Niger, and Chad. Their ultimate aim was to have an uninterrupted colonial empire from the Niger River to the Nile, thus controlling all trade to and from the Sahel region, by virtue of their existing control over the Caravan routes through the Sahara. The British, on the other hand, wanted to link their possessions in Southern Africa (modern South Africa, Botswana, Zimbabwe, Lesotho, Swaziland, and Zambia), with their territories in East Africa (modern Kenya), and these two areas with the Nile basin.

The Sudan (which in those days included most of present-day Uganda) was the key to the fulfillment of these ambitions, especially since Egypt was already under British control. This "red line" through Africa is made most famous by Cecil Rhodes. Along with Lord Milner, the British colonial minister in South Africa, Rhodes advocated such a "Cape to Cairo" empire, linking the Suez Canal to the mineral-rich Southern part of the continent by rail. Though hampered by German occupation of Tanganyika until the end of World War I, Rhodes successfully lobbied on behalf of such a sprawling African empire.

If one draws a line from Cape Town to Cairo (Rhodes's dream), and one from Dakar to the Horn of Africa (now Ethiopia, Eritrea, Djibouti and Somalia), (the French ambition), these two lines intersect somewhere in eastern Sudan near Fashoda, explaining its strategic importance. In short, Britain had sought to extend its East African empire contiguously from Cairo to the Cape of Good Hope, while France had sought to extend its own holdings from Dakar to the

Figure 113: *Muhammad Ahmad, leader of the Mahdists. This fundamentalist group of Muslim dervishes over-ran much of Sudan and fought British forces.*

Sudan, which would enable its empire to span the entire continent from the Atlantic Ocean to the Red Sea.

A French force under Jean-Baptiste Marchand arrived first at the strategically located fort at Fashoda, soon followed by a British force under Lord Kitchener, commander in chief of the British Army since 1892. The French withdrew after a standoff and continued to press claims to other posts in the region. In March 1899, the French and British agreed that the source of the Nile and Congo Rivers should mark the frontier between their spheres of influence.Wikipedia:Citation needed

Moroccan Crisis

Although the 1884–85 Berlin Conference had set the rules for the Scramble for Africa, it had not weakened the rival imperialists. The 1898 Fashoda Incident, which had seen France and the British Empire on the brink of war, ultimately led to the signature of the *Entente Cordiale* of 1904, which countered the influence of the European powers of the Triple Alliance. As a result, the new German Empire decided to test the solidity of such influence, using the contested territory of Morocco as a battlefield.

Figure 114: *The Moroccan Sultan Abdelhafid, who led the resistance to French expansionism during the Agadir Crisis*

Thus, Kaiser Wilhelm II visited Tangiers on 31 March 1905 and made a speech in favor of Moroccan independence, challenging French influence in Morocco. France's influence in Morocco had been reaffirmed by Britain and Spain in 1904. The Kaiser's speech bolstered French nationalism, and with British support the French foreign minister, Théophile Delcassé, took a defiant line. The crisis peaked in mid-June 1905, when Delcassé was forced out of the ministry by the more conciliation-minded premier Maurice Rouvier. But by July 1905 Germany was becoming isolated and the French agreed to a conference to solve the crisis. Both France and Germany continued to posture up until the conference, with Germany mobilizing reserve army units in late December and France actually moving troops to the border in January 1906.

The 1906 Algeciras Conference was called to settle the dispute. Of the thirteen nations present, the German representatives found their only supporter was Austria-Hungary. France had firm support from Britain, the US, Russia, Italy and Spain. The Germans eventually accepted an agreement, signed on 31 May 1906, whereby France yielded certain domestic changes in Morocco but retained control of key areas.

However, five years later the Second Moroccan Crisis (or Agadir Crisis) was sparked by the deployment of the German gunboat *Panther* to the port of Agadir on 1 July 1911. Germany had started to attempt to surpass Britain's naval supremacy—the British navy had a policy of remaining larger than the

Figure 115: *Statue of Sayyid Mohammed Abdullah Hassan (the "Mad Mullah"), leader of the Dervish movement*

next two naval fleets in the world combined. When the British heard of the *Panther*'s arrival in Morocco, they wrongly believed that the Germans meant to turn Agadir into a naval base on the Atlantic.

The German move was aimed at reinforcing claims for compensation for acceptance of effective French control of the North African kingdom, where France's pre-eminence had been upheld by the 1906 Algeciras Conference. In November 1911 a convention was signed under which Germany accepted France's position in Morocco in return for territory in the French Equatorial African colony of Middle Congo (now the Republic of the Congo).

France and Spain subsequently established a full protectorate over Morocco (30 March 1912), ending what remained of the country's formal independence. Furthermore, British backing for France during the two Moroccan crises reinforced the Entente between the two countries and added to Anglo-German estrangement, deepening the divisions that would culminate in the First World War.

Dervish resistance

Following the Berlin Conference at the end of the 19th century, the British, Italians, and Ethiopians sought to claim lands owned by the Somalis such as

Figure 116: *Surviving Herero, emaciated, after their escape through the Omaheke desert*

the Warsangali Sultanate, the Ajuran Sultanate and the Gobroon Dynasty.

The Dervish movement was a state established by Mohammed Abdullah Hassan, a Somali religious leader who gathered Muslim soldiers from across the Horn of Africa and united them into a loyal army known as the *Dervishes*. This Dervish army enabled Hassan to carve out a powerful state through conquest of lands sought after by the Ethiopians and the European powers. The Dervish movement successfully repulsed the British Empire four times and forced it to retreat to the coastal region.[518] Due to these successful expeditions, the Dervish movement was recognised as an ally by the Ottoman and German empires. The Turks also named Hassan Emir of the Somali nation,[519] and the Germans promised to officially recognise any territories the Dervishes were to acquire.[520]

After a quarter of a century of holding the British at bay, the Dervishes were finally defeated in 1920 as a direct consequence of Britain's use of aircraft.

Herero Wars and the Maji-Maji Rebellion

Between 1904 and 1908, Germany's colonies in German South-West Africa and German East Africa were rocked by separate, contemporaneous native revolts against their rule. In both territories the threat to German rule was quickly defeated once large-scale reinforcements from Germany arrived, with the Herero rebels in German South-West Africa being defeated at the Battle

Figure 117: *Pygmies and a European. Some pygmies would be exposed in human zoos, such as Ota Benga displayed by eugenicist Madison Grant in the Bronx Zoo.*

of Waterberg and the Maji-Maji rebels in German East Africa being steadily crushed by German forces slowly advancing through the countryside, with the natives resorting to guerrilla warfare. German efforts to clear the bush of civilians in German South-West Africa then resulted in a genocide of the population.

In total, as many as 65,000 Herero (80% of the total Herero population), and 10,000 Namaqua (50% of the total Namaqua population) either starved, died of thirst, or were worked to death in camps such as Shark Island Concentration Camp between 1904 and 1908. Characteristic of this genocide was death by starvation and the poisoning of the population's wells whilst they were trapped in the Namib Desert.

Colonial encounter

Colonial consciousness and exhibitions

Colonial lobby

In its earlier stages, imperialism was generally the act of individual explorers as well as some adventurous merchantmen. The colonial powers were a long way from approving without any dissent the expensive adventures carried out abroad. Various important political leaders, such as Gladstone, opposed colonisation in its first years. However, during his second premiership between 1880 and 1885 he could not resist the colonial lobby in his cabinet, and thus did not execute his electoral promise to disengage from Egypt. Although Gladstone was personally opposed to imperialism, the social tensions caused by the Long Depression pushed him to favor jingoism: the imperialists had become the "parasites of patriotism" (John A. Hobson).[521] In France, then Radical politician Georges Clemenceau also adamantly opposed himself to it: he thought colonisation was a diversion from the "blue line of the Vosges" mountains, that is revanchism and the patriotic urge to reclaim the Alsace-Lorraine region which had been annexed by the German Empire with the 1871 Treaty of Frankfurt. Clemenceau actually made Jules Ferry's cabinet fall after the 1885 Tonkin disaster. According to Hannah Arendt in *The Origins of Totalitarianism* (1951), this expansion of national sovereignty on overseas territories contradicted the unity of the nation state which provided citizenship to its population. Thus, a tension between the universalist will to respect human rights of the colonised people, as they may be considered as "citizens" of the nation state, and the imperialist drive to cynically exploit populations deemed inferior began to surface. Some, in colonising countries, opposed what they saw as unnecessary evils of the colonial administration when left to itself; as described in Joseph Conrad's *Heart of Darkness* (1899)—published around the same time as Kipling's *The White Man's Burden*—or in Louis-Ferdinand Céline's *Journey to the End of the Night* (1932).

Colonial lobbies emerged to legitimise the Scramble for Africa and other expensive overseas adventures. In Germany, France, and Britain, the middle class often sought strong overseas policies to ensure the market's growth. Even in lesser powers, voices like Enrico Corradini claimed a "place in the sun" for so-called "proletarian nations", bolstering nationalism and militarism in an early prototype of fascism.

Colonial propaganda and jingoism

Colonial exhibitions

However, by the end of World War I the colonial empires had become very popular almost everywhere in Europe: public opinion had been convinced of the needs of a colonial empire, although most of the metropolitans would never see a piece of it. Colonial exhibitions had been instrumental in this change of popular mentalities brought about by the colonial propaganda, supported by the colonial lobby and by various scientists. Thus, the conquest of territories were inevitably followed by public displays of the indigenous people for scientific and leisure purposes. Karl Hagenbeck, a German merchant in wild

Figure 118: *Poster for the 1906 Colonial Exhibition in Marseilles (France)*

animals and a future entrepreneur of most Europeans zoos, thus decided in 1874 to exhibit Samoa and Sami people as "purely natural" populations. In 1876, he sent one of his collaborators to the newly conquered Egyptian Sudan to bring back some wild beasts and Nubians. Presented in Paris, London, and Berlin these Nubians were very successful. Such "human zoos" could be found in Hamburg, Antwerp, Barcelona, London, Milan, New York City, Paris, etc., with 200,000 to 300,000 visitors attending each exhibition. Tuaregs were exhibited after the French conquest of Timbuktu (visited by René Caillié, disguised as a Muslim, in 1828, thereby winning the prize offered by the French *Société de Géographie*); Malagasy after the occupation of Madagascar; Amazons of Abomey after Behanzin's mediatic defeat against the French in 1894. Not used to the climatic conditions, some of the indigenous exposed died, such as some Galibis in Paris in 1892.[522]

Geoffroy de Saint-Hilaire, director of the Parisian Jardin d'acclimatation, decided in 1877 to organise two "ethnological spectacles", presenting Nubians and Inuit. The public of the Jardin d'acclimatation doubled, with a million paying entrances that year, a huge success for these times. Between 1877 and 1912, approximately thirty "ethnological exhibitions" were presented at the Jardin zoologique d'acclimatation.[523] "Negro villages" would be presented in Paris' 1878 and 1879 World's Fair; the 1900 World's Fair presented the famous diorama "living" in Madagascar, while the Colonial Exhibitions in

Marseilles (1906 and 1922) and in Paris (1907 and 1931) would also display human beings in cages, often nudes or quasi-nudes. Nomadic "Senegalese villages" were also created, thus displaying the power of the colonial empire to all the population.

In the US, Madison Grant, head of the New York Zoological Society, exposed Pygmy Ota Benga in the Bronx Zoo alongside the apes and others in 1906. At the behest of Grant, a prominent scientific racist and eugenicist, zoo director Hornaday placed Ota Benga in a cage with an orangutan and labeled him "The Missing Link" in an attempt to illustrate Darwinism, and in particular that Africans like Ota Benga are closer to apes than were Europeans. Other colonial exhibitions included the 1924 British Empire Exhibition and the successful 1931 Paris "Exposition coloniale".

Countering disease

From the beginning of the 20th century onward, the elimination or control of disease in tropical countries became a driving force for all colonial powers.[524] The sleeping sickness epidemic in Africa was arrested due to mobile teams systematically screening millions of people at risk. In the 20th century, Africa saw the biggest increase in its population due to lessening of the mortality rate in many countries due to peace, famine relief, medicine, and above all, the end or decline of the slave trade. Africa's population has grown from 120 million in 1900 to over 1 billion today.[525]

Slavery abolition

The continuing anti-slavery movement in Europe became a reason and an excuse for the conquest and colonization of the Africa. It was the central theme of the Brussels Anti-Slavery Conference 1889-90. During the Scramble for Africa, an early but secondary focus of all colonial regimes was the suppression of slavery and the slave trade. In French West Africa, following conquest and abolition by the French, over a million slaves fled from their masters to earlier homes between 1906 and 1911. In Madagascar, the French abolished slavery in 1896 and approximately 500,000 slaves were freed. Slavery was abolished in the French controlled Sahel by 1911. Independent nations attempting to westernize or impress Europe sometimes cultivated an image of slavery suppression. In response to European pressure, the Sokoto Caliphate abolished slavery in 1900 and Ethiopia officially abolished slavery in 1932. Colonial powers were mostly successful in abolishing slavery, though slavery remained active in Africa even though it has gradually moved to a wage economy. Slavery was never fully eradicated in Africa.[526,527,528]

Figure 119: *German Cameroon, painting by R. Hellgrewe, 1908*

Colonialism leading to World War I

During the New Imperialism period, by the end of the 19th century, Europe added almost 9,000,000 square miles (23,000,000 km^2) – one-fifth of the land area of the globe – to its overseas colonial possessions. Europe's formal holdings now included the entire African continent except Ethiopia, Liberia, and Saguia el-Hamra, the latter of which would be integrated into Spanish Sahara. Between 1885 and 1914, Britain took nearly 30% of Africa's population under its control; 15% for France, 11% for Portugal, 9% for Germany, 7% for Belgium and 1% for Italy.Wikipedia:Citation needed Nigeria alone contributed 15 million subjects, more than in the whole of French West Africa or the entire German colonial empire. It was paradoxical that Britain, the staunch advocate of free trade, emerged in 1914 with not only the largest overseas empire thanks to its long-standing presence in India, but also the greatest gains in the "scramble for Africa", reflecting its advantageous position at its inception. In terms of surface area occupied, the French were the marginal victors but much of their territory consisted of the sparsely populated Sahara.

The political imperialism followed the economic expansion, with the "colonial lobbies" bolstering chauvinism and jingoism at each crisis in order to legitimise the colonial enterprise. The tensions between the imperial powers led to a succession of crises, which finally exploded in August 1914, when previous rivalries and alliances created a domino situation that drew the major European nations into World War I. Austria-Hungary attacked Serbia to avenge the murder by Serbian agents of Austrian crown prince Francis Ferdinand, Russia would mobilise to assist allied Serbia, Germany would intervene to support Austria-Hungary against Russia. Since Russia had a military alliance with France against Germany, the German General Staff, led by General von Moltke decided to realise the well prepared Schlieffen Plan to invade and quickly knock France out of the war before turning against Russia in what was expected to be a long campaign. This required an invasion of Belgium which brought Britain into the war against Germany, Austria-Hungary and their allies. German U-Boat campaigns against ships bound for Britain eventually drew the United States into what had become World War I. Moreover, using the Anglo-Japanese Alliance as an excuse, Japan leaped onto this opportunity to conquer German interests in China and the Pacific to become the dominating power in the Western Pacific, setting the stage for the Second Sino-Japanese War (starting in 1937) and eventually World War II.

African colonies listed by colonising power

Belgium

- Congo Free State and Belgian Congo (today's Democratic Republic of the Congo)
- Ruanda-Urundi (comprising modern Rwanda and Burundi, 1922–62)

France

- French West Africa:
  - Mauritania
  - Senegal
  - Albreda (1681–1857, now part of Gambia)
  - French Sudan (now Mali)
  - French Guinea (now Guinea)
  - Ivory Coast
  - Niger
  - French Upper Volta (now Burkina Faso)
  - French Dahomey (now Benin)
  - French Togoland (1916–60, now Togo)
  - Enclaves of Forcados and Badjibo (in modern Nigeria)
- French Equatorial Africa:
  - Gabon
  - French Cameroun (1922–60)
  - French Congo (now Republic of the Congo)
  - Oubangui-Chari (now Central African Republic)
  - Chad
- French North Africa:
  - French Algeria
  - French Protectorate of Tunisia
  - French Morocco
  - Fezzan-Ghadames (1943–1951) (administration given by the UNO after its conquest by Charles de Gaulle)
  - Egypt (ownership (1798–1801)) (Condominium of France and the United Kingdom) (1876–1882)
- French East Africa:
  - French Madagascar
  - Comoros
  - Scattered islands in the Indian Ocean
  - French Somaliland (now Djibouti)
  - Isle de France (1715-1810) (now Mauritius)

Germany

- German Kamerun (now Cameroon and part of Nigeria, 1884–1916)
- German East Africa (now Rwanda, Burundi and most of Tanzania, 1885–1919)
- German South-West Africa (now Namibia, 1884–1915)
- German Togoland (now Togo and eastern part of Ghana, 1884–1914)

After the First World War, Germany's possessions were partitioned among Britain (which took a sliver of western Cameroon, Tanzania, western Togo, and Namibia), France (which took most of Cameroon and eastern Togo) and Belgium (which took Rwanda and Burundi).

Italy

- Italian Libya
- Italian Eritrea
- Italian Somaliland

Later, during the Interwar period, with the Second Italo-Ethiopian War Italy would annex Ethiopia, which formed together with Eritrea and Italian Somaliland the Italian East Africa (A.O.I., "Africa Orientale Italiana", also defined by the fascist government as *L'Impero*).

Figure 120: *The Senegalese Tirailleurs, led by Colonel Alfred-Amédée Dodds, conquered Dahomey (present-day Benin) in 1892*

Portugal

- Portuguese West Africa
  (now Angola)
  - Mainland Angola
  - Portuguese Congo
    (now Cabinda Province of Angola)
- Portuguese East Africa
  (now Mozambique)
- Portuguese Guinea
  (now Guinea-Bissau)
- Portuguese Cape Verde
- Portuguese São Tomé and Príncipe
  - São Tomé Island
  - Príncipe Island
  - Fort of São João Baptista de Ajudá
    (now Ouidah, in Benin)

Figure 121: *Marracuene in Portuguese Mozambique was the site of a decisive battle between Portuguese and Gaza king Gungunhana in 1895*

Spain

- Spanish North Africa
  - Northern Spanish Morocco
    - Chefchaouen (*Chauen*)
    - Jebala (*Yebala*)
    - Kert
    - Loukkos (*Lucus*)
    - Rif
- Spanish West Africa
  - Southern Spanish Morocco
    - Cape Juby
    - Ifni
  - Spanish Sahara (now Western Sahara)
    - Río de Oro
    - Saguia el-Hamra
- Spanish Guinea (now Equatorial Guinea)
  - Fernando Pó
  - Río Muni
  - Annobón

Figure 122: *Opening of the railway in Rhodesia, 1899*

Figure 123: *Following the Fourth Anglo-Ashanti War in 1896, the British proclaimed a protectorate over the Ashanti Kingdom.*

United Kingdom

The British were primarily interested in maintaining secure communication lines to India, which led to initial interest in Egypt and South Africa. Once these two areas were secure, it was the intent of British colonialists such as Cecil Rhodes to establish a Cape-Cairo railway and to exploit mineral and agricultural resources. Control of the Nile was viewed as a strategic and commercial advantage.

- Egypt
- British Mauritius
- British West Africa
  - Gambia Colony and Protectorate
  - Sierra Leone
  - Nigeria
  - British Togoland (1916–56, today part of Ghana)
  - Cameroons (1922–61, now parts of Cameroon and Nigeria)
  - Gold Coast (British colony) (now Ghana)
- Anglo-Egyptian Sudan (1899–1956)
- British Somaliland (now part of Somalia)
- British East Africa:
  - Kenya Colony
  - Uganda Protectorate
  - Tanzania :
    - Tanganyika Territory (1919–61)
    - Zanzibar
- Bechuanaland (now Botswana)
- Southern Rhodesia (now Zimbabwe)
- Northern Rhodesia (now Zambia)
- Nyasaland (now Malawi)
- Basutoland (now Lesotho)
- Swaziland
- British Seychelles
- British South Africa
  - South Africa :
    - Transvaal Colony
    - Cape Colony
    - Colony of Natal
    - Orange River Colony
  - South-West Africa (from 1915, now Namibia)

Independent states

Liberia was the only nation in Africa that was a colony and a protectorate of the United States. Liberia was founded, colonised, established and controlled by the American Colonization Society, a private organisation established in order to relocate freed African-American and Caribbean slaves from the United States and the Caribbean islands in 1821. Liberia declared its independence from the American Colonization Society on July 26, 1847. Liberia is Africa's oldest democratic republic, and the second-oldest black republic in the world (after Haiti).

Ethiopia maintained its independence from Italy after the Battle of Adwa which resulted in the Treaty of Addis Ababa. With the exception of the occupation between 1936 and 1941 by Benito Mussolini's military forces, Ethiopia is Africa's oldest independent nation.

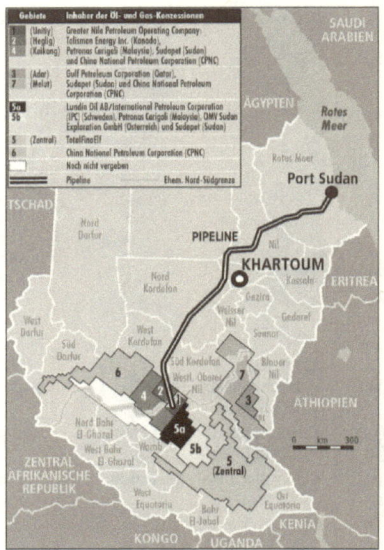

Figure 124: *Oil and gas concessions in Sudan – 2004*

Modern Scramble for Africa

The new scramble for Africa began with the emergence of the Afro-Neo-Liberal capitalist movement in Post-Colonial Africa.[529] When African nations began to gain independence during the Post World War II Era, their post colonial economic structures remained undiversified and linear. In most cases, the bulk of a nation's economy relied on cash crops or natural resources. The decolonisation process kept independent African nations at the mercy of colonial powers due to structurally-dependent economic relations. Structural adjustment programs led to the privatization and liberalization of many African political and economic systems, forcefully pushing Africa into the global capitalist market. The economic decline in the 1990s fostered democratization by the World Bank intervening in the political and economic affairs of Africa once again. All of these factors led to Africa's forced development under Western ideological systems of economics and politics.[530]

Petro-states

In the era of globalization, many African countries have emerged as petro-states (for example Sudan, Cameroon, Nigeria, Angola). These are nations with an economic and political partnership between transnational oil companies and the ruling elite class in oil-rich African nations.[531] Numerous countries have entered into a neo-imperial relationship with Africa during this time period. Mary Gilmartin notes that "material and symbolic appropriation of space [is] central to imperial expansion and control"; nations in the globalization era who invest in controlling land internationally are engaging in neo-imperialism.[532] Chinese (and other Asian countries) state oil companies have entered Africa's highly competitive oil sector. China National Petroleum Corporation purchased 40% of Greater Nile Petroleum Operating Company. Furthermore, Sudan exports 50–60% of its domestically produced oil to China, making up 7% of China's imports. China has also been purchasing equity shares in African oil fields, invested in industry related infrastructure development and acquired continental oil concessions throughout Africa.[533]

Further reading

- Aldrich, Robert. *Greater France: A History of French Overseas Expansion* (1996)
- Atkinson, David. "Constructing Italian Africa: Geography and Geopolitics." *Italian colonialism* (2005): 15–26.
- Axelson, Eric. *Portugal and the Scramble for Africa: 1875–1891* (Johannesburg, Witwatersrand UP, 1967)
- Boddy-Evans, Alistair. "What Caused the Scramble for Africa?" *African History* (2012). online[534]
- Brantlinger, Patrick. "Victorians and Africans: The genealogy of the myth of the dark continent." *Critical Inquiry* (1985): 166–203. online[535]
- Chamberlain, Muriel Evelyn. *The scramble for Africa* (4th ed. Routledge, 2014) excerpt and text search[536]
- Curtin, Philip D. *Disease and empire: The health of European Troops in the Conquest of Africa* (Cambridge University Press, 1998)
- Darwin, John. "Imperialism and the Victorians: The dynamics of territorial expansion." *English Historical Review* (1997) 112#447 pp: 614–642.
- Finaldi, Giuseppe. *Italian National Identity in the Scramble for Africa: Italy's African Wars in the Era of Nation-building, 1870–1900* (Peter Lang, 2009)
- Gifford, Prosser and William Roger Louis. *France and Britain in Africa: Imperial Rivalry and Colonial Rule* (1971)
- Gifford, Prosser and William Roger Louis. *Britain and Germany in Africa: Imperial rivalry and colonial rule* (1967).
- Gjersø, Jonas Fossli (2015). "The Scramble for East Africa: British Motives Reconsidered, 1884-95"[537]. *Journal of Imperial and Commonwealth History*. Taylor & Francis. **43** (5): 831–60. doi:

10.1080/03086534.2015.1026131[538]. Retrieved 4 March 2016.<templatestyles src="Module:Citation/CS1/styles.css"></templatestyles>
- Hammond, Richard James. *Portugal and Africa, 1815–1910: a study in uneconomic imperialism* (Stanford University Press, 1966)
- Henderson, W. O. *The German Colonial Empire, 1884–1919* (London: Frank Cass, 1993)
- Hinsley, F. H. ed. *The New Cambridge Modern History, Vol. 11: Material Progress and World-Wide Problems, 1870-98* (1962) contents[539] pp 593-40.
- Hochschild, Adam (2006) [1998]. *King Leopold's Ghost: A Story of Greed, Terror, and Heroism in Colonial Africa.* London: Pan Books. ISBN 978-0-330-44198-8.<templatestyles src="Module:Citation/CS1/styles.css"></templatestyles>
- Klein, Martin A. *Slavery and colonial rule in French West Africa* (Cambridge University Press, 1998)
- Lovejoy, Paul E. *Transformations in slavery: a history of slavery in Africa* (Cambridge University Press, 2011)
- Lloyd, Trevor Owen. *Empire: the history of the British Empire* (2001).
- Mackenzie J. M. *The Partition of Africa, 1880–1900, and European Imperialism in the Nineteenth Century* (London 1983).
- Oliver, Roland, *Sir Harry Johnston and the Scramble for Africa* (1959) online[540]
- Pakenham, Thomas (1992) [1991]. *The Scramble for Africa.* London: Abacus. ISBN 978-0-349-10449-2.<templatestyles src="Module:Citation/CS1/styles.css"></templatestyles>
- Penrose E. F., ed. *European Imperialism and the Partition of Africa* (London 1975).
- Perraudin, Michael, and Jürgen Zimmerer, eds. *German colonialism and national identity* (London: Taylor & Francis, 2010)
- Robinson R,. and J. Gallagher, "The partition of Africa", in *The New Cambridge Modern History* vol XI, pp 593–640 (Cambridge, 1962).
- Rotberg, Robert I. *The Founder: Cecil Rhodes and the Pursuit of Power* (1988) excerpt and text search[541]; online[542]
- Sanderson G. N., "The European partition of Africa: Coincidence or conjuncture?" *Journal of Imperial and Commonwealth History* (1974) 3#1 pp 1–54.
- Stoecker, Helmut. *German imperialism in Africa: From the beginnings until the Second World War* (Hurst & Co., 1986.)
- Thomas, Antony. *Rhodes: The Race for Africa* (1997) excerpt and text search[543]
- Thompson, Virginia, and Richard Adloff. *French West Africa* (Stanford University Press, 1958)

- Wesseling, H.L. and Arnold J. Pomerans. *Divide and rule: The partition of Africa, 1880–1914* (Praeger, 1996.) online[544]

External links

- "Belgium exhumes its colonial demons"[545]. *The Guardian*. 13 July 2002.<templatestyles src="Module:Citation/CS1/styles.css"></templatestyles>
- Gülstorff, Torben (2016). "Trade follows Hallstein? Deutsche Aktivitäten im zentralafrikanischen Raum des Second Scramble"[546]. Berlin.<templatestyles src="Module:Citation/CS1/styles.css"></templatestyles>

Geography of Africa

Geography of Africa

Africa is a continent comprising 63 political territories, representing the largest of the great southward projections from the main mass of Earth's surface. Within its regular outline, it comprises an area of 30,368,609 km² (11,725,385 sq mi), excluding adjacent islands. Its highest mountain is Mount Kilimanjaro, its largest lake is Lake Victoria[547]

Separated from Europe by the Mediterranean Sea and from much of Asia by the Red Sea, Africa is joined to Asia at its northeast extremity by the Isthmus of Suez (which in transected by the Suez Canal), 130 km (81 mi) wide. For geopolitical purposes, the Sinai Peninsula of Egypt – east on the Suez Canal – is often considered part of Africa. From the most northerly point, Ras ben Sakka in Tunisia, at 37°21′ N, to the more southerly point, Cape Agulhas in South Africa, 34°51′15" S, is a distance approximately of 8,000 km

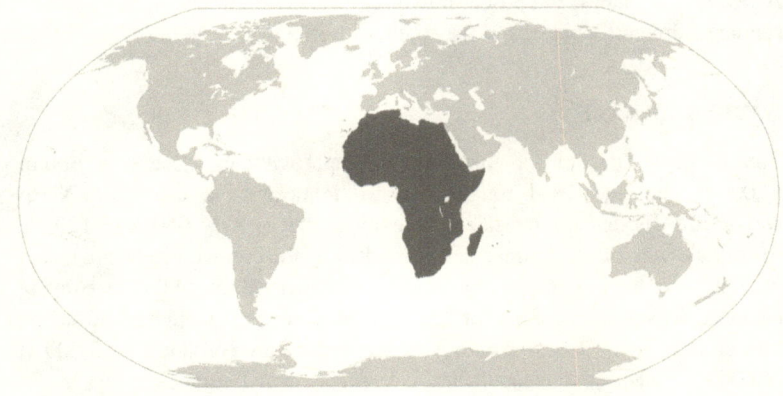

Figure 125: *Satellite view of Africa*

(5,000 mi); from Cap-Vert, 17°31′13″W, the westernmost point, to Ras Hafun in Somalia, 51°27′52″ E, the most easterly projection, is a distance (also approximately) of 7,400 km (4,600 mi).

The main structural lines of the continent show both the east-to-west direction characteristic, at least in the eastern hemisphere, of the more northern parts of the world, and the north-to-south direction seen in the southern peninsulas. Africa is thus mainly composed of two segments at right angles, the northern running from east to west, and the southern from north to south.

Main features

The average elevation of the continent approximates closely to 600 m (2,000 ft) above sea level, roughly near to the mean elevation of both North and South America, but considerably less than that of Asia, 950 m (3,120 ft). In contrast with other continents, it is marked by the comparatively small area of either very high or very low ground, lands under 180 m (590 ft) occupying an unusually small part of the surface; while not only are the highest elevations inferior to those of Asia or South America, but the area of land over 3,000 m (9,800 ft) is also quite insignificant, being represented almost entirely by individual peaks and mountain ranges. Moderately elevated tablelands are thus the characteristic feature of the continent, though the surface of these is broken by higher peaks and ridges. (So prevalent are these isolated peaks and ridges that a specialised term [*Inselberg-Landschaft*, island mountain landscape] has been adopted in Germany to describe this kind of country, thought to be in great part the result of wind action.)

As a general rule, the higher tablelands lie to the east and south, while a progressive diminution in altitude towards the west and north is observable. Apart from the lowlands and the Atlas mountain range, the continent may be divided into two regions of higher and lower plateaus, the dividing line (somewhat concave to the north-west) running from the middle of the Red Sea to about 6 deg. S. on the west coast.

Africa can be divided into a number of geographic zones:

- The coastal plains — often fringed seawards by mangrove swamps — never stretching far from the coast, apart from the lower courses of streams. Recent alluvial flats are found chiefly in the delta of the more important rivers. Elsewhere, the coastal lowlands merely form the lowest steps of the system of terraces that constitutes the ascent to the inner plateaus.
- The Atlas range — orthographically distinct from the rest of the continent, being unconnected with and separated from the south by a depressed and desert area (the Sahara).

Plateau region

The high southern and eastern plateaus, rarely falling below 600 m (2,000 ft), have a mean elevation of about 1,000 m (3,300 ft). The South African Plateau, as far as about 12° S, is bounded east, west and south by bands of high ground which fall steeply to the coasts. On this account South Africa has a general resemblance to an inverted saucer. Due south, the plateau rim is formed by three parallel steps with level ground between them. The largest of these level areas, the Great Karoo, is a dry, barren region, and a large tract of the plateau proper is of a still more arid character and is known as the Kalahari Desert.

The South African Plateau is connected towards East African plateau, with probably a slightly greater average elevation, and marked by some distinct features. It is formed by a widening out of the eastern axis of high ground, which becomes subdivided into a number of zones running north and south and consisting in turn of ranges, tablelands and depressions. The most striking feature is the existence of two great lines of depression, due largely to the subsidence of whole segments of the Earth's crust, the lowest parts of which are occupied by vast lakes. Towards the south the two lines converge and give place to one great valley (occupied by Lake Nyasa), the southern part of which is less distinctly due to rifting and subsidence than the rest of the system.

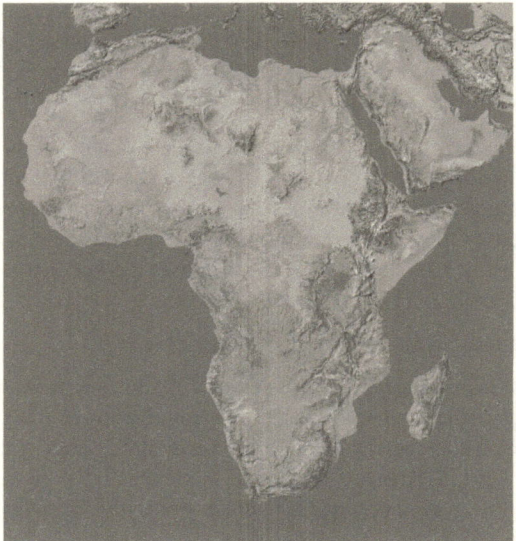

Figure 126: *Topography of Africa*

Farther north the western hollow, known as the Albertine Rift, is occupied for more than half its length by water, forming the Great Lakes of Tanganyika, Kivu, Lake Edward and Lake Albert, the first-named over 400 miles (640 km) long and the longest freshwater lake in the world. Associated with these great valleys are a number of volcanic peaks, the greatest of which occur on a meridional line east of the eastern trough. The eastern branch of the East African Rift, contains much smaller lakes, many of them brackish and without outlet, the only one comparable to those of the western trough being Lake Turkana or Basso Norok.

A short distance east of this rift-valley is Mount Kilimanjaro — with its two peaks Kibo and Mawenzi, the latter being 5,889 m (19,321 ft), and the culminating point of the whole continent — and Mount Kenya, which is 5,184 m (17,008 ft). Hardly less important is the Ruwenzori Range, over 5,060 m (16,600 ft), which lies east of the western trough. Other volcanic peaks rise from the floor of the valleys, some of the Kirunga (Mfumbiro) group, north of Lake Kivu, being still partially active. This could cause most of the cities and states to be flooded with lava and ash.

The third division of the higher region of Africa is formed by the Ethiopian Highlands, a rugged mass of mountains forming the largest continuous area of its altitude in the whole continent, little of its surface falling below 1,500 m

(4,900 ft), while the summits reach heights of 4400 m to 4550 m. This block of country lies just west of the line of the great East African Trough, the northern continuation of which passes along its eastern escarpment as it runs up to join the Red Sea. There is, however, in the centre a circular basin occupied by Lake Tsana.

Both in the east and west of the continent the bordering highlands are continued as strips of plateau parallel to the coast, the Ethiopian mountains being continued northwards along the Red Sea coast by a series of ridges reaching in places a height of 2,000 m (6,600 ft). In the west the zone of high land is broader but somewhat lower. The most mountainous districts lie inland from the head of the Gulf of Guinea (Adamawa, etc.), where heights of 1,800 to 2,400 m (5,900 to 7,900 ft) are reached. Exactly at the head of the gulf the great peak of the Cameroon, on a line of volcanic action continued by the islands to the south-west, has a height of 4,075 m (13,369 ft), while Clarence Peak, in Fernando Po, the first of the line of islands, rises to over 2,700 m (8,900 ft). Towards the extreme west the Futa Jallon highlands form an important diverging point of rivers, but beyond this, as far as the Atlas chain, the elevated rim of the continent is almost wanting.

Plains

Much of Africa is made up of plains of the pediplain and etchplain type often occurring as steps. The etchplains are commonly associated with laterite soil and inselbergs. Inselberg-dotted plains are common in Africa including Tanzania,[548] the Anti-Atlas of Morocco, Namibia, and the interior of Angola.[549] One of the most wideaspread plain is the African Surface, a composite etchplain occurring across much of the continent.

The area between the east and west coast highlands, which north of 17° N is mainly desert, is divided into separate basins by other bands of high ground, one of which runs nearly centrally through North Africa in a line corresponding roughly with the curved axis of the continent as a whole. The best marked of the basins so formed (the Congo basin) occupies a circular area bisected by the equator, once probably the site of an inland sea.

Running along the south of desert is the plains region known as the Sahel.

The arid region, the Sahara — the largest hot desert in the world, covering 9,000,000 km^2 (3,500,000 sq mi) — extends from the Atlantic to the Red Sea. Though generally of slight elevation, it contains mountain ranges with peaks rising to 2,400 m (7,900 ft) Bordered N.W. by the Atlas range, to the northeast a rocky plateau separates it from the Mediterranean; this plateau gives place at the extreme east to the delta of the Nile. That river (see below) pierces the desert without modifying its character. The Atlas range, the north-westerly part of the continent, between its seaward and landward heights encloses elevated steppes in places 160 km (99 mi) broad. From the inner slopes of the plateau numerous wadis take a direction towards the Sahara. The greater part of that now desert region is, indeed, furrowed by old water-channels.

Mountains

The following table gives the details of the chief mountains and ranges of the continent:

Mountain	Range	Country	Height (m)	Height (ft)	Prominence (m)	Isolation (km)
Kilimanjaro	Eastern Rift volcanoes	Tanzania	5895	19,340	5885	5510
Mt Kenya	Eastern Rift volcanoes	Kenya	5199	17,058	3825	323
Mt Stanley	Rwenzori Mtns	Uganda/-DRC	5109	16,762	3951	830
Mt Meru	Eastern Rift volcanoes	Tanzania	4566	14,980	3170	70
Ras Dashen	Semien Mountains	Ethiopia	4533	14,872	3997	1483
Mt Karisimbi	Virunga mountains	Rwanda/-DRC	4507	14,787	3312	207
Mt Elgon	Eastern Rift volcanoes	Uganda	4321	14,178	2458	339
Toubkal	Atlas mountains	Morocco	4167	13,671	3755	2078
Mt Cameroon	Cameroon line	Cameroon	4095	13,435	3901	2338
Mt Satima	Aberdare range	Kenya	4001	13,120	2081	77
Thabana Ntlenyana	Drakensberg	Lesotho	3482	11,422	2390	3003
Emi Koussi	Tibesti mountains	Chad	3445	11,302	2934	2001
Sapitwa Peak	Mulanje Massif	Malawi	3002	9,849	2319	1272

Rivers

From the outer margin of the African plateaus, a large number of streams run to the sea with comparatively short courses, while the larger rivers flow for long distances on the interior highlands, before breaking through the outer ranges.

Figure 127: *Drainage basins of Africa*

The main drainage of the continent is to the north and west, or towards the basin of the Atlantic Ocean.

To the main African rivers belong: Nile (the longest river of Africa), Congo (river with the highest water discharge on the continent) and the Niger, which flows half of its length through the arid areas. The largest lakes are the following: Lake Victoria (Lake Ukerewe), Lake Chad, in the centre of the continent, Lake Tanganyika, lying between the Democratic Republic of Congo, Burundi, Tanzania and Zambia. There is also the considerably large Lake Malawi stretching along the eastern border of one of the poorest countries in the world -Malawi. There are also numerous water dams throughout the continent: Kariba on the river of Zambezi, Asuan in Egypt on the river of Nile and the biggest dam of the continent lying completely in The republic of Ghana is called Akosombo on the Volta river (Fobil 2003). The high lake plateau of the African Great Lakes region contains the headwaters of both the Nile and the Congo.

The break-up of Gondwana in Late Cretaceous and Cenozoic times led to a major reorganization of the river courses of various large African rivers including the Congo, Niger, Nile, Orange, Limpopo and Zambezi rivers.

Flowing to the Mediterranean Sea

The upper Nile receives its chief supplies from the mountainous region adjoining the Central African trough in the neighborhood of the equator. From there, streams pour eastward into Lake Victoria, the largest lake in Africa (covering over 26,000 square m.), and to the west and north into Lake Edward and Lake Albert. To the latter of these, the effluents of the other two lakes add their waters. Issuing from there, the Nile flows northward, and between the latitudes of 7 and 10 degrees north it traverses a vast marshy level, where its course is liable to being blocked by floating vegetation. After receiving the Bahr-el-Ghazal from the west and the Sobat, Blue Nile and Atbara from the Ethiopian Highlands (the chief gathering ground of the flood-water), it separates the great desert with its fertile watershed, and enters the Mediterranean at a vast delta.

Flowing to the Atlantic Ocean

The most remote head-stream of the Congo is the Chambezi, which flows southwest into the marshy Lake Bangweulu. From this lake issues the Congo, known in its upper course by various names. Flowing first south, it afterwards turns north through Lake Mweru and descends to the forest-clad basin of west equatorial Africa. Traversing this in a majestic northward curve, and receiving vast supplies of water from many great tributaries, it finally turns southwest and cuts a way to the Atlantic Ocean through the western highlands. The area of the Congo basin is greater than that of any other river except the Amazon, while the African inland drainage area is greater than that of any continent but Asia, where the corresponding area is 1,000,000 km^2 (390,000 sq mi).

West of Lake Chad is the basin of the Niger, the third major river of Africa. With its principal source in the far west, it reverses the direction of flow exhibited by the Nile and Congo, and ultimately flows into the Atlantic — a fact that eluded European geographers for many centuries. An important branch, however — the Benue—flows from the southeast.

These four river basins occupy the greater part of the lower plateaus of North and West Africa — the remainder consists of arid regions watered only by intermittent streams that do not reach the sea.

Of the remaining rivers of the Atlantic basin, the Orange, in the extreme south, brings the drainage from the Drakensberg on the opposite side of the continent, while the Kunene, Kwanza, Ogowe and Sanaga drain the west coastal highlands of the southern limb; the Volta, Komoe, Bandama, Gambia and Senegal the highlands of the western limb. North of the Senegal, for over 1,500 km (930 mi) of coast, the arid region reaches to the Atlantic. Farther north are the streams, with comparatively short courses, reaching the Atlantic and Mediterranean from the Atlas mountains.

Flowing to the Indian Ocean

Of the rivers flowing to the Indian Ocean, the only one draining any large part of the interior plateaus is the Zambezi, whose western branches rise in the western coastal highlands. The main stream has its rise in 11°21'3" S 24°22' E, at an elevation of 1,500 m (4,900 ft). It flows to the west and south for a considerable distance before turning eastward. All the largest tributaries, including the Shire, the outflow of Lake Nyasa, flow down the southern slopes of the band of high ground stretching across the continent from 10° to 12° S. In the southwest, the Zambezi system interlaces with that of the Taukhe (or Tioghe), from which it at times receives surplus water. The rest of the water of the Taukhe, known in its middle course as the Okavango, is lost in a system of swamps and saltpans that was formerly centred in Lake Ngami, now dried up.

Farther south, the Limpopo drains a portion of the interior plateau, but breaks through the bounding highlands on the side of the continent nearest its source. The Rovuma, Rufiji and Tana principally drain the outer slopes of the African Great Lakes highlands.

In the Horn region to the north, the Jubba and the Shebelle rivers begin in the Ethiopian Highlands. These rivers mainly flow southwards, with the Jubba emptying in the Indian Ocean. The Shebelle River reaches a point to the southwest. After that, it consists of swamps and dry reaches before finally disappearing in the desert terrain near the Jubba River. Another large stream, the Hawash, rising in the Ethiopian mountains, is lost in a saline depression near the Gulf of Aden.

Inland basins

Between the basins of the Atlantic and Indian Oceans, there is an area of inland drainage along the centre of the Ethiopian plateau, directed chiefly into the lakes in the Great Rift Valley. The largest river is the Omo, which, fed by the rains of the Ethiopian highlands, carries down a large body of water into Lake Rudolf. The rivers of Africa are generally obstructed either by bars at their mouths, or by cataracts at no great distance upstream. But when these obstacles have been overcome, the rivers and lakes afford a vast network of navigable waters.

North of the Congo basin, and separated from it by a broad undulation of the surface, is the basin of Lake Chad – a flat-shored, shallow lake filled principally by the Chari coming from the southeast.

Lakes

The principal lakes of Africa are situated in the African Great Lakes plateau. As a rule, the lakes found within the Great Rift Valley have steep sides and are very deep. This is the case with the two largest of the type, Tanganyika and Nyasa, the latter with depths of 800 m (2,600 ft).

Others, however, are shallow, and hardly reach the steep sides of the valleys in the dry season. Such are Lake Rukwa, in a subsidiary depression north of Nyasa, and Eiassi and Manyara in the system of the Great Rift Valley. Lakes of the broad type are of moderate depth, the deepest sounding in Lake Victoria being under 90 m (300 ft).

Besides the African Great Lakes, the principal lakes on the continent are: Lake Chad, in the northern inland watershed; Bangweulu and Mweru, traversed by the head-stream of the Congo; and Lake Mai-Ndombe and Ntomba (Mantumba), within the great bend of that river. All, except possibly Mweru, are more or less shallow, and Lake Chad appears to be drying up.

Divergent opinions have been held as to the mode of origin of the African Great Lakes, especially Tanganyika, which some geologists have considered to represent an old arm of the sea, dating from a time when the whole central Congo basin was under water; others holding that the lake water has accumulated in a depression caused by subsidence. The former view is based on the existence in the lake of organisms of a decidedly marine type. They include jellyfish, molluscs, prawns, crabs, etc.

Lake	m	ft
Chad	259	850
Mai-Ndombe	335	1100
Turkana	381	1250
Malawi	501	1645
Albert	618	2028
Tanganyika	800	2624
Ngami	899	2950
Mweru	914	3000
Edward	916	3004
Bangweulu	1128	3700
Victoria	1134	3720
Abaya	1280	4200
Kivu	1472	4829
Tana	1734	5690
Naivasha	1870	6135

Islands

With the exception of Madagascar, the African islands are small. Madagascar, with an area of 587,041 km² (226,658 sq mi), is, after Greenland, New Guinea and Borneo, the fourth largest island on the Earth. It lies in the Indian Ocean, off the S.E. coast of the continent, from which it is separated by the deep Mozambique channel, 400 km (250 mi) wide at its narrowest point.[550] Madagascar in its general structure, as in flora and fauna, forms a connecting link between Africa and southern Asia. East of Madagascar are the small islands of Mauritius and Réunion. There are also islands in the Gulf of Guinea on which lies the Republic of Sao Tomé and Príncipe (islands of São Tomé and Príncipe). Part of the Republic of Equatorial Guinea is lying on the island of Bioko (with the capital Malabo and the town of Lubu) and the island of Annobón. Socotra lies E.N.E. of Cape Guardafui. Off the north-west coast are the Canary and Cape Verde archipelagoes. which, like some small islands in the Gulf of Guinea, are of volcanic origin. The South Atlantic Islands of Saint Helena and Ascension are classed as Africa but are situated on the Mid-Atlantic Ridge half way to South America.

Climatic conditions

<templatestyles src="Multiple_image/styles.css" />

Africa mean annual temperature

Africa mean annual precipitation

Lying almost entirely within the tropics, and equally to north and south of the equator, Africa does not show excessive variations of temperature.

Great heat is experienced in the lower plains and desert regions of North Africa, removed by the great width of the continent from the influence of the ocean, and here, too, the contrast between day and night, and between summer and

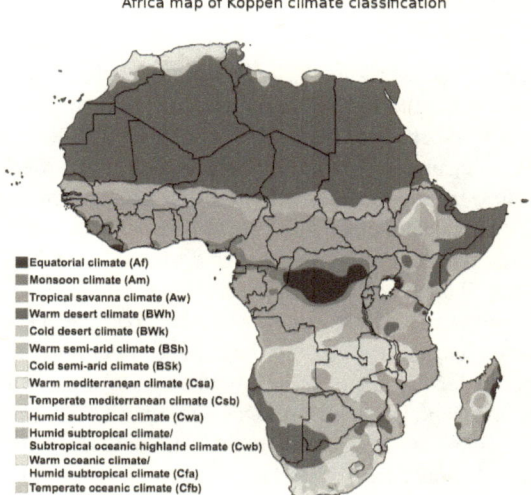

Figure 128: *Africa map of Köppen climate classification.*

winter, is greatest. (The rarity of the air and the great radiation during the night cause the temperature in the Sahara to fall occasionally to freezing point.)

Farther south, the heat is to some extent modified by the moisture brought from the ocean, and by the greater elevation of a large part of the surface, especially in East Africa, where the range of temperature is wider than in the Congo basin or on the Guinea coast.

In the extreme north and south the climate is a warm temperate one, the northern countries being on the whole hotter and drier than those in the southern zone; the south of the continent being narrower than the north, the influence of the surrounding ocean is more felt.

The most important climatic differences are due to variations in the amount of rainfall. The wide heated plains of the Sahara, and in a lesser degree the corresponding zone of the Kalahari in the south, have an exceedingly scanty rainfall, the winds which blow over them from the ocean losing part of their moisture as they pass over the outer highlands, and becoming constantly drier owing to the heating effects of the burning soil of the interior; while the scarcity of mountain ranges in the more central parts likewise tends to prevent condensation. In the inter-tropical zone of summer precipitation, the rainfall is greatest when the sun is vertical or soon after. It is therefore greatest of all near the equator, where the sun is twice vertical, and less in the direction of both tropics.

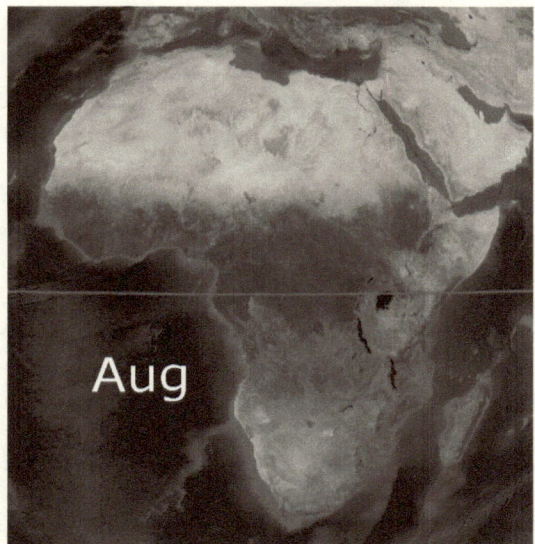

Figure 129: *Vegetation in February and August*

The rainfall zones are, however, somewhat deflected from a due west-to-east direction, the drier northern conditions extending southwards along the east coast, and those of the south northwards along the west. Within the equatorial zone certain areas, especially on the shores of the Gulf of Guinea and in the upper Nile basin, have an intensified rainfall, but this rarely approaches that of the rainiest regions of the world. The rainiest district in all Africa is a strip of coastland west of Mount Cameroon, where there is a mean annual rainfall of about 10,000 mm (394 in) as compared with a mean of 11,600 mm (457 in) at Cherrapunji, in Meghalaya, India.

The two distinct rainy seasons of the equatorial zone, where the sun is vertical at half-yearly intervals, become gradually merged into one in the direction of the tropics, where the sun is overhead but once. Snow falls on all the higher mountain ranges, and on the highest the climate is thoroughly Alpine.

The countries bordering the Sahara are much exposed to a very dry wind, full of fine particles of sand, blowing from the desert towards the sea. Known in Egypt as the khamsin, on the Mediterranean as the sirocco, it is called on the Guinea coast the harmattan. This wind is not invariably hot; its great dryness causes so much evaporation that cold is not infrequently the result. Similar dry winds blow from the Kalahari Desert in the south. On the eastern coast the monsoons of the Indian Ocean are regularly felt, and on the southeast hurricanes are occasionally experienced.

Health

The climate of Africa lends itself to certain environmental diseases, the most serious of which are: malaria, sleeping sickness and yellow fever. Malaria is the most deadly environmental disease in Africa. It is transmitted by a genus of mosquito (anopheles mosquito) native to Africa, and can be contracted over and over again. There is not yet a vaccine for malaria, which makes it difficult to prevent the disease from spreading in Africa. Recently, the dissemination of mosquito netting has helped lower the rate of malaria.

Yellow fever is a disease also transmitted by mosquitoes native to Africa. Unlike malaria, it cannot be contracted more than once. Like chicken pox, it is a disease that tends to be severe the later in life a person contracts the disease.

Sleeping sickness, or African trypanosomiasis, is a disease that usually affects animals, but has been known to be fatal to some humans as well. It is transmitted by the tsetse fly and is found almost exclusively in Sub-Saharan Africa. This disease has had a significant impact on African development not because of its deadly nature, like Malaria, but because it has prevented Africans from pursuing agriculture (as the sleeping sickness would kill their livestock).

Extreme points

These are the points that are farther north, south, east or west than any other location on the continent.

Africa

- Northernmost point — Iles des Chiens, Tunisia (37°32'N)
- Southernmost point — Cape Agulhas, South Africa (34°51'15"S)[551]
- Westernmost point — Santo Antão, Cape Verde Islands (25°25'W)
- Easternmost point — Rodrigues, Mauritius (63°30'E)
- The African pole of inaccessibility is close to the border of Central African Republic, South Sudan and Congo, near the town of Obo.

Africa (mainland)

- Northernmost point — Ras ben Sakka (Ra's al Abyad) (Cape Blanc), Tunisia
- Southernmost point — Cape Agulhas, South Africa
- Westernmost point — Pointe des Almadies, Cap Vert Peninsula, Ngor, Dakar, Senegal (17°33'22"W)
- Easternmost point — Ras Hafun (Raas Xaafuun), Somalia (51°27'52"E)

The highest point in Africa is Mount Kilimanjaro, 5,891.8 m (19,330 ft) in Tanzania. The lowest point is Lake Asal, 153 m (502 ft) below sea level, in Djibouti.

Figure 130: *Westernmost Point (mainland) — Pointe des Almadies*

External links

 Wikimedia Commons has media related to *Maps of Africa*.

- Wikimedia Atlas of Africa
- Africa: The Human Footprint[552]. Interactive map of human impact on Africa by National Geographic.
- Africa - Interactive Map with demographics and geopolitical information[553] from the United States Army Africa

African Plate

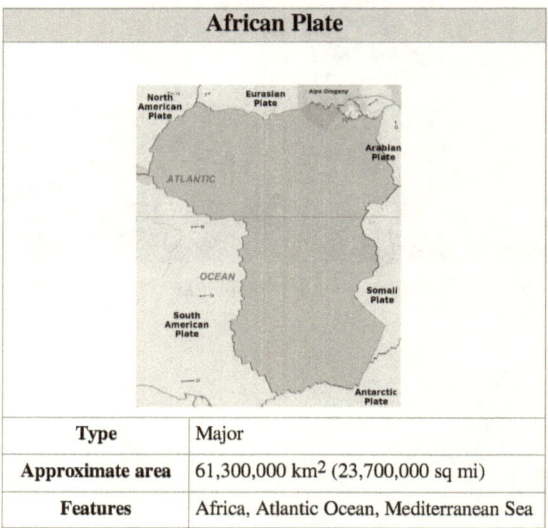

African Plate	
Type	Major
Approximate area	61,300,000 km² (23,700,000 sq mi)
Features	Africa, Atlantic Ocean, Mediterranean Sea

The **African Plate** is a major tectonic plate straddling the equator as well as the prime meridian. It includes much of the continent of Africa, as well as oceanic crust which lies between the continent and various surrounding ocean ridges. Between 60[554] million years ago and 10[555] million years ago, the Somali Plate began rifting from the African Plate along the East African Rift. Since the continent of Africa consists of crust from both the African and the Somali plates, some literature refers to the African Plate as the **Nubian Plate** to distinguish it from the continent as a whole.

Boundaries

The western edge of the African Plate is a divergent boundary with the North American Plate to the north and the South American Plate to the south which forms the central and southern part of the Mid-Atlantic Ridge. The African plate is bounded on the northeast by the Arabian Plate, the southeast by the

Somali Plate, the north by the Eurasian Plate, the Aegean Sea Plate, and the Anatolian Plate, and on the south by the Antarctic Plate. All of these are divergent or spreading boundaries with the exception of the northern boundary and a short segment near the Azores known as the Terceira Rift.

Components

The African Plate includes several cratons, stable blocks of old crust with deep roots in the subcontinental lithospheric mantle, and less stable terranes, which came together to form the African continent during the assembly of the supercontinent Pangea around 550 million years ago. The cratons are, from south to north, the Kalahari Craton, Congo Craton, Tanzania Craton and West African Craton. The cratons were widely separated in the past, but came together during the Pan-African orogeny and stayed together when Gondwana split up. The cratons are connected by orogenic belts, regions of highly deformed rock where the tectonic plates have engaged. The Saharan Metacraton has been tentatively identified as the remains of a craton that has become detached from the subcontinental lithospheric mantle, but alternatively may consist of a collection of unrelated crustal fragments swept together during the Pan-African orogeny.

In some areas, the cratons are covered by sedimentary basins, such as the Tindouf Basin, Taoudeni Basin and Congo Basin, where the underlying archaic crust is overlaid by more recent Neoproterozoic sediments. The plate includes shear zones such as the Central African Shear Zone (CASZ) where, in the past, two sections of the crust were moving in opposite directions, and rifts such as the Anza Trough where the crust was pulled apart, and the resulting depression filled with more modern sediment.

Modern movements

The African Plate is rifting in the eastern interior of the African continent along the East African Rift. This rift zone separates the African Plate to the west from the Somali Plate to the east. One hypothesis proposes the existence of a mantle plume beneath the Afar region, whereas an opposing hypothesis asserts that the rifting is merely a zone of maximum weakness where the African Plate is deforming as plates to its east are moving rapidly northward.

The African Plate's speed is estimated at around 2.15 cm (0.85 in) per year. It has been moving over the past 100 million years or so in a general northeast direction. This is drawing it closer to the Eurasian Plate, causing subduction where oceanic crust is converging with continental crust (e.g. portions of the central and eastern Mediterranean). In the western Mediterranean, the relative

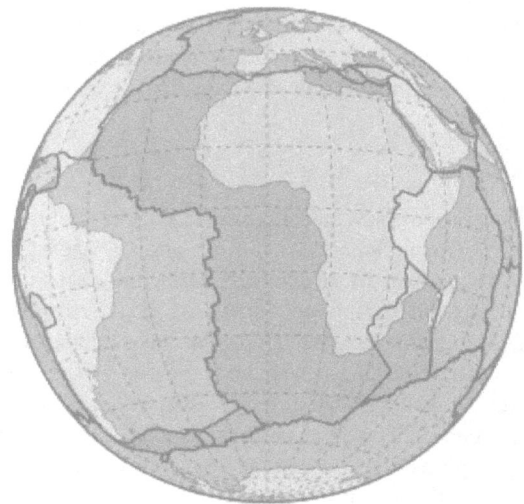

Figure 131: *Today, the African Plate is moving over Earth's surface at a speed of 0.292° ± 0.007° per million years, relative to the "average" Earth (NNR-MORVEL56)Wikipedia:Please clarify*

motions of the Eurasian and African plates produce a combination of lateral and compressive forces, concentrated in a zone known as the Azores–Gibraltar Fault Zone. Along its northeast margin, the African Plate is bounded by the Red Sea Rift where the Arabian Plate is moving away from the African Plate.

The New England hotspot in the Atlantic Ocean has probably created a short line of mid- to late-Tertiary age seamounts on the African Plate but appears to be currently inactive.

External links

- USGS - Understanding plate motions[556]
- Meijer, P. Th.; Wortel, M. J. R. (1999). "Cenozoic dynamics of the African plate with emphasis on the Africa-Eurasia collision"[557]. *Journal of Geophysical Research: Solid Earth*. **104** (B4): 7405–7418. Bibcode: 1999JGR...104.7405M[558]. doi: 10.1029/1999JB900009[559]. Retrieved 30 June 2015.<templatestyles src="Module:Citation/CS1/styles.css"></templatestyles>

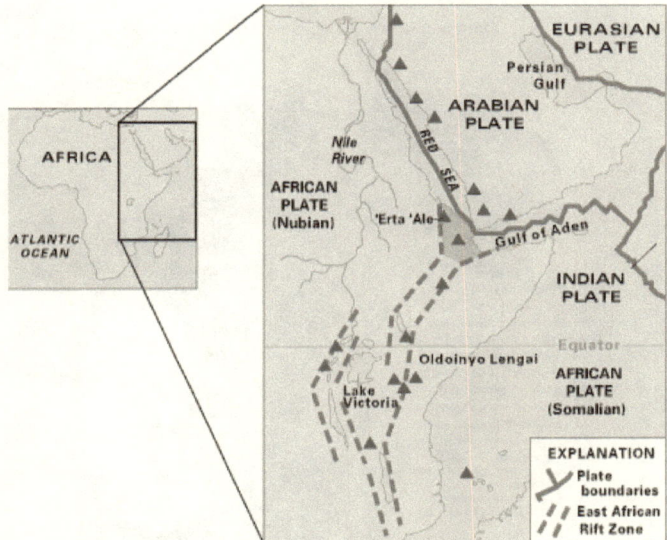

Figure 132: *Map of East Africa showing some of the historically active volcanoes (red triangles) and the Afar Triangle (shaded, center) – a triple junction where three plates are pulling away from one another: the Arabian Plate, the African Plate, and the Somali Plate (USGS).*

Climate of Africa

Owing to Africa's position across equatorial and subtropical latitudes in both the northern and southern hemisphere, several different climate types can be found within it. The continent mainly lies within the intertropical zone between the Tropic of Cancer and the Tropic of Capricorn. Hence, it's interesting density of humidity intensity is always high, and it is a hot continent. Warm and hot climates prevail all over Africa, but the northern part is that most marked by aridity and high temperatures. Only the northernmost and the southernmost fringes of the continent have a Mediterranean climate. The equator runs through the middle of Africa, as do the Tropic of Cancer and the Tropic of Capricorn, making Africa the most tropical continent.

The **climate of Africa** is a range of climates such as the equatorial climate, the tropical wet and dry climate, the tropical monsoon climate, the semi-desert climate (semi-arid), the desert climate (hyper-arid and arid), the subtropical highland climate etc. Temperate climates are rare across the continent except at very high elevations and along the fringes. In fact, the climate of Africa is more variable by rainfall amount than by temperatures, which are consistently

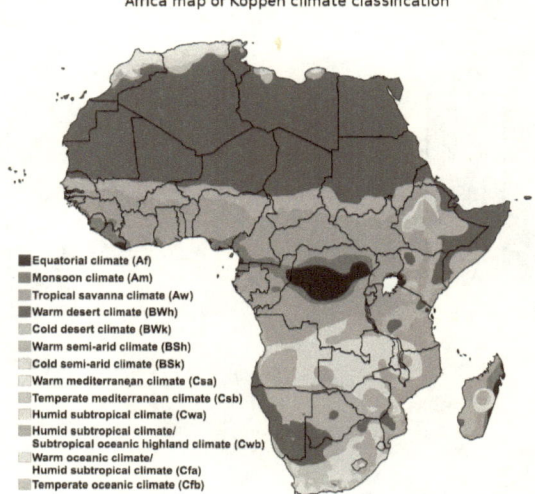

Figure 133: *Climate zones of Africa, showing the ecological break between the hot desert climate of the Sahara Desert (red), the hot semi-arid climate of the Sahel (orange) and the tropical climate of Central and Western Africa (blue). Southern Africa has a transition to semi-tropical or temperate climates (green), and more desert or semi-arid regions, centered on Namibia, Botswana, and South Africa.*

high. African deserts are the sunniest and the driest parts of the continent, owing to the prevailing presence of the subtropical ridge with subsiding, hot, dry air masses. Africa holds many heat-related records: the continent has the hottest extended region year-round, the areas with the hottest summer climate, the highest sunshine duration etc.

Temperatures

Globally, heating of the earth near the equator leads to large amounts of upward motion and convection along the monsoon trough or Intertropical Convergence Zone. The divergence over the near-equatorial trough leads to air rising and moving away from the equator aloft. As it moves towards the Mid-Latitudes, the air cools and sinks, which leads to subsidence near the 30th parallel of both hemispheres. This circulation is known as the Hadley cell and leads to the formation of the subtropical ridge.[560] Many of the world's deserts are caused by these climatological high-pressure areas,[561] including the Sahara Desert.

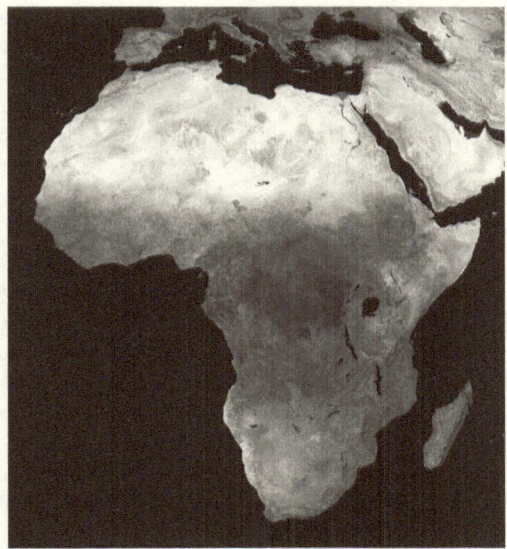

Figure 134: *A map of Africa showing the ecological break around the Sahara Desert*

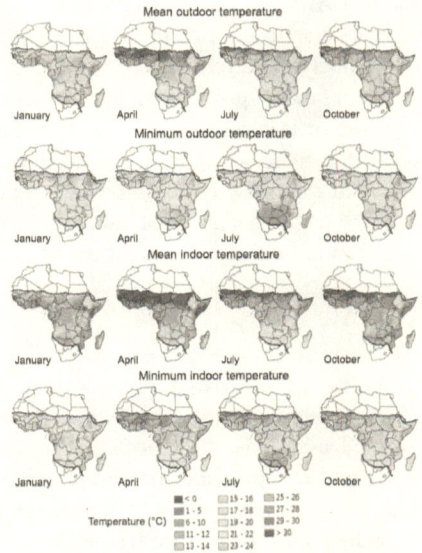

Figure 135: *Monthly mean and minimum outdoor and indoor temperatures throughout Africa*

Temperatures are hottest within the Sahara regions of Algeria and Mali, and coolest across the south and at elevation within the topography across the eastern and northwest sections of the continent. The hottest average temperature on Earth is at Dallol, Ethiopia, which averages a temperature of 33.9 °C (93.0 °F) throughout the year. The hottest temperature recorded within Africa, which was also the world record, was 57.8 °C (136.0 °F) at 'Aziziya, Libya on September 13, 1922. This was later proven to be false, and to derive from an inaccurate reading of a thermometer. The world's hottest place is in fact Death Valley, in California.[562,563] Apparent temperatures, combining the effect of the temperature and humidity, along the Red Sea coast of Eritrea and Gulf of Aden coast of Somalia range between 57 °C (135 °F) and 63 °C (145 °F) during the afternoon hours. The lowest temperature measured within Africa was −24 °C (−11 °F) at Ifrane, Morocco on February 11, 1935. Nevertheless, the major part of Africa experiences extreme heat during much of the year, especially the deserts, steppes and savannas. The African deserts are arguably the hottest places on Earth, especially the Sahara Desert and the Danakil Desert, located in the Horn of Africa.

Wind

The low-level easterly African jet stream is considered to play a crucial role in the southwest monsoon of Africa,[564] and helps form the tropical waves which march across the tropical Atlantic and eastern Pacific oceans during the warm season.[565] The jet exhibits both barotropic and baroclinic instability, which produces synoptic-scale, westward-propagating disturbances in the jet known as African easterly waves, or tropical waves. A small number of mesoscale storm systems embedded in these waves develop into tropical cyclones after they move from west Africa into the tropical Atlantic, mainly during August and September. When the jet lies south of normal during the peak months of the Atlantic hurricane season, tropical cyclone formation is suppressed.

Precipitation

Great parts of North Africa and Southern Africa as well as the whole Horn of Africa mainly have a hot desert climate, or a hot semi-arid climate for the wetter locations. The Sahara Desert in North Africa is the largest hot desert in the world and is one of the hottest, driest and sunniest places on Earth. Located just south of the Sahara is a narrow steppe (a semi-arid region) called the Sahel, while Africa's most southern areas contain both savanna plains, and its central portion contains very dense jungle (rainforest) regions. The equatorial region near the Intertropical Convergence Zone is the wettest portion of the continent. Annually, the rain belt across the country moves northward into Sub-Saharan

Climate of Africa

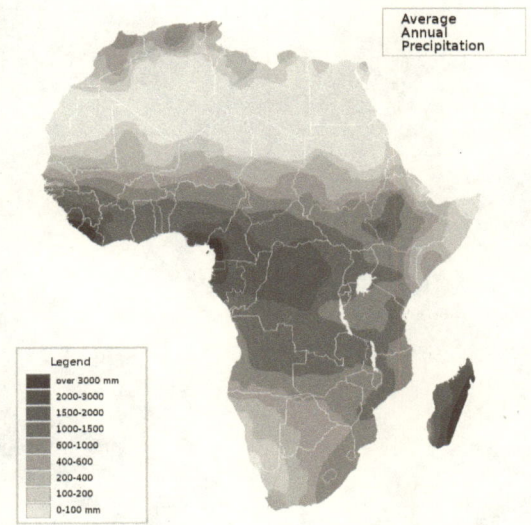

Figure 136: *Mean precipitation map*

Africa by August, then passes back southward into south-central Africa by March. Areas with a savannah climate in Sub-Saharan Africa, such as Ghana, Burkina Faso,[566,567] Darfur,[568] Eritrea,[569] Ethiopia,[570] and Botswana have a distinct rainy season.[571] El Nino results in drier-than-normal conditions in Southern Africa from December to February, and wetter-than-normal conditions in equatorial East Africa over the same period.[572]

In Madagascar, trade winds bring moisture up the eastern slopes of the island, which is deposited as rainfall, and bring drier downsloped winds to areas south and west, leaving the western sections of the island in a rain shadow. This leads to significantly more rainfall over northeast sections of Madagascar than its southwestern portions. Southern Africa receives most of its rainfall from summer convective storms and with extratropical cyclones moving through the Westerlies. Once a decade, tropical cyclones lead to excessive rainfall across the region.

Snow and glaciers

Snow is an almost annual occurrence on some of the mountains of South Africa, including those of the Cedarberg and around Ceres in the South-Western Cape, and on the Drakensberg in Natal and Lesotho. Tiffendell Resort in the Drakensberg is the only commercial skiing that takes place in South

Figure 137: *Snow in the Atlas Mountains in Morocco*

Africa, and has "advanced snow-making capability" allowing skiing for three months of the year. The Mountain Club of South Africa (MCSA) and the Mountain and Ski Club (MSC) of the University of Cape Town both have equipped ski huts in the Hex River mountains. Skiing including snowboarding in the Cape is a hit-and-miss affair, both in terms of timing of snowfalls, and whether there is sufficient snow to cover the rocks.

Table Mountain gets a light dusting of snow on the Front Table and also at Devil's Peak every few years. Snowfalls on Table Mountain took place on 20 September 2013; 30 Aug 2013; 5 August 2011; and on 15 June 2010.

Snow is a rare occurrence in Johannesburg; it fell in May 1956, August 1962, June 1964, September 1981, August 2006, and on 27 June 2007, accumulating up to 10 centimetres (3.9 in) in the southern suburbs.

Additionally, snow regularly falls in the Atlas Mountains in the Maghreb. Snowfall is also a regular occurrence at Mount Kilimanjaro in Tanzania.

There have been permanent glaciers on the Rwenzori Mountains, on the border of Uganda and the Democratic Republic of the Congo. However, by the 2010s, the glaciers were in retreat, and they are under threat of disappearing through rising temperatures.[573]

Fauna of Africa

The **fauna of Africa**, in its broader sense, is all the animals living in Africa and its surrounding seas and islands. The more characteristic African fauna is found in the Afrotropical ecoregion.[574] Lying almost entirely within the tropics, and equally to north and south of the equator creates favourable conditions for rich wildlife.

Origins of African fauna

Whereas the earliest traces of life in fossil record of Africa date back to the earliest times,[575] the formation of African fauna as we know it today, began with the splitting up of the Gondwana supercontinent in the mid-Mesozoic era.

After that, four to six faunal assemblages, the so-called African Faunal Strata (AFSs) can be distinguished. The isolation of Africa was broken intermittently by discontinuous "filter routes" that linked it to some other Gondwanan continents (Madagascar, South America, and perhaps India), but mainly to Laurasia. Interchanges with Gondwana were rare and mainly "out-of-Africa" dispersals, whereas interchanges with Laurasia were numerous and bidirectional, although mainly from Laurasia to Africa. Despite these connections, isolation resulted in remarkable absences, poor diversity, and emergence of endemic taxa in Africa.[576] Madagascar separated from continental Africa during the break-up of Gondwanaland early in the Cretaceous, but was probably connected to the mainland again in the Eocene.[577]

The first Neogene faunal interchange took place in the Middle Miocene (the introduction of Myocricetodontinae, Democricetodontinae, and Dendromurinae).[578] A major terrestrial faunal exchange between North Africa and Europe began at about 6.1 Ma, some 0.4 Myr before the beginning of the Messinian salinity crisis[579](for example introduction of Murinae, immigrants from southern Asia)[580]

During the early Tertiary, Africa was covered by a vast evergreen forest inhabited by an endemic forest fauna with many types common to southern Asia. In the Pliocene the climate became dry and most of the forest was destroyed, the forest animals taking refuge in the remaining forest islands. At the same time a broad land-bridge connected Africa with Asia and there was a great invasion of animals of the steppe fauna into Africa. At the beginning of the Pleistocene a moist period set in and much of the forest was renewed while the grassland fauna was divided and isolated, as the forest fauna had previously been. The present forest fauna is therefore of double origin, partly descended of the endemic fauna and partly from steppe forms that adapted themselves to forest life, while the present savanna fauna is similarly explained. The isolation in

Figure 138: *Spotted hyenas at the carcass of an impala that they had stolen from a cheetah at Masai Mara National Park, Kenya*

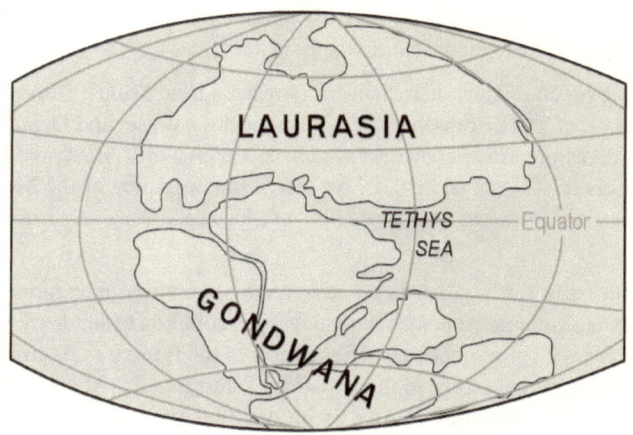

Figure 139: *The continents Laurasia-Gondwana 200 million years ago*

Figure 140: *Giant East African Snail*

past times has resulted in the presence of closely related subspecies in widely separated regions[581,582] Africa, where humans originated, shows much less evidence of loss in the Pleistocene megafaunal extinction, perhaps because co-evolution of large animals alongside early humans provided enough time for them to develop effective defenses.[583] Its situation in the tropics spared it also from Pleistocene glaciations and the climate has not changed much.[584]

Invertebrates

There are large gaps in human knowledge about African invertebrates. East Africa has a rich coral fauna[585] with about 400 known species. More than 400 species of Echinoderms and 500 species of Bryozoa live there too,[586] as well as one Cubozoan species (*Carybdea alata*). Of Nematodes, the *Onchocerca volvulus*, *Necator americanus*, *Wuchereria bancrofti* and *Dracunculus medinensis* are human parasites. Some of important plant-parasitic nematodes of crops include *Meloidogyne*, *Pratylenchus*, *Hirschmanniella*, *Radopholus*, *Scutellonema* and *Helicotylenchus*.[587,588,589,590] Of the few Onychophorans, *Peripatopsis* and *Opisthopatus* live in Africa.[591] Greatest diversity of freshwater mollusks is found in East African lakes. Of marine snails, less diversity is present in Atlantic coast, more in tropical Western Indian Ocean region (over 3000 species of gastropods with 81 endemic species).[592,593] Cowry shells have been used as a money by native Africans. The land snail fauna is especially rich in Afromontane regions, and there are some endemic families in Africa (e.g. Achatinidae, Chlamydephoridae) but other tropical families are common

Figure 141: *A termite mound in Botswana*

too (Charopidae, Streptaxidae, Cyclophoridae, Subulinidae, Rhytididae). 156 tardigrade species have been found,[594,595] and about 8000 species of arachnids. The African millipede *Archispirostreptus gigas* is one of the largest in the world. 20 genera of freshwater crabs are present.[596]

The soil animal communities tropical Africa are poorly known. A few ecological studies have been undertaken on macrofauna, mainly in West Africa.[597] Earthworms are being extensively studied in West and South Africa.[598,599]

Insects

Approximately 100,000 species of insects have been described from sub-Saharan Africa, but there are very few overviews of the fauna as a whole[600] (it has been estimated that the African insects make up about 10-20% of the global insect species richness,[601] and about 15% of new species descriptions come from Afrotropics[602]). The only endemic African insect order is Mantophasmatodea.

About 875 African species of dragonflies have been recorded.

The migratory locust and desert locust have been serious threats to African economies and human welfare.

Figure 142: *A citrus swallowtail from Tanzania*

Africa has the biggest number of termite genera of all continents,[603] and over 1,000 termite species.

Of Diptera, the number of described African species is about 17,000.[604] Natalimyzidae, a new family of acalyptrate flies has been recently described from South Africa.[605] *Anopheles gambiae*, *Aedes aegypti* and Tsetse fly are important vectors of diseases. 1600 species of bees[606] and 2000 species of ants[607] among other Hymenopterans are known from Africa.

There live also 3,607 species of butterflies, being the best known group of insects.[608] The caterpillars of mopani moth are part of the South African cuisine. Among the numerous species of African beetles are the famous sacred scarab, the centaurus beetle, the manticora tiger beetle and enormous Goliath beetles.

Butterflies

Hotspots for butterflies include the Congolian forests and the Guinean forest-savanna mosaic. Some butterflies (*Hamanumida daedalus*, *Precis*, *Eurema*) are grassland or savannah specialists. Many of these have very large populations and a vast range. South Africa has one of the highest proportions of

Figure 143: *Latimeria, a living member of a long-thought-extinct group of fish*

Lycaenid butterflies (48%) for any region in the world with many species restricted in range. North Africa is in the Palaearctic region and has a different species assemblage.

Genera which are species rich in Africa include *Charaxes*, *Acraea*, *Colotis* and *Papilio*, most notably *Papilio antimachus* and *Papilio zalmoxis*. The subfamily Lipteninae is endemic to the Afrotropics and includes species rich genera such as *Ornipholidotos*, *Liptenara*, *Pentila*, *Baliochila*, *Hypophytala*, *Teriomima*, *Deloneura* and *Mimacraea*. The Miletinae are mostly African, notably *Lachnocnema*. Endemic Nymphalidae include *Euphaedra*, *Bebearia*, *Heteropsis*, *Precis*, *Pseudacraea*, *Bicyclus* and *Euxanthe*. Endemic Pieridae include *Pseudopontia paradoxa* and *Mylothris*. Endemic skippers include *Sarangesa*and *Kedestes*. The highest species diversity is in the Democratic Republic of the Congo, home to 2,040 species 181 of which are endemic.

Fish

Africa is the richest continent of freshwater fish, with about 3000 species.[609,610] The East African Great Lakes (Victoria, Malawi, and Tanganyika) are the center of biodiversity of many fish, especially cichlids (they harbor more than two-thirds of the estimated 2000 species in the family).[611] The West African coastal rivers region covers only a fraction of West Africa, but harbours 322 of West African's fish species, with 247 restricted to this area and 129 restricted even to smaller ranges. The central rivers fauna comprises 194 fish species, with 119 endemics and only 33 restricted to small areas.[612] The marine diversity is greatest near the Indian Ocean shore with about 2000 species.[613]

Characteristic to African fauna are Perciformes (*Lates*, tilapias, Dichistiidae, Anabantidae, Mudskippers, *Parachanna, Acentrogobius, Croilia, Glossogobius, Hemichromis, Nanochromis, Oligolepis, Oreochromis, Redigobius, Sarotherodon, Stenogobius* and others), Gonorhynchiformes (Kneriidae, Phractolaemidae), some lungfishes (*Protopterus*), many Characiformes (Distichodontidae, Hepsetidae, Citharinidae, Alestiidae), Osteoglossiformes (African knifefish, Gymnarchidae, Mormyridae, Pantodontidae), Siluriformes (Amphiliidae, Anchariidae, Ariidae, Austroglanididae, Clariidae, Claroteidae, Malapteruridae, Mochokidae, Schilbeidae), Osmeriformes (Galaxiidae), Cyprinodontiformes (Aplocheilidae, Poeciliidae) and Cypriniformes (*Labeobarbus, Pseudobarbus, Tanakia* and others).

Amphibians

Endemic to Africa are the families Arthroleptidae, Astylosternidae, Heleophrynidae, Hemisotidae, Hyperoliidae, Petropedetidae, Mantellidae. Also widespread are Bufonidae (*Bufo, Churamiti, Capensibufo, Mertensophryne, Nectophryne, Nectophrynoides, Schismaderma, Stephopaedes, Werneria, Wolterstorffina*), Microhylidae (*Breviceps, Callulina, Probreviceps,* Cophylinae, *Dyscophus,* Melanobatrachinae, Scaphiophryninae), Rhacophoridae (*Chiromantis*), Ranidae (*Afrana, Amietia, Amnirana, Aubria, Conraua, Hildebrandtia, Lanzarana, Ptychadena, Strongylopus, Tomopterna*) and Pipidae (*Hymenochirus, Pseudhymenochirus, Xenopus*). The 2002–2004 'Global Amphibian Assessment' by IUCN, Conservation International and NatureServe revealed that for only about 50% of the Afrotropical amphibians, there is least concern about their conservation status; approximately 130 species are endangered, about one-fourth of which are at a critical stage. Almost all of the amphibians of Madagascar (238 species[614]) are endemic to that region. The West African goliath frog is the largest frog species in the world.

Reptiles

The center of chameleon diversity is Madagascar. Snakes found in Africa include atractaspidids, elapids (cobras, *Aspidelaps, Boulengerina, Dendroaspis, Elapsoidea, Hemachatus, Homoroselaps* and *Paranaja*), causines, viperines (*Adenorhinos, Atheris, Bitis, Cerastes, Echis, Macrovipera, Montatheris, Proatheris, Vipera*), colubrids (*Dendrolycus, Dispholidus, Gonionotophis, Grayia, Hormonotus, Lamprophis, Psammophis, Leioheterodon, Madagascarophis, Poecilopholis, Dasypeltis* etc.), the pythonids (*Python*), typhlopids (*Typhlops*) and leptotyphlopids (*Leptotyphlops, Rhinoleptus*).

Of the lizards, many species of geckos (day geckos, *Afroedura, Afrogecko, Colopus, Pachydactylus, Hemidactylus, Narudasia, Paroedura, Pristurus,*

Figure 144: *Western green mamba, a venomous snake*

Quedenfeldtia, Rhoptropus, Tropiocolotes, Uroplatus), Cordylidae, as well as Lacertidae (*Nucras, Lacerta, Mesalina, Acanthodactylus, Pedioplanis*), Agamas, skinks, plated lizards and some monitor lizards are common. There are 12 genera and 58 species of African amphisbaenians (e.g. *Chirindia, Zygaspis, Monopeltis, Dalophia*).[615]

Several genera of tortoises (*Kinixys, Pelusios, Psammobates, Geochelone, Homopus, Chersina*), turtles (Pelomedusidae, *Cyclanorbis, Cycloderma, Erymnochelys*), and three species of crocodiles (the Nile crocodile, slender-snouted crocodile and dwarf crocodile) are also present.

Birds

There live (temporarily or permanently) more than 2600 bird species in Africa (about 1500 of them passerines). Some 114 of them are threatened species.[616] The Afrotropic has various endemic bird families, including ostriches (Struthionidae), mesites, sunbirds, secretary bird (Sagittariidae), guineafowl (Numididae), and mousebirds (Coliidae). Also, several families of passerines are limited to the Afrotropics. These include rock-jumpers (Chaetopidae), bushshrikes (Malaconotidae), wattle-eyes, (Platysteiridae) and rockfowl (Picathartidae). Other common birds include parrots (lovebirds, *Poicephalus, Psittacus*), various cranes (crowned canes, blue crane, wattled

Figure 145: *The grey parrot is native to West-African rainforests.*

crane), storks (slaty egret, black heron, marabous, Abdim's stork, shoebill), bustards (kori bustard, *Neotis*, *Eupodotis*, *Lissotis*), sandgrouse (*Pterocles*), Coraciiformes (bee-eaters, hornbills, *Ceratogymna*), phasianids (francolins, Congo peafowl, blue quail, harlequin quail, stone partridge, Madagascar partridge). The woodpeckers and allies include honeyguides, African barbets, African piculet, ground woodpecker, *Dendropicos* and *Campethera*. The birds of prey include the buzzards, harriers, Old World vultures, bateleur, *Circaetus*, *Melierax* and others. Trogons are represented by one genus (*Apaloderma*). African penguin is the only penguin species. Madagascar was once home to the now extinct elephant birds.

Africa is home to numerous songbirds (pipits, orioles, antpeckers, brubrus, cisticolas, negrofinches, olivebacks, pytilias, green-backed twinspot, crimson-wings, seedcrackers, bluebills, firefinches, waxbills, amandavas, quailfinches, munias, weavers, tit-hylia, *Amadina*, *Anthoscopus*, *Mirafra*, *Hypargos*, *Eremomela*, *Euschistospiza*, *Erythrocercus*, *Malimbus*, *Pitta*, *Uraeginthus*, pied crow, white-necked raven, thick-billed raven, Cape crow and others). The red-billed quelea is the most abundant bird species in the world.

Of the 589 species of birds (excluding seabirds) that breed in the Palaearctic (temperate Europe and Asia), 40% spend the winter elsewhere. Of those species that leave for the winter, 98% travel south to Africa.[617] See also: Endemic birds of western and central Africa, Endemic birds of southern Africa.

Figure 146: *A herd of African elephants*

Mammals

More than 1100 mammal species live in Africa.[618] Africa has three endemic orders of mammals, the Tubulidentata (aardvarks), Afrosoricida (tenrecs and golden moles), and Macroscelidea (elephant shrews). The current research of mammalian phylogeny has proposed an Afrotheria clade (including the exclusively African orders).[619] The East-African plains are well known for their diversity of large mammals.

African Soricomorpha include the Myosoricinae and Crocidurinae subfamilies. Hedgehogs include desert hedgehogs, *Atelerix* and others. The rodents are represented by African bush squirrels, African ground squirrels, African striped squirrels, gerbils, cane rats, acacia rats, Nesomyidae, springhare, mole rats, dassie rats, striped grass mice, sun squirrels, thicket rats, Old World porcupines, target rats, maned rats, Deomyinae, *Aethomys*, *Arvicanthis*, *Colomys*, *Dasymys*, *Dephomys*, *Epixerus*, *Grammomys*, *Graphiurus*, *Hybomys*, *Hylomyscus*, *Malacomys*, *Mastomys*, *Mus*, *Mylomys*, *Myomyscus*, *Oenomys*, *Otomys*, *Parotomys*, *Pelomys*, *Praomys*, *Rhabdomys*, *Stenocephalemys* and many others. African rabbits and hares include riverine rabbit, Bunyoro rabbit, Cape hare, scrub hare, Ethiopian highland hare, African savanna hare, Abyssinian hare and several species of *Pronolagus*. Among the marine mammals there are several species of dolphins, 2 species of sirenians and seals (e.g. Cape fur seals). Of the carnivorans there are 60 species, including the conspicuous hyenas, lions, leopards, cheetahs, serval, as well as the less prominent bat-eared fox, striped polecat, African striped weasel, caracal, honey badger, speckle-throated otter, several mongooses, jackals and civets. The family Eupleridae is restricted to Madagascar.

The African list of ungulates is longer than in any other continent. The largest number of modern bovids is found in Africa (African buffalo, duikers, impala, rhebok, Reduncinae, oryx, dik-dik, klipspringer, oribi, gerenuk, true gazelles, hartebeest, wildebeest, dibatag, eland, *Tragelaphus*, *Hippotragus*, *Neotragus*, *Raphicerus*, *Damaliscus*). Other even-toed ungulates include giraffes, hippopotamuses, warthogs, giant forest hogs, red river hogs and bushpigs. Odd-toed ungulates are represented by three species of zebras, African wild ass, black and white rhinoceros. The biggest African mammal is the African bush elephant, the second largest being its smaller counterpart, the African forest elephant. Four species of pangolins can be found in Africa.[620]

African fauna contains 64 species of primates.[621] Four species of great apes (Hominidae) are endemic to Africa: both species of gorilla (western gorilla, *Gorilla gorilla*, and eastern gorilla, *Gorilla beringei*) and both species of chimpanzee (common chimpanzee, *Pan troglodytes*, and bonobo, *Pan paniscus*). Humans and their ancestors originated in Africa. Other primates include colobuses, baboons, geladas, vervet monkeys, guenons, macaques, mandrills, crested mangabeys, white-eyelid mangabeys, kipunji, Allen's swamp monkeys, Patas monkeys and talapoins. Lemurs and aye-aye are characteristic of Madagascar. See also Lists of mammals of Africa.

External links

- *African Invertebrates*[622]
- *FAUNA(French)FRI - A tool to assess and monitor the distribution of fresh and brackish waters fish species in Africa*[623]
- *PPEAO - An information system on fish communities and artisanal fisheries in estuarine and lagoon ecosystems in West Africa (in French)*[624]

Politics

List of political parties in Africa by country

Part of the Politics series
Party politics
Political spectrum
Left-wing
• Far-left • Centre-left
Centre
• Centre-left • Radical centre • Centre-right
Right-wing
• Centre-right • Far-right
Party platform
• Extremist • Radical
• Progressive • Reformist • Liberal
• Moderate • Syncretic • Third Position
• Conservative • Reactionary • Traditionalist
Party system

- Non-partisan
- One-party
- Dominant-party
- Two-party
- Multi-party

Coalition

- Hung parliament
- Confidence and supply
- Minority government
- Rainbow coalition
- Grand coalition
- Full coalition
- National unity government
- Majority government

Lists

- Ruling parties by country
- Political parties by UN geoscheme
- Political ideologies

Politics portal

- v
- t
- e[625]

This is a **List of political parties in Africa by country**, linking to the country list of parties and the political system of each country in the region.

Northern Africa

	Country	Multi party	Two party	Dominant party	Single party	No party
	Algeria	•				
	Egypt	•				
	Libya	•				
	Morocco	•				
	Sudan			•		
	Tunisia	•				
	Western Sahara				•	

Central Africa

	Country	Multi party	Two party	Dominant party	Single party	No party
	Angola			•		
	Cameroon			•		
	Central African Republic	•				
	Chad			•		
	Congo (Kinshasa)	•				
	Congo (Brazzaville)	•				
	Equatorial Guinea			•		
	Gabon			•		
	São Tomé and Príncipe	•				

Southern Africa

	Country	Multi party	Two party	Dominant party	Single party	No party
	Botswana			•		
	Lesotho	•				
	Namibia			•		
	South Africa			•		
	Swaziland					•
	Zimbabwe			•		

Western Africa

	Country	Multi party	Two party	Dominant party	Single party	No party
	Benin	•				
	Burkina Faso	•				
	Cape Verde		•			
	Ivory Coast			•		
	Gambia			•		
	Ghana	•				
	Guinea			•		
	Guinea-Bissau	•				
	Liberia	•				
	Mali	•				
	Mauritania	•[626]				
	Niger	•				
	Nigeria	•				
	Senegal	•				
	Sierra Leone	•				
	Togo			•		

Eastern Africa

	Country	Multi party	Two party	Dominant party	Single party	No party
	Burundi	•				
	Comoros	•[627]				
	Djibouti			•		
	Eritrea				•	
	Ethiopia			•		
	Kenya	•				
	Madagascar	•				
	Malawi	•				
	Mauritius	•				
	Mozambique	•				
	Rwanda	•				

	Somalia	•				
	Seychelles		•			
	South Sudan			•		
	Tanzania	•				
	Uganda			•		
	Zambia	•				
	Zimbabwe			•		

African Union

African Union
Flag
Emblem
Motto: "A United and Strong Africa"
Anthem: "Let Us All Unite and Celebrate Together"
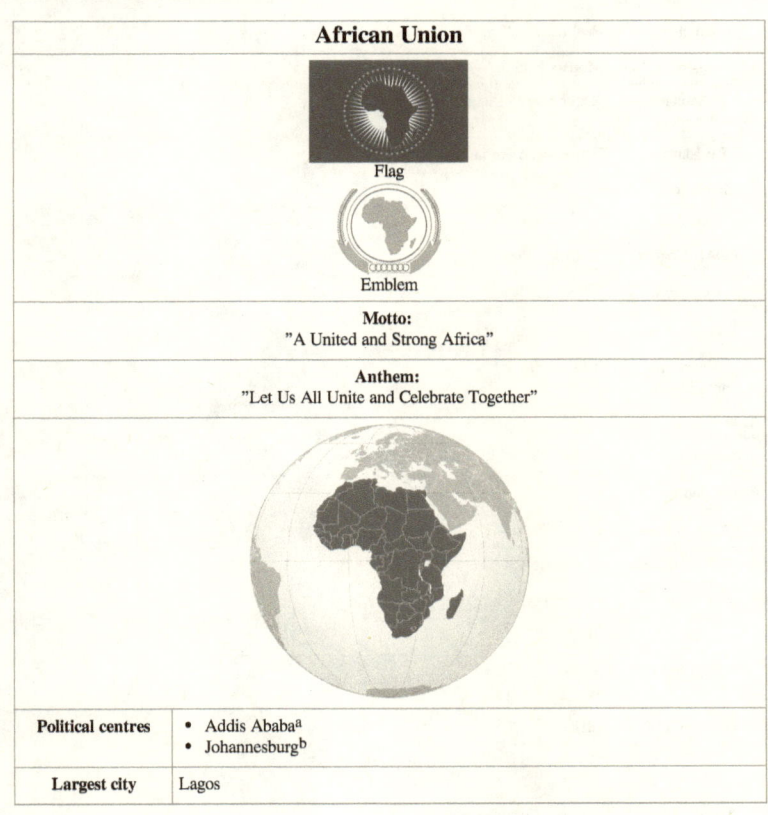

Political centres	• Addis Ababa[a] • Johannesburg[b]
Largest city	Lagos

Official languages	• Amharic • Arabic • French • English • Portuguese • Spanish • Swahili • African languagesWikipedia:Please clarify
Demonym	African
Type	Continental union
Membership	55 member states
Leaders	
• Assembly Chair	Paul Kagame[628]
• Commission Chair	Moussa Faki
• Parliamentary President	Roger Nkodo Dang
Legislature	Pan-African Parliament
Establishment	
• OAU Charter	25 May 1963
• Abuja Treaty	3 June 1991
• Sirte Declaration	9 September 1999
• African Union founded	9 July 2002
Area	
• Total	29,922,059[629] km^2 (11,552,972 sq mi)
Population	
• 2016 estimate	1,225,080,510
GDP (nominal)	2017 estimate
• Total	$2.2 trillion[630]
• Per capita	$1,800
HDI (2014)	0.524 low
Internet TLD	.africa c
Website au<wbr/>.int[631]	

- a Seat of the African Union Commission.
- b Seat of the Pan-African Parliament.
- c Proposed.

Life in the African Union
• Economy
• Enlargement
• Foreign relations
• Geography
• History
• Languages
• v • t • e[632]

The **African Union** (**AU**) is a continental union consisting of all 55 countries on the continent of Africa, extending slightly into geographical Asia via the Sinai Peninsula in Egypt, except for territories of European countries located in Africa. It was established on 26 May 2001 in Addis Ababa, Ethiopia and launched on 9 July 2002 in South Africa with the aim of replacing the Organisation of African Unity (OAU), established on 25 May 1963 in Addis Ababa with 32 signatory governments. The most important decisions of the AU are made by the Assembly of the African Union, a semi-annual meeting of the heads of state and government of its member states. The AU's secretariat, the African Union Commission, is based in Addis Ababa.

In result of its geographical location, the African Union has an area of around 29 million km^2 (11 million sq mi) and includes popular world landmarks, including the Sahara and the Nile. They have adopted a gold, green and red based emblem and flag to represent the continental union, where they held a competition for citizens to design a flag in which they chose a submission to replace the old flag. Their main celebration occurs on Africa Day on 25 May. The primary languages spoken include Arabic, English, French and Portuguese and the languages of Africa. Within the African Union, there are official bodies such as the Peace and Security Council and the Pan-African Parliament. Each individual state organises their own international relations and will work with each other to develop their foreign policy. However, it was not until recently did the AU form continent-wide passports.

Overview

The objectives of the AU are the following:

1. To achieve greater unity and solidarity between the African countries and Africans.
2. To defend the sovereignty, territorial integrity and independence of its Member States.

3. To accelerate the political and social-economic integration of the continent.
4. To promote and defend African common positions on issues of interest to the continent and its peoples.
5. To encourage international cooperation, taking due account of the Charter of the United Nations and the Universal Declaration of Human Rights.
6. To promote peace, security, and stability on the continent.
7. To promote democratic principles and institutions, popular participation and good governance.
8. To promote and protect human and peoples' rights in accordance with the African Charter on Human and Peoples' Rights and other relevant human rights instruments.
9. To establish the necessary conditions which enable the continent to play its rightful role in the global economy and in international negotiations.
10. To promote sustainable development at the economic, social and cultural levels as well as the integration of African economies.
11. To promote co-operation in all fields of human activity to raise the living standards of African peoples.
12. To coordinate and harmonize the policies between the existing and future Regional Economic Communities for the gradual attainment of the objectives of the Union.
13. To advance the development of the continent by promoting research in all fields, in particular in science and technology.
14. To work with relevant international partners in the eradication of preventable diseases and the promotion of good health on the continent.

The African Union is made up of both political and administrative bodies. The highest decision-making organ is the Assembly of the African Union, made up of all the heads of state or government of member states of the AU. The Assembly is chaired by Paul Kagame, President of Rwanda. The AU also has a representative body, the Pan African Parliament, which consists of 265 members elected by the national legislatures of the AU member states. Its president is Roger Nkodo Dang.

Other political institutions of the AU include:

- the Executive Council, made up of foreign ministers, which prepares decisions for the Assembly;
- the Permanent Representatives Committee, made up of the ambassadors to Addis Ababa of AU member states; and
- the Economic, Social, and Cultural Council (ECOSOCC), a civil society consultative body.

The AU Commission, the secretariat to the political structures, is chaired by Nkosazana Dlamini-Zuma of South Africa. On 15 July 2012, Ms. Dlamini-Zuma won a tightly contested vote to become the first female head of the African Union Commission, replacing Jean Ping of Gabon.

Other AU structures are hosted by different member states:

- the African Commission on Human and Peoples' Rights is based in Banjul, the Gambia; and
- the New Partnership for Africa's Development (NEPAD) and APRM Secretariats and the Pan-African Parliament are in Midrand, South Africa.

The AU covers the entire continent except for several territories held by Spain (Canary Islands, Plazas de soberanía), France (Mayotte, Réunion, Scattered Islands in the Indian Ocean), Portugal (Madeira, Savage Islands) and the United Kingdom (Saint Helena, Ascension and Tristan da Cunha).

The AU's first military intervention in a member state was the May 2003 deployment of a peacekeeping force of soldiers from South Africa, Ethiopia, and Mozambique to Burundi to oversee the implementation of the various agreements. AU troops were also deployed in Sudan for peacekeeping during Darfur conflict, before the mission was handed over to the United Nations on 1 January 2008 UNAMID. The AU has also sent a peacekeeping mission to Somalia, of which the peacekeeping troops are from Uganda and Burundi.

The AU has adopted a number of important new documents establishing norms at continental level, to supplement those already in force when it was created. These include the African Union Convention on Preventing and Combating Corruption (2003), the African Charter on Democracy, Elections and Governance (2007), the New Partnership for Africa's Development (NEPAD) and its associated Declaration on Democracy, Political, Economic and Corporate Governance.[633]

History

The historical foundations of the African Union originated in the Union of African States, an early confederation that was established by Kwame Nkrumah in the 1960s, as well as subsequent attempts to unite Africa, including the Organisation of African Unity (OAU), which was established on 25 May 1963, and the African Economic Community in 1981. Critics argued that the OAU in particular did little to protect the rights and liberties of African citizens from their own political leaders, often dubbing it the "Dictators' Club".[634]

The idea of creating the AU was revived in the mid-1990s under the leadership of Libyan head of state Muammar al-Gaddafi: the heads of state and government of the OAU issued the Sirte Declaration (named after Sirte, in Libya) on 9 September 1999, calling for the establishment of an African Union. The Declaration was followed by summits at Lomé in 2000, when the Constitutive Act of the African Union was adopted, and at Lusaka in 2001, when the plan for the implementation of the African Union was adopted. During the same period, the initiative for the establishment of the New Partnership for Africa's Development (NEPAD), was also established.

The African Union was launched in Durban on 9 July 2002, by its first chairperson, South African Thabo Mbeki, at the first session of the Assembly of the African Union. The second session of the Assembly was in Maputo in 2003, and the third session in Addis Ababa on 6 July 2004.

Since 2010, the African Union eyes the establishment of a joint African space agency.

Barack Obama was the first ever sitting United States president to speak in front of the African Union in Addis Ababa, on 29 July 2015. With his speech, he encouraged the world to increase economic ties via investments and trade with the continent, and lauded the progresses made in education, infrastructure and economy. But he also criticized lacks of democracy and leaders who refuse to step down, discrimination against minorities (LGBT people, religious groups and ethnicities) and corruption. He suggested an intensified democratization and free trade, to significantly increase living quality for Africans.

Treaties

Signed	1961	1963	1991	1999
In force	1962	1965	N/A	2002
Document		OAU Charter	Abuja Treaty	Sirte Declaration

Organisation of African Unity (OAU)	African Economic Community: (AEC)
	Community of Sahel-Saharan States (CEN-SAD)
	Common Market for Eastern and Southern Africa (COMESA)
	East African Community (EAC)
	Economic Community of Central African States (ECCAS)
	Economic Community of West African States (ECOWAS)

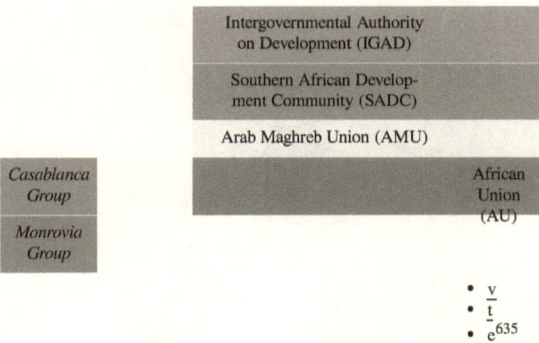

- v
- t
- e⁶³⁵

Geography

Member states of the African Union cover almost the entirety of continental Africa, excluding only Spanish North Africa (disambiguation), and several offshore islands. Consequently, the geography of the African Union is wildly diverse, including the world's largest hot desert (the Sahara), huge jungles and savannas, and the world's longest river (the Nile).

The AU presently has an area of 29,922,059 square kilometres (11,552,972 sq mi), with 24,165 kilometres (15,015 mi) of coastline. The vast majority of this area is on continental Africa, while the only significant territory off the mainland is the island of Madagascar (the world's fourth largest island), accounting for slightly less than 2% of the total.

Demographics

Languages

According to the Constitutive Act of the African Union, its working languages are Arabic, English, French and Portuguese, and African languages "if possible".[636] A protocol amending the Constitutive Act, adopted in 2003 but as of June 2016 not yet ratified by a two-thirds majority of member states, would add Spanish, Swahili and "any other African language" and declare all "official" (rather than "working") languages of the African Union. The Executive Council shall determine the process and practical modalities for the use of official languages as working languages.

Founded in 2001 under the auspices of the AU, the African Academy of Languages promotes the usage and perpetuation of African languages among African people. The AU declared 2006 the Year of African Languages. 2006 also marked Ghana's 55th anniversary since it founded the Bureau of Ghana Languages originally known as Gold Coast Vernacular Literature Bureau.

Politics

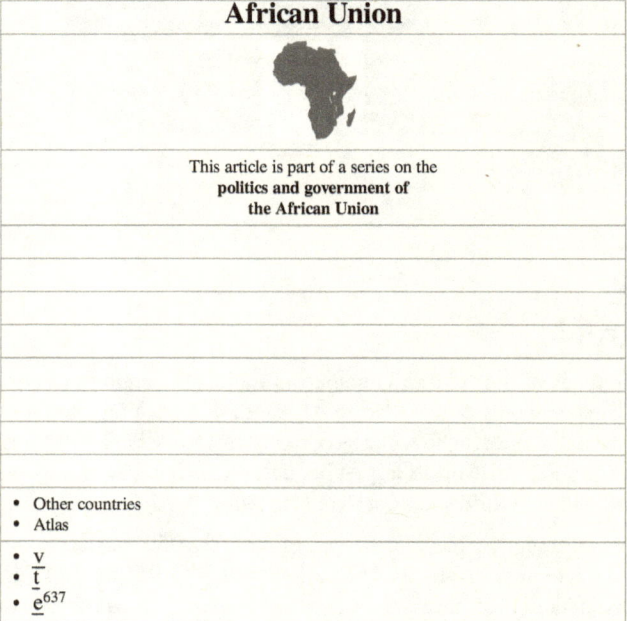

African Union

This article is part of a series on the
**politics and government of
the African Union**

- Other countries
- Atlas
- v
- t
- e[637]

The African Union has a number of official bodies:

Pan-African Parliament (PAP)
To become the highest legislative body of the African Union. The seat of the PAP is at Midrand, South Africa. The Parliament is composed of 265 elected representatives from all 55 AU states, and intended to provide popular and civil-society participation in the processes of democratic governance. Its president is Roger Nkodo Dang, of Cameroon.

Assembly of the African Union
Composed of heads of state and heads of government of AU states, the Assembly is currently the supreme governing body of the African Union. It is gradually devolving some of its decision-making powers to the Pan African Parliament. It meets once a year and makes its decisions by consensus or by a two-thirds majority. The current chair of the AU is Rwandan President Paul Kagame.

African Union Commission (or Authority)
The secretariat of the African Union, composed of ten commissioners and supporting staff and headquartered in Addis Ababa, Ethiopia. In a similar fashion to its European counterpart, the European Commission, it is responsible for the administration and co-ordination of the AU's activities and meetings.

Court of Justice of the African Union
The Constitutive Act provides for a Court of Justice to rule on disputes over interpretation of AU treaties. A protocol to set up this Court of Justice was adopted in 2003 and entered into force in 2009. It was, however, superseded by a protocol creating an African Court of Justice and Human Rights, which will incorporate the already established African Court on Human and Peoples' Rights (see below) and have two chambers: one for general legal matters and one for rulings on the human rights treaties.

Executive Council
Composed of ministers designated by the governments of member states. It decides on matters such as foreign trade, social security, food, agriculture and communications, is accountable to the Assembly, and prepares material for the Assembly to discuss and approve.It is chaired by Mr Shawn Makuyana of Zimbabwe (2015–).

Permanent Representatives' Committee
Consisting of nominated permanent representatives of member states, the Committee prepares the work for the Executive Council, similar the role of the Committee of Permanent Representatives in the European Union.

Peace and Security Council (PSC)
Proposed at the Lusaka Summit in 2001 and established in 2004 under a protocol to the Constitutive Act adopted by the AU Assembly in July 2002. The protocol defines the PSC as a collective security and early warning arrangement to facilitate timely and effective response to conflict and crisis situations in Africa. Other responsibilities conferred to the PSC by the protocol include prevention, management and resolution of conflicts, post-conflict peace building and developing common defence policies. The PSC has fifteen members elected on a regional basis by the Assembly. Similar in intent and operation to the United Nations Security Council.

Economic, Social and Cultural Council
An advisory organ composed of professional and civic representatives, similar to the European Economic and Social Committee. The chair of ECOSOCC, elected in 2008, is Cameroonian lawyer Akere Muna of the Pan-African Lawyers Union (PALU).

Specialised Technical Committees

Both the Abuja Treaty and the Constitutive Act provide for Specialised Technical Committees to be established made up of African ministers to advise the Assembly. In practice, they have never been set up. The ten proposed themes are: Rural Economy and Agricultural Matters; Monetary and Financial Affairs; Trade, Customs, and Immigration; Industry, Science and Technology; Energy, Natural Resources, and Environment; Transport, Communications, and Tourism; Health; Labour, and Social Affairs; Education, Culture, and Human Resources.

Financial institutions

- African Central Bank – Abuja, Nigeria
- African Investment Bank – Tripoli, Libya
- African Monetary Fund – Yaoundé, Cameroon

These institutions have not yet been established, however, the Steering Committees working on their founding have been constituted. Eventually, the AU aims to have a single currency (the Afro).

Human rights

The African Commission on Human and Peoples' Rights, in existence since 1986, is established under the African Charter on Human and Peoples' Rights (the African Charter) rather than the Constitutive Act of the African Union. It is the premier African human rights body, with responsibility for monitoring and promoting compliance with the African Charter. The African Court on Human and Peoples' Rights was established in 2006 to supplement the work of the Commission, following the entry into force of a protocol to the African Charter providing for its creation. It is planned that the African Court on Human and Peoples' Rights will be merged with the Court of Justice of the African Union (see above).

African Energy Commission

Membership

All UN member states based in Africa and on African waters are members of the AU, as is the disputed Sahrawi Arab Democratic Republic (SADR). Morocco, which claims sovereignty over the SADR's territory, withdrew from the Organisation of African Unity, the AU's predecessor, in 1984 due to the admission of the SADR as a member. However, on 30 January 2017, the AU admitted Morocco as a member state.

Members

- Algeria
- Angola
- Benin
- Botswana
- Burkina Faso
- Burundi
- Cape Verde
- Cameroon
- Central African Republic
- Chad
- Comoros
- Democratic Republic of the Congo
- Djibouti
- Egypt
- Equatorial Guinea
- Eritrea
- Ethiopia
- Gabon
- Gambia
- Ghana
- Guinea
- Guinea-Bissau
- Ivory Coast
- Kenya
- Lesotho
- Liberia
- Libya
- Madagascar
- Malawi
- Mali
- Mauritania
- Mauritius
- Morocco
- Mozambique
- Namibia
- Niger
- Nigeria
- Republic of the Congo
- Rwanda
- Sahrawi Arab Democratic Republic
- São Tomé and Príncipe
- Senegal
- Seychelles
- Sierra Leone
- Somalia
- South Africa
- South Sudan
- Sudan
- Swaziland
- Tanzania
- Togo
- Tunisia
- Uganda
- Zambia
- Zimbabwe

Governance

The principal topic for debate at the July 2007 AU summit held in Accra, Ghana, was the creation of a Union Government,[638] with the aim of moving towards a United States of Africa. A study on the Union Government was adopted in late 2006,[639] and proposes various options for "completing" the African Union project. There are divisions among African states on the proposals, with some (notably Libya) following a maximalist view leading to a common government with an AU army; and others (especially the southern African states) supporting rather a strengthening of the existing structures, with some reforms to deal with administrative and political challenges in making the AU Commission and other bodies truly effective.[640]

Following a heated debate in Accra, the Assembly of Heads of State and Government agreed in the form of a declaration to review the state of affairs of the AU with a view to determining its readiness towards a Union Government.[641] In particular, the Assembly agreed to:

- Accelerate the economic and political integration of the African continent, including the formation of a Union Government of Africa;

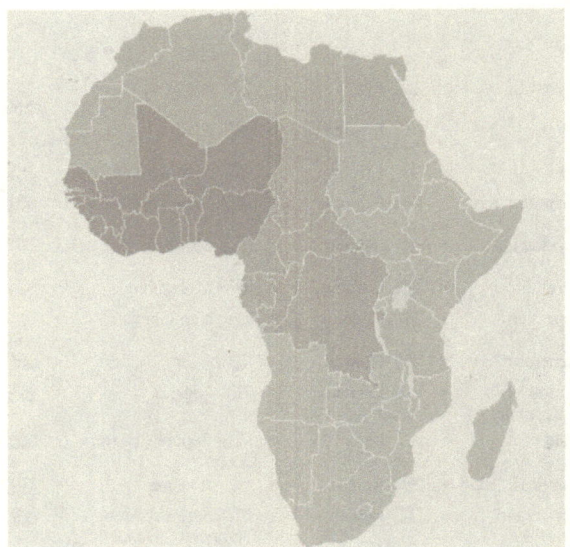

Figure 147: *Regions of the African Union*
***Northern Region** (Sahara)*   ***Southern Region** (Kalahari)*   ***Eastern Region** (Nile)*
***Western Regions A and B** (Niger and Volta Niger)*   ***Central Region** (Congo)*

- Conduct an audit of the institutions and organs of the AU; review the relationship between the AU and the RECs; find ways to strengthen the AU and elaborate a timeframe to establish a Union Government of Africa.

The declaration lastly noted the "importance of involving the African peoples, including Africans in the Diaspora, in the processes leading to the formation of the Union Government."

Following this decision, a panel of eminent persons was set up to conduct the "audit review". The review team began its work on 1 September 2007. The review was presented to the Assembly of Heads of State and Government at the January 2008 summit in Addis Ababa. No final decision was taken on the recommendations, however, and a committee of ten heads of state was appointed to consider the review and report back to the July 2008 summit to be held in Egypt. At the July 2008 summit, a decision was once again deferred, for a "final" debate at the January 2009 summit to be held in Addis Ababa.

African Union

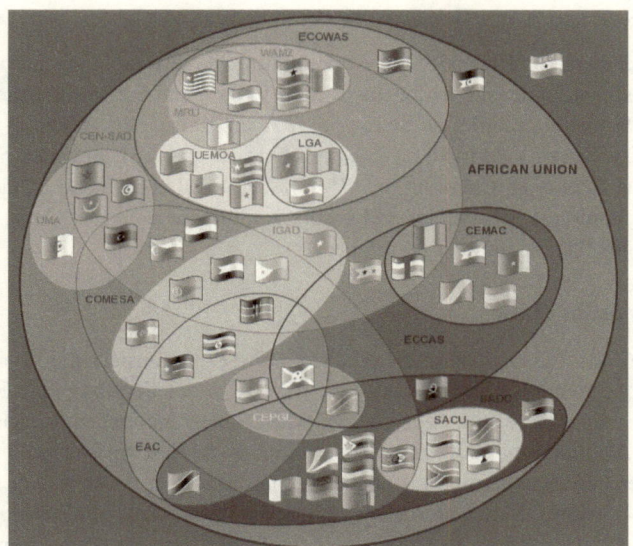

Figure 148: *The image above contains clickable links Euler diagram showing the relationships between various multinational African entities* v · d · e[642]

Role of African Union

One of the key debates in relation to the achievement of greater continental integration is the relative priority that should be given to integration of the continent as a unit in itself or to integration of the sub-regions. The 1980 Lagos Plan of Action for the Development of Africa and the 1991 treaty to establish the African Economic Community (also referred to as the Abuja Treaty), proposed the creation of Regional Economic Communities (RECs) as the basis for African integration, with a timetable for regional and then continental integration to follow.[643]

Currently, there are eight RECs recognised by the AU, each established under a separate regional treaty. They are:

- the Arab Maghreb Union (AMU)
- the Common Market for Eastern and Southern Africa (COMESA)
- the Community of Sahel-Saharan States (CEN-SAD)
- the East African Community (EAC)
- the Economic Community of Central African States (ECCAS)
- the Economic Community of West African States (ECOWAS)
- the Intergovernmental Authority on Development (IGAD)

* the Southern Africa Development Community (SADC)

The membership of many of the communities overlaps, and their rationalisation has been under discussion for several years – and formed the theme of the 2006 Banjul summit. At the July 2007 Accra summit the Assembly finally decided to adopt a Protocol on Relations between the African Union and the Regional Economic Communities.[644] This protocol is intended to facilitate the harmonisation of policies and ensure compliance with the Abuja Treaty and Lagos Plan of Action time frames.

Selection of chair

In 2006, the AU decided to create a Committee "to consider the implementation of a rotation system between the regions" in relation to the presidency. Controversy arose at the 2006 summit when Sudan announced its candidacy for the AU's chairmanship, as a representative of the East African region. Several member states refused to support Sudan because of tensions over Darfur (see also below). Sudan ultimately withdrew its candidacy and President Denis Sassou-Nguesso of the Republic of the Congo was elected to a one-year term. At the January 2007 summit, Sassou-Nguesso was replaced by President John Agyekum Kufuor of Ghana, despite another attempt by Sudan to gain the chair. 2007 was the 50th anniversary of Ghana's independence, a symbolic moment for the country to hold the chair of the AU—and to host the mid-year summit at which the proposed Union Government was also discussed. In January 2008, President Jakaya Kikwete of Tanzania took over as chair, representing the East African region and thus apparently ending Sudan's attempt to become chair—at least till the rotation returns to East Africa.[645] The current chair is Benin

List of chairpersons

Name	Beginning of term	End of term	Country
Thabo Mbeki	9 July 2002	10 July 2003	South Africa
Joaquim Chissano	10 July 2003	6 July 2004	Mozambique
Olusegun Obasanjo	6 July 2004	24 January 2006	Nigeria
Denis Sassou-Nguesso	24 January 2006	24 January 2007	Congo
John Kufuor	30 January 2007	31 January 2008	Ghana
Jakaya Kikwete	31 January 2008	2 February 2009	Tanzania

Muammar al-Gaddafi	2 February 2009	31 January 2010	Libya
Bingu wa Mutharika[646,647]	31 January 2010	31 January 2011	Malawi
Teodoro Obiang Nguema Mbasogo[648]	31 January 2011	29 January 2012	Equatorial Guinea
Yayi Boni	29 January 2012	27 January 2013	Benin
Hailemariam Desalegn	27 January 2013	30 January 2014	Ethiopia
Mohamed Ould Abdel Aziz	30 January 2014	30 January 2015	Mauritania
Robert Mugabe	30 January 2015	30 January 2016	Zimbabwe
Idriss Déby	30 January 2016	30 January 2017	Chad
Alpha Condé	30 January 2017	28 January 2018	Guinea
Paul Kagame	28 January 2018	Incumbent	Rwanda

l+Chairpersons of the African Union

Headquarters

The main administrative capital of the African Union is in Addis Ababa, Ethiopia, where the African Union Commission is headquartered. A new headquarters complex, the AU Conference Center and Office Complex (AUCC), was inaugurated on 28 January 2012, during the 18th AU summit.[649] The complex was built by China State Construction Engineering Corporation as a gift from the Chinese government, and accommodates, among other facilities, a 2,500-seat plenary hall and a 20-story office tower. The tower is 99.9 meters high to signify the date 9 September 1999, when the Organization of African Unity voted to become the African Union. The building cost US$200 million to construct.

On 26 January 2018, five years after the building's completion, the French Newspaper *Le Monde* published an article stating that the Chinese government had heavily bugged the building, installing listening devices in the walls and furniture and setting up the computer system to copy data to servers in Shanghai daily. The Chinese government denied that they bugged the building, stating that the accusations were "utterly groundless and ridiculous." Ethiopian Prime Minister Hailemariam Desalegn rejected the French media report. Moussa Faki Mahamat, head of the African Union Commission, said the allegations in the Le Monde's report were false. "These are totally false allegations and I believe that we are completely disregarding them."

Figure 149: *Muammar Gaddafi embracing Tanzanian President Kikwete after assuming the chairmanship*

Figure 150: *The African Union's headquarters complex in Addis Ababa*

African Union Summits

Session	Host country	Host city	Date	Theme	Notes
30th	Ethiopia	Addis Ababa	22–29 January 2018	"Winning the Fight against Corruption: A Sustainable Path to Africa's Transformation"	
29th	Ethiopia	Addis Ababa	27 June–4 July 2017	"Harnessing the Demographic Dividend through Investments in Youth"	
28th	Ethiopia	Addis Ababa	22–31 January 2017	"Harnessing the Demographic Dividend through investments in Youth"	Morocco rejoins the AU after 33 years
27th	Rwanda	Kigali	10–18 July 2016	"African Year of Human Rights with particular focus on the Rights of Women"	Launch of African Union Passport
26th	Ethiopia	Addis Ababa	21–31 January 2016	"African Year of Human Rights with particular focus on the Rights of Women"	
Third India-Africa Forum Summit	India	New Delhi	26–29 October 2015	Reinvigorated Partnership-Shared Vision	
25th	South Africa	Johannesburg	7–15 June 2015	"Year of Women Empowerment and Development Towards Africa's Agenda 2063"	Featured Angelina Jolie
24th	Ethiopia	Addis Ababa	23–31 January 2015	"Year of Women Empowerment and Development Towards Africa's Agenda 2063"	
2nd Africa-Turkey Summit	Equatorial Guinea	Malabo	19–21 November 2014	"A new model of partnership to enhance a sustainable development and integration of Africa"	
23rd	Equatorial Guinea	Malabo	20–27 June 2014	"Year of Agriculture and food security"	

22nd	Ethiopia	Addis Ababa	21–31 January 2014	"Year Agriculture and food security, Marking 10th Anniversary of the Adoption of the Comprehensive Africa Agriculture Development Programme (CAADP)"	
ICC – Extraordinary Summit	Ethiopia	Addis Ababa	11–12 October 2013	"Africa's relationship with the ICC"	This was in regards to the ICC's non-adherence to AU calls to drop certain charges against sitting leaders and that it was disproportionally targeting Africans.
21st	Ethiopia	Addis Ababa	19–27 May 2013	"Panafricanism and African Renaissance"	50th Anniversary of the Establishment of the Organisation of African Unity
20th	Ethiopia	Addis Ababa	27–28 January 2013	"Panafricanism and African Renaissance"	
Diaspora Summit	South Africa	Sandton	23–25 May 2012	"Towards the realisation of a united and integrated Africa and its diaspora"	
19th	Ethiopia	Addis Ababa	9–16 July 2012	"Boosting Intra-African trade"	
18th	Ethiopia	Addis Ababa	23–30 January 2012	"Boosting Intra-African trade"	
17th	Equatorial Guinea	Malabo	23 June–1 July 2011	"Youth empowerment for sustainable development"	
2nd Africa-India Summit	Ethiopia	Addis Ababa	20–25 May 2011	"Enhancing partnership: shared vision"	
16th	Ethiopia	Addis Ababa	24–31 January 2011	"Towards greater unity and integration through shared values"	
15th	Uganda	Kampala	19–27 July 2010	"Maternal, Infant, and Child Health and Development in Africa"	
14th	Ethiopia	Addis Ababa	25 January–2 February 2010	"Information and Communication Technologies (ICT) in Africa: Challenges and Prospects for Development"	

13th	Libya	Sirte	24 June–3 July 2009	"Investing in Agriculture for Economic Growth and Food Security"	
12th	Ethiopia	Addis Ababa	26 January–3 February 2009	"Infrastructure Development in Africa"	
11th	Egypt	Sharm el-Sheikh	24 June–1 July 2008	"Meeting the Millennium Development Goals on Water and Sanitation"	
10th	Ethiopia	Addis Ababa	25 January–2 February 2008	"Industrial Development of Africa"	
9th	Ghana	Accra	25 June–6 July 2007	"Grand Debate on the Union Government"	
8th	Ethiopia	Addis Ababa	22–30 January 2007	1. Science, Technology and Scientific Research for Development 2. Climate change in Africa	
7th	Gambia	Banjul	25 June–2 July 2006	"Rationalisation of Recs and Regional Integration"	
6th	Sudan	Khartoum	16–24 January 2006	"Education and Culture"	
5th	Libya	Sirte	28–29 June 2005		
Extraordinary summit on UN Reform	Ethiopia	Addis Ababa	4 August 2005		
4th	Nigeria	Abuja	24–31 January 2005		
3rd	Ethiopia	Addis Ababa	6–8 July 2004		
2nd	Mozambique	Maputo	2–12 July 2003		
1st	South Africa	Durban	28–10 July 2002	"Peace, Development and Prosperity: The African Century"	Notable events include the launch of the African Union.

Foreign relations

The individual member states of the African Union coordinate foreign policy through this agency, in addition to conducting their own international relations on a state-by-state basis. The AU represents the interests of African peoples at large in intergovernmental organisations (IGOs); for instance, it is a permanent observer at the United Nations General Assembly. Both the African Union and the United Nations work in tandem to address issues of common concerns in various areas. The African Union Mission in United Nations aspires to serve as a bridge between the two Organisations.

Membership of the AU overlaps with other IGOs and occasionally these third-party organisations and the AU will coordinate matters of public policy. The African Union maintains special diplomatic representation with the United States and the European Union.

In 2016, the Union introduced continent-wide passports.

Upon the election of Donald Trump for the presidency of the U.S., in 2017, the latter passed an executive order for a ban on citizens from seven countries with suspected links to terrorism, that concerns three African countries. During the 28th African Union Summit, in Ethiopia, African leaders criticized the ban as they expressed their growing concerns for the African Economy, under Trump's policies.

Africa–China relations

One of the leading economic partners of the continent has been the People's Republic of China (PRC). In September 2018, the bloc held its third Forum on China–Africa Cooperation summit in Beijing, China.

Economy

The AU's future goals include the creation of a free trade area, a customs union, a single market, a central bank, and a common currency (see African Monetary Union), thereby establishing economic and monetary union. The current plan is to establish an African Economic Community with a single currency by 2023.

Indicators

The following table shows various data for AU member states, including area, population, economic output and income inequality, as well as various indices, including human development, viability of the state, perception of corruption, economic freedom, state of peace, freedom of the press and democratic level.

Country	Land Area (km²) 2015	Population 2016	GDP (PPP) (Intl. $) 2015	GDP (PPP) per capita (Intl. $) 2015	HDI 2014	FSI 2016	CPI 2016	IEF 2016	GPI 2016	WPFI 2016	DI 2016
Algeria	2,381,741	40,606,052	548,293,085,686	13,823	0.736	78.3	34	50.06	2.21	41.69	3.56
Angola	1,246,700	28,813,463	173,593,223,667	6,938	0.532	90.5	18	48.94	2.14	39.89	3.40
Benin	112,760	10,872,298	21,016,184,357	1,932	0.48	78.9	36	59.31	2.00	28.97	5.67
Botswana	566,730	2,250,260	33,657,545,969	14,876	0.698	63.5	60	71.07	1.64	22.91	7.87
Burkina Faso	273,600	18,646,433	28,840,666,622	1,593	0.402	89.4	42	59.09	2.06	22.66	4.70
Burundi	25,680	10,524,117	7,634,578,343	300	0.4	100.7	20	53.91	2.50	54.10	2.40
Cape Verde	4,030	539,560	3,205,197,585	6,158	0.646	71.5	59	66.46	N/A	19.82	7.94
Cameroon	472,710	23,439,189	68,302,439,597	2,926	0.512	97.8	26	54.18	2.36	40.53	3.46
Central African Republic	622,980	4,594,621	2,847,726,468	581	0.35	112.1	20	45.23	3.35	33.60	1.61
Chad	1,259,200	14,452,543	28,686,194,920	2,044	0.392	110.1	20	46.33	2.46	40.59	1.50
Comoros	1,861	795,601	1,098,546,195	1,393	0.503	83.8	24	52.35	N/A	24.33	3.71
Congo, Democratic Republic of the	2,267,050	78,736,153	56,920,935,460	300	0.433		21	46.38	3.11	50.97	1.93
Congo, Republic of the	341,500	5,125,821	27,690,345,067	5,993	0.591	92.2	20	42.80	2.25	35.84	2.91
Côte d'Ivoire	318,000	23,695,919	74,916,780,423	3,300	0.462	97.9	34	60.01	2.28	30.17	3.81
Djibouti	23,180	942,333	2,911,406,226	3,279	0.47	89.7	30	55.96	2.29	70.90	2.83
Egypt	1,010,407	95,688,681	1,173,000,000,000	10,250	0.69	90.2	34	55.96	2.57	54.45	3.31

Equatorial Guinea	28,050	1,221,490	32,317,928,931	38,243	0.587	85.2	N/A	43.67	1.94	66.47	1.70
Eritrea	101,000	4,954,645	8,845,000,000[b]	600[b]	0.391	98.6	18	42.7	2.46	83.92	2.37
Ethiopia	1,104,300	102,403,196	152,057,290,468	1,530	0.442	97.2	34	51.52	2.28	45.13	3.60
Gabon	257,670	1,979,786	32,539,376,597	18,860	0.684	72	35	58.96	2.03	32.20	3.74
Gambia, The	10,120	2,038,501	3,140,820,062	1,578	0.441	86.8	26	57.14	2.09	46.53	2.91
Ghana	227,540	28,206,728	108,393,071,924	3,955	0.579	71.2	43	63.00	1.81	17.95	6.75
Guinea	245,720	12,395,924	14,316,884,358	1,135	0.411	103.8	27	53.33	2.15	33.08	3.14
Guinea-Bissau	28,120	1,815,698	2,521,743,682	1,367	0.42	99.8	16	51.81	2.26	29.03	1.98
Kenya	569,140	48,461,567	133,592,522,053	2,901	0.548	98.3	26	57.51	2.38	31.16	5.33
Lesotho	30,360	2,203,821	5,914,437,068	2,770	0.497	80.9	39	50.62	1.94	28.78	6.59
Liberia	96,320	4,613,823	3,533,313,381	500	0.43	95.5	37	52.19	2.00	30.71	5.31
Libya	1,759,540	6,293,253	94,010,000,000[b]	14,900[b]	0.724	96.4	14	N/A	3.20	57.89	2.25
Madagascar	581,800	24,894,551	33,354,200,458	1,376	0.51	84.2	26	61.06	1.76	27.04	5.07
Malawi	94,280	18,091,575	19,137,290,349	1,112	0.445	87.6	31	51.8	1.82	28.12	5.55
Mali	1,220,190	17,994,837	33,524,899,739	1,905	0.419	95.2	32	56.54	2.49	39.83	5.70
Mauritania	1,030,700	4,301,018	16,190,000,000[b]	4,400[b]	0.506	95.4	27	54.8	2.30	24.03	3.96
Mauritius	2,030	1,262,132	23,817,914,134	18,864	0.777	43.2	54	74.73	1.56	27.69	8.28
Morocco	446,300	35,276,786	257,398,957,178	7,365	0.628	74.2	37	61.27	2.09	42.64	4.77
Mozambique	786,380	28,829,476	31,326,751,237	1,120	0.416	87.8	27	53.19	1.96	30.25	4.02
Namibia	823,290	2,479,713	24,043,436,006	9,778	0.628	71.1	52	61.85	1.87	15.15	6.31

Country										
Niger	1,266,700	20,672,987	17,857,377,171	897	0.348	98.4	35	54.26	2.24	24.62	3.96
Nigeria	910,770	185,989,640	1,168,000,000,000	5,639	0.514	103.5	28	57.46	2.88	35.90	4.50
Rwanda	24,670	11,917,508	19,216,033,048	1,655	0.483	91.3	54	63.07	2.32	54.61	3.07
São Tomé and Príncipe	960	199,910	575,391,345	3,023	0.555	72.9	46	56.71	N/A	N/A	N/A
Senegal	192,530	15,411,614	34,398,281,018	2,274	0.466	83.6	45	58.09	1.98	27.99	6.21
Seychelles	460	94,228	2,384,515,771	25,525	0.772	60.2	N/A	62.2	N/A	30.60	N/A
Sierra Leone	72,180	7,396,190	9,511,431,824	1,474	0.413	91	30	52.31	1.81	29.94	4.55
Somalia	627,340	14,317,996	5,900,000,000ᶜ	600ᶜ	N/A	114	10	N/A	3.41	65.35	N/A
South Africa	1,213,090	56,015,473	742,461,000,000	12,393	0.666	69.9	45	61.9	2.32	21.92	7.41
South Sudan	619,745	12,230,730	21,484,823,398	1,741	0.467	113.8	11	N/A	3.59	44.87	N/A
Sudan	1,886,086	39,578,828	165,813,461,495	4,121	0.479	111.5	14	N/A	3.27	72.53	2.37
Swaziland	17,200	1,343,098	10,452,834,007	8,122	0.531	87.6	N/A	59.65	2.07	52.37	3.03
Tanzania	885,800	55,572,201	130,297,806,032	2,510	0.521	81.8	32	58.46	1.90	28.65	5.76
Togo	54,390	7,606,374	10,018,697,437	1,372	0.484	85.8	32	53.64	1.95	30.31	3.32
Tunisia	155,360	11,403,248	121,200,025,401	10,770	0.721	74.6	41	57.55	1.95	31.60	6.40
Uganda	200,520	41,487,965	67,856,334,117	1,738	0.483	97.7	25	59.26	2.15	32.58	5.26
Western Sahara	266,000	538,755	906,500,000ᵈ	2,500ᵈ	N/A	N/A	N/A	N/A	N/A	N/A	N/A
Zambia	743,390	16,591,390	58,400,082,027	3,602	0.586	86.3	38	58.79	1.78	35.08	5.99
Zimbabwe	386,850	16,150,362	26,180,942,292	500	0.509	100.5	22	38.23	2.32	40.41	3.05

African Union

African Union	30,370,000	1,225,080,510	5,457,724,064,668	4,602	0.524d	88.99d	31.51d	55.55d	2.27	37.89	4.30
Country	Land Area (km²) 2015	Population 2016	GDP (PPP) (Intl. $) 2015	GDP (PPP) per capita (Intl. $) 2015	HDI 2014	FSI 2016	CPI 2016	IEF 2016	GPI 2016	WPFI 2016	DI 2016

ª External data from 2016. ᵇ External data from 2015. ᶜ External data from 2014. ᵈ AU total used for indicators 1 through 3; AU weighted average used for indicator 4; AU unweighted average used for indicators 5 through 12.

Culture

Symbols

The emblem of the African Union consists of a gold ribbon bearing small interlocking red rings, from which palm leaves shoot up around an outer gold circle and an inner green circle, within which is a gold representation of Africa. The red interlinked rings stand for African solidarity and the blood shed for the liberation of Africa; the palm leaves for peace; the gold, for Africa's wealth and bright future; the green, for African hopes and aspirations. To symbolise African unity, the silhouette of Africa is drawn without internal borders.

The African Union adopted its new flag at its 14th Ordinary Session of the Assembly of Heads of State and Government taking place in Addis Ababa 2010. During the 8th African Union Summit which took place in Addis Ababa on 29 and 30 January 2007, the Heads of State and Government decided to launch a competition for the selection of a new flag for the Union. They prescribed a green background for the flag symbolising hope of Africa and stars to represent Member States.

Pursuant to this decision, the African Union Commission (AUC) organised a competition for the selection of a new flag for the African Union. The AUC received a total of 106 entries proposed by citizens of 19 African countries and 2 from the Diaspora. The proposals were then examined by a panel of experts put in place by the African Union Commission and selected from the five African regions for short listing according to the main directions given by the Heads of State and Government.

At the 13th Ordinary Session of the Assembly, the Heads of State and Government examined the report of the Panel and selected one among all the proposals. The flag is now part of the paraphernalia of the African Union and replaces the old one.

The old flag of the African Union bears a broad green horizontal stripe, a narrow band of gold, the emblem of the African Union at the centre of a broad white stripe, another narrow gold band and a final broad green stripe. Again, the green and gold symbolise Africa's hopes and aspirations as well as its wealth and bright future, and the white represents the purity of Africa's desire for friends throughout the world. The flag has led to the creation of the "national colours" of Africa of gold and green (sometimes together with white). These colours are visible in one way or another in the flags of many African

Figure 151: *Emblem of the African Union*

nations. Together the colours green, gold, and red constitute the Pan-African colours.

The African Union has adopted the anthem, "Let Us All Unite and Celebrate Together".

Celebration

Africa Day, formerly African Freedom Day and African Liberation Day, is an annual commemoration regarding the founding of the Organisation of African Unity (OAU), on 25 May 1963, and occurring on the same date of the month each year. Other celebrations include the following:

- The Fez Festival of World Sacred Music: a week long celebration for harmony between cultures with dancing, Moroccan music, art exhibitions and films.
- The Knysna Oyster festival: held in Knysna and focused around sport, food and their oyster heritage.
- Lake of Stars Festival: three-day celebration that takes place in Lake Malawi, showcasing African music and welcoming people from around the world.

- Fête du Vodoun: also known as the Ouidah Voodoo Festival. It is centred around their rituals on voodoo temples, with entertainment that includes horse races and traditional drum performances.
- Umhlanga (ceremony): is mainly a private event for young women but on the sixth and seventh days the traditions are done publicly.
- Marsabit Lake Turkana Cultural Festival: held in Kenya and celebrates harmony amongst tribes with their culture, singing, dancing and traditional costumes.

Current issues

The AU faces many challenges, including health issues such as combating malaria and the AIDS/HIV epidemic; political issues such as confronting undemocratic regimes and mediating in the many civil wars; economic issues such as improving the standard of living of millions of impoverished, uneducated Africans; ecological issues such as dealing with recurring famines, desertification, and lack of ecological sustainability; as well as the legal issues regarding Western Sahara.

AIDS in Africa

The AU has been active in addressing the AIDS pandemic in Africa. In 2001, the AU established AIDS Watch Africa to coordinate and mobilize a continent-wide response. Sub-Saharan Africa, especially southern and eastern Africa, is the most affected area in the world. Though this region is home to only 6.2% of the world's population, it is also home to half of the world's population infected with HIV.[650] While the measurement of HIV prevalence rates has proved methodologically challenging, more than 20% of the sexually active population of many countries of southern Africa may be infected, with South Africa, Botswana, Kenya, Namibia, and Zimbabwe all expected to have a decrease in life expectancy by an average of 6.5 years. The pandemic has had massive implications for the economy of the continent, reducing economic growth rates by 2–4% across Africa.

In July 2007, the AU endorsed two new initiatives to combat the AIDS crisis, including a push to recruit, train and integrate 2 million community health workers into the continent's healthcare systems.

Libya

The AU attempted to mediate in the early stages of the 2011 Libyan civil war, forming an *ad hoc* committee of five presidents (Congolese President Denis Sassou Nguesso, Malian President Amadou Toumani Touré, Mauritanian President Mohamed Ould Abdel Aziz, South African President Jacob Zuma, and Ugandan President Yoweri Museveni) to broker a truce. However, the beginning of the NATO-led military intervention in March 2011 prevented the committee from traveling to Libya to meet with Libyan leader and former head of the AU until 2010 Muammar Gaddafi. As a body, the AU sharply dissented from the United Nations Security Council's decision to create a no-fly zone over Libya, though a few member states, such as Botswana, Gabon, Zambia, and others expressed support for the resolution.

As a result of Gaddafi's defeat at the Battle of Tripoli, the decisive battle of the war, in August 2011, the Arab League voted to recognise the anti-Gaddafi National Transitional Council as the legitimate government of the country pending elections, yet although the council has been recognised by several AU member states, including two countries that are also members of the Arab League, the AU Peace and Security Council voted on 26 August 2011 not to recognise it, insisting that a ceasefire be agreed to and a national unity government be formed by both sides in the civil war. A number of AU member states led by Ethiopia, Nigeria, and Rwanda requested that the AU recognise the NTC as Libya's interim governing authority, and several other AU member states have recognised the NTC regardless of the Peace and Security Council's decision. However, AU member states Algeria and Zimbabwe have indicated they will not recognise the NTC, and South Africa has expressed reservations as well.

On 20 September 2011, the African Union officially recognised the National Transitional Council as the legitimate representative of Libya.

Military

Togo

In response to the death of Gnassingbé Eyadéma, President of Togo, on 5 February 2005, AU leaders described the naming of his son Faure Gnassingbé the successor as a military coup. Togo's constitution calls for the speaker of parliament to succeed the president in the event of his death. By law, the parliament speaker must call national elections to choose a new president within sixty days. The AU's protest forced Gnassingbé to hold elections. Under heavy allegations of election fraud, he was officially elected President on 4 May 2005.

Mauritania

On 3 August 2005, a coup in Mauritania led the African Union to suspend the country from all organisational activities. The Military Council that took control of Mauritania promised to hold elections within two years.Wikipedia:Citation needed These were held in early 2007, the first time that the country had held elections that were generally agreed to be of an acceptable standard. Following the elections, Mauritania's membership of the AU was restored. However, on 6 August 2008, a fresh coup overthrew the government elected in 2007. The AU once again suspended Mauritania from the continental body. The suspension was once again lifted in 2009 after the military junta agreed with the opposition to organize elections

Mali

The Malian army was formed on 1 October 1960 and was supported by the Soviet Union. In March 2012, a military coup was staged in Mali, when an alliance of Touareg and Islamist forces conquered the north, resulting in a coming to power of the Islamists. This resulted in the deaths of hundreds of Malian soldiers and the loss of control over their camps and positions. After a military intervention with help from French troops, the region was in control of the Malian army. To reinstall local authorities, the AU helped to form a caretaker government, supporting it and holding presidential elections in Mali in July 2013.[651]

Regional conflicts and peacekeeping

One of the objectives of the AU is to "promote peace, security, and stability on the continent".[652] Among its principles is "Peaceful resolution of conflicts among Member States of the Union through such appropriate means as may be decided upon by the Assembly".[653] The primary body charged with implementing these objectives and principles is the Peace and Security Council. The PSC has the power, among other things, to authorise peace support missions, to impose sanctions in case of unconstitutional change of government, and to "take initiatives and action it deems appropriate" in response to potential or actual conflicts. The PSC is a decision-making body in its own right, and its decisions are binding on member states.

Article 4(h) of the Constitutive Act, repeated in article 4 of the Protocol to the Constitutive Act on the PSC, also recognises the right of the Union to intervene in member state in circumstances of war crimes, genocide and crimes against humanity. Any decision to intervene in a member state under article 4 of the Constitutive Act will be made by the Assembly on the recommendation of the PSC.

Figure 152: *South Sudanese independence referendum, 2011*

Since it first met in 2004, the PSC has been active in relation to the crises in Darfur, Comoros, Somalia, Democratic Republic of Congo, Burundi, Côte d'Ivoire and other countries. It has adopted resolutions creating the AU peace-keeping operations in Somalia and Darfur, and imposing sanctions against persons undermining peace and security (such as travel bans and asset freezes against the leaders of the rebellion in Comoros). The Council is in the process of overseeing the establishment of a "standby force" to serve as a permanent African peacekeeping force.Wikipedia:Citation needed Institute for Security Studies, South Africa, March 2008.

The founding treaty of the AU also called for the establishment of the African Peace and Security Architecture (APSA), including the African Standby Force (ASF), which is to be deployed in emergencies. That means, in cases of genocide or other serious human-rights violations, an ASF mission can be launched even against the wishes of the government of the country concerned, as long as it is approved by the AU General Assembly. In the past AU peacekeeping missions, the concept was not yet applied, forces had to be mobilised from member states. The AU is planning on putting the concept into practise by 2015 at the earliest.Wikipedia:Manual of Style/Dates and numbers#Chronological items

Darfur, Sudan

In response to the ongoing Darfur conflict in Sudan, the AU has deployed 7,000 peacekeepers, many from Rwanda and Nigeria, to Darfur. While a donor's conference in Addis Ababa in 2005 helped raise funds to sustain the peacekeepers through that year and into 2006, in July 2006 the AU said it would pull out at the end of September when its mandate expires. Critics of the AU peacekeepers, including Dr. Eric Reeves, have said these forces are largely ineffective due to lack of funds, personnel, and expertise. Monitoring an area roughly the size of France has made it even more difficult to sustain an effective mission. In June 2006, the United States Congress appropriated US $173 million for the AU force. Some, such as the Genocide Intervention Network, have called for UN or NATO intervention to augment and/or replace the AU peacekeepers. The UN has considered deploying a force, though it would not likely enter the country until at least October 2007. The under-funded and badly equipped AU mission was set to expire on 31 December 2006 but was extended to 30 June 2007 and merged with the United Nations African Union Mission in Darfur in October 2007. In July 2009 the African Union ceased cooperation with the International Criminal Court, refusing to recognise the international arrest warrant it had issued against Sudan's leader, Omar al-Bashir, who was indicted in 2008 for war crimes.

The AU struggled to have a strategic role in the independence talks and the reconciliation process of South Sudan, anyway due to overwhelming interests of African and non-African powers, its influence is still limited and not consistent.

Somalia

From the early 1990s up until 2000, Somalia was without a functioning central government. A peace agreement aimed at ending the civil war that broke out following the collapse of the Siad Barre regime was signed in 2006 after many years of peace talks. However, the new government was almost immediately threatened by further violence. To temporarily shore up the government's military base, starting in March 2007, AU soldiers began arriving in Mogadishu as part of a peacekeeping force that was intended by the AU to eventually be 8,000 strong. Eritrea recalled its ambassadors to the African Union on 20 November 2009[654] after the African Union called on the United Nations Security Council to impose sanctions on them due to their alleged support of Somali Islamists attempting to topple the Transitional Federal Government of Somalia, the internationally recognised government of Somalia which holds Somalia's seat on the African Union.[655] On 22 December 2009, the United Nations Security Council passed UNSCR 1907, which imposed an arms embargo on Eritrea, travel bans on Eritrean leaders, and asset freezes on Eritrean officials. Eritrea strongly criticised the resolution. In January 2011, Eritrea reestablished their mission to the AU in Addis Ababa.

Anjouan, Comoros

A successful 2008 invasion of Anjouan by AU and Comoros forces to stop self-declared president Mohamed Bacar, whose 2007 re-election was declared illegal. Prior to the invasion, France helped transport Tanzanian troops but their position in the disagreement was questioned when a French police helicopter was suspected of attempting to sneak Bacar into French exile. The first wave of troops landed on Anjouan Bay on 25 March and soon took over the airfield in Ouani, ultimately aiming to locate and remove Bacar from office. On the same day, the airport, capital, and second city were overrun and the presidential palace was deserted. Bacar escaped and sought asylum in France and the government of Comoros demanded they return him so they may determine his consequence. Many of Bacar's primary supporters were arrested by the end of March, including Caabi El-Yachroutu Mohamed and Ibrahim Halidi. His asylum request was rejected in 15 May as France agreed to cooperate with the Comoran governments demand. His presendential position was then occupied by Moussa Toybou adter winning the election in 29 June.

Bibliography

- *Strengthening Popular Participation in the African Union: A Guide to AU Structures and Processes*[656], AfriMAP and Oxfam GB, 2010.
- *Towards a People Driven African Union: Current Challenges and New Opportunities*[657] AfriMAP, AFRODAD and Oxfam GB, January 2007.
- The New African Initiative and the African Union: A Preliminary Assessment and Documentation by Henning Melber, Publisher: Nordiska Afrikainstitutet, Sweden; <templatestyles src="Module:Citation/CS1/styles.css" />ISBN 91-7106-486-9; (October 2002).
- "The African Union, NEPAD and Human Rights: The Missing Agenda" *Human Rights Quarterly* Vol.26, No.4, November 2004.
- Bibliography on the AU at the Peace Palace Library[658].

External links

- Official website[659]
- African Union Mission in the United Nations[660]
- 1st African Union Summit July 2002[661] in Durban, South Africa, website created by SA government
- Southern Africa Regional Poverty Network[662] Page on the AU and NEPAD – many useful links
- Pan-African Perspective[663] Background on Union Government debate
- BBC Profile: African Union[664]

- African Union[665] at Curlie (based on DMOZ)
- Africa: 50 years of independence[666] Radio France Internationale in English
- "The broken dream of African unity, Jean-Karim Fall"[667], Radio France Internationale in English

Economy

Economy of Africa

Economy of Africa

Statistics	
Population	1.25 billion (15%; 2017)
GDP	$3.52 trillion (Nominal; 2017) $6.36 trillion (PPP; 2017)
GDP growth	3.7%
GDP per capita	$2,820 (2017; 6th)
Millionaires (US$)	140,000 (0.011%)
Unemployment	15%
Most numbers are from the International Monetary Fund. All values, unless otherwise stated, are in US dollars.	

World economy
<ul><li>Africa</li><li>Americas<ul><li>Central America</li><li>North America</li><li>South America</li></ul></li><li>Asia<ul><li>East Asia</li></ul></li><li>Europe</li><li>Oceania</li></ul>
<ul><li>v</li><li>t</li><li>e[668]</li></ul>

Figure 153: *Ancient Egyptian units of measurement also served as units of currency.*

The **economy of Africa** consists of the trade, industry, agriculture, and human resources of the continent. As of 2012[669], approximately 1.07 billion people were living in 54 different countries in Africa. Africa is a resource-rich continent. Recent growth has been due to growth in sales in commodities, services, and manufacturing. Sub-Saharan Africa, in particular, is expected to reach a GDP of $29 trillion by 2050.

In March 2013, Africa was identified as the world's poorest inhabited continent: Africa's entire combined GDP is barely a third of the United States' GDP; however, the World Bank expects that most African countries will reach "middle income" status (defined as at least US$1,000 per person a year) by 2025 if current growth rates continue. In 2013, Africa was the world's fastest-growing continent at 5.6% a year, and GDP is expected to rise by an average of over 6% a year between 2013 and 2023. In 2017, the African Development Bank reported Africa to be the world's second-fastest growing economy, and estimates that average growth will rebound to 3.4% in 2017, while growth is expected to increase by 4.3% in 2018.

Growth has been present throughout the continent, with over one-third of Sub-Saharan Africa countries posting 6% or higher growth rates, and another 40% growing between 4% to 6% per year. Several international business observers have also named Africa as the future economic growth engine of the world.

History

Africa's economy was diverse, driven by extensive trade routes that developed between cities and kingdoms. Some trade routes were overland, some involved navigating rivers, still others developed around port cities. Large African empires became wealthy due to their trade networks, for example Ancient Egypt, Nubia, Mali, Ashanti, and the Oyo Empire.

Some parts of Africa had close trade relationships with Arab kingdoms, and by the time of the Ottoman Empire, Africans had begun converting to Islam in large numbers. This development, along with the economic potential in finding a trade route to the Indian Ocean, brought the Portuguese to sub-Saharan

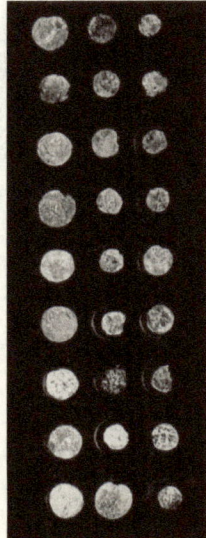

Figure 154: *The Sultanate of Mogadishu's medieval currency.*

Africa as an imperial force. Colonial interests created new industries to feed European appetites for goods such as palm oil, rubber, cotton, precious metals, spices, cash crops other goods, and integrated especially the coastal areas with the Atlantic economy.

Following the independence of African countries during the 20th century, economic, political and social upheaval consumed much of the continent. An economic rebound among some countries has been evident in recent years, however.

The dawn of the African economic boom (which is in place since the 2000s) has been compared to the Chinese economic boom that had emerged in Asia since late 1970's. In 2013, Africa was home to seven of the world's fastest-growing economies.

As of 2018, Nigeria is the biggest economy in terms of nominal GDP, followed by South Africa; in terms of PPP, Egypt is second biggest after Nigeria.. Equatorial Guinea possessed Africa's highest GDP per capita albeit allegations of human rights violations. Oil-rich countries such as Algeria, Libya and Gabon, and mineral-rich Botswana emerged among the top economies since the 21st century, while Zimbabwe and the Democratic Republic of Congo, potentially among the world's richest nations, have sunk into the list of the world's poorest

Figure 155: *The National Cement Share Company of Ethiopia's new plant in Dire Dawa*

nations due to pervasive political corruption, warfare and braindrain of workforce. Botswana remains the site of Africa's longest and one of the world's longest periods of economic boom (1966–1999).

Current conditions

The United Nations predicts Africa's economic growth will reach 3.5% in 2018 and 3.7% in 2019. As of 2007, growth in Africa had surpassed that of East Asia. Data suggest parts of the continent are now experiencing fast growth, thanks to their resources and increasing political stability and 'has steadily increased levels of peacefulness since 2007'. The World Bank reports the economy of Sub-Saharan African countries grew at rates that match or surpass global rates. According to the United Nations Department of Economic and Social Affairs, the improvement in the region's aggregate growth is largely attributable to a recovery in Egypt, Nigeria and South Africa, three of Africa's largest economies.

The economies of the fastest growing African nations experienced growth significantly above the global average rates. The top nations in 2007 include Mauritania with growth at 19.8%, Angola at 17.6%, Sudan at 9.6%, Mozambique at 7.9% and Malawi at 7.8%. Other fast growers include Rwanda, Mozambique, Chad, Niger, Burkina Faso, Ethiopia. Nonetheless, growth has been dismal, negative or sluggish in many parts of Africa including Zimbabwe, the Democratic Republic of the Congo, the Republic of the Congo and Burundi. Many international agencies are increasingly interested in investing in emerging African economies. especially as Africa continues to maintain high economic growth despite current global economic recession. The rate of return on investment in Africa is currently the highest in the developing world.

Debt relief is being addressed by some international institutions in the interests of supporting economic development in Africa. In 1996, the UN sponsored the Heavily Indebted Poor Countries (HIPC) initiative, subsequently taken up by the IMF, World Bank and the African Development Fund (AfDF) in the form of the Multilateral Debt Relief Initiative (MDRI). As of 2013, the initiative has given partial debt relief to 30 African countries.

Trade growth

Trade has driven much of the growth in Africa's economy in the early 21st century. China and India are increasingly important trade partners; 12.5% of Africa's exports are to China, and 4% are to India, which accounts for 5% of China's imports and 8% of India's. The Group of Five (Indonesia, Malaysia, Saudi Arabia, Thailand, and the United Arab Emirates) are another increasingly important market for Africa's exports.

Future

Africa's economy—with expanding trade, English language skills (official in many Sub-Saharan countries), improving literacy and education, availability of splendid resources and cheaper labour force—is expected to continue to perform better into the future. Trade between Africa and China stood at US $166 billion in 2011.

Africa will only experience a "demographic dividend" by 2035, when its young and growing labour force will have fewer children and retired people as dependents as a proportion of the population, making it more demographically comparable to the US and Europe. It is becoming a more educated labour force, with nearly half expected to have some secondary-level education by 2020. A consumer class is also emerging in Africa and is expected to keep booming. Africa has around 90 million people with household incomes exceeding $5,000, meaning that they can direct more than half of their income towards discretionary spending rather than necessities. This number could reach a projected 128 million by 2020.

During the President of the United States Barack Obama's visit to Africa in July 2013, he announced a US$7 billion plan to further develop infrastructure and work more intensively with African heads of state. A new program named

Figure 156: *A mobile phone advertisement on the side of a van, Kampala, Uganda.*

Trade Africa, designed to boost trade within the continent as well as between Africa and the U.S., was also unveiled by Obama.

Causes of the economic underdevelopment over the years

The seemingly intractable nature of Africa's poverty has led to debate concerning its root causes. Endemic warfare and unrest, widespread corruption, and despotic regimes are both causes and effects of the continued economic problems. The decolonization of Africa was fraught with instability aggravated by cold war conflict. Since the mid-20th century, the Cold War and increased corruption and despotism have also contributed to Africa's poor economy.

Infrastructure

According to the researchers at the Overseas Development Institute, the lack of infrastructure in many developing countries represents one of the most significant limitations to economic growth and achievement of the Millennium Development Goals (MDGs).[670] Infrastructure investments and maintenance can be very expensive, especially in such areas as landlocked, rural and sparsely populated countries in Africa.

Figure 157: *The Trans-African Highway network*

It has been argued that infrastructure investments contributed to more than half of Africa's improved growth performance between 1990 and 2005 and increased investment is necessary to maintain growth and tackle poverty. The returns to investment in infrastructure are very significant, with on average 30–40% returns for telecommunications (ICT) investments, over 40% for electricity generation, and 80% for roads.

In Africa, it is argued that to meet the MDGs by 2015, infrastructure investments would need to reach about 15% of GDP (around $93 billion a year). Currently, the source of financing varies significantly across sectors. Some sectors are dominated by state spending, others by overseas development aid (ODA) and yet others by private investors. In sub-Saharan Africa, the state spends around $9.4 billion out of a total of $24.9 billion.

In irrigation, SSA states represent almost all spending; in transport and energy a majority of investment is state spending; in Information and communication technologies and water supply and sanitation, the private sector represents the majority of capital expenditure. Overall, aid, the private sector and non-OECD financiers between them exceed state spending. The private sector spending alone equals state capital expenditure, though the majority is focused on ICT infrastructure investments. External financing increased from $7 billion (2002) to $27 billion (2009). China, in particular, has emerged as an important investor.

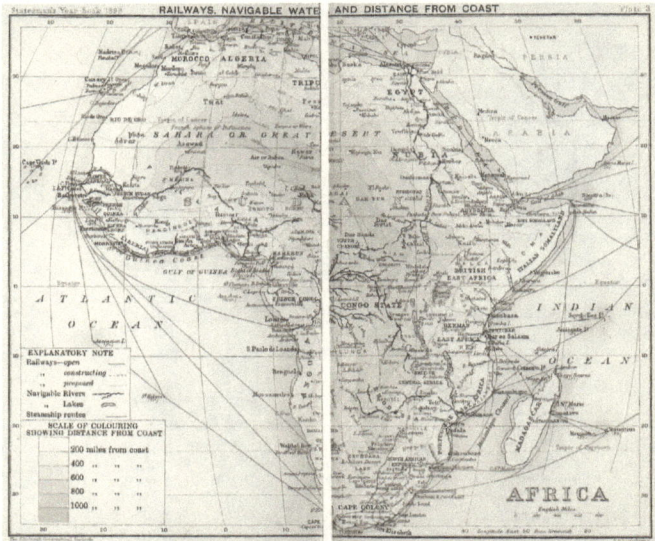

Figure 158: *Railway map of Africa, including tracks proposed and under construction, The Statesman's Yearbook, 1899.*

Colonialism

The economic impact of the colonization of Africa has been debated. In this matter, the opinions are biased between researchers, some of them consider that Europeans had a positive impact on Africa; others affirm that Africa's development was slowed down by colonial rule. The principal aim of colonial rule in Africa by European colonial powers was to exploit natural wealth in the African continent at a low cost. Some writers, such as Walter Rodney in his book *How Europe Underdeveloped Africa*, argue that these colonial policies are directly responsible for many of Africa's modern problems. Critics of colonialism charge colonial rule with injuring African pride, self-worth and belief in themselves. Other post-colonial scholars, most notably Frantz Fanon continuing along this line, have argued that the true effects of colonialism are psychological and that domination by a foreign power creates a lasting sense of inferiority and subjugation that creates a barrier to growth and innovation. Such arguments posit that a new generation of Africans free of colonial thought and mindset is emerging and that this is driving economic transformation.[671]

Historians L. H. Gann and Peter Duignan have argued that Africa probably benefited from colonialism on balance. Although it had its faults, colonialism was probably "one of the most efficacious engines for cultural diffusion in world history".[672] These views, however, are controversial and are rejected by some who, on balance, see colonialism as bad. The economic historian David Kenneth Fieldhouse has taken a kind of middle position, arguing that the effects of colonialism were actually limited and their main weakness wasn't in deliberate underdevelopment but in what it failed to do.[673] Niall Ferguson agrees with his last point, arguing that colonialism's main weaknesses were *sins of omission*.[674] Analysis of the economies of African states finds that independent states such as Liberia and Ethiopia did not have better economic performance than their post-colonial counterparts. In particular the economic performance of former British colonies was better than both independent states and former French colonies.[675]

Africa's relative poverty predates colonialism. Jared Diamond argues in Guns, Germs, and Steel that Africa has always been poor due to a number of ecological factors affecting historical development. These factors include low population density, lack of domesticated livestock and plants and the North-South orientation of Africa's geography.[676] However Diamond's theories have been criticized by some including James Morris Blaut as a form of environmental determinism. Historian John K. Thornton argues that sub-Saharan Africa was relatively wealthy and technologically advanced until at least the seventeenth century.[677] Some scholars who believe that Africa was generally poorer than the rest of the world throughout its history make exceptions for certain parts of Africa. Acemoglue and Robinson, for example, argue that most of Africa has always been relatively poor, but "Aksum, Ghana, Songhay, Mali, [and] Great Zimbabwe... were probably as developed as their contemporaries anywhere in the world."[678] A number of people including Rodney and Joseph E. Inikori have argued that the poverty of Africa at the onset of the colonial period was principally due to the demographic loss associated with the slave trade as well as other related societal shifts.[679] Others such as J. D. Fage and David Eltis have rejected this view.[680]

Language diversity

African countries suffer from communication difficulties caused by language diversity. Greenberg's diversity index is the chance that two randomly selected people would have different mother tongues. Out of the most diverse 25 countries according to this index, 18 (72%) are African. This includes 12 countries for which Greenberg's diversity index exceeds 0.9, meaning that a pair of randomly selected people will have less than 10% chance of having the same mother tongue. However, the primary language of government, political debate, academic discourse, and administration is often the language of the former colonial powers; English, French, or Portuguese.

Figure 159: *A randomly selected pair of people in Ghana has only an 8.1% chance of sharing a mother tongue.*

Trade based theories

Dependency theory asserts that the wealth and prosperity of the superpowers and their allies in Europe, North America and East Asia is dependent upon the poverty of the rest of the world, including Africa. Economists who subscribe to this theory believe that poorer regions must break their trading ties with the developed world in order to prosper.[681]

Less radical theories suggest that economic protectionism in developed countries hampers Africa's growth. When developing countries have harvested agricultural produce at low cost, they generally do not export as much as would be expected. Abundant farm subsidies and high import tariffs in the developed world, most notably those set by Japan, the European Union's Common Agricultural Policy, and the United States Department of Agriculture, are thought to be the cause. Although these subsidies and tariffs have been gradually reduced, they remain high.

Local conditions also affect exports; state over-regulation in several African nations can prevent their own exports from becoming competitive. Research in Public Choice economics such as that of Jane Shaw suggest that protectionism operates in tandem with heavy State intervention combining to depress economic development. Farmers subject to import and export restrictions cater to localized markets, exposing them to higher market volatility and fewer opportunities. When subject to uncertain market conditions, farmers press for governmental intervention to suppress competition in their markets, resulting in competition being driven out of the market. As competition is driven out of the market, farmers innovate less and grow less food further undermining economic performance.

Governance

Political corruption Concepts

- Bribery
- Cronyism
- Kleptocracy
- Economics of corruption
- Electoral fraud
- Legal plunder
- Nepotism
- Slush fund
- Political scandal

Corruption by country Europe

- Albania
- Armenia
- Austria
- Azerbaijan
- Belgium
- Bosnia
- Bulgaria
- Croatia
- Cyprus
- Czech Republic
- Denmark
- Finland
- France

- Germany
- Georgia
- Greece
- Iceland
- Ireland
- Italy
- Kosovo
- Latvia
- Lithuania
- Luxembourg
- Macedonia
- Moldova
- Montenegro
- Netherlands
- Poland
- Portugal
- Romania
- Serbia
- Slovakia
- Slovenia
- Spain
- Sweden
- Switzerland
- Ukraine

Asia
- Afghanistan
- Bahrain
- Bangladesh
- Cambodia
- China
- India

- Indonesia
- Iran
- Iraq
- Israel
- Jordan
- Kuwait
- Kyrgyzstan
- Malaysia
- Myanmar
- North Korea
- Pakistan
- Philippines
- Singapore
- South Korea
- Sri Lanka
- Tajikistan
- Thailand
- Turkmenistan
- Uzbekistan
- Vietnam
- Yemen

Africa
- Angola
- Botswana
- Cameroon
- Congo
- Egypt
- Equatorial Guinea
- Eritrea
- Ethiopia
- Ghana

- Guinea-Bissau
- Kenya
- Liberia
- Mauritius
- Morocco
- Nigeria
- Senegal
- Somalia
- South Africa
- South Sudan
- Sudan
- Tanzania
- Tunisia
- Uganda
- Zambia
- Zimbabwe

North America
- Canada
- Cuba
- Haiti
- Mexico
- Nicaragua
- United States

South America
- Argentina
- Bolivia
- Brazil
- Chile
- Colombia
- Ecuador
- Paraguay

- Peru
- Venezuela

Oceania and the Pacific
- Australia
- New Zealand
- Papua New Guinea

Transcontinental countries
- Russia
- Turkey
- v̱
- ṯ
- e̱[682]

Although Africa and Asia had similar levels of income in the 1960s, Asia has since outpaced Africa, with the exception of a few extremely poor and wartorn countries like Afghanistan and Yemen. One school of economists argues that Asia's superior economic development lies in local investment. Corruption in Africa consists primarily of extracting economic rent and moving the resulting financial capital overseas instead of investing at home; the stereotype of African dictators with Swiss bank accounts is often accurate. University of Massachusetts Amherst researchers estimate that from 1970 to 1996, capital flight from 30 sub-Saharan countries totalled $187bn, exceeding those nations' external debts. This disparity in development is consistent with the model theorized by economist Mancur Olson. Because governments were politically unstable and new governments often confiscated their predecessors' assets, officials would stash their wealth abroad, out of reach of any future expropriation.

Socialist governments influenced by Marxism, and the land reform they have enacted, have also contributed to economic stagnation in Africa. For example, the regime of Robert Mugabe in Zimbabwe, particularly the land seizures from white farmers, led to the collapse of the country's agricultural economy, which had formerly been one of Africa's strongest;[683] Mugabe had been previously supported by the USSR during the Rhodesian Bush War. In Tanzania, socialist President Julius Nyerere resigned in 1985 after his policies of agricultural collectivisation in 1971 led to economic collapse, with famine only being averted by generous aid from the IMF and other foreign entities.[684] Tanzania was left as one of the world's poorest and most aid-dependent nations, and has taken decades to recover.[685] Since the abolition of the socialist one-party state in 1992 and the transition to democracy, Tanzania has experienced rapid economic growth, with growth of 6.5% in 2017.[686]

Foreign aid

Food shipments in case of dire local shortage are generally uncontroversial; but as Amartya Sen has shown, most famines involve a local lack of income rather than of food. In such situations, food aid—as opposed to financial aid—has the effect of destroying local agriculture and serves mainly to benefit Western agribusiness which are vastly overproducing food as a result of agricultural subsidies.

Historically, food aid is more highly correlated with excess supply in Western countries than with the needs of developing countries. Foreign aid has been an integral part of African economic development since the 1980s.

The aid model has been criticized for supplanting trade initiatives. Growing evidence shows that foreign aid has made the continent poorer. One of the biggest critics of the aid development model is economist Dambiso Moyo (a Zambian economist based in the US), who introduced the Dead Aid model, which highlights how foreign aid has been a deterrent for local development.

Today, Africa faces the problem of attracting foreign aid in areas where there is potential for high income from demand. It is in need of more economic policies and active participation in the world economy. As globalization has heightened the competition for foreign aid among developing countries, Africa has been trying to improve its struggle to receive foreign aid by taking more responsibility at the regional and international level. In addition, Africa has created the 'Africa Action Plan' in order to obtain new relationships with development partners to share responsibilities regarding discovering ways to receive aid from foreign investors.[687]

Trade blocks and multilateral organizations

The African Union is the largest international economic grouping on the continent. The confederation's goals include the creation of a free trade area, a customs union, a single market, a central bank, and a common currency (see African Monetary Union), thereby establishing economic and monetary union. The current plan is to establish an African Economic Community with a single currency by 2023. The African Investment Bank is meant to stimulate development. The AU plans also include a transitional African Monetary Fund leading to an African Central Bank. Some parties support development of an even more unified United States of Africa.

International monetary and banking unions include:

- Central Bank of West African States
- Bank of Central African States
- Common Monetary Area

Major economic unions are shown in the chart below.

African Economic Community				
Pillars regional blocs (REC)[1]	Area (km²)	Population	GDP (PPP) ($US)		Member states
			in millions	per capita	
AEC	29,910,442	853,520,010	2,053,706	2,406	54
ECOWAS	5,112,903	349,154,000	1,322,452	3,888	15
ECCAS	6,667,421	121,245,958	175,928	1,451	11
SADC	9,882,959	233,944,179	737,335	3,152	15
EAC	2,440,409	169,519,847	411,813	2,429	6
COMESA	12,873,957	406,102,471	735,599	1,811	20
IGAD	5,233,604	187,969,775	225,049	1,197	7
Other African blocs	Area (km²)	Population	GDP (PPP) ($US)		Member states
			in millions	per capita	
CEMAC [2]	3,020,142	34,970,529	85,136	2,435	6
SACU	2,693,418	51,055,878	541,433	10,605	5
UEMOA [1]	3,505,375	80,865,222	101,640	1,257	8
UMA [2]	5,782,140	84,185,073	491,276	5,836	5
GAFTA [3]	5,876,960	166,259,603	635,450	3,822	5

[1] Economic bloc inside a pillar REC
[2] Proposed for pillar REC, but objecting participation
[3] Non-African members of GAFTA are excluded from figures
 smallest value among the blocs compared
 largest value among the blocs compared
During 2004. Source: CIA World Factbook 2005, IMF WEO Database
This box:
- view
- talk
- edit[688]

Economic variants and indicators

After an initial rebound from the 2009 world economic crisis, Africa's economy was undermined in the year 2011 by the Arab uprisings. The continent's growth fell back from 5% in 2010 to 3.4% in 2011. With the recovery of North African economies and sustained improvement in other regions, growth across the continent is expected to accelerate to 4.5% in 2012 and 4.8% in 2013. Short-term problems for the world economy remain as Europe confronts its debt crisis. Commodity prices—crucial for Africa—have declined from their peak due to weaker demand and increased supply, and some could fall further. But prices are expected to remain at levels favourable for African exporter.

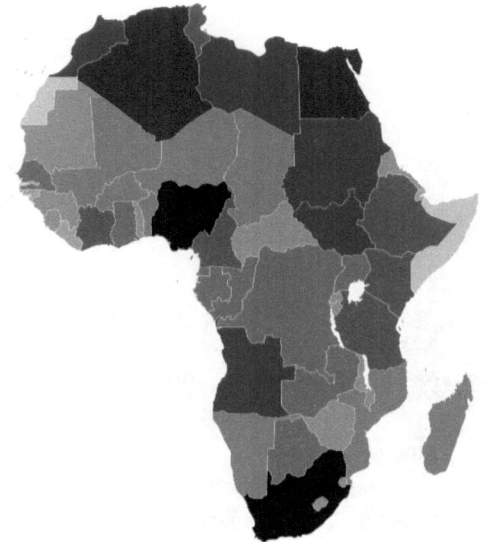

Figure 160:
Map of Africa by nominal GDP in billions USD (2008).
200+
100–200
50–100
20–50
10–20
5–10
1–5
0–1

Regions

Economic activity has rebounded across Africa. However, the pace of recovery was uneven among groups of countries and subregions. Oil-exporting countries generally expanded more strongly than oil-importing countries. West Africa and East Africa were the two best-performing subregions in 2010.

Intra-African trade has been slowed by protectionist policies among countries and regions. Despite this, trade between countries belonging to the Common Market for Eastern and Southern Africa (COMESA), a particularly strong economic region, grew six-fold over the past decade up to 2012. Ghana and Kenya, for example, have developed markets within the region for construction materials, machinery, and finished products, quite different from the mining and agriculture products that make up the bulk of their international exports.

The African Ministers of Trade agreed in 2010 to create a Pan-Africa Free Trade Zone. This would reduce countries' tariffs on imports and increase intra-African trade, and it is hoped, the diversification of the economy overall.

African nations

Country	Total GDP (nominal)[689] (billion US$)	GDP per capita[690] (US$, PPP)	GDP Growth, 2007-2011 (in %)	HDI 2017[691]
Algeria	188.7	15,758	2.7	0.754
Angola	124.1	6,850	9.1	0.581
Benin	8.3	2,405	3.9	0.515
Botswana	14.8	18,843	3.0	0.712
Burkina Faso	10.2	1,994	4.9	0.423
Burundi	2.3	731	4.3	0.417
Cameroon	29.6	3,799	3.1	0.556
Cape Verde	1.9	7,316	5.8	0.654
Central African Republic	2.2	706	2.8	0.367
Chad	9.5	2,420	2.9	0.404
Comoros	0.6	1,629	1.5	0.503
Democratic Republic of the Congo	32.7	813	5.9	0.457
Congo	14.7	6,676	4.9	0.606
Ivory Coast	24.1	4,155	1.1	0.492
Djibouti	1.0 (2009)	3,778	5.3	0.476
Egypt	229.5	13,330	5.2	0.696
Equatorial Guinea	19.8	32,855	8.8	0.591
Eritrea	2.6	1,653	1.3	0.440
Ethiopia	47.5	2,361	9.7	0.463
Gabon	19.3	19,952	3.6	0.702
Gambia	0.9	1,790	6.0	0.460
Ghana	48.1	5,013	8.3	0.592
Guinea	5.1	2,154	2.4	0.459
Guinea-Bissau	1.0	1,948	3.6	0.455
Kenya	55.2	3,664	4.2	0.590
Lesotho	2.4	3,713	4.9	0.520
Liberia	2.0	1,396	11.6	0.435

Libya	62.4 (2009)	11,774	4.0	0.706
Madagascar	10.6	1,622	2.3	0.519
Malawi	5.7	1,201	6.8	0.477
Mali	10.6	2,256	4.5	0.427
Mauritania	4.1	4,564	2.8	0.520
Mauritius	11.9	22,910	4.5	0.790
Morocco	100.2	8,936	4.3	0.667
Mozambique	15.6	1,275	6.9	0.437
Namibia	13.1	11,613	3.7	0.647
Niger	6.0	1,214	4.3	0.354
Nigeria	568.5	6,027	6.8	0.532
Réunion (France)	15.98	8,233 (nominal)		0.850 (2003)
Rwanda	7.5	2,225	7.3	0.524
São Tomé and Príncipe	0.3	3,338	5.7	0.589
Senegal	14.3	2,901	3.5	0.505
Seychelles	1.4	30,084	4.2	0.797
Sierra Leone	2.2	1,608	5.2	0.419
Somalia	(N/A)	(N/A)	(N/A)	0.364 (2008)[692]
South Africa	349.8	13,840	2.7	0.699
South Sudan	11.8	1,420		0.388
Sudan	55.1	4,725	4.1	0.502
Swaziland	4.0	9,894	2.1	0.588
Tanzania	43.6	3,457	6.8	0.538
Togo	4.3	1,736	3.1	0.503
Tunisia	45.9	12,186	3.0	0.735
Uganda	24.7	2,458	7.4	0.516
Zambia	26.8	4,124	6.4	0.588
Zimbabwe	13.5	2,330	0.6	0.535

Economic sectors and industries

Because Africa's export portfolio remains predominantly based on raw material, its export earnings are contingent on commodity price fluctuations. This exacerbates the continent's susceptibility to external shocks and bolsters the need for export diversification. Trade in services, mainly travel and tourism,

Figure 161: *A Kenyan farmer at work in the Mount Kenya region*

continued to rise in year 2012, underscoring the continent's strong potential in this sphere.[693,693]

Agriculture

The situation whereby African nations export crops to the West while millions on the continent starve has been blamed on developed countries including Japan, the European Union and the United States. These countries protect their own agricultural sectors with high import tariffs and offer subsidies to their farmers, which many contend leads the overproduction of such commodities as grain, cotton and milk. The result of this is that the global price of such products is continually reduced until Africans are unable to compete, except for cash crops that do not grow easily in a northern climate.

In recent years countries such as Brazil, which has experienced progress in agricultural production, have agreed to share technology with Africa to increase agricultural production in the continent to make it a more viable trade partner. Increased investment in African agricultural technology in general has the potential to reduce poverty in Africa. The demand market for African cocoa has experienced a price boom in 2008. The Nigerian, South African and Ugandan governments have targeted policies to take advantage of the increased demand for certain agricultural products and plan to stimulate agricultural sectors. The African Union has plans to heavily invest in African agriculture and the situation is closely monitored by the UN.

Figure 162: *The Athlone Power Station in Cape Town, South Africa*

Energy

Africa has significant resources for generating energy in several forms (hydroelectric, reserves of petroleum and gas, coal production, uranium production, renewable energy such as solar and geothermal). The lack of development and infrastructure means that little of this potential is actually in use today. The largest consumers of electric power in Africa are South Africa, Libya, Namibia, Egypt, Tunisia, and Zimbabwe, which each consume between 1000 and 5000 KWh/m^2 per person, in contrast with African states such as Ethiopia, Eritrea, and Tanzania, where electricity consumption per person is negligible.

Petroleum and petroleum products are the main export of 14 African countries. Petroleum and petroleum products accounted for a 46.6% share of Africa's total exports in 2010; the second largest export of Africa as a whole is natural gas, in its gaseous state and as liquified natural gas, accounting for a 6.3% share of Africa's exports.

Infrastructure

Lack of infrastructure creates barriers for African businesses. Although it has many ports, a lack of supporting transportation infrastructure adds 30–40% to costs, in contrast to Asian ports. Many large infrastructure projects are underway across Africa. By far, most of these projects are in the production and

Figure 163: *Lagos, Nigeria, Africa's largest city*

transportation of electric power. Many other projects include paved highways, railways, airports, and other construction.

Telecommunications infrastructure is also a growth area in Africa. Although Internet penetration lags other continents, it has still reached 9%. As of 2011, it was estimated that 500,000,000 mobile phones of all types were in use in Africa, including 15,000,000 "smart phones".

Mining and drilling

Oil production by country[694]

Rank	Area	bb/day	Year	Like...
–	W: World	85540000	2007 est.	
01	E: Russia	9980000	2007 est.	
02	Ar: Saudi Arb	9200000	2008 est.	
04	As: Libya	4725000	2008 est.	Iran
10	Af: Nigeria	2352000	2011 est.	Norway
15	Af: Algeria	2173000	2007 est.	
16	Af: Angola	1910000	2008 est.	

17	Af: Egypt	1845000	2007 est.	
27	Af: Tunisia	664000	2007 est.	Australia
31	Af: Sudan	466100	2007 est.	Ecuador
33	Af: Eq. Guinea	368500	2007 est.	Vietnam
38	Af: DR Congo	261000	2008 est.	
39	Af: Gabon	243900	2007 est.	
40	Af: Sth Africa	199100	2007 est.	
45	Af: Chad	156000	2008 est.	Germany
53	Af: Cameroon	87400	2008 est.	France
56	E: France	71400	2007	
60	Af: Ivory Coast	54400	2008 est.	
–	**Af: Africa**	**10780400**	**2011**	**Russia**

The mineral industry of Africa is one of the largest mineral industries in the world. Africa is the second biggest continent, with 30 million km² of land, which implies large quantities of resources. For many African countries, mineral exploration and production constitute significant parts of their economies and remain keys to future economic growth. Africa is richly endowed with mineral reserves and ranks first or second in quantity of world reserves of bauxite, cobalt, industrial diamond, phosphate rock, platinum-group metals (PGM), vermiculite, and zirconium. Gold mining is Africa's main mining resource.

African mineral reserves rank first or second for bauxite, cobalt, diamonds, phosphate rocks, platinum-group metals (PGM), vermiculite, and zirconium. Many other minerals are also present in quantity. The 2005 share of world production from African soil is the following: bauxite 9%; aluminium 5%; chromite 44%; cobalt 57%; copper 5%; gold 21%; iron ore 4%; steel 2%; lead (Pb) 3%; manganese 39%; zinc 2%; cement 4%; natural diamond 46%; graphite 2%; phosphate rock 31%; coal 5%; mineral fuels (including coal) & petroleum 13%; uranium 16%.

Figure 164: *The Soucreye sugar factory in Sidi Bennour (Doukkala), Morocco*

Manufacturing

Both the African Union and the United Nations have outlined plans in modern years on how Africa can help itself industrialize and develop significant manufacturing sectors to levels proportional to the African economy in the 1960s with 21st-century technology. This focus on growth and diversification of manufacturing and industrial production, as well as diversification of agricultural production, has fueled hopes that the 21st century will prove to be a century of economic and technological growth for Africa. This hope, coupled with the rise of new leaders in Africa in the future, inspired the term "the African Century", referring to the 21st century potentially being the century when Africa's vast untapped labor, capital, and resource potentials might become a world player.

This hope in manufacturing and industry is helped by the boom in communications technology and local mining industry in much of sub-Saharan Africa. Namibia has attracted industrial investments in recent years and South Africa has begun offering tax incentives to attract foreign direct investment projects in manufacturing.

Countries such as Mauritius have plans for developing new "green technology" for manufacturing. Developments such as this have huge potential to open new markets for African countries as the demand for alternative "green" and clean technology is predicted to soar in the future as global oil reserves dry up and fossil fuel-based technology becomes less economically viable.

Figure 165: *Many financial firms have offices in downtown Johannesburg, South Africa.*

Nigeria in recent years has been embracing industrialization, It currently has an indigenous vehicle manufacturing company, *Innoson Vehicle Manufacturing (IVM)* which manufactures Rapid Transit Buses, Trucks and SUVs with an upcoming introduction of Cars. Their various brands of vehicle are currently available in Nigeria, Ghana and other West African Nations. Nigeria also has few Electronic manufacturers like Zinox, the first Branded Nigerian Computer and Electronic gadgets (like tablet PCs) manufacturers. In 2013, Nigeria introduced a policy regarding import duty on vehicles to encourage local manufacturing companies in the country. In this regard, some foreign vehicle manufacturing companies like Nissan have made known their plans to have manufacturing plants in Nigeria. Apart from Electronics and vehicles, most consumer, pharmaceutical and cosmetic products, building materials, textiles, home tools, plastics and so on are also manufactured in the country and exported to other west African and African countries. Nigeria is currently the largest manufacturer of cement in Sub-saharan Africa. and Dangote Cement Factory, Obajana is the largest cement factory in sub-saharan Africa. Ogun is considered to be Nigeria's industrial hub (as most factories are located in Ogun and even more companies are moving there), followed by Lagos.

The manufacturing sector is small but growing in East Africa. The main industries are textile and clothing, leather processing, agribusiness, chemical products, electronics and vehicles. East African countries like Uganda also produce motorcycles for the domestic market.

Investment and banking

Africa's US$107 billion financial services industry will log impressive growth for the rest of the decadeWikipedia:Avoid weasel words as more banks target the continent's emerging middle class. The banking sector has been experiencing record growth, among others due to various technological innovations.

China and India have showed increasing interest in emerging African economies in the 21st century. Reciprocal investment between Africa and China increased dramatically in recent years amidst the current world financial crisis.

The increased investment in Africa by China has attracted the attention of the European Union and has provoked talks of competitive investment by the EU. Members of the African diaspora abroad, especially in the EU and the United States, have increased efforts to use their businesses to invest in Africa and encourage African investment abroad in the European economy.

Remittances from the African diaspora and rising interest in investment from the West will be especially helpful for Africa's least developed and most devastated economies, such as Burundi, Togo and Comoros. However, experts lament the high fees involved in sending remittances to Africa due to a duopoly of Western Union and MoneyGram that is controlling Africa's remittance market, making Africa is the most expensive cash transfer market in the world. According to some experts, the high processing fees involved in sending money to Africa are hampering African countries' development.

Angola has announced interests in investing in the EU, Portugal in particular. South Africa has attracted increasing attention from the United States as a new frontier of investment in manufacture, financial markets and small business, as has Liberia in recent years under their new leadership.

There are two African currency unions: the West African Banque Centrale des États de l'Afrique de l'Ouest (BCEAO) and the Central African Banque des États de l'Afrique Centrale (BEAC). Both use the CFA franc as their legal tender. The idea of a single currency union across Africa has been floated, and plans exist to have it established by 2020, though many issues, such as bringing continental inflation rates below 5 percent, remain hurdles in its finalization.

Stock exchanges

As of 2012, Africa has 23 stock exchanges, twice as many as it had 20 years earlier. Nonetheless, African stock exchanges still account for less than 1% of the world's stock exchange activity. The top ten stock exchanges in Africa by stock capital are (amounts are given in billions of United States dollars):

- South Africa (82.88)(2014)

Figure 166: *The Bourse de Tunis headquarters in Tunis, Tunisia*

- Egypt ($73.04 billion (30 November 2014 est.))
- Morocco (5.18)
- Nigeria (5.11) (Actually has a market capitalisation value of $39.27Bln)
- Kenya (1.33)
- Tunisia (0.88)
- BRVM (regional stock exchange whose members include Benin, Burkina Faso, Guinea-Bissau, Ivory Coast, Mali, Niger, Senegal and Togo: 6.6)
- Mauritius (0.55)
- Botswana (0.43)
- Ghana (.38)

Between 2009 and 2012, a total of 72 companies were launched on the stock exchanges of 13 African countries.

Trade blocs and multilateral organizations

The African Union is the largest international economic grouping on the continent. The confederation's goals include the creation of a free trade area, a customs union, a single market, a central bank, and a common currency (see African Monetary Union), thereby establishing economic and monetary union. The current plan is to establish an African Economic Community with a single currency by 2023. The African Investment Bank is meant to stimulate development. The AU plans also include a transitional African Monetary Fund leading to an African Central Bank. Some parties support development of an even more unified United States of Africa.

International monetary and banking unions include:

- Central Bank of West African States
- Bank of Central African States
- Common Monetary Area

Major economic unions are shown in the chart below.

African Economic Community					
Pillars regional blocs (REC)[1]	**Area** (km²)	**Population**	**GDP (PPP) ($US)**		**Member states**
			in millions	per capita	
AEC	29,910,442	853,520,010	2,053,706	2,406	54
ECOWAS	5,112,903	349,154,000	1,322,452	3,888	15
ECCAS	6,667,421	121,245,958	175,928	1,451	11
SADC	9,882,959	233,944,179	737,335	3,152	15
EAC	2,440,409	169,519,847	411,813	2,429	6
COMESA	12,873,957	406,102,471	735,599	1,811	20
IGAD	5,233,604	187,969,775	225,049	1,197	7
Other African blocs	**Area** (km²)	**Population**	**GDP (PPP) ($US)**		**Member states**
			in millions	per capita	
CEMAC [2]	3,020,142	34,970,529	85,136	2,435	6
SACU	2,693,418	51,055,878	541,433	10,605	5
UEMOA [1]	3,505,375	80,865,222	101,640	1,257	8
UMA [2]	5,782,140	84,185,073	491,276	5,836	5
GAFTA [3]	5,876,960	166,259,603	635,450	3,822	5

[1] Economic bloc inside a pillar REC
[2] Proposed for pillar REC, but objecting participation
[3] Non-African members of GAFTA are excluded from figures
  smallest value among the blocs compared
  largest value among the blocs compared
During 2004. Source: CIA World Factbook 2005, IMF WEO Database
This box:
- view
- talk
- edit[688]

Regional economic organizations

During the 1960s, Ghanaian politician Kwame Nkrumah promoted economic and political union of African countries, with the goal of independence. Since then, objectives, and organizations, have multiplied. Recent decades have brought efforts at various degrees of regional economic integration. Trade between African states accounts for only 11% of Africa's total commerce as of 2012, around five times less than in Asia. Most of this intra-Africa trade originates from South Africa and most of the trade exports coming out of South Africa goes to abutting countries in Southern Africa.

There are currently eight regional organizations that assist with economic development in Africa:

Name of organization	Date created	Member countries	Cumulative GDP (in millions of US dollars)
Economic Community of West African States	28 May 1975	Benin, Burkina Faso, Cape Verde, Gambia, Ghana, Guinea-Bissau, Guinea, Ivory Coast, Liberia, Mali, Niger, Nigeria, Senegal, Sierra Leone, Togo	657
East African Community	30 November 1999	Burundi, Kenya, Uganda, Rwanda, Tanzania	232
Economic Community of Central African States	18 October 1983	Angola, Burundi, Cameroon, Central African Republic, Congo, Democratic Republic of Congo, Gabon, Guinea, São Tomé and Príncipe, Chad	289
Southern African Development Community	17 August 1992	Angola, Botswana, Lesotho, Madagascar, Malawi, Mauritius, Mozambique, Namibia, Democratic Republic of Congo, Seychelles, South Africa, Swaziland, Tanzania, Zambia, Zimbabwe	909
Intergovernmental Authority on Development	25 November 1996	Djibouti, Ethiopia, Kenya, Uganda, Somalia, Sudan, South Sudan	326
Community of Sahel-Saharan States	4 February 1998	Benin, Burkina Faso, Central African Republic, Comores, Djibouti, Egypt, Eritrea, Gambia, Ghana, Guinea, Guinea-Bissau, Ivory Coast, Kenya, Liberia, Libya, Mali, Morocco, Mauritania, Niger, Nigeria, São Tomé and Príncipe, Senegal, Sierra Leone, Somalia, Sudan, Chad, Togo, Tunisia	1,692
Common Market for Eastern and Southern Africa	5 November 1993	Burundi, Comores, Djibouti, Egypt, Eritrea, Ethiopia, Kenya, Liberia, Madagascar, Malawi, Mauritius, Uganda, Democratic Republic of Congo, Rwanda, Seychelles, Sudan, Swaziland, Zambia, Zimbabwe	1,011

| Arab Maghreb Union | 17 February 1989 | Algeria, Libya, Morocco, Mauritania, Tunisia | 579 |

References

<templatestyles src="Template:Refbegin/styles.css" />

- Goldsmith, Arthur A. "Foreign Aid and Statehood in Africa"[695]. The MIT Press 55.1 (2001): 123–48. JSTOR. Web. 25 March 2012.
- Fage, J. D. *A History of Africa* (Routledge, 4th edition, 2001 <templatestyles src="Module:Citation/CS1/styles.css" />ISBN 0-415-25247-4) (Hutchinson, 1978, <templatestyles src="Module:Citation/CS1/styles.css" />ISBN 0-09-132851-9) (Knopf 1st American edition, 1978, <templatestyles src="Module:Citation/CS1/styles.css" />ISBN 0-394-32277-0)
- Kayizzi-Mugerwa, Steve *The African Economy: Policy, Institutions and the Future*[696] (Routledge, 1999, <templatestyles src="Module:Citation/CS1/styles.css" />ISBN 0-415-18323-5)
- Moshomba, Richard E. *Africa in the Global Economy*[697] (Lynne Rienner, 2000, <templatestyles src="Module:Citation/CS1/styles.css" />ISBN 1-55587-718-4)
- OECD. *African Economic Outlook 2006/2007*[698] (OECD, 2007, <templatestyles src="Module:Citation/CS1/styles.css" />ISBN 978-92-64-03313-9)
- Rodney, Walter. *How Europe Underdeveloped Africa.* (Washington: Howard UP, 1982, <templatestyles src="Module:Citation/CS1/styles.css" />ISBN 0-88258-096-5)
- Sahn, David E., Paul A. Dorosh, Stephen D. Younger, *Structural Adjustment Reconsidered: Economic Policy and Poverty in Africa* (Cambridge University Press, 1997, <templatestyles src="Module:Citation/CS1/styles.css" />ISBN 0-521-58451-5)
- Laouisset, Djamel (2009). A Retrospective Study of the Algerian Iron and Steel Industry. New York City: Nova Publishers. <templatestyles src="Module:Citation/CS1/styles.css" />ISBN 978-1-61761-190-2

External links

- Economy of Africa[699] at Curlie (based on DMOZ)

Wikimedia Commons has media related to *Economy of Africa*.

- The Age of the Dragon: China's Conquest of Africa[700]
- Howard W. French's book "China's Second Continent" – On China's increasing African presence[701]
- Holding the door open for multinationals to extract Africa's wealth[702], *Foreign Policy in Focus*
- Africa in the World Economy: the national, regional and international challenges[703] by Jan Joost Teunissen and Age Akkerman
- Africa: Living on the Fringe[704], *Monthly Review*. Samir Amin offers a Marxist analysis of Africa's continued economic crisis
- BBC: Africa's Economy[705]
- OECD work on African economy[706]
- Africa Economic Analysis[707]
- World Economic Forum – Africa[708]
- African Development Bank Group[709]
- IMF World Economic Outlook (WEO) – September 2003 – Public Debt in Emerging Markets[710]
- Language and Africa[711]
- Africa's economy: A glimmer of light at last?[712] – The Economist
- Africa and the Knowledge Economy[713] – World Bank Institute report.
- Economic analysis of Middle Africa[714]
- From Aid to Trade with Africa[715] News and analysis by Inter Press Service
- African Development Hindered by Vast US Corporate Interests in Continent's Resources[716] – video report by *Democracy Now!*
- Africa: Going Forward or Backward?[717] from the Dean Peter Krogh Foreign Affairs Digital Archives[718]

Economy of the African Union

Life in the African Union
• Economy • Enlargement • Foreign relations • Geography • History • Languages
• v • t • e[719]

The combined states of the **African Union** (AU) constitute the world's 11th largest economy with a nominal gross domestic product (GDP) of US$2263 billion.Wikipedia:Citation needed By measuring GDP by purchasing power parity (PPP), the African Union's economy totals US$1.515 trillion, ranking it 11th after Russia. At the same time, they have a combined total debt of US $200 billion.

The AU has only 2% of the world's international trade. But because over 90% of international trade consists of currency futuresWikipedia:Citation needed, Africa's 2% actually makes up the bulk of real commodity traded worldwide to include about 70% of the world's strategic minerals, including gold and aluminium. Africa is also a large market for European, American and Chinese industry.

The AU future confederation's goals include the creation of a free trade area, a customs union, a single market, a central bank, and a common currency, thereby establishing economic and monetary union. The current plan is to establish an African Economic Community with a single currency by 2023.

African Economic Community

African Economic Community						
Pillars regional blocs (REC)[1]	Area (km²)	Population	GDP (PPP) ($US)		Member states
			in millions	per capita	
AEC	29,910,442	853,520,010	2,053,706	2,406	54
ECOWAS	5,112,903	349,154,000	1,322,452	3,888	15
ECCAS	6,667,421	121,245,958	175,928	1,451	11
SADC	9,882,959	233,944,179	737,335	3,152	15

EAC	2,440,409	169,519,847	411,813	2,429	6
COMESA	12,873,957	406,102,471	735,599	1,811	20
IGAD	5,233,604	187,969,775	225,049	1,197	7
Other African blocs	Area (km²)	Population	GDP (PPP) ($US)		Member states
			in millions	per capita	
CEMAC [2]	3,020,142	34,970,529	85,136	2,435	6
SACU	2,693,418	51,055,878	541,433	10,605	5
UEMOA [1]	3,505,375	80,865,222	101,640	1,257	8
UMA [2]	5,782,140	84,185,073	491,276	5,836	5
GAFTA [3]	5,876,960	166,259,603	635,450	3,822	5

[1] Economic bloc inside a pillar REC
[2] Proposed for pillar REC, but objecting participation
[3] Non-African members of GAFTA are excluded from figures
smallest value among the blocs compared
largest value among the blocs compared
During 2004. Source: CIA World Factbook 2005, IMF WEO Database

This box:
- view
- talk
- edit[720]

Demographics

Demographics of Africa

Demographics of Africa	
Population	1.256 billion (2017 est.)
Density	1/sq km (2017 est.)
Growth rate	2.5% per annum (2017 est.)

The **population of Africa** has grown rapidly over the past century[721] and consequently shows a large youth bulge, further reinforced by a low life expectancy of below 50 years in some African countries.[722] Total population as of 2017 is estimated at more than 1.25 billion, with a growth rate of more than 2.5% p.a. The most populous African country is Nigeria with 191 million inhabitants as of 2017 and a growth rate of 2.6% p.a.

Population growth

As of 2016[723], the total population of Africa is estimated at 1.225 billion, representing 17% of the world's population. According to UN estimates, the population of Africa may reach 2.5 billion by 2050 (about 26% of the world's total) and nearly 4.5 billion by 2100 (about 40% of the world's total).

The population of Africa first surpassed one billion in 2009, with a doubling time of 27 years (growth rate 2.6% p.a.).[724]

Population growth has continued at almost the same pace, and total population is expected to surpass 2 billion by 2038 (doubling time 29 years, 2.4% p.a.).

The reason for the uncontrolled population growth since the mid 20th century is the decrease of infant mortality and general increase of life expectancy without a corresponding reduction in fertility rate, due to a very limited use

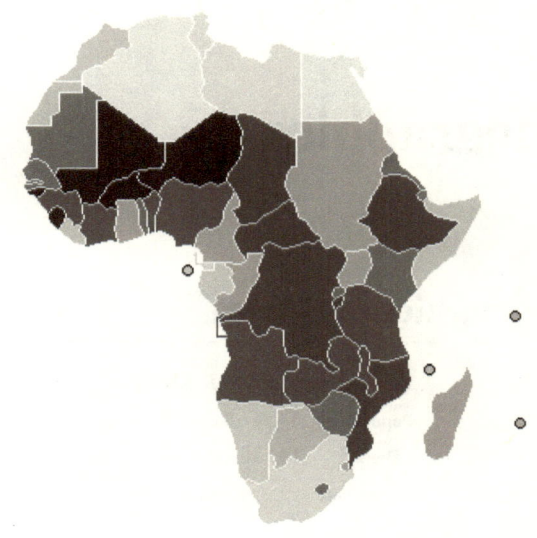

Figure 167: *Most African countries have annual population growth rates above 2%.*

Figure 168:
Life expectancy by region in 2015

of contraceptives. Uncontrolled population growth threatens to overwhelm infrastructure development and crippling economic development.[725] Kenya and Zambia are pursuing programs to promote family planning in an attempt to curb growth rates.[726]

The extreme population growth in Africa is driven by East Africa, Middle Africa and West Africa, which regions are projected to more than quintuple their populations over the 21st century. The most extreme of these is Middle Africa, with an estimated population increase by 680%, from less than 100 million in 2000 to more than 750 million in 2100 (more than half of this figure is driven by the Democratic Republic of the Congo, projected to increase from 47 million in 2000 to 379 million in 2100). Projected population growth is less extreme in Southern Africa and North Africa, which are expected, respectively, to not quite double and triple their populations over the same period.

Population estimates by region (in billions):

	2000	2050	2100
Eastern Africa	0.26	0.89 (+242%, +2.5% p.a.)	1.58 (+507%, +1.8% p.a.)
Middle Africa	0.096	0.38 (+300%, +2.8% p.a.)	0.75 (+680%, +2.1% p.a.)
North Africa	0.17	0.36 (+112%, +1.5% p.a.)	0.47 (+176%, +1.0% p.a.)
Southern Africa	0.052	0.086 (+65%, +1.0% p.a.)	0.092 (+77%, +0.6% p.a.)
West Africa	0.24	0.81 (+238%, +2.5% p.a.)	1.58 (+558%, +1.9% p.a.)

Africa	0.82	2.53 (+209%, +2.3% p.a.)	4.47 (+454%, +1.7% p.a.)
World	6.15	9.77 (+60%, +0.9% p.a.)	11.18 (+82%, +0.6% p.a.)

Health

History of health care development in sub-Saharan Africa

In September 1987, UNICEF and the World Health Organization (WHO) Regional Committee announced the launching of the Bamako Initiative— chartered in response to financial issues occurring in the region during the 1980s, and with the aim of increasing access to vital medications through community involvement in revolving drug funds. The 1987 Bamako Initiative conference, organized by the WHO was held in Bamako, the capital of Mali, and helped reshape the health policy of sub-Saharan Africa. The meeting was attended by African Ministers of Health who advocated for improvement of healthcare access through the revitalization of primary healthcare. The new strategy substantially increased accessibility through community-based healthcare reform, resulting in more efficient and equitable provision of services. The public health community within the region raised issues in response to the initiative, of which included: equity, access, affordability, integration issues, relative importance given to medications, management, dependency, logistics, and sustainability. As a result of these critiques, the Initiative later transformed to address the increase of accessibility of health services, the enhancement of quality of health services, and the overall improvement of health system management. A comprehensive approach strategy was extended to all areas of health care, with subsequent improvement in the health care indicators and improvement in health care efficiency and cost.

Period	Life expectancy in Years
1950–1955	37.46
1955–1960	39.95
1960–1965	42.32
1965–1970	44.42
1970–1975	46.51
1975–1980	48.66
1980–1985	50.45
1985–1990	51.72
1990–1995	51.71

1995–2000	52.33
2000–2005	53.67
2005–2010	56.97
2010–2015	60.23

Source: *World Population Prospects*

Major health challenges

The sub-Saharan African region experiences disproportionate rates of infectious and chronic diseases in comparison to other global regions.

Diabetes

Type 2 diabetes persists as an epidemic in the region posing a public health and socioeconomic crisis for sub-Saharan Africa. Scarcity of data for pathogenesis and subtypes for diabetes in sub-Saharan African communities has led to gaps in documenting epidemiology for the disease. High rates of undiagnosed diabetes in many countries leaves individuals at a high risk of chronic health complications, thus, posing a high risk of diabetes-related morbidity and mortality in the region.

HIV/AIDS

In 2011, sub-Saharan Africa was home to 69% of all people living with HIV/AIDS worldwide. In response, a number of initiatives have been launched to educate the public on HIV/AIDS. Among these are combination prevention programmes, considered to be the most effective initiative, the abstinence, be faithful, use a condom campaign, and the Desmond Tutu HIV Foundation's outreach programs. According to a 2013 special report issued by the Joint United Nations Programme on HIV/AIDS (UNAIDS), the number of HIV positive people in Africa receiving anti-retroviral treatment in 2012 was over seven times the number receiving treatment in 2005, with an almost 1 million added in the last year alone. The number of AIDS-related deaths in sub-Saharan Africa in 2011 was 33 percent less than the number in 2005. The number of new HIV infections in sub-Saharan Africa in 2011 was 25 percent less than the number in 2001.

Malaria

Malaria is an endemic illness in sub-Saharan Africa, where the majority of malaria cases and deaths worldwide occur.

Figure 169: *World map indicating infant mortality rates per 1000 births in 2006.*

Maternal and infant mortality

Studies show that more than half of the world's maternal deaths occur in sub-Saharan Africa. However, progress has been made in this area, as maternal mortality rates have decreased for multiple countries in the region by about half since 1990. Additionally, the African Union in July 2003 ratified the Maputo Protocol, which pledges to prohibit female genital mutilation(FGM).

The sub-Saharan African region alone accounts for about 45% of global infant and child mortalities. Studies have shown a relationship between infant survival and the education of mothers, as years of education positively correlate with infant survival rates. Geographic location is also a factor, as child mortality rates are higher in rural areas in comparison to urban regions.

Measles

Routine immunization has been introduced to countries within sub-Saharan Africa in order to prevent measles outbreaks within the region.

Neglected tropical diseases

Neglected tropical diseases such as hookworm infection encompass some of the most common health conditions which affect an estimated 500 million individuals in the sub-Saharan African region.

Non-communicable diseases

Results of Global Burden of Disease studies reveal that the age-standardized death rates of non-communicable diseases in at least four sub-Saharan countries including South Africa, Democratic Republic of Congo, Nigeria, and Ethiopia supersede that of identified high-income countries. Improvement in statistics systems and increase in epidemiological studies with in-depth analysis of disease risk factors could improve the understanding of non-communicable diseases (i.e.: diabetes, hypertension, cancer, cardiovascular disease, obesity, etc.) in sub-Saharan Africa as well as better inform decisions surrounding healthcare policy in the region.

Onchocerciasis

Onchocerciasis ("river blindness"), a common cause of blindness, is also endemic to parts of the region. More than 99% of people affected by the illness worldwide live in 31 countries therein. In response, the African Programme for Onchocerciasis Control (APOC) was launched in 1995 with the aim of controlling the disease.

Tuberculosis

Tuberculosis is a leading cause of morbidity and mortality on a global scale, especially in high HIV-prevalent populations in the sub-Saharan African region, with a high case fatality rate.

National healthcare systems

National health systems vary between countries. In Ghana, most health care is provided by the government and largely administered by the Ministry of Health and Ghana Health Services. The healthcare system has five levels of providers: health posts which are first level primary care for rural areas, health centers and clinics, district hospitals, regional hospitals and tertiary hospitals. These programs are funded by the government of Ghana, financial credits, Internally Generated Fund (IGF), and Donors-pooled Health Fund.

A shortage of health professionals compounded by migration of health workers from sub-Saharan Africa to other parts of the world (namely English-speaking nations such as the United States and the United Kingdom) has negatively impacted productivity and efficacy of the region's health systems.

More than 85% of individuals in Africa use traditional medicine as an alternative to often expensive allopathic medical health care and costly pharmaceutical products. The Organization of African Unity (OAU) Heads of State and Government declared the 2000s decade as the African Decade on African Traditional Medicine in an effort to promote The WHO African Region's adopted resolution for institutionalizing traditional medicine in health care systems across the continent. Public policy makers in the region are challenged with consideration of the importance of traditional/indigenous health systems and whether their coexistence with the modern medical and health sub-sector would improve the equitability and accessibility of health care distribution, the health status of populations, and the social-economic development of nations within sub-Saharan Africa.

Figure 170: *Map of Africa colored according to the percentage of the adult (ages 15–49) population with HIV/AIDS. UNIQ-ref-0-47d5f3b6a4f7ba0c-QINU*

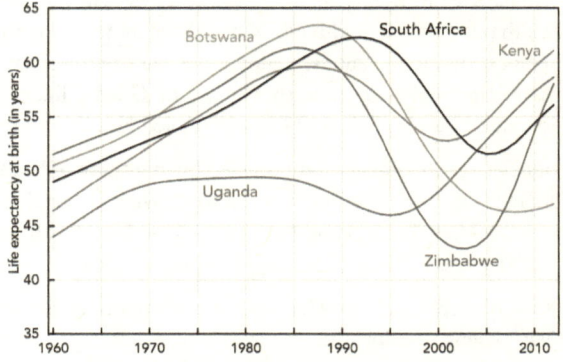

Figure 171: *Life expectancy has fallen drastically in Southern Africa a result of HIV/AIDS.*

Figure 172: *San man from Botswana.*

Ethnicity

Speakers of Bantu languages (part of the Niger–Congo family) predominate in southern, central and southeast Africa. The Bantu farmers from West Africa's inland savanna progressively expanded over most of Africa.[727] But there are also several Nilotic groups in South Sudan and East Africa, the mixed Swahili people on the Swahili Coast, and a few remaining indigenous Khoisan (San and Khoikhoi) and Pygmy peoples in southern and central Africa, respectively. Bantu-speaking Africans also predominate in Gabon and Equatorial Guinea, and are found in parts of southern Cameroon. In the Kalahari Desert of Southern Africa, the distinct people known as the "San" have long been present. Together with the Khoikhoi, they form the Khoisan. The San are the pre-Bantu indigenous people of southern Africa, while Pygmies are the pre-Bantu indigenous African peoples of Central Africa.[728] The peoples of West Africa primarily speak Niger–Congo languages belonging mostly, though not exclusively, to its non-Bantu branches, though some Nilo-Saharan and Afroasiatic-speaking groups are also found. The Niger–Congo-speaking Yoruba, Igbo, Fulani, Akan and Wolof ethnic groups are the largest and most influential. In the central Sahara, Mandinka or Mande groups are most significant. Chadic-speaking groups, including the Hausa, are found in the more northerly parts of the region nearest to the Sahara and Nilo-Saharan communities such as the

Figure 173: *Yoruba drummers in Kwara State, Nigeria (2004).*

Figure 174: *Mongo family in the Province of Équateur, DRC*

Figure 175: *Beja nomads from Northeast Africa*

Kanuri, Zarma and Songhai are present in eastern parts of West Africa bordering Central Africa.

The peoples of North Africa comprise three main groups: Berbers in the northwest, Egyptians and Libyans in northeast, and Nilo-Saharan-speaking peoples in the east. The Muslim settlers who arrived in the 7th century introduced the Arabic language and Islam to the region, initiating a process of linguistic Arabization of the region's inhabitants. The Semitic Phoenicians (who founded Carthage) and Hyksos, the Indo-Iranian Alans, the Indo-European Greeks, Romans and Vandals settled in North Africa as well. Berber-speaking populations still make significant communities within Morocco and Algeria and are still also present in smaller numbers in Tunisia and Libya.[729] The Berber-speaking Tuareg and other often-nomadic peoples are the principal inhabitants of the Saharan interior of North Africa. In Mauritania, there is a small Berber community and Niger–Congo-speaking peoples in the South, though in both regions Arabic and Arab culture predominates. In Sudan, although Arabic and Arab culture predominates, it is also inhabited by originally Nilo-Saharan-speaking groups such as the Nubians, Fur, Masalit and Zaghawa[730] who over the centuries have variously intermixed with migrants from the Arabian peninsula. Small communities of Afro-Asiatic-speaking Beja nomads can also be found in Egypt and Sudan.

Figure 176: *An Afrikaner family from South Africa, 1886.*

In the Horn of Africa, Afro-Asiatic-speaking groups predominate. Ethiopian and Eritrean groups like the Amhara and Tigrayans (collectively known as Habesha) speak languages from the Semitic branch of Afro-Asiatic language family, while the Oromo and Somali speak languages from the Cushitic branch of Afro-Asiatic. In southern Ethiopia and Eritrea, Nilotic peoples related to those in South Sudan are also found, while Bantu and Khoisan ethnic minorities inhabit parts of southern Somalia.

Prior to the decolonization movements of the post-World War II era, Europeans were represented in every part of Africa.[731] Decolonisation during the 1960s and 1970s often resulted in the mass emigration of European-descended settlers out of Africa – especially from Algeria and Morocco (1.6 million *pieds-noirs* in North Africa),[732] Kenya, Congo,[733] Rhodesia, Mozambique and Angola.[734] By the end of 1977, more than one million Portuguese were thought to have returned from Africa.[735] Nevertheless, White Africans remain a minority in many African states, particularly South Africa, Zimbabwe, Namibia and Réunion. The African country with the largest native European African population is South Africa.[736] The Afrikaners, the British diaspora and the Coloureds are the largest native European-descended groups in Africa today.

Native European colonization also brought sizable groups of Asians, particularly people from the Indian subcontinent, to British colonies. Large Indian communities are found in South Africa, and smaller ones are present in Kenya, Tanzania, and some other southern and East African countries. The large Indian community in Uganda was expelled by the dictator Idi Amin in 1972, though many have since returned. The islands in the Indian Ocean are also populated primarily by people of Asian origin, often mixed with Africans and Europeans. The Malagasy people of Madagascar are Austronesian people and native African people, but those along the coast are generally mixed with Bantu, Arab, Indian and European origins. Malay and Indian ancestries are also important components in the group of people known in South Africa as Cape Coloureds (people with origins in two or more races and continents). Beginning with the 21st century many Hispanics, primarily Mexicans, Central Americans, Chileans, Peruvians, and Colombians, have immigrated to Africa. Around 500,000 Hispanics have immigrated to Africa, most of whom live in South Africa, Kenya, Nigeria, Uganda, and Ghana. During the 20th century, small but economically important communities of Lebanese and Chinese[737] have also developed in the larger coastal cities of West and East Africa, respectively.[738]

Languages

There are three major linguistic phyla native to Africa: Niger–Congo languages (including Bantu) in West, Central, Southeast and Southern Africa; Nilo-Saharan languages (unity debated) spoken from Tanzania to Sudan and from Chad to Mali; Khoisan languages (probably no phylogenetic unit, see Khoe languages), concentrated in the Kalahari Desert of Namibia and Botswana; There are several other small families and language isolates, as well as languages that have yet to be classified.

In addition, the Afroasiatic languages are spread throughout Western Asia, North Africa, the Horn of Africa and parts of the Sahel. The Afroasiatic homeland may be either in Western Asia or in Africa.

More recently introduced to Africa are Austronesian languages spoken in Madagascar, as well as Indo-European languages spoken in South Africa and Namibia (Afrikaans, English, German), which were used as lingua francas in former European colonies.

The total number of languages natively spoken in Africa is variously estimated (depending on the delineation of language vs. dialect) at between 1,250 and 2,100, and by some counts at "over 3,000", Nigeria alone has over 500 languages (according to the count of SIL Ethnologue),

Around a hundred languages are widely used for inter-ethnic communication. Arabic, Somali, Berber, Amharic, Oromo, Igbo, Swahili, Hausa, Manding,

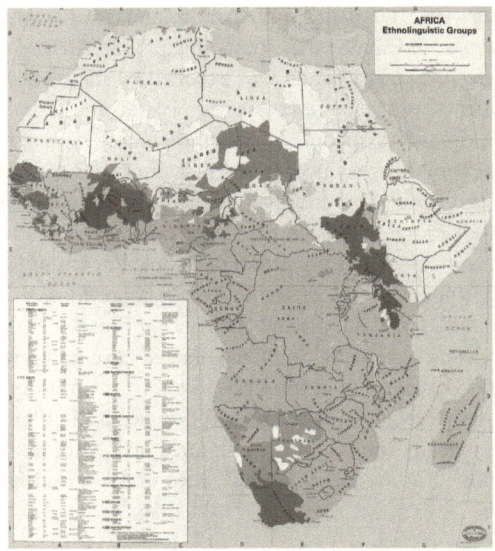

Figure 177: *1996 map of the major ethnolinguistic groups of Africa, by the Library of Congress Geography and Map Division (substantially based on G.P. Murdock, Africa, its peoples and their cultural history, 1959). Colour-coded are 15 major ethnolinguistic super-groups, as follows:* ***Afroasiatic*** *Hamitic (Berber, Cushitic) + Semitic (Ethiopian, Arabic) Hausa (Chadic)* ***Niger–Congo*** *Bantu "Guinean" (Volta-Niger, Kwa, Kru) "Western Bantoid" (Atlantic) "Central Bantoid" (Gur, Senufo) "Eastern Bantoid" (Southern Bantoid) Mande* ***Nilo-Saharan*** *(unity debated) Nilotic Central Sudanic, Eastern Sudanic (besides Nilotic) Kanuri Songhai* ***other*** *Khoi-San (unity doubtful; Khoikhoi, San, Sandawe + Hadza) Malayo-Polynesian (Malagasy) Indo-European (Afrikaaner)*

Fulani and Yoruba are spoken by tens of millions of people. Twelve dialect clusters (which may group up to a hundred linguistic varieties) are spoken by 75 percent, and fifteen by 85 percent, of Africans as a first or additional language.

Niger–Congo is the largest phylum of African languages, with more than 500 million speakers (2017); it is dominated by the Bantu branch, spread throughout sub-Saharan Africa in the Bantu expansion, Bantu speakers accounting for about half of Niger–Congo speakers. Arabic is the most widely spoken single language in Africa by far, with a population of Arab Africa of the order of 330 million (2017). Other Afroasiatic languages are spoken by of the order of 100 million speakers in Africa (2017). Nilo-Saharan are spoken by of the order of 100 million speakers (2017). Khoisan groups a number of mostly endangered click languages, the largest being Khoekhoe with of the order of 300,000 speakers (2016).

Languages

Languages of Africa

The **languages of Africa** are divided into six major language families:

- Afroasiatic languages are spread throughout Western Asia, North Africa, the Horn of Africa and parts of the Sahel.
- Austronesian languages are spoken in Madagascar.
- Indo-European languages are spoken in South Africa and Namibia (Afrikaans, English, German) and are used as lingua francas in the former colonies of Britain (English), former colonies of France and of Belgium (French), former colonies of Portugal and remaining Afro-Portuguese islands (Portuguese), and the current Spanish territories of Ceuta, Melilla and the Canary Islands (Spanish).
- Khoe languages are concentrated in the Kalahari Desert of Namibia and Botswana.
- Niger–Congo languages (Bantu and non-Bantu) cover West, Central, Southeast and Southern Africa.
- Nilo-Saharan languages (unity debated) are spoken from Tanzania to Sudan and from Chad to Mali.

There are several other small families and language isolates, as well as languages that have yet to be classified. In addition, Africa has a wide variety of sign languages, many of which are language isolates (see below).

The total number of languages natively spoken in Africa is variously estimated (depending on the delineation of language vs. dialect) at between 1,250 and 2,100, and by some counts at "over 3,000". Nigeria alone has over 500 languages (according to the count of SIL Ethnologue), one of the greatest concentrations of linguistic diversity in the world. However, "One of the notable differences between Africa and most other linguistic areas is its relative uniformity. With few exceptions, all of Africa's languages have been gathered into four major phyla."[739]

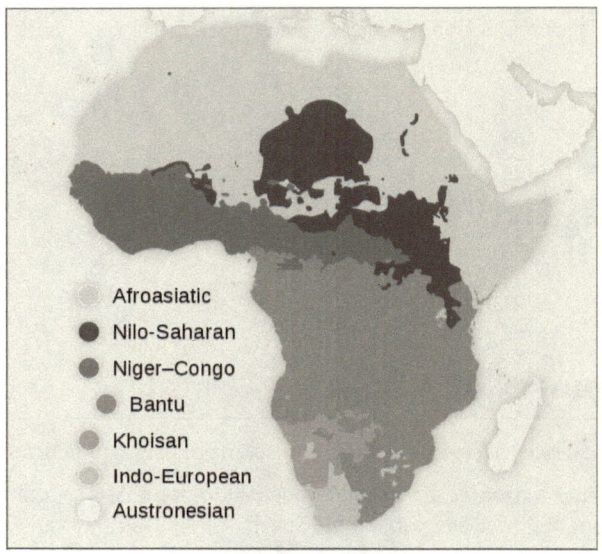

Figure 178:
The traditional language families spoken in Africa:
Afroasiatic
Nilo-Saharan
Niger–Congo
Bantu
Khoisan
Indo-European
Austronesian

Around a hundred languages are widely used for inter-ethnic communication. Arabic, Somali, Berber, Amharic, Oromo, Igbo, Swahili, Hausa, Manding, Fulani and Yoruba are spoken by tens of millions of people. Twelve dialect clusters (which may group up to a hundred linguistic varieties) are spoken by 75 percent, and fifteen by 85 percent, of Africans as a first or additional language. Although many mid-sized languages are used on the radio, in newspapers and in primary-school education, and some of the larger ones are considered national languages, only a few are official at the national level. The African Union declared 2006 the "Year of African Languages".[740]

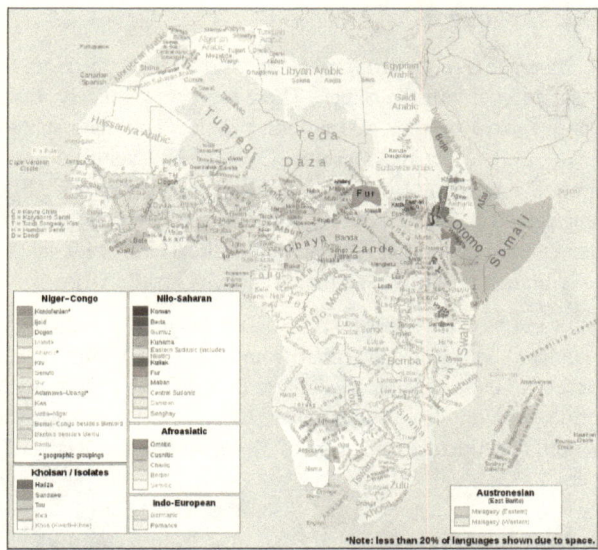

Figure 179: *Clickable map showing the traditional language families, subfamilies and major languages spoken in Africa*

Language groups

Most languages spoken in Africa belong to one of three large language families: Afroasiatic, Nilo-Saharan and Niger–Congo. Another hundred belong to small families such as Ubangian (sometimes grouped within Niger-Congo) and the various families called Khoisan, or the Indo-European and Austronesian language families mainly spoken outside Africa; the presence of the latter two dates to 2,600 and 1,500 years ago, respectively. In addition, the languages of Africa languages include several unclassified languages and sign languages.

The earliest Afroasiatic languages are associated with the Capsian culture, the Nilo-Saharan languages are linked with the Khartoum Mesolithic/Neolithic, the Niger-Congo languages are correlated with the west and central African hoe-based farming traditions and the Khoisan languages are matched with the south and southeastern Wilton industries. More broadly, the Afroasiatic family is tentatively grouped within the Nostratic superfamily, and the Nilo-Saharan and Niger-Congo phyla form the Niger-Saharan macrophylum.

Afroasiatic languages

Afroasiatic languages are spoken throughout North Africa, the Horn of Africa, Western Asia and parts of the Sahel. There are approximately 375 Afroasiatic languages spoken by over 400 million people. The main subfamilies of Afroasiatic are Berber, Chadic, Cushitic, Egyptian and Semitic. The Afroasiatic Urheimat is uncertain. However, the family's most extensive branch, the Semitic languages (including Arabic, Amharic and Hebrew among others), seems to have developed in the Arabian peninsula. The Semitic languages are now the only branch of Afroasiatic that is spoken outside Africa.

Some of the most widely spoken Afroasiatic languages include Arabic (a Semitic language, and a recent arrival from West Asia), Somali (Cushitic), Berber (Berber), Hausa (Chadic), Amharic (Semitic) and Oromo (Cushitic). Of the world's surviving language families, Afroasiatic has the longest written history, as both the Akkadian language of Mesopotamia and Ancient Egyptian are members.

Nilo-Saharan languages

Nilo-Saharan languages consist of a hundred diverse languages. The family has a speech area that stretches from the Nile Valley to northern Tanzania and into Nigeria and DR Congo, with the Songhay languages along the middle reaches of the Niger River as a geographic outlier. Genetic linkage between these languages has not been conclusively demonstrated, and among linguists, support for the proposal is sparse.[741,742] The languages share some unusual morphology, but if they are related, most of the branches must have undergone major restructuring since diverging from their common ancestor. The inclusion of the Songhay languages is questionable, and doubts have been raised over the Koman, Gumuz and Kadu branches.

Some of the better known Nilo-Saharan languages are Kanuri, Fur, Songhay, Nobiin and the widespread Nilotic family, which includes the Luo, Dinka and Maasai. The Nilo-Saharan languages are tonal.

Niger–Congo languages

The Niger–Congo languages constitute the largest language family spoken in Africa and perhaps the world in terms of the number of languages. One of its salient features is an elaborate noun class system with grammatical concord. A large majority of languages of this family are tonal such as Yoruba and Igbo, Ashanti and Ewe language. A major branch of Niger–Congo languages is the Bantu phylum, which has a wider speech area than the rest of the family (see Niger–Congo B (Bantu) in the map above).

Languages of Africa 343

The Niger–Kordofanian language family, joining Niger–Congo with the Kordofanian languages of south-central Sudan, was proposed in the 1950s by Joseph Greenberg. Today, linguists often use "Niger–Congo" to refer to this entire family, including Kordofanian as a subfamily. One reason for this is that it is not clear whether Kordofanian was the first branch to diverge from rest of Niger–Congo. Mande has been claimed to be equally or more divergent. Niger–Congo is generally accepted by linguists, though a few question the inclusion of Mande and Dogon, and there is no conclusive evidence for the inclusion of Ubangian.

Other language families

Several languages spoken in Africa belong to language families concentrated or originating outside the African continent.

Austronesian

Malagasy belongs to the Austronesian languages and is the westernmost branch of the family. It is the national and co-official language of Madagascar and one of Malagasy dialects called Bushi is also spoken in Mayotte.

The ancestors of the Malagasy people migrated to Madagascar around 1,500 years ago from Southeast Asia, more specifically the island of Borneo. The origins of how they arrived to Madagascar remains a mystery, however the Austronesians are known for their seafaring culture. Despite the geographical isolation, Malagasy still has strong resemblance to Barito languages especially the Ma'anyan language of southern Borneo.

With more than 20 million speakers, Malagasy is one of the most widely spoken of the Austronesian languages.

Indo-European

Afrikaans is Indo-European, as is most of the vocabulary of most African creole languages. Afrikaans evolved from the Dutch vernacular[743] of South Holland (Hollandic dialect)[744,745] spoken by the mainly Dutch settlers of what is now South Africa, where it gradually began to develop distinguishing characteristics in the course of the 18th century. Most Afrikaans speakers live in South Africa. In Namibia it is the lingua franca and in Botswana and Zimbabwe it is a minority language of roughly several ten thousand people. Overall 15 to 20 million people are estimated to speak Afrikaans.

Since the colonial era, Indo-European languages such as Afrikaans, English, French, (Italian - lost official status in 1939), Portuguese and (Spanish - official still in Equatorial Guinea - Canary Islands, Melilla, Ceuta are part of Spain) still hold official status in many countries, and/or are widely spoken, generally as lingua francas. (*See African French and African Portuguese*.) German was once used in Germany's colonies there from the late 1800s until World War I, when Britain and France took over and revoked German's official status. Despite this, German is still spoken in Namibia, mostly among the white population. Although it lost its official status in the 1990s, it has been redesignated as a national language. Indian languages such as Gujarati are spoken by South Asian expatriates exclusively. In earlier historical times, other Indo-European languages could be found in various parts of the continent, such as Old Persian and Greek in Egypt, Latin and Vandalic in North Africa and Modern Persian in the Horn of Africa.

Small families

The three small Khoisan families of southern Africa have not been shown to be closely related to any other major language family. In addition, there are various other families that have not been demonstrated to belong to one of these families. (The questionable branches of Nilo-Saharan were covered above, and are not repeated here.)

- Mande, some 70 languages, including the major languages of Mali and Guinea. These are generally thought to be divergent Niger–Congo, but debate persists.
- Ubangian, some 70 languages, centered on the languages of the Central African Republic; may be Niger–Congo
- Khoe, around 10 languages, the primary family of Khoisan languages of Namibia and Botswana
- Sandawe, an isolate of Tanzania, possibly related to Khoe
- Kx'a, a language of Southern Africa
- Tuu, or Taa-!Kwi, two surviving languages
- Hadza, an isolate of Tanzania
- Bangime, a likely isolate of Mali
- Jalaa, a likely isolate of Nigeria
- Laal, a possible isolate of Chad

Khoisan is a term of convenience covering some 30 languages spoken by around 300,000–400,000 people. There are five Khoisan families that have not been shown to be related to each other: Khoe, Tuu and Kx'a, which are found mainly in Namibia and Botswana, as well as Sandawe and Hadza of Tanzania, which are language isolates. A striking feature of Khoisan languages, and the reason they are often grouped together, is their use of click consonants. Some neighbouring Bantu languages (notably Xhosa and Zulu) have clicks as well, but these were adopted from Khoisan languages. The Khoisan languages are also tonal.

Creole languages

Due partly to its multilingualism and its colonial past, a substantial proportion of the world's creole languages are to be found in Africa. Some are based on Indo-European languages (e.g. Krio from English in Sierra Leone and the very similar Pidgin in Nigeria; Ghana and parts of Cameroon; Cape Verdean Creole in Cape Verde and Guinea-Bissau Creole in Guinea-Bissau and Senegal, all from Portuguese; Seychellois Creole in the Seychelles and Mauritian Creole in Mauritius, both from French); some are based on Arabic (e.g. Juba Arabic in the southern Sudan, or Nubi in parts of Uganda and Kenya); some are based on local languages (e.g. Sango, the main language of the Central African Republic); while in Cameroon a creole based on French, English and local African languages known as Camfranglais has started to become popular.

Unclassified languages

A fair number of unclassified languages are reported in Africa. Many remain unclassified simply for lack of data; among the better-investigated ones that continue to resist easy classification are:

- possibly Afroasiatic: Ongota, Gomba
- possibly Nilo-Saharan: Shabo
- possibly Niger–Congo: Jalaa, Mbre, Bayot
- possibly Khoe: Kwadi
- unknown: Laal, Mpre

Of these, Jalaa is perhaps the most likely to be an isolate.

Less-well investigated languages include Irimba, Luo, Mawa, Rer Bare (possibly Bantu), Bete (evidently Jukunoid), Bung (unclear), Kujarge (evidently Chadic), Lufu (Jukunoid), Meroitic (possibly Afroasiatic), Oropom (possibly spurious) and Weyto (evidently Cushitic). Several of these are extinct, and adequate comparative data is thus unlikely to be forthcoming. Hombert & Philippson (2009)[746] list a number of African languages that have been classified as language isolates at one point or another. Many of these are simply unclassified, but Hombert & Philippson believe Africa has about twenty language families, including isolates. Beside the possibilities listed above, there are:

- Aasax or Aramanik (Tanzania) (South Cushitic? contains non-Cushitic lexicon)
- Imeraguen (Mauritania) - Hassaniyya Arabic restructured on an Azêr (Soninke) base
- Kara (Fer?) (Central African Republic)
- Oblo (Cameroon) (Adamawa? Extinct?)

Roger Blench notes a couple additional possibilities:

- Defaka (Nigeria)
- Dompo (Ghana)

Sign languages

Many African countries have national sign languages, such as Algerian Sign Language, Tunisian Sign Language, Ethiopian Sign Language. Other sign languages are restricted to small areas or single villages, such as Adamorobe Sign Language in Ghana. Tanzania has seven, one for each of its schools for the Deaf, all of which are discouraged. Not much is known, since little has been published on these languages

Sign language systems extant in Africa include the Paget Gorman Sign System used in Namibia and Angola, the Sudanese Sign languages used in Sudan and South Sudan, the Arab Sign languages used across the Arab Mideast, the Francosign languages used in Francophone Africa and other areas such as Ghana and Tunisia, and the Tanzanian Sign languages used in Tanzania.

Language in Africa

Throughout the long multilingual history of the African continent, African languages have been subject to phenomena like language contact, language expansion, language shift and language death. A case in point is the Bantu expansion, in which Bantu-speaking peoples expanded over most of Sub-Equatorial Africa, displacing Khoi-San speaking peoples from much of Southeast Africa and Southern Africa and other peoples from Central Africa. Another example is the Arab expansion in the 7th century, which led to the extension of Arabic from its homeland in Asia, into much of North Africa and the Horn of Africa.

Trade languages are another age-old phenomenon in the African linguistic landscape. Cultural and linguistic innovations spread along trade routes and languages of peoples dominant in trade developed into languages of wider communication (lingua franca). Of particular importance in this respect are Berber (North and West Africa), Jula (western West Africa), Fulfulde (West Africa), Hausa (West Africa), Lingala (Congo), Swahili (Southeast Africa), Somali (Horn of Africa) and Arabic (North Africa and Horn of Africa).

After gaining independence, many African countries, in the search for national unity, selected one language, generally the former colonial language, to be used in government and education. However, in recent years, African countries have become increasingly supportive of maintaining linguistic diversity. Language policies that are being developed nowadays are mostly aimed at multilingualism.

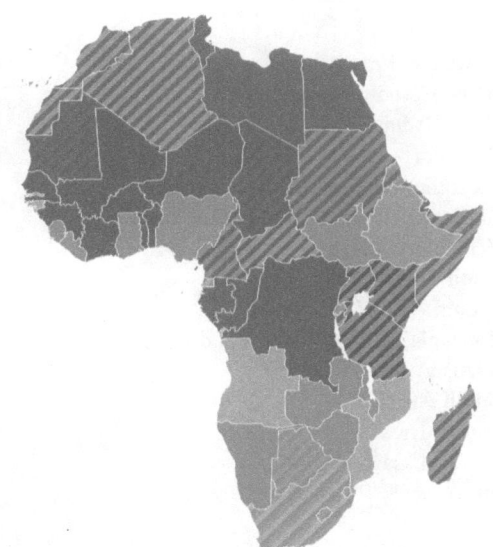

Figure 180:
Official languages in Africa:

Official Languages

Besides the former colonial languages of English, French, Portuguese and Spanish, the following languages are official at the national level in Africa (non-exhaustive list):

Afroasiatic

- Arabic in Comoros, Chad, Djibouti, Egypt, Eritrea, Mauritania,[747] Somalia,[748] Sudan, Tunisia, Algeria, Libya, Morocco and Zanzibar (Tanzania)
- Berber in Morocco and Algeria
- Amharic in Ethiopia
- Somali in Somalia
- Tigrinya in Eritrea and Ethiopia

Austronesian

- Malagasy in Madagascar

Indo-European

- Afrikaans

Niger-Congo

- Chewa in Malawi and Zimbabwe
- Comorian in the Comoros
- Kinyarwanda in Rwanda
- Kirundi in Burundi
- Sesotho in Lesotho, South Africa and Zimbabwe
- Setswana/Tswana in Botswana and South Africa
- Shona, Sindebele in Zimbabwe
- Sepedi in South Africa
- Ndebele in South Africa[749]
- Swahili in Tanzania, Kenya, Rwanda and Uganda
- Swati in Swaziland and South Africa
- Tsonga in South Africa
- Venda in South Africa
- Xhosa in South Africa
- Zulu in South Africa

Cross-border languages

The colonial borders established by European powers following the Berlin Conference in 1884–1885 divided a great many ethnic groups and African language speaking communities. In a sense, "cross-border languages" is a misnomerWikipedia:Citation needed—the speakers did not divide themselves. Nevertheless, it describes the reality of many African languages, which has implications for divergence of language on either side of a border (especially when the official languages are different), standards for writing the language, etc. Some notable cross-border languages include Berber (which stretches across much of North Africa and some parts of West Africa), Somali (stretches across most of the Horn of Africa), Swahili (spoken in the African Great Lakes region), Fula (in the Sahel and West Africa) and Luo languages (in Democratic Republic of the Congo, Ethiopia, Kenya, Tanzania, Uganda, South Sudan and Sudan).

Some prominent Africans such as former Malian president and former Chairman of the African Commission, Alpha Oumar Konaré, have referred to cross-border languages as a factor that can promote African unity.[750]

Language change and planning

Language is not static in Africa any more than on other continents. In addition to the (likely modest) impact of borders, there are also cases of dialect levelling (such as in Igbo and probably many others), koinés (such as N'Ko and possibly Runyakitara) and emergence of new dialects (such as Sheng). In some countries, there are official efforts to develop standardized language versions.

There are also many less widely spoken languages that may be considered endangered languages.

Demographics

Of the 1 billion Africans (in 2009), about 17 percent speak an Arabic dialectWikipedia:Citation needed. About 10 percent speak SwahiliWikipedia:Citation needed, the lingua franca of Southeast Africa; about 5 percent speak a Berber dialectWikipedia:Citation needed; and about 5 percent speak Hausa, which serves as a lingua franca in much of the Sahel. Other important West African languages are Yoruba, Igbo and Fula. Major Horn of Africa languages are Amharic, Oromo and Somali. Important South African languages are Zulu, Xhosa and Afrikaans.[751]

English, French and Portuguese are important languages in Africa. About 130 million, 115 million and 30 million Africans, respectively, speak them as either native or secondary languages. Portuguese has become the national language of Angola, and Portuguese is the official language of Mozambique. The economies of Angola and Mozambique are quickly becoming economic powerhouses in Africa. Through (among other factors) sheer demographic weight, Africans are increasingly taking ownership Wikipedia:Citation needed of these three world languages as they are having an ever-greater influence on the research, economic growth and development in the African countries where English, French and Portuguese are spoken.

Linguistic features

Some linguistic features are particularly common among languages spoken in Africa, whereas others are less common. Such shared traits probably are not due to a common origin of all African languages. Instead, some may be due to language contact (resulting in borrowing) and specific idioms and phrases may be due to a similar cultural background.

Phonological

Some widespread phonetic features include:

- certain types of consonants, such as implosives (/ɓa/), ejectives (/k'a/), the labiodental flap and in southern Africa, clicks (/ǂa/, /ǁ!a/). True implosives are rare outside Africa, and clicks and the flap almost unheard of.
- doubly articulated labial-velar stops like /k͡pa/ and /ɡ͡ba/ are found in places south of the Sahara.

- prenasalized consonants, like /mpa/ and /ŋga/, are widespread in Africa but not common outside it.
- sequences of stops and fricatives at the beginnings of words, such as /fsa/, /pta/ and /d͡sk͡x'a/.
- nasal stops which only occur with nasal vowels, such as [ba] vs. [mã] (but both [pa] and [pã]), especially in West Africa.
- vowels contrasting an advanced or retracted tongue, commonly called "tense" and "lax".
- simple tone systems which are used for grammatical purposes.

Sounds that are relatively uncommon in African languages include uvular consonants, diphthongs and front rounded vowels

Tonal languages are found throughout the world but are predominantly used in Africa. Both the Nilo-Saharan and the Khoi-San phyla are fully tonal. The large majority of the Niger–Congo languages is also tonal. Tonal languages are also found in the Omotic, Chadic and South & East Cushitic branches of Afroasiatic. The most common type of tonal system opposes two tone levels, High (H) and Low (L). Contour tones do occur, and can often be analysed as two or more tones in succession on a single syllable. *Tone melodies* play an important role, meaning that it is often possible to state significant generalizations by separating tone sequences ("melodies") from the segments that bear them. Tonal sandhi processes like tone spread, tone shift, downstep and downdrift are common in African languages.

Syntactic

Widespread syntactical structures include the common use of adjectival verbs and the expression of comparison by means of a verb 'to surpass'. The Niger–Congo languages have large numbers of genders (noun classes) which cause agreement in verbs and other words. Case, tense and other categories may be distinguished only by tone.

Semantic

Quite often, only one term is used for both animal and meat; the word *nama* or *nyama* for animal/meat is particularly widespread in otherwise widely divergent African languages.

Number of speakers

The following is a table displaying the number of speakers of given languages within Africa:

Languages of Africa

Language	Family	Native speakers (L1)	Official status per country
Afrikaans	Indo-European	7,200,000	National language in Namibia, co-official in South Africa
Akan	Niger–Congo	11,000,000[752]	None. Government sponsored language of Ghana
Amharic	Afroasiatic	21,800,000	Ethiopia
Arabic	Afroasiatic	150,000,000 but with separate mutually unintelligible varieties	Algeria, Chad, Comoros, Djibouti, Egypt, Eritrea, Libya, Mauritania, Morocco, Sahrawi Arab Democratic Republic, Somalia, Sudan, Tanzania (Zanzibar), Tunisia
Berber	Afroasiatic	16,000,000 (estimated) (including separate mutually unintelligible varieties)	Morocco, Algeria
Chewa	Niger–Congo	9,700,000	Malawi, Zimbabwe
English	Indo-European	6,500,000 (estimated)	See List of territorial entities where English is an official language
Fon	Niger–Congo		Benin
French	Indo-European	700,000 (estimated)	see List of territorial entities where French is an official language and African French
Fulani	Niger–Congo	25,000,000	national language of Senegal
German	Indo-European		national language of Namibia, special status in South Africa
Gikuyu	Niger–Congo	6,600,000	
Hausa	Afroasiatic	34,000,000[753]	recognized in Nigeria, Ghana, Niger
Igbo	Niger–Congo	27,000,000	native in Nigeria
Italian	Indo-European		recognized in Libya, Eritrea, Somalia
Khoekhoe	Khoe	300,000[754]	national language of Namibia
Kimbundu	Niger–Congo		Angola
Kinyarwanda	Niger–Congo	9,800,000	Rwanda
Kirundi	Niger–Congo	8,800,000	Burundi
Kituba	Kongo-based creole		Democratic Republic of Congo, Republic of Congo
Kongo	Niger–Congo	5,600,000	Angola, recognised national language of Republic of Congo and Democratic Republic of Congo

Lingala	Niger–Congo	5,500,000	National language of Democratic Republic of the Congo
Luganda	Niger–Congo	4,100,000	Native language of Uganda
Luo	Nilo-Saharan (probable)	4,200,000	
Malagasy	Austronesian	18,000,000	Madagascar
Mauritian Creole	Indo-European	1,100,000	Native language of Mauritius
Mossi	Niger–Congo	7,600,000	Recognised regional language in Burkina Faso
Ndebele	Niger–Congo	1,100,000	Statutory national language in South Africa
Noon	Niger–Congo		Senegal
Northern Sotho	Niger–Congo	4,600,000	South Africa
Oromo	Afroasiatic	26,000,000	Ethiopia
Portuguese	Indo-European	13,700,000 (estimated)	Angola, Cape Verde, Guinea-Bissau, Equatorial Guinea, Mozambique, São Tomé and Príncipe
Sena	Niger-Congo		Zimbabwe
Sepedi	Niger–Congo		South Africa
Sesotho	Niger–Congo	5,600,000	Lesotho, South Africa, Zimbabwe
Shona	Niger–Congo	7,200,000	Zimbabwe
Somali	Afroasiatic	16,600,000	Somalia, Djibouti
Northern Ndebele	Niger–Congo		Zimbabwe
Spanish	Indo-European	1,100,000	Equatorial Guinea, still marginally spoken in Sahrawi Arab Democratic Republic, recognized in Morocco
Southern Ndebele	Niger–Congo		South Africa
Swahili	Niger–Congo	15,000,000	Official in Tanzania, Kenya, Uganda, Rwanda, Democratic Republic of the Congo
Tigrinya	Afroasiatic	7,000,000	Eritrea, regional language in Ethiopia
Tsoa	Khoe		Zimbabwe
Tshiluba	Niger–Congo	6,300,000 (1991)	National language of Democratic Republic of the Congo
Tsonga	Niger–Congo	5,000,000[755]	South Africa, Zimbabwe (as 'as Shangani'), Mozambique

Tshivenda	Niger–Congo		South Africa, Zimbabwe
Tswana	Niger–Congo	5,800,000	South Africa, Botswana
Umbundu	Niger–Congo	6,000,000	Angola
Xhosa	Niger–Congo	7,600,000	South Africa, Zimbabwe
Yoruba	Niger–Congo	28,000,000	recognized in Nigeria, Benin, Togo
Zulu	Niger–Congo	10,400,000	South Africa

By region

Below is a list of the major languages of Africa by region, family and total number of primary language speakers in millions.

Central Africa	Horn of Africa	North Africa	Southeast Africa	Southern Africa	West Africa

• Niger–Congo, Bantu
  • Lingala
  • Kinyarwanda:12
  • Kongo:5+
  • Tshiluba
  • Kirundi
	• Afroasiatic
	  • Semitic
	    • Amharic: 20+
	    • Tigrinya: 5
	  • Cushitic
	    • Somali: 10–15
	    • Oromo: 30–35
	• Nilo-Saharan: 1
	  • Gumuz
	  • Anuak
	  • Kunama
	  • Nara
	• Niger–Congo: 1
	  • Zigula
		• Afroasiatic
		  • Semitic
		    • Arabic: 200
		  • Berber: 30–40
		    • Kabyle
		    • Atlas
		    • Tuareg
		    • Zenaga
		• Nilo-Saharan
		  • Nubian: 5+
		  • Fur: 5+[756]
		  • Zaghawa[757]
		  • Masalit
		• Niger–Congo
		  • Kordofanian languages
		    • Nuba
			• Niger–Congo, Bantu:
			  • Swahili: 5–10
			  • Gikuyu: 9
			  • Ganda:6
			  • Luhya: 6
			• Austronesian
			  • Malagasy: 20+
			• Niger–Congo, Ubangian
			  • Gbaya:2
			  • Banda:1-2
			  • Zande
			• Nilo-Saharan
			  • Kanuri:10
			  • Sara:3-4
			  • Kalenjin:5
			  • Luo:5
			  • Dinka
			  • Nuer
			  • Shilluk
			  • Maasai:1-2
				• Niger–Congo, Bantu
				  • Zulu: 10
				  • Xhosa: 8
				  • Shona: 7
				  • Sotho: 5
				  • Tsonga: 12
				  • Tswana: 4
				  • Umbundu: 4
				  • Northern Sotho: 4
				  • Chichewa: 8
				  • Makua: 8
				• Indo-European
				  • Germanic
				    • Afrikaans: 7
				    • English: 5
				  • Romance
				    • Portuguese: 14	

- Niger–Congo
  - Benue–Congo
    - Ibibio (Nigeria): 7
  - Volta–Niger
    - Igbo (Nigeria): 30–35
    - Yoruba: 40
  - Kwa:
    - Akan (Ghana, Côte d'Ivoire): 20–25
  - Gur
    - More: 5
  - Senegambian
    - Fula (West Africa): 40
  - Wolof: 8
- Afroasiatic
  - Chadic
    - Hausa: 50
- Nilo-Saharan
  - Saharan
    - Kanuri: 10
  - Songhai:5
  - Zarma:5

References

- Childs, G. Tucker (2003). *An Introduction to African Languages*. Amsterdam: John Benjamin.
- Chimhundu, Herbert (2002). *Language Policies in Africa*. (Final report of the Intergovernmental Conference on Language Policies in Africa.) Revised version. UNESCO.
- Cust, Robert Needham (1883). *Modern Languages of Africa*.
- Ellis, Stephen (ed.) (1996). *Africa Now: People - Policies - Institutions*. The Hague: Ministry of Foreign Affairs (DGIS).
- Elugbe, Ben (1998) "Cross-border and major languages of Africa." In K. Legère (editor), *Cross-border Languages: Reports and Studies, Regional Workshop on Cross-Border Languages, National Institute for Educational Development (NIED), Okahandja, 23–27 September 1996*. Windhoek: Gamsberg Macmillan.
- Ethnologue.com's Africa[758]: A listing of African languages and language families.
- Greenberg, Joseph H. (1983). 'Some areal characteristics of African languages.' In Ivan R. Dihoff (editor), *Current Approaches to African Linguistics*, Vol. 1 (*Publications in African Languages and Linguistics*, Vol. 1), Dordrecht: Foris, 3-21.
- Greenberg, Joseph H. (1966). *The Languages of Africa* (2nd edition with additions and corrections). Bloomington: Indiana University.
- Heine, Bernd and Derek Nurse (editors) (2000). *African Languages: An Introduction*. Cambridge: Cambridge University Press.
- Webb, Vic and Kembo-Sure (editors) (1998). *African Voices: An Introduction to the Languages and Linguistics of Africa*. Cape Town: Oxford University Press Southern Africa.
- Wedekind, Klaus (Oxford University Press.

External links

- African language resources for children[759]
- Web resources for African languages[760]
- Linguistic maps of Africa from Muturzikin.com[761]
- Online Dictionaries[762], e-books[763] and other online fulltexts[764] in or on African languages

Culture

Culture of Africa

The **culture of Africa** is varied and manifold, consisting of a mixture of countries with various tribes that each have their own unique characteristic from the continent of Africa. It is a product of the diverse populations that today inhabit the continent of Africa and the African Diaspora. African culture is expressed in its arts and crafts, folklore and religion, clothing, cuisine, music and languages. Expressions of culture are abundant within Africa, with large amounts of cultural diversity being found not only across different countries but also within single countries. Even though African cultures are widely diverse, it is also, when closely studied, seen to have many similarities. For example, the morals they uphold, their love and respect for their culture as well as the strong respect they hold for the aged and the important i.e. Kings and Chiefs.

Africa has influenced and been influenced by other continents. This can be portrayed in the willingness to adapt to the ever-changing modern world rather than staying rooted to their static culture. The Westernized few, persuaded by European culture and Christianity, first denied African traditional culture, but with the increase of African nationalism, a cultural recovery occurred. The governments of most African nations encourage national dance and music groups, museums, and to a lower degree, artists and writers.

Historical overview

Africa is divided into a great number of ethnic cultures.[765,766,767] The continent's cultural regeneration has also been an integral aspect of post-independence nation-building on the continent, with a recognition of the need to harness the cultural resources of Africa to enrich the process of education, requiring the creation of an enabling environment in a number of ways. In recent times, the call for a much greater emphasis on the cultural dimension in

Figure 181: *An Ethiopian woman preparing Ethiopian coffee at a traditional ceremony. She roasts, crushes and brews the coffee on the spot.*

Figure 182: *Sample of the Egyptian Book of the Dead of the scribe Nebqed, c. 1300 BC.*

all aspects of development has become increasingly vocal. During the Roman colonization of North Africa,(parts of Algeria, Libya, Egypt and the whole of Tunisia) provinces such as Tripolitania became major producers of food for the republic and the empire, this generated much wealth in these places for their 400 years of occupation. During colonialism in Africa, Europeans possessed attitudes of superiority and a sense of mission. The French were able to accept an African as French if that person gave up their African culture and adopted French ways. Knowledge of the Portuguese language and culture and abandonment of traditional African ways defined one as civilized.[768] Kenyan social commentator Mwiti Mugambi argues that the future of Africa can only be forged from accepting and mending the sociocultural present. For Mugambi, colonial cultural hangovers, pervasive Western cultural inundation, and aid-giving arm-twisting donors are, he argues, here to stay and no amount of looking into Africa's past will make them go away. However, Maulana Karenga states: <templatestyles src="Template:Quote/styles.css"/>

> *Our culture provides us with an ethos we must honor in both thought and practice. By ethos, we mean a people's self-understanding as well as its self-presentation in the world through its thought and practice in the other six areas of culture. It is above all a cultural challenge. For culture is here defined as the totality of thought and practice by which a people creates itself, celebrates, sustains and develops itself and introduces itself to history and humanity*
>
> *—Maulana Karenga, African Culture and the Ongoing Quest for Excellence*[769]

African arts and crafts

Africa has a rich tradition of arts and crafts. African arts and crafts find expression in a variety of woodcarvings, brass and leather art works. African arts and crafts also include sculpture, paintings, pottery, ceremonial and religious headgear and dress. Maulana Karenga states that in African art, the object was not as important as the soul force behind the creation of the object. He also states that All art must be revolutionary and in being revolutionary it must be collective, committing, and functional.Wikipedia:Citation needed

Certain African cultures have always placed emphasis on personal appearance and jewelry has remained an important personal accessory. Many pieces of such jewelry are made of cowry shells and similar materials. Similarly, masks are made with elaborate designs and are an important part of some cultures in Africa. Masks are used in various ceremonies depicting ancestors and spirits, mythological characters and deities.

Figure 183: *SUDAN basket -tray, Tabar of weaved natural plant fiber, colored in different colors*

Figure 184: *A Yombe sculpture (Louvre, Paris).*

Figure 185: *BaKongo voodoo masks from the Kongo Central region*

In many traditional arts and craft traditions in Africa, certain themes significant to those particular cultures recur, including a couple, a woman with a child, a male with a weapon or animal, and an outsider or a stranger. Couples may represent ancestors, community founder, married couple or twins. The couple theme rarely exhibits intimacy of men and women. The mother with the child or children reveals intense desire of the women to have children. The theme is also representative of mother mars and the people as her children. The man with the weapon or animal theme symbolizes honor and power. A stranger may be from some other tribe or someone from a different country, and more distorted portrayal of the stranger indicates proportionately greater gap from the stranger.

Folklore and religion

Like all human cultures, African folklore and religion represents a variety of social facets of the various cultures in Africa.Wikipedia:Citation needed Like almost all civilizations and cultures, flood myths have been circulating in different parts of Africa. Culture and religion share space and are deeply intertwined in African cultures. In Ethiopia, Christianity and Islam form the core aspects of Ethiopian culture and inform dietary customs as well as rituals and rites.[770] According to a Pygmy myth, Chameleon, hearing a strange noise in a

Figure 186: *Central mosque in Nouakchott, Mauritania.*

tree, cut open its trunk and water came out in a great flood that spread all over the land.

Folktales also play an important role in many African cultures. Stories reflect a group cultural identity and preserving the stories of Africa will help preserve an entire culture. Storytelling affirms pride and identity in a culture. In Africa, stories are created by and for the ethnic group telling them. Different ethnic groups in Africa have different rituals or ceremonies for storytelling, which creates a sense of belonging to a cultural group. To outsiders hearing an ethnic group's stories, it provides an insight into the community's beliefs, views, and customs. For people within the community, it allows them to encompass their group's uniqueness. They show the human desires and fears of a group, such as love, marriage, and death. Folktales are also seen as a tool for education and entertainment. They provide a way for children to understand the material and social environment. Every story has a moral to teach people, such as goodwill prevail over evil. For entertainment, stories are set in fantastic, non-human worlds. Often, the main character of the story would be a talking animal or something unnatural would happen to a human character. Even though folktales are for entertainment, they bring a sense of belonging and pride to communities in Africa.[771]

There are different types of African stories: animal tales and day-to-day tales. Animal tales more oriented towards entertainment, but still have morals and

Figure 187: *Kenyan boys and girls performing a traditional folklore dance.*

lessons to them. Animal tales are normally divided into trickster tales and ogre tales. In the animal tales, a certain animal would always have the same character or role in each story so the audience does not have to worry about characterization. The Hare was always the trickster, clever and cunning, while the Hyena was always being tricked by the Hare. Ogres are always cruel, greedy monsters. The messengers in all the stories were the Birds. Day-to-Day tales are the most serious tales, never including humor, that explained the everyday life and struggles of an African community. These tales take on matters such as famine, escape from death, courtship, and family matters, using a song form when the climax of the story was being told.

African stories all have a certain structure to them. Villagers would gather around a common meeting place at the end of the day to listen and tell their stories. Storytellers had certain commands to start and end the stories, "Ugai Itha" to get the audience's attention and begin the story, and "Rukirika" to signal the end of a tale. Each scene of a story is depicted with two characters at a time, so the audience does not get overwhelmed. In each story, victims are able to overcome their predators and take justice out on the culprit. Certain tools were used in African folktales. For example, idiophones, such as drums, were used to make the sounds of different animals. Repetition and call-back techniques in the form of prose or poem were also used to get the audience involved in the stories.[772,773]

Figure 188: *Ashanti Kente cloth patterns.*

Clothing

Women's traditional clothes in Ethiopia are made from cloth called *shemma* and are used to make *habesha kemis*. The latter garment is basically cotton cloth, about 90 cm wide, woven in long strips which are then sewn together. Sometimes shiny threads are woven into the fabric for an elegant effect. Men wear pants and a knee-length shirt with a white collar, and perhaps a sweater. Men often wear knee-high socks, while women might not wear socks at all. Men as well as women wear shawls, the *netela*.

Zulus wear a variety of attire, both traditional for ceremonial or culturally celebratory occasions, and modern westernised clothing for everyday use. Traditional male clothing is usually light, consisting of a two-part apron (similar to a loincloth) used to cover the genitals and buttocks. The front piece is called the *umutsha* (pronounced Zulu pronunciation: [umtifash]), and is usually made of springbok or other animal hide twisted into different bands which cover the genitals. The rear piece, called the *ibheshu* [ibeːʃu], is made of a single piece of springbok or cattle hide, and its length is usually used as an indicator of age and social position; longer amabheshu (plural of ibheshu) are worn by older men. Married men will usually also wear a headband, called the *umqhele* [umˈǃʰɛle], which is usually also made of springbok hide, or leopard hide by men of higher social status, such as chiefs. Zulu men will also wear cow tails as bracelets and

Figure 189: *A woman in Kenya wearing kanga*

Figure 190: *Maasai wearing traditional clothes named Matavuvale while performing Adumu, a traditional dance*

Figure 191: *Fufu (right) is a staple meal in West Africa and Central Africa. It is served here with some peanut soup.*

anklets called *imishokobezi* [imiʃoɡobɛːzi] during ceremonies and rituals, such as weddings or dances.

In the Muslim parts of Africa, daily attire also often reflects Islamic tradition.Wikipedia:Citation needed

Cuisine

The various cuisines of Africa use a combination of locally available fruits, cereal grains and vegetables, as well as milk and meat products. In some parts of the continent, the traditional diet features a preponderance of milk, curd and whey products. In much of tropical Africa, however, cow's milk is rare and cannot be produced locally (owing to various diseases that affect livestock). The continent's diverse demographic makeup is reflected in the many different eating and drinking habits, dishes, and preparation techniques of its manifold populations.

In Central Africa, the basic ingredients are plantains and cassava. Fufu-like starchy foods (usually made from fermented cassava roots) are served with grilled meat and sauces. A variety of local ingredients are used while preparing other dishes like spinach stew, cooked with tomato, peppers, chillis,

Figure 192: *Fresh Moroccan couscous with vegetables and chickpeas.*

onions, and peanut butter. Cassava plants are also consumed as cooked greens. Groundnut (peanut) stew is also prepared, containing chicken, okra, ginger, and other spices. Another favorite is Bambara, a porridge of rice, peanut butter, and sugar. Beef and chicken are favorite meat dishes, but game meat preparations containing crocodile, monkey, antelope and warthog are also served occasionally.

The cuisine of the African Great Lakes region varies from area to area. In the inland savannah, the traditional cuisine of cattle-keeping peoples is distinctive in that meat products are generally absent. Cattle, sheep and goats were regarded as a form of currency and a store of wealth, and are not generally consumed as food. In some areas, traditional peoples consume the milk and blood of cattle, but rarely the meat. Elsewhere, other peoples are farmers who grow a variety of grains and vegetables. Maize (corn) is the basis of ugali, the East African version of West Africa's fufu. Ugali is a starch dish eaten with meats or stews. In Uganda, steamed, green bananas called matoke provide the starch filler of many meals.

In the Horn of Africa, the main traditional dishes in Ethiopian cuisine and Eritrean cuisine are *tsebhis* (stews) served with *injera*[774] (flatbread made from teff, wheat, or sorghum), and hilbet (paste made from legumes, mainly lentil, faba beans). Eritrean and Ethiopian cuisine (especially in the northern half) are very similar, given the shared history of the two countries. The related Somali

Figure 193: *Potjiekos is a traditional Afrikaner stew made with meat and vegetables and cooked over coals in cast-iron pots.*

cuisine consists of an exotic fusion of diverse culinary influences. Varieties of *bariis* (rice), the most popular probably being basmati, usually serve as the main dish. *Xalwo* (halwo) or halva is a popular confection served during special occasions such as Eid celebrations or wedding receptions.[775] After meals, homes are traditionally perfumed using frankincense (*lubaan*) or incense (*cuunsi*), which is prepared inside an incense burner referred to as a *dabqaad*. All food is served halal.

The roots of North African cuisine can be traced back to the ancient empires of North Africa, particularly in Egypt where many of the country's dishes and culinary traditions date back to ancient Egypt. Over several centuries traders, travelers, invaders, migrants and immigrants all have influenced the cuisine of North Africa. Most of the North African countries today have several similar dishes, sometimes almost the same dish with a different name (the Moroccan *tangia* and the Tunisian *coucha* are both essentially the same dish: a meat stew prepared in an urn and cooked overnight in a public oven), sometimes with a slight change in ingredients and cooking style. To add to the confusion, two completely different dishes may also share the same name (for example, a "tajine" dish is a slow-cooked stew in Morocco, whereas the Tunisian "tajine" is a baked omelette/quiche-like dish). There are noticeable differences between the cooking styles of different nations – there's the sophisticated, full-bodied flavours of Moroccan palace cookery, the fiery dishes of Tunisian cuisine, and the humbler, simpler cuisines of Egypt and Algeria.

The cooking of Southern Africa is sometimes called 'rainbow cuisine', as the food in this region is a blend of many culinary traditions, including those of the Khoisan, Bantu, European and Asian populations. Basic ingredients include seafood, meat products (including wild game), poultry, as well as grains, fresh fruits and vegetables. Fruits include apples, grapes, mangoes, bananas and papayas, avocado, oranges, peaches and apricots. Desserts may simply be fruit. However, there are some more western style puddings, such as the Angolan Cocada amarela, which was inspired by Portuguese cuisine. Meat products include lamb, as well as game like venison, ostrich, and impala. The seafood includes a wide variety such as crayfish, prawns, tuna, mussels, oysters, calamari, mackerel, and lobster. There are also several types of traditional and modern alcoholic beverages including many European-style beers.

A typical West African meal is heavy with starchy items, meat, spices, and flavors. A wide array of staples are eaten across the region, including those of Fufu, Banku and Kenkey (originating from Ghana), Foutou, Couscous, Tô, and Garri, which are served alongside soups and stews. Fufu is often made from starchy root vegetables such as yams, cocoyams, or cassava, but also from cereal grains like millet, sorghum or plantains. The staple grain or starch varies region to region and ethnic group to ethnic group, although corn has gained significant ground as it is cheap, swells to greater volumes and creates a beautiful white final product that is greatly desired. Banku and Kenkey are maize dough staples, and Gari is made from dried grated cassavas. Rice-dishes are also widely eaten in the region, especially in the dry Sahel belt inland. Examples of these include Benachin from The Gambia and Jollof rice, a pan-West African rice dish similar to Arab kabsah.

African music

Traditional Sub-Saharan African music is as diverse as the region's various populations. The common perception of Sub-Saharan African music is that it is rhythmic music centered on the drums, and indeed, a large part of Sub-Saharan music, mainly among speakers of Niger–Congo and Nilo-Saharan languages, is rhythmic and centered on the drum. Sub-Saharan music is polyrhythmic, usually consisting of multiple rhythms in one composition. Dance involves moving multiple body parts. These aspects of Sub-Saharan music were transferred to the new world by enslaved Sub-Saharan Africans and can be seen in its influence on music forms as Samba, Jazz, Rhythm and Blues, Rock & Roll, Salsa, and Rap music.[776]

Figure 194: *Yoruba drummers at celebration in Ojumo Oro, Kwara State, Nigeria.*

Other African musical traditions also involve strings, horns, and very little poly-rhythms. Music from the eastern Sahel and along the Nile, among the Nilo-Saharan, made extensive use of strings and horns in ancient times. Dancing involve swaying body movements and footwork. Among the Khoisans extensive use of string instruments with emphasis on footwork.[777]

Modern Sub-Saharan African music has been influenced by music from the New World (Jazz, Salsa, Rhythm and Blues etc.). Popular styles include Mbalax in Senegal and Gambia, Highlife in Ghana, Zoblazo in Côte d'Ivoire, Makossa in Cameroon, Soukous in the Democratic Republic of Congo, Kizomba in Angola, and Mbaqanga in South Africa. New World styles like Salsa, R&B/Rap, Reggae, and Zouk also have widespread popularity.

Like the musical genres of the Nile Valley and the Horn of Africa, North African music has close ties with Middle Eastern music and utilizes similar melodic modes (*maqamat*). It has a considerable range, from the music of ancient Egypt to the Berber and the Tuareg music of the desert nomads. The region's art music has for centuries followed the outline of Arabic and Andalusian classical music. Its popular contemporary genres include the Algerian Raï. Somali music is typically pentatonic, using five pitches per octave in contrast to a heptatonic (seven note) scale such as the major scale. In Ethiopia, the music of the highlands uses a fundamental modal system called *qenet*, of which there are four main modes: *tezeta*, *bati*, *ambassel*, and *anchihoy*. Three additional modes are variations on the above: tezeta minor, bati major, and bati minor.[778] Some songs take the name of their qenet, such as tizita, a song of reminiscence.

Languages

The main ethnolinguistic divisions in Africa are Afro-Asiatic (North Africa, Horn of Africa), Niger–Congo (including speakers from the Bantu branch) in most of Sub-Saharan Africa, Nilo-Saharan in parts of the Sahara and the Sahel and parts of Eastern Africa, and Khoisan (indigenous minorities of Southern Africa).[779] The continent of Africa speaks hundreds of languages, and if dialects spoken by various ethnic groups are also included, the number is much higher. These languages and dialects do not have the same importance: some are spoken by only few hundred people, others are spoken by millions. Among the most prominent languages spoken are Arabic, Swahili and Hausa. Very few countries of Africa use any single language and for this reason, several official languages coexist, African and European. Some Africans speak various European languages such as English, Spanish, French, Portuguese, Italian, German and Dutch.

External links

- Unesco African Website[780]
- Squinti African Art[781]
- culture africaine[782]

Music of Africa

Music of Africa

The traditional **music of Africa**, given the vastness of the continent, is historically ancient, rich and diverse, with different regions and nations of Africa having many distinct musical traditions. Music in Africa is very important when it comes to religion. Songs and music are used in rituals and religious ceremonies, to pass down stories from generation to generation, as well as to sing and dance to.

Traditional music in most of the continent is passed down orally (or aurally) and is not written. In Sub-Saharan African music traditions, it frequently relies on percussion instruments of every variety, including xylophones, djembes, drums, and tone-producing instruments such as the mbira or "thumb piano."

The music and dance of the African diaspora, formed to varying degrees on African musical traditions, include American music and many Caribbean genres, such as soca, calypso (see kaiso) and zouk. Latin American music genres such as the rumba, conga, bomba, cumbia, salsa and samba were founded on the music of enslaved Africans, and have in turn influenced African popular music.

Like the music of Asia, India and the Middle East, it is a highly rhythmic music. African music consists of complex rhythmic patterns, often involving one rhythm played against another to create a *polyrhythm*. The most common polyrhythm plays three beats on top of two, like a triplet played against straight notes. Beyond the rhythmic nature of the music, African music differs from Western music in that the various parts of the music do not necessarily combine in a harmonious fashion. African musicians unlike Western musicians, do not seek to combine different sounds in a way that is pleasing to the ear. Instead their aim is to express life, in all its aspects, through the medium of sound. Each instrument or part may represent a particular aspect of life, or a different character; the through-line of each instrument/part matters more than how the

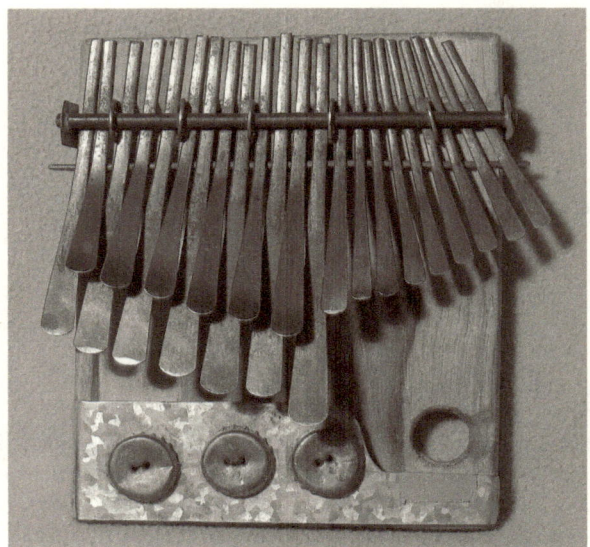

Figure 195: *The lamellophone thumb piano or mbira, a popular instrument in the African Great Lakes*

different instruments and parts fit together. Understanding African music gets even more difficult when you consider that it does not have a written tradition; there is little or no written music to study or analyze. This makes it almost impossible to notate the music – especially the melodies and harmonies – using the Western staff. There are subtle differences in pitch and intonation that do not easily translate to Western notation. That said, African music most closely adheres to Western tetratonic (three-notes), pentatonic (five-note), hexatonic (six-note), and heptatonic (seven-note) scales. Harmonization of the melody is accomplished by singing in parallel thirds, fourths, or fifths. Another distinguishing form of African music is its call-and-response nature: one voice or instrument plays a short melodic phrase, and that phrase is echoed by another voice or instrument. The call-and-response nature extends to the rhythm, where one drum will play a rhythmic pattern, echoed by another drum playing the same pattern. African music is also highly improvised. (This speaks to the lack of a written tradition.) A core rhythmic pattern is typically played, with drummers then improvising new patterns over the static original patterns.

Figure 196: *Aar Maanta performing with his band at Pier Scheveningen Strandweg in The Hague, Netherlands*

Music by regions

North Africa and the Horn of Africa

North Africa is the seat of ancient Egypt and Carthage, civilizations with strong ties to the ancient Near East and which influenced the ancient Greek and Roman cultures. Eventually, Egypt fell under Persian rule followed by Greek and Roman rule, while Carthage was later ruled by Romans and Vandals. North Africa was later conquered by the Arabs, who established the region as the Maghreb of the Arab world.

Like the musical genres of the Nile Valley and the Horn of Africa *(sky-blue and dark green region on map)*, its music has close ties with Middle Eastern music and utilizes similar melodic modes *(maqamat)*. North African music has a considerable range, from the music of ancient Egypt to the Berber and the Tuareg music of the desert nomads. The region's art music has for centuries followed the outline of Arabic and Andalusian classical music: its popular contemporary genres include the Algerian Raï.

With these may be grouped the music of Sudan and of the Horn of Africa, including the music of Eritrea, Ethiopia, Djibouti and Somalia. Somali music is typically pentatonic, using five pitches per octave in contrast to a heptatonic (seven note) scale such as the major scale. The music of the Ethiopian highlands uses a fundamental modal system called *qenet*, of which there are four main modes: *tezeta*, *bati*, *ambassel*, and *anchihoy*. Three additional modes are variations on the above: tezeta minor, bati major, and bati minor.[783] Some songs take the name of their qenet, such as tizita, a song of reminiscence.

West, Central, Southeast and South Africa

The ethnomusicological pioneer Arthur Morris Jones (1889–1980) observed that the shared rhythmic principles of Sub-Saharan African music traditions constitute *one main system*.[784] Similarly, master drummer and scholar C. K. Ladzekpo affirms the "profound homogeneity" of sub-Saharan African rhythmic principles.[785]

African traditional music is frequently functional in nature. Performances may be long and often involve the participation of the audience.[786] There are, for example, little different kinds of work songs, songs accompanying childbirth, marriage, hunting and political activities, music to ward off evil spirits and to pay respects to good spirits, the dead and the ancestors. None of this is performed outside its intended socialess context and much of it is associated with a particular dance. Some of it, performed by professional musicians, is sacral music or ceremonial and courtly music performed at royal courts.

Musicologically, Sub-Saharan Africa may be divided into four regions:

- The **eastern** region *(light green regions on map)* includes the music of Uganda, Kenya, Rwanda, Burundi, Tanzania, Malawi, Mozambique and Zimbabwe as well as the islands of Madagascar, the Seychelles, Mauritius and Comor. Many of these have been influenced by Arabic music and also by the music of India, Indonesia and Polynesia, though the region's indigenous musical traditions are primarily in the mainstream of the sub-Saharan Niger–Congo-speaking peoples.
- The **southern** region *(brown region on map)* includes the music of South Africa, Lesotho, Swaziland, Botswana, Namibia and Angola.
- The **central** region *(dark blue region on map)* includes the music of Chad, the Central African Republic, the Democratic Republic of the Congo and Zambia, including Pygmy music.
- West African music *(yellow region on map)* includes the music of Senegal and the Gambia, of Guinea and Guinea-Bissau, Sierra Leone and Liberia, of the inland plains of Mali, Niger and Burkina Faso, the coastal nations of Cote d'Ivoire, Ghana, Togo, Benin, Nigeria, Cameroon, Gabon and the Republic of the Congo as well as islands such as Sao Tome and Principe.

Southern, Central and West Africa are similarly in the broad Sub-Saharan musical tradition. They also have several ancillary influences, from the Muslim regions of Africa, and in modern times, the Americas and Western Europe.

Figure 197: *Azande song from the Congo performed with xylophone.*

West African music has regional variations, with Muslim regions incorporating elements of Islamic music and non-Muslim regions more influenced by indigenous traditions, according to the historian Sylviane Diouf and ethnomusicologist Gerhard Kubik. According to Diouf, traditional Muslim West African Music incorporates elements of the Islamic call to prayer (originating from Bilal ibn Rabah, an Abyssinian African Muslim in the early 7th century), including lyrics praising God, melody, note changes, "words that seem to quiver and shake" in the vocal chords, dramatic changes in musical scales, and nasal intonation. According to Kubik, the vocal style of Muslim West African singers "using melisma, wavy intonation, and so forth is a heritage of that large region of West Africa that had been in contact with the Arabic-Islamic world of the Maghreb since the seventh and eighth centuries." In terms of instrumentation, Kubik notes that stringed instruments (including ancestors of the banjo) were traditionally favored by Muslim West Africans, while drumming was traditionally favored by non-Muslim West Africans.

Musical instruments

Besides vocalisation, which uses various techniques such as complex hard melisma and yodel, a wide array of musical instruments are used. African musical instruments include a wide range of drums, slit gongs, rattles and double bells, different types of harps, and harp-like instruments such as the Kora and the ngoni, as well as fiddles, many kinds of xylophone and lamellophone such as the mbira, and different types of wind instrument like flutes and trumpets. Additionally, string instruments are also used, with the lute-like oud and Ngoni serving as musical accompaniment in some areas.

Figure 198: *Algerian musician Abderrahmane Abdelli playing the oud*

There are five groups of sub-Saharan African musical instruments: membranophones, chordophones, aerophones, idiophones, and percussion. Membranophones are the drums, including kettles, clay pots, and barrels. Chordophones are stringed instruments like harps and fiddles. Aerophones are another name for wind instruments. These can include flutes and trumpets, similar to the instruments you hear in American music. Idiophones are rattles and shakers, while percussion can be sounds like foot-stomping and hand-clapping.[787] Many of the wooden instruments have shapes or pictures carved out into them to represent ancestry. Some are decorated with feathers or beads.[788]

Drums used in African traditional music include talking drums, bougarabou and djembe in West Africa, water drums in Central and West Africa, and the different types of ngoma drums (or engoma) in Central and Southern Africa. Other percussion instruments include many rattles and shakers, such as the kosika (kashaka), rain stick, bells and wood sticks. Also, Africa has lots of other types of drums, and lots of flutes, and lots of stringed and wind instruments.

The playing of polyrhythms is one of the most universal characteristics of Sub-Sarahan music, in contrast to polyphony in Western music. Several uniquely designed instruments have evolved there over time to facilitate the playing of simultaneous contrasting rhythms. The mbira, kalimba, Kora, Ngoni and

Figure 199: *Traditional drummers in Ghana*

dousn'gouni are examples of these instruments which organize notes not in the usual single linear order from bass to treble, but in two separated rank arrays which allows additional ease in playing cross rhythms. The continuing influence of this principle can be seen in the 20th century American instruments the gravi-kora and gravikord which are new modern examples.

Relationship to language

Many languages spoken in Africa are tonal languages, leading to a close connection between music and language in some local cultures. These particular communities use vocal sounds and movements with their music as well. In singing, the tonal pattern or the text puts some constraints on the melodic patterns. On the other hand, in instrumental music a native speaker of a language can often perceive a text or texts in the music. This effect also forms the basis of drum languages (talking drums).[789]

Influences on African music

Historically, several factors have influenced the traditional music of Africa. The music has been influenced by language, the environment, a variety of cultures, politics, and population movement, all of which are intermingled. Each African group evolved in a different area of the continent, which means that

Figure 200: *Steve Winwood's progressive rock/jazz rock band Traffic often used West African rhythms*

they ate different foods, faced different weather conditions, and came in contact with different groups than other societies did. Each group moved at different rates and to different places than others, and thus each was influenced by different people and circumstances. Furthermore, each society did not necessarily operate under the same government, which also significantly influenced their music styles.[790]

Influence on North American music

Although African American music is widely known and loved, and much popular North American music emerged from it, White American music also has strong African roots. The musical traditions of the Irish and Scottish settlers merged with African-American musical elements to become old-time and bluegrass, among other genres.

African music has been a major factor in the shaping of what we know today as Dixieland, the blues and jazz. These styles have all borrowed from African rhythms and sounds, brought over the Atlantic Ocean by slaves. African music in Sub-Saharan Africa is mostly upbeat polyrhythmic and joyful, whereas the blues should be viewed as an aesthetic development resulting from the conditions of slavery in the new world.

On his album *Graceland*, the American folk musician Paul Simon employs African bands, rhythms and melodies as a musical backdrop for his own lyrics;

especially Ladysmith Black Mambazo. In the early 1970s, Remi Kabaka, an Afro-rock avant-garde drummer, laid the initial drum patterns that created the Afro-rock sounds in bands such as Ginger Baker's Airforce, The Rolling Stones, and Steve Winwood's Traffic. He continued to work with Winwood, Paul McCartney, and Mick Jagger throughout the decade.[791]

Certain Sub-Saharan African musical traditions also had a significant influence on such works as Disney's *The Lion King* and *The Lion King II: Simba's Pride*, which blend traditional music with Western music. Songs such as "Circle of Life" and "He Lives in You" combine of Zulu and English lyrics, as well as traditional African styles of music with more modern western styles. Additionally, the Disney film incorporates numerous words from the Bantu Swahili language. The phrase *hakuna matata*, for example, is an actual Swahili phrase that does in fact mean "no worries". Characters such as Simba, Kovu, and Zira are also Swahili words, meaning "lion", "scar", and "hate", respectively.[792]

Babatunde Olatunji, Miriam Makeba, and Hugh Masakela were among the earliest African performing artists to develop sizable fan bases in the United States. Non-commercial African American radio stations promoted African music as part of their cultural and political missions in the 1960s and 1970s. African music also found eager audiences at Historically Black colleges and universities (HBCUs) and appealed particularly to activists in the civil rights and Black Power movements.[793]

Popular music

African popular music, like African traditional music, is vast and varied. Most contemporary genres of African popular music build on cross-pollination with western popular music. Many genres of popular music, including blues, jazz and rumba, derive to varying degrees from musical traditions from Africa, taken to the Americas by enslaved Africans. These rhythms and sounds have subsequently been adapted by newer genres like rock and rhythm and blues. Similarly, African popular music has adopted elements, particularly the musical instruments and recording studio techniques of western music.

One of the most important 20th century singers of South African popular music was Miriam Makeba, who played a key-role, in the 60s, in drawing global audience's attention to African music and its meaning. Zenzile Miriam Makeba was said to have been one of the most influential and popular musicians of Africa, beginning in the 1950s. She was a part of three bands, including one all-woman band and two others. She performed all types of jazz music, traditional African music, and music that was popular in western Africa at the time. Miriam played a majority of her music in the form of "mbube", which was "a style of vocal harmony which drew on American jazz, ragtime,

Figure 201: *Miriam Makeba during a performance*

and Anglican church hymns, as well as indigenous styles of music." After she moved to the U.S., problems with Makeba's passport occurred and she had to stay in America, it was said that she put an American twist on most of her African music. She had a very diverse scale of her vocal range and could hit almost any note.[794]WP:NOTRS "The Empress of African Music" passed away at the age of 76.[795]

The Afro-Euro hybrid style, the Cuban son, has had an influence on certain popular music in Africa. Some of the first guitar bands on the continent played covers of Cuban songs.[796] The early guitar-based bands from the Congo called their music *rumba* (although it was son rather than rumba-based). The Congolese style eventually evolved into what became known as soukous.

Music industry

For African artists concerts were the one of the fews ways to earn in the industry. Piracy and changing consumer behavior are behind declining sales of records. Enforcement of copyright law remains weak in Africa. MusikBi is the first legal music download website of Africa. It does not offer streaming and is limited by internet speeds in Africa. African countries (Kenya, Gambia and South Africa) have seen protest over airtime given to American music. In Zimbabwe 75% of airtime has to be given to local music. Protective actions have seen the growth of new genres like Urban Grooves emerge in Zimbabwe.

In 2016 Sony Music launched in Africa by opening an office in Nigeria, traditionally services of western major international studios have not been available in Africa, the local demand for their music being met through piracy.

Further reading

- Joshua Clark Davis, "African Sounds in the American South: Community Radio, Historically Black Colleges, and Musical Pan Africanism,"[797] The Journal of Popular Music Studies, December 2015
- Graeme Ewens. *Africa O-Yé: a Celebration of African Music*. 1992, cop. 1991. New York: Da Capo Press. <templatestyles src="Module:Citation/CS1/styles.css" />ISBN 0-306-80461-1
- Ruth M. Stone, ed. *The Garland handbook of African Music* 2nd ed., 2008. NY & Oxford: Routledge. <templatestyles src="Module:Citation/CS1/styles.css" />ISBN 978-0-415-96102-8 (Abridged paperback edition of vol."Africa", vol. 1 of *The Garland Encyclopedia of World Music* with additional articles)
- Rhythms of the Continent[798] from the BBC
- International Library of African Music[799] at Rhodes University
- Recordings of African music from the British Library's collections[800]

External links

- Glossary of African music styles[801]
- Historical Notes on African Melodies[802]
- Music of Africa[803] at Curlie (based on DMOZ)
- Lecture on music and politics in contemporary Mali[804]

Religion

Religion in Africa

Religion by country
✿ Religion portal
• v • t • e⁸⁰⁵

Religion in Africa (2015 Study)

Christianity (47.31%)

Islam (44.29%)

Others/None (8.40%)

Religion in Africa is multifaceted and has been a major influence on art, culture and philosophy. Today, the continent's various populations and individuals are mostly adherents of Christianity, Islam, and to a lesser extent several

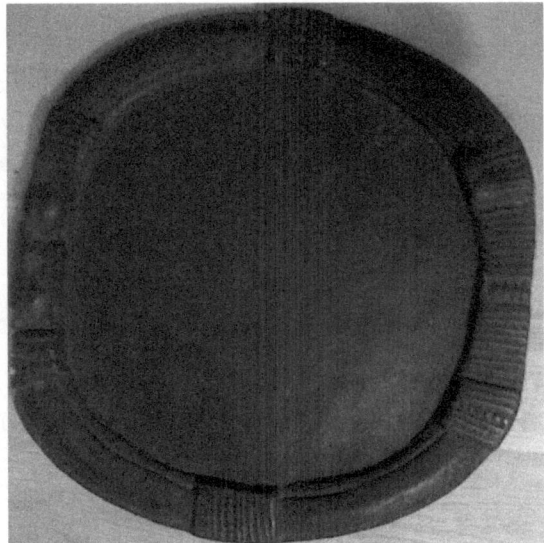

Figure 202: *Early 20th-century Yoruba divination board*

Traditional African religions. In Christian or Islamic communities, religious beliefs are also sometimes characterized with syncretism with the beliefs and practices of traditional religions.[806,807]

African Traditional Religion

Africa encompasses a wide variety of traditional beliefs. Although religious customs are sometimes shared by many local societies, they are usually unique to specific populations or geographic regions.[808]

According to Dr J Omosade Awolalu, The "traditional" in this context means indigenous, that which is foundational, handed down from generation to generation, meant as to be upheld and practised today and forevermore. A heritage from the past, yet not treated as a thing of the past but that which connects the past with the present and the present with eternity.

Often spoken of in the terms of a singularity, deliberate; yet conscious of the fact that Africa is a large continent with multitudes of nations who have complex cultures, innumerable languages and myriad dialects.

The essence of this school of thought is based mainly on oral transmission; that which is written in people's hearts, minds, oral history, customs, temples and religious functions.[809] It has no founders or leaders like Gautama Buddha,

Figure 203: *Vodun altar in Abomey, Benin*

Jesus, or Muhammed.[810] It has no missionaries or the intent to propagate or to proselytise.[811] Some of the African traditional religions are those of the Serer of Senegal, the Yoruba and Igbo of Nigeria, and the Akan of Ghana and the Ivory Coast. The religion of the Gbe peoples (mostly the Ewe and Fon) of Benin, Togo and Ghana is called Vodun and is the main source for similarly named religions in the diaspora, such as Louisiana Voodoo, Haitian Vodou, Cuban Vodú, Dominican Vudú and Brazilian Vodum

Abrahamic religions

The majority of Africans are adherents of Christianity or Islam. African people often combine the practice of their traditional belief with the practice of Abrahamic religions.[812,813,814,815,816] Abrahamic religions are widespread throughout Africa. They have both spread and replaced indigenous African religions, but are often adapted to African cultural contexts and belief systems. The World Book Encyclopedia has estimated that in 2002 Christians formed 40% of the continent's population, with Muslims forming 45%. It was also estimated in 2002 that Christians form 45% of Africa's population, with Muslims forming 40.6%.[817]

Figure 204: *The Hanging Church of Cairo, Egypt.*

Christianity

Christianity is now one of the most widely practiced religions in Africa along with Islam and is the largest religion in Sub-Saharan Africa. Most adherents outside Egypt, Ethiopia and Eritrea are Roman Catholic or Protestant. Wikipedia:Citation needed Several syncretistic and messianic sects have formed throughout much of the continent, including the Nazareth Baptist Church in South Africa and the Aladura churches in Nigeria.There is also fairly widespread populations of Seventh-day Adventists and Jehovah's Witnesses. The oldest Christian denominations in Africa are the Coptic church in Egypt and the Ethiopian Orthodox Tewahedo Church and the Eritrean Orthodox Tewahedo Church, all Oriental Orthodox, which rose to prominence in the fourth century AD after King Ezana the Great made Ethiopia one of the first Christian nations.[818]

In the first few centuries of Christianity, Africa produced many figures who had a major influence outside the continent, including St Augustine of Hippo, St Maurice, Origen, Tertullian, and three Roman Catholic popes (Victor I, Miltiades and Gelasius I), as well as the Biblical characters Simon of Cyrene and the Ethiopian eunuch baptised by Philip the Evangelist. Christianity existed in Ethiopia before the rule of King Ezana the Great of the Kingdom of Axum, but the religion took a strong foothold when it was declared a state religion in 330 AD, becoming one of the first Christian nations. The earliest and best known reference to the introduction of Christianity to Africa is mentioned in the Christian Bible's Acts of the Apostles, and pertains to the evangelist Phillip's conversion of an Ethiopian traveler in the 1st century AD. Although the Bible refers to them as Ethiopians, scholars have argued that Ethiopia was a common term encompassing the area South-Southeast of Egypt.

Other traditions have the convert as a Jew who was a steward in the Queen's court.Wikipedia:Please clarify All accounts do agree on the fact that the traveler was a member of the royal court who successfully succeeded in converting the Queen, which in turn caused a church to be built. Tyrannius Rufinus, a noted church historian, also recorded a personal account as do other church historians such as Socrates and Sozemius.[819] Some experts predict the shift of Christianity's center from the European industrialized nations to Africa and Asia in modern times. Yale University historian Lamin Sanneh stated, that "African Christianity was not just an exotic, curious phenomenon in an obscure part of the world, but that African Christianity might be the shape of things to come."[820] The statistics from the World Christian Encyclopedia (David Barrett) illustrate the emerging trend of dramatic Christian growth on the continent and supposes, that in 2025 there will be 633 million Christians in Africa.[821]

A 2015 study estimates 2,161,000 Christian believers from a Muslim background in Africa, most of them belonging to some form of Protestantism.

Islam

Islam is the other major religion in Africa alongside Christianity,[822] with 47% of the population being Muslim, accounting for 1/4 of the world's Muslim population.Wikipedia:Citation needed The faith's historic roots on the continent stem from the time of the Prophet Muhammad, whose early disciples migrated to Abyssinia (hijira) in fear of persecution from the pagan Arabs.

The spread of Islam in North Africa came with the expansion of Arab empire under Caliph Umar, through the Sinai Peninsula. Spread of Islam in West Africa was through Islamic traders and sailors.

Islam is the dominant religion in North Africa and the Horn of Africa. It has also become the predominant religion on the Swahili Coast as well as the West African seaboard and parts of the interior. There have been several Muslim empires in Western Africa which exerted considerable influence, notably the Mali Empire, which flourished for several centuries and the Songhai Empire, under the leadership of Mansa Musa, Sunni Ali and Askia Mohammed.

The vast majority of Muslims in Africa are Sunni, belonging to either Maliki or Shafi schools of jurisprudence. However, Hanafi school of jurisprudence is

Figure 205: *The Great Mosque of Kairouan, erected in 670 by the Arab general Uqba Ibn Nafi, is the oldest mosque in North Africa, Kairouan, Tunisia.*

Figure 206: *Abuja National Mosque in Nigeria.*

Figure 207: *Bahá'í House of Worship, Kampala, Uganda.*

also represented, mainly in Egypt. There are also sizeable minorities of Shias, Ahmadis, Ibadi and Sufis.[823]

Judaism

Adherents of Judaism can be found scattered in a number of countries across Africa; including North Africa, Ethiopia, Uganda, Kenya, Cameroon, Gabon, Ghana, Ivory Coast, Sierra Leone, Nigeria and Southern Africa.

Bahá'í Faith

The Bahá'í Faith in Africa has a diverse history. It especially had wide-scale growth in the 1950s which extended further in the 1960s. The Association of Religion Data Archives (relying on World Christian Encyclopedia) lists many large and smaller populations in Africa with Kenya, the Democratic Republic of the Congo, South Africa and Zambia among the top ten numerical populations of Bahá'ís in the world in 2005 (each with over 200,000 adherents), and Mauritius in terms of percentage of the national population.

All three individual heads of the religion, Bahá'u'lláh, 'Abdu'l-Bahá, and Shoghi Effendi, were in Africa at various times. More recently the roughly 2000 Bahá'ís of Egypt have been embroiled in the Egyptian identification card

Figure 208: *Ganga Talao in Mauritius*

controversy from 2006 through 2009. Since then there have been homes burned down and families driven out of towns. On the other hand, Sub-Saharan Bahá'ís were able to mobilize for nine regional conferences called for by the Universal House of Justice 20 October 2008 to celebrate recent achievements in grassroots community-building and to plan their next steps in organizing in their home areas.

Hinduism

Hinduism has existed in Africa mainly since the late 19th century. It is the largest religion in Mauritius, and several other countries have Hindu temples.Wikipedia:Citation needed

Buddhism and Chinese religions

Buddhism is a tiny religion in Africa with around 250,000 practicing adherents, and up to nearly 400,000 if combined with Taoism and Chinese Folk Religion as a common traditional religion of mostly new Chinese migrants (significant minority in Mauritius, Réunion, and South Africa). About half of African Buddhists are now living in South Africa, while Mauritius has the highest Buddhist percentage in the continent, between 1.5% to 2% of the total population.

Figure 209: *Nan Hua Temple in Bronkhorstspruit, South Africa.*

Other religions

Other faiths are practiced in Africa, including Sikhism, Jainism, Zoroastrianism and Rastafarianism among others.

Irreligion

A Gallup poll shows that the irreligious comprise 20% in South Africa, 16% in Botswana, 13% in Mozambique, 13% in Togo, 12% in Libya and Côte d'Ivoire, 10% in Ethiopia and Angola, 9% in Sudan, Zimbabwe and Algeria, 8% in Namibia and 7% in Madagascar.[824]

Syncretism

Syncretism is the combining of different (often contradictory) beliefs, often while melding practices of various schools of thought. In the commonwealth of Africa syncretism with indigenous beliefs is practiced throughout the region. It is believed by some to explain religious tolerance between different groups. Kwesi Yankah and John Mbiti argue that many African peoples today have a 'mixed' religious heritage to try to reconcile traditional religions with Abrahamic faiths. Jesse Mugambi claims that the Christianity taught to Africans by missionaries had a fear of syncretism, which was carried on by current African Christian leadership in an attempt to keep Christianity "pure." Syncretism in Africa is said by others to be overstated, and due to a misunderstanding of the abilities of local populations to form their own orthodoxies and also confusion over what is culture and what is religion.Wikipedia:Citation needed Others state that the term syncretism is a vague one,[825] since it can be applied to refer to substitution or modification of the central elements of Christianity or Islam with beliefs or practices from somewhere else. The consequences under this definition, according to missiologist Keith Ferdinando, are a fatal compromise of the religion's integrity. However, communities in Africa (e.g. Afro-Asiatic) have many common practices which are also found in Abrahamic faiths, and thus these traditions do not fall under the category of some definitions of syncretism.

Religious distribution

Religion in Africa by country and region, as percentage of national population[n1]

Country	Population	Christianity	Christian Population	Islam	Muslim Population	Other	Other Religions
Angola	29,250,009	95	27,787,508	0.5	146,250	4.5	1,316,250
Cameroon	23,794,164	69	16,417,973	21	4,996,774	10	2,379,416
Central African Republic	4,737,423	50	2,368,711	15	710,613	35	1,658,098
Chad	15,353,184	41	6,294,805	58	8,904,846	1	153,531
Democratic Republic of the Congo	84,004,989	80	67,203,991	10	8,400,498	10	8,400,498
Republic of the Congo[826]	5,399,895	79	4,265,917	1.6	86,398	19.4	1,047,579
Equatorial Guinea	1,222,442	91	1,112,422	4.1	50,120	4.9	59,899
Gabon	2,067,561	73	1,509,319	10	206,756	17	351,485
São Tomé and Príncipe	197,700	97	191,769	2	3,954	1	1,977
Burundi	10,681,186	75	8,010,889	5	534,059	20	2,136,237
Comoros	850,688	0.7	5,954	98.3	836,226	1	8,506
Kenya	50,950,879	83	42,289,229	11.2	5,706,498	5.8	2,955,150
Madagascar	26,262,810	41	10,767,752	7	1,838,396	52	13,656,661
Malawi	17,931,637	79.9	14,327,377	12.8	2,295,249	7.3	1,309,009
Mauritius	1,264,887	32.7	413,618	17.3	218,825	50	632,443
Mayotte	256,518	1.2	3,078	98.8	253,439	0	0
Mozambique	28,861,863	54.1	15,614,267	22.8	6,580,504	23.1	6,667,090

Country							
Réunion<wbr />	865,826	84.8	734,220	4.2	36,364	11	95,240
Rwanda<wbr />	12,001,136	93.4	11,209,061	4.8	576,054	1.8	216,020
Seychelles<wbr />	94,205	93.1	87,704	1.1	1,036	5.8	5,463
South Sudan	12,323,419	60.5	7,455,668	6.2	764,051	32.9	4,054,404
Tanzania<wbr />	54,199,163	61.4	33,278,286	35.2	19,078,105	1.8	975,584
Uganda<wbr />[827]	38,823,100	84.4	32,766,696	13.7	5,318,764	1.8	698,815
Zambia<wbr />[828]	16,887,720	87	14,692,316	1	168,877	12	2,026,526
Djibouti<wbr />[829]	1,049,001	3	31,470	97	1,017,530	0	0
Eritrea<wbr />	5,187,948	46.4	2,407,207	51.6	2,676,981	2	103,758
Ethiopia<wbr />	107,534,882	63	67,746,975	35	37,637,208	2	2,150,697
Somalia<wbr />	15,181,925	0	0	100	15,181,925	0	0
Algeria<wbr />[830]	42,545,964	0.5	212,729	99	42,120,504	0.5	212,729
Egypt<wbr />[831]	97,521,500	10	9,752,150	90	87,769,350	0	0
Libya<wbr />[832]	6,470,956	2.4	155,302	96.6	6,250,943	1	64,709
Morocco<wbr />[833]	34,779,400	0.9	313,014	99.1	34,466,385	0	0
Sudan<wbr />[834]	40,810,080	3	1,224,302	97	39,585,777	0	0
Tunisia<wbr />	11,446,300	0	0	99.8	11,423,407	0.2	22,892
Botswana<wbr />[835]	2,302,878	79.1	1,821,576	0.6	13,817	20.3	467,484
Lesotho<wbr />[836]	2,263,010	80	1,810,408	0.1	2,263	19.9	450,338
Namibia<wbr />[837]	2,413,643	85	2,051,596	0.4	9,654	15	362,046

Country							
South Africa<wbr />[838]	57,725,600	79.7	46,007,303	1.9	1,096,786	18.5	10,679,236
Swaziland<wbr />	1,159,250	85	985,362	10	115,925	5	57,962
Zimbabwe<wbr />	14,848,905	84	12,473,080	3	445,467	13	1,930,357
Benin<wbr />	11,362,269	48.5	5,510,700	27.7	3,147,348	22.6	2,567,872
Burkina Faso<wbr />	20,244,080	29.8	6,032,735	61.5	12,450,109	8.7	1,761,234
Cape Verde<wbr />	544,081	85	462,468	2	10,881	13	70,730
Côte d'Ivoire<wbr />	24,571,044	33.9	8,329,583	42.9	10,540,977	23.2	5,700,482
The Gambia<wbr />	2,163,765	4.2	90,878	95.7	2,070,723	0.2	4,327
Ghana[839]	29,614,337	71	21,026,179	18	5,330,580	11	3,257,577
Guinea<wbr />	11,883,516	9.7	1,152,701	86.2	10,243,590	4.1	487,224
Guinea-Bissau<wbr />	1,584,763	22.1	350,232	45.1	714,728	32.8	519,802
Liberia<wbr />	4,382,387	85	3,725,028	12.8	560,945	2.1	92,030
Mali<wbr />	19,107,706	2.4	458,584	95	18,152,320	2.6	496,800
Mauritania<wbr />	3,984,233	0	0	100	3,984,233	0	0
Niger<wbr />	21,466,863	1	214,668	98.3	21,101,926	0.7	150,268
Nigeria<wbr />[840]	191,000,000	48.3	92,250,000	48.9	93,400,000	2.8	5,350,000
Senegal<wbr />	15,726,037	3.6	566,137	96.1	15,112,721	0.3	47,178
Sierra Leone<wbr />	7,719,729	20.8	1,605,703	78.6	6,067,706	0.5	38,598
Western Sahara	567,421	0	0	100	567,421	0	0
Togo<wbr />[841]	7,352,000	29	2,132,080	20	1,470,400	51	3749520

| Africa | 1,257,190,394 | 47.31 | 594,815,686 | 44.29 | 556,783,726 | 8.40 | 105,590,982 |

1. ^ The most recent census data are used.

Further reading

- Bongmba, Elias Kifon, ed. *The Wiley-Blackwell Companion to African Religions* (2012) excerpt[842]
- Engel, Elisabeth. *Encountering Empire: African American Missionaries in Colonial Africa, 1900–1939* (Stuttgart: Franz Steiner, 2015). 303 pp.
- Mbiti, John S. *Introduction to African religion* (2nd ed. 1991) excerpt[843]
- Olupona, Jacob K. *African Religions: A Very Short Introduction* (2014) excerpt[844]
- Parrinder, Geoffrey. *African Traditional Religion*. (3rd ed. London: Sheldon Press, 1974) <templatestyles src="Module:Citation/CS1/styles.css" />ISBN 0-85969-014-8
- Parinder, E. Geoffrey. *Africa's Three Religions*. (2nd ed. London: Sheldon Press, 1976). The three religions are traditional religions (grouped), Christianity, and Islam. <templatestyles src="Module:Citation/CS1/styles.css" />ISBN 0-85969-096-2
- Ray, Benjamin C. *African Religions: Symbol, Ritual, and Community* (2nd ed. 1999)

External links

- African Beliefs[845]
- "African Traditional Religion" in "The Story of Africa" from the BBC World Service[846]
- Text of *Atoms and Ancestors*, considered a classic study[847]
- Stanford Page[848]
- African Religions at Africa Missions Resource Center[849]
- Tutelary deities of the Akan people of West Africa[850]

Territories and regions

List of regions of Africa

The continent of Africa is commonly divided into five regions or subregions, four of which are in Sub-Saharan Africa, though some definitions may contain four (removing Central Africa).

List of subregions in Africa

The five UN subregions:

- **Northern Africa**
- **Eastern Africa**
- **Central Africa**
- **Western Africa**
- **Southern Africa**

Region	Country
Northern Africa	
	Algeria
	Canary Islands
	Ceuta
	Egypt
	Libya
	Madeira
	Melilla
	Morocco
	Sudan
	Tunisia
	Western Sahara

Eastern Africa	
	Burundi
	Comoros
	Djibouti
	Eritrea
	Ethiopia
	Kenya
	Madagascar
	Malawi
	Mauritius
	Mayotte
	Mozambique
	Reunion
	Rwanda
	Seychelles
	Somalia
	South Sudan
	Tanzania
	Uganda
	Zambia
	Zimbabwe
Central Africa	
	Angola
	Cameroon
	Central African Republic
	Chad
	Democratic Republic of the Congo
	Republic of the Congo
	Equatorial Guinea
	Gabon
	São Tomé and Príncipe
Western Africa	
	Benin
	Burkina Faso
	Cape Verde
	Ivory Coast

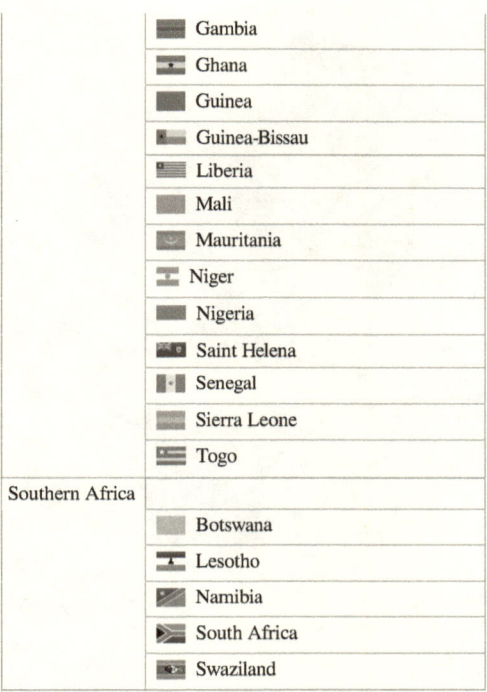

		Gambia
		Ghana
		Guinea
		Guinea-Bissau
		Liberia
		Mali
		Mauritania
		Niger
		Nigeria
		Saint Helena
		Senegal
		Sierra Leone
		Togo
Southern Africa		
		Botswana
		Lesotho
		Namibia
		South Africa
		Swaziland

Directional approach

One common approach categorises Africa directionally, e.g., by cardinal direction (compass direction):

- North Africa lies north of the Sahara and runs along the Mediterranean coast.
- West Africa is the portion roughly west of 10° east longitude, excluding Northern Africa and the Maghreb. West Africa contains large portions of the Sahara Desert and the Adamawa Mountains.
- East Africa stretches from the Red Sea and the Horn of Africa to Mozambique, including Madagascar
- Central Africa is the large mass at the center of Africa which either does not fall squarely into any other region or only partially does so.
- Southern Africa consists of the portion generally south of -10° latitude and the great rainforests of Congo.

This approach is taken, for example, in the United Nations geoscheme for Africa and the regions of the African Union.

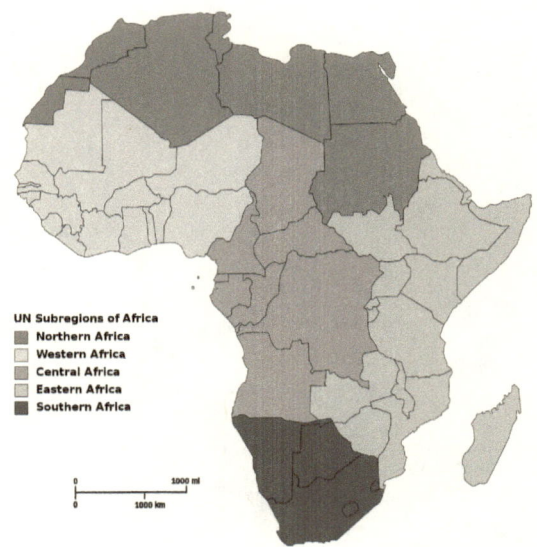

Figure 210: *The five regions according to the United Nations geoscheme for Africa.*

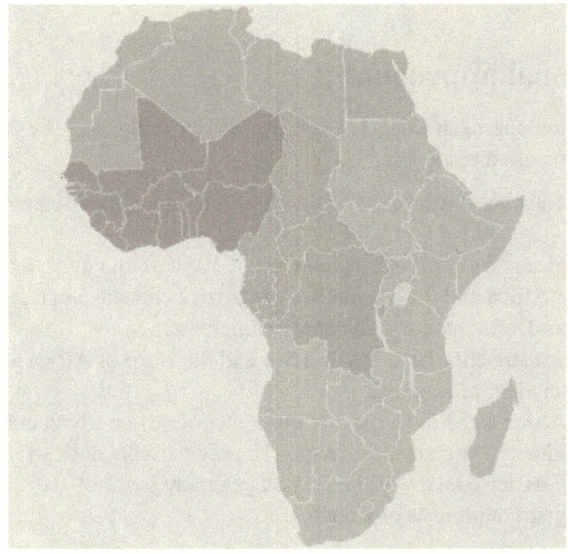

Figure 211: *The five regions of the African Union.*

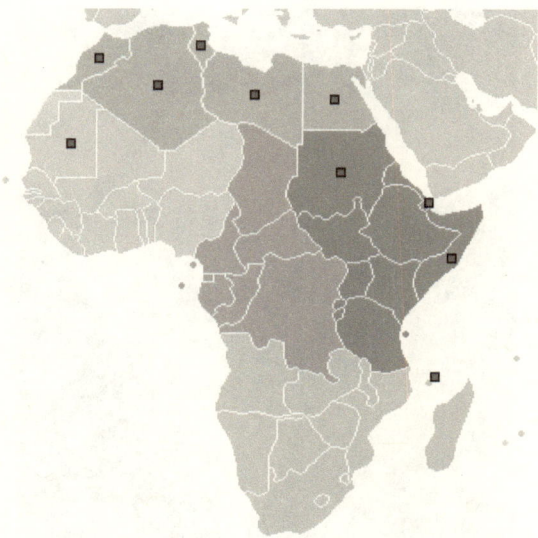

Figure 212: *The five regions of the Confederation of African Football.*

Physiographic approach

Another common approach divides Africa by using features such as landforms, climatic regions, or vegetation types:

- Nile Valley
- Nile Delta
- Atlas Mountains
- Nubia (Lower Nubia)
- The Sahara Desert is the massive but largely empty region in North Africa that contains the world's largest hot deserts
- The Maghreb is a region of northwest Africa encompassing the coastlands and Atlas Mountains of Morocco, Algeria, and Tunisia.
- The Sahel region covers a belt of grasslands south of the Sahara stretching from Senegal to Sudan.
- The Sudan region lies just below the Sahel but is slightly more humid and arable.
- Sudanian Savanna
- The Horn of Africa is a peninsula in East Africa that juts for hundreds of kilometers into the Arabian Sea, and lies along the southern side of the Gulf of Aden. It encompasses Ethiopia, Eritrea, Somalia and Djibouti.
- Ethiopian Highlands (Roof of Africa)

Figure 213: *Satellite image of Africa, showing the ecological break that defines the sub-Saharan area*

- Sub-Saharan Africa is the area of the African continent which lies south of the Sahara.
- The Guinea region is distinguished from the neighboring Sudan region by its rainforests and runs along the Atlantic coast from Guinea to Nigeria.
- Sudan (region)
- Negroland
- Rhodesia (region) (Northern Rhodesia, Southern Rhodesia)
- Mayombe
- The Congo Basin is the rainforest region
- The Chad Basin The Chad Basin is the largest endorheic drainage basin in Africa, centered on Lake Chad.
- East African Rift. The region contains Tanzania, Kenya, Uganda.
- Eastern Rift mountains
- Rift Valley Lakes
- African Great Lakes
- Swahili Coast
- Pepper Coast
- Gold Coast
- Slave Coast
- Ivory Coast

- Barbary Coast
- Mittelafrika
- Igboland (Mbaise)
- Maputaland

Linguistic approach

By official language

- Anglophone Africa includes five countries in West Africa (The Gambia, Sierra Leone, Liberia, Ghana, and the most populous African country Nigeria, as well as a part of Cameroon) that are separated by Francophone countries, South Sudan, and a large continuous area in Southern Africa and the African Great Lakes.
- Arabophone Africa includes the four most populous Arabic-speaking countries (Egypt, Sudan, Morocco, Algeria) as well as Tunisia, Mauritania and Chad, and includes a majority of both the population and the area of the Arabic-speaking countries. French has also kept a strong role in the Maghreb countries, though this has receded somewhat with official Arabization.
- Francophone Africa is a continuous area in West Africa and Central Africa, plus Madagascar and Djibouti.
- Lusophone Africa consists of the widely separated countries of Cabo Verde, Guinea-Bissau, Sao Tome and Principe, Angola, and Mozambique.
- Equatorial Guinea is the only African country where the Spanish language is official, though French and more recently Portuguese have also been added as official languages.
- Swahili is widely used as an inter language in East Africa; its use for official and educational functions is greatest in Tanzania.
- Ethiopia and Somalia use the Afro-Asiatic Amharic and Somali languages, respectively, as their official languages, although Arabic also serves as a secondary language in Somalia. Eritrea and parts of Ethiopia use the Tigrinya language and Arabic language as working languages.

By indigenous language family

- Niger–Congo languages and Nilo-Saharan languages are spoken in most of Sub-Saharan Africa. Nilo-Saharan occupies a smaller area but is highly diverse, and may be related as a parent or sibling of Niger–Congo.
- Afro-Asiatic languages are spoken in North Africa, the Horn of Africa, as well as parts of the Sahel.

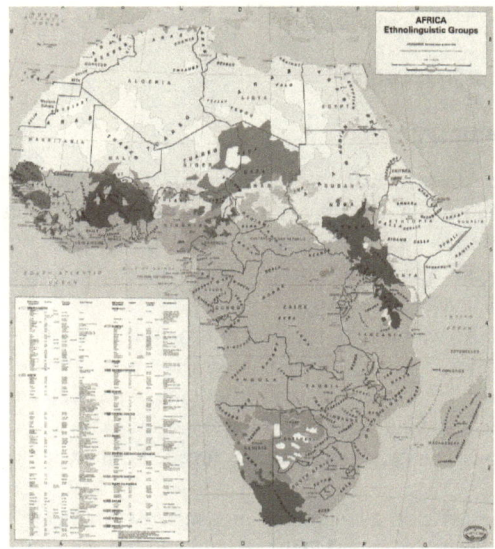

Figure 214:
Map showing the traditional language families represented in Africa:
Afroasiatic (Semitic-Hamitic)
Austronesian (Malay-Polynesian)
Indo-European
Khoisan
Niger-Congo:
Bantu
Central and Eastern Sudanese
Central Bantoid
Eastern Bantoid
Guinean
Mande
Western Bantoid
Nilo-Saharan:
Kanuri
Nilotic
Songhai

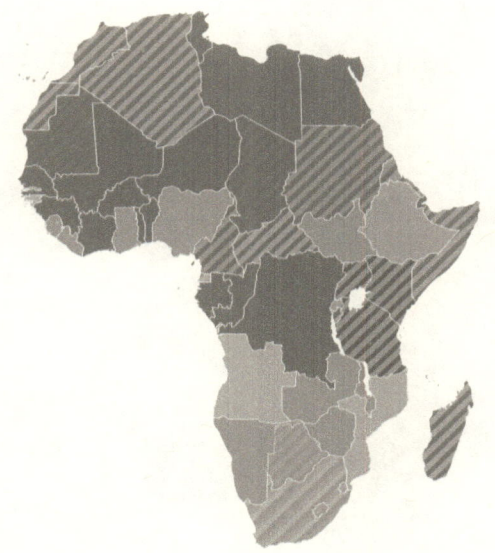

Figure 215:
Official languages in Africa

- Khoisan languages are spoken in desert areas of Southern Africa, but were formerly spoken over a larger area, and are thought to include two small languages (Hadza and Sandawe) in the African Great Lakes.
- Austronesian languages originating from Southeast Asia are spoken in Madagascar.

Investment approach

A slightly less common, but equally important method of division of the continent is by investment factors. For the purposes of investing, Africa is not a single destination with a single set of standardized risk factors and homogeneous potential for reward. Although some high-level similarities are evident, digging into the specifics of certain regions and countries shows that Africa comprises a range of distinct investment destinations, each with its own attractions, flaws, cultural differences and business practices.

The investment approach was first developed by global, independent financial analytics provider and investment consultant, RisCura[851].

- Maghreb region

Figure 216: *Investment divisions of Africa. Source: RisCura*[851]

Otherwise known as the western portion of Northern Africa, these countries form the Arab Maghreb Union, established in 1989. The region was established with the goal of functioning as a unified political and economic grouping. Political unrest in the region has stunted progress since its inception but hope still remains that the Union will fulfill its purpose in years to come. Algeria, Libya, Mauritania, Morocco and Tunisia are included in this region.

- Egypt and Sudan

  Previously united under British rule, these countries still share strong ties, as well as one significant commonality – the trade facilitation through transport on the Nile River. As Egypt does not fall within the Arab Maghreb Union, it is separated from the rest of North Africa. However, Egypt's strong economic and cultural ties with the Middle East bring natural trading partners, and it is often seen grouped with the Middle East for investment purposes.

- Francophone West Africa

  This is a commonly recognized region on the continent, and typically includes Mauritania. However, Mauritania is sometimes allocated to the Maghreb region as it is found to have closer ties to the North African countries. These French-speaking countries share more than just a language. Due to their common history as French colonies, they

also share similar legal and socio-political systems. The countries in this group are Benin, Burkina Faso, Cape Verde, Côte d'Ivoire, Guinea, Mali, Niger, São Tomé and Príncipe, Senegal and Togo.
- Nigeria
  On its own, Nigeria is the size of the entire Maghreb region on an aggregated-GDP basis. While Nigeria is traditionally grouped with the rest of West Africa, its reliance on the rest of the region is less pronounced, likely as a result of its massive standalone GDP, its access to international markets via its six large ports, and its population of over 170 million people.
- East Africa
  This is a combination of the East African Community (Kenya, Tanzania, Uganda, Rwanda and Burundi), the LAPSSET corridor (Kenya, South Sudan and Ethiopia) as well as Djibouti, a crucial link to the Indian Ocean for Ethiopia and South Sudan. Kenya has traditionally headlined this region through consistently generating the largest GDP and acts as the primary route to international trade through the Mombasa port.
- Central Africa
  This market is the same as that defined by the African Development Bank with the exception of Madagascar, which here is classified as Southern Africa (ex-SA). On a GDP basis (USD) and by population, the Central Africa region is on par with the Francophone West African region. Countries included here are Cameroon, Central African Republic, Chad and the Democratic Republic of Congo, as well as Equatorial Guinea and Gabon.
- Southern Africa excluding South Africa (ex-SA)
  This incorporates countries south of central and eastern Africa, and north of the South African border. The region has support from the most developed economy on the continent from the south, and access to capital coming out of South Africa as large companies look to expand into the rest of the continent. The group comprises Angola (which offers substantial oil resources), Botswana, Comoros, Madagascar, Malawi, Mauritius, Mozambique, Namibia, Reunion, Zambia (substantial supply of copper) and Zimbabwe.
- South Africa
  Like Nigeria, South Africa is a large African economy on a standalone basis. Due to the developed nature of South Africa relative to the rest of the continent, it has not been included in the Southern African region. South Africa boasts the largest GDP per capita of all the regions (double that of Nigeria) and is the most advanced investment destination on the continent. The South African market includes Lesotho

and Swaziland due to their reliance and proximity to SA. The Swazi lilangeni is pegged to the South African rand, which is also accepted as currency within the country.
- Other West Africa
  This region includes Ghana, Liberia, Sierra Leone, Guinea-Bissau and The Gambia.

Appendix

References

[1] From 1984 to 2003, an alternative scientific hypothesis was the multiregional origin of modern humans, which envisioned a wave of *Homo sapiens* migrating earlier from Africa and interbreeding with local *Homo erectus* populations in varied regions of the globe.Robert Jurmain; Lynn Kilgore; Wenda Trevathan (20 March 2008). *Essentials of Physical Anthropology* https://books.google.com/books?id=TSaSPza9LMYC&pg=PA266. Cengage Learning. pp. 266–. ISBN 978-0-495-50939-4. Retrieved 14 June 2011.<templatestyles src="Module:Citation/CS1/styles.css"></templatestyles>

[2] See also *Modern humans in China ~80,000 years ago (?)* http://dienekes.blogspot.nl/2015/10/modern-humans-in-china-80000-years-ago.html, Dienekes' Anthropology Blog.

[3] McChesney: "...genetic evidence suggests that a small band with the marker M168 migrated out of Africa along the coasts of the Arabian Peninsula and India, through Indonesia, and reached Australia very early, between 60,000 and 50,000 years ago. This very early migration into Australia is also supported by Rasmussen et al. (2011).

[4] Young McChesney 2015.

[5] See also *mtDNA from 55 hunter-gatherers across 35,000 years in Europe* http://dienekes.blogspot.nl/2016/02/mtdna-from-55-hunter-gatherers-across.html, Dienekes' Anthroplogy Bog.

[6] Beyin (2011).

[7] ; see also .

[8] Appenzeller (2012).

[9] Kay Young McChesney: "Wells (2003) divided the descendants of men who left Africa into a genealogical tree with 11 lineages. Each genetic marker represents a single-point mutation (SNP) at a specific place in the genome. First, genetic evidence suggests that a small band with the marker M168 migrated out of Africa along the coasts of the Arabian Peninsula and India, through Indonesia, and reached Australia very early, between 60,000 and 50,000 years ago. This very early migration into Australia is also supported by Rasmussen et al. (2011). Second, a group bearing the marker M89 moved out of northeastern Africa into the Middle East 45,000 years ago. From there, the M89 group split into two groups. One group that developed the marker M9 went into Asia about 40,000 years ago. The Asian (M9) group split three ways: into Central Asia (M45), 35,000 years ago; into India (M20), 30,000 years ago; and into China (M122), 10,000 years ago. The Central Asian (M45) group split into two groups: toward Europe (M173), 30,000 years ago and toward Siberia (M242), 20,000 years ago. Finally, the Siberian group (M242) went on to populate North and South America (M3), about 10,000 years ago.<ref name="FOOTNOTEYoungMcChesney2015">Young McChesney 2015.

[10] The researchers used radiocarbon dating techniques on pollen grains trapped in lake-bottom mud to establish vegetation over the ages of the Malawi lake in Africa, taking samples at 300-year-intervals. Samples from the megadrought times had little pollen or charcoal, suggesting sparse vegetation with little to burn. The area around Lake Malawi, today heavily forested, was a desert approximately 135,000 to 90,000 years ago.<ref name="U of AZ">

[11] Finlayson (2009), p. 68.

[12] Liu, Prugnolle et al. (2006).

[13] See also *Ancestors of Eastern Neandertals admixed with modern humans 100 thousand years ago* http://dienekes.blogspot.nl/2016/02/ancestors-of-eastern-neandertals.html, Dienekes'Anthropology Blog.

[14]

See also 55,000-Year-Old Skull Fossil Sheds New Light on Human Migration out of Africa http://www.sci-news.com/othersciences/anthropology/science-55000-year-old-skull-fossil-manot-cave-israel-02443.html, Science News.

[15] Groucutt et al. (2015).

[16] ; summary in Kliman (ed.), *Encyclopedia of Evolutionary Biology* (2016), p. 451 https://books.google.com/books?id=_r4OCAAAQBAJ&pg=PA451#v=onepage&q&f=false

[17] Elizabeth Matisoo-Smith, K. Ann Horsburgh, *DNA for Archaeologists*, Routledge (2016).

[18] East Asians 2.3-2.6%, Western Eurasians 1.8-2.4% ()

[19]

Stringer, C. B. (1992). "Replacement, continuity and the origin of Homo sapiens". In: *Continuity or replacement? Controversies in Homo sapiens evolution*. F. H. Smith (ed). Rotterdam: Balkema. pp. 9–24.

Bräuer, G.; Stringer, C. (1997). "Models, polarization, and perspectives on modern human origins". In: *Conceptual issues in modern human origins research*. New York: Aldine de Gruyter. pp. 191–201.

[20] Liu Wu in Zhisheng, Weijian Zhou (eds.), *Quaternary Geology* VSP (1997), p. 24 https://books.google.com/books?id=QZym919tNigC&pg=PA24.

[21] "evidence that our species arose in Africa about 150 000 years before present (YBP), migrated out of Africa into Asia about 60 000 to 70 000 YBP and into Europe about 40 000 to 50 000 YBP, and migrated from Asia and possibly Europe to the Americas about 20 000 to 30 000 YBP."

[22] http://www.nature.com/news/human-migrations-eastern-odyssey-1.10560

[23] //doi.org/10.4061%2F2011%2F615094

[24] //www.ncbi.nlm.nih.gov/pmc/articles/PMC378623

[25] //doi.org/10.1086%2F345487

[26] //www.ncbi.nlm.nih.gov/pubmed/12478481

[27] https://books.google.com/books?id=EzBV3OPb5mAC&pg=PA68

[28] //doi.org/10.1002%2Fevan.21455

[29] //www.ncbi.nlm.nih.gov/pmc/articles/PMC1288200

[30] //doi.org/10.1086%2F302863

[31] //www.ncbi.nlm.nih.gov/pubmed/10733465

[32] http://adsabs.harvard.edu/abs/2015Natur.520..216H

[33] //doi.org/10.1038%2Fnature14134

[34] //www.ncbi.nlm.nih.gov/pubmed/25629628

[35] //www.ncbi.nlm.nih.gov/pmc/articles/PMC4933530

[36] http://adsabs.harvard.edu/abs/2016Natur.530..429K

[37] //doi.org/10.1038%2Fnature16544

[38] //www.ncbi.nlm.nih.gov/pubmed/26886800

[39] //www.ncbi.nlm.nih.gov/pmc/articles/PMC1559480

[40] //doi.org/10.1086%2F505436

[41] //www.ncbi.nlm.nih.gov/pubmed/16826514

[42] http://www.nature.com/doifinder/10.1038/nature15696

[43] http://adsabs.harvard.edu/abs/2015Natur.526..696L

[44] //doi.org/10.1038%2Fnature15696

[45] //www.ncbi.nlm.nih.gov/pubmed/26466566

[46] http://adsabs.harvard.edu/abs/2005Sci...308.1034M

[47] //doi.org/10.1126%2Fscience.1109792

[48] //www.ncbi.nlm.nih.gov/pubmed/15890885

[49] https://books.google.com/books?id=WrR9OShae2wC&pg=PT148

[50] http//www.cell.com

[51] //doi.org/10.1016%2Fj.cub.2016.01.037

[52] //www.ncbi.nlm.nih.gov/pubmed/26853362

[53] //www.ncbi.nlm.nih.gov/pmc/articles/PMC1617318

[54] //doi.org/10.1128%2FJVI.00441-06

[55] //www.ncbi.nlm.nih.gov/pubmed/17005670

[56] //doi.org/10.1006%2Fjhev.2002.0601

[57] //www.ncbi.nlm.nih.gov/pubmed/12473485
[58] http://sgo.sagepub.com/content/5/4/2158244015611712
[59] //doi.org/10.1177%2F2158244015611712
[60] http://www.britannica.com/EBchecked/topic/275670/human-evolution
[61] http://humanorigins.si.edu/evidence/human-evolution-timeline-interactive
[62] Africa Information
[63] http://www.eyewitnesstohistory.com/slavetrade.htm
[64] //en.wikipedia.org/w/index.php?title=Template:Human_history&action=edit
[65] Shillington, Kevin (2005), *History of Africa*, p. 2. Rev. 2nd ed. New York: Palgrave Macmillan.
[66] Shillington (2005), p. 2.
[67] Shillington (2005), p. 2-3.
[68] Shillington (2005), p. 3.
[69] Ehret, Christopher (2002), *The Civilizations of Africa*, p. 22. Charlottesville: University of Virginia.
[70] Genetic studies by Luca Cavalli-Sforza pioneered tracing the spread of modern humans from Africa.
[71] Sarah A. Tishkoff,* Floyd A. Reed, Françoise R. Friedlaender, Christopher Ehret, Alessia Ranciaro, Alain Froment, Jibril B. Hirbo, Agnes A. Awomoyi, Jean-Marie Bodo, Ogobara Doumbo, Muntaser Ibrahim, Abdalla T. Juma, Maritha J. Kotze, Godfrey Lema, Jason H. Moore, Holly Mortensen, Thomas B. Nyambo, Sabah A. Omar, Kweli Powell, Gideon S. Pretorius, Michael W. Smith, Mahamadou A. Thera, Charles Wambebe, James L. Weber, Scott M. Williams. The Genetic Structure and History of Africans and African Americans http://www.sciencemag.org/cgi/content/full/1172257/DC1. Published 30 April 2009 on Science Express.
[72] Diamond, Jared (1997), *Guns, Germs, and Steel: The Fates of Human Societies*, pp. 126–127.
[73] Ehret (2002), pp. 64–75, 80–81, 87–88.
[74] Ehret (2002), pp. 64–75.
[75] https://www.britannica.com/topic/Mande
[76] Ehret (2002), pp. 82–84.
[77] Ehret (2002), pp. 94, 95.
[78] Orbit: Earth's Extraordinary Journey documentary
[79] Dr. Stuart Tyson Smith http://www.anth.ucsb.edu/faculty/stsmith/research/nubia_history.html
[80] PlanetQuest Education http://www.planetquest.org/learn/nabta.html
[81] Late Neolithic megalithic structures at Nabta Playa http://www.comp-archaeology.org/WendorfSAA98.html – Wendorf (1998)
[82] Peter Mitchell et al., The Oxford Handbook of African Archeology (2013), p. 855: "The relatively recent discovery of extensive walled settlements at the transition from the Neolithic to the Early Iron Age in the Chad Basin (Magnavita et al., 2006) indicates what enormous sites and processes may still await recognition."
[83] Appiah & Gates 2010, p. 254.
[84] Nicholson, Paul T, and Ian Shaw (2000), *Ancient Egyptian Materials and Technology*, p. 168. Cambridge University Press.
[85] Nicholson and Shaw (2000), pp. 149–160
[86] Swami, Bhaktivejanyana (2013), *Ithihaasa: The Mystery of Story Is My Story of History*, p. 98. Author House. , 9781477242735.
[87] Nicholson and Shaw (2000), pp. 161–165, 170.
[88] Ehret (2002), pp. 136–137.
[89] Martin and O'Meara. "Africa, 3rd Ed." http://princetonol.com/groups/iad/lessons/middle/history1.htm#Irontechnology Indiana: Indiana University Press, 1995.
[90] É. Zangato & A.F.C. Holl. On the Iron Front: New Evidence from North-Central Africa Journal of African Archaeology http://www.african-archaeology.de/index.php?page_id=154&journal_id=24&pdf_id=172 , Volume 8 (1), 2010, pages 7–23,
[91] Iron in Africa: Revising the History, UNESCO http://portal.unesco.org/en/ev.php-URL_ID=3432&URL_DO=DO_PRINTPAGE&URL_SECTION=201.html Aux origines de la métallurgie du fer en Afrique, Une ancienneté méconnue: Afrique de l'Ouest et Afrique centrale.

[92] Shillington (2005), pp. 37–39.
[93] O'Brien, Patrick Karl (2002), *Atlas of World History*, pp. 22–23. Oxford: Oxford University Press.
[94] Simson Najovits, *Egypt, trunk of the tree, Volume 2*, (Algora Publishing: 2004), p.258.
[95] Ehret (2002), pp. 143–46.
[96] Davidson, Basil (1991), *Africa In History: Themes and Outlines*, pp. 30–33. Revised and expanded ed. New York: Simon & Schuster
[97] Davidson (1991), pp. 30–33.
[98] Grimal. (1988) p. 155
[99] Grimal. (1988) p. 156
[100] Habachi. (1963) pp. 16–52
[101] Ehret (2002), pp. 144, 145.
[102] Alberge, Dalya. "Tomb Reveals Ancient Egypt's Humiliating Secret", *The Times*{London}, 28 July 2003(Monday).
[103] Ehret (2002), pp. 148–151.
[104] Shillington (2005), pp. 40–41.
[105] Shillington (2005), pp. 42–45.
[106] Iliffe, John (2007), *Africans: The History of a Continent*, p. 30. 2nd ed. New York:Cambridge University Press.
[107] Shillington (2005), pp. 63–65.
[108] Shillington (2005), pp. 65.
[109] Phoenicia, pg. 199.
[110] Rose, Jeanne, and John Hulburd, *The Aromatherapy Book*, p. 94.
[111] Vine, Peter, *Oman in History*, p. 324.
[112] Collins, Robert O., and James M. Burns (2007), *A History of Sub-Saharan Africa*, pp. 66–71. New York City: Cambridge University Press.
[113] Iliffe (2007), p. 41.
[114] Shillington (2005), pp. 66–71.
[115] Collins and Burns (2007), pp. 79–80.
[116] Iliffe, John (2007). pp. 49,50
[117] Collins and Burns (2007), p. 78.
[118] Shillington, Kevin (2005), p. 39.
[119] after Derek Nurse and Gérrard Philipsian: The Bantu Languages. Routledge, London 2003.
[120] life (2007), pp. 34, 35.
[121] Fanso 19.
[122] Fanso 19; Hudgens and Trillo 1051.
[123] Barth, *Travels*, II, 16–17.
[124] Falola 2008, p. 26.
[125] Shillington (2005), pp. 182–183.
[126] Collins and Burns (2007), p. 90.
[127] Falola 2008, p. 27.
[128] Shillington (2005), pp. 183–184.
[129] Collins and Burns (2007), p. 91.
[130] Davidson (1991), p. 96.
[131] Falola 2008, p. 47.
[132] Udo 1970, p. 178.
[133] Shillington (2005), p. 138, 139.
[134] Davidson (1991), p. 159, 160.
[135] Shillington (2005), p. 141.
[136] Davidson (1991), p. 161.
[137] Shillington (2005), p. 139, 141.
[138] Collins and Burns (2007), pp. 185–188
[139] Shillington (2005), p. 196–198
[140] Davidson (1991), pp. 156–157
[141] Shillington (2005), p. 198, 199.
[142] Davidson (1991), p. 158.

[143] David D. Laitin, Said S. Samatar, *Somalia: Nation in Search of a State*, (Westview Press: 1987), p. 15.
[144] I.M. Lewis, *A modern history of Somalia: nation and state in the Horn of Africa*, 2nd edition, revised, illustrated, (Westview Press: 1988), p.20
[145] Brons, Maria (2003), *Society, Security, Sovereignty and the State in Somalia: From Statelessness to Statelessness?*, p. 116.
[146] Morgan, W. T. W. (1969), *East Africa: Its Peoples and Resources*, p. 18.
[147] *Journal of African History* p. 50, by John Donnelly Fage and Roland Anthony Oliver.
[148] Da Gama's First Voyage p. 88.
[149] *East Africa and its Invaders*, p. 38.
[150] Gujarat and the Trade of East Africa pg.35
[151] The return of Cosmopolitan Capital:Globalization, the State and War, p. 22.
[152] *The Arabian Seas: The Indian Ocean World of the Seventeenth Century*, by R. J. Barendse.
[153] *Gujarat and the Trade of East Africa*, p. 30.
[154] Chinese Porcelain Marks from Coastal Sites in Kenya: aspects of trade in the Indian Ocean, XIV-XIX centuries. Oxford: British Archaeological Reports, 1978 p. 2.
[155] *East Africa and its Invaders*, p. 37.
[156] Gujarat and the Trade of East Africa, p. 45.
[157] Ian Mortimer, *The Fears of Henry IV* (2007), p.111
[158] Girma Beshah and Merid Wolde Aregay, *The Question of the Union of the Churches in Luso-Ethiopian Relations (1500–1632)* (Lisbon: Junta de Investigações do Ultramar and Centro de Estudos Históricos Ultramarinos, 1964), pp. 13–4.
[159] Girma and Merid, *Question of the Union of the Churches*, pp. 25.
[160] Girma and Merid, *Question of the Union of the Churches*, pp. 45–52.
[161] Girma and Merid, *Question of the Union of the Churches*, pp. 91, 97–104.
[162] Girma and Merid, *Question of the Union of the Churches*, p. 105.
[163] van Donzel, Emeri, "Fasilädäs" in Siegbert Uhlig, ed., *Encyclopaedia Aethiopica: D-Ha* (Wiesbaden: Harrassowitz Verlag, 2005), p. 500.
[164] Shillington (2005), pp. 65–67, 72–75.
[165] Shillington (2005), pp. 75, 76.
[166] Shillington, Kevin (2005). p 90.
[167] Shillington, Kevin (2005), pp. 156, 157
[168] Shillington (2005), pp. 88–92.
[169] Shillington, Kevin (2005), pp. 166,167
[170] Shillington (2005), pp. 167–168.
[171] Shillington, Kevin (2005), p. 157.
[172] Shillington (2005), p. 158.
[173] Shillington, Kevin (2005), pp. 158,159
[174] Shillington (2005), pp. 159–161.
[175] Shillington (2005), p. 161.
[176] Shillington (2005), p. 162.
[177] Shillington (2005), p. 67
[178] Ehret (2002), p. 305.
[179] Collins and Burns (2007), p. 77.
[180] Collins and Burns 2007, p. 77.
[181] Page, Willie F.(2001). Encyclopedia of African History and Culture:From Conquest to Colonization (1500–1850). New York:Learning Source Books, p. 88, .
[182] Ehret, Christopher (2002). p. 252.
[183] Ehret (2002), pp. 252–254.
[184] Shillington (2005), pp. 147–153.
[185] Davidson (1991), pp. 252–254.
[186] Davidson (1991), pp. 252–154.
[187] Shillington (2005), p. 218.
[188] Shillington (2005), pp. 153–155.
[189] Worden, Nigel. The Making of Modern South Africa, Oxford UK/Cambridge USA: Blackwell Publishers, 1995, p. 13.

[190] Shillington (2005), pp. 210–213.
[191] Shillington (2005), pp. 213, 214.
[192] Daniel Don Nanjira, African Foreign Policy and Diplomacy: From Antiquity to the 21st Century, ABC-CLIO, 2010, p.114
[193] Jens Finke, The Rough Guide to Tanzania https://books.google.com/books?isbn=1405380187 (2010)
[194] Casson, Lionel (1989). The Periplus Maris Erythraei. Lionel Casson. (Translation by H. Frisk, 1927, with updates and improvements and detailed notes). Princeton, Princeton University Press.
[195] Chami, F. A. (1999). "The Early Iron Age on Mafia island and its relationship with the mainland." Azania Vol. XXXIV 1999, pp. 1–10.
[196] Chami, Felix A. 2002. "The Egypto-Graeco-Romans and Paanchea/Azania: sailing in the Erythraean Sea." From: Red Sea Trade and Travel. The British Museum. Sunday 6 October 2002. Organised by The Society for Arabian Studies
[197] Yu Huan, *The Weilue* in *The Peoples of the West http://depts.washington.edu/silkroad/texts/weilue/weilue.html*, translation by John E. Hill
[198] Miller, J. Innes. 1969. Chapter 8: "The Cinnamon Route". In: The Spice Trade of the Roman Empire. Oxford: University Press.
[199] Hill, John E. 2004. *The Peoples of the West from the Weilue by Yu Huan : A Third Century Chinese Account Composed between 239 and 265 CE.* https://web.archive.org/web/20050315032618/http://depts.washington.edu/uwch/silkroad/texts/weilue/weilue.html Draft annotated English translation. See especially Section 15 on *Zesan* = Azania and notes.
[200] Zanzibar: Its History and Its People https://books.google.com/books?isbn=0714611026 (1967), page 24, W.H. Ingrams
[201] Lonely Planet, Mary Fitzpatrick, Tim Bewer, Lonely Planet Tanzania https://books.google.com/books?isbn=1743213026 (2012)
[202] Rhonda M. Gonzales, Societies, religion, and history: central-east Tanzanians https://books.google.com/books?id=o6owAQAAIAAJ (2009), Page 222
[203] Collins and Burns (2007), p. 103.
[204] "Eastern and Southern Africa 500–1000 CE" http://www.metmuseum.org/toah/ht/06/sfe/ht06sfe.htm.
[205] Tanzanian dig unearths ancient secret by Tira Shubart http://news.bbc.co.uk/2/hi/africa/1924318.stm.
[206] Ibn Battuta: Travels in Asia and Africa 1325–1354 http://www.fordham.edu/halsall/source/1354-ibnbattuta.html.
[207] Page, Willie F. (2001). p. 263,264
[208] Shillington (2005), p. 135.
[209] Lye, Keith (2002). pp. 242,243
[210] Roland Oliver, et al. "Africa South of the Equator", in Africa Since 1800. Cambridge, UK: Cambridge University Press, 2005, pp. 24–25.
[211] Collins and Burns (2007), pp. 122–123.
[212] Lye, Keith (2002). p. 121,122.
[213] Collins and Burns (2007), pp. 123–124.
[214] Collins and Burns (2007), p. 124.
[215] Davidson (1991), pp. 164–165.
[216] Shillington (2005), pp. 80–85.
[217] Iliffe, John(2007). p. 51–53.
[218] Collins and Burns (2007), p. 83.
[219] Davidson (1991), pp. 173, 174.
[220] The Story of Africal BBC World Service http://www.bbc.co.uk/worldservice/africa/features/storyofafrica/4chapter1.shtml
[221] Collins and Burns (2007), pp. 83–84.
[222] Collins and Burns (2007), pp. 83–87.
[223] Davidson, Basil (1971), *Great Ages of Man: African Kingdoms*, p. 83. New York City: Time Life Books. Library of Congress 66-25647.
[224] Davidson (1971), pp. 84–85.

[225] Collins and Burns (2007), p. 87.
[226] Shillington (2005), pp. 100–101.
[227] Collins and Burns (2007), p. 88.
[228]
[229] Shillington (2005), pp. 100–102, 179–181.
[230] Lye, Keith (2002). p. 188
[231] Collins and Burns (2007), p. 139.
[232] Collins and Burns (2007), p. 140.
[233] Davidson (1991), p. 240.
[234] Collins and Burns (2007), pp. 140–141.
[235] Davidson (1991), p. 242.
[236] Shillington (2005), pp. 191, 192.
[237] Collins and Burns (2007), pp. 131–132.
[238] Davidson (1991), pp. 173–174.
[239] Collins and Burns (2007), p. 134.
[240] Stride, G.T. & C. Ifeka (1971). *Peoples and Empires of West Africa: West Africa in History 1000–1800*. Edinburgh: Nelson.
[241] Collins and Burns (2007), pp. 134–135.
[242] Shillington (2005), pp. 188–189.
[243] Collins and Burns (2007), pp. 136–137.
[244] Martin, Phyllis M. and O'Meara, Patrick(1995). p. 95.
[245] Collins and Burns (2007), p. 137.
[246] Shillington (2005), pp. 218, 327–329, 340–342.
[247] Shillington (2005), pp. 218, 327
[248] Shillington (2005), pp. 218, 327.
[249] Shillington (2005), pp. 256, 257, 270.
[250] Shillington (2005), pp. 256, 257.
[251] Davidson (1991), pp. 274–275.
[252] Shillington (2005), pp. 261–262, 271.
[253] Shillington (2005), pp. 215–216.
[254] Shillington (2005), pp. 268–271.
[255] Collins and Burns (2007), pp. 268–269.
[256] Collins and Burns (2007), p. 269.
[257] Collins and Burns (2007), p. 265.
[258] Shillington (2005), p. 295.
[259] Collins and Burns (2007), pp. 254–257.
[260] Lovejoy, Paul E. 2012
[261] D. W. Brogan, *France under the Republic: The Development of Modern France (1870–1930)* (1940) pp 321–26
[262] William L. Langer, *The diplomacy of imperialism: 1890–1902* (1951) pp 537–80
[263] Martin, Phyllis M. and O'Meara, Patrick (1995). p. 135–138.
[264] Alistair Horne, *A savage war of peace: Algeria 1954–1962* (1977).
[265] David Anderson, *Histories of the hanged: The dirty war in Kenya and the end of empire* (2005).
[266] Gabriel Almond and James S. Coleman, *The Politics of the Developing Areas* (1971)
[267] Festus Ugboaja Ohaegbulam, *Nationalism in colonial and post-colonial Africa* (University Press of America, 1977).
[268] Thomas Hodgkin, *Nationalism in Colonial Africa* (1956)
[269] Ashley Jackson, *The British Empire and the Second World War* (2006) 171-239.
[270] David Killingray and Richard Rathbone, edfs. *Africa and the Second World War* (1986).
[271] Jackson, *The British Empire and the Second World War* (2006) 175-77.
[272] Jackson, *The British Empire and the Second World War* (2006) pp 180-189.
[273] Jackson, *The British Empire and the Second World War* (2006) pp 240-45.
[274] Robert Aldrich, *Greater France: A History of French Overseas Expansion* (1996) p 223.
[275] Raffael Scheck, "French African Soldiers in World War II." in Thomas W.Zeiler, ed., *A Companion to World War II* (2012): vol 1:501-515.

[276] Ruth Ginio, *The French Army and Its African Soldiers: The Years of Decolonization* (U of Nebraska Press, 2017).
[277] Arthur L. Funk, "Negotiating the 'Deal with Darlan'." *Journal of Contemporary History* 8.2 (1973): 81-117.
[278] Arthur Layton Funk, *Charles de Gaulle: the crucial years, 1943-1944* (1959).
[279] Henry S. Wilson, *African decolonization* (E. Arnold, 1994).
[280] Daniel Branch, *Defeating Mau Mau, creating Kenya: Counterinsurgency, civil war, and decolonization* (Cambridge UP, 2009).
[281] Christopher C. Taylor, *Sacrifice as terror: the Rwandan genocide of 1994* (Berg Publishers, 1999).
[282] Thomas K. Park and Aomar Boum, *Historical dictionary of Morocco* (Scarecrow Press, 2006).
[283] Alistair Horne, *A savage war of peace: Algeria 1954–1962* (1977).
[284] Lye, Keith (2002). pp. 97, 264.
[285] Joseph Finklestone, *Anwar Sadat: visionary who dared* (Routledge, 2013).
[286] Leonard Thompson, *A history of South Africa* (Yale Up, 2001.
[287] Rita Barnard, ed. *The Cambridge Companion to Nelson Mandela* (Cambridge UP, 2014).
[288] J.F. Ade Ajayi and Michael Crowder. *History of West Africa* (2 vol. 1970–87)
[289] David Apter, *Ghana in transition* (Princeton University Press, 2015).
[290] David Owusu-Ansah, *Historical dictionary of Ghana* (Rowman & Littlefield, 2014)
[291] Roberts, "The British Empire in Tropical Africa"
[292] Ronald Robinson, John Gallagher, Alice Denny. *Africa and the Victorians: The Climax of Imperialism in the Dark Continent* (1961)
[293] www.amazon.com https://www.amazon.com/Oxford-history-South-Africa-Vol-1/dp/0195003829
[294] www.oxfordhandbooks.com http://www.oxfordhandbooks.com/view/10.1093/oxfordhb/9780199572472.001.0001/oxfordhb-9780199572472
[295] https://www.questia.com/library/journal/1P3-3335703931/the-african-diaspora-slavery-modernity-and-globalization
[296] //www.worldcat.org/oclc/644651969
[297] https://archive.org/details/in.ernet.dli.2015.84402
[298] https://archive.org/details/in.ernet.dli.2015.89466
[299] https://www.amazon.com/Penguin-Atlas-African-History-Revised/dp/0140513213/
[300] http://www.manning.pitt.edu/pdf/2013.Manning.JAH.pdf
[301] //doi.org/10.1017%2FS0021853713000753
[302] https://web.archive.org/web/20100815022804/http://www.worldtimelines.org.uk/world/africa
[303] http://historyscoper.com/africahistoryscope.html
[304] http://africanhistory.about.com/od/countryhistoryatoz/u/PeoplePlaces.htm
[305] http://www.bbc.co.uk/worldservice/africa/features/storyofafrica/index.shtml
[306] https://www.pbs.org/wonders/fr_wn.htm
[307] http://www.wsu.edu:8080/~dee/CIVAFRCA/ABOUT.HTM#Purpose
[308] http://www.metmuseum.org/toah/hi/te_index.asp?i=Africa
[309] http://www.africankingdoms.com/
[310] https://web.archive.org/web/20120401181050/http://web.up.ac.za/default.asp?ipkCategoryID=12651%2F
[311] //en.wikipedia.org/w/index.php?title=Template:Slavery&action=edit
[312] Based on "records for 27,233 voyages that set out to obtain slaves for the Americas". Stephen Behrendt, "Transatlantic Slave Trade", *Africana: The Encyclopedia of the African and African American Experience* (New York: Basic Civitas Books, 1999), .
[313]
[314] Shaban 1976, pp. 101-02.
[315] Noel King (ed.), *Ibn Battuta in Black Africa*, Princeton 2005, p. 54
[316] Based on "records for 27,233 voyages that set out to obtain slaves for the Americas". Stephen Behrendt, "Transatlantic Slave Trade", *Africana: The Encyclopedia of the African and African American Experience* (New York: Basic Civitas Books, 1999), .
[317] Muhammad A. J. Beg, The "serfs" of Islamic society under the Abbasid regime, Islamic Culture, 49, 2, 1975, p. 108

[318] Manning (1990) p.10
[319] Murray Gordon, *Slavery in the Arab World,* New Amsterdam Press, New York, 1989. Originally published in French by Editions Robert Laffont, S.A. Paris, 1987, page 28.
[320] "Know about Islamic Slavery in Africa" https://www.amazon.com/gp/richpub/syltguides/fullview/22NTE7XMTJIHE
[321] Irfan Shahid, *Byzantium and the Arabs in the Sixth Century,* Dumbarton Oaks, 2002, p. 364 documents; Ghassanid Arabs seizing and selling 20,000 Samaritans as slaves in the year 529, before the rise of Islam.
[322]
[323] Mintz, S. *Digital History Slavery, Facts & Myths*
[324] Jay Spaulding. "Medieval Christian Nubia and the Islamic World: A Reconsideration of the Baqt Treaty," *International Journal of African Historical Studies* XXVIII, 3 (1995)
[325] Gwyn Campbell, *The Structure of Slavery in Indian Ocean Africa and Asia,* 1 edition, (Routledge: 2003), p.ix
[326] Bridget Anderson, *World Directory of Minorities,* (Minority Rights Group International: 1997), p. 456.
[327] Catherine Lowe Besteman, *Unraveling Somalia: Race, Class, and the Legacy of Slavery,* (University of Pennsylvania Press: 1999), p. 116.
[328] Refugee Reports, November 2002, Volume 23, Number 8
[329] Alistair Boddy-Evans. Central Africa Republic Timeline – Part 1: From Prehistory to Independence (13 August 1960), A Chronology of Key Events in Central Africa Republic http://africanhistory.about.com/od/car/l/bl-CAR-Timeline-1.htm. About.com
[330] Catherine Coquery-Vidrovitch, in *Les Collections de l'Histoire* (April 2001) says: *"la traite vers l'Océan indien et la Méditerranée est bien antérieure à l'irruption des Européens sur le continent"*
[331] Davis, Robert. *Christian Slaves, Muslim Masters: White Slavery in the Mediterranean, the Barbary Coast and Italy, 1500-1800.*https://www.amazon.com/dp/1403945519
[332] The Cambridge World History of Slavery: Volume 3, AD 1420–AD 1804
[333] David Livingstone (2006). " *The Last Journals of David Livingstone, in Central Africa, from 1865 to His Death https://books.google.com/books?id=AA75Tx77sHwC*". Echo Library. p. 46.
[334] Stanley Henry M., *How I Found Livingstone; travels, adventures, and discoveries in Central Africa, including an account of four months' residence with Dr. Livingstone.* (1871)
[335] "The Abolition season" http://www.bbc.co.uk/worldservice/specials/1458_abolition/page4.shtml, BBC World Service
[336] A. J. Toynbee, *Civilization on Trial,* New York, 1948, p. 205
[337] Noel King (ed.), *Ibn Battuta in Black Africa,* Princeton 2005, p. 54
[338] Please note : The numbers occurring in the source, and repeated here on Wikipedia include both Arab and European trade.
[339] Nehemia Levtzion, Randall Lee Pouwels, The History of Islam in Africa, (Ohio University Press, 2000), p.255.
[340] Pankhurst, Richard. *The Ethiopian Borderlands: Essays in Regional History from Ancient Times to the End of the 18th Century* (Asmara, Eritrea: Red Sea Press, 1997), pp.416
[341] Pankhurst. *Ethiopian Borderlands,* pp.432
[342] Pankhurst. *Ethiopian Borderlands,* pp.59 & 435
[343] Emery Van Donzel, "Primary and Secondary Sources for Ethiopian Historiography. The Case of Slavery and Slave-Trade in Ethiopia," in Claude Lepage, ed., *Études éthiopiennes,* vol I. France: Société française pour les études éthiopiennes, 1994, pp.187-88.
[344]
[345] Mohamed Diriye Abdullahi, *Culture and Customs of Somalia,* (Greenwood Press: 2001), p.13
[346] James Hastings, *Encyclopedia of Religion and Ethics Part 12: V. 12,* (Kessinger Publishing, LLC: 2003), p.490
[347] Henry Louis Gates, *Africana: The Encyclopedia of the African and African American Experience,* (Oxford University Press: 1999), p.1746
[348] David D. Laitin, *Politics, Language, and Thought: The Somali Experience,* (University Of Chicago Press: 1977), p.52

[349] Catherine Lowe Besteman, *Unraveling Somalia: Race, Class, and the Legacy of Slavery*, (University of Pennsylvania Press: 1999), p. 51
[350] Luiz Felipe de Alencastro, "Traite", in *Encyclopædia Universalis* (2002), corpus 22, page 902.
[351] Ralph Austen, *African Economic History* (1987)
[352] Quoted in Ronald Segal's *Islam's Black Slaves* http://necrometrics.com/pre1700b.htm#ISlave
[353] Maddison, Angus. *Contours of the world economy 1-2030 AD: Essays in macro-economic history*. Oxford University Press, 2007.
[354] https://www.newscientist.com/article/dn25051-empires-and-slave-trading-left-their-mark-on-our-genes/
[355] https://books.google.com/books?id=Wkqlp-lHllcC&pg=PA101
[356] https://books.google.com/books?id=cL_jRqPmQN8C
[357] http://www.bbc.co.uk/history/british/empire_seapower/white_slaves_01.shtml
[358] http://www.bbc.co.uk/religion/religions/islam/history/slavery_1.shtml
[359] https://web.archive.org/web/20141006131931/http://www.britannica.com/blackhistory/article-24157
[360] http://www.britannica.com/blackhistory/article-24157
[361] http://www.iAbolish.org/
[362] //en.wikipedia.org/w/index.php?title=Template:Slavery&action=edit
[363] Klein, Herbert S., and Jacob Klein. *The Atlantic Slave Trade*. Cambridge University Press, 1999, pp. 103–139.
[364] Ronald Segal, *The Black Diaspora: Five Centuries of the Black Experience Outside Africa* (New York: Farrar, Straus and Giroux, 1995), , p. 4. "It is now estimated that 11,863,000 slaves were shipped across the Atlantic." (Note in original: Paul E. Lovejoy, "The Impact of the Atlantic Slave Trade on Africa: A Review of the Literature", in *Journal of African History* 30 (1989), p. 368.)
[365] Eltis, David and Richardson, David, "The Numbers Game". In: Northrup, David: *The Atlantic Slave Trade*, 2nd edn, Houghton Mifflin Co., 2002, p. 95.
[366] Basil Davidson. *The African Slave Trade*.
[367] Thornton 1998, pp. 15–17.
[368] Christopher 2006, p. 127.
[369] Thornton 1998, p. 13.
[370] Chaunu 1969, pp. 54–58.
[371] Thornton 1998, p. 24.
[372] Thornton 1998, pp. 24–26.
[373] Thornton 1998, p. 27.
[374] Ferro, Mark (1997). *Colonization: A Global History*. Routledge, p. 221, .
[375] Elikia M'bokolo, "The impact of the slave trade on Africa", *Le Monde diplomatique*, 2 April 1998. http://mondediplo.com/1998/04/02africa
[376] Thornton, p. 112.
[377] Thornton, p. 310.
[378] *Slave Trade Debates 1806*, Colonial History Series, Dawsons of Pall Mall, London 1968, pp. 203-204.
[379] Thornton, p. 45.
[380] Thornton, p. 94.
[381] Thornton 1998, pp. 28–29.
[382] Thornton 1998, p. 31.
[383] Thornton 1998, pp. 29–31.
[384] Thornton 1998, pp. 37.
[385] Thornton 1998, p. 38.
[386] Thornton 1998, p. 39.
[387] Thornton 1998, p. 40.
[388] Rodney 1972, pp. 95-113.
[389] Austen 1987, pp. 81–108.
[390] Thornton 1998, p. 44.

[391] Anne C. Bailey, *African Voices of the Atlantic Slave Trade: Beyond the Silence and the Shame* https://books.google.com/books?id=YrIjNMu5_vsC&q=Africans+were+equal+partners#v=snippet&q=Africans%20were%20equal%20partners&f=false, Beacon Press, 2005, p. 62.
[392] Anstey, Roger: *The Atlantic Slave Trade and British abolition, 1760–1810*. London: Macmillan, 1975, p. 5.
[393] P. C. Emmer, *The Dutch in the Atlantic Economy, 1580–1880. Trade, Slavery and Emancipation* (1998), p. 17.
[394] Klein 2010.
[395] Lovejoy, Paul E., "The Volume of the Atlantic Slave Trade. A Synthesis". In: Northrup, David (ed.): *The Atlantic Slave Trade*. D.C. Heath and Company, 1994.
[396] "Skeletons Discovered: First African Slaves in New World" http://www.livescience.com/history/060131_first_slaves.html, 31 January 2006, LiveScience.com. Accessed September 27, 2006.
[397] Solow, Barbara (ed.). Slavery and the Rise of the Atlantic System, Cambridge: Cambridge University Press, 1991.
[398]
[399] Thornton, p. 304.
[400] Thornton, p. 305.
[401] Thornton, p. 311.
[402] Thornton, p. 122.
[403] Howard Winant (2001), *The World is a Ghetto: Race and Democracy Since World War II*, Basic Books, p. 58.
[404] Catherine Lowe Besteman, *Unraveling Somalia: Race, Class, and the Legacy of Slavery* (University of Pennsylvania Press: 1999), pp. 83–84.
[405] Kevin Shillington, ed. (2005), *Encyclopedia of African History*, CRC Press, vol. 1, pp. 333–34; Nicolas Argenti (2007), *The Intestines of the State: Youth, Violence and Belated Histories in the Cameroon Grassfields*, University of Chicago Press, p. 42.
[406] Rights & Treatment of Slaves http://www.accessgambia.com/information/slave-treatment-rights-privileges.html . Gambia Information Site.
[407] Mungo Park, *Travels in the Interior of Africa* v. II, Chapter XXII - War and Slavery. http://www.gutenberg.org/etext/5305
[408] The Negro Plot Trials: A Chronology. http://www.law.umkc.edu/faculty/projects/ftrials/negroplot/plotchronology.html
[409] Lovejoy, Paul E. *Transformations in Slavery*. Cambridge University Press, 2000.
[410] Quick guide: The slave trade; Who were the slaves? http://news.bbc.co.uk/1/hi/world/africa/6445941.stm BBC News, 15 March 2007.
[411] Stannard, David. *American Holocaust*. Oxford University Press, 1993.
[412] *Paths of the Atlantic Slave Trade: Interactions, Identities, and Images.*
[413] Patrick Manning, "The Slave Trade: The Formal Dermographics of a Global System" in Joseph E. Inikori and Stanley L. Engerman (eds), *The Atlantic Slave Trade: Effects on Economies, Societies and Peoples in Africa, the Americas, and Europe* (Duke University Press, 1992), pp. 117-44, online at pp. 119-20. https://books.google.com/books?id=abvkqNGSTZ0C&pg=PA119
[414] Maddison, Angus. *Contours of the world economy 1-2030 AD: Essays in macro-economic history*. Oxford University Press, 2007.
[415] Gomez, Michael A. *Exchanging Our Country Marks*. Chapel Hill, 1998
[416] Thornton, John. *Africa and Africans in the Making of the Atlantic World, 1400–1800*, Cambridge University Press, 1998.
[417] Stride, G. T., and C. Ifeka. *Peoples and Empires of West Africa: West Africa in History 1000–1800*. Nelson, 1986.
[418] Winthrop, reading by John Thornton, "African Political Ethics and the Slave Trade" http://www.millersville.edu/~winthrop/Thornton.html , Millersville College.
[419] Museum Theme: The Kingdom of Dahomey http://www.museeouidah.org/Theme-Dahomey.htm, Musee Ouidah.
[420] "Dahomey (historical kingdom, Africa)" http://www.britannica.com/eb/topic-149772/Dahomey, *Encyclopædia Britannica*.

[421] "Benin seeks forgiveness for role in slave trade" http://www.finalcall.com/national/slave_trade10-08-2002.htm, *Final Call*, 8 October 2002.

[422] Le Mali précolonial. http://www.histoire-afrique.org/article76.html?artsuite=5

[423] *The Story of Africa* http://www.bbc.co.uk/worldservice/africa/features/storyofafrica/4chapter7.shtml, BBC.

[424] African Slave Owners http://www.bbc.co.uk/worldservice/africa/features/storyofafrica/9chapter2.shtml, BBC.

[425]

[426] Cohn, Raymond L. "Deaths of Slaves in the Middle Passage", *Journal of Economic History*, September 1985.

[427] Health In Slavery. http://www.ukcouncilhumanrights.co.uk/webbook-chap1.html

[428] Elkins, Stanley: *Slavery*. New York: Universal Library, 1963, p. 48.

[429] Rawley, James: *London, Metropolis of the Slave Trade*, 2003.

[430] Anstey, Roger: *The Atlantic Slave Trade and British Abolition, 1760–1810*. London: Macmillan, 1975.

[431] "Slave-grown cotton in greater Manchester" http//www.revealinghistories.org.uk, Revealing Histories.

[432] Stephen D. Behrendt, David Richardson, and David Eltis, W. E. B. Du Bois Institute for African and African-American Research, Harvard University. Based on "records for 27,233 voyages that set out to obtain slaves for the Americas".

[433] Curtin, *The Atlantic Slave Trade*, 1972, p. 88.

[434] Daudin 2004.

[435] Digital History. http://www.digitalhistory.uh.edu/topic_display.cfm?tcid=104

[436] UN report. https://www.un.org/esa/population/publications/sixbillion/sixbilpart1.pdf

[437] Walter Rodney, *How Europe Underdeveloped Africa*.

[438] Manning, Patrick: "Contours of Slavery and Social change in Africa". In: Northrup, David (ed.): *The Atlantic Slave Trade*. D.C. Heath & Company, 1994, pp. 148-160.

[439] Thornton, John. *A Cultural History of the Atlantic World 1250-1820*. 2012, p. 64.

[440] Fage, J. D. "Slavery and the Slave Trade in the Context of West African History", *The Journal of African History*, Vol. 10. No 3, 1969, p. 400.

[441] Eric Williams, *Capitalism & Slavery* (University of North Carolina Press, 1944), pp. 98–107, 169–177.

[442] David Richardson, "The British Empire and the Atlantic Slave Trade, 1660-1807," in P. J. Marshall, ed. *The Oxford History of the British Empire: Volume II: The Eighteenth Century* (1998), pp. 440-64.

[443] J.R. Ward, "The British West Indies in the Age of Abolition," in P. J. Marshall, ed. *The Oxford History of the British Empire: Volume II: The Eighteenth Century* (1998), pp. 415-39.

[444] David Eltis, *Economic Growth and the Ending of the Transatlantic Slave Trade*.

[445] Thornton, John. *Africa and Africans in the Making of the Atlantic World, 1400-1800*. Cambridge University Press, 1992.

[446] Joseph E. Inikori, "Ideology versus the Tyranny of Paradigm: Historians and the Impact of the Atlantic Slave Trade on African Societies", *African Economic History*, 1994.

[447] David Brion Davis, *The Problem of Slavery in the Age of Revolution: 1770–1823* (1975), p. 129.

[448] Library of Society of Friends Subject Guide: Abolition of the Slave Trade.

[449] Paul E. Lovejoy (2000). *Transformations in Slavery: a history of slavery in Africa*, Cambridge University Press, p. 290.

[450] John E. Selby and Don Higginbotham, *The Revolution in Virginia, 1775–1783* (2007), p. 158.

[451] Erik S. Root, *All Honor to Jefferson?: The Virginia Slavery Debates and the Positive Good Thesis* (2008), p. 19.

[452] Marcyliena H. Morgan (2002). *Language, Discourse and Power in African American Culture* https//books.google.com, Cambridge University Press, 2002, p. 20.

[453] Huw Lewis-Jones, "The Royal Navy and the Battle to End Slavery" http://www.bbc.co.uk/history/british/abolition/royal_navy_article_02.shtml, BBC, 17 February 2011.

[454] Jo Loosemore, "Sailing against slavery" http://www.bbc.co.uk/devon/content/articles/2007/03/20/abolition_navy_feature.shtml, BBC, 24 September 2014.

[455] Caroline Davies, "William Wilberforce 'condoned slavery', Colonial Office papers reveal...Rescued slaves forced into unpaid 'apprenticeships'" https://www.theguardian.com/uk/2010/aug/02/wilberforce-condoned-slavery-files-claim, *The Guardian*, 2 August 2010.
[456] Hardt, M., and A. Negri(2000), *Empire*, Cambridge, Mass, Harvard University Press, pp. 114-128.
[457] Handley 2006, pp. 21–23.
[458] Handley 2006, pp. 23–25.
[459] Osei-Tutu 2006.
[460] Handley 2006, p. 21.
[461] "Reggae and slavery" http://www.bbc.co.uk/religion/religions/rastafari/history/reggae.shtml, BBC, 9 October 2009.
[462] " Ending the Slavery Blame-Game" https://www.nytimes.com/2010/04/23/opinion/23gates.html?pagewanted=all&_r=0, *The New York Times*, 22 April 2010.
[463] " Benin Officials Apologize For Role In U.S. Slave Trade" http://articles.chicagotribune.com/2000-05-01/news/0005010158_1_slave-trade-benin-president-mathieu-kerekou. *Chicago Tribune*, 1 May 2000.
[464] "Chirac names slavery memorial day" http://news.bbc.co.uk/2/hi/europe/4662442.stm. BBC News, 30 January 2006. Accessed 22 July 2009.
[465] National Museums Liverpool, "Liverpool and the transatlantic slave trade" http://www.liverpoolmuseums.org.uk/ism/srd/liverpool.aspx. Accessed 31 August 2010.
[466] "Blair 'sorrow' over slave trade" http://news.bbc.co.uk/1/hi/uk_politics/6185176.stm. BBC News, 27 November 2006. Accessed 15 March 2007.
[467] "Blair 'sorry' for UK slavery role" http://news.bbc.co.uk/1/hi/uk_politics/6451793.stm. BBC News, 14 March 2007. Accessed 15 March 2007.
[468] "Livingstone breaks down in tears at slave trade memorial" http://www.dailymail.co.uk/pages/live/articles/news/news.html?in_article_id=477337&in_page_id=1770. *Daily Mail*, 24 August 2007. Accessed 22 July 2009.
[469] House Joint Resolution Number 728 http://leg1.state.va.us/cgi-bin/legp504.exe?071+ful+HJ728H2. Commonwealth of Virginia. Accessed 22 July 2009.
[470] Associated Press. "Alabama Governor Joins Other States in Apologizing For Role in Slavery" http://www.foxnews.com/story/0,2933,276724,00.html. Fox News, 31 May 2007. Accessed 22 July 2009.
[471] Fears, Darryl. "House Issues An Apology For Slavery" https://www.washingtonpost.com/wp-dyn/content/article/2008/07/29/AR2008072902279.html. *The Washington Post*, 30 July 2008, p. A03. Accessed 22 July 2009.
[472] Agence France-Presse. "Obama praises 'historic' Senate slavery apology" https://www.google.com/hostednews/afp/article/ALeqM5iyMeHvk7WyJys7iAyehSzik11Yqg. Google News, 18 June 2009. Accessed 22 July 2009.
[473] http//www.revealinghistories.org.uk
[474] https://www.worldcat.org/oclc/46413
[475] //www.worldcat.org/oclc/46413
[476] https//www.cambridge.org
[477] //doi.org/10.1017%2FS0022050704002633
[478] //www.worldcat.org/issn/1471-6372
[479] https://www.worldcat.org/oclc/39897280
[480] //www.worldcat.org/oclc/39897280
[481] https://www.jstor.org/stable/2674417
[482] https://books.google.com/books?id=1ySu0sQRv-MC
[483] https://books.google.com/books?id=abvkqNGSTZ0C
[484] https://web.archive.org/web/20120331141713/http://www.marcusrediker.com/Books/Slave_Ship/Synopsis_of_Slave_Ship.htm
[485] http://www.marcusrediker.com/Books/Slave_Ship/Synopsis_of_Slave_Ship.htm
[486] https://books.google.com/books/about/Public_Memory_of_Slavery.html?id=kymzngEACAAJ
[487] https://web.archive.org/web/20130325095837/http://www.slavevoyages.org/tast/index.faces
[488] http://news.bbc.co.uk/1/hi/world/africa/6445941.stm

[489] http://www.blackhistory4schools.com/slavetrade/
[490] http://fax.libs.uga.edu/HT857xA1/stamenu.html
[491] https://unequalscenes.com/
[492] https://web.archive.org/web/20140904081130/http://trace.tennessee.edu/cgi/viewcontent.cgi?article=1182&context=utk_chanhonoproj
[493] https://web.archive.org/web/20040203145656/http://www.africana.com/articles/daily/index_20021014.asp
[494] https://www.theguardian.com/world/2002/jul/13/humanities.artsandhumanities
[495] //en.wikipedia.org/w/index.php?title=Template:New_Imperialism&action=edit
[496] R. Robinson, J. Gallagher and A. Denny, *Africa and the Victorians*, London, 1965, p. 175.
[497] Kevin Shillington, *History of Africa*. Revised second edition (New York: Macmillan Publishers Limited, 2005), 301.
[498] Thomas Pakenham, *The Scramble for Africa: White Man's Conquest of the Dark Continent from 1876 to 1912* (1991) ch 1
[499] Compare:
[500] Ewout Frankema, Jeffrey Williamson, and Pieter Woltjer, "An Economic Rationale for the West African Scramble? The Commercial Transition and the Commodity Price Boom of 1835–1885," *Journal of Economic History* 78#1 (2018), pp. 231-267.
[501] Lynn Hunt, *The Making of the West*: volume C, Bedford: St. Martin, 2009.
[502] Darwin, John. "Imperialism and the Victorians: The dynamics of territorial expansion." *English Historical Review* (1997) 112#447 pp: 614–642. http://ehr.oxfordjournals.org/content/CXII/447/614.full.pdf+html
[503] H. R. Cowie, *Imperialism and Race Relations*. Revised edition, Nelson Publishing, Vol. 5, 1982.
[504] Thomas Pakenham, *The Scramble for Africa: White Man's Conquest of the Dark Continent from 1876 to 1912* (1991).
[505] Robert Aldrich, *Greater France: A history of French overseas expansion* (1996).
[506] German colonial imperialism: a late and short-term phenomenon http://www.paris4.sorbonne.fr/fr/IMG/pdf/navette-7.pdf (PDF) by Bernard Poloni, in "Imperialism, hegemony, leadership", 26 March 2004 Conference in the Sorbonne University, Paris .
[507] Hartmut Pogge von Strandmann. "Domestic Origins of Germany's Colonial Expansion under Bismarck." *Past & Present* (Feb 1969), Issue 42, pp. 140–59 in JSTOR https://www.jstor.org/pss/650184.
[508] Alfred von Tirpitz, *Erinnerungen* (1919), quoted by Hannah Arendt, *The Origins of Totalitarianism*, section on Imperialism, chapter I, part 3.
[509] Ullendorff, Edward. *The Ethiopians: An Introduction to Country and People* 2nd ed., p. 90. Oxford University Press (London), 1965.
[510] Enrico Corradini, *Report to the First Nationalist Congress*, Florence, 3 December 1919.
[511] Hochschild 2006, pp. 226–32.
[512] John D. Fage, *The Cambridge History of Africa: From the earliest times to c. 500 BC*, https://books.google.com/books?id=8DSa_viBgsgC&pg=&dq&hl=en#v=onepage&q=&f=false Cambridge University Press, 1982, p. 748.
[513] "Report of the British Consul, Roger Casement, on the Administration of the Congo Free State". http://www.urome.be/fr2/reflexions/casemrepo.pdf
[514] Rubinstein, W. D. (2004). *Genocide: a history* https://books.google.com/books?id=nMMAk4VwLLwC&pg=&dq&hl=en#v=onepage&q=&f=false. Pearson Education. pp. 98–99.
[515] Hochschild 2006, pp. 280–1.
[516] L'Aventure Humaine: *Le canal de Suez*, Article de l'historien Uwe Oster http://www.arte.tv/fr/connaissance-decouverte/aventure-humaine/Cette_20semaine/1291022.html .
[517] BBC News website:The Suez Crisis — Key maps http://news.bbc.co.uk/2/hi/middle_east/5195068.stm.
[518] Kevin Shillington, *Encyclopedia of African History* (CRC Press, 2005), p. 1406.
[519] I. M. Lewis, *The Modern History of Somaliland: from nation to state* (Weidenfeld & Nicolson: 1965), p. 78.
[520] Thomas P. Ofcansky, *Historical Dictionary of Ethiopia* (The Scarecrow Press, Inc.: 2004), p. 405.

[521] John A. Hobson, *Imperialism*, 1902, p. 61 (quoted by Arendt).
[522] Pascal Blanchard, Nicolas Bancel, and Sandrine Lemaire, "From human zoos to colonial apotheoses: the era of exhibiting the Other". http://www.ces.uc.pt/formacao/materiais_racismo_pos_racismo/From_human_zoos_to_colonial_apotheoses_the_era_of_exhibiting_the_Other.htm
[523] "These human zoos of the Colonial Republic" http://www.monde-diplomatique.fr/2000/08/BANCEL/14145.html, *Le Monde diplomatique*, August 2000 . (Translation http://mondediplo.com/2000/08/07humanzoo)
[524] Conquest and Disease or Colonialism and Health? http://www.gresham.ac.uk/event.asp?PageId=45&EventId=696 , Gresham College I Lectures and Events.
[525] "Africa's population now 1 billion" http://www.africanews.com/site/Africas_population_now_1_billion/list_messages/26588 . AfricaNews. August 25, 2009.
[526] Shillington, Kevin (2005). Encyclopedia of African history. New York: CRC Press, p. 878
[527] Lovejoy, Paul E. (2012). Transformations of Slavery: A History of Slavery in Africa. London: Cambridge University Press.
[528] Martin Klein, 'Slave Descent and Social Status in Sahara and Sudan', in Reconfiguring Slavery: West African Trajectories, ed. Benedetta Rossi (Liverpool: Liverpool University Press, 2009), 29.
[529] Southall, Roger and Melber, Henning. *A New Scramble For Africa?: Imperialism, Investment and Development*, (University of KwaZulu-Natal Press, 2009) p 40
[530] Southall and Melber, *A New Scramble For Africa?: Imperialism, Investment and Development*, pp 41-45
[531] Southall, Roger and Melber, Henning. "A New Scramble For Africa?: Imperialism, Investment and Development," South Africa: University of KwaZulu-Natal Press, 2009: 46/47
[532] Gallaher, Carolyn et al. "Key Concepts in Political Geography," London: Sage Printing Press, 2009: 123
[533] Southall, Roger and Melber, Henning. "A New Scramble For Africa?: Imperialism, Investment and Development," South Africa: University of KwaZulu-Natal Press, 2009: 192
[534] https//www.seal-pa.org
[535] http://www.uwf.edu/dearle/imperialadventure/imperial%20adventure/documents/brantlinger%20victorians%20and%20africans.pdf
[536] https://www.amazon.com/Scramble-Africa-Seminar-Studies/dp/1408220148/
[537] https://dx.doi.org/10.1080/03086534.2015.1026131
[538] //doi.org/10.1080%2F03086534.2015.1026131
[539] http://library.mpib-berlin.mpg.de/toc/z2010_334.pdf
[540] https://www.questia.com/library/3879535/sir-harry-johnston-the-scramble-for-africa
[541] https://www.amazon.com/The-Founder-Cecil-Rhodes-Pursuit/dp/0195066685/
[542] https://www.questia.com/library/3036853/the-founder-cecil-rhodes-and-the-pursuit-of-power
[543] https://www.amazon.com/Rhodes-Race-Africa-Antony-Thomas/dp/0312169825/
[544] https://www.questia.com/library/71854045/divide-and-rule-the-partition-of-africa-1880-1914
[545] https://www.theguardian.com/world/2002/jul/13/humanities.artsandhumanities
[546] https://edoc.hu-berlin.de/docviews/abstract.php?id=42990
[547] kedcfjsuhk
[548] Sundborg, Å., & Rapp, A. (1986). Erosion and sedimentation by water: problems and prospects. *Ambio*, 215-225.
[549] DEVELOPMENT OF A SOIL AND TERRAIN MAP/DATABASE FOR ANGOLA https://library.wur.nl/isric/fulltext/isricu_i27864_001.pdf
[550] Physical map of Africa http://africa.zoom-maps.com/ by National Geographic
[551] If the Prince Edward Islands are included in Africa, then Marion Island is the southernmost point at 46°54'S.
[552] http://plasma.nationalgeographic.com/ngm/0509/feature1/zoomify/index.html
[553] https://web.archive.org/web/20100117005910/http://www.usaraf.army.mil/MAP_INTERACTIVE/INTERACTIVE_MAP.swf
[554] http://tools.wmflabs.org/timescale/?Ma=60

[555] http://tools.wmflabs.org/timescale/?Ma=10
[556] http://pubs.usgs.gov/publications/text/understanding.html
[557] http://onlinelibrary.wiley.com/doi/10.1029/1999JB900009/pdf
[558] http://adsabs.harvard.edu/abs/1999JGR...104.7405M
[559] //doi.org/10.1029%2F1999JB900009
[560] Dr. Owen E. Thompson (1996). Hadley Circulation Cell. http://www.atmos.umd.edu/~owen/CHPI/IMAGES/circs02.html Channel Video Productions. Retrieved on 2007-02-11.
[561] ThinkQuest team 26634 (1999). The Formation of Deserts. http://library.thinkquest.org/26634/desert/formation.htm Oracle ThinkQuest Education Foundation. Retrieved on 2009-02-16.
[562] Global Measured Extremes of Temperature and Precipitation. http://www.ncdc.noaa.gov/oa/climate/globalextremes.html National Climatic Data Center. Retrieved on 2007-06-21.
[563] (The 136 °F (57.8 °C), claimed by 'Aziziya, Libya, on September 13, 1922, has been officially deemed invalid by the World Meteorological Organization.)
[564] Kerry H. Cook. Generation of the African Easterly Jet and Its Role in Determining West African Precipitation. http://ams.allenpress.com/perlserv/?request=get-abstract&doi=10.1175%2F1520-0442(1999)012%3C1165%3AGOTAEJ%3E2.0.CO%3B2 Retrieved on 2008-05-08.
[565] Chris Landsea. AOML Frequently Asked Questions. Subject: A4) What is an easterly wave? http://www.aoml.noaa.gov/hrd/tcfaq/A4.html Retrieved on 2008-05-08.
[566] Patrick Laux et al. (2008): Predicting the regional onset of the rainy season in West Africa. International Journal of Climatology, 28 (3), 329-342.
[567] Patrick Laux et al. (2009): Modelling daily precipitation features in the Volta Basin of West Africa. International Journal of Climatology, 29 (7), 937-954.,
[568] David Vandervort (2009). Darfur: getting ready for the rainy season. http://www.icrc.org/Web/Eng/siteeng0.nsf/html/sudan-feature-060707 International Committee of the Red Cross. Retrieved on 2009-02-06.
[569] Mehari Tesfazgi Mebrhatu, M. Tsubo, and Sue Walker (2004). A Statistical Model for Seasonal Rainfall Forecasting over the Highlands of Eritrea. http://www.cropscience.org.au/icsc2004/poster/2/6/580_mebrhatumt.htm New directions for a diverse planet: Proceedings of the 4th International Crop Science Congress. Retrieved on 2009-02-08.
[570] Alex Wynter (2009). Ethiopia: March rainy season "critical" for southern pastoralists. http://www.alertnet.org/thenews/fromthefield/218536/123391195425.htm Thomson Reuters Foundation. Retrieved on 2009-02-06.
[571] The Voice (2009). Botswana: Rainy Season Fills Up Dams. http://allafrica.com/stories/200901270599.html allAfrica.com. Retrieved on 2009-02-06.
[572] http://www.scoop.co.nz/stories/WO1010/S00173/la-nina-weather-likely-to-last-for-months.htm
[573] Dalsy Carrington, CNN, April,3, 2014 "Last chance to see: Disappearing glaciers in the 'Mountains of the Moon'" http://www.cnn.com/2014/04/03/world/africa/last-chance-disappearing-glaciers/
[574] R.W. Crosskey, G.B. White, The Afrotropical Region. A recommended term in zoogeography, Journal of Natural History, Vol.11, 5 (1977)
[575] F. Westall et al., Implications of a 3.472-3.333Gyr-old subaerial microbial mat from the Barberton greenstone belt, South Africa for the UV environmental conditions on the early Earth, Philosophical Transactions of The Royal Society B, Vol.361, No.1474 (2006)
[576] E. Gheerbrant, J.-C. Rage, Paleobiogeography of Africa: How distinct from Gondwana and Laurasia?. Palaeogeography, Palaeoclimatology, Palaeoecology, Vol 241, 9 Nov. 2006
[577] R. McCall, Implications of recent geological investigations of the Mozambique Channel for the mammalian colonization of Madagascar, Proc. R. Soc. Lond. B (1997) 264
[578] A. J. Winkler, Neogene paleobiogeography and East African paleoenvironments: contributions from the Tugen Hills rodents and lagomorphs. Journal of Human Evolution, Vol 42, January 2002
[579] M. Benammi et al., Magnetostratigraphy and paleontology of Aït Kandoula basin (High Atlas, Morocco) and the African-European late Miocene terrestrial fauna exchanges. Earth and Planetary Science Letters, Vol 145, Dec 1996

[580] A. J. Winkler, Neogene paleobiogeography and East African paleoenvironments: contributions from the Tugen Hills rodents and lagomorphs. Journal of Human Evolution, Vol 42, January 2002

[581] E. Lönnberg, The Development and Distribution of the African Fauna in Connection with and Depending upon Climatic Changes. Arkiv for Zoologi, Band 21 A. No.4.1929. pp. 1-33.

[582] J. Fjeldsaå and J.C. Lovett, Geographical patterns of old and young species in African forest biota: the significance of specific montane areas as evolutionary centres. Biodiversity and Conservation, Vol 6, No 3 March 1997

[583] Owen-Smith,N. Pleistocene extinctions; the pivotal role of megaherbivores. Paleobiology; July 1987; v. 13; no. 3; p. 351-362

[584] P. Brinck. The Relations between the South African Fauna and the Terrestrial and Limnic Animal Life of the Southern Cold Temperate Zone.Proc. Royal Soc. of London. Series B, Vol. 152, No. 949 (1960)

[585] M.H. Schleyer&L.Celliers. Modelling reef zonation in the Greater St Lucia Wetland Park, South Africa. Estuarine, Coastal and Shelf Science,Vol. 63, May 2005

[586] Richmond, M. D., 2001. The marine biodiversity of the western Indian Ocean and its biogeography. How much do we know? In: Marine Science Development in Eastern Africa. Proc. of the 20th Anniversary Conference on Marine Science in Tanzania. Institute of Marine Sciences/WIOMSA, Zanzibar

[587] M. Luc et al. (Esd.), Plant Parasitic Nematodes in Subtropical and Tropical Agriculture. CABI Publishing, 2005

[588] Fourie, H et al. Plant-parasitic nematodes in field crops in South Africa. 6. Soybean. Nematology, vol. 3, 5 (2001)

[589] J. Bridge, Nematodes of Bananas and Plantains in Africa, ISHS Acta Horticulturae 540

[590] Marais, M., Swart, A. Plant nematodes in South Africa. 6. Tzaneen area, Limpopo Province, African Plant Protection, 2003 (Vol. 9) (No. 2) 99-107

[591] R.C. Brusca and G.J. Brusca, Invertebrates, Sinauer Associates; 2 ed.(2003)

[592] S.M. Goodman et al. (eds.) The Natural History of Madagascar, University Of Chicago Press, 2007

[593] Kilburn, R.N. 2009. Genus *Kermia* (Mollusca: Gastropoda: Conoidea: Conidae: Raphitominae) in South African waters, with observations on the identities of related extralimital species. *African Invertebrates* **50** (2): 217-236.

[594] A. Jörgensen, Graphical Presentation from the African Tardigrade FaunaUsing GIS with the Description of *Isohypsibius malawiensis* sp. n. (Eutardigrada: Hypsibiidae) from Lake Malawi, Zoologischer Anzeiger Vol 240,2001

[595] Meyer, H.A. & Hinton, J.G. 2009. The Tardigrada of southern Africa, with the description of *Minibiotus harrylewisi*, a new species from KwaZulu-Natal, South Africa (Eutardigrada: Macrobiotidae). *African Invertebrates* **50** (2): 255-268.

[596] Cumberlidge, N. et al. 2008. A revision of the higher taxonomy of the Afrotropical freshwater crabs (Decapoda: Brachyura) with a discussion of their biogeography. *Biological Journal of the Linnean Society* **93**: 399–413.

[597] Okwakol, M.J.N. & Sekamatte, M.B. 2007. Soil macrofauna research in ecosystems in Uganda. *African Journal of Ecology* **45** Suppl. 2.

[598] Plisko, J.D. 2006. The Oligochaeta type material housed at the Natal Museum, South Africa. *African Invertebrates* **47**: 57-61.

[599] Plisko, J.D. 2009. Pre-testical spermathecal pores and unusual setal arrangement in the South African endemic microchaetid earthworms of presumed Gondwanan origin (Oligochaeta: Microchaetidae). *African Invertebrates* **50** (2): 237-254.

[600] S.E. Miller, & L.M. Rogo, Challenges and opportunities in understanding and utilisation of African insect diversity. Cimbebasia 17: 197-218, 2001

[601] K.J. Gaston and E. Hudson, Regional patterns of diversity and estimates of global insect species richness. Biodiversity and Conservation 3,493-500 (1994)

[602] Gaston, K. J. 1991. The magnitude of global insect species richness. Conserv. Biol. 5:283-296.

[603] Eggleton, P., P. H. Williams, and K. J. Gaston. 1994. Explaining global termite diversity: productivity or history? Biodiversity and Conservation, 3: 318-330

[604] Crosskey,R.W.(Ed.) Catalogue of the Diptera of the Afrotropical Region. London, British Museum, 1980

[605] Barraclough, D. A. & McAlpine, D. K. Natalimyzidae, a new African family of acalyptrate flies (Diptera: Schizophora: Sciomyzoidea). African Invertebrates 47: 117-134.

[606] Eardley, C.D., Diversity and endemism of southern African bees. Plant Protection News 18: 1-2. (1989)

[607] The Ants of Africa - 2005 http://antbase.org/ants/africa/

[608] Ackery, P. R. et al., (eds.) 1995. Carcasson's African Butterflies. An Annotated Catalogue of the Papilionoidea and Hesperioidea of the Afrotropical Region. CSIRO, Canberra

[609] N. Myers, The Rich Diversity of Biodiversity Issues. (In:Biodiversity II, ed. E.O. Wilson et al., National Academy Press, 1997)

[610] Lévêque et al. (2008). Global diversity of fish (Pisces) in freshwater. Hydrobiologia, 595, 545–567

[611] I.P. Farias et al., Total Evidence: Molecules, Morphology, and the Phylogenetics of Cichlid Fishe Journal of Experimental Zoology (Mol Dev Evol) 288:76–92 (2000)

[612] T. Moritz and K. E. Linsenmair, West African fish diversity – distribution patterns and possible conclusions for conservation strategies (in African Biodiversity: Molecules, Organisms, Ecosystems, Springer, 2001)

[613] Richmond, M.D. (ed.) 1997. A Guide to the Seashores of Eastern Africa and the Western Indian Ocean Islands. Sida/Department for Research Cooperation, SAREC

[614] Andreone F, Carpenter AI, Cox N, du Preez L, Freeman K, et al. (2008) The Challenge of Conserving Amphibian Megadiversity in Madagascar. PLoS Biol 6(5): e118

[615] C. Gans, D. Kraklau, Studies on Amphisbaenians (Reptilia) 8. Two Genera of Small Species from East Africa 8. Two Genera of Small Species from East AfricaAm. Mus. Novitates 2944, 1989

[616] De Klerk, H. M, Gaps in the protected area network for threatened Afrotropical birds. Biological Conservation 117 (2004) 529–537

[617] M. Begon et al., *Ecology: From Individuals to Ecosystems*, Wiley-Blackwell (2006) pp.169

[618] A. Anton, M. Anton. Evolving Eden: An Illustrated Guide to the Evolution of the African Large Mammal Fauna, Columbia Univ. Press,2007

[619] Tabuce, R, et al., Early Tertiary mammals from North Africa reinforce the molecular Afrotheria clade. Proceedings of the Royal Society B, Vol.274, No.1614 (2007)

[620] J. Dorst and P. Dandelot, A Field Guide to the Larger Mammals of Africa, Collins, London 1983

[621] Colin A. et al., What hope for African primate diversity? African Journal of Ecology 44 (2), 116-133.(2006)

[622] https://web.archive.org/web/20080820143549/http://www.africaninvertebrates.org.za/

[623] http://www.poissons-afrique.ird.fr/faunafri/

[624] http://vmppeao-proto.mpl.ird.fr/index.php

[625] //en.wikipedia.org/w/index.php?title=Template:Party_politics&action=edit

[626] The party system is in transition

[627] The Comoros have two main "camps," federalists (supporters of the central government) and autonomists (supporters of the three island presidents).

[628] Kagame takes over AU leadership, commits to visa-free regime http://www.africanews.com/2018/01/28/kagame-takes-over-au-leadership-commits-to-visa-free-regime/ Africa News

[629] Corresponds to the terrestrial surface. Including the Exclusive Economic Zones of each member state, the total area is 43 434 569 km².

[630] http://www.imf.org/external/datamapper/NGDPD@WEO?year=2017

[631] http://au.int

[632] //en.wikipedia.org/w/index.php?title=Template:Life_in_the_African_Union&action=edit

[633] Africa-union.org http://www.africa-union.org/root/au/Documents/Treaties/treaties.htm

[634] African Union replaces dictators' club http://news.bbc.co.uk/2/hi/africa/2115736.stm, BBC, 8 July 2002.

[635] //en.wikipedia.org/w/index.php?title=Template:AU_evolution_timeline&action=edit

[636] Article 25, Constitutive Act of the African Union.

[637] //en.wikipedia.org/w/index.php?title=Template:Politics_of_the_African_Union&action=edit

[638] Decision on the Report of the 9th Extraordinary session of the executive council on the proposals for the Union Government, DOC.Assembly/AU/10 (VIII), Assembly/AU/Dec.156 (VIII).
[639] Study on an African Union Government: Towards a United States of Africa, 2006. See also, Decision on the Union Government, Doc. Assembly/AU/2(VII).
[640] Pambazuka.org http://www.pambazuka.org/aumonitor/
[641] Accra Declaration, Assembly of the Union at its 9th Ordinary session in Accra, Ghana, 1–3 July 2007.
[642] //en.wikipedia.org/w/index.php?title=Template:Supranational_African_Bodies&action=edit
[643] See note on The Role of the Regional Economic Communities (RECs) as the Building Blocks of the African Union https://web.archive.org/web/20040906140832/http://www.dfa.gov.za/docs/2003/au0815.htm prepared by the South African Department of Foreign Affairs.
[644] Decision on the Protocol on Relations between the African Union and the Regional Economic Communities (RECs), Assembly/AU/Dec.166 (IX).
[645] See *Towards a People-Driven African Union: Current Obstacles and New Opportunities* http://www.afrimap.org/english/images/report/AU_People-DrivenNov07.pdf , AfriMAP, AFRODAD and Oxfam GB, Updated Edition November 2007, pp. 45–46, and *Strengthening Popular Participation in the African Union: A Guide to AU Structures and Processes* http://www.afrimap.org/english/images/report/AfriMAP-AU-Guide-EN.pdf , AfriMAP and Oxfam GB, 2010, pp. 8–9.
[646] Gaddafi fails in bid to remain African Union chair https://af.reuters.com/article/topNews/idAFJOE60U05O20100131l, Reuters, 31 January 2010
[647] Malawi president takes over as AU president https://web.archive.org/web/20111230205627/http://www.google.com/hostednews/afp/article/ALeqM5g8cvj3048f4WEB6UQuim80MKqhVA, AFP, 31 January 2010
[648] According to the AU http://www.au.int/en/dp/cp/biography , his official style is *Son Excellence Obiang Nguema Mbasogo, Président de la République, Chef de l'État et Président Fondateur du Parti Démocratique de Guinée Equatoriale* . Retrieved 4 October 2011.
[649] Press release No 13 / 18th AU Summit : Inauguration of the new African Union Conference Center http://www.au.int/en/sites/default/files/28%2001%202012_18SUMMIT_PR_INAUGURATION.pdf . Directorate of Information and Communication. African Union Commission (28 January 2012).
[650] http://www.unaids.org/sites/default/files/media_asset/2016-prevention-gap-report_en.pdf
[651] Bernadette Schulz, Ruth Langer, "Peace missions – The long haul" http://www.dandc.eu/en/article/african-peace-and-security-architecture-already-proving-useful-even-though-it-still-work, D+C, 27 August 2013.
[652] Article 3(f) of the Constitutive Act.
[653] Article 4(e) of the Constitutive Act.
[654] Afro News http://www.afrol.com/articles/10577 *Eritrea breaks with African Union*, 20 November 2009.
[655] "AU calls for sanctions on Eritrea" http://news.bbc.co.uk/2/hi/africa/8064939.stm BBC.co.uk 23 May 2009. Retrieved 23 May 2009
[656] https://web.archive.org/web/20130927110741/http://www.afrimap.org/english/images/report/AfriMAP-AU-Guide-EN.pdf
[657] https://web.archive.org/web/20080216054523/http://www.afrimap.org/english/images/report/AU_People-DrivenNov07.pdf
[658] https://web.archive.org/web/20070927195414/http://www.ppl.nl/catalogue.php?ppn=241754658&keyword=African%20Union&pagename=keyword-catalogue
[659] http://www.au.int/
[660] https://web.archive.org/web/20121104044706/http://www.aumission-ny.org/
[661] https://web.archive.org/web/20161022142733/http://www.au2002.gov.za/
[662] https://web.archive.org/web/20070609115441/http://www.sarpn.org.za/nepad.php
[663] http://www.panafricanperspective.com/youtube_USofAfrica.html
[664] http://news.bbc.co.uk/1/hi/world/africa/country_profiles/3870303.stm
[665] https://curlie.org/Society/Government/Multilateral/Regional/African_Union
[666] http://www.english.rfi.fr/africa/20100212-africa-50-years-independence
[667] http://www.english.rfi.fr/africa/20100225-broken-dream-african-unity

[668] //en.wikipedia.org/w/index.php?title=Template:World_economy&action=edit
[669] //en.wikipedia.org/w/index.php?title=Economy_of_Africa&action=edit
[670] Christian K.M. Kingombe 2011. Mapping the new infrastructure financing landscape http//www.odi.org.uk . London: Overseas Development Institute
[671] Nick Mead, "African Economic Outlook 2012" https://www.theguardian.com/global-development/datablog/interactive/2012/may/28/african-economic-outlook-2012, *The Guardian*, 28 May 2012.
[672] Lewis H. Gann and Peter Duignan, *The Burden of Empire: A Reappraisal of Western Colonialism South of the Sahara*
[673] D. K. Fieldhouse, *The West and the Third World*
[674] Niall Ferguson, Empire: How Britain Made the Modern World and Colossus: The Rise and Fall of the American Empire
[675] http://pure.au.dk/portal-asb-student/files/41656700/alexandra_hrituleac_thesis_1_dec.pdf
[676] 1997: *Guns, Germs, and Steel: The Fates of Human Societies*. W.W. Norton & Co. (). Also published with the title *Guns, germs and steel: A short history of everybody for the last 13,000 years*.
[677] Africa and Africans in the Formation of the Atlantic World, 1400–1680 (New York and London: Cambridge University Press, 1992, second expanded edition, 1998).
[678] Why is Africa Poor? (Economic History of Developing Regions Vol. 25: 2010)
[679] Rodney, Walter. *How Europe Underdeveloped Africa*. London: Bogle-L'Ouverture Publications, 1972.
[680] David Eltis, *Economic Growth and the Ending of the Transatlantic Slave Trade*
[681] See, for example, Frank, A. G. (1979), *Dependent Accumulation and Underdevelopment*, New York: Monthly Review Press.; Köhler, G., and A. Tausch (2001), *Global Keynesianism: unequal exchange and global exploitation*, Nova Publishers; Amin, S. (1976), *Unequal Development: An Essay on the Social Formations of Peripheral Capitalism*, New York: Monthly Review Press.
[682] //en.wikipedia.org/w/index.php?title=Template:Political_corruption_sidebar&action=edit
[683] http://newzimbabwe.com/columns-40850-The+costs+of+the+Robert+Mugabe+era/columns.aspx
[684] Philip Wayland Porter. Challenging nature: local knowledge, agroscience, and food security in Tanga.
[685] Skinner, Annabel (2005). Tanzania & Zanzibar. New Holland Publishers. p. 19.
[686] http://www.imf.org/external/pubs/ft/weo/2017/02/weodata/download.aspx
[687] http://www.uneca.org/atpc/Work%20in%20progress/21.pdf
[688] //en.wikipedia.org/w/index.php?title=Template:African_Economic_Community&action=edit
[689] World Bank Development Indicators http://data.worldbank.org/indicator/, World Bank, 2011, accessed Nov. 2012
[690] https//www.imf.org
[691] Source http://hdr.undp.org/en/media/hdr_20072008_en_complete.pdf , 2005
[692] https://www.unescap.org/sites/default/files/wp-09-02.pdf
[693] John J. Saul and Colin Leys, Sub-Saharan Africa in Global Capitalism http://monthlyreview.org/1999/07/01/sub-saharan-africa-in-global-capitalism, *Monthly Review*, 1999, Volume 51, Issue 03 (July–August)
[694] https://web.archive.org/web/20120512233445/https://www.cia.gov/library/publications/the-world-factbook/rankorder/2173rank.html
[695] https//www.jstor.org
[696] https://books.google.com/books?vid=ISBN0415183235&id=YiLaMsvQMBQC&printsec=toc&dq=ISBN0415183235
[697] https://books.google.com/books?vid=ISBN1555874436&id=IQJNU72KQykC&printsec=toc&dq=ISBN1555877184
[698] http://www.oecd.org/bookshop?9789264033139
[699] https://curlie.org/Regional/Africa/Business_and_Economy
[700] http://www.spiegel.de/international/world/0,1518,484603,00.html
[701] http://www.counterpunch.org/2014/07/25/chinas-increasing-african-presence/
[702] http://fpif.org/obama-africa/

[703] http://www.fondad.org/publications/africaworld/contents.htm
[704] http://www.osisa.org/sites/default/files/sup_files/africa_-_living_on_the_fringe_0.pdf
[705] http://news.bbc.co.uk/1/shared/spl/hi/africa/05/africa_economy/html/poverty.stm
[706] http://www.oecd.org/dev/publications/africanoutlook
[707] http://www.africaeconomicanalysis.org/
[708] http://www.weforum.org/site/homepublic.nsf/Content/Africa+Economic+Summit+2004
[709] http://www.afdb.org/
[710] http://www.imf.org/external/pubs/ft/weo/2003/02/index.htm
[711] http://damnsw.net/~matt/pdf/africa.pdf
[712] http://www.economist.com/world/africa/displaystory.cfm?story_id=7089006
[713] http//web.worldbank.org
[714] https://web.archive.org/web/20070509005812/http://www.guinea.aha.ru/
[715] http://www.ipsnews.net/new_focus/trade_af_eu/index.asp
[716] http://www.democracynow.org/2009/8/12/land
[717] http://repository.library.georgetown.edu/handle/10822/552501
[718] http://repository.library.georgetown.edu/handle/10822/549457
[719] //en.wikipedia.org/w/index.php?title=Template:Life_in_the_African_Union&action=edit
[720] //en.wikipedia.org/w/index.php?title=Template:African_Economic_Community&action=edit
[721] Zinkina J., Korotayev A. Explosive Population Growth in Tropical Africa: Crucial Omission in Development Forecasts (Emerging Risks and Way Out). *World Futures* 70/2 (2014): 120–139 http://cliodynamics.ru/index.php?option=com_content&task=view&id=360&Itemid=1.
[722] See List of countries by life expectancy; according to the 2012 CIA Factbook, 4 of 53 countries show a life expectancy at birth below 50 years
[723] //en.wikipedia.org/w/index.php?title=Demographics_of_Africa&action=edit
[724] "World Population Prospects: The 2004 Revision" https://www.un.org/esa/population/publications/WPP2004/2004Highlights_finalrevised.pdf United Nations (Department of Economic and Social Affairs, population division)
[725] Eliya Zulu, "How to defuse sub-Saharan Africa's population bomb" https://www.newscientist.com/article/dn21745-how-to-defuse-sub-saharan-africas-population-bomb/, *New Scientist*, 26 April 2012. Jeffrey Gutman and Nirav Patel, "Urban Africa: Avoiding the perfect storm" https://www.brookings.edu/blog/africa-in-focus/2018/01/26/foresight-africa-viewpoint-urban-africa-avoiding-the-perfect-storm/, *Foresight Africa*, 26 January 2018.
[726] Joseph J Bish, "Population growth in Africa: grasping the scale of the challenge" https://www.theguardian.com/global-development-professionals-network/2016/jan/11/population-growth-in-africa-grasping-the-scale-of-the-challenge, *The Guardian*, 11 January 2016. "African fertility has not fallen as expected. Precipitous declines in fertility in Asia and Latin America, from five children per woman in the 1970s to around 2.5 today, led many to believe Africa would follow a similar course. [...] Unfortunately, since the early 1990s, family planning programmes in Africa have not had the same attention [as in other parts of the world], resulting in slow, sometimes negligible, fertility declines. In a handful of countries, previous declines have stalled altogether and are reversing. [...] A few heroic efforts, such as Family Planning 2020, are attempting to stimulate family planning programmes across the continent, and there are some signs of success. Recent figures from Kenya and Zambia show substantial strengthening of contraceptive use among married women. In Kenya, 58% of married women now use modern contraception, and in Zambia this measure has risen from 33% to 45% in the last three years. In both cases, the catalysts for improvements were government commitment and commensurate budget financing. The virtuous circle may not be completely out of reach, but many more African governments must make haste and make substantial investments in contraceptive information and access for their people."
[727] Luc-Normand Tellier (2009). " *Urban world history: an economic and geographical perspective* https://books.google.com/books?id=cXuCjDbxC1YC&pg=&dq&hl=en#v=onepage&q=&f=false". PUQ. p.204.
[728] Pygmies struggle to survive in war zone where abuse is routine http://www.timesonline.co.uk/tol/news/world/article402970.ece. Times Online. 16 December 2004.
[729] Q&A: The Berbers http://news.bbc.co.uk/2/hi/africa/3509799.stm. BBC News. 12 March 2004.

[730] John A. Shoup, Ethnic Groups of Africa and the Middle East (2011), p. 333, : "The Zaghawa is one of the major divisions of the Beri peoples who live in western Sudan and eastern Chad, and their language, also called Zaghawa, belongs to the Saharan branch of the Nilo-Saharan language group."

[731] "We Want Our Country" (3 of 10) http://www.time.com/time/magazine/article/0,9171, 901759-3,00.html. Time. 5 November 1965

[732] Raimondo Cagiano De Azevedo (1994). *Migration and development co-operation. https: //books.google.com/books?id=N8VHizsqaH0C&pg=PA25&dq&hl=en#v=onepage&q= &f=false*". Council of Europe. p.25.

[733] Jungle Shipwreck http://www.time.com/time/magazine/article/0,9171,826488-4,00.html. *Time*. 25 July 1960

[734] Flight from Angola http://www.economist.com/world/mideast-africa/displayStory.cfm?story_ id=12079340, *The Economist*, 16 August 1975

[735] Portugal - Emigration http://countrystudies.us/portugal/48.htm, Eric Solsten, ed. Portugal: A Country Study. Washington: GPO for the Library of Congress, 1993.

[736] South Africa: People: Ethnic Groups. https://www.cia.gov/library/publications/the-world-factbook/geos/sf.html#People World Factbook of CIA

[737] " China and Africa: Stronger Economic Ties Mean More Migration http://www. migrationinformation.org/Feature/display.cfm?id=690". By Malia Politzer, *Migration Information Source*. August 2008.

[738] " Lebanese Immigrants Boost West African Commerce http://www1.voanews.com/english/ news/a-13-2007-07-10-voa46.html", By Naomi Schwarz, VOANews.com, 10 July 2007

[739] Blench, Roger. 2017. African language isolates. In *Language Isolates*, edited by Lyle Campbell, pp. 176-206. Routledge.

[740] African Union Summit 2006 http://www.sarpn.org.za/documents/d0001850/index.php Khartoum, Sudan. SARPN.

[741] Lyle Campbell & Mauricio J. Mixco, *A Glossary of Historical Linguistics* (2007, University of Utah Press)

[742] P.H. Matthews, *Oxford Concise Dictionary of Linguistics* (2007, 2nd edition, Oxford)

[743] K. Pithouse, C. Mitchell, R. Moletsane, Making Connections: Self-Study & Social Action, p.91

[744] Herkomst en groei van het Afrikaans - G.G. Kloeke (1950) http://www.dbnl.org/tekst/ kloe004herk01_01/kloe004herk01_01.pdf

[745] The origin of Afrikaans pronunciation: a comparison to west Germanic languages and Dutch dialects - Wilbert Heeringa, Febe de Wet (2007) http://citeseerx.ist.psu.edu/viewdoc/download? rep=rep1&type=pdf&doi=10.1.1.222.5044

[746] Jean-Marie Hombert & Gérard Philippson. 2009. " The linguistic importance of language isolates: the African case http://www.ddl.ish-lyon.cnrs.fr/fulltext/hombert/Hombert_2009_ LDLT2.pdf." In Peter K. Austin, Oliver Bond, Monik Charette, David Nathan & Peter Sells (eds). *Proceedings of Conference on Language Documentation and Linguistic Theory 2*. London: SOAS.

[747] CIA – The World Factbook https://www.cia.gov/library/publications/the-world-factbook/ geos/mr.html.

[748] According to article 7 of *The Transitional Federal Charter of the Somali Republic* http: //www.chr.up.ac.za/hr_docs/countries/docs/charterfeb04.pdf : "The official languages of the Somali Republic shall be Somali (Maay and Maxaatiri) and Arabic. The second languages of the Transitional Federal Government shall be English and Italian."

[749] "The languages of South Africa" http://www.southafrica.info/about/people/language.htm. *southafrica.info*.

[750] African languages for Africa's development http://www.acalan.org/ ACALAN (French & English).

[751] *The Economist*, "Tongues under threat", 22 January 2011, p. 58.

[752] Nationalencyklopedin "Världens 100 största språk 2007" The World's 100 Largest Languages in 2007

[753] *Ethnologue* (2009) cites 18,5 million L1 and 15 million L2 speakers in Nigeria in 1991; 5.5 million L1 speakers and half that many L2 speakers in Niger in 2006, 0.8 million in Benin in 2006, and just over 1 million in other countries.

[754] Brenzinger, Matthias (2011) "The twelve modern Khoisan languages." In Witzlack-Makarevich & Ernszt (eds.), *Khoisan languages and linguistics: proceedings of the 3rd International Symposium, Riezlern / Kleinwalsertal* (Research in Khoisan Studies 29). Cologne: Rüdiger Köppe Verlag.
[755] https://www.ethnologue.com/language/tso
[756] http://www.darfurcentre.ch/images/00_DRDC_documents/DRDC_Reports_Briefing_Papers/DRDC_Report_on_the_5th_Population_Census_in_Sudan.pdf
[757] John A. Shoup, Ethnic Groups of Africa and the Middle East (2011), p. 333, : "The Zaghawa is one of the major divisions of the Beri peoples who live in western Sudan and eastern Chad, and their language, also called Zaghawa, belongs to the Saharan branch of the Nilo-Saharan language group."
[758] http://www.ethnologue.com/country_index.asp?place=Africa
[759] http://kasahorow.org
[760] http://www.africanlanguages.com/
[761] http://www.muturzikin.com/carteafrique.htm
[762] http://www.ilissafrica.de/en/als/iliss-advanced.html?query=&tt=&kw=&sbj=0700300&geo=&res=3020&search=1
[763] http://www.ilissafrica.de/en/als/iliss-advanced.html?query=&tt=&kw=&sbj=0700300&geo=&res=6082&search=1
[764] http://www.ilissafrica.de/en/als/iliss-advanced.html?query=&tt=&kw=&sbj=0700300&geo=&res=6170&search=1
[765] Khair El-Din Haseeb et al., *The Future of the Arab Nation: Challenges and Options*, 1 edition (Routledge: 1991), p.54
[766] Halim Barakat, *The Arab World: Society, Culture, and State*, (University of California Press: 1993), p.80
[767] Tajudeen Abdul Raheem, ed., Pan Africanism: Politics, Economy and Social Change in the Twenty-First Century, Pluto Press, London, 1996.
[768] Khapoya, op. cit. p. 126f
[769] African culture and the ongoing quest for excellence: dialog, principles, practice.: An article from: The Black Collegian : Maulana Karenga
[770] Richard Pankhurst, 1997, 'History of the Ethiopian Borderlands: Essays in Regional History, Lawrenceville, New Jersey.
[771] Florence, Namulundah. The Bukusu of Kenya: Folktales, Culture and Social Identities. Durham, NC: Carolina Academic, 2011. Print.
[772] Mwangi, Rose. Kikuyu Folktales. Nairobi: East African Literature Bureau, 1970. Print.
[773] Strong, Polly, and Rodney Wimer. African Tales: Folklore of the Central African Republic. Mogadore, OH: Telcraft, 1992. Print.
[774] "Eritrean Food Practices." https://www.webcitation.org/query?url=http://www.geocities.com/WARSAISANDIEGO/our_culture.htm&date=2009-10-25+11:44:57 Webcitation.org https://www.webcitation.org. Accessed July 2011.
[775] Barlin Ali, *Somali Cuisine*, (AuthorHouse: 2007), p.79
[776] Bowden, Rob(2007). Africa South of the Sahara. Coughlan Publishing: p. 40, .
[777] Christopher Ehret, (2002). The Civilizations of Africa. Charlottesville: University of Virginia, p. 103, .
[778] Abatte Barihun, liner notes of the album Ras Deshen, 200.
[779] Greenberg, Joseph H. (1966). The Languages of Africa (2nd ed.). Bloomington: Indiana University.
[780] https://web.archive.org/web/20100625061742/http://www.unescobreda.org/
[781] https://archive.is/20130202231209/http://squinti.com/?page_id=932
[782] https://web.archive.org/web/20170801050454/http://afrika-culture.com/
[783] Abatte Barihun, liner notes of the album Ras Deshen, 200.
[784] Jones, A. M. (1959). *Studies in African Music*. London: Oxford University Press. 1978 edition:

[785] Ladzekpo, C. K. (1996). "Cultural Understanding of Polyrhythm" http://www.richardhodges.com/ladzekpo/Developmental.html. Foundation Course in African Music.
[786] *GCSE Music – Edexcel Areas of Study*, Coordination Group Publications, UK, 2006, p. 36.
[787] http://www.contemporary-african-art.com/african-musical-instruments.html

[788] http://www.contemporary-african-art.com/african-musical-instruments.html
[789] *GCSE Music – Edexcel Areas of Study*, Coordination Group Publications, UK, 2006, p. 35, quoting examination board syllabus.
[790] Nketia, J. H. Kwabena. *The Music of Africa*. New York: Norton and Company, 1974. Print.
[791] Azam, O. A. (1993), "The recent influence of African Music on the American music scene and music market". http://azam.org/archives/geocities/www.geocities.com/omarazam/papers/afrMusic.htm
[792] "The Characters." *Lion King Pride*. 2008. Disney, 1997–2008. Web. 1 February 2010.
[793] "African Sounds in the American South: Community Radio, Historically Black Colleges, and Musical Pan Africanism," https://www.academia.edu/19649475/African_Sounds_in_the_American_South_Community_Radio_Historically_Black_Colleges_and_Musical_Pan-Africanism The Journal of Popular Music Studies, December 2015
[794] Miriam Makeba#Musical style and themes
[795] https://www.theguardian.com/music/2008/nov/11/miriam-makeba-obituary
[796] Roberts, John Storm (1986: cassette) *Afro-Cuban Comes Home: The Birth and Growth of Congo Music*, Original Music.
[797] https://www.academia.edu/19649475/African_Sounds_in_the_American_South_Community_Radio_Historically_Black_Colleges_and_Musical_Pan-Africanism
[798] http://www.bbc.co.uk/worldservice/africa/features/rhythms/index.shtml
[799] http://sounds.ru.ac.za/ilam/
[800] http://sounds.bl.uk/World-and-traditional-music/
[801] http://archive.kubatana.net/html/archive/artcul/030521music.asp?sector=ARTCUL
[802] http://imslp.org/wiki/User:Clark_Kimberling/Historical_Notes_11
[803] https://curlie.org/Regional/Africa/Arts_and_Entertainment/Music
[804] https://archive.is/20121215121058/http://ias.umn.edu/2012/10/11/skinner-ryan/
[805] //en.wikipedia.org/w/index.php?title=Template:Religions_by_country_sidebar&action=edit
[806] Restless Spirits: Syncretic Religion http://www.jpanafrican.com/docs/vol3no5/3.5-6newRestless.pdf Yolanda Pierce, Ph.D. Associate Professor of African American Religion & Literature
[807] Dr J.O. Awolalu, Studies in Comparative Religion Vol. 10, No. 2. (Spring, 1976). http://www.studiesincomparativereligion.com/uploads/ArticlePDFs/268.pdf
[808] Cheikh Anta Diop The African Origin of Civilization: Myth or Reality, Chicago, L.Hill, 1974.
[809] Leo Frobenius on African History, Art, and Culture: An Anthology, 2007
[810] Bolaji Idowu African Traditional Religion: A Definition, Maryknoll, N.Y., Orbis Books (1973)
[811] J S Mbiti*African Religions and Philosophy*, African Writers Series, Heinemann [1969] (1990).
[812] When Africans are converted to other religions, they often mix their traditional religion with the one to which they are converted. In this way they are not losing something valuable, but are gaining something from both religious customs
[813] Although a large proportion of Africans have converted to Islam an Christianity, these two world religions have been assimilated into African culture, and many African Christians and Muslims maintain traditional spiritual beliefs
[814] Even in the adopted religions of Islam and Christianity, which on the surface appear to have converted millions of Africans from their traditional religions, many aspect of traditional religions are still manifest
[815] t doesn't seem to be an either-or for many people. They can describe themselves primarily as Muslim or Christian and continue to practice many of the traditions that are characteristic of African traditional religion," Luis Lugo, executive director of the Pew Forum, told AFP.
[816] Even though the two religions are monotheistic, most African Christians and Muslims convert to them and still retain some aspects of their traditional religions
[817] Encyclopædia Britannica. Britannica Book of the Year 2003. Encyclopædia Britannica, (2003) p.306
According to the Encyclopædia Britannica, as of mid-2002, there were 376,453,000 Christians, 329,869,000 Muslims and 98,734,000 people who practiced traditional religions in Africa. Ian S. Markham,(A World Religions Reader. Cambridge, Massachusetts: Blackwell Publishers, 1996.) http://www.greenwoodsvillage.com/gor/islam.htm is cited by Morehouse University as giving the mid-1990s figure of 278,250,800 Muslims in Africa, but still as 40.8% of the total.

These numbers are estimates, and remain a matter of conjecture. See Amadu Jacky Kaba. The spread of Christianity and Islam in Africa: a survey and analysis of the numbers and percentages of Christians, Muslims and those who practice indigenous religions. The Western Journal of Black Studies, Vol 29, Number 2, June 2005. Discusses the estimations of various almanacs and encyclopedium, placing Britannica's estimate as the most agreed figure. Notes the figure presented at the World Christian Encyclopedia, summarized here http://www.afrikaworld.net/afrel/Statistics.htm, as being an outlier. On rates of growth, Islam and Pentecostal Christianity are highest, see: The List: The World's Fastest-Growing Religions https://foreignpolicy.com/story/cms.php?story_id=3835, Foreign Policy, May 2007.

[818] http://www.kebranegast.com Kebra Negast

[819] Hansberry, William Leo. *Pillars in Ethiopian History; the William Leo Hansberry African History Notebook*. Washington: Howard University Press, 1934.

[820] *Historian Ahead of His Time, Christianity Today Magazine*, February 2007

[821] *World Council of Churches Report, August 2004*

[822] Encyclopædia Britannica. Britannica Book of the Year 2003. Encyclopædia Britannica, (2003) p.306

According to the Encyclopædia Britannica, as of mid-2002, there were 480,453,000 Christians, 479,869,000 Muslims and 98,734,000 people who practiced traditional religions in Africa. Ian S. Markham, (A World Religions Reader. Cambridge, Massachusetts: Blackwell Publishers, 1996.) http://www.greenwoodsvillage.com/gor/islam.htm is cited by Morehouse University as giving the mid-1990s figure of 278,250,800 Muslims in Africa, but still as 40.8% of the total. These numbers are estimates, and remain a matter of conjecture (see Amadu Jacky Kaba). The spread of Christianity and Islam in Africa: a survey and analysis of the numbers and percentages of Christians, Muslims and those who practice indigenous religions. The Western Journal of Black Studies, Vol 29, Number 2, June 2005. Discusses the estimations of various almanacs and encyclopedium, placing Britannica's estimate as the most agreed figure. Notes the figure presented at the World Christian Encyclopedia, summarized here http://www.afrikaworld.net/afrel/Statistics.htm, as being an outlier. On rates of growth, Islam and Pentecostal Christianity are highest, see: The List: The World's Fastest-Growing Religions https://foreignpolicy.com/story/cms.php?story_id=3835, Foreign Policy, May 2007.

[823] Pew Forum on Religious & Public life. 9 August 2012. Retrieved 29 October 2013

[824] GALLUP WorldView https://worldview.gallup.com/default.aspx - data accessed on 14 September 2011

[825] http://www.missiology.org.uk/pdf/cotterell-fs/15_ferdinando.pdf

[826] Global Religious Landscape Table - Percent of Population - Pew Forum on Religion & Public Life http://features.pewforum.org/grl/population-percentage.php. Features.pewforum.org (2012-12-18). Retrieved on 2013-07-28.

[827] http://www.ubos.org/onlinefiles/uploads/ubos/pdf%20documents/2002%20Census%20Final%20Reportdoc.pdf

[828] Zambia https://www.state.gov/g/drl/rls/irf/2010/148728.htm. State.gov. Retrieved on 2013-07-28.

[829] The World Factbook https://www.cia.gov/library/publications/the-world-factbook/geos/dj.html. Cia.gov. Retrieved on 2013-07-28.

[830] The World Factbook https://www.cia.gov/library/publications/the-world-factbook/geos/ag.html. Cia.gov. Retrieved on 2013-07-28.

[831] The World Factbook https://www.cia.gov/library/publications/the-world-factbook/geos/eg.html. Cia.gov. Retrieved on 2013-07-28.

[832] The World Factbook https://www.cia.gov/library/publications/the-world-factbook/geos/ly.html. Cia.gov. Retrieved on 2013-07-28.

[833] The World Factbook https://www.cia.gov/library/publications/the-world-factbook/geos/mo.html. Cia.gov. Retrieved on 2013-07-28.

[834] The World Factbook https://www.cia.gov/library/publications/the-world-factbook/geos/su.html. Cia.gov. Retrieved on 2013-07-28.

[835] Botswana https://www.state.gov/g/drl/rls/irf/2007/90083.htm. State.gov (2007-09-14). Retrieved on 2013-07-28.

[836] Lesotho https://www.state.gov/g/drl/rls/irf/2007/90104.htm. State.gov (2007-09-14). Retrieved on 2013-07-28.
[837] Namibia https://www.state.gov/g/drl/rls/irf/2010/148710.htm. State.gov (2010-11-17). Retrieved on 2013-07-28.
[838] The World Factbook https://www.cia.gov/library/publications/the-world-factbook/geos/sf.html. Cia.gov. Retrieved on 2013-07-28.
[839] 2010 Population and Housing Census http://www.statsghana.gov.gh/docfiles/2010phc/Census2010_Summary_report_of_final_results.pdf
[840] {{cite web|url= Pew Forum on Religion http://features.pewforum.org/grl/population-percentage.php
[841] Togo https://www.cia.gov/library/publications/the-world-factbook/geos/to.html\. CIA – The World Factbook. Cia.gov.
[842] https://www.amazon.com/The-Wiley-Blackwell-Companion-African-Religions/dp/1405196904
[843] https://books.google.com/books?hl=en&lr=&id=f6e3BgAAQBAJ
[844] https://www.amazon.com/African-Religions-Short-Introduction-Introductions/dp/0199790582/
[845] http://africanbelief.com/
[846] http://www.bbc.co.uk/worldservice/africa/features/storyofafrica/index_section6.shtml
[847] https://www.ucalgary.ca/%7Enurelweb/books/atoms/fred.html
[848] http://www-sul.stanford.edu/depts/ssrg/africa/religion/african-traditional-religion.html
[849] http://www.africamissions.org/africa/african_religion.html
[850] http://www.scn.org/rdi/kw-gods.htm
[851] http://www.riscura.com/

Article Sources and Contributors

The sources listed for each article provide more detailed licensing information including the copyright status, the copyright owner, and the license conditions.

Recent African origin of modern humans *Source:* https://en.wikipedia.org/w/index.php?oldid=861640379 *License:* Creative Commons Attribution-Share Alike 3.0 *Contributors:* 3primetime3, Adam9007, AfricaQuest, AldezD, Alex Bardill, Alexandermcnabb, Archaon, Bahudhara, BatteryIncluded, Ben MacDui, Beyond My Ken, BibleScholar, Boghog, Brett, CLCStudent, Carlotm, CenfusRex, Cgx8253, Chakazul, Chhandama, ClueBot NG, Cuchullan, Dbachmann, Dcirovic, Ddumv, Drbogdan, Dudley Miles, Ebizur, Emowe1, Favonian, Fixer88, Flyer22 Reborn, FreeKnowledgeCreator, Frietjes, Gap9551, General Ization, Geo1un, Goodtiming8871, Goustien, Groogle, Haeinous, Hairy Dude, Headbomb, IQ125, Javantea, Jdaloner, Jim1138, Joe Roe, Jonesey95, Jonkerz, Joshua Jonathan, Just a guy from the KP, Keith-264, Kgrad, Lampshade Maker, Magioladitis, Marek69, Maunus, Me, Myself, and I are Here, Mikalra, Monochrome Monitor, Moxy, Nihiltres, Omnipaedista, Onel5969, Oshwah, PLawrence99cx, Pavel Vozenilek, Phuzion, PlyrStar93, Precious Feelings, Quercus solaris, Rednblu, Rich Farmbrough, Richard Keatinge, Rjwilmsi, Sakaimover, Scarpy, Scratplays, Smhanes, TAnthony, The Blade of the Northern Lights, Thine Antique Pen, TiMike, TimidGuy, Titus III, Tobus, TomS TDotO, Triggerhippie4, Twinsday, User000name, Utcursch, 75 anonymous edits 3

History of Africa *Source:* https://en.wikipedia.org/w/index.php?oldid=863389027 *License:* Creative Commons Attribution-Share Alike 3.0 *Contributors:* A.Savin, Alfie Gandon, Ananias Kantene, Anarchyte, Andre Kritzinger, AntiCompositeNumber, Any Armadillo, Arjayay, Artistology, BD2412, Bgwhite, Blpower380, CAPTAIN RAJU, CLCStudent, Ceosad, CharlesWhite4321, ChiefPrinceAndDuke, ChocolateCity, Christinatoma, Citizen Canine, Classybluepower, ClueBot NG, Cnwilliams, Colonel Wilhelm Klink, Colonies Chris, CommonsDelinker, Connor Behan, Conor2004, Cooperporter, Coryphantha, Dan6hell66, Daniel Power of God, Dave Dial, Dawnseeker2000, Dimadick, DivermanAU, Donner60, Doug Weller, Egsan Bacon, Endriksohn, Ermahgerd9, Excirial, FT2, Fama Clamosa, Fluppeteer, GSS, Gadfium, Gap9551, Gareth Griffith-Jones, Gillh2017, Gilliam, Graham87, Grayfell, GreenC, GünniX, Hanif Al Husaini, Highpeaks35, Hillbillyholiday, Hmains, Horseless Headman, HrEkstedt, Hypergeek14, INKA000, InspectorTiger, Iridescent, Isis Hillenberg, JamDeodato, Jayjg, Jim1138, Jmb900, John of Reading, Jokjokjokjok, Jonathan Tweet, Jonesey95, Katunku joshua, Keith D, Kevt2002, Kuru, KylieTastic, LittleWink, LizardJr8, Look2See1, M2545, Marcocapelle, Marcus Cyron, Marek69, Martamirazonlahr, Materialscientist, Maximajorian Viridio, My Chemistry romantic, Natuur12, NewEnglandYankee, Nihiltres, Ninafundisha, Northamerica1000, Onel5969, Orenburg1, Oshwah, Pepper, PericlesofAthens, PlanespotterA320, Prinsipe Ybarro, Quenhitran, Rjensen, Rjwilmsi, Rodw, Russ3Z, Samf4u, Ser Amantio di Nicolao, Serols, Shellwood, Simplexity22, Sorcc, StaceyC16, Stryn, Stumink, Sunriseshore, The Transhumanist, The ed17, Timbuktu123, Tommynewsnetwork, Uğurkent, Vai2fc, WBVT, Weegeeweeg, Wiae, Widr, XXGfHXx, Yamaguchi先生 , YeOldeGentleman, Yohira, 162 anonymous edits 18

Arab slave trade *Source:* https://en.wikipedia.org/w/index.php?oldid=863637840 *License:* Creative Commons Attribution-Share Alike 3.0 *Contributors:* AManWithNoPlan, Acroterion, Alayambo, Anticla rutila, Arminden, Barry Prescott, Bayesedam, Bender235, Bgwhite, Bigdan201, BrettAllen, CAPTAIN RAJU, CaliphoShah, CambridgeBayWeather, Checkmate55, Classicwiki, ClueBot NG, Contributor451, Cplakidas, Crowtow849, Cuddly Visionary, DA1, David.moreno72, Davidxnull, Dcirovic, Deisenbe, DoABarrelRoll.dev, Donner60, Dsp13, Dubito, ergo cogito, ergo sum, EconomicHisorianinTraining, Egsan Bacon, Eik Corell, El C, Enthusiast01, Eperoton, Esszet, Favonian, Flyer22 Reborn, FoCuSandLeArN, Guccisamsclub, HampsteadCoffee, HerbertMacuse, Highpeaks35, Homeguard2387, Hondatabian, I dream of horses, Ibadibam, Illegitimate Barrister, Jakecasablanca, JamesAM, JamesBWatson3, Jennica, Jprg1966, Kahtar, Kaiger, Kaled Fattah, Kintetsubuffalo, Knujra1, Kpgjhpjm, L3X1, Lebob, Loaka1, MONGO, MShabazz, Marco.natalino, Materialscientist, Mccapra, Milktaco, MosheA, Motherfan, NaijaBond, Nizil Shah, NoToleranceForIntolerance, Node-0, Non-dropframe, Nunya is cool, Nyttend, Oshwah, Piotrus, Qohen, Regulov, RolandR, Roncon1, Rosalina523, Rouge000, Rupert loup, Saxiwashere, Seraphim System, Serols, Shamalyguy, Shawnqual, Skilla1st, Slightsmile, Soupforone, Swingoswingo, TantraYum, TerraCodes, Tobby72, Tom.Reding, Topbookclub, Trappist the monk, Troublesome octopus person, Txjo 115173, Ursurtra, Vidyadunk, Will Resources, Winner 42, Wywyit, XPTO, Xxproslikemexx, הורון, יניב 182 anonymous edits 101

Atlantic slave trade *Source:* https://en.wikipedia.org/w/index.php?oldid=861408249 *License:* Creative Commons Attribution-Share Alike 3.0 *Contributors:* 0xF8E8, 97531martin, Absbanana, AgnosticPreachersKid, Alanscottwalker, Alexb102072, Alfie Gandon, Alonso de Mendoza, Amax1701, Aquillion, Arch dude, Battleofalma, Beauty School Dropout, Bender235, Benjamin Lawless, Bgwhite, BiologicalMe, Cadillac000, Cannolis, Caprockranger, Carrite, Catsmeat, Ceolirbi, Cindcind1208, ClueBot NG, CuriousMind01, Cush, Cyberbot II, Dan Koehl, Dcbernar, Dcirovic, DePiep, Dhurst456, Diannaa, Dissident93, DivineAlpha, Donner60, Doug Weller, Dsp13, Dungbeetle2, EVDiam, EconomicHisorianinTraining, EdJohnston, Egsan Bacon, Enthusiast01, Epicmeman, Esszet, Eumolpo, Excirial, FabulousFerd, Fdsdh1, Fentener van Vlissingen, FiendYT, Floridasand, Fluous, Gabbe, General Ization, Gilliam, Graham87, GreenCows, Gwillhickers, Hairy Dude, Hazmat2, Helenabella, Higher Ground 1, Hmains, I dream of horses, IAmACelt, Illegitimate Barrister, Inayity, Incendiary Iconoclasm, J 1982, Jabberjaw, JambhalaKalasha, Jandalhandler, Jayjayhansard, Jejsmekeksdmdjek, Jessica.dyer, Jmertel23, Jobas, JoetheMoe25, John, Johnny3001, Jonesey95, JordanGero, Josephohara69, Juanma Campano, KH-1, KaJunl, Kku, L1ttleTr33, LawrenceScafuri, LilHelpa, Lotje, MShabazz, MaeseLeon, Mais oui!, Malerooster, Malik Shabazz, Mandruss, Materialscientist, Mberglund32, Mcc1789, Me, Myself, and I are Here, Mean as custard, Meltdown627, Mx. Granger, My Chemistry romantic, Natalia Maier, Natg 19, Nerdcatcher, Niceguyedc, Nihiltres, North Shoreman, OG17, Omo Obatalá, Oshwah, PMLF, Petermirnitchenko, Pincrete, Poiuytre, Proscribe, Pwoodfor, Quinnpin536, RHParish, Rajkumar 1 02, Rayholou, Rjensen, Rjwilmsi, Rupert loup, Russ3Z, Savvyjack23, Sean aislabiee, Senegambianamestudy, Shiftyrye27, ShorinBJ, SimonP, Skjoldbro, Someguywhat, Starwire, Stesmo, Student7, Stumink, Superwoman 007, TaqPol, TheFreeWorld, Tobby72, Toxic Native, Tristancoolio, True220, Ucmercedstudent209, Velteau, Waqob, Widefox, Wikidea, YeOldeGentleman, Yopienso, 105 anonymous edits 123

Colonisation of Africa *Source:* https://en.wikipedia.org/w/index.php?oldid=864220119 *License:* Creative Commons Attribution-Share Alike 3.0 *Contributors:* Acather96, Ale jrb, Annabelmiltond, Anniepresto, ArnoldPlaton, Atamajhidatakli, Autacoid, AvalerionV, BD2412, Beland, Bender235, Bongwarrior, Boomer Vial, Brigade Piron, BritAc, Calabe1992, Carlstak, Chipmunkdavis, Clintville, ClueBot NG, Cocolexis, Dairy501, DavideVeloria88, Dbensous, Dcirovic, Denisarona, Dewritech, Dfqml1997, Discospinster, Donner60, Edward, Empirecoins, Epicgenius, Fama Clamosa, Fat&Happy, Gabbybandit, Gembres, Gilderien, GoobMooch, HCPUNXKID, Hayman30, Horseless Headman, I dream of horses, Inayity, Isarra (HG), Jim1138, Jschnur, K6ka, KH-1, Kanoem12, Katniss240, Kintetsubuffalo, Koavf, KylieTastic, Lakun.patra, LilHelpa, Liquidmetalrob, Look2See1, Magicmike69, Magioladitis, Malcolm77, Marcocapelle, Marianna251, Materialscientist, Middayexpress, Millejoh, MjolnirPants, NewEnglandYankee, NittyG, Ocean Skyler, Ogbumegmt, Omo Obatalá, Onel5969, Oshwah, OttawaAC, Proofreader, Proscribe, Psihedelisto, Pyrotle, Raymondwinn, Robertgreer, Rodw, Rs24, Runehelmet, Ryan Vesey, SMcCandlish, Sam Sailor, Samf4u, SamuelOdinga, Serols, ShakespeareFan00, Shellwood, Simplexity22, Slightsmile, Smalljim, Snake668771, Snori, Spellcast, Stemonitis, Sundgauvien38, Superbad52, Titodutta, VMS Mosaic, Vieque, Warofdreams, Wdchk, Widr, Wikina17, Wikipelli, Wikishovel, XPTO, Yamaguchi先生 , Yvwv, 225 anonymous edits 167

Scramble for Africa *Source:* https://en.wikipedia.org/w/index.php?oldid=863853994 *License:* Creative Commons Attribution-Share Alike 3.0 *Contributors:* 2minty, AcidSnow, Acroterion, Actualist, Akl;sdht;alsdIAHSDGOADIHS, Albertnorman, Alfie, Andy M. Wang, Anotherclown, Asha.abukar, Avoided, BD2412, BU Rob13, Balikaldsim, Barjimoa, Bender235, Binabik80, Blame whitey, Blue Edits, Bobrayner, Bongwarrior, Breana howell, Brees43, CLCStudent, Camdennator11, Chris troutman, Cjrother, Closeralph44, ClueBot NG, Cyberbot II, Danielmbarlow, DavidLeighEllis, Dcirovic, Derpman1020, Discospinster, DisillusionedBitterAndKnackered, Donner60, E5150-00000000000, Edokter, Egsan Bacon, Ehrbar, El C, Elinruby, Embu wiki, Emmanuel178, Excirial, Finnusertop, FoCuSandLeArN, Gob Lofa, Grant65, GreenCows, Hairy Dude, Harfarhs, Hayek79, Hello71, Home Lander, I dream of horses, Imreallygays, IronGargoyle, Isrefaee, Iwilsonp, J 1982, J'espère69, Jandalhandler, Jchmrt, JeanVivian, Jiten D, John, JorisvS, Josve05a, Juan-Riley, Juliand, KSFT, Kintetsubuffalo, KylieTastic, Kzl55, L293D, LakesideMiners, Laszlo Panaflex, Lel420scrubz, Liance, LuizLSNeto, Mariam.essack, Materialscientist, Mccapra, MelbourneStar, Mojoworker, MusikAnimal, MxcDangerous, Narky Blert, Niceguyedc, Nyttend, Oshwah, P. S. Burton, Philip Trueman, Piledhigheranddeeper, Pimpdaddy8697, Prinsgezinde, R'n'B, RA0808, Redgro, Rjensen, RufusTheEditor, SUM1, Sarr Cat, Shrek33sander, Simplexity22, Smalljim, Soupforone, SquidHomme, Srnec, Steve Quinn, Suhailpurkar, SushiGod, SvenAERTS, Tamwin, The Transhumanist, The wub, TheFreeWorld, Thermocycler, Thomas.W, Thylacoop5, Tobby72, Torben Gülstorff, TrestonGay, Tsanku, Uriel1022, Vanjagenije, Vsmith, Wikidushyant, Winner 42, XPTO, ZappaOMati, Zarcademan123456, Zoozaz1, 217 anonymous edits 179

Geography of Africa *Source:* https://en.wikipedia.org/w/index.php?oldid=859173007 *License:* Creative Commons Attribution-Share Alike 3.0 *Contributors:* A520, Acather96, Amit6, Art LaPella, Atethnekos, Aymatth2, Banjopat, Bapreme, Bgwhite, Bohancheng, Bold Clone, Borgendorf, CBM, Carioca, Choij, ChrisGualtieri, ClueBot NG, Coinmanj, CommonsDelinker, Dale Arnett, Danblakemore, David Edgar, Derpaherpaderp, Diannaa, DivermanAU, Don4of4, Donner60, Drmies, Durova, Elizium23, Epicgenius, Fama Clamosa, Flyer22 Reborn, Fraggle81, Fredddie, GVnayR, Gaius Cornelius, GeneralizationsAreBad, Gilliam, Giorgiogp2, Goustien, Graham87, GünniX, HMSLavender, Hello71, HolsteinPommern, Howcheng, Iancaddy, Idkidk02, Jack Merridew, Jarble, Jdkelly12, Jim1138, JimVC3, Jmg38, John of Reading, Junglecat, JustAGal, Khalid Mahmood, Ktagaro, Lappspira, Leeheonjin, Lightmouse, Loraof, MaghrebiLove, Magioladitis, Maranello10, Markan80, Marqaz, Melanauts, Mentifisto, Middayexpress, Mifter, Mild Bill Hiccup, Minecraft 2727, Monty845, MrPanyGoff, NAHID, NetherlandishYankee, Nikkimaria, Oganesson007, Onel5969, Originalwana, Oshwah, Papa Lima Whiskey, Patdagolfboy, Penskins, Pepper, Peter B., Peter Horn, Phenolla, PhnomPencil, Pinethicket, Pitt the elder, Pocketthis, Postdlf, Prvc, R'n'B, RA0808, Ramaksoud2000, RenamedUser01302013, Rich Farmbrough, Richard Trillo, Runehelmet, Sdrawkcab, Serols, Shaded0, Shadowjams, Shirik, Sideways713, Snow Blizzard, Someguy1221, SoxBot III, Stfg, Thane, The Thing That Should Not Be, The Transhumanist, Theenragedgamerz, Thingg, Tonyfv, Trevor MacInnis, Ttwaring, VLADIMIR Skokan, VX, Vaccine skeptic, Vanished User 1004, Wavelength, WereSpielChequers, WikiCopter, Wikipelli, WoodyWerm, Woohookitty, Www06035, YUL89YYZ, Yowanvista, Zdtrlik, Zoe Bertrand, زرشک, 228 anonymous edits 215

African Plate *Source:* https://en.wikipedia.org/w/index.php?oldid=857330451 *License:* Creative Commons Attribution-Share Alike 3.0 *Contributors:* Ahoerstemeier, Alataristarion, AlexiusHoratius, Alro, Atif.t2, Aymatth2, Bdewaele, Ben Ben, Blackguard SF, Blanchardb, CLCStudent, ClueBot NG, CommonsDelinker, DARIO SEVERI, Dawnseeker2000, Download, El C, Elert, Eric-Wester, Faigl.ladislav, Fama Clamosa, Florian Huber, Flyer22 Reborn, GeoWriter, Geologyguy, Glacialfox, Gorthian, Gwernol, HMSLavender, Hadal, Hayman30, Hede2000, Hellbus, Hmains, Howard the Duck, Hunnjazal, I dream of horses, ImperatorExercitus, Interiot, Invitamia, Ivan Štambuk, Jackfork, JorisvS, Khalid Mahmood, Kipala, Korbnep, Littleteddy, Magioladitis, Magus732, Maine12329, Materialscientist, Merovingian, Middayexpress, Mikenorton, Morel, NTBot~enwiki, Naraht, NatureA16, Nightstallion, Omgitslily, Oshwah, Ouro, Pbsouthwood, Peter SamFan, Quadell, Quintote, Ratemonth, Raven in Orbit, RekishiEJ, RexNL, Rich Farmbrough, Rjwilmsi, Rmashhadi, Rollingfrenzy, Runefrost, Rémih, Sammalin, Serols, Seth Ilys, Sfaddeam, Solarra, Some jerk on the Internet, StuRat, Swid, Synergy, Tmangray, Tonyfaull, Vegaswikian, Volcanoguy, Vsmith, WadeSimMiser, Wk muriithi, Wtmitchell, Xaosflux, Yamaguchi先生 , Yunshui, Zvn, الدبوني, 135 anonymous edits 230

Climate of Africa *Source:* https://en.wikipedia.org/w/index.php?oldid=863569026 *License:* Creative Commons Attribution-Share Alike 3.0 *Contributors:* 0xF8E8, A.Minkowiski, AKS.9955, Acroterion, Ajaxfiore, Alan Liefting, Antandrus, Bentogoa, BethNaught, Bgwhite, Bluerasberry, Cadillac000, Capebio, Certes, ChrisGualtieri, ClueBot NG, Cnwilliams, DVdm, Dcirish11, Dcirovic, Discospinster, Dogru144, Drewmutt, Epicgenius, Erutuon, Flyer22 Reborn, Frosty, Gilliam, Hackerszzz, Harfarhs, Iamcooldude1999, IronGargoyle, Jarble, Jeancey, John of Reading, Katieh5584, Kieranskillan16, Kinetic37, Kopiersperre, Layla, the remover, Lexusuns, Lugia2453, MadGuy7023, Materialscientist, Middayexpress, Mightymights, Mike the G.O.A.T, MusikAnimal, NicoScribe, Northamerica1000, Oganesson007, Oshwah, Pablomartinez, Paul tk, PlyrStar93, Pratyya Ghosh, ProprioMe OW, RA0808, Racerx11, Robevans123, Serols, Seujan, ShelfSkewed, Simplexity22, Sjö, Smalljim, Stesmo, Technopat, TerryAlex, ThePlatypusofDoom, Thegreatdr, Tolly4bolly, Velella, Widr, Will102, William2001, Winterierword94, Wyatt3623, Yamaguchi先生 , Zabshk, 148 anonymous edits 233

Fauna of Africa *Source:* https://en.wikipedia.org/w/index.php?oldid=862190878 *License:* Creative Commons Attribution-Share Alike 3.0 *Contributors:* Angrytoast, BD2412, Belovedfreak, Bender235, BocoROTH, Bongwarrior, Caltas, Captain-tucker, Chris the speller, Clpo13, ClueBot NG, Coffinfly, CommonsDelinker, Dbfirs, DeadEyeArrow, Denisarona, Dewritech, Ecangola, Edward321, Floquenbeam, GalileoCope, Hans Dunkelberg, Headbomb, Hidayatsrf, Iamthecheese44, J 1982, JDCMAN, JamesAM, JamesEG, Julius Sahara, Justintime516, Jwinius, Kaarel, Ken Gallager, Look2See1, Lord Opeth, Ltdm, Lugia2453, MBlaze Lightning, Maias, Mgiganteus1, Middayexpress, MoodyNormal, Morel, Northamerica1000, Notafly, Nsaa, OlEnglish, Olly150, Orestek, Parent5446, Pro bug catcher, Qwertsar, RexNL, Rich Farmbrough, Richard001, Rjwilmsi, RolandR, SchreiberBike, Shellwood, Snoito, Spartaz, Starbois, Stemonitis, Subidei, Tbhotch, The Emirr, The Thing That Should Not Be, Topbanana, Ucucha, Ulric1313, WWGB, WolfmanSF, YUL89YYZ, Ypna, Zrno, 103 anonymous edits 239

List of political parties in Africa by country *Source:* https://en.wikipedia.org/w/index.php?oldid=804549447 *License:* Creative Commons Attribution-Share Alike 3.0 *Contributors:* Bgwhite, Bhuyquang1, Blondeguynative, BrownHairedGirl, ESkog, Frietjes, Garam, Kwamikagami, LibyaDragoon, Mannerheimo, Meno25, Middayexpress, Northamerica1000, Tim!, Tsarisco, WeifengYang, 8 anonymous edits 251

African Union *Source:* https://en.wikipedia.org/w/index.php?oldid=864550674 *License:* Creative Commons Attribution-Share Alike 3.0 *Contributors:* 011nyegagh, Adûnâi, Africanlog, Aisteco, Ajverink, Albertoeda, Alifazal, Alligators1974, Anonymous from the 21st century, Anuxicus, ApolloCarmb, Aquintero82, Arjayay, Atlantic306, Auguel, Axeman89, B.S. Lawrence, Badlander2019, BarrelProof, BedrockPerson, BegbertBiggs, Bonzolive, Buttons0603, CASSIOPEIA, CaribDigita, Cathrynpate108, ChasedSpade, Chipmunkdavis, Classicwiki, Clifffonte, ClueBot NG, CollinsTheRock, Cynulliad3, Danachos, Danlaycock, Daydreamers, Demmo, Denisarona, Discott, Drewmutt, Dthomsen8, Ecangola, Enciclopediaenlinea2, Eno Lirpa, EthanMagnuson, Etothepi, Euro1994ltu, FDMS4, Fleetwood Mac and Gary Dust.mp3, Floatjon, FreeKnowledgeCreator, Frietjes, GELongstreet, Georgia guy, Geraldshields11, Gilliam, Hairy Dude, HershelJunior, Hmains, Horst-schlaemma, Huon, Huritisho, Illegitimate Barrister, J 1982, JJMC89, Jaqoc, Jeff531, John of Reading, Jwkozak91, Keith D, Koavf, Ksanata, Largoplazo, Last edited by:, Leoberacai, Lepsyleon, Leschnei, LittleWink, Loginnigol, Lopifalko, Mandruss, Mannerheimo, Marquisbaai, Materialscientist, Mathdino, MazabukaBloke, Mohatatou, Mpjmcevoybeta, Mr Minchin, Neptune's Trident, Newslack, NinjaRobotPirate, Orthopraxia, Oshwah, PanchoS, Paul K., Penguin, Phoenix7777, Phuzion, Pizzafuer, Polopolus, Prioryman, ProprioMe OW, Proscribe, Pussayt, Quasar G., R'n'B, Radom1967, Rlong29, Rreagan007, Rsz19, Rubbish computer, RudyReis, Rui Gabriel Correia, SUM1, Sam Sailor, Searingjet, Shellwood, ShockandAwe, Shotats70, Sjö, Skyblue100, Skycycle, Smjg, Soulsisder, Spintendo, Sputink, Stefanodekiabi, SteveStrummer, Sureshkhole, Surjection, TenorTwelve, The Optimistic One, The Watchtower, Thekiller160, Tim!, Tom991, Turismond, User000name, Vmavanti, Vpab15, Wcam, WillemBK, Wimmiden, XavierGreen, Yahya el kouchi, X, 195 anonymous edits 255

Economy of Africa *Source:* https://en.wikipedia.org/w/index.php?oldid=862853980 *License:* Creative Commons Attribution-Share Alike 3.0 *Contributors:* 0x0077BE, AcidSnow, Afif Brika1, Alfie Gandon, AlfonsoHermoso, Andajara120000, Archon 2488, Ashley thomas80, Assasinzex, BadaBoom, Badlander2019, Batternut, Bgwhite, Btec233, Chris the speller, ChrisGualtieri, CircleAdrian, ClueBot NG, CommonsDelinker, Cyberbot II, DVdm, Dane, DavidLeighEllis, Davisrich1, Dcirovic, Delta343, Denisarona, Dewritech, Dl2000, DoABarrelRoll.dev, Drewmutt, Ecangola, EdmundIJones, El C, Emefaush, Frietjes, Funandtrvl, Gadget850, Gilliam, GoingBatty, Graham87, Guy1890, Hagato, Hftf, IjonTichyIjonTichy, Ita140188, Jamie Tubers, Jarble, Joshvd, Joy-historian, Katieh5584, Keith D, Kevin12xd, Kku, Kswag23, Le Grand Bleu, LeeLuce, LilHelpa, Lojbanist, Lor, Loriendrew, Lotje, M2545, Magioladitis, Medical physician, Middayexpress, MrOllie, Mrt3366, Msamaria190, NeilN, Nick Moyes, Nihiltres, Nikkimaria, Oshwah, OttawaAC, Outaouaisregina, Palove, PanchoS, Praxidicae, PriceDL, Proscribe, Psychonaut, Rachmat04, Rigorosho, Secretkeeper12, Serols, Sfgabe, Shaded0, Shellwood, SheriffIsInTown, Smalljim, Solarra, Soulman78, Soulparadox, Srich32977, Stumink, Thanmark412, ThePlatypusofDoom, Tommaso12345678910, Widr, Wjfox2005, XXGfHXx, Yamada Taro, Yintan, Youaretheoneinmymind, Youssefbhy, Zarcadia, 164 anonymous edits 289

Economy of the African Union *Source:* https://en.wikipedia.org/w/index.php?oldid=860698563 *License:* Creative Commons Attribution-Share Alike 3.0 *Contributors:* Alifazal, Briaboru, CieloEstrellado, Hemlock Martinis, Northamerica1000, Panoramalama, Shaded0, Subho2017, TFCforever, Toussaint, Wiz9999, 8 anonymous edits 321

Demographics of Africa *Source:* https://en.wikipedia.org/w/index.php?oldid=861464890 *License:* Creative Commons Attribution-Share Alike 3.0 *Contributors:* 22merlin, AcidSnow, Adavidb, Afus199620, AlternativesLebensglück, Andajara120000, BD2412, BDD, Ben Bezuidenhout, BigBoii2k17, Bishop Harrington, Black Falcon, Boghog, BrittneyWright, Callinus, Chris the speller, ClueBot NG, Cnwilliams, Coinmanj, Colonies Chris, CommonsDelinker, Cyberbot II, Davidcannon, Dbachmann, Dcljr, De728631, Demmo, Doc James, Doug Weller, DrLewisphd, Dudzy cant nut, Ecangola, Edgar181, Edward, Elmokicksass.poo, Fobos92, FrancessO, Funandtrvl, GVnayR, Giraffedata, Gooseflesh12, Gun jack 5000, Hamusteele, Hddty., HelenOnline, Hibernian, JMK, JMM The Killer, Jay D. Easy, Jdcollins13, Jennica, JesseRafe, KT-RICHARD, Kwamikagami, KylieTastic, Lihaas, Lotje, Magioladitis, Malcolmxl5, Materialscientist, Michael Devore, Michael Jester, Michael696969696969696969696696, Middayexpress, Mightymights, Mutos124, My name is not dave, NBKraskal, Narky Blert, Neptune's Trident, Niceguyedc, Oshwah, PhnomPencil, PlyrStar93, Political Rebel, PorfirioJFK, R'n'B, Rachmat04, Red-eyed demon, Robertiki, Rsrikanth05, SeoMac, Shellwood, Soupforone, Splette, Stanleytux, Stephen G. Brown, Stevey7788, TAnthony, Tajotep, The Anome, The Banner, Tony Tan, TranquilHope, Troyoleg, Urgemont999role, WikiPuppies, Wikipelli, Wingbowingbo, 82 anonymous edits 323

Languages of Africa *Source:* https://en.wikipedia.org/w/index.php?oldid=864535610 *License:* Creative Commons Attribution-Share Alike 3.0 *Contributors:* A lad insane, AKS.9955, AcidSnow, Adavidb, Aketch, Alumnum, Animalparty, Awilson107, BD2412, Batternut, Bearsca, Bender235, Bgwhite, Blame whitey, Booleund, Boomer Vial, Brookeaskew, Caballero1967, Carstensen, ChemicalyImbalanced, Chris the speller, Citizen Canine, Clarinetguy097, Cliveolsen121, ClueBot NG, ConfusedCollie8, Danachos, Daniel Chmielnicki, Danijuyusuf, Dbachmann, Dcirovic, DemocraticLuntz, Doug Weller, Dpm12, Elinruby, ElpasoWIKI, Epicnesss724, Evansmuchesa, Excirial, Flyer22 Reborn, Gatemansgc, GeekEmad, Graham11, Graham87, Greenman, GregKaye, GünniX, Haminoon, Holliniv, IceBrotherhood, Ie899, Iridescent, Iñaki Salazar, Jairoken10, Jellyman, Jeppiz, Jiten D, John of Reading, JorisvS, Katangais, Kintetsubuffalo, Knisfo, Koavf, LReditor, Largoplazo, Last edited by:, LightandDark2000, LilHelpa, LittleWink, Loup Solitaire 81, Lucarubis, Luciano.nyc, Mahmudmasri, MaxEnt, Medhat1997, Michiel1607, Middayexpress, Money money tickle parsnip, Moyogo, Mrgoodbytes84, Munci, MusikAnimal, NoToleranceForIntolerance, Omni Flames, Oramfe, Oshwah, Otache Ratara, Peacelovecamle, Pete unseth, Pratyya Ghosh, R'n'B, Rajkumar 1 02, Rui Gabriel Correia, SUM1, Shellwood, Smalljim, Soupforone, Starts, The Spartan 003, The Transhumanist, TheEsb, Trixte23, Troyoleg, Tumast22, Wahrheit28, Wakuran, Yassinelahboubi, Youssefbhy, ￼, 180 anonymous edits 339

Culture of Africa *Source:* https://en.wikipedia.org/w/index.php?oldid=864480729 *License:* Creative Commons Attribution-Share Alike 3.0 *Contributors:* AKS.9955, AddWittyNameHere, Addshore, Andajara120000, Andrewaskew, Avoided, BD2412, Berean Hunter, Berth the Great, BethNaught, Bgwhite, BigNib27, Bladesmulti, BranStark, Classicmike, ClueBot NG, CommonsDelinker, Cooldrd102, Cryptic Canadian, Crystallizedcarbon, DVdm, Darwinek, Darylgolden, Dash9Z, DavidLeighEllis, Derek R Bullamore, Dewritech, DferDaisy, Earflaps, Elinruby, Epicgenius, Excirial, FaithJael, Flooded with them hundreds, FlyingLeopard2014, FoCuSandLeArN, Gareth Griffith-Jones, Gilliam, Gobonobo, Gooseflesh12, Gyrofrog, Haminoon, HickoryOughtShirt?4, Hy Brasil, Hyacinth, I dream of horses, INeedSupport, IceBrotherhood, Imminent77, Inayity, Jayjg, Jcartone, Jim Carter, Jim1138, Jith12, Jon Kolbert, Jonathanjaydusturrubiarte, JustAGal, Justlettersandnumbers, K6ka, Kanguole, King muh, Kpgjhpjm, KylieTastic, L293D, LilHelpa, LoveTano, Lugia2453, Marianna251, Mark Arsten, Mark Ironie, MelbourneStar, Metalello, Middayexpress, Moonman3K, Music Boy50, NJRobbie, Ndoto ya Afrika, NewEnglandYankee, Nonchalant77, Optakeover, Oshwah, PCHS-NJROTC, PRehse, Prisencolin, Rsrikanth05, Rupert loup, Samee, Seaphoto, Serols, Shellwood, Simplexity22, Siuenti, Skizzik, Skr15081997, Sro23, Swedishelitev2, TI. Gracchus, TeaLover1996, The Anonymouse, The Transhumanist, The oof group leader, TheRepositioner, Theinstantmatrix, Thine Antique Pen, Thomas.W, Tolly4bolly, Toshisafagboy, TranquilHope, Trappist the monk, User With A Name, Vexations, WOSlinker, Whalestate, Wiae, Widr, Winner 42, Yr9sgrp1, 222 anonymous edits 357

Music of Africa *Source:* https://en.wikipedia.org/w/index.php?oldid=864189205 *License:* Creative Commons Attribution-Share Alike 3.0 *Contributors:* 18cyang, 26oo, Alphathon, Anniepoopshoot, Anthere, Anupmehra, Apap04, Arthur1124, AuthorAuthor, BabbaQ, Bgwhite, BigEditor15, Boomer Vial, C185, CLCStudent, Callanecc, Cboucher97, ChasedSpade, Checkingfax, Cherubinirules, Clelia albano, ClueBot NG, Contirbuter, Danieljones013, Davey2010, David.moreno72, Dawnseeker2000, Dbachmann, Dcmo, Dellenbaugh, Devlo12, Dewritech, DferDaisy, Discospinster, Dl2000, Donner60, Doworks000, Ducknish, Dwanyewest, Epicgenius, Ezeu, Faizan, Fraggle81, Frosty, Frze, General Ization, Gilliam, Giraffedata, GorillaWarfare, HMSLavender, Happysailor, Hedwig in Washington, HelenOnline, Hyacinth, I dream of horses, Ilovepinkthings, Iridescent, JC7V7DC5768, JackintheBox, JaconaFrere, James1011R, Jcd79, Jim1138, JimVC3, Joedandridge11, Joefromrandb, Jtoppfargion, K6ka, KH-1, Kinetic37, KylieTastic, Largoplazo, Lolitartine, Lopifalko, Loriendrew, Magioladitis, Marco Ngoni, Materialscientist, Mean as custard, MelbourneStar, Michael Bednarek, Middayexpress,

Mogism, Mough7, Mrjulesd, Munsick21, Musicology~enwiki, Nasedil Genio, Neodop, Nick Number, Northamerica1000, NottNott, Numuse37, Ohnoitsjamie, OnBeyondZebrax, Optakeover, Oshwah, Patient Zero, Plantdrew, Prisencolin, Proscribe, Qwerty6811, RA0808, ReconditeRodent, Rsrikanth05, Rystheguy, Sam Sailor, Samsbanned, Schmit829, Serial Number 54129, Serols, Simplexity22, Smalljim, Stanleytux, Thathatpokemon, TheNMF, Thomasfulton, Tom.Hakwkins23, Tonytoesmith, Trivialist, Trusilver, TwoTwoHello, Vinegarymass911, WNYY98, Widr, Woovee, 207 anonymous edits ... 373

Religion in Africa *Source:* https://en.wikipedia.org/w/index.php?oldid=863694883 *License:* Creative Commons Attribution-Share Alike 3.0 *Contributors:* A. Parrot, AcidSnow, Adavidb, Alifazal, Alina Haidar, Amortias, Andajara120000, Angelo De La Paz, Arabeditor11786, Arjayay, BU Rob13, Bgwhite, Billytnjng, Boing! said Zebedee, Bruce1ee, Catlemur, Chris the speller, Citizen Canine, ClueBot NG, Cnilep, Collosoll, Compfreak7, Cookiemohnsta, Coreduverna2020, DARIO SEVERI, Dayzle, Dbachmann, Dcirovic, Delusion23, Design, Dewritech, DocYako, Donner60, Dont belittle245, Dwanyewest, Emmette Hernandez Coleman, Erp, Excirial, Favonian, Fixwikimaps, Fontema, Galactic-Radiance, Gareth Griffith-Jones, Girl1704, Gregpierce2, Grunners, Helpsome, Hesnotblack, Hume42, INeedSupport, Ian.thomson, IceBrotherhood, Igoldste, Inayity, Iodalach93, Iridescent, IronGargoyle, Ivanvector, Jamie Tubers, Jeffholton, Jim1138, JimRenge, Jobas, Jodosma, John of Reading, Jonkerz, Jose de Souza Ribeiro, K6ka, Khazar2, Koavf, Krizpo, Kuru, KylieTastic, Last edited by:, Leoboudv, Liam haffernan, Madooo12, MaghrebiLove, Mannerheimo, Massinissaking123, Materialscientist, Matt Fitzpatrick, Matthew rutland, Middayexpress, Mightymights, Mignoscoper42069blazeit, Mr.motown, MusikAnimal, NeilN, Nicholas.Horsey, NicoScribe, Nikhil1234567, Nillurcheier, No longer a penguin, Non-dropframe, North Atlanticist Usonian, Ohnoitsjamie, Omar-toons, Otelemuyen, Peaceworld111, Porter16, Portillo, Pratyya Ghosh, Pritsindhar, Prof. Mc, Puttingfacts, Qwyrxian, Rich Farmbrough, Rise of power, Rjensen, Rupert loup, Saddhiyama, Saif78692, Schreiber-Bike, Seaphoto, Septate, Sfan00 IMG, Skylo Frost, Stormmeteo, Superprrrt, Takeaway, The Mighty Glen, TheSuave, This lousy T-shirt, Vanquisher.UA, VibeScepter, Widr, Wiki-uk, ⌐, 202 anonymous edits 385

List of regions of Africa *Source:* https://en.wikipedia.org/w/index.php?oldid=861240900 *License:* Creative Commons Attribution-Share Alike 3.0 *Contributors:* A phantom to lead u into the city, A12n, Alansohn, Alexf, Alifazal, Amaury, Arkuat, Ashley Pomeroy, Aymatth2, AzryckAnin, Belovedfreak, Bgwhite, Black Falcon, Blanchardb, Boreas74, Can't sleep, clown will eat me, Carstensen, ChristianCT95, ClueBot NG, CommonsDelinker, Corticopia, Deljr, Dewritech, Dooky, Dwo, Elemented9, Excirial, Eyesnore, Fuper, Geekdiva, Giraffedata, Gzornenplatz, Hibernian, JWB, Jarble, Jim1138, Jon2857092, Jurema Oliveira, Keisyz, Kintetsubuffalo, Kwamikagami, L Kensington, LeonardoMelchior, Loginnigol, Lord Roem, Lucidity, Mahagaja, Malayo-Filipino, Marshall Williams2, Middayexpress, Museagle, Mvc, Narky Blert, Neelix, Nick C, Nick Number, NielsenGW, Onel5969, Onifpaz, Oranjelo100, Otis182, PranksterTurtle, Quest for Truth, Rexparry sydney, Ryanoo, Saimdusan, SeeSchloss, Serols, SimonP, SoxBot III, Tbhotch, Telfordbuck, The Thing That Should Not Be, Thewikipopo, Tide rolls, Trusilver, Valenciano, Vesperius, VoABot II, WVRMad, Warofdreams, Webclient101, XXN, Zazaban, 140 anonymous edits 401

Image Sources, Licenses and Contributors

The sources listed for each image provide more detailed licensing information including the copyright status, the copyright owner, and the license conditions.

Figure 1 *Source:* https://en.wikipedia.org/w/index.php?title=File:Map-of-human-migrations.jpg *License:* GNU Free Documentation License *Contributors:* 84user, AnRe photography, ArachanoxReal, Atamari, Aude, Avsa, Chronus, Cwbm (commons), DEm, Dbachmann, DieBuche, Dudley Miles, Eleassar, Exsabuta, Fabartus, Glenn, Goustien, Ies, JMCC1, Jameslwoodward, Janbies, Joey-das-WBF, Joostik, Karlfk, Kintetsubuffalo, MGA73bot2, Noisy, Paulmallet, Phirosiberia, Ranveig, Rednblu, Themightyquill, VIGNERON, Verdy p, W!B:, Was a bee, Zemant, 16 anonymous edits 4

Figure 2 *Source:* https://en.wikipedia.org/w/index.php?title=File:Red_Sea2.png *License:* Creative Commons Attribution 2.0 *Contributors:* en:user:Muntuwandi 7

Figure 3 *Source:* https://en.wikipedia.org/w/index.php?title=File:African_Mitochondrial_descent.PNG *License:* Creative Commons Attribution 3.0 *Contributors:* Maulucioni 9

Figure 4 *Source:* https://en.wikipedia.org/w/index.php?title=File:Huxley_-_Mans_Place_in_Nature.jpg *License:* Public Domain *Contributors:* Benjamin Waterhouse Hawkins (1807–94) 12

Figure 5 *Source:* https://en.wikipedia.org/w/index.php?title=File:African-civilizations-map-pre-colonial.svg *License:* Creative Commons Attribution-Sharealike 3.0,2.5,2.0,1.0 *Contributors:* Jeff Israel (ZyMOS) 19

Figure 6 *Source:* https://en.wikipedia.org/w/index.php?title=File:Obelisk_Luxor.JPG *License:* GNU Free Documentation License *Contributors:* Ben Pirard, BotMultichillT, JMCC1, Juiced lemon, Kilom691, Neithsabes, OgreBot 2, 1 anonymous edits 19

Figure 7 *Source:* https://en.wikipedia.org/w/index.php?title=File:Rytter_fra_Bagirmi.jpg *License:* Public Domain *Contributors:* Daniel Bruun 20

Figure 8 *Source:* https://en.wikipedia.org/w/index.php?title=File:Pieza_foliácea_africana.jpg *License:* Public Domain *Contributors:* José-Manuel Benito Álvarez —> Locutus Borg 22

Figure 9 *Source:* https://en.wikipedia.org/w/index.php?title=File:Bronze_ornamental_staff_head,_9th_century,_Igbo-Ukwu.JPG *License:* Creative Commons Attribution-Sharealike 3.0 *Contributors:* User:Ochiwar 25

Figure 10 *Source:* https://en.wikipedia.org/w/index.php?title=File:Lower_Egypt_Nomes_01.png *License:* Creative Commons Attribution-Sharealike 3.0,2.5,2.0,1.0 *Contributors:* Jeff Dahl 27

Figure 11 *Source:* https://en.wikipedia.org/w/index.php?title=File:All_Gizah_Pyramids.jpg *License:* Creative Commons Attribution-Sharealike 2.0 *Contributors:* Ricardo Liberato 27

Figure 12 *Source:* https://en.wikipedia.org/w/index.php?title=File:Kushite_empire_700bc.jpg *License:* Public domain *Contributors:* Scott Free (talk) 29

Figure 13 *Source:* https://en.wikipedia.org/w/index.php?title=File:Naqa_Apedamak_temple.jpg *License:* Creative Commons Attribution-Share Alike *Contributors:* User:LassiHU 30

Figure 14 *Source:* https://en.wikipedia.org/w/index.php?title=File:Carthaginianempire.PNG *License:* Public domain *Contributors:* JavierV1212 (talk) 31

Figure 15 *Source:* https://en.wikipedia.org/w/index.php?title=File:Ruines_de_Carthage.jpg *Contributors:* Patrick Verdier, Free On Line Photos 32

Figure 16 *Source:* https://en.wikipedia.org/w/index.php?title=File:Qableh1.JPG *License:* Creative Commons Attribution-Sharealike 3.0 *Contributors:* Abdirisak 34

Figure 17 *Source:* https://en.wikipedia.org/w/index.php?title=File:Roman_Africa.JPG *License:* Public Domain *Contributors:* H. Kiepert 35

Image *Source:* https://en.wikipedia.org/w/index.php?title=File:Altes_Museum-Memnon.jpg *License:* Public Domain *Contributors:* User:Capillon 34

Image *Source:* https://en.wikipedia.org/w/index.php?title=File:Antakya_Arkeoloji_Muzesi_1250320_nevit_cr.jpg *License:* Creative Commons Attribution 2.5 *Contributors:* Nevit Dilmen (talk) 34

Figure 18 *Source:* https://en.wikipedia.org/w/index.php?title=File:The_Mummy_of_Demetrios,_95-100_C.E.,_11.600.jpg *Contributors:* Ashashyou, JMCC1, Kaitlyn153 36

Figure 19 *Source:* https://en.wikipedia.org/w/index.php?title=File:LocationAksumiteEmpire.png *License:* Creative Commons Attribution-Sharealike 2.5 *Contributors:* Gauravjuvekar, Karlfk, Koavf, Runehelmet, Spiridon Ion Cepleanu, Yom~commonswiki, Zheim~commonswiki 38

Figure 20 *Source:* https://en.wikipedia.org/w/index.php?title=File:ET_Axum_asv2018-01_img37_Stelae_Park.jpg *License:* Creative Commons Attribution *Contributors:* A.Savin 39

Figure 21 *Source:* https://en.wikipedia.org/w/index.php?title=File:Nok_sculpture_Louvre_70-1998-11-1.jpg *License:* Public Domain *Contributors:* User:Jastrow 40

Figure 22 *Source:* https://en.wikipedia.org/w/index.php?title=File:Bantu_Phillipson.png *License:* Public Domain *Contributors:* Bender235, Bibi Saint-Pol, Botev, Dbachmann, FogueraC, Karlfk, Kenmayer, Orrling, Runehelmet, Ulamm, Verdy p, Visite fortuitement prolongée, Waffles9761, Was a bee, 1 anonymous edits 41

Figure 23 *Source:* https://en.wikipedia.org/w/index.php?title=File:Borno_in_1810.svg *License:* Creative Commons Attribution 3.0 *Contributors:* Arrantzaleak 43

Figure 24 *Source:* https://en.wikipedia.org/w/index.php?title=File:CentralEastAfrica1750.png *License:* Creative Commons Attribution 3.0 *Contributors:* Gabagool 44

Figure 25 *Source:* https://en.wikipedia.org/w/index.php?title=File:La_ville_d'Abéché,_vue_du_poste_Français.jpg *License:* Public Domain *Contributors:* Ferrandi 45

Figure 26 *Source:* https://en.wikipedia.org/w/index.php?title=File:Luba_pottery-1908.jpg *License:* Public Domain *Contributors:* Johnston, Harry Hamilton, Sir, 1858-1927 46

Figure 27 *Source:* https://en.wikipedia.org/w/index.php?title=File:Lunda_houses-1854.jpg *License:* Public Domain *Contributors:* JMK, Ji-Elle, Jim Derby 47

Figure 28 *Source:* https://en.wikipedia.org/w/index.php?title=File:KingdomKongo1711.png *License:* Creative Commons Attribution-Sharealike 2.5 *Contributors:* Electionworld, Happenstance, Karlfk, Koavf, Razorbliss, Roke~commonswiki, 2 anonymous edits 49

Figure 29 *Source:* https://en.wikipedia.org/w/index.php?title=File:Gondereshe2008.jpg *License:* Creative Commons Attribution-Sharealike 3.0 *Contributors:* Warya 50

Figure 30 *Source:* https://en.wikipedia.org/w/index.php?title=File:Ancient-Almnara.jpg *License:* Creative Commons Attribution-Sharealike 3.0 *Contributors:* Vascoscream 50

Figure 31 *Source:* https://en.wikipedia.org/w/index.php?title=File:ET_Gondar_asv2018-02_img03_Fasil_Ghebbi.jpg *Contributors:* A.Savin .. 52

Figure 32 *Source:* https://en.wikipedia.org/w/index.php?title=File:Almohad1200.png *License:* Creative Commons Attribution 3.0 *Contributors:* Gabagool 53

Figure 33 *Source:* https://en.wikipedia.org/w/index.php?title=File:Great_Mosque_of_Kairouan_Panorama_-_Grande_Mosquée_de_Kairouan_Panorama.jpg *License:* Creative Commons Attribution-Sharealike 2.0 *Contributors:* MAREK SZAREJKO from CLONMEL, IRELAND - POLAND 54

Figure 34 *Source:* https://en.wikipedia.org/w/index.php?title=File:Safi_minaret.png *License:* Creative Commons Attribution *Contributors:* FSII, Masen, N. Wadjid, OgreBot 2, Poulos~commonswiki, Stegop, Yabroq 55

Figure 35 *Source:* https://en.wikipedia.org/w/index.php?title=File:Fatimid_Caliphate.PNG *Contributors:* User:Omar-toons 56

Figure 36 *Source:* https://en.wikipedia.org/w/index.php?title=File:Christian_Nubia.png *License:* Creative Commons Attribution-Sharealike 2.0 *Contributors:* SimonP 58

Figure 37 *Source:* https://en.wikipedia.org/w/index.php?title=File:Tower,_Great_Zimbabwe1.jpg *License:* Creative Commons Attribution-ShareAlike 3.0 Unported *Contributors:* JackyR 60

Figure 38 *Source:* https://en.wikipedia.org/w/index.php?title=File:Realnam.JPG *License:* Creative Commons Zero *Contributors:* Kacembepower 61

Figure 39 *Source:* https://en.wikipedia.org/w/index.php?title=File:Realzulu.JPG *License:* Creative Commons Zero *Contributors:* Kacembepower 62

Figure 40 *Source:* https://en.wikipedia.org/w/index.php?title=File:SouthAfrica1885.png *License:* Public Domain *Contributors:* John George Bartholomew (1860-1920) 63

Figure 41 *Source:* https://en.wikipedia.org/w/index.php?title=File:Swahili_door_Zanzibar.jpg *License:* Creative Commons Attribution-Sharealike 3.0 *Contributors:* Rotsee2 64

Figure 42 *Source:* https://en.wikipedia.org/w/index.php?title=File:Slaves_ruvuma.jpg *License:* Public Domain *Contributors:* Béka~commonswiki, Checkmate55, FSII, G.dallorto, JMCC1, JotaCartas, Mircea, Santosga, Underlying lk, חורין ייני 65

Figure 43 *Source:* https://en.wikipedia.org/w/index.php?title=File:Maravi_Kingdom_map_c._1650s.svg *License:* Creative Commons Attribution-ShareAlike 3.0 Unported *Contributors:* Africa_map_blank.svg: Eric Gaba (Sting - fr:Sting) derivative work: moyogo (talk) 69

442

Figure 44 *Source:* https://en.wikipedia.org/w/index.php?title=File:Ghana_empire_map.png *License:* GNU Free Documentation License *Contributors:* Luxo ... 70

Figure 45 *Source:* https://en.wikipedia.org/w/index.php?title=File:MALI_empire_map.PNG *License:* Creative Commons Attribution-ShareAlike 3.0 Unported *Contributors:* 4shizzal, BotMultichill, Electionworld, Helt, Karlfk, Roke∼commonswiki, Sven-steffen arndt, 2 anonymous edits ... 71

Figure 46 *Source:* https://en.wikipedia.org/w/index.php?title=File:SONGHAI_empire_map.PNG *License:* Creative Commons Attribution-Sharealike 2.5 *Contributors:* User:Roke∼commonswiki ... 73

Figure 47 *Source:* https://en.wikipedia.org/w/index.php?title=File:Kent_wove.jpg *License:* Creative Commons Attribution-Sharealike 3.0 *Contributors:* User:Bottracker ... 75

Figure 48 *Source:* https://en.wikipedia.org/w/index.php?title=File:Dahomey_amazon2.jpg *License:* Public Domain *Contributors:* Biologo32, Magog the Ogre ... 77

Figure 49 *Source:* https://en.wikipedia.org/w/index.php?title=File:WestAfrica1625.png *License:* Creative Commons Attribution 3.0 *Contributors:* Gabagool ... 78

Figure 50 *Source:* https://en.wikipedia.org/w/index.php?title=File:Benin_bronze_Louvre_A97-14-1.jpg *License:* Public Domain *Contributors:* User:Jastrow ... 79

Figure 51 *Source:* https://en.wikipedia.org/w/index.php?title=File:Maxim_machine_gun_Megapixie.jpg *License:* Public domain *Contributors:* Ain92, Atirador, BotMultichill, Hohum, Kleon3, Morio, Nemo5576, Soerfm ... 83

Figure 52 *Source:* https://en.wikipedia.org/w/index.php?title=File:Davidlivingstone_cropped.jpg *License:* Public Domain *Contributors:* User:Infrogmation ... 84

Figure 53 *Source:* https://en.wikipedia.org/w/index.php?title=File:Fashoda_Incident_map_-_en.svg *License:* Creative Commons Attribution-Sharealike 3.0 *Contributors:* User:14nu5, User:Domie, User:Mozzan ... 86

Figure 54 *Source:* https://en.wikipedia.org/w/index.php?title=File:Colonial_Africa_1913_map.svg *License:* Creative Commons Attribution-ShareAlike 3.0 Unported *Contributors:* Eric Gaba (Sting - fr:Sting) ... 87

Figure 55 *Source:* https://en.wikipedia.org/w/index.php?title=File:Map_of_Africa_in_1939.png *License:* Creative Commons Attribution-Sharealike 3.0 *Contributors:* User:Brigade Piron ... 91

Figure 56 *Source:* https://en.wikipedia.org/w/index.php?title=File:Africa_independence_dates.svg *License:* GNU Free Documentation License *Contributors:* Original uploader was Mehmetaergun; recreated by Nobelium (talk) 2010-05-10 ... 94

Image *Source:* https://en.wikipedia.org/w/index.php?title=File:Wikisource-logo.svg *License:* Creative Commons Attribution-Sharealike 3.0 *Contributors:* ChrisiPK, Guillom, INeverCry, Jarekt, JuTa, Leyo, Lokal Profil, MichaelMaggs, NielsF, Rei-artur, Rocket000, Romaine, Steinsplitter ... 98

Image *Source:* https://en.wikipedia.org/w/index.php?title=File:Lock-green.svg *License:* Creative Commons Zero *Contributors:* User:Trappist the monk ... 99

Figure 57 *Source:* https://en.wikipedia.org/w/index.php?title=File:Slaves_ruvuma.jpg *License:* Public Domain *Contributors:* Béka∼commonswiki, Checkmate55, FSII, G.dallorto, JMCC1, JotaCartas, Mircea, Santosga, Underlying lk, הורון יניב ... 102

Image *Source:* https://en.wikipedia.org/w/index.php?title=File:IJzeren_voetring_voor_gevangenen_transparent_background.png *License:* Creative Commons Attribution-Sharealike 3.0 *Contributors:* Chatsam, Ies, RaphaelQS ... 101

Figure 58 *Source:* https://en.wikipedia.org/w/index.php?title=File:Arabslavers.jpg *License:* Public Domain *Contributors:* User:SreeBot ... 103

Figure 59 *Source:* https://en.wikipedia.org/w/index.php?title=File:Purchase_of_Christian_captives_from_the_Barbary_States.jpg *License:* Public Domain *Contributors:* Anonymous 17th century ... 107

Figure 60 *Source:* https://en.wikipedia.org/w/index.php?title=File:Slavezanzibar2.JPG *License:* Public Domain *Contributors:* BotMultichill, Ecummenic, File Upload Bot (Magnus Manske), Frank C. Müller, Geekdiva, Jarekt, Jbarta, Joostik, Kintetsubuffalo, Lioneldecoster, Mjrmtg, MrMrM, OgreBot 2, Olivier, Pierpao, Sfan00 IMG, Wouterhagens, ВоенТех, 3 anonymous edits ... 109

Figure 61 *Source:* https://en.wikipedia.org/w/index.php?title=File:Slaves_Zadib_Yemen_13th_century_BNF_Paris.jpg *License:* Public Domain *Contributors:* Aa77zz, AndreasPraefcke, Ashashyou, Ashrf1979, Bricou, Calame, Dcoetzee, Dsmdgold, G.dallorto, Gryffindor, Mel22, Moez, Urban∼commonswiki ... 110

Figure 62 *Source:* https://en.wikipedia.org/w/index.php?title=File:Zanzslgwch.jpg *License:* Public Domain *Contributors:* Middayexpress ... 113

Figure 63 *Source:* https://en.wikipedia.org/w/index.php?title=File:A_slave_market_in_Cairo-David_Roberts.jpg *License:* Public Domain *Contributors:* Ashashyou, Bastique, Dudu90, Fentener van Vlissingen, JMCC1, Martin H., Mister EM, 3 anonymous edits ... 114

Figure 64 *Source:* https://en.wikipedia.org/w/index.php?title=File:African_slave_trade.png *License:* Creative Commons Attribution-Sharealike 3.0 *Contributors:* User:Aliesin, User:Runehelmet ... 115

Figure 65 *Source:* https://en.wikipedia.org/w/index.php?title=File:Boutre_indien.jpg *Contributors:* Hervé Cozanet ... 115

Figure 66 *Source:* https://en.wikipedia.org/w/index.php?title=File:Different_cowries.jpg *License:* Creative Commons Attribution-ShareAlike 3.0 Unported *Contributors:* Allforrous, Bricktop, Medium69 ... 117

Figure 67 *Source:* https://en.wikipedia.org/w/index.php?title=File:Slave_market_Khartoum_19th_c.png *License:* Public Domain *Contributors:* Artist unknown ... 117

Figure 68 *Source:* https://en.wikipedia.org/w/index.php?title=File:Captain_walter_croker_horror_stricken_at_algiers_1815.jpg *License:* Public Domain *Contributors:* Walker Croker ... 120

Image *Source:* https://en.wikipedia.org/w/index.php?title=File:Padlock-silver.svg *Contributors:* AzaToth, BotMultichill, BotMultichillT, Gurch, Jarekt, Kallerna, Multichill, Perhelion, Rd232, Riana, Sarang, Siebrand, Steinsplitter, 4 anonymous edits ... 123

Figure 69 *Source:* https://en.wikipedia.org/w/index.php?title=File:Slaveshipposter_(cropped).jpg *Contributors:* Plymouth Chapter of the Society for Effecting the Abolition of the Slave Trade ... 124

Figure 70 *Source:* https://en.wikipedia.org/w/index.php?title=File:Slave_Auction_Ad.jpg *License:* Public Domain *Contributors:* Hilohello, Jdx, Magog the Ogre, Wikihistorian, Wwbread, 4 anonymous edits ... 124

Figure 71 *Source:* https://en.wikipedia.org/w/index.php?title=File:Group_of_men_and_women_being_taken_to_a_slave_market_Wellcome_V0050647.jpg *Contributors:* Fæ, Jim.henderson ... 127

Figure 72 *Source:* https://en.wikipedia.org/w/index.php?title=File:Kongo_audience.jpg *License:* Public Domain *Contributors:* 4shizzal, Jarekt, Magog the Ogre ... 128

Figure 73 *Source:* https//en.wikipedia.org *License:* Public Domain *Contributors:* BotMultichill, Fæ, Jan Arkesteijn, Jbribeiro1, MrMrM, Orrling, Parabolooidal, Poeticbent, Sailko, Shakko, Wmpearl, Wolfmann ... 130

Figure 74 *Source:* https://en.wikipedia.org/w/index.php?title=File:The_Slave_Trade_by_Auguste_Francois_Biard.jpg *License:* Public Domain *Contributors:* Bapti, Botaurus, Infrogmation, Jonund, Oursana, Poulpy, Trzęsacz, 1 anonymous edits ... 132

Figure 75 *Source:* https://en.wikipedia.org/w/index.php?title=File:BLAKE10.JPG *Contributors:* - ... 133

Figure 76 *Source:* https://en.wikipedia.org/w/index.php?title=File:Marchands_d'esclaves_de_Gorée-Jacques_Grasset_de_Saint-Sauveur_mg_8526.jpg *License:* Public Domain *Contributors:* Rama ... 134

Figure 77 *Source:* https://en.wikipedia.org/w/index.php?title=File:The_inspection_and_sale_of_a_slave.jpg *License:* Public Domain *Contributors:* Brantz Mayer ... 135

Figure 78 *Source:* https://en.wikipedia.org/w/index.php?title=File:Africa_slave_Regions.svg *License:* Creative Commons Attribution-ShareAlike 3.0 Unported *Contributors:* Africa_map_no_countries.svg: *Africa_map_blank.svg: Eric Gaba (Sting - fr:Sting) derivative work: User:Zscout370 (Return 136

Figure 79 *Source:* https://en.wikipedia.org/w/index.php?title=File:Gezo_(2).jpg *License:* Public Domain *Contributors:* Forbes, Frederick E. . 137

Figure 80 *Source:* https://en.wikipedia.org/w/index.php?title=File:Slave_ship_diagram.png *Contributors:* Bongoman, BoringHistoryGuy, Dittaeva, G.dallorto, Ibn Battuta, JMCC1, Korrigan, Mdd, Paroxysm∼commonswiki, Quibik, Rd232, Stunteltje, Túrelio, 3 anonymous edits ... 139

Figure 81 *Source:* https://en.wikipedia.org/w/index.php?title=File:Thomas-Clarkson-De-kreet-der-Afrikanen_MG_1315.tif *Contributors:* Finavon, Hansmuller, Steinsplitter ... 140

Figure 82 *Source:* https://en.wikipedia.org/w/index.php?title=File:A_Liverpool_Slave_Ship_by_William_Jackson.jpg *License:* Public Domain *Contributors:* MarmadukePercy, Tangopaso ... 142

Figure 83 *Source:* https://en.wikipedia.org/w/index.php?title=File:Punishing_negroes_at_Calabouco.jpg *License:* Public Domain *Contributors:* FastilyClone, Jahoe, Peripitus, Quissamã, Wmpearl, 1 anonymous edits ... 144

Figure 84 *Source:* https://en.wikipedia.org/w/index.php?title=File:Slaves_resting_by_Rugendas_01.jpg *License:* Public Domain *Contributors:* Allforrous, Lecen ... 145

Figure 85 *Source:* https://en.wikipedia.org/w/index.php?title=File:Tropenmuseum_Royal_Tropical_Institute_Objectnumber_3581-33h_Ingekleurde_litho_voorstellende_de_oo.jpg *Contributors:* BotMultichill, Botaurus-stellaris, GerardM, Minerv, Takeaway, Wolfmann, Ymnes ... 146

Figure 86 *Source:* https://en.wikipedia.org/w/index.php?title=File:1670_virginia_tobacco_slaves.jpg *License:* Public Domain *Contributors:* EChastain, MarmadukePercy, Morgan Riley, Tangopaso, 1 anonymous edits ... 149

Figure 87 *Source:* https://en.wikipedia.org/w/index.php?title=File:Different_cowries.jpg *License:* Creative Commons Attribution-ShareAlike 3.0 Unported *Contributors:* Allforrous, Bricktop, Medium69 ... 149

Figure 88 *Source:* https://en.wikipedia.org/w/index.php?title=File:Joseph_Cross,_The_Impolicy_of_Slavery,_1823_Cornell_CUL_PJM_1039_01.jpg *Contributors:* EVDiam ... 151

Figure 89 *Source:* https//en.wikipedia.org *License:* Public Domain *Contributors:* BotMultichillT, BronHiggs, Ixtzib, Laura1822, Michael Barera 152

Figure 90 *Source:* https://en.wikipedia.org/w/index.php?title=File:Agostino_Brunias_-_West_Indian_Creole_woman,_with_her_Black_Servant_-_Google_Art_Project.jpg *License:* Public Domain *Contributors:* BotMultichillT, Laura1822, Man vyi, Tamba52, Wolfmann ... 154
Figure 91 *Source:* https://en.wikipedia.org/w/index.php?title=File:Wilberforce_john_rising.jpg *License:* Public Domain *Contributors:* John Rising (1753–1817) ... 155
Figure 92 *Source:* https://en.wikipedia.org/w/index.php?title=File:SisterSlave.jpg *License:* Public Domain *Contributors:* Unknown; uploaded by en:User:Dumarest to en.wikipedia ... 156
Figure 93 *Source:* https://en.wikipedia.org/w/index.php?title=File:HMS_Black_Joke_(1827).jpg *License:* Public Domain *Contributors:* Badzil, BotMultichill, Botaurus, Chase me ladies, I'm the Cavalry, Docu, File Upload Bot (Magnus Manske), JMCC1, Mattes, Off2riorob, OgreBot 2, Stunteltje, Takeaway ... 157
Figure 94 *Source:* https://en.wikipedia.org/w/index.php?title=File:Debret_casa_ciganos.jpg *License:* Public Domain *Contributors:* André Koehne, DarwIn, Origamiemensch ... 158
Image *Source:* https://en.wikipedia.org/w/index.php?title=File:Commons-logo.svg *License:* logo *Contributors:* Anomie, Callanecc, CambridgeBayWeather, Jo-Jo Eumerus, RHaworth ... 165
Image *Source:* https://en.wikipedia.org/w/index.php?title=File:Wikivoyage-Logo-v3-icon.svg *License:* Creative Commons Attribution-Sharealike 3.0 *Contributors:* User:AleXXw ... 165
Figure 95 *Source:* https://en.wikipedia.org/w/index.php?title=File:1910_map_of_Africa.png *License:* Public Domain *Contributors:* File Upload Bot (Magnus Manske), Michael Barera, Zhuyifei1999 ... 168
Figure 96 *Source:* https://en.wikipedia.org/w/index.php?title=File:Negroland_and_Guinea_with_the_European_Settlements,_1736.jpg *License:* Public Domain *Contributors:* Herman Moll ... 169
Figure 97 *Source:* https://en.wikipedia.org/w/index.php?title=File:Colonial_Africa_1913_map.svg *License:* Creative Commons Attribution-ShareAlike 3.0 Unported *Contributors:* Eric Gaba (Sting - fr:Sting) ... 170
Figure 98 *Source:* https://en.wikipedia.org/w/index.php?title=File:Africa1940.png *License:* Creative Commons Attribution-Sharealike 3.0,2.5,2.0,1.0 *Contributors:* Jackaranga ... 171
Figure 99 *Source:* https://en.wikipedia.org/w/index.php?title=File:Mahmood_Mamdani.jpg *License:* Creative Commons Attribution-Sharealike 2.0 *Contributors:* Alifazal, 1 anonymous edits ... 174
Figure 100 *Source:* https://en.wikipedia.org/w/index.php?title=File:Achille_Mbembe_2.JPG *Contributors:* User:Heike Huslage-Koch ... 175
Figure 101 *Source:* https://en.wikipedia.org/w/index.php?title=File:Colonial_Africa_1913_map.svg *License:* Creative Commons Attribution-ShareAlike 3.0 Unported *Contributors:* Eric Gaba (Sting - fr:Sting) ... 181
Image *Source:* https://en.wikipedia.org/w/index.php?title=File:Punch_Rhodes_Colossus.png *License:* Public Domain *Contributors:* Edward Linley Sambourne (1844–1910) ... 179
Figure 102 *Source:* https://en.wikipedia.org/w/index.php?title=File:Preaching_from_a_Waggon_(David_Livingstone)_by_The_London_Missionary_Society.jpg *License:* anonymous-EU *Contributors:* See filename/description ... 182
Figure 103 *Source:* https://en.wikipedia.org/w/index.php?title=File:Scramble-for-Africa-1880-1913.png *Contributors:* User:Somebody500 . 182
Figure 104 *Source:* https://en.wikipedia.org/w/index.php?title=File:LeCommandantMarchand.jpg *License:* Creative Commons Attribution-Sharealike 2.5 *Contributors:* Airelle, BotMultichill, DITWIN GRIM, Jianhui67, Kilom691, World Imaging, 2 anonymous edits ... 184
Figure 105 *Source:* https://en.wikipedia.org/w/index.php?title=File:Bundesarchiv_Bild_105-DOA6364,_Deutsch-Ostafrika,_Polizeiaskaris.jpg *License:* Creative Commons Attribution-Sharealike 3.0 Germany *Contributors:* BotMultichill, Charlesdrakew, Chrischerf, Martin H., Pibwl, Ras67 . 185
Figure 106 *Source:* https://en.wikipedia.org/w/index.php?title=File:Detail,_Battle_of_Adwa_(2872663780).jpg *License:* Creative Commons Attribution 2.0 *Contributors:* A. Davey from Where I Live Now: Pacific Northwest ... 187
Figure 107 *Source:* https://en.wikipedia.org/w/index.php?title=File:Henry_Morton_Stanley.jpg *License:* Public Domain *Contributors:* Deadstar, Finavon, Jmabel, Malo, Mike Hayes, Paobac~commonswiki, Ruthven ... 188
Figure 108 *Source:* https://en.wikipedia.org/w/index.php?title=File:Pierre_Savorgnan_de_Brazza.jpg *License:* Public Domain *Contributors:* Arria Belli, Ashashyou, Jipre, Tholme, 1 anonymous edits ... 189
Figure 109 *Source:* https://en.wikipedia.org/w/index.php?title=File:MutilatedChildrenFromCongo.jpg *License:* Public Domain *Contributors:* Alice Harris, Daniel Danielson, others. ... 190
Figure 110 *Source:* https://en.wikipedia.org/w/index.php?title=File:Port_Said_Suez_Canal.jpg *License:* Public Domain *Contributors:* JMCC1, Kilom691 ... 191
Figure 111 *Source:* https://en.wikipedia.org/w/index.php?title=File:Kongokonferenz.jpg *License:* Public Domain *Contributors:* Adalbert von Rößler (†1922) ... 192
Figure 112 *Source:* https://en.wikipedia.org/w/index.php?title=File:LizzieVanZyl.jpg *License:* Public Domain *Contributors:* Brinkie, Hannolans, JMK, Julien Carnot, Kelson, Perseus25, Ruff tuff cream puff, Sgconlaw, SunOfErat, Timeshifter, 1 anonymous edits ... 193
Figure 113 *Source:* https://en.wikipedia.org/w/index.php?title=File:Muhammad_Ahmad.jpg *License:* Public Domain *Contributors:* Not identified 195
Figure 114 *Source:* https://en.wikipedia.org/w/index.php?title=File:Si_Kaddour_ben_Ghabrit_et_le_sultan_Moulay_Hafid.jpg *License:* Public Domain *Contributors:* Bissorte, Clindberg, Havang(nl), Yann ... 196
Figure 115 *Source:* https://en.wikipedia.org/w/index.php?title=File:Sayyid_Mohammed_Abdullah_Hassan.jpeg *Contributors:* Somali government 197
Figure 116 *Source:* https://en.wikipedia.org/w/index.php?title=File:Surviving_Herero.jpg *License:* Public Domain *Contributors:* FA2010, Foundert~commonswiki, GrumpyTroll~commonswiki, Nv8200pa, Richard-of-Earth, Sgconlaw, Tano4595, Wikieditoroftoday, Wolfmann, Zantastik~commonswiki, 2 anonymous edits ... 198
Figure 117 *Source:* https://en.wikipedia.org/w/index.php?title=File:African_Pigmies_CNE-v1-p58-B.jpg *License:* Public Domain *Contributors:* Keystone View Company ... 199
Figure 118 *Source:* https://en.wikipedia.org/w/index.php?title=File:Dellepiane-exposition-nationale-coloniale-1906.jpg *License:* Public Domain *Contributors:* User:Bloody-libu ... 201
Figure 119 *Source:* https://en.wikipedia.org/w/index.php?title=File:Victoria_(Cameroon).jpg *License:* Public Domain *Contributors:* Aschroet, Jcb, Ji-Elle, JuTa, LSDSL, Lotje, Rémih, Soranoch ... 203
Figure 120 *Source:* https://en.wikipedia.org/w/index.php?title=File:Desembarco_en_Cotonou_de_tropas_senegalesas._Le_Petit_Journal,_21may1892.jpg *License:* Creative Commons Zero *Contributors:* BernardinoMendoza, Funke, Humboldt, M2545, Soerfm, Zykasaa ... 206
Figure 121 *Source:* https://en.wikipedia.org/w/index.php?title=File:Combat_de_marracuene.jpg *License:* Public Domain *Contributors:* AnRo0002, Barbe-Noire, Jcornelius, JotaCartas, Santosga, 1 anonymous edits ... 207
Figure 122 *Source:* https://en.wikipedia.org/w/index.php?title=File:1899railroad_salisbury.jpg *License:* Public Domain *Contributors:* Beira railroad 208
Figure 123 *Source:* https://en.wikipedia.org/w/index.php?title=File:Prempeh-124-palaver-and-submission.jpg *License:* Public Domain *Contributors:* Ahanta, FSII, Katharinaiv, Nerika, Zykasaa, 2 anonymous edits ... 208
Figure 124 *Source:* https://en.wikipedia.org/w/index.php?title=File:Sudan_Map_Oelgas.png *License:* Public Domain *Contributors:* Ammar1ah, Danzig88, Dinsdagskind, Muhammad adel007, Seb az86556, Sven-steffen arndt, Zykasaa ... 210
Image *Source:* https://en.wikipedia.org/w/index.php?title=File:LocationAfrica.png *License:* Public Domain *Contributors:* see above ... 215
Figure 125 *Source:* https://en.wikipedia.org/w/index.php?title=File:Africa_(satellite_image).jpg *License:* Public Domain *Contributors:* NASA 216
Figure 126 *Source:* https://en.wikipedia.org/w/index.php?title=File:Topography_of_africa.png *License:* Public Domain *Contributors:* Dbachmann, JeffyP, TUBS, Tomdo08 ... 218
Figure 127 *Source:* https://en.wikipedia.org/w/index.php?title=File:Karte_der_Einzugsgebiete_der_großen_Gewässer_Afrikas.png *License:* Creative Commons Attribution-Sharealike 2.0 *Contributors:* Maximilian Dörrbecker (Chumwa) ... 221
Image *Source:* https://en.wikipedia.org/w/index.php?title=File:Africa_1971_2000_mean_temperature.png *License:* Creative Commons Attribution-Sharealike 3.0 *Contributors:* Giorgiogp2 ... 225
Image *Source:* https://en.wikipedia.org/w/index.php?title=File:Africa_1971-2000_mean_precipitation.png *License:* Creative Commons Attribution-Sharealike 3.0 *Contributors:* Giorgiogp2 ... 225
Figure 128 *Source:* https://en.wikipedia.org/w/index.php?title=File:Africa_map_of_Köppen_climate_classification.svg *Contributors:* User:Ali Zifan ... 226
Figure 129 *Source:* https://en.wikipedia.org/w/index.php?title=File:Africa_FebAug.gif *License:* Public Domain *Contributors:* User:Interiot~commonswiki ... 227
Figure 130 *Source:* https://en.wikipedia.org/w/index.php?title=File:Pointe_des_Almadies_-_Senegal.jpg *License:* Creative Commons Attribution 2.0 *Contributors:* User:MrPanyGoff ... 229
Image *Source:* https://en.wikipedia.org/w/index.php?title=File:Gnome-globe.svg *Contributors:* Abu badali~commonswiki, Adambro, Cathy Richards, Lijealso, Odder, Perhelion, Reseletti, Sarang, Seahen, Steinsplitter, Thibaut120094, Thomas Linard, Tkgd2007, Tulsi Bhagat, 4 anonymous edits ... 230
Image *Source:* https://en.wikipedia.org/w/index.php?title=File:AfricanPlate.png *Contributors:* User:Alataristarion ... 230
Figure 131 *Source:* https://en.wikipedia.org/w/index.php?title=File:Motion_of_Nubia_Plate.gif *Contributors:* User:Rollingfrenzy ... 232
Figure 132 *Source:* https://en.wikipedia.org/w/index.php?title=File:EAfrica.png *License:* Public Domain *Contributors:* USGS ... 233

Figure 133 *Source:* https://en.wikipedia.org/w/index.php?title=File:Africa_map_of_Köppen_climate_classification.svg *Contributors:* User:Ali Zifan ... 234
Figure 134 *Source:* https://en.wikipedia.org/w/index.php?title=File:Africa_satellite_orthographic.jpg *License:* Public Domain *Contributors:* Anomie, Jo-Jo Eumerus ... 235
Figure 135 *Source:* https://en.wikipedia.org/w/index.php?title=File:Africa_temperature.png *License:* Creative Commons Attribution 3.0 *Contributors:* Alan Liefting, Allforrous, Bluerasberry, Daniel Mietchen, Treisijs ... 235
Figure 136 *Source:* https://en.wikipedia.org/w/index.php?title=File:Africa_Precipitation_Map.svg *Contributors:* Alex Great, Bigbossfarin, Delphi234, Kopiersperre, Sarang, Scarlett Creeper, TFerenczy, Wylve ... 237
Figure 137 *Source:* https://en.wikipedia.org/w/index.php?title=File:Atlas_Mountains_snow_cover.jpg *License:* Creative Commons Attribution-Sharealike 2.0 *Contributors:* notcreative123 ... 238
Figure 138 *Source:* https://en.wikipedia.org/w/index.php?title=File:Hyenas_at_stolen_impala_kill.jpg *License:* Creative Commons Attribution-ShareAlike 3.0 Unported *Contributors:* JerryFriedman ... 240
Figure 139 *Source:* https://en.wikipedia.org/w/index.php?title=File:Laurasia-Gondwana.png *License:* Public Domain *Contributors:* AndreR, Chris.urs-o, Funandtrvl, Glenn, Kevmin, LennyWikipedia∼commonswiki, Leyo, Liftarn, Maksim, McPot, Phe, TomCatX, 4 anonymous edits ... 240
Figure 140 *Source:* https://en.wikipedia.org/w/index.php?title=File:Achatina_fulica_Hawaii.jpg *License:* GNU Free Documentation License *Contributors:* / Eric Guinther ... 241
Figure 141 *Source:* https://en.wikipedia.org/w/index.php?title=File:H17termound.jpg *License:* Public Domain *Contributors:* John Walker ... 242
Figure 142 *Source:* https://en.wikipedia.org/w/index.php?title=File:Citrus_swallowtail_Tanzania.JPG *License:* GNU Free Documentation License *Contributors:* Muhammad_Mahdi_Karim (talk) (Uploads) ... 243
Figure 143 *Source:* https://en.wikipedia.org/w/index.php?title=File:Latimeria_chalumnae01.jpg *License:* Creative Commons Attribution-ShareAlike 3.0 Unported *Contributors:* User:JoJan ... 244
Figure 144 *Source:* https://en.wikipedia.org/w/index.php?title=File:Dendroaspis_viridisPCCA20051227-1885B.jpg *License:* Creative Commons Attribution-Sharealike 2.5 *Contributors:* Patrick Coin (Patrick Coin) ... 246
Figure 145 *Source:* https://en.wikipedia.org/w/index.php?title=File:Psittacus_erithacus_-upper_body-8c.jpg *License:* Creative Commons Attribution-ShareAlike 3.0 Unported *Contributors:* L.Miguel Bugallo Sánchez (http://commons.wikimedia.org/wiki/User:Lmbuga) ... 247
Figure 146 *Source:* https://en.wikipedia.org/w/index.php?title=File:Makuleke6.JPG *License:* Creative Commons Attribution 2.5 *Contributors:* Attis1979, JMK, Kersti Nebelsiek, MGA73bot2, Mario1952, OgreBot 2, Simisa, Themightyquill, Winterkind ... 248
Image *Source:* https://en.wikipedia.org/w/index.php?title=File:Flag_of_Algeria.svg *License:* Public Domain *Contributors:* This graphic was originaly drawn by User:SKopp. ... 252
Image *Source:* https://en.wikipedia.org/w/index.php?title=File:Flag_of_Egypt.svg *License:* Public Domain *Contributors:* Open Clip Art ... 252
Image *Source:* https://en.wikipedia.org/w/index.php?title=File:Flag_of_Libya.svg *License:* Public Domain *Contributors:* Various ... 252
Image *Source:* https://en.wikipedia.org/w/index.php?title=File:Flag_of_Morocco.svg *License:* Public Domain *Contributors:* Anime Addict AA, AymanFlad, Barryob, Bgag, Cimoi, Cycn, Denelson83, Denniss, Djampa, Doodledoo, Earth Resident, EugeneZelenko, Fastily, Flad, Foroa, Fred J, Fry1989, Gmaxwell, Herbythyme, J. Patrick Fischer, Klemen Kocjancic, Krinkle, Leyo, Mattes, Meno25, Mindspillage, Myself488, Odder, Offnfopt, Omar-toons, Orrling, OsamaK, Permjak, Ppntori, Reisio, Rodejong, Sangjinhwa, Sarang, SiBr4, Steinsplitter, Str4nd, TFCforever, ThomasPusch, Vispec, Xiquet, Yougarten, Zscout370, ∼riley, 11 anonymous edits ... 252
Image *Source:* https://en.wikipedia.org/w/index.php?title=File:Flag_of_Sudan.svg *License:* Public Domain *Contributors:* Vzb83 ... 252
Image *Source:* https://en.wikipedia.org/w/index.php?title=File:Flag_of_Tunisia.svg *License:* Public Domain *Contributors:* entraîneur: BEN KHALIFA WISSAM ... 252
Image *Source:* https://en.wikipedia.org/w/index.php?title=File:Flag_of_the_Sahrawi_Arab_Democratic_Republic.svg *License:* Public Domain *Contributors:* El Uali Mustapha Sayed ... 252
Image *Source:* https://en.wikipedia.org/w/index.php?title=File:Flag_of_Angola.svg *License:* Public Domain *Contributors:* User:SKopp ... 253
Image *Source:* https://en.wikipedia.org/w/index.php?title=File:Flag_of_Cameroon.svg *License:* Public Domain *Contributors:* User:SKopp ... 253
Image *Source:* https://en.wikipedia.org/w/index.php?title=File:Flag_of_the_Central_African_Republic.svg *License:* Public Domain *Contributors:* User:Nightstallion ... 253
Image *Source:* https://en.wikipedia.org/w/index.php?title=File:Flag_of_Chad.svg *License:* Public Domain *Contributors:* SKopp & others (see upload log) ... 253
Image *Source:* https://en.wikipedia.org/w/index.php?title=File:Flag_of_the_Democratic_Republic_of_the_Congo.svg *Contributors:* User:Nightstallion ... 253
Image *Source:* https://en.wikipedia.org/w/index.php?title=File:Flag_of_the_Republic_of_the_Congo.svg *License:* Public Domain *Contributors:* Andres gb.ldc, Anime Addict AA, Antemister, Benzoyl, Blackcat, Courcelles, Denelson83, Erlenmeyer, Estrilda, FischersFritz, Fry1989, HoheHoffnungen, Homo lupus, Klemen Kocjancic, LA2, Madden, Mattes, Moyogo, Neq00, Nightstallion, Persiana, Pitke, Ratatosk, Reisio, Romaine, SiBr4, ThomasPusch, Thuresson, 6 anonymous edits ... 253
Image *Source:* https://en.wikipedia.org/w/index.php?title=File:Flag_of_Equatorial_Guinea.svg *License:* Public Domain *Contributors:* Allforrous, Andres gb.ldc, Anime Addict AA, Antonsusi, Benzoyl, Cathy Richards, Cycn, Duschgeldrache2, Emc2, Fastily, Fred the Oyster, Fry1989, Homo lupus, Klemen Kocjancic, Maks Stirlitz, Mattes, Neq00, NeverDoING, Nightstallion, OAlexander∼commonswiki, Permjak, Pitke, SiBr4, SouthSudan, ThomasPusch, 4 anonymous edits ... 253
Image *Source:* https://en.wikipedia.org/w/index.php?title=File:Flag_of_Gabon.svg *License:* Public Domain *Contributors:* User:Gabbe, User:SKopp 253
Image *Source:* https://en.wikipedia.org/w/index.php?title=File:Flag_of_Sao_Tome_and_Principe.svg *License:* Public Domain *Contributors:* User:Gabbe ... 253
Image *Source:* https://en.wikipedia.org/w/index.php?title=File:Flag_of_Botswana.svg *License:* Public Domain *Contributors:* Andres gb.ldc, Antemister, Benzoyl, Blackcat, Cathy Richards, Charlesjsharp, Cycn, Denelson83, Fry1989, Gabbe, GoldenRainbow, HoheHoffnungen, Ilfga, Klemen Kocjancic, Koefbac, Madden, Mattes, Neq00, Reisio, Rodejong, SKopp, Sangjinhwa, Sarang, Smaug the Golden, Stasyan117, TFerenczy, ThomasPusch, Torstein, Xoristzatziki, Zscout370, 1 anonymous edits ... 253
Image *Source:* https://en.wikipedia.org/w/index.php?title=File:Flag_of_Lesotho.svg *License:* Public Domain *Contributors:* Benzoyl, Cathy Richards, CommonsDelinker, Denelson83, Erlenmeyer, FSII, Fry1989, Homo lupus, JuTa, Klemen Kocjancic, Liftarn, Mattes, Nightstallion, OgreBot 2, Patricia.fidi, Pumbaa80, Rodejong, Sangjinhwa, Sarang, Shervinafshar, SiBr4, Sphilbrick, ThomasPusch, Typokorrektör, VulpesVulpes42, Zscout370, 6 anonymous edits ... 253
Image *Source:* https://en.wikipedia.org/w/index.php?title=File:Flag_of_Namibia.svg *License:* Public Domain *Contributors:* User:Vzb83 ... 253
Image *Source:* https://en.wikipedia.org/w/index.php?title=File:Flag_of_South_Africa.svg *Contributors:* Adriaan, Anime Addict AA, AnonMoos, Aumars, BRUTE, Benzoyl, Cathy Richards, Charlesjsharp, Daemonic Kangaroo, Dnik, Duduziq, Dzordzm, Fry1989, Golden Bosnian Lily, Homo lupus, Illegitimate Barrister, Jappalang, Juliancolton, Kam Solusar, Klemen Kocjancic, Klymene, Lexxyy, MAXXX-309, Mahahahaneapneap, Manuelt15, Moviedefender, Mwtoews, NeverDoING, Nilli, Ninane, Pitke, Poznaniak, Przemub, Ricordisamoa, SKopp, Sarang, SiBr4, Stïnger, ThePCKid, ThomasPusch, Tvdm, Ultratomio, VulpesVulpes42, Vzb83∼commonswiki, Watchduck, Zscout370, 41 anonymous edits ... 253
Image *Source:* https://en.wikipedia.org/w/index.php?title=File:Flag_of_Swaziland.svg *License:* Public Domain *Contributors:* CemDemirkartal, Cycn, EugeneZelenko, Fry1989, Homo lupus, JMK, Klemen Kocjancic, Lojbanist, Mogelzahn, Nightstallion, OAlexander∼commonswiki, Ratatosk, Sangjinhwa, SiBr4, ThomasPusch, Wieralee, 1 anonymous edits ... 253
Image *Source:* https://en.wikipedia.org/w/index.php?title=File:Flag_of_Zimbabwe.svg *License:* Public Domain *Contributors:* User:Madden ... 253
Image *Source:* https://en.wikipedia.org/w/index.php?title=File:Flag_of_Benin.svg *License:* Public Domain *Contributors:* Drawn by User:SKopp, rewritten by User:Gabbe ... 254
Image *Source:* https://en.wikipedia.org/w/index.php?title=File:Flag_of_Burkina_Faso.svg *License:* Public Domain *Contributors:* User:Gabbe, User:SKopp ... 254
Image *Source:* https://en.wikipedia.org/w/index.php?title=File:Flag_of_Cape_Verde.svg *License:* Public Domain *Contributors:* Drawn by User:SKopp ... 254
Image *Source:* https://en.wikipedia.org/w/index.php?title=File:Flag_of_Côte_d'Ivoire.svg *License:* Public Domain *Contributors:* User:Jon Harald Søby ... 254
Image *Source:* https://en.wikipedia.org/w/index.php?title=File:Flag_of_The_Gambia.svg *License:* Public Domain *Contributors:* Andres gb.ldc, Atamari, Avala, Cathy Richards, Courcelles, Denniss, Erlenmeyer, FischersFritz, Fry1989, HoheHoffnungen, INeverCry, Klemen Kocjancic, Materialscientist, Mattes, Neq00, Nightstallion, OAlexander∼commonswiki, Porao, Rkt2312, Rodejong, Sangjinhwa, Sarang, SiBr4, ThomasPusch, Vzb83∼commonswiki, WikipediaMaster, Xoristzatziki, Zscout370, 4 anonymous edits ... 254
Image *Source:* https://en.wikipedia.org/w/index.php?title=File:Flag_of_Ghana.svg *License:* Public Domain *Contributors:* AFBorchert, Benchill, Cathy Richards, Charlesjsharp, Cycn, Fry1989, Gunnex, Henswick, HoheHoffnungen, Homo lupus, Indolences, Jarekt, Kangseijoon, Klemen Kocjancic, Magasjukur2, MassiveEartha, Neq00, OAlexander∼commonswiki, Roberto Fiadone, SKopp, Sangjinhwa, SiBr4, ThomasPusch, Threecharlie, Torstein, Tulsi Bhagat, Vyacheslav Nasretdinov, Zscout370, 11 anonymous edits ... 254
Image *Source:* https://en.wikipedia.org/w/index.php?title=File:Flag_of_Guinea.svg *License:* Public Domain *Contributors:* User:SKopp ... 254
Image *Source:* https://en.wikipedia.org/w/index.php?title=File:Flag_of_Guinea-Bissau.svg *License:* Public Domain *Contributors:* User:SKopp 254
Image *Source:* https://en.wikipedia.org/w/index.php?title=File:Flag_of_Liberia.svg *License:* Public Domain *Contributors:* Government of Liberia 254

Image *Source:* https://en.wikipedia.org/w/index.php?title=File:Flag_of_Mali.svg *License:* Public Domain *Contributors:* User:SKopp ... 254

Image *Source:* https://en.wikipedia.org/w/index.php?title=File:Flag_of_Mauritania.svg *Contributors:* Ahmedsalem22, BrendonTheWizard, Cathy Richards, Fry1989, Guanaco, Gumruch, Hedwig in Washington, Herr chagall, Jcb, Jdx, JoaoPedro10029, Jon Harald Søby, Kimjiho2015, Sangjinhwa, Taivo, Todofai, Zscout370, 3 anonymous edits ... 254

Image *Source:* https://en.wikipedia.org/w/index.php?title=File:Flag_of_Niger.svg *License:* Public Domain *Contributors:* Made by: Philippe Verdy User:verdy_p, see also fr:Utilisateur:verdy_p. ... 254

Image *Source:* https://en.wikipedia.org/w/index.php?title=File:Flag_of_Nigeria.svg *License:* Public Domain *Contributors:* User:Jhs ... 254

Image *Source:* https://en.wikipedia.org/w/index.php?title=File:Flag_of_Senegal.svg *License:* Public Domain *Contributors:* Original upload by Nightstallion ... 254

Image *Source:* https://en.wikipedia.org/w/index.php?title=File:Flag_of_Sierra_Leone.svg *License:* Public Domain *Contributors:* Zscout370 ... 254

Image *Source:* https://en.wikipedia.org/w/index.php?title=File:Flag_of_Togo.svg *License:* Public Domain *Contributors:* Aaker, Ahsoous, Alkari, Benzoyl, Camervan, Cycn, Denniss, EugeneZelenko, File Upload Bot (Magnus Manske), Fry1989, Homo lupus, Klemen Kocjancic, Mattes, Mxn, Neq00, Nightstallion, Reisio, SiBr4, ThomasPusch, Vzb83∼commonswiki ... 254

Image *Source:* https://en.wikipedia.org/w/index.php?title=File:Flag_of_Burundi.svg *License:* Public Domain *Contributors:* Alkari, Bast64∼commonswiki, Benzoyl, Cathy Richards, Cycn, Denelson83, Fry1989, GoldenRainbow, HoheHoffnungen, Illegitimate Barrister, Klemen Kocjancic, Ludger1961, Mattes, Neq00, Persiana, Pixeltoo, Pumbaa80, Ricordisamoa, Rodejong, SKopp, Sarang, SiBr4, Smaug the Golden, Smooth O, ThomasPusch, Yeenosaurus, 3 anonymous edits ... 254

Image *Source:* https://en.wikipedia.org/w/index.php?title=File:Flag_of_the_Comoros.svg *License:* Public Domain *Contributors:* User:SKopp 254

Image *Source:* https://en.wikipedia.org/w/index.php?title=File:Flag_of_Djibouti.svg *License:* Public Domain *Contributors:* Andres gb.ldc, EugeneZelenko, Fry1989, Homo lupus, Klemen Kocjancic, Martin H., Mattes, MyriamThyes, Neq00, Nielshoogvliet, Nightstallion, Nishkid64, Pymouss, Ratatosk, Sangjinhwa, Smaug the Golden, Str4nd, TFCforever, ThomasPusch, Tomasdd, Zaccarias, Zscout370, Ö, Şêr, Владимир турчанинов, 8 anonymous edits ... 254

Image *Source:* https://en.wikipedia.org/w/index.php?title=File:Flag_of_Eritrea.svg *License:* Public Domain *Contributors:* Alkari, Bukk, Cathy Richards, Counny, Crasstun, Fry1989, HJ Mitchell, HoheHoffnungen, Homo lupus, Klemen Kocjancic, Mattes, Michael seium, Moipaulochon, Neq00, Nightstallion, Ninane, Persiana, Ratatosk, Rodejong, SiBr4, TFerenczy, ThomasPusch, VulpesVulpes42, Vzb83∼commonswiki, WikipediaMaster, Zscout370, 8 anonymous edits ... 254

Image *Source:* https://en.wikipedia.org/w/index.php?title=File:Flag_of_Ethiopia.svg *Contributors:* Aaker, Anime Addict AA, Antemister, Benzoyl, BotMultichill, BotMultichillT, Cathy Richards, Cycn, Djampa, F l a n k e r, Fry1989, GoodMorningEthiopia, Happenstance, Homo lupus, Huhsunqu, INeverCry, Ixfd64, Klemen Kocjancic, Ludger1961, MartinThoma, Mattes, Mozzan, Neq00, OAlexander∼commonswiki, Pumbaa80, Rainforest tropicana, Reisio, Ricordisamoa, SKopp, SiBr4, Smooth O, Spiritia, ThomasPusch, Torstein, Wsiegmund, Xoristzatziki, Zscout370, 16 anonymous edits ... 254

Image *Source:* https://en.wikipedia.org/w/index.php?title=File:Flag_of_Kenya.svg *License:* Public Domain *Contributors:* User:Pumbaa80 ... 254

Image *Source:* https://en.wikipedia.org/w/index.php?title=File:Flag_of_Madagascar.svg *License:* Public Domain *Contributors:* User:SKopp ... 254

Image *Source:* https://en.wikipedia.org/w/index.php?title=File:Flag_of_Malawi.svg *License:* Public Domain *Contributors:* Achim1999, AnonMoos, Antonsusi, Awadewit, BartekChom, Cathy Richards, Erlenmeyer, Fred J, Fry1989, Gddea, GoldenRainbow, Homo lupus, IvanLanin, Klemen Kocjancic, Mattes, Phlegmatic, Rodejong, SKopp, Sangjinhwa, Sarang, Sebjarod, SiBr4, Sweeper tamonten, Theo10011, ThomasPusch, Zscout370, 6 anonymous edits 254

Image *Source:* https://en.wikipedia.org/w/index.php?title=File:Flag_of_Mauritius.svg *License:* Public Domain *Contributors:* User:Zscout370 254

Image *Source:* https://en.wikipedia.org/w/index.php?title=File:Flag_of_Mozambique.svg *License:* Public Domain *Contributors:* User:Nightstallion 254

Image *Source:* https://en.wikipedia.org/w/index.php?title=File:Flag_of_Rwanda.svg *License:* Public Domain *Contributors:* Achim1999, Albedo-ukr, Alkari, CemDemirkartal, Charlesjsharp, Erlenmeyer, EugeneZelenko, Fred J, Fry1989, Gmaxwell, GoldenRainbow, Homo lupus, Illegitimate Barrister, J Milburn, Klemen Kocjancic, Mattes, Perhelion, Persiana, Reisio, Rfc1394, Sangjinhwa, Sarang, SiBr4, Sixflashphoto, Smooth O, Steinsplitter, Sweeper tamonten, Theo10011, ThomasPusch, Vyacheslav Nasretdinov, Wester, Zscout370, Zzyzx11, 3 anonymous edits ... 254

Image *Source:* https://en.wikipedia.org/w/index.php?title=File:Flag_of_Somalia.svg *License:* Public Domain *Contributors:* see upload history 255

Image *Source:* https://en.wikipedia.org/w/index.php?title=File:Flag_of_the_Seychelles.svg *Contributors:* - ... 255

Image *Source:* https://en.wikipedia.org/w/index.php?title=File:Flag_of_South_Sudan.svg *License:* Public Domain *Contributors:* User:Achim1999 255

Image *Source:* https://en.wikipedia.org/w/index.php?title=File:Flag_of_Tanzania.svg *License:* Public Domain *Contributors:* User:Alkari, User:Madden, User:SKopp ... 255

Image *Source:* https://en.wikipedia.org/w/index.php?title=File:Flag_of_Uganda.svg *License:* Creative Commons Zero *Contributors:* tobias ... 255

Image *Source:* https://en.wikipedia.org/w/index.php?title=File:Flag_of_Zambia.svg *License:* Public Domain *Contributors:* User:Zscout370 ... 255

Image *Source:* https://en.wikipedia.org/w/index.php?title=File:African_Union_flag.svg *Contributors:* Bearcat, Danlaycock, Exorix Adfjk, Eyesnore, Fry1989, Glentamara, Illegitimate Barrister, Marchjuly, MifterBot I, Ronhjones, Sphilbrick, Wcam ... 255

Image *Source:* https://en.wikipedia.org/w/index.php?title=File:Emblem_of_the_African_Union.svg *Contributors:* Beao, Dharmadhyaksha, Ebonelm, Ed veg, Luciandrei, Skier Dude ... 255

Image *Source:* https://en.wikipedia.org/w/index.php?title=File:African_Union_(orthographic_projection).svg *License:* GNU Free Documentation License *Contributors:* Brightgalrs, Chipmunkdavis, Cwbm (commons), DanPMK, Danlaycock, Flappiefh, Forward Unto Dawn, Heraldry, Hossam Baligh, Keepscases, Kmusser, Koavf, Look2See1, Magog the Ogre, McBernik, NickK, Sarang, Seb az86556, Sisyphos23, TUBS, TownDown, 3 anonymous edits 255

Image *Source:* https://en.wikipedia.org/w/index.php?title=File:Pix.gif *License:* Public Domain *Contributors:* BotMultichill, Ectoplasmic, Fastilysock (usurped), Justass, Krdan, Mdd, Paradoctor, Penubag, Pepetps, Themightyquill, 1 anonymous edits ... 260

Image *Source:* https://en.wikipedia.org/w/index.php?title=File:Map_of_the_African_Union.svg *License:* Creative Commons Attribution-Share Alike *Contributors:* Mangwanani ... 262

Figure 147 *Source:* https://en.wikipedia.org/w/index.php?title=File:Regions_of_the_African_Union.png *License:* Creative Commons Attribution-Sharealike 3.0 *Contributors:* User:Alifazal ... 266

Figure 148 *Source:* https://en.wikipedia.org/w/index.php?title=File:Supranational_African_Bodies-en.svg *License:* GNU Lesser General Public License *Contributors:* Nuvola_Algerian_flag.svg: Antigoni Nuvola_Angolan_flag.svg: Antigoni Nuvola_Botswana_flag.svg: arz Nuvola_Burkina_Faso_f 267

Figure 149 *Source:* https://en.wikipedia.org/w/index.php?title=File:Jakaya_Kikwete_and_Muammar_al-Gaddafi,_12th_AU_Summit,_090202-N-0506A-678.jpg *License:* Public Domain *Contributors:* U.S. Navy photo by Mass Communication Specialist 2nd Class Jesse B. Awalt/Released ... 270

Image *Source:* https://en.wikipedia.org/w/index.php?title=File:Flag_of_Libya_(1977–2011).svg *License:* Public Domain *Contributors:* User:Zscout370 ... 269

Image *Source:* https://en.wikipedia.org/w/index.php?title=File:Flag_of_Malawi_(2010-2012).svg *License:* Public Domain *Contributors:* Fornax, Zscout370, Phlegmatic ... 269

Image *Source:* https://en.wikipedia.org/w/index.php?title=File:Flag_of_Mauritania_(1959–2017).svg *License:* Public Domain *Contributors:* Aaa men ändå, Alkari, Anime Addict AA, AnonMoos, Bast64∼commonswiki, Beko, CAPTAIN RAJU, Cactus26, Cycn, Docu, File Upload Bot (Magnus Manske), Flad, Fred J, Fry1989, Gabbe, GeneralAdmiralAladeen, Herbythyme, Homo lupus, Illegitimate Barrister, Itatch, Jarould, Jelloud Najem, Juiced lemon, Klemen Kocjancic, Mattes, Panam2014, ProloSozz, SKopp, Sangjinhwa, SiBr4, SpiderMum, Sportsguy17, Squidville1, TFCforever, Takeaway, Tcfc2349, ThomasPusch, 11 anonymous edits ... 269

Figure 150 *Source:* https://en.wikipedia.org/w/index.php?title=File:African_Union_conference_center_and_office_complex,_AUCC.jpg *License:* Creative Commons Attribution-Sharealike 3.0 *Contributors:* Atlasowa, Danmichaelo, Joppa Chong ... 270

Image *Source:* https://en.wikipedia.org/w/index.php?title=File:Flag_of_India.svg *License:* Public Domain *Contributors:* Anomie, Jo-Jo Eumerus, Mifter ... 271

Figure 151 *Source:* https://en.wikipedia.org/w/index.php?title=File:Emblem_of_the_African_Union.svg *Contributors:* Beao, Dharmadhyaksha, Ebonelm, Ed veg, Luciandrei, Skier Dude ... 280

Figure 152 *Source:* https://en.wikipedia.org/w/index.php?title=File:Eritrea_-_Flickr_-_Al_Jazeera_English.jpg *License:* Creative Commons Attribution-Sharealike 2.0 *Contributors:* Al Jazeera English ... 284

Image *Source:* https://en.wikipedia.org/w/index.php?title=File:Blue_pencil.svg *License:* Public Domain *Contributors:* User:VasilievVV and user:Jarekt ... 286

Figure 153 *Source:* https://en.wikipedia.org/w/index.php?title=File:Coudée-turin.jpg *License:* Creative Commons Attribution-Sharealike 3.0,2.5,2.0,1.0 *Contributors:* Bakha ... 290

Figure 154 *Source:* https://en.wikipedia.org/w/index.php?title=File:Mogadishan_currency.JPG *License:* Creative Commons Attribution-Sharealike 2.0 *Contributors:* Regio Governo Della Somalia ... 291

Figure 155 *Source:* https://en.wikipedia.org/w/index.php?title=File:Factory_of_National_Cement_Share_Company.jpg *License:* Creative Commons Attribution 2.0 *Contributors:* DFID - UK Department for International Development ... 292

Figure 156 *Source:* https://en.wikipedia.org/w/index.php?title=File:Uganda_-_ad_on_van_in_Kampala.jpg *License:* Creative Commons Attribution 2.0 *Contributors:* futureatlas.com ... 294

Figure 157 *Source:* https://en.wikipedia.org/w/index.php?title=File:Map_of_Trans-African_Highways.PNG *License:* Creative Commons Attribution-ShareAlike 3.0 Unported *Contributors:* Rex Parry ... 295

Figure 158 *Source:* https://en.wikipedia.org/w/index.php?title=File:Map_of_railways_in_Africa_1899.jpg *License:* Public Domain *Contributors:* LA2, Vysotsky 296
Figure 159 *Source:* https://en.wikipedia.org/w/index.php?title=File:TamaleGhana2.jpg *License:* Public domain *Contributors:* en:User:MichaelLeonhard 298
Figure 160 *Source:* https://en.wikipedia.org/w/index.php?title=File:Africa-GDP.svg *License:* Public Domain *Contributors:* Jklamo 306
Image *Source:* https://en.wikipedia.org/w/index.php?title=File:Flag_of_France.svg *License:* Public Domain *Contributors:* Anomie, Fastily, Jo-Jo Eumerus 308
Figure 161 *Source:* https://en.wikipedia.org/w/index.php?title=File:2DU_Kenya_86_(5367322642).jpg *License:* Creative Commons Attribution-Sharealike 2.0 *Contributors:* CIAT 309
Figure 162 *Source:* https://en.wikipedia.org/w/index.php?title=File:Greater_Cape_Town_12.02.2007_16-41-31.2007_16-41-33.JPG *License:* Creative Commons Attribution-Sharealike 3.0 *Contributors:* Simisa 310
Figure 163 *Source:* https://en.wikipedia.org/w/index.php?title=File:Lagos_Island.jpg *License:* Creative Commons world66 *Contributors:* Photograph by Benji Robertson 311
Figure 164 *Source:* https://en.wikipedia.org/w/index.php?title=File:Soucreye_Sidi_Bennour.jpg *License:* GNU Free Documentation License *Contributors:* L. Mahin 313
Figure 165 *Source:* https://en.wikipedia.org/w/index.php?title=File:South_Africa-Johannesburg-Skyline02.jpg *License:* Creative Commons Attribution-Share Alike *Contributors:* MGA73bot2, NJR ZA, OgreBot 2 314
Figure 166 *Source:* https://en.wikipedia.org/w/index.php?title=File:Bvmt_headquarters.JPG *License:* Creative Commons Attribution-Sharealike 3.0 *Contributors:* Ashoola 316
Image *Source:* https://en.wikipedia.org/w/index.php?title=File:HDImap_spectrum2006_Africa.png *License:* Public Domain *Contributors:* Dbachmann, Delusion23, Hoshie, Igna, Luan, Maphobbyist, Slomox, 1 anonymous edits 324
Figure 167 *Source:* https://en.wikipedia.org/w/index.php?title=File:Population_growth_rate_world_2013.svg *License:* Creative Commons Attribution-Sharealike 3.0 *Contributors:* User:Kwamikagami 324
Figure 168 *Source:* https://en.wikipedia.org/w/index.php?title=File:Expectancy_of_life.svg *Contributors:* De728631 325
Figure 169 *Source:* https://en.wikipedia.org/w/index.php?title=File:Infantmortalityrate.jpg *License:* Public Domain *Contributors:* User:Electionworld 328
Image *Source:* https://en.wikipedia.org/w/index.php?title=File:Increase2.svg *License:* Public Domain *Contributors:* Sarang 326
Image *Source:* https://en.wikipedia.org/w/index.php?title=File:Decrease2.svg *License:* Public Domain *Contributors:* Sarang 326
Figure 170 *Source:* https://en.wikipedia.org/w/index.php?title=File:Africa_HIV-AIDS_2002.svg *License:* Creative Commons Attribution 3.0 *Contributors:* Reuvenk 330
Figure 171 *Source:* https://en.wikipedia.org/w/index.php?title=File:Life_expectancy_in_select_Southern_African_countries_1960-2012.svg *Contributors:* User:Splette 330
Figure 172 *Source:* https://en.wikipedia.org/w/index.php?title=File:San_tribesman.jpg *License:* Creative Commons Attribution-Sharealike 2.0 *Contributors:* Ian Beatty from Amherst, MA, USA 331
Figure 173 *Source:* https://en.wikipedia.org/w/index.php?title=File:Kwarastatedrummers.jpg *License:* Creative Commons Attribution 2.0 *Contributors:* Melvin "Buddy" Baker from St. Petersburg, Florida, United States 332
Figure 174 *Source:* https://en.wikipedia.org/w/index.php?title=File:Mongo_family_in_Equateur_Province.jpg *License:* Creative Commons Attribution-Sharealike 3.0 *Contributors:* User:Francish7 332
Figure 175 *Source:* https://en.wikipedia.org/w/index.php?title=File:Bedscha.jpg *License:* GNU Free Documentation License *Contributors:* () 333
Figure 176 *Source:* https://en.wikipedia.org/w/index.php?title=File:Boerfamily1886.jpg *License:* Public Domain *Contributors:* Georgio 334
Figure 177 *Source:* https://en.wikipedia.org/w/index.php?title=File:Africa_ethnic_groups_1996.jpg *License:* Public Domain *Contributors:* United States. Central Intelligence Agency. 336
Figure 178 *Source:* https://en.wikipedia.org/w/index.php?title=File:Map_of_African_language_families.svg *Contributors:* User:Mark Dingemanse, User:SUM1, User:Sting 340
Figure 179 *Source:* https://en.wikipedia.org/w/index.php?title=File:Map_of_African_languages.svg *Contributors:* User:Alphathon, User:SUM1, User:Sting 341
Figure 180 *Source:* https://en.wikipedia.org/w/index.php?title=File:Official_languages_in_Africa.svg *License:* Public Domain *Contributors:* B25es, Cycn, Delusion23, Kanguole, MacedonianBoy, NordNordWest, Pitthée, Sarang, VulpesVulpes42, Wmq, 1 anonymous edits 347
Figure 181 *Source:* https://en.wikipedia.org/w/index.php?title=File:Ethcofcerm.jpg *License:* Creative Commons Attribution-Sharealike 2.0 *Contributors:* sameffron 358
Figure 182 *Source:* https://en.wikipedia.org/w/index.php?title=File:Egypt_bookofthedead.jpg *License:* Public Domain *Contributors:* User:Fredduf 358
Figure 183 *Source:* https://en.wikipedia.org/w/index.php?title=File:African_Sudan_Art_Basket-Tray.jpg *Contributors:* User:King muh 360
Figure 184 *Source:* https://en.wikipedia.org/w/index.php?title=File:African_Art,_Yombe_sculpture,_Louvre.jpg *License:* Creative Commons Attribution-Sharealike 3.0 *Contributors:* CherryX 360
Figure 185 *Source:* https://en.wikipedia.org/w/index.php?title=File:Masques_BaKongo.JPG *License:* Creative Commons Attribution-Sharealike 3.0 *Contributors:* User:Ndoto ya Afrika 361
Figure 186 *Source:* https://en.wikipedia.org/w/index.php?title=File:Central_mosque_in_Nouakchott.jpg *License:* Creative Commons Attribution-Sharealike 3.0 *Contributors:* Александра Пугачевская (Alexandra Pugachevsky) 362
Figure 187 *Source:* https://en.wikipedia.org/w/index.php?title=File:Kenyan_dancers.jpg *License:* Creative Commons Attribution 2.0 *Contributors:* Angela Sevin 363
Figure 188 *Source:* https://en.wikipedia.org/w/index.php?title=File:Kent_wove.jpg *License:* Creative Commons Attribution-Sharealike 3.0 *Contributors:* User:Bottracker 364
Figure 189 *Source:* https://en.wikipedia.org/w/index.php?title=File:KangaSiyu1.jpg *License:* Public Domain *Contributors:* Petr Berka (Petrberka) 365
Figure 190 *Source:* https://en.wikipedia.org/w/index.php?title=File:Traditional_Maasai_Dance.jpg *License:* Creative Commons Attribution 2.5 *Contributors:* Original uploader was en:User: at en.wikipedia 365
Figure 191 *Source:* https://en.wikipedia.org/w/index.php?title=File:Fufu.jpg *License:* Creative Commons Attribution-Sharealike 3.0 *Contributors:* Londonsista 366
Figure 192 *Source:* https://en.wikipedia.org/w/index.php?title=File:Couscous-1.jpg *License:* Creative Commons Attribution-ShareAlike 3.0 Unported *Contributors:* Apalsola, Bohème, BotMultichill, Jdx, Juiced lemon, Octave.H, Opponent, Rainer Zenz, Saber68, Smiller933, Takeaway, Waldir, 28 anonymous edits 367
Figure 193 *Source:* https://en.wikipedia.org/w/index.php?title=File:Potjiekos2.jpg *License:* Creative Commons Attribution-Sharealike 3.0 *Contributors:* Borisgorelik 368
Figure 194 *Source:* https://en.wikipedia.org/w/index.php?title=File:Kwarastatedrummers.jpg *License:* Creative Commons Attribution 2.0 *Contributors:* Melvin "Buddy" Baker from St. Petersburg, Florida, United States 370
Figure 195 *Source:* https://en.wikipedia.org/w/index.php?title=File:Mbira_dzavadzimu.jpg *License:* GNU Free Documentation License *Contributors:* BotAdventures, BotMultichillT, Foroa, HSMusic, Ji-Elle, Juiced lemon, Moyogo, Villanueva 374
Figure 196 *Source:* https://en.wikipedia.org/w/index.php?title=File:Aar_maanta.jpg *License:* Public Domain *Contributors:* Xaawotaako 375
Figure 197 *Source:* https//en.wikipedia.org *Contributors:* Anthere, Ji-Elle, Pdproject 377
Figure 198 *Source:* https://en.wikipedia.org/w/index.php?title=File:Abderrahmane_Abdelli.jpg *License:* Creative Commons Attribution-Sharealike 2.5 *Contributors:* Michel Vuijlsteke 378
Figure 199 *Source:* https://en.wikipedia.org/w/index.php?title=File:Drumming_(7250728078).jpg *License:* Public Domain *Contributors:* USAID Africa Bureau 379
Figure 200 *Source:* https://en.wikipedia.org/w/index.php?title=File:Traffic_1973.jpg *License:* Creative Commons Attribution-Sharealike 2.0 *Contributors:* Heinrich Klaffs 380
Figure 201 *Source:* https://en.wikipedia.org/w/index.php?title=File:Miriam_Makeba_2011.jpg *License:* Creative Commons Attribution 2.0 *Contributors:* Tom Beetz 382
Image *Source:* https://en.wikipedia.org/w/index.php?title=File:P_religion_world.svg *License:* GNU Free Documentation License *Contributors:* Achim55, Anime Addict AA, AnonMoos, Cathy Richards, Chris-martin, Gerrit Erasmus, Herbythyme, Jean-Frédéric, Jonund, Little Savage, MGA73bot2, Marcus Cyron, 3 anonymous edits 385
Figure 202 *Source:* https://en.wikipedia.org/w/index.php?title=File:Early_20th_century_Yoruba_divination_board.jpg *License:* Creative Commons Attribution-Sharealike 3.0 *Contributors:* Tamsier 386
Figure 203 *Source:* https://en.wikipedia.org/w/index.php?title=File:Voodo-altar.jpg *License:* Creative Commons Attribution-Sharealike 3.0 *Contributors:* Dominik Schwarz 387
Figure 204 *Source:* https://en.wikipedia.org/w/index.php?title=File:Kairo_Hanging_Church_BW_1.jpg *License:* Creative Commons Attribution-Sharealike 3.0,2.5,2.0,1.0 *Contributors:* Berthold Werner 388
Figure 205 *Source:* https://en.wikipedia.org/w/index.php?title=File:Kairouan_Mosque_Courtyard.jpg *License:* Creative Commons Attribution-Sharealike 2.0 *Contributors:* Colin Hepburn 390

Figure 206 *Source:* https://en.wikipedia.org/w/index.php?title=File:AbujaNationalMosque.jpg *License:* Creative Commons Attribution-Sharealike 2.0 *Contributors:* Shiraz Chakera 390
Figure 207 *Source:* https://en.wikipedia.org/w/index.php?title=File:Africa's_Bahai_temple_in_Kampala.jpg *License:* Creative Commons Attribution-Sharealike 2.0 *Contributors:* Shiraz Chakera 391
Figure 208 *Source:* https://en.wikipedia.org/w/index.php?title=File:GangaTalaoLake.jpg *License:* Free Art License *Contributors:* Girish10, Peter in s, Roland zh 392
Figure 209 *Source:* https://en.wikipedia.org/w/index.php?title=File:Nan_Hua_Temple.jpg *License:* Creative Commons Attribution 2.0 *Contributors:* Ivan Fourie from South Africa 393
Figure 210 *Source:* https://en.wikipedia.org/w/index.php?title=File:Africa_map_regions.svg *License:* Public Domain *Contributors:* User:Andreas 06 404
Figure 211 *Source:* https://en.wikipedia.org/w/index.php?title=File:Regions_of_the_African_Union.png *License:* Creative Commons Attribution-Sharealike 3.0 *Contributors:* User:Alifazal 404
Figure 212 *Source:* https://en.wikipedia.org/w/index.php?title=File:Carte_Afrique_CAF.png *License:* GNU Free Documentation License *Contributors:* (지금은) 소년시대, 44Charles, Chtrede, Faycal.09, File Upload Bot (Magnus Manske), Fry1989, Hpyounes, Kilom691, MGA73bot2, OgreBot 2, TFCforever, 1 anonymous edits 405
Image *Source:* https://en.wikipedia.org/w/index.php?title=File:Flag_of_the_Canary_Islands.svg *License:* Public Domain *Contributors:* User:Zirland 401
Image *Source:* https://en.wikipedia.org/w/index.php?title=File:Flag_Ceuta.svg *License:* Creative Commons Attribution-Share Alike *Contributors:* - jkb-, Benzoyl, BotMultichill, Charlik, Denniss, HansenBCN, Joanbanjo, Jürgen Krause, Manxruler, Mattes, QuimGil, Sarang, Ulaidh∽commonswiki, 2 anonymous edits 401
Image *Source:* https://en.wikipedia.org/w/index.php?title=File:Flag_of_Madeira.svg *Contributors:* Brian Boru, Clemix2345, Denelson83, Fry1989, Homo lupus, INeverCry, Jarekt, JotaCartas, Lusitana, Mattes, Nightstallion, Permjak, Pfctdayelise, Pmsyyz, Sarang, Tarkattack, VulpesVulpes42, Waldir, Zscout370, 1 anonymous edits 401
Image *Source:* https://en.wikipedia.org/w/index.php?title=File:Flag_of_Melilla.svg *License:* Creative Commons Attribution-Sharealike 3.0,2.5,2.0,1.0 *Contributors:* Arnapha, Denelson83, DenghiûComm, G.dallorto, Gabri, HansenBCN, Joanbanjo, Jose Garzón, Jymus, Lokal Profil, Mattes, Monarchy, Patricia Rios, Quibik, Sarang, SiBr4, Xinese-v, 1 anonymous edits 401
Image *Source:* https://en.wikipedia.org/w/index.php?title=File:Flag_of_Saint_Helena.svg *License:* Public Domain *Contributors:* Patricia Fidi 403
Figure 213 *Source:* https://en.wikipedia.org/w/index.php?title=File:Africa_satellite_orthographic.jpg *License:* Public Domain *Contributors:* Anomie, Jo-Jo Eumerus 406
Figure 214 *Source:* https://en.wikipedia.org/w/index.php?title=File:Africa_ethnic_groups_1996.jpg *License:* Public Domain *Contributors:* United States. Central Intelligence Agency. 408
Figure 215 *Source:* https://en.wikipedia.org/w/index.php?title=File:Official_languages_in_Africa.svg *License:* Public Domain *Contributors:* B25es, Cycn, Delusion23, Kanguole, MacedonianBoy, NordNordWest, Pitthée, Sarang, VulpesVulpes42, Wmq, 1 anonymous edits 409
Figure 216 *Source:* https://en.wikipedia.org/w/index.php?title=File:African_economic_division_investments.png *Contributors:* User:ChristianCT95 410

License

Creative Commons Attribution-Share Alike 3.0
//creativecommons.org/licenses/by-sa/3.0/

Index

'Abdul-Bahá, 391
.africa, 256

Aardvark, 248
Aasax language, 345
Abakaliki, 80
Aba, Nigeria, 80
Abatte Barihun, 435
Abbasid Caliphate, 53, 73, 103
Abdallah ibn Yasin, 54
Abd al-Mumin, 55
Abdelhafid of Morocco, 196
Abderrahmane Abdelli, 378
Abdims stork, 247
Abéché, 45
Aberdare range, 220
Abjection, 167, 176
Abolitionism, 111, 150, 202
Abolitionism in the United States, 156
Abomey, 201, 387
Aboriginal Australians, 11
Abraham ben Jacob, 120
Abstinence, be faithful, use a condom, 327
Abu-Bakr Ibn-Umar, 54
Abuja, 264, 273
Abuja National Mosque, 390
Abuja Treaty, 256, 260
Abu Yusuf Yaqub al-Mansur, 105
Abyssinia Crisis, 89
Abyssinian–Adal War, 52
Abyssinian hare, 248
Abyssinian people, 377
Acacia rat, 248
Acanthodactylus, 246
Accra, 265, 273
Acentrogobius, 245
Achaemenid Empire, 28
Achatinidae, 241
Acheulean, 22
Achille Mbembe, 175
Acraea (genus), 244
Act Prohibiting Importation of Slaves, 131, 155
Acts of the Apostles, 389
AD, 18

Adal Sultanate, 18, 52, 112, 121
Adam Hochschild, 190, 212
Adamorobe Sign Language, 346
Addis Ababa, 90, 255, 257, 258, 260, 263, 269–273
Aden, 116, 119
Adenorhinos, 245
Adhan, 377
Adulis, 38
Advanced tongue root, 350
Aedes aegypti, 243
Aegean Sea Plate, 231
Aethomys, 248
Afar people, 112
Afar Triangle, 231, 233
Afghanistan, 303
Afonso I of Kongo, 48, 129, 140, 141
Afrana, 245
Africa, 98, 104, 126, 127, 167, 174–176, 215, 216, 230, 239, 249, 257, 290, 294, 323, 335, 357, 373, 401
Africa Day, 257, 280
African Academy of Languages, 261
African-American, 158, 209
African art, 385
African barbet, 247
African buffalo, 249
African bush elephant, 249
African bush squirrel, 248
African Central Bank, 264, 304, 317
African Century, 313
African Charter on Democracy, Elections and Governance, 259
African Charter on Human and Peoples Rights, 258, 264
African Commission on Human and Peoples Rights, 259, 264
African Continental Free Trade Area, 274
African Court of Justice and Human Rights, 263
African Court on Human and Peoples Rights, 263, 264
African culture, 394
African Development Bank, 411

African Development Fund, 293
African diaspora, 158, 315, 357, 373, 387
African Economic Community, 259, 260, 274, 304, 305, 316, 317, 321
African elephant, 248
African Empires, 138
African Energy Commission, 264
African forest elephant, 249
African French, 339, 344, 351
African Great Lakes, 24, 26, 41, 103, 106, 221, 367, 374, 406, 407, 409
African ground squirrel, 248
African Invertebrates, 429, 430
African Investment Bank, 264, 304, 317
African Iron Age, 66
African Monetary Fund, 264, 304, 317
African Monetary Union, 274, 304, 316
African National Congress, 96
African penguin, 247
African people, 256
African philosophy, 385
African piculet, 247
African Plate, **230**
African popular music, 373
African Portuguese, 339
African rice, 23
African Rumba, 381
African savanna hare, 248
African slave trade, 182, 373
African Standby Force, 284
African striped squirrel, 248
African striped weasel, 249
African Surface, 219
African trypanosomiasis, 83, 190, 202, 228
African Union, **255**, 257, 261, 262, 304, 313, 316, 321, 328, 340
African Union Commission, 256, 257, 259, 263, 431
African Union Convention on Preventing and Combating Corruption, 259
African Union Passport, 271
African wild ass, 249
African Writers Series, 436
Africa Province, 169
Africa (Roman province), 32, 375
Afrikaaner, 336
Afrikaans, 335, 339, 343, 347, 349, 351, 354
Afrikaans language, 82
Afrikaner, 194, 334, 368
Afrikaners, 82, 343
Afro-Arab, 64
Afroasiatic, 336
Afro-Asiatic, 394
Afroasiatic language, 351
Afroasiatic languages, 331, 335, 339–342, 351, 352, 354, 355, 371, 408

Afro-Asiatic languages, 334, 407
Afroasiatic Urheimat, 335, 342
Afro (currency), 264
Afroedura, 245
Afro-Eurasia, 22, 125
Afrogecko, 245
Afromontane, 241
Afro-rock, 381
Afrosoricida, 248
Afrotheria, 248
Afrotropical, 239
Afrotropical ecozone, 244
Agadir, 196
Agadir Crisis, 186, 196
Agadja, 77
Agama (lizard), 246
Agaw people, 51
Agbome, 76
Agbor, 80
Agence France-Presse, 425
Agreement (linguistics), 342
Agricultural collectivisation, 303
Agricultural diversification, 313
Agricultural subsidies, 304
Agricultural subsidy, 298
Agriculture, 36, 103, 290
A-Group Culture, 29
Ahmad al-Mansur, 56, 73
Ahmad ibn Ibrahim al-Ghazi, 52
Ahmadiyya, 391
Ahoada, 80
AIDS, 327
Aïr Mountains, 25
Ajam, 121
Aja people, 76
Ajuran Empire, 18
Ajuran Sultanate, 50, 51, 198
Akan language, 342, 351, 355
Akan people, 44, 75, 76, 138, 331
Akan religion, 387
Aka people, 12
Akere Muna, 263

Åke Sundborg, 427

Akkadian language, 342
Aksum, 30
Aksumite Empire, 18
Aksum Obelisk, 39
Akwamu, 75, 76
Akyem, 75
Al-Adid, 57
Aladura, 388
Al-Andalus, 105
Alans, 333
Alaouite Dynasty, 56

452

Al-Bakri, 120
Albertine Rift, 218
Albreda, 205
Alcoholic beverage, 193, 369
Alestiidae, 245
Alexander the Great, 29, 168
Alexandre de Serpa Pinto, 84
Alexandria, 32, 168
Alex Haley, 158
Al-Farazi, 70
Alfonso V of Aragon, 51
Alfred-Amédée Dodds, 206
Alfred Milner, 194
Alfred Sharpe, 189
Alfred von Tirpitz, 186, 426
Algebra, 55
Algeciras Conference, 186, 196
Algeria, 31, 87, 95, 119, 236, 265, 275, 282, 291, 307, 319, 333, 347, 351, 369, 378, 393, 396, 401, 405, 407, 410
Algerian Sign Language, 346
Algerian War, 95, 173
Algiers, 55, 108, 118–120
Ali Gazi, 44
Allada, 76, 77
Allan Wilson, 14
Alldeutscher Verband, 183, 186
Allens swamp monkey, 249
Allied landings in North Africa, 93
Al-Maqrizi, 105, 121
Al-Masudi, 120
Almohad, 33
Almohad Caliphate, 105
Almohad dynasty, 55
Almoravid dynasty, 33, 54, 71
Almoravids, 55
Alodia, 58, 59
Alpha Condé, 269
Alpha Oumar Konaré, 348
Al-Rashid of Morocco, 56
Alsace-Lorraine, 200
Al Sahili, 72
Aluminium, 321

Álvaro I of Kongo, 48

Amadina, 247
Amadou Toumani Touré, 282
Amandava, 247
Amartya Sen, 304
Amasis II, 168
Ambassadors from the United States, 274
Ambassel scale, 371, 376
Ambergris, 51
AMBIO, 427
American Broadcasting Company, 158

American Civil War, 156
American Colonization Society, 89, 159, 209
American Journal of Human Genetics, 15
Americans, 108
Americas, 123, 125, 139, 376
Amhara people, 334
Amharic, 256, 335, 340, 342, 347, 351, 354
Amharic language, 349, 407
Amietia, 245
Am I Not a Man and a Brother?, 133
Amnirana, 245
Amphiliidae, 245
Amphisbaenia, 246
Amun, 30
Anabantidae, 245
Ana Lucia Araujo, 139
Anatolian Plate, 231
Anatomically modern human, 3
Anatomically modern humans, 3, 4, 18
Anchariidae, 245
Ancient Carthage, 18, 32
Ancient Egypt, 18, 26, 290, 375
Ancient Egyptian religion, 26
Ancient Egyptians, 33
Ancient Egyptian units of measurement, 290
Ancient Greece, 30, 32, 168, 333, 375
Ancient history, 20
Ancient Libya, 31
Ancient Near East, 20, 26, 375
Ancient Rome, 32, 114, 333, 375
Andalusian classical music, 370, 375
Andaman Islands, 10
Anders Rapp, 427
Anglo-Ashanti wars, 76
Anglo-Egyptian Sudan, 45, 88, 93, 209
Anglo-Zulu War, 82, 194
Angola, 24, 42, 47, 88, 94, 131, 137, 138, 206, 219, 265, 275, 292, 307, 318, 346, 351–353, 370, 393, 395, 402, 407, 411
Angola (Portugal), 180
Animal, 239
Anioma, 80
Anjouan, 286
Annibale Carracci, 130
Annobon, 88
Annobón, 207
Anopheles gambiae, 243
Anopheles mosquito, 228
Ant, 243
Antarctic Plate, 231
Antelope, 367
Anthoscopus, 247
Anti-Atlas, 219
Antioch, 35
Antiquity, 20
António I of Kongo, 48

António Silva Porto, 84
Antpecker, 247
Antsiranana, 67
Anuak language, 354
Anwar Sadat, 95
Anza trough, 231
Aoudaghost, 70, 119
Apaloderma, 247
Apartheid, 95
Apedemak, 30
Apes, 13
Aplocheilidae, 245
Apoidea, 243
Apple, 369
Apricot, 369
APRM, 259
Arab, 49, 53, 64, 169
Arab Africa, 336
Arab classical music, 370, 375
Arab culture, 59
Arabia, 6, 10, 51
Arabian Peninsula, 26, 49, 54, 103, 119
Arabian Plate, 230, 232
Arabian Sea, 405
Arabic, 59, 65, 256, 333, 336, 342, 347, 351, 354
Arabic language, 55, 169, 342, 346, 371, 407
Arabic music, 376
Arabic world, 377
Arabization, 55, 333, 407
Arab League, 282
Arab Maghreb Union, 261, 267, 305, 317, 319, 322, 410
Arab people, 102
Arabs, 39
Arab sign-language family, 346
Arab slave trade, 18, 65, **101**
Arab Spring, 410
Arab states, 95
Arab world, 101, 116, 375
Arachnid, 242
Archaeoastronomy, 24
Archaeogenetics, 14
Archaeological record, 6
Archaeology of Africa, 20
Archaeology of Igbo-Ukwu, 25
Archaic human, 11, 18
Archaic human admixture with modern humans, 3, 6, 11, 14
Archaic humans, 3
Archibald Dalzel, 149
Archispirostreptus gigas, 242
Ariidae, 245
Arma people, 74
Armor, 90
Arms race, 186

Arnold J. Pomerans, 213
Arnold J. Toynbee, 111
Aro Confederacy, 140
Art, 359
Arthroleptidae, 245
Arthur Morris Jones, 376
Article One of the United States Constitution, 155
Artillery, 83
Arvicanthis, 248
Asante Empire, 135
Asanteman, 140
Asante royal thrones, 76
Ascension Island, 225
Ashanti Empire, 18, 290
Ashanti Kingdom, 208
Ashanti people, 75, 364
Asia, 8, 106, 153, 215, 216, 239, 257
Asian cuisine, 369
Asian people, 8, 334
Asiento, 130
Askari, 185
Askia Daoud, 73
Askia Mohammad I, 73
Askia Mohammed, 389
Askiya, 73
Askiya Dynasty, 73
Aspidelaps, 245
Assab, 119
Assassination of Anwar Sadat, 95
Assembly of the African Union, 257, 258, 262, 265
Associated Press, 425
Association Internationale Africaine, 188
Association of Religion Data Archives, 391
Assyria, 25, 30
Astronomy, 22
Astylosternidae, 245
Aswan, 119
Atbarah River, 30, 222
Atelerix, 248
Atheris, 245
Athlone Power Station, 310
Atlantic, 406
Atlantic hurricane season, 236
Atlantic languages, 336
Atlantic Ocean, 80, 127, 195, 219, 221, 230, 232
Atlantic slave trade, 18, **123**
Atlas languages, 354
Atlas Mountains, 55, 217, 220, 238, 405
Atractaspididae, 245
Aubria, 245
AU Conference Center and Office Complex, 269
Auguste François Biard, 132

Augustine of Hippo, 37
Augustus, 169
Aus87, 422
Australasia, 11
Australia, 183
Australopithecus, 21
Austria-Hungary, 185, 196, 204
Austroglanididae, 245
Austronesian language, 354
Austronesian languages, 67, 335, 339–341, 343, 352, 408, 409
Austronesian people, 335
Autonomous Regions of Portugal, 339
Autosome, 11
Avocado, 369
Awgu, 80
Awka, 80
Axumite Empire, 33
Aye-aye, 249
Ayyubid Dynasty, 57
Azania, 65
Aziziya, 236, 428
Azores, 231
Azores–Gibraltar Transform Fault, 232
Aztec, 131

Bab al Mandab, 4
Bab-el-Mandeb straits, 7
Baboon, 249
Babylonians, 33
Badi II, 59
Badi IV, 59
Bagamoyo, 119
Baghdad, 53
Baháí Faith, 391
Baháulláh, 391
Bakt, 58
Balance of power in international relations, 184
Balance of trade, 181
Balearica, 246
Baliochila, 244
Ballana, 58
Bamako, 326
Bamako Initiative, 326
Bambara Empire, 74, 141
Bambouk, 70, 72
Banana, 67, 367, 369
Banda languages, 354
Bangime language, 344
Banjo, 377
Banjul, 259, 273
Bank of Central African States, 304, 317
Banku, 369
Bantoid, 336
Bantu expansion, 18, 41, 62, 64, 66, 336, 346

Bantu languages, 41, 59, 62, 64, 67, 331, 335, 336, 339, 340, 342, 354, 371, 381, 408
Bantu migration, 167
Bantu people, 135
Bantu peoples, 24, 62, 65, 102, 106, 331, 336, 369
Banu Hilal, 55
Banu Sulaym, 55
Baqt, 106
Barack Obama, 162, 260
Barawa, 49, 51
Barbados, 147
Barbary Coast, 407
Barbary pirate, 143
Barbary pirates, 104
Barbary slave trade, 108
Barbary states, 107
Barito languages, 343
Barley, 23
Baroclinity, 236
Barotropic fluid, 236
Barter, 114
Bas-Congo, 361
Basil Davidson, 97, 98
Basimba people, 47
Basmati, 368
Basra, 103, 104
Basutoland, 82, 89, 209
Bat-eared fox, 249
Bateleur, 247
Battle of Adwa, 187, 209
Battle of Ain Jalut, 57
Battle of Dakar, 92, 93
Battle of Gabon, 92, 93
Battle of Isandlwana, 82
Battle of Kirina, 71
Battle of Königgrätz, 185
Battle of Mbwila, 48
Battle of Tondibi, 73
Battle of Ulundi, 82
Battle of Waterberg, 81, 199
Bayot language, 345
Bazaar, 111
BBC, 383, 430
BBC News, 425
Beachcombing, 7
Bebearia, 244
Bechuanaland, 88, 209
Bedouin, 54, 59
Bee-eater, 247
Beer, 369
Beetles, 243
Behanzin, 201
Beijing, 274
Beira, Mozambique, 119
Beja people, 333

Belgian colonial empire, 170
Belgian Congo, 86, 190, 204
Belgian Empire, 339
Belisarius, 37
Belize, 146
Bemba people, 47
Benachin, 369
Benguela, 48, 142
Benin, 41, 74, 87, 88, 137, 138, 140, 160, 205, 206, 265, 269, 275, 307, 318, 351, 353, 387, 397, 402, 411
Benin city, 80
Benin Empire, 18, 79, 141
Benito Mussolini, 187, 209
Benjamin Disraeli, 192
Benue–Congo, 355
Benue River, 222
Berbera, 49
Berber language, 346
Berber languages, 55, 333, 335, 336, 340, 342, 347–349, 351, 354
Berber music, 370, 375
Berber people, 31, 33, 53, 56
Berbers, 120, 333
Berghahn Books, 122
Berlin, 193
Berlin Conference, 167, 171, 180, 185, 197
Berlin Conference (1884), 85, 348
Bernard Lewis, 122
Bete language (Nigeria), 345
Bey, 57
Bia Expedition, 189
Bicyclus, 244
Bight of Benin, 80, 137, 160
Bight of Biafra, 137
Bight of Bonny, 80
Bigo, 67
Bilala people, 42, 44
Bilal ibn Rabah, 377
Bilateral trade, 101
Bilma, 44, 119
Bingu wa Mutharika, 269
Bini people, 41
Biodiversity hotspot, 243
Bioko, 88, 207
Biped, 21
Bird, 246
Birmingham, 145
Biskra, 35
Bissagos Islands, 129
Bitis, 245
Black-eyed pea, 23
Black heron, 247
Black rhinoceros, 249
Black Sea, 38, 108
Black Volta, 76

Blindness, 329
Blood River, 82
Bluebill, 247
Blue crane, 246
Blue grass music, 380
Blue Nile, 30, 84, 222
Blue quail, 247
Blues, 380, 381
Bob Riley, 161
Boer, 63, 82, 85, 193
Boers, 194
Bogle-LOuverture, 178
Bogle-LOuverture Publications, 432
Bolaji Idowu, 436
Bomba (Puerto Rico), 373
Bonny, Nigeria, 142
Bonobo, 249
Bonoman, 75
Book of Roads and Kingdoms (al-Bakrī), 120
Book of the Dead, 358
Borneo, 225
Borno State, 55
Bornu Empire, 24, 42, 43, 45, 55, 74
Botswana, 61, 88, 194, 209, 237, 242, 265, 275, 282, 291, 307, 318, 331, 335, 339, 343, 344, 348, 353, 393, 396, 403, 411
Bougarabou, 378
Boulengerina, 245
Bourse de Tunis, 316
Bovid, 249
Brackish water, 218
Brass, 359
Brass, Nigeria, 80
Brazil, 125, 131, 138, 144, 157, 158
Brazilian Vodum, 387
Brazzaville, 188
Breviceps, 245
Bribery, 299
Bristol, 144
British Cape Colony, 88
British diaspora in Africa, 334
British East Africa, 85, 88, 173, 209
British Egypt, 209
British Empire, 57, 125, 155, 170
British Empire Exhibition, 202
British Gold Coast, 88
British Guiana, 147
British India, 183
British Malaya, 183
British Mauritius, 209
British North America, 146
British people, 197
British Raj, 203
British rule, 209
British Somaliland, 88, 93, 209
British South Africa Company, 189

British Togoland, 209
British West Africa, 85, 209
Bronkhorstspruit, 393
Bronx Zoo, 199, 202
Bronze, 25, 42
Brooklyn Museum, 36
Brubru, 247
Brussels Anti-Slavery Conference 1889-90, 202
Bryozoa, 241
Bufo, 245
Bufonidae, 245
Buganda, 67
Buganda kingdom, 68
Bung language, 345
Bunyoro, 68
Bunyoro kingdom, 67
Bunyoro rabbit, 248
Bureaucracy, 26
Bureau of Ghana Languages, 261
Burkina Faso, 87, 96, 205, 237, 265, 275, 292, 307, 318, 352, 397, 402, 411
Burundi, 47, 66, 86, 88, 95, 204, 205, 259, 265, 275, 293, 307, 318, 348, 351, 395, 402, 411
Burundian monarchy, 68
Bushi language, 343
Bushpig, 249
Bushshrike, 246
Bus rapid transit, 314
Bustard, 247
Butterflies, 243
Buzzard, 247
Byzantine Empire, 37, 169

Caabi El-Yachroutu Mohamed, 286
Cabinda Province, 88, 206
Cabo Verde, 407
Cairo, 43, 57, 119, 121, 194, 388
Calabar, 80
California, 236
Caliphate, 53, 375
Callulina, 245
Calypso music, 373
Cambria Press, 165
Cambridge Reference Sequence, 14
Cambridge University, 97
Cambridge University Press, 178, 426
Cameroon, 18, 23, 25, 41, 42, 74, 88, 135, 137, 138, 175, 205, 209, 220, 262, 265, 275, 307, 318, 345, 370, 391, 395, 402, 407, 411
Cameroon line, 220
Cameroons, 88, 185, 209
Camfranglais, 345
Camp David Accords, 95

Campeche, Campeche, 131
Campethera, 247
Canary Islands, 116, 128, 173, 225, 259, 339, 401
Cancer, 329
Cane rat, 248
Cannon, 57
Cape Agulhas, 215, 228
Cape Colony, 180, 193, 209
Cape Coloured, 335
Cape Coloureds, 82
Cape crow, 247
Cape fur seal, 249
Cape Guardafui, 33
Cape hare, 248
Cape Juby, 207
Capensibufo, 245
Cape of Good Hope, 194
Cape Province, 62, 82
Cape to Cairo Red Line, 86
Cape Town, 194, 310
Cape Verde, 170, 225, 228, 265, 275, 307, 318, 345, 352, 397, 402, 411
Cape Verdean Creole, 345
Cape Verde Islands, 88
Capital flight, 303
Capitalism, 183
Capsian culture, 341
Cap Vert, 228
Cap-Vert, 216
Car, 314
Caracal, 249
Caravan (travellers), 111
Cardinal direction, 403
Cardiovascular disease, 329
Caribbean, 131
Caribbean music, 373
Carleton S. Coon, 13
Carnivora, 249
Carthage, 26, 31, 36, 168, 333, 375
Carybdea alata, 241
Casablanca Group, 261
Case fatality rate, 329
Casement Report, 190
Cash crops, 210
Cassava, 48, 75, 369
Cast-iron, 368
Castor bean, 23
Cataract, 58
Cataracts of the Nile, 26, 58
Category:New Imperialism, 179
Category:Politics, 251
Catholic Church, 32, 52
Cattle, 364, 367
Causinae, 245
Cayor, 18

Cecil Rhodes, 183, 189, 194, 208
Cedarberg, 237
Cenozoic, 221
Censer, 368
Centaurus beetle, 243
Central Africa, 18, 21, 26, 47, 75, 112, 132, 180, 333, 335, 339, 346, 366, 376, 378, 401–403, 407, 411
Central African Republic, 25, 42, 45, 87, 205, 228, 265, 275, 307, 318, 344, 345, 395, 402, 411
Central African Shear Zone, 231
Central Asia, 110
Central bank, 274, 304, 316, 321
Central Bank of West African States, 304, 317
Central Sudanic, 336
Centre-left politics, 251
Centre-right politics, 251
Centrism, 251
Cerastes (genus), 245
Ceratogymna, 247
Cereal grain, 366
Ceremonial, 359
Ceres, Western Cape, 237
Ceuta, 55, 173, 339, 401
CFA franc, 315
Cha69, 422
Chad, 24, 42, 45, 185, 194, 220, 265, 269, 275, 292, 307, 318, 335, 339, 347, 351, 395, 402, 407, 411
Chad Basin, 42, 406
Chadic languages, 331, 336, 342, 355
Chairperson of the African Union, 256, 262
Chairperson of the African Union Commission, 256, 348
Chamba people, 138
Chambezi River, 222
Chameleon, 245
Characiformes, 245
Charaxes, 244
Chariot, 28
Chari River, 42, 223
Charles Darwin, 13
Charles de Gaulle, 93, 173, 205
Charleston, South Carolina, 124
Charopidae, 242
Charter of the United Nations, 258
Chattel slavery, 101
Chauvinism, 203
Cheetah, 240, 249
Cheikh Anta Diop, 98, 436
Cherrapunji, 227
Chersina, 246
Chewa language, 351
Chibuene, 59
Chicago Tribune, 425

Chichewa language, 348, 354
Chicken (food), 367
Childbirth, 376
Chimpanzee, 13, 21, 249
China, 8, 103, 183, 204, 211, 295
China National Petroleum Corporation, 211
China State Construction Engineering Corporation, 269
Chinese economic reform, 291
Chinese Folk Religion, 392
Chinese language, 6, 51
Chinese people, 107
Chirindia, 246
Chiromantis, 245
Chlamydephoridae, 241
Chobe District, 61
Chokwe people, 48
Cholera, 191
Chris Landsea, 428
Christ, 37
Christendom, 126, 388
Christian, 37, 108
Christian Bible, 389
Christianity, 32, 67, 85, 385, 387
Christianity in Africa, 385
Christianization, 37, 66
Christopher Ehret, 97, 435
Chronological items, 41, 284
Churamiti, 245
CIA Factbook, 433
Cichlid, 244
Circaetus, 247
Circle of Life, 381
Cisticola, 247
Citadel, 50
CITEREFAppenzeller2012, 413
CITEREFAppiahGates2010, 415
CITEREFBeyin2011, 413
CITEREFChristopher2006, 422
CITEREFEndicott et al.2003, 11
CITEREFFalola2008, 416
CITEREFFinlayson2009, 413
CITEREFGroucutt et al.2015, 8, 414
CITEREFHochschild2006, 426
CITEREFLiu, Harding et al.2000, 11
CITEREFLiu, Martinón-Torres et al.2015, 6
CITEREFLiu, Prugnolle et al.2006, 413
CITEREFMacaulay et al.2005, 5, 8
CITEREFPosth et al.2016, 5, 8
CITEREFShaban1976, 420
CITEREFShackleton et al.2006, 11
CITEREFUdo1970, 416
CITEREFWells2003, 5, 6
CITEREFYoung McChesney2015, 413
Citharinidae, 245
Citrus swallowtail, 243

City-state, 80
Civet, 249
Civil war, 96
Clariidae, 245
Claroteidae, 245
Class conflict, 200
Classical African civilization, 18, 26
Classical antiquity, 20, 26, 33, 167
Claudius, 36
Click consonant, 62, 344, 349
Click language, 337
Climate of Africa, 228, **233**
Climate zone, 234
Cloth, 364
Clothing, 359
Clotilde (slave ship), 156
Coalition, 252
Coalition government, 252
Coast, 108
Cocada amarela, 369
Cocoa bean, 183
Co-evolution, 241
Coffee ceremony, 358
Coffee house, 145
Cold War, 294
Collar (clothing), 364
Colobinae, 249
Colombia, 145
Colomys, 248
Colonial Chad, 87, 205
Colonial empire, 335
Colonial exhibition, 200, 201
Colonialism, 18, 167, 180, 183, 343
Colonialism in Africa, 359
Colonial Nigeria, 88, 209
Colonisation of Africa, **167**
Colonization, 167
Colony, 85, 202
Colony of Natal, 88, 209
Colony of Niger, 87, 205
Colopus, 245
Colotis, 244
Coloured, 334
Colubrid, 245
Commando, 82
Committee of Permanent Representatives, 263
Common Agricultural Policy, 298
Common chimpanzee, 249
Common Market for Eastern and Southern Africa, 260, 267, 305, 306, 317, 318, 322
Common Monetary Area, 304, 317
Commons:Atlas of Africa, 230
Commons:Atlas of the African Union, 262
Commons:Category:Colonial Africa, 179
Commons:Category:Economy of Africa, 320

Commons:Category:Maps of Africa, 229
Commons:Category:Slavery, 165
Commonwealth of Nations, 393
Community of Sahel-Saharan States, 260, 267, 318
Comores, 318
Comorian language, 348
Comorian music, 376
Comoros, 87, 205, 265, 275, 286, 307, 347, 348, 351, 395, 402, 411
Concentration camp, 193
Concubinage, 106, 111
Concubine, 118
Condominium (international law), 205
Confederation, 82, 259
Confederation of African Football, 405
Confidence and supply, 252
Confiscation, 303
Conga (music), 373
Congo Basin, 113, 188, 231, 382, 403, 406
Congo Craton, 231
Congo Free State, 86, 172, 183, 184, 188, 191, 204
Congolian forests, 243
Congo peafowl, 247
Congo Reform Association, 190
Congo River, 48, 190, 195, 219, 221
Conquest of the Canary Islands, 128
Conraua, 245
Conscription, 176
Conservatism, 251
Constantine the Great, 37
Constantinople, 37
Constitutive Act of the African Union, 260
Contemporary history, 21
Continent, 215, 230
Continental crust, 231
Continental union, 256, 257
Contraceptives, 325
Convergent evolution, 11
Cophylinae, 245
Copper, 25, 42, 183, 411
Coptic language, 58
Coptic Orthodox Church of Alexandria, 32, 58, 388
Coraciiformes, 247
Córdoba, Andalusia, 105
Cordylidae, 246
Corruption in Afghanistan, 300
Corruption in Albania, 299
Corruption in Angola, 301
Corruption in Argentina, 302
Corruption in Armenia, 299
Corruption in Australia, 303
Corruption in Austria, 299
Corruption in Azerbaijan, 299

459

Corruption in Bahrain, 300
Corruption in Bangladesh, 300
Corruption in Belgium, 299
Corruption in Bolivia, 302
Corruption in Bosnia and Herzegovina, 299
Corruption in Botswana, 301
Corruption in Brazil, 302
Corruption in Bulgaria, 299
Corruption in Cambodia, 300
Corruption in Cameroon, 301
Corruption in Canada, 302
Corruption in Chile, 302
Corruption in China, 300
Corruption in Colombia, 302
Corruption in Croatia, 299
Corruption in Cuba, 302
Corruption in Cyprus, 299
Corruption in Denmark, 299
Corruption in Ecuador, 302
Corruption in Egypt, 301
Corruption in Equatorial Guinea, 301
Corruption in Eritrea, 301
Corruption in Ethiopia, 301
Corruption in Finland, 299
Corruption in France, 299
Corruption in Georgia, 300
Corruption in Germany, 300
Corruption in Ghana, 301
Corruption in Guinea-Bissau, 302
Corruption in Haiti, 302
Corruption in Iceland, 300
Corruption in India, 300
Corruption in Indonesia, 301
Corruption in Iran, 301
Corruption in Iraq, 301
Corruption in Ireland, 300
Corruption in Israel, 301
Corruption in Italy, 300
Corruption in Jordan, 301
Corruption in Kenya, 302
Corruption in Kosovo, 300
Corruption in Kuwait, 301
Corruption in Kyrgyzstan, 301
Corruption in Latvia, 300
Corruption in Liberia, 302
Corruption in Lithuania, 300
Corruption in Luxembourg, 300
Corruption in Macedonia, 300
Corruption in Malaysia, 301
Corruption in Mauritius, 302
Corruption in Mexico, 302
Corruption in Moldova, 300
Corruption in Montenegro, 300
Corruption in Morocco, 302
Corruption in Myanmar, 301
Corruption in New Zealand, 303

Corruption in Nicaragua, 302
Corruption in Nigeria, 302
Corruption in North Korea, 301
Corruption in Pakistan, 301
Corruption in Papua New Guinea, 303
Corruption in Paraguay, 302
Corruption in Peru, 303
Corruption in Poland, 300
Corruption in Portugal, 300
Corruption in Romania, 300
Corruption in Russia, 303
Corruption in Senegal, 302
Corruption in Serbia, 300
Corruption in Singapore, 301
Corruption in Slovakia, 300
Corruption in Slovenia, 300
Corruption in Somalia, 302
Corruption in South Africa, 302
Corruption in South Korea, 301
Corruption in South Sudan, 302
Corruption in Spain, 300
Corruption in Sri Lanka, 301
Corruption in Sudan, 302
Corruption in Sweden, 300
Corruption in Switzerland, 300
Corruption in Tajikistan, 301
Corruption in Tanzania, 302
Corruption in Thailand, 301
Corruption in the Czech Republic, 299
Corruption in the Democratic Republic of the Congo, 301
Corruption in the Netherlands, 300
Corruption in the Philippines, 301
Corruption in the United States, 302
Corruption in Tunisia, 302
Corruption in Turkey, 303
Corruption in Turkmenistan, 301
Corruption in Uganda, 302
Corruption in Ukraine, 300
Corruption in Uzbekistan, 301
Corruption in Venezuela, 303
Corruption in Vietnam, 301
Corruption in Yemen, 301
Corruption in Zambia, 302
Corruption in Zimbabwe, 302
Corruption Perceptions Index, 275, 278
Costa Rica, 145
Côte dIvoire, 370, 393
Cotton, 23, 131
Council of Carthage (256), 37
Country code top-level domain, 256
Coup détat, 96, 282
Court of Justice of the African Union, 263
Couscous, 367, 369
Cowrie, 149
Cowry, 116, 117, 241, 359

Craft, 359
Crane (bird), 246
Craton, 231
Crayfish, 369
Creole language, 343, 345, 351
Creole peoples, 154
Crested mangabey, 249
Cretaceous, 239
Crime against humanity, 160
Crimson-wing, 247
Crisis of the Third Century, 36
Crocidurinae, 248
Crocodile, 246, 367
Croilia mossambica, 245
Cronyism, 299
Cross-border language, 348
Cross rhythm, 379
Cross River State, 80
Crusades, 57
Cuba, 144, 145
Cuban rumba, 373
Cuban Vodú, 387
Cubozoa, 241
Cudjoe Lewis, 156
Culture of Africa, **357**, 385
Cumbia, 373
Cunene River, 81
Curd, 366
Currency, 367
Currency union, 315
Cushitic, 334
Cushitic languages, 23, 51, 336, 342, 354
Customs union, 274, 304, 316, 321
Cyclanorbis, 246
Cycloderma, 246
Cyclophoridae, 242
Cypriniformes, 245
Cyprinodontiformes, 245
Cyrenaica, 168, 186
Cyrene, Libya, 168

Dabqaad, 368
Dahlak Archipelago, 112
Dahomey, 76, 79, 137, 140, 141, 150, 160
Dahomey Amazons, 201
Daily Mail, 425
Dakar, 194
Dallol, Ethiopia, 236
Dalophia, 246
Damaliscus, 249
Damascus, 53
Dangote Cement, 314
Danish West Indies, 147
Darfur, 44, 237, 268, 284
Darfur conflict, 259, 284
Darwinism, 202

Das Kapital, 152
Dassie rat, 248
Dasymys, 248
Dasypeltis, 245
David Kenneth Fieldhouse, 297
David Livingstone, 84, 108, 113, 121, 150, 182, 188
David Roberts (painter), 114
David Stannard, 140
Dawit II of Ethiopia, 52
Day gecko, 245
Dead Aid, 304
Death Valley, 236
Debal, 119
De Beers Mining Company, 183
Debt bondage, 110
Decimal, 55
Decolonisation, 167, 173
Decolonization, 18, 180, 334
Decolonization of Africa, 94, 294
Defaka language, 346
Deity, 72
Delcommune Expedition, 189
Deloneura, 244
Democracy Index, 275, 278
Democracy Now, 320
Democratic republic, 209
Democratic Republic of Congo, 137, 138, 284, 291, 318, 370
Democratic Republic of the Congo, 66, 86, 190, 204, 228, 238, 265, 275, 293, 307, 312, 325, 329, 332, 342, 351, 352, 391, 395, 402, 411
Democratization, 260
Democricetodontinae, 239
Demographics of Africa, **323**
Demographics of Nigeria, 323
Demonym, 256
Dendi Kingdom, 74
Dendroaspis, 245
Dendrolycus, 245
Dendromurinae, 239
Dendropicos, 247
Denisova hominin, 11
Denis Sassou Nguesso, 282
Denis Sassou-Nguesso, 268
Denkyira, 75
Denmark, 155
Deomyinae, 248
Dependency theory, 298
Dephomys, 245
Dervish movement (Somali), 197, 198
Descent of Man, 13
Desert climate, 233
Desert hedgehog, 248
Desertification, 18, 26, 281

461

Desert locust, 242
Desmond Tutu HIV Foundation, 327
Despotism, 294
Deutscher Kolonialverein, 186
Developing countries, 294
Development aid, 295
D'mt, 38
Dhar Tichitt, 40
Dhow, 114, 115
Diabetes mellitus, 329
Dialect, 335, 339
Dialect cluster, 336, 340
Dialect levelling, 348
Dibatag, 249
Dichistiidae, 245
Dik-dik, 249
Dingane kaSenzangakhona, 82
Dingiswayo, 81
Dinka language, 342, 354
Diocletian, 37
Diorama, 201
Dioula language, 346
Diphthong, 350
Diptera, 243
Dire Dawa, 292
Dispholidus, 245
Disputed statement, 6, 106, 108
Distichodontidae, 245
Divergent boundary, 230
Divination, 386
Dixieland, 380
Djembe, 373, 378
Djémila, 36
Djenné, 72
Djenné-Djenno, 40
Djibouti, 26, 87, 89, 94, 119, 194, 205, 228, 265, 275, 307, 318, 347, 351, 352, 396, 402, 405, 407, 411
DMOZ, 287, 319, 383
Dmt, 18
Dogon languages, 343
Dolphin, 248
Domestication, 23
Dominant-party system, 252
Dominican Republic, 145
Dominican Vudú, 387
Dompo language, 346
Donatism, 32, 37
Dongola, 26, 58
Donkey, 23
Double bell, 377
Doubling time, 323
Doudou Diène, 122
Doukkala, 313
Dracunculus medinensis, 241
Drakensberg, 62, 220, 222, 237

Drum, 370
Drum (communication), 379
Drum (musical instrument), 377
Drums, 373
Dryopithecus, 13
Dual Alliance, 1879, 184, 185
Duarte Barbosa, 51
Duiker, 249
Dunama Dabbalemi, 43
Durban, 42, 159, 260
Durban, South Africa, 273
Dutch East India Company, 63
Dutch Empire, 125
Dutch language, 343
Dutch West Indies, 147
Dwarf crocodile, 246
Dyscophus, 245
Dysentery, 143

Early historical era, 20
Early hominin expansions out of Africa, 4
Early human migrations, 3
Early modern period, 21
Early Muslim conquests, 37
Earth, 215
East Africa, 6, 18, 21, 64, 75, 103, 167, 180, 194, 325, 401–403, 411
East African Campaign (World War I), 90
East African Campaign (World War II), 93
East African Community, 260, 267, 305, 317, 318, 322, 411
East African plateau, 217
East African Rift, 218, 220, 230, 231, 406
East Asia, 6, 298
Eastern Africa, 325, 371
Eastern Cape, 59
Eastern Lunda, 48
Eastern Rift mountains, 406
Eastern Sudanic, 336
Ebony, 29
Echinoderms, 241
Echis, 245
Ecology: From Individuals to Ecosystems, 430
Economic and Monetary Community of Central Africa, 305, 317, 322
Economic and monetary union, 274, 304, 316, 321
Economic and Social Committee, 263
Economic Community of Central African States, 260, 267, 305, 317, 318, 321
Economic Community of West African States, 260, 267, 305, 317, 318, 321
Economic development, 303
Economic growth, 294
Economic history, 143
Economic history of Britain, 147

Economic history of the United Kingdom, 151
Economic potential, 290
Economic rent, 303
Economic, Social and Cultural Council, 263
Economic, Social, and Cultural Council, 258
Economic, social and cultural rights, 258
Economics of corruption, 299
Economy of Africa, 260, 289, **289**
Economy of Asia, 289, 291
Economy of Botswana, 292
Economy of Central America, 289
Economy of East Asia, 289
Economy of Europe, 289
Economy of North America, 289
Economy of Oceania, 289
Economy of South America, 289
Economy of the African Union, 257, 321, **321**
Economy of the Americas, 289
Edict of Milan, 32
Edo people, 79
Education in Africa, 260
Edward Ullendorff, 426
Egypt, 88, 94, 103, 108, 119, 168, 183, 185, 193, 205, 208, 215, 227, 265, 273, 275, 291, 292, 307, 318, 347, 351, 369, 375, 388, 391, 396, 401, 407, 410
Egyptian identification card controversy, 392
Egyptian Islamic Jihad, 95
Egyptian language, 342
Egyptian Revolution of 1952, 95
Egyptians, 32, 333
Egypt (Roman province), 29, 375
Eid ul-Fitr, 368
Eighteenth Dynasty of Egypt, 28, 30
Ejective consonant, 349
Elaeis guineensis, 23
El Alamein, 93
Elapidae, 245
Elapsoidea, 245
Electoral fraud, 299
Electricity, 295
Elele, 80
Elephant bird, 247
Elephant shrew, 248
Eleventh Dynasty of Egypt, 28
Elmina, 142
El Nino, 237
El Salvador, 145
Emblem of the African Union, 255, 279
Emigration, 153
Emi Koussi, 220
Emir, 57, 198
Emirate of Granada, 55
Emirate of Sharjah, 5
Emperor of Ethiopia, 51, 114
Empire of Ashanti, 75

Empire of Kitara, 67
En:Bibcode, 15, 16, 232
Enclave, 173
Enclaves of Forcados and Badjibo, 205
Encyclopaedia Aethiopica, 417
Encyclopædia Britannica, 123
Encyclopædia Britannica Eleventh Edition, 98
Encyclopedia of World History, 98
Endangered language, 349
Endemic birds of southern Africa, 247
Endemic birds of western and central Africa, 247
Endemic species, 244
Endemic warfare, 127, 294
En:Digital object identifier, 15–17, 99, 163, 211, 232
Endnote n1, 395
England, 104
English colonial empire, 161
English colonies, 125
English language, 256, 297, 335, 339, 343, 351, 354, 407
En:International Standard Serial Number, 163
Enlargement of the African Union, 257, 321
Ennarea, 114
En:OCLC, 98, 163
En:PubMed Central, 15–17
Enrico Corradini, 186, 200, 426
Ensete, 23
Entente cordiale, 186, 195
Enugu, 80
Environmental determinism, 297
Eocene, 239
Epidemics, 144
Epixerus, 248
Equator, 230
Equatorial climate, 233
Equatorial Guinea, 88, 137, 207, 265, 269, 271, 272, 276, 291, 307, 352, 395, 402, 407, 411
Eremomela, 247
Eric Reeves, 285
Eric Williams, 151, 154, 165
Eritrea, 7, 26, 38, 88, 90, 94, 119, 185, 186, 194, 237, 265, 276, 307, 318, 334, 347, 351, 352, 388, 396, 402, 405, 407
Eritrean cuisine, 367
Eritrean Orthodox Tewahedo Church, 388
Ernst Haeckel, 13
Erymnochelys, 246
Erythrocercus, 247
Esigie, 79
Estrilda, 247
Estuarine, Coastal and Shelf Science, 429
Etchplain, 219

Ethiopia, 26, 38, 84, 94, 103, 180, 187, 194, 197, 203, 209, 220, 237, 257, 259, 265, 269, 271–273, 276, 282, 292, 307, 318, 329, 334, 347, 351, 352, 358, 364, 388, 389, 391, 393, 396, 402, 405, 407, 411
Ethiopian cuisine, 367
Ethiopian Empire, 51, 89, 180
Ethiopian eunuch, 388
Ethiopian highland hare, 248
Ethiopian Highlands, 23, 38, 218, 222, 223, 405
Ethiopian Orthodox Tewahedo Church, 52, 388
Ethiopian Semitic languages, 336
Ethiopian Sign Language, 346
Ethnic groups in Europe, 174
Ethnic groups of Europe, 334
Ethnomusicological, 376
Ethnomusicologist, 377
Eugenicist, 199, 202
Euler diagram, 267
Eunuch, 118
Euphaedra, 244
Eupleridae, 249
Eupodotis, 247
Eurasian Plate, 231
Eurema, 243
Europe, 101, 110, 141, 153, 168, 171, 175, 215, 298
European colonialism, 167
European colonization of the Americas, 126
European Commission, 263
European cuisine, 369
European Union, 263, 309
European Union Special Representative, 274
Euschistospiza, 247
Euxanthe, 244
Eva, Arcadia, 35
Evidence as to Mans Place in Nature, 12
Ewe language, 342
Ewe people, 387
Ewuare, 79
Examples, 365
Exclusive Economic Zones, 430
Executive Council of the African Union, 258, 263
Expansionism, 186
Exploitation of labour, 200
Expulsion of Asians in Uganda in 1972, 335
Extratropical cyclone, 237
Extremism, 251
Ezana, 31, 39, 388
Ezana of Axum, 58

Faber and Faber, 178
Fakir, 59

Fall of France, 93
Family history, 159
Family planning, 325
Faras, 58
Far East, 103
Far-left politics, 251
Farm, 23
Far-right politics, 251
Fascism, 200
Fascist, 90
Fascist regime (1922–1943), 205
Fashion accessory, 359
Fashoda, 45, 194
Fashoda Incident, 86, 184, 186, 195
Fasilides of Ethiopia, 52
Fatimah, 53
Fatimid Caliphate, 56
Fatimid Dynasty, 53
Fauna of Africa, **239**
Faure Gnassingbé, 282
Fayum mummy portraits, 36
Fealty, 185
Félix Nadar, 189
Fellah, 56
Female genital mutilation, 328
Ferdinand de Lesseps, 191
Fer language, 345
Fernando Po (island), 219
Fertility rate, 323
Fes, 32, 56
Fête du Vodoun, 281
Fezzan, 43
Fezzan-Ghadames (French Administration), 205
Fiddle, 377
Financial capital, 303
Finger millet, 23
Fiqh, 111
Firearm, 44, 77
Firefinch, 247
First Boer War, 194
First Dynasty of Egypt, 29
First Intermediate Period of Egypt, 28
First Italo-Ethiopian War, 90
First Italo–Ethiopian War, 186
First Moroccan Crisis, 186
First Punic War, 32, 33
Fishing, 23
Five southernmost capes, 228
Flag of the African Union, 255, 279
Fleet Acts, 186
Florida, 145
Flute, 377
Fon language, 351
Fon people, 76, 387
Foreign minister, 258

Foreign Policy in Focus, 320
Foreign relations of the African Union, 257, 321
Fort, 170
Fort of São João Baptista de Ajudá, 88, 206
Forum on China–Africa Cooperation, 274
Foster child, 34
Founder effect, 10, 11
Fourth Anglo-Ashanti War, 208
Fourth Dynasty of Egypt, 28
Fouta Djallon, 74
Fox News Channel, 425
Fragile States Index, 275, 278
Françafrique, 339
France, 104, 141, 160, 170, 205, 259
France in the nineteenth century, 180
Francesco Crispi, 183
Franco-Hova War, 67
François Darlan, 93
Francolin, 247
Francophone Africa, 346, 407
Franco-Prussian War, 171, 185
Frankincense, 28, 33, 368
Frantz Fanon, 296
Frederick Selous, 189
Freedman, 72
Free France, 92
Free French, 93
Free trade area, 304, 316, 321
French Algeria, 85, 87, 205
French Cameroun, 205
French campaign in Egypt and Syria, 57
French colonial empire, 77, 125, 170, 410
French Congo, 205
French Dahomey, 87, 205
French East Africa, 205
French Equatorial Africa, 87, 172, 185, 197, 205
French Gabon, 92
French Guinea, 87, 205
French language, 256, 297, 343, 351, 410
French Madagascar, 201, 205
French Morocco, 87, 205
French North Africa, 93, 205
French occupation of Tunisia, 87
French people, 134
French protectorate in Morocco, 197
French Protectorate of Tunisia, 205
French rule in Algeria, 180
French Sign Language family, 346
French Somaliland, 87, 89, 205
French Sudan, 87, 205
French Third Republic, 181, 200
French Togoland, 205
French Upper Volta, 87, 205

French West Africa, 87, 92–94, 172, 185, 203, 205
French West Africa in World War II, 92
French West Indies, 134
Freshwater, 244
Freshwater crab, 242
Friedrich Gerhard Rohlfs, 84
Friedrich List, 185
Front vowel, 350
Fr:Traite musulmane, 122
Fruit, 366
Frumentius, 39
Fufu, 366, 367, 369
Fula language, 346, 348, 349, 351, 355
Fulani Empire, 74
Fulani Jihad, 46
Fulani language, 336, 340
Fulani people, 331
Fulani War, 74
Fula people, 72, 74, 112
Funj people, 59
Fur, 333
Fur language, 342, 354
Fusion cuisine, 368
Futa Tooro, 74
Future, 21
Futures studies, 21

Gabon, 87, 137, 205, 259, 265, 276, 282, 291, 307, 318, 391, 395, 402, 411
Gaetuli, 31
Gaius Gracchus, 169
Galaxiidae, 245
Galibis, 201
Gamal Abdel Nasser, 95
Gambeson, 20
Gambia, 159, 205, 318, 370
Gambia Colony and Protectorate, 209
Gambia River, 222
Game (food), 21
Ganda language, 354
Ganga Talao, 392
Gao, 72, 119, 120
Garamantes, 32
Garri, 369
Gaza Empire, 207
Gazella, 249
Gbaya languages, 354
Gbe languages, 138, 387
GDP per capita .28nominal.29 by continents, 289
Geary–Khamis dollar, 275, 278
Gecko, 245
Geez, 38
Geez script, 38
Gelada, 249

Gelasius I, 388
Gelawdewos of Ethiopia, 52
General History of Africa, 99
Genetic admixture, 6
Genetic drift, 10
Genetic marker, 14
Genetics, 20, 22
Genocide Intervention Network, 285
Gentlemanly capitalism, 180
Genus, 244
Geochelone, 246
Geoffrey Parrinder, 399
Geography and cartography in medieval Islam, 120
Geography of Africa, **215**
Geography of the African Union, 256, 257, 321
Geology, 219
Geopolitics, 215
George Schweinfurth, 84
Georges Clemenceau, 200
Gerbil, 248
Gerenuk, 249
Gerhard Kubik, 377
German Cameroon, 203
German colonial empire, 81, 170, 344
German East Africa, 88, 172, 185, 198, 205
German Empire, 181, 198
German General Staff, 204
Germanic languages, 354
German Kamerun, 88, 205
German language, 335, 339, 344, 351
German South West Africa, 81, 88
German South-West Africa, 198, 205
German Togoland, 88, 205
Germany, 185, 217
Ghana, 76, 88, 96, 137, 138, 160, 205, 209, 237, 265, 268, 273, 276, 307, 318, 329, 345, 346, 351, 369, 370, 379, 387, 391, 397, 403, 407, 412
Ghana Empire, 18, 40, 54, 70
Ghana Health Services, 329
Ghanzi, 61
Ghassanids, 421
Ghezo, 137
Giant East African Snail, 241
Giant forest hog, 249
Gikuyu language, 351, 354
Ginger, 367
Ginger Baker, 381
Ginger Bakers Air Force, 381
Giraffe, 249
Girgam, 42
Glacier, 238
Global Burden of Disease, 329
Global financial crisis of 2008–2009, 293
Globalization, 210, 211

Global Peace Index, 275, 278, 292
Glossogobius, 245
Gnassingbé Eyadéma, 282
Goat, 367
Gobir, 74
Gobroon Dynasty, 198
Gold, 25, 126, 321
Gold Coast (British colony), 137, 209
Gold Coast (region), 406
Golden mole, 248
Goliath frog, 245
Goliathus, 243
Gomba language, 345
Gondershe, 50
Gondwana, 221, 239
Gondwanan, 429
Gonimbrasia belina, 243
Gonionotophis, 245
Gonja people, 76
Gonorhynchiformes, 245
Google News, 425
Gorée, 134
Gorilla, 13, 21, 249
Gourd, 23
Government, 174
Government of the Peoples Republic of China, 269
Governor of Alabama, 161
Graceland (album), 380
Grammatical case, 350
Grammatical tense, 350
Grammomys, 248
Granada War, 55
Grand coalition, 252
Grape, 369
Graphiurus, 248
Gravi-kora, 379
Gravikord, 379
Grayia (snake), 245
Great apes, 21
Great Coastal Migration, 10
Great Depression, 90
Greater Arab Free Trade Area, 305, 317, 322
Greater Maghreb, 409
Great Fish River, 59, 82
Great Karoo, 217
Great Kei River, 42
Great Lakes (Africa), 67, 218
Great Rift Valley, 223
Great Socialist Peoples Libyan Arab Jamahiriya, 265, 282
Great Zimbabwe, 59, 60
Greco-Roman, 33
Greek language, 58
Greeks, 116
Green-backed twinspot, 247

Greenland, 225
Green Sahara, 24
Grey parrot, 247
Grimal1988, 416
Griqua people, 82
Gross domestic product, 256, 289, 321, 411
Ground woodpecker, 247
Guanches, 128
Guangzhou, 116
Guatemala, 145
Guenon, 249
Guerrilla warfare, 63
Guinea, 78, 87, 137, 138, 173, 205, 265, 269, 276, 307, 318, 344, 397, 403, 406, 411
Guinea-Bissau, 88, 94, 137, 206, 265, 276, 307, 318, 345, 352, 397, 403, 407, 412
Guinea-Bissau Creole, 345
Guineafowl, 246
Guinean forest-savanna mosaic, 243
Guinea (region), 406
Gujarati language, 344
Gulf of Aden, 236, 405
Gulf of Guinea, 113, 219
Gumuz language, 342, 354
Gungunhana, 207
Gun Quarter, Birmingham, 145
Guns, Germs, and Steel, 98, 297, 432
Gur languages, 336, 355
Gustav Nachtigal, 84
Gyaaman, 76
Gymnarchidae, 245

Habachi1963, 416
Habesha kemis, 364
Habesha people, 334
Habib Bourguiba, 95
Hadley cell, 234
Hadza language, 344, 409
Hadza people, 12, 336
Hailemariam Desalegn, 269
Hair, 10
Haiti, 145, 209
Haitian Revolution, 158
Haitian Vodou, 387
Hajj, 72, 105
Halal, 368
Halva, 368
Hamanumida daedalus, 243
Hamitic, 336
Hamoud bin Mohammed of Zanzibar, 113
Han06, 425
Hanafi, 389
Handgun, 57
Hanging Church, 388
Hannah Arendt, 200, 426
Hannibal, 32

Hanno the Great, 169
Haplogroup L0 (mtDNA), 9
Haplogroup L1 (mtDNA), 9
Haplogroup L2 (mtDNA), 9
Haplogroup L3 (mtDNA), 6, 9
Haplogroup M1, 9
Haplogroup M (mtDNA), 9, 10
Haplogroup N (mtDNA), 9
Harlequin quail, 247
Harmattan, 227
Harp, 377
Harpoon, 23
Harrier (bird), 247
Hartebeest, 249
Harvard University, 424
Hassaniyya, 345
Hausa Kingdoms, 44, 46, 73, 112
Hausaland, 44
Hausa language, 77, 335, 340, 342, 346, 349, 351, 355, 371
Hausa people, 331, 336
Hawash river, 223
Headgear, 359
Healthcare reform, 326
Health minister, 326
Heart of Darkness, 200
Heavily Indebted Poor Countries, 293
Hebrew, 342
Hedgehog, 248
Hegemony, 180
Heinrich Barth, 42, 84, 121
Heleophrynidae, 245
Helicotylenchus, 241
He Lives in You, 381
Helmuth von Moltke the Younger, 204
Hemachatus, 245
Hemichromis, 245
Hemidactylus, 245
Hemisotidae, 245
Hennchir Besseriani, 35
Henotheism, 26
Henri Giraud, 93
Henry IV of England, 51
Henry Morton Stanley, 84, 121, 184, 188
Hepsetidae, 245
Heptatonic scale, 370, 375
Herero and Namaqua genocide, 81, 172, 199
Herero people, 61, 81, 198
Heresy, 37
Hernán Cortés, 131
Herodes Atticus, 34
Heteropsis (butterfly), 244
Highlife, 370
High-pressure area, 234
Highveld, 62
Hildebrandtia (animal), 245

Hindu, 51, 103
Hippopotamus, 249
Hippo Regius, 37
Hippotragus, 249
Hiram S. Maxim, 83
Hirschmanniella, 241
Hispaniola, 144, 145
Historical linguistics, 20
Historiography, 167
Historiography of the British Empire, 179
Historiography of the fall of the Western Roman Empire, 36
History of Africa, **18**
History of East Asia, 20, 21
History of Egypt under the British, 410
History of Islam, 49
History of Oceania, 21
History of Oman, 6
History of Persian Egypt, 375
History of South Africa in the Apartheid Era, 95
History of the African Union, 257, 260, 321
History of the Jews in the Roman Empire, 36
History of the Royal Navy, 196
History of the world, 20
History of writing, 20
HIV, 281
HMS Black Joke (1827), 157
Hobyo, 51
Hollandic dialect, 343
Holocene, 10
Hominid, 18
Hominidae, 21, 249
Homo erectus, 14, 22, 413
Homo ergaster, 22
Homo floresiensis, 22
Homo georgicus, 22
Homo habilis, 21
Homo heidelbergensis, 11
Homopus, 246
Homoroselaps, 245
Homo sapiens, 3, 4, 18, 22
Honduras, 145
Honey badger, 249
Honeyguide, 247
Hookworm infection, 328
Hor-Aha, 29
Horatio Kitchener, 195
Hormonotus, 245
Horn of Africa, 3, 10, 18, 26, 33, 64, 101, 119, 194, 198, 223, 236, 334, 335, 339, 342, 344, 367, 370, 375, 389, 403, 405, 407
Hot desert climate, 234, 236
Hot semi-arid climate, 234, 236
Houegbadja, 76
Houghton Mifflin, 178

Howard Winant, 423
How Europe Underdeveloped Africa, 178, 296, 424
Human, 249
Human Development Index, 256, 275, 278, 281
Human resources, 290
Human Y-chromosome DNA haplogroup, 14
Human zoo, 199
Human zoos, 201
Hummay, 43
Hung parliament, 252
Hunting, 376
Hutu, 68, 95
Hybomys, 248
Hyena, 249
Hyksos, 28, 30, 333
Hylobates, 13
Hylomyscus, 248
Hymenochirus, 245
Hymenoptera, 243
Hypargos (bird), 247
Hyperoliidae, 245
Hypertension, 329
Hypophytala, 244
Hypothesis, 231

Ibadi, 391
Iberian Peninsula, 55
Iberian Union, 130
Ibibio language, 355
Ibn Battuta, 66, 72, 104, 111, 120
Ibn Butlan, 105
Ibn Khaldun, 121, 122
Ibrahim Halidi, 286
Ice age, 241
Iceland, 104
Idi Amin, 335
Idris Alooma, 44
Idris of Libya, 95
Idriss Déby, 269
Ife, 41, 77
Ifni, 88, 207
Ifrane, 236
Igala people, 140
Igboland, 80, 407
Igbo language, 335, 340, 342, 348, 349, 351, 355
Igbo people, 80, 135, 331
Igbo religion, 387
Igbo-Ukwu, 80
Igrita, 80
Ihiala, 80
Ile Ife, 18
Iles des Chiens, 228
Ilunga Tshibinda, 47

Imamate of Futa Toro, 72
Imam (Sunni Islam), 52
Imbangala, 47, 49, 140
Imeraguen language, 345
IMF, 293, 303
Impala, 240, 249, 369
Imperial cult, 26
Imperialism, 180, 183
Imperialism (Hobson), 180, 183, 427
Imperialism, the Highest Stage of Capitalism, 180
Imperial Japan, 93
Implosive consonant, 349
Import tariff, 309
Incense, 368
Indentured servants, 101, 125
Indentured servitude, 132
Index of Economic Freedom, 275, 278
India, 33, 103, 119, 208, 227, 239, 271
Indian Ocean, 18, 42, 57, 102, 119, 127, 223, 225, 290, 411
Indians in Uganda, 335
Indian subcontinent, 334
Indigenous Australians, 10
Indigenous people, 200
Indigenous peoples of Africa, 331
Indigenous peoples of the Americas, 8, 132
Indo-European languages, 335, 336, 339–341, 343, 351, 352, 354, 408
Indonesia, 63
Industrial Revolution, 84, 147, 151
Industry, 290
Infant mortality, 323, 328
Information and communication technologies, 295
Ingombe Ilede, 60
Injera, 367
Innoson Vehicle Manufacturing, 314
In political and religious discourse, 251
Inselberg, 219
Intergovernmental Authority on Development, 261, 267, 305, 317, 318, 322
Intergovernmental organisation, 274
Internal slave trade, 155
International Criminal Court, 272, 285
International crisis, 186
International Day for the Remembrance of the Slave Trade and its Abolition, 159
International human rights instruments, 258
International law, 281
International migration, 143
International Monetary Fund, 289
International recognition of the Sahrawi Arab Democratic Republic, 264
International relations, 274

International Standard Book Number, 15–17, 97–99, 122, 162–165, 178, 179, 212, 286, 319, 383, 399, 413
Intertropical Convergence Zone, 234, 236
Interwar period, 205
Intonation (music), 377
Introduction, 1
Inuit, 201
Iraq, 103
Ireland, 104
Iron, 26, 42
Iron Age, 26, 40
Iron working, 25
Ishango bone, 22
Islam, 18, 39, 43, 67, 70, 72, 74, 126, 169, 333, 385, 387, 389
Islam by country, 105
Islamic, 389
Islamic music, 377
Islamic views on slavery, 105
Islamic world, 49, 376, 377
Islam in Africa, 105, 377, 385
Islam in Somalia, 49
Islamism, 95
Islamization, 55, 59
Isle de France (Mauritius), 205
Ismail ibn Sharif, 56
Ismail Pasha, 191
Israel, 95
Istanbul, 55, 57
Istiqlal Party, 95
Italian Colonial Empire, 170
Italian East Africa, 90, 205
Italian Eritrea, 89, 186, 205
Italian invasion of Greece, 93
Italian language, 343, 351
Italian Libya, 205
Italian North Africa, 88
Italian people, 197
Italian Somaliland, 88, 90, 186, 205
Italo-Turkish War, 186
Italy, 104, 184, 203
IUCN, 245
Ivory, 188
Ivory Coast, 76, 87, 96, 137, 138, 205, 265, 275, 307, 318, 387, 391, 397, 402, 406, 411
Ivory trade, 29

Jackal, 249
Jacob Zuma, 282
Jacques Chirac, 160
Jaga (people), 48
Jainism, 393
Jaja of Opobo, 133
Jakaya Kikwete, 268, 270

Jalaa language, 344, 345
Jalba, 116
Jamaica, 143, 145, 147, 159
James Bruce, 84, 121
James Madison, 157
James Morris Blaut, 297
Jameson Raid, 194
Jamestown, Virginia, 146, 161
James Watt, 148
Jan Smuts, 92
Japan, 8, 204
Jardin dAcclimatation, 201
Jared Diamond, 98, 297
Java, 103
Javanese people, 107
Jazz, 369, 380, 381
Jazz rock, 380
JC virus, 11
J. D. Fage, 153, 297
Jean-Baptiste Debret, 158
Jean-Baptiste Marchand, 184, 195
Jean Ping, 259
Jebel Faya, 5
Jeddah, 119
Jehovahs Witnesses, 388
Jerry Rawlings, 160
Jesse Jackson, 161
Jesse Mugambi, 393
Jesus, 37
Jewelry, 359
Jihad, 55, 73, 74
Jingoism, 200, 203
João de Castro, 121
João III of Portugal, 140
Joaquim Chissano, 268
Johannesburg, 238, 255, 271
Johannesburg Reform Committee, 194
Johannesburg, South Africa, 194
Johann Ludwig Burckhardt, 108, 121
John Agyekum Kufuor, 268
John A. Hobson, 183, 200, 427
John Andrew Gallagher, 97
John Darwin (historian), 183
John Desmond Clark, 98
John Hanning Speke, 84
John Hawkins (naval commander), 131
John Henrik Clarke, 163
John K. Thornton, 297
John Kufuor, 268
John Mbiti, 393, 436
John Thornton (historian), 126, 162
Jollof rice, 369
Jomo Kenyatta, 94
Joseph C. Miller, 148
Joseph Conrad, 200
Joseph E. Inikori, 297

Joseph Greenberg, 343
Joseph Thomson (explorer), 84, 189
Josiah Wedgwood, 133
Jos Plateau, 26, 40
Journal of Human Evolution, 17
Journey to the End of the Night, 200
Juba Arabic, 345
Jubba River, 223
Judaism, 37
Judea, 28, 36
Jules Ferry, 183, 200
Julius Caesar, 169
Julius Nyerere, 173, 303
Jungle, 236
Jurisprudence, 389
Justinian I, 37

Kaabu, 18, 140
Kabaka of Buganda, 68
Kabsah, 369
Kabyle language, 354
Kadu languages, 342
Kagera Region, 66
Kairouan, 54, 390
Kaiso, 373
Kalabari Kingdom, 80
Kalahari Craton, 231
Kalahari Desert, 81, 217, 227, 331, 335, 339
Kalala Ilunga, 46
Kalenjin language, 354
Kalimba, 378
Kamerun Campaign, 90
Kampala, 176, 272, 391
Kampala, Uganda, 294
Kanem-Bornu Empire, 45
Kanem Empire, 24, 42, 112
Kanga (African garment), 365
Kano, 119
Kanuri language, 342, 354, 355, 408
Kanuri people, 42, 43, 333, 336
Karachi, 119
Karagwe, 67
Karl Marx, 152
Kasanje Kingdom, 49
Kashaka, 378
Kashta, 28
Katanga Province, 189
Kato Kintu, 68
Kavango Region, 61
Kebra Nagast, 121
Kedestes, 244
Kenkey, 369
Ken Livingstone, 161
Kente cloth, 364
Kenya, 23, 42, 65, 66, 88, 93, 94, 102, 119, 173, 174, 193, 194, 220, 240, 265, 276,

281, 307, 309, 318, 325, 345, 348, 352, 359, 363, 365, 391, 395, 402, 406, 411
Kenya Colony, 209
Ketu (Benin), 78
Kevin Shillington, 98
Khalid Islambouli, 95
Khambhat, 51
Khami, 61
Khamsin, 227
Kharijites, 53
Khartoum, 117, 273
Khasso, 141
Khedive, 191
Khedive of Egypt, 86
Khoekhoe language, 337, 351
Khoe languages, 335, 339, 344, 351, 352
Khoikhoi, 63, 331, 336
Khoikhoi-Dutch Wars, 63
Khoisan, 23, 42, 62, 331, 336, 344, 370
Khoi-San, 336
Khoisan languages, 59, 61, 62, 335, 340, 341, 344, 371, 408, 409
Khoisan people, 369
Khūzestān Province, 104
Kigali, 68, 271
Kigeli IV of Rwanda, 68
Kilindini Harbour, 411
Kilwa District, 119
Kilwa Empire, 60, 69
Kilwa Kisiwani, 66, 121
Kilwa Sultanate, 51, 67
Kimbundu, 351
Kingdom of Aksum, 26, 112
Kingdom of Aragon, 55
Kingdom of Baguirmi, 20, 24
Kingdom of Baol, 18
Kingdom of Bonny, 80
Kingdom of Butua, 61
Kingdom of Castile, 55, 128
Kingdom of Dahomey, 135
Kingdom of Kano, 46
Kingdom of Kerma, 29
Kingdom of Kongo, 18, 48, 128, 129, 141
Kingdom of Kush, 18, 28–30
Kingdom of Makuria, 18, 58
Kingdom of Mapungubwe, 18, 59
Kingdom of Matamba, 49
Kingdom of Mutapa, 60, 61
Kingdom of Ndongo, 48
Kingdom of Nri, 18, 80
Kingdom of Portugal, 52, 55
Kingdom of Rwanda, 68
Kingdom of Saloum, 18
Kingdom of Sine, 18
Kingdom of Warri, 80
Kingdom of Whydah, 77
Kingdom of Zimbabwe, 18
King Leopolds Ghost: A Story of Greed, Terror, and Heroism in Colonial Africa, 212
Kinixys, 246
Kinshasa, 189
Kinyarwanda, 348, 351, 354
Kipunji, 249
Kirundi, 348, 351, 354
Kisangani, 189
Kismayo, 119
Kituba, 351
Kivu, 66
Kizomba, 370
Kleptocracy, 299
Klipspringer, 249
Kneriidae, 245
Knysna, 280
Koine Greek, 344
Koiné language, 348
Kola nut, 23, 75
Koman languages, 342
Kongo Civil War, 134
Kongo Empire, 188
Kongo Kingdom, 184
Kongo language, 351, 354
Kongolo Mwamba, 46
Kongo people, 48, 138, 361
Kora (instrument), 377, 378
Kordofanian languages, 343, 354
Kori bustard, 247
Koumbi Saleh, 40, 70
Kru languages, 336
Kuhane language, 61
Kujargé language, 345
Kunama language, 354
Kurdish people, 57
Kurdufan, 59
Kusi Obodom, 76
Kutch, 119
Kwadi language, 345
Kwa languages, 75, 79, 336, 355
Kwame Nkrumah, 96, 259, 318
Kwango River, 48
Kwara State, 332, 370
KwaZulu-Natal, 59, 61
Kxa languages, 344

Laal language, 344, 345
Labeobarbus, 245
Labial-velar consonant, 349
Labiodental flap, 349
Labour shortage, 132
Lacerta, 246
Lacertidae, 246
Lachnocnema, 244
Ladysmith Black Mambazo, 381

Lagos, 255, 314
Lagos, Nigeria, 311
Lagos Plan of Action for the Development of Africa, 267
Lake Abaya, 224
Lake Albert (Africa), 218, 222, 224
Lake Asal (Djibouti), 228
Lake Bangweulu, 222, 224
Lake Chad, 24, 26, 43, 45, 222–224
Lake Edward, 218, 222, 224
Lake Fitri, 42
Lake Kisale, 46
Lake Kivu, 68, 218, 224
Lake Mai-Ndombe, 224
Lake Malawi, 69, 224, 280, 413
Lake Mweru, 222, 224
Lake Naivasha, 224
Lake Ngami, 223, 224
Lake No, 45
Lake Nyasa, 217, 223
Lake of Stars Festival, 280
Lake Plateau, 67
Lake Rudolf, 223
Lake Rukwa, 224
Lake Tana, 224
Lake Tanganyika, 84, 218, 224
Lake Toba, 7
Lake Tsana, 219
Lake Turkana, 218, 224
Lake Victoria, 66, 68, 84, 215, 222, 224, 244
Lamellophone, 374, 377
Lamin Sanneh, 389
Lamprophis, 245
Lamtuna, 54
Lamu Port and Lamu-Southern Sudan-Ethiopia Transport Corridor, 411
Landed nobility, 57
Land of Punt, 26, 28
Land reform, 303
Language, 335, 339
Language contact, 349
Language family, 339, 341
Language isolate, 335, 339, 344, 345
Languages of Africa, 167, 256, 257, 261, **339**, 379
Languages of India, 344
Languages of the African Union, 257, 321
Lanzarana, 245
Late Cretaceous, 221
Late modern period, 21
Laterite, 219
Lates, 245
Latimeria, 244
Latin, 344
Latin American music, 373
Latitude, 45

Laurasia, 239
Lazarus taxon, 244
Lead, 25
Leaf vegetable, 367
Leather, 359
Leeward Islands, 147
Left-wing politics, 251
Legal plunder, 299
Legal status of Western Sahara, 281
Legume, 367
Leioheterodon, 245
Le Marinel Expedition, 189
Le Monde, 269
Le Monde diplomatique, 112, 126, 422, 427
Lemur, 249
Lentil, 367
Leo Africanus, 73, 121
Leo Frobenius, 436
Leopard, 249, 364
Leopold II of Belgium, 172
Léopold II of Belgium, 183, 184, 188, 193
Leprosy, 83
Leptotyphlopidae, 245
Leptotyphlops, 245
Lesotho, 82, 89, 194, 209, 220, 237, 265, 276, 307, 318, 348, 352, 396, 403, 411
Let Us All Unite and Celebrate Together, 255, 280
Levallois technique, 5
Levant, 28
LGBT, 260
Liberalism, 251
Liberia, 85, 89, 94, 96, 137, 159, 180, 203, 209, 265, 276, 307, 318, 397, 403, 407, 412
Library of Congress, 336, 418
Libya, 42, 88, 94, 119, 186, 236, 265, 269, 273, 276, 282, 291, 308, 318, 319, 333, 347, 351, 393, 396, 401, 410, 428
Libyan Civil War (2011), 95
Libyans, 333
Life expectancy, 281, 323
Life in the African Union, 257, 321
Limpopo River, 59, 62, 189, 221, 223
Lingala, 354
Lingala language, 346, 352
Lingua franca, 343, 344, 346
Lingua francas, 335, 339
Linguistic Diversity Index, 297
Lion, 249
Liptenara, 244
Lisbon, 105
Lissotis, 247
List of African countries, 373
List of African countries by population, 290
List of Beys of Tunis, 95

List of butterflies of South Africa, 243
List of butterflies of the Democratic Republic of the Congo, 244
List of continents by GDP (nominal), 289
List of countries and outlying territories by total area, 275, 278
List of countries by GDP (nominal), 307, 321
List of countries by GDP (nominal) per capita, 411
List of countries by GDP (PPP), 275, 278, 321
List of countries by GDP (PPP) per capita, 275, 278, 307
List of countries by Human Development Index, 307
List of countries by life expectancy, 433
List of countries by population, 275, 278
List of countries where Arabic is an official language, 407
List of ethnic groups of Africa, 123
List of former German colonies, 90
List of hominina fossils, 13
List of islands by area, 261
List of islands in the Indian Ocean, 103
List of Ottoman conquests, sieges and landings, 104
List of political ideologies, 252
List of political parties by region, 252
List of political parties in Africa by country, **251**
List of political parties in Algeria, 252
List of political parties in Benin, 254
List of political parties in Botswana, 253
List of political parties in Burkina Faso, 254
List of political parties in Burundi, 254
List of political parties in Cameroon, 253
List of political parties in Cape Verde, 254
List of political parties in Chad, 253
List of political parties in Comoros, 254
List of political parties in Djibouti, 254
List of political parties in Egypt, 252
List of political parties in Equatorial Guinea, 253
List of political parties in Eritrea, 254
List of political parties in Ethiopia, 254
List of political parties in Gabon, 253
List of political parties in Ghana, 254
List of political parties in Guinea, 254
List of political parties in Guinea-Bissau, 254
List of political parties in Ivory Coast, 254
List of political parties in Kenya, 254
List of political parties in Lesotho, 253
List of political parties in Liberia, 254
List of political parties in Madagascar, 254
List of political parties in Malawi, 254
List of political parties in Mali, 254
List of political parties in Mauritania, 254
List of political parties in Mauritius, 254
List of political parties in Morocco, 252
List of political parties in Mozambique, 254
List of political parties in Namibia, 253
List of political parties in Niger, 254
List of political parties in Nigeria, 254
List of political parties in Rwanda, 254
List of political parties in São Tomé and Príncipe, 253
List of political parties in Senegal, 254
List of political parties in Seychelles, 255
List of political parties in Sierra Leone, 254
List of political parties in Somalia, 255
List of political parties in South Africa, 253
List of political parties in South Sudan, 255
List of political parties in Sudan, 252
List of political parties in Swaziland, 253
List of political parties in Tanzania, 255
List of political parties in the Central African Republic, 253
List of political parties in the Gambia, 254
List of political parties in the Republic of the Congo, 253
List of political parties in Togo, 254
List of political parties in Tunisia, 252
List of political parties in Uganda, 255
List of political parties in Western Sahara, 252
List of political parties in Zambia, 255
List of political parties in Zimbabwe, 253, 255
List of political parties of the Democratic Republic of the Congo, 253
List of popular music genres, 381
List of Presidents of Egypt, 95
List of Prime Ministers of Egypt, 95
List of Prime Ministers of Israel, 95
List of regions of Africa, **401**
List of rulers of Baguirmi, 45
List of ruling political parties by country, 252
List of sultans of the Ottoman Empire, 44
List of territorial entities where English is an official language, 351
List of territorial entities where French is an official language, 351
Literacy, 55, 72
Liujiang man, 6, 8
Liverpool, 144, 161
Liverpool City Council, 161
Living standard, 258
Lizards, 245
Loanword, 65
Lobster, 369
Lomé, 260
London, 144
London School of Economics, 97
London Zoo, 13
Long Depression, 181, 200

Longitude, 403
Lord Mansfield, 154
Lothar von Trotha, 81
Louis-Ferdinand Céline, 200
Louisiana Voodoo, 387
Louvre, 40
Lovebird, 246
Lower Egypt, 26
Lower Nubia, 405
Lozi people, 48, 61
Lualaba River, 189
Luanda, 48, 84, 116
Luapula River, 48
Luba Empire, 47
Luba-Kasai language, 352
Luba people, 46
Luca Cavalli-Sforza, 415
Luc Gnacadja, 160
Luena people, 48
Lufu language, 345
Luganda, 352
Luhya languages, 354
Lunar calendar, 22
Lunda Empire, 47
Lunda people, 47
Lungfishes, 245
Luo dialect, 342, 352
Luo language, 354
Luo language (Cameroon), 345
Luo languages, 348
Luo peoples, 67
Lusaka, 260
Lusophone Africa, 407
Lute, 377
Luxor Temple, 19

Maanyan language, 343
Maasai language, 342, 354
Maba people, 46
Macaque, 249
Machine gun, 83
Macina, Mali, 74
Mackerel, 369
Macro-haplogroup L (mtDNA), 9
Macroscelidea, 248
Macrovipera, 245
Madagascar, 63, 67, 87, 137, 167, 201, 225, 237, 239, 249, 261, 265, 276, 308, 318, 335, 339, 343, 347, 352, 393, 395, 402, 403, 407, 409, 411
Madagascarophis, 245
Madagascar partridge, 247
Madeira, 173, 259, 401
Madison Grant, 199, 202
Madjedbebe, 8

Maghreb, 18, 25, 32, 53, 105, 114, 238, 375, 377, 403, 405, 407
Mahdi, 192
Mahdist revolt, 192
Mahdist War, 195
Mahmood Mamdani, 174
Maize, 48, 75, 367
Majindo, 106
Majority government, 252
Major plates, 230
Major scale, 370, 375
Makossa, 370
Makua language, 354
Makua people, 106
Makua (people), 138
Makuria, 59, 106
Malabo, 271, 272
Malacca, 51
Malacomys, 248
Malagasy language, 343, 347, 352, 354
Malagasy people, 201, 335, 336
Malao, 33
Malapteruridae, 245
Malaria, 83, 181, 228, 281, 327
Malawi, 42, 47, 89, 106, 209, 220, 244, 265, 269, 276, 292, 308, 318, 348, 351, 395, 402, 411, 413
Malay language, 169
Malayo-Polynesian languages, 336
Malay people, 169
Mali, 40, 74, 75, 87, 119, 194, 205, 236, 265, 276, 282, 290, 308, 318, 326, 335, 339, 344, 348, 397, 403, 411
Mali Empire, 18, 71, 104, 111, 389
Maliki, 389
Malimbus, 247
Malindi, 51
Mamluk, 57, 59, 110
Mamluk Sultanate (Cairo), 57, 72
Mammal, 248
Mammals, 13
Manchester, 144
Mancur Olson, 303
Mande languages, 343, 344, 408
Mandé peoples, 23, 40, 71, 138, 331, 336
Manding languages, 335, 340
Mandinka people, 331
Mandrillus, 249
Mandvi, 119
Maned rat, 248
Mango, 369
Manikongo, 48, 128, 140
Manot 1, 8
Manot Cave, 8
Mansa Musa, 389
Mansa (title), 71

Mantellidae, 245
Manticora (genus), 243
Mantle (geology), 231
Mantle plume, 231
Mantophasmatodea, 242
Maputaland, 407
Maputo, 42, 260, 273
Maputo Protocol, 328
Marabou stork, 247
Maravi, 47, 69
Marcus Rediker, 164
Marine Isotope Stage 5, 6
Marion Island, 427
Mark Stoneking, 14
Marracuene, 207
Marrakesh, 56, 119
Marriage, 376
Marseilles, 201
Martin Meredith, 16
Marxism, 303
Marxist, 320
Maryland, 161
Mary Leakey, 66
Masai Mara National Park, 240
Masalit language, 354
Masalit people, 333
Mashriq, 105
Masinissa, 33
Mask, 359
Massawa, 107, 112, 119
Mastomys, 248
Matabeleland, 189
Maternal death, 328
Mathieu Kerekou, 160
Matoke, 367
Maulana Karenga, 359, 435
Mau Mau Uprising, 94
Mauretania, 18, 31, 35
Maurice Rouvier, 196
Mauri (people), 31
Mauritania, 40, 54, 74, 87, 110, 119, 205, 265, 269, 276, 282, 283, 292, 308, 318, 319, 345, 347, 351, 362, 397, 403, 407, 410
Mauritian Creole, 345, 352
Mauritius, 205, 225, 228, 265, 276, 308, 318, 345, 352, 391, 392, 395, 402, 411
Mawa language (Nigeria), 345
Maxim gun, 83
Maya civilization, 131
Mayombe, 406
Mayor of London, 161
Mayotte, 259, 343, 395, 402
Mbaise, 407
Mbalax, 370
Mbanderu people, 61, 81
Mbanza-Kongo, 48

Mbaqanga, 370
Mbira, 373, 374, 377, 378
Mbre language, 345
Mbukushu, 61
Mbuti, 9
MC1R, 11
Measles, 328
Meat, 366
Mecca, 43, 57, 72, 116
Medieval history, 21
Medieval Near East, 21
Medieval slavery, 144
Medina, 57
Mediterranean, 168, 403
Mediterranean climate, 233
Mediterranean Sea, 108, 215, 219, 230, 231
Megadrought, 5
Megalith, 24
Meghalaya, 227
Melanesians, 11
Melanobatrachinae, 245
Melanocortin 1 receptor, 11
Melierax, 247
Melilla, 173, 339, 401
Melisma, 377
Meloidogyne, 241
Member states of the African Union, 256
Member states of the United Nations, 264
Memphis, Egypt, 28
Menachem Begin, 95
Mende people, 12
Menes, 26
Menouthias, 65
Merca, 51
Mercantilism, 186
Meridional line, 218
Merina, 67
Merka, 49
Meroe, 26, 58
Meröe, 30
Meroitic alphabet, 30
Meroitic language, 345
Merseyside Maritime Museum, 142
Mertensophryne, 245
Mesalina, 246
Mesite, 246
Mesopotamia, 104
Mesozoic era, 239
Messaâd, 35
Messianism, 388
Messinian salinity crisis, 239
Metalworking, 26
Metropolis, 65
Metropolitan Museum of Art, 100
Mexico, 131
Mfecane, 81, 82

Mick Jagger, 381
Microhylidae, 245
Microlith, 12
Mid-Atlantic Ridge, 225, 230
Middens, 7
Middle Africa, 123, 325
Middle Ages, 18, 21, 105, 115, 167
Middle class, 186
Middle Congo, 87, 197
Middle East, 18, 106, 126, 410
Middle Eastern music, 370, 375
Middle Kingdom of Egypt, 28
Middle kingdoms of India, 21
Middle Passage, 123, 142
Midrand, 259, 262
Migration to Abyssinia, 389
Migratory locust, 242
Miletinae, 244
Milford Wolpoff, 14
Militarism, 200
Military conquests of Umars era, 389
Milk, 366
Millennium Development Goals, 294
Millet, 39, 48, 71
Millionaire, 289
Milton Meltzer, 142
Mimacraea, 244
Minatogawa Man, 8
Ming Empire, 51
Miniature (illuminated manuscript), 121
Ministry of Health, Ghana, 329
Minority government, 252
Mirafra, 247
Miriam Makeba, 381, 382
Misliya cave, 5
Missiology, 394
Missionary, 67
Mitochondrial DNA, 4, 9, 14
Mitochondrial Eve, 9, 14
Mittelafrika, 407
Mleiha Archaeological Centre, 5
Mobile, Alabama, 156
Mochokidae, 245
Mode (music), 370, 375
Moderate, 251
Modern, 202
Modern Era, 167
Modern history, 21
Modernity, 21
Modern period, 110
Mogadishu, 49, 119, 285
Mogadishu currency, 291
Mohamed Bacar, 286
Mohamed Ould Abdel Aziz, 269, 282
Mohammed Abdullah Hassan, 197, 198
Mohammed V of Morocco, 95

Molasses, 131
Mombasa, 51, 65, 67, 119, 411
Monarchies in Africa, 357
Monarchy, 169
Monetary union, 321
Mongol Empire, 57
Mongoose, 249
Mongo people, 332
Monitor lizard, 246
Monkey, 367
Monopeltis, 246
Monophysitism, 32, 58
Monrovia Group, 261
Monsoon, 236
Monsoon trough, 234
Montatheris, 245
Monthly Review, 320, 432
Montserrat, 146
Moral universalism, 200
More language, 355
Mormyridae, 245
Moroccan cuisine, 367, 369
Morocco, 31, 56, 73, 86, 95, 119, 120, 173,
    195, 219, 220, 236, 238, 264, 265, 276,
    308, 313, 318, 319, 333, 347, 351, 352,
    396, 401, 405, 407, 410
Morphology (biology), 8
Morphology (linguistics), 342
Mortality rate, 143, 202
Moshoeshoe I, 82
Mosque of Uqba, 54, 390
Mossi Kingdoms, 18
Mossi language, 352
Mossi people, 72
Mosylon, 33
Mother tongue, 297
Moulouya River, 33
Mountain Club of South Africa, 238
Mount Cameroon, 220, 227
Mount Elgon, 220
Mount Karisimbi, 220
Mount Kenya, 218, 220, 309
Mount Kilimanjaro, 215, 218, 220, 228, 238
Mount Meru (Tanzania), 220
Mount Satima, 220
Mount Stanley, 220
Mousebird, 246
Moussa Faki, 256, 269
Moussa Toybou, 286
Mozambique, 42, 60, 63, 65, 88, 94, 102, 137,
    138, 206, 259, 265, 268, 273, 276, 292,
    308, 318, 352, 393, 395, 402, 403, 407,
    411
Mozambique channel, 225
Mozambique (Portugal), 180
Mpande, 82

Mpre language, 345
Msiri, 189
Mthethwa Paramountcy, 81
Mt-MRCA, 14
Muammar al-Gaddafi, 260, 269
Muammar Gaddafi, 95, 270, 282
Mudskipper, 245
Muhammad, 120, 389
Muhammad Ahmad, 89, 192, 195
Muhammad Ahmed Ben Bella, 95
Muhammad al-Amin al-Kanemi, 44
Muhammad al-Idrisi, 120
Muhammad Ali of Egypt, 59
Muhammed Bello, 74
Mukātaba, 111
Mulanje Massif, 220
Multilateral Debt Relief Initiative, 293
Multi-party system, 252
Multiregional origin of modern humans, 14, 413
Mungo Lake remains, 8
Mungo Man, 14
Mungo Park (explorer), 84, 121, 135
Munia, 247
Muqaddimah, 121
Murinae, 239
Murray Gordon, 122
Murud-Janjira, 119
Musa I of Mali, 72
Muscat, Oman, 119
Mus (genus), 248
Music, 373
Musical instrument, 377
Musical scale, 377
Musical style and themes, 436
Music of Africa, **373**
Music of Algeria, 370, 375
Music of Angola, 376
Music of Benin, 376
Music of Botswana, 376
Music of Burkina Faso, 376
Music of Burundi, 376
Music of Cameroon, 376
Music of Chad, 376
Music of Cote dIvoire, 376
Music of Djibouti, 375
Music of Egypt, 370, 375
Music of Eritrea, 375
Music of Ethiopia, 370, 375
Music of Gabon, 376
Music of Ghana, 376
Music of Guinea, 376
Music of Guinea-Bissau, 376
Music of India, 376
Music of Indonesia, 376
Music of Kenya, 376

Music of Lesotho, 376
Music of Liberia, 376
Music of Madagascar, 376
Music of Malawi, 376
Music of Mali, 376
Music of Mauritius, 376
Music of Mozambique, 376
Music of Namibia, 376
Music of Niger, 376
Music of Nigeria, 376
Music of Polynesia, 376
Music of Rwanda, 376
Music of Sao Tome and Principe, 376
Music of Senegal, 376
Music of Sierra Leone, 376
Music of Somalia, 370, 375
Music of South Africa, 376
Music of Sudan, 375
Music of Swaziland, 376
Music of Tanzania, 376
Music of the Central African Republic, 376
Music of the Democratic Republic of the Congo, 376
Music of The Gambia, 376
Music of the Republic of the Congo, 376
Music of the Seychelles, 376
Music of the United States, 373
Music of Togo, 376
Music of Uganda, 376
Music of Zambia, 376
Music of Zimbabwe, 376, 382
Musket, 83, 127
Muslim, 64, 102, 333, 377, 389
Muslim conquest of Egypt, 56, 58
Muslim conquests, 375
Muslim empire, 103
Muslim world, 65, 72, 110, 127
Mussel, 369
Mutapa Empire, 18
Mutara II of Rwanda, 68
Mwami, 68
Mwata Kazembe, 48
Mycenaean Greece, 33
Mylomys, 248
Mylothris, 244
Myocricetodontinae, 239
Myomyscus, 248
Myosoricinae, 248
Myrrh, 33

Nabta Playa, 24
Nairobi, 174
Naja, 245
Nama people, 61, 81
Namib Desert, 199

Namibia, 42, 61, 81, 88, 94, 173, 205, 209, 219, 265, 276, 308, 318, 334, 335, 339, 343, 344, 351, 393, 396, 403, 411
Nan Hua Temple, 393
Nanochromis, 245
Napata, 30
Napoleon, 57
Nara language, 354
Narmer, 26, 29
Narudasia, 245
Natal (region), 237
Nataruk, 23
National Climatic Data Center, 428
National colours, 279
Nationalencyklopedin, 434
National Fascist Party, 186
National Geographic Magazine, 230
Nationalism, 89, 184, 186, 200, 357
National language, 340
National Liberal Party (Germany), 186
National Liberation Front (Algeria), 95
National Museum of Natural History, 17
National Museums Liverpool, 425
National Party (South Africa), 95
National Transitional Council, 282
National unity government, 252
Nation state, 18, 200
NATO, 282, 285
Natural resource, 175
Natural resources, 210
Natural selection, 11
Naucratis, 168
Nazareth Baptist Church, 388
Ndwandwe, 81
Neanderthal, 6, 14
Neanderthals, 11
Near East, 6, 105
Necator americanus, 241
Nectophryne, 245
Nectophrynoides, 245
Nefasit, 119
Neglected tropical diseases, 328
Negritos, 11
Negrofinch, 247
Negroland, 406
Nelson Mandela, 96
Nematode, 241
Nemencha, 35
Neo-Assyrian Empire, 28
Neocolonialism, 211
Neo Destour, 95
Neolithic revolution, 24
Neoproterozoic, 231
Neotis, 247
Neotragus, 249
Nepotism, 299

Nerva, 36
Nesomyidae, 248
Netherlands, 104, 159, 375
New Delhi, 271
New England hotspot, 232
New France, 146
New Guinea, 225
New Imperialism, 171, 179, 180
New Kingdom of Egypt, 28
New Partnership for Africas Development, 259, 260
New World, 75, 125, 138
New York Herald, 109
New York Zoological Society, 202
New Zealand, 183
Ngazargamu, 43
Ngoma drums, 378
Ngoni (instrument), 377, 378
Ngor, Dakar, 228
Nguni languages, 62
Nguni people, 61, 62
Niall Ferguson, 178, 297, 432
Niani, Mali, 71
Niani, Mali Empire, 72
Niger, 25, 42, 119, 194, 265, 277, 292, 308, 318, 351, 397, 403, 411
Niger-Congo languages, 352, 354, 408
Niger Delta, 79, 80, 137
Niger–Congo, 77, 79, 336, 369, 371
Niger–Congo language, 376
Niger–Congo languages, 23, 41, 331, 335, 336, 339-342, 351-355, 407
Niger–Kordofanian languages, 343
Nigeria, 40, 42, 74, 80, 88, 96, 119, 137, 138, 141, 160, 193, 203, 205, 209, 265, 268, 273, 277, 282, 291, 292, 308, 318, 323, 329, 332, 335, 339, 342, 345, 346, 351, 353, 370, 387, 390, 391, 397, 403, 406, 407, 411
Niger River, 40, 71, 72, 80, 84, 127, 194, 221, 222, 342
Nile, 84, 209, 221, 261, 410
Nile crocodile, 246
Nile Delta, 26, 405
Nile River, 193
Nile Valley, 24, 26, 342, 370, 375, 405
Nilo-Saharan, 331, 333, 336, 370, 371
Nilo-Saharan languages, 23, 58, 72, 331, 335, 336, 339-342, 352, 354, 355, 369, 407, 408
Nilotes, 336
Nilotic, 64, 331
Nilotic languages, 342, 408
Nilotic peoples, 112
Nissan, 314
Njimi, 42

NKo language, 348
Nkosazana Dlamini-Zuma, 259
Nobadia, 59
Nobatia, 58
Nobiin language, 342
No-fly zone, 282
Nok culture, 18, 26, 40
Nomad, 333
Nome (Egypt), 28
Non-communicable disease, 329
Non-partisan democracy, 252
Non-resident Indian and person of Indian origin, 335
Noon language, 352
North Africa, 10, 101, 119, 167, 168, 197, 236, 325, 335, 339, 342, 375, 389, 391, 401, 403, 407, 410
North African cuisine, 368
North African Monsoon, 24
North America, 216, 298
North American Plate, 230
North Carolina, 161
Northeast Africa, 23, 106, 333
Northern Mbundu people, 48, 138
Northern Ndebele language, 348, 352
Northern Rhodesia, 85, 88, 209, 406
Northern Sotho language, 352, 354
Nostratic languages, 341
Nouakchott, 362
Noun class, 342, 350
Nsukka, 80
Ntare I Kivimira Savuyimba Semunganzashamba Rushatsi Cambarantama, 68
Ntare IV Rutaganzwa Rugamba, 68
Ntusi, 67
Nuba, 354
Nubia, 25, 26, 58, 108, 290, 405
Nubian language, 354
Nubians, 201, 333
Nubi language, 345
Nucras, 246
Nuer language, 354
Numidia, 18, 31, 33, 35
Numidians, 31
Nupe people, 78
Nyanza Province, 66
Nyasaland, 89, 209
Nyasa people, 106
Nyoro people, 67
Nzinga of Ndongo and Matamba, 49

Oasis, 111
Obelisk, 19
Obesity, 329
Obiaruku, 80
Oblo language, 345

Obo, 228
Obolo (town), 80
Oceanic crust, 231
Octave, 370, 375
Odonata, 242
Oduduwa, 77
Oenomys, 248
Official language, 167, 340
Ofin, 75
Ogun State, 314
Oil, 411
Okavango River, 223
Okigwe, 80
Okinawa, 8
Okomfo Anokye, 76
Okra, 23, 367
Old Kingdom of Egypt, 24, 28, 29
Old Nubian language, 58
Oldowan, 21
Old Persian language, 344
Old-time music, 380
Old World, 125, 132
Old World oriole, 247
Old World porcupine, 248
Old World vulture, 247
Oligolepis, 245
Olive, 32
Oliveback, 247
Olive oil, 32
Olusegun Obasanjo, 268
Omaheke, 198
Oman, 66, 119
Omani, 51
Omar al-Bashir, 285
Omelette, 368
Omo River (Ethiopia), 223
Omotic languages, 23
Onchocerca volvulus, 241
Onchocerciasis, 329
One-party state, 252, 303
Ongota language, 345
Onitsha, 80
Onychophora, 241
On the Postcolony, 175, 177
Oorlams creole, 82
Operation Torch, 93
Opisthopatus, 241
Opoku Ware I, 76
Opone, 33
Oral history, 20
Oral tradition, 121
Orang Asli, 10
Orange Free State, 82, 88, 194
Orange (fruit), 369
Orange River, 81, 221, 222
Orange River Colony, 209

Orbis Books, 436
Oreochromis, 245
Organisation of African Unity, 256, 257, 259, 260, 272
Organization of African Unity, 269
Oribi, 249
Oriental Orthodox, 388
Origen, 388
Ornipholidotos, 244
Orogeny, 231
Oromo language, 335, 340, 342, 349, 352, 354
Oromo people, 334
Orompoto, 78
Oropom language, 345
Orthodox Tewahedo, 39
Oryx, 249
Ose06, 425
Osei Kofi Tutu I, 76
Osei Kwadwo, 76
Osei Kwame Panyin, 76
Osmeriformes, 245
Osteoglossiformes, 245
Ostrich, 246, 369
Ota Benga, 199, 202
Otomys, 248
Ottoman Empire, 44, 45, 52, 55, 57, 104, 185, 198, 290
Ottoman–Mamluk War (1516–17), 57
Otto von Bismarck, 171, 185, 193
Oualata, 23, 40, 112
Oualia, 74
Ouani, 286
Oubangi-Chari, 87
Oud, 377, 378
Ouidah, 88, 206
Outline of Africa, 260
Outline of South Asian history, 20
Out of Africa I, 4, 13
Out of Asia theory, 13
Ovambo people, 61
Overproduction, 309
Overseas Chinese, 335, 392
Overseas Development Institute, 294, 432
Owerri, 80
Oxford University, 97
Oxford University Press, 416, 426
Oyo Empire, 18, 77, 135, 140, 290
Oyster, 369
Oyster festival, 280

Pachydactylus, 245
Pacific, 204
Pact of Steel, 93
Pagan, 389
Paget Gorman Sign System, 346
Painting, 359

Pakistan, 10, 119
Palaearctic, 247
Palaearctic region, 244
Paleoanthropology, 3
Paleontological, 5
Paleontology, 21
Palestine (region), 30, 36
Palm oil, 183
Pan-African colours, 280
Pan-African Lawyers Union, 263
Pan-African orogeny, 231
Pan African Parliament, 258
Pan-African Parliament, 256, 257, 259, 262
Pangaea, 231
Pan-Germanism, 186
Pangolin, 249
Pantodontidae, 245
Papaya, 369
Papilio, 244
Papilio antimachus, 244
Papilio zalmoxis, 244
Papua New Guinea, 10
Parachanna, 245
Parallel evolution, 3
Paranaja, 245
Paroedura, 245
Parotomys, 248
Parrot, 246
Parthia, 33
Partus sequitur ventrem, 146
Party platform, 251
Party system, 251
Pasha, 57
Pashas, 55
Passerine, 246
Patas monkey, 249
Pate Island, 51
Patrick Manning, 122
Patrick Manning (professor), 105
Patriotism, 200
Paul Kagame, 256, 258, 262, 269
Paul McCartney, 381
Paul Simon, 380
PBS, 100
Peace and Security Council, 257, 263, 282
Peach, 369
Peanut soup, 366
Peasant, 56
Pedioplanis, 246
Pediplain, 219
Pelomedusidae, 246
Pelomys, 248
Pelusios, 246
Pemba Island, 102
Pende people, 48
Penguin, 247

Penguin Books, 178
Peninsula, 405
Pentatonic scale, 370, 375
Pentila, 244
Peoples Republic of China, 274
Pepper Coast, 137, 406
Perciformes, 245
Peripatopsis, 241
Periplus of the Erythraean Sea, 116
Permanent Representatives Committee of the African Union, 258, 263
Persia, 6, 10, 38, 51, 106
Persian Gulf, 39, 103, 116
Persian language, 344
Persian people, 64
Peter Stearns, 98
Petite bourgeoisie, 172
Petropedetidae, 245
Pharaoh, 26, 28
Phasianidae, 247
Philippines, 185
Philip the Evangelist, 388
Phoenicia, 26, 31, 168, 333
Phoenicians, 33
Phractolaemidae, 245
Piciformes, 247
Pied crow, 247
Pied-Noir, 95, 334
Pierre Chaunu, 126
Pierre Savorgnan de Brazza, 184, 188, 189
Pioneer Column, 189
Pipidae, 245
Pipit, 247
Piracy, 55, 67, 104, 155
Pitch (music), 370, 375
Pitta (bird), 247
Piye, 28
Plain, 236
Plantation, 102
Plantation economy, 103
Plantations, 125
Plated lizard, 246
Plazas de soberanía, 207, 259
Pleistocene, 14, 239
Pleistocene megafauna, 241
Pliocene, 239
Ploceidae, 247
Poeciliidae, 245
Poecilopholis, 245
Poicephalus, 246
Pointe des Almadies, 228, 229
Pole of inaccessibility, 228
Political consciousness, 186
Political corruption, 96, 294, 299
Political parties and elections, 252
Political parties in Angola, 253

Political party, 251
Political radicalism, 251
Political scandal, 299
Political spectrum, 251
Politics by region, 262
Politics of the African Union, 262
Polyomavirus, 11
Polyphony, 378
Polyrhythm, 378, 380
Pool Malebo, 48
Pope Miltiades, 388
Pope Victor I, 388
Population bottleneck, 10, 11
Population genetics, 3, 9
Population growth, 323
Porcelain, 51
Poritiinae, 244
Porridge, 367
Portal:Politics, 252
Portal:Religion, 385
Porter–MacKenzie debate, 180
Port Harcourt, 80
Port Said, 191
Portugal, 104, 130, 140, 144, 159, 170
Portuguese America, 146
Portuguese Angola, 129
Portuguese Cape Verde, 206
Portuguese Congo, 88, 206
Portuguese cuisine, 369
Portuguese East Africa, 88, 206
Portuguese Empire, 48, 125, 170
Portuguese Guinea, 88, 206
Portuguese in Africa, 344
Portuguese language, 256, 297, 343, 352, 354
Portuguese Mozambique, 207
Portuguese People, 128, 129, 141, 143
Portuguese São Tomé and Príncipe, 206
Portuguese-speaking African countries, 339
Portuguese West Africa, 88, 206
Post-classical history, 20
Postcolonialism, 175
Potjiekos, 368
Pottery, 23, 359
Poverty in Africa, 294
POW, 141
Praomys, 248
Pra River (Ghana), 75
Pratylenchus, 241
Prawn, 369
Precession, 23
Precis (butterfly), 243, 244
Pre-Columbian era, 20, 21
Predynastic Egypt, 25
Prehistoric Australia, 3
Prehistory, 20
Prenasalized consonant, 350

Présence Africaine, 99
President of Algeria, 95
President of Kenya, 94
President of the United States, 162
President of Tunisia, 95
Presidents of the Pan-African Parliament, 256
Press Freedom Index, 275
Primary language, 353
Prime meridian, 230
Prime Minister of the United Kingdom, 192
Primogeniture, 76
Prince Edward Islands, 427
Príncipe Island, 88, 206
Pristurus, 245
Privateer, 55
Proatheris, 245
Probreviceps, 245
Progressive rock, 380
Progressivism, 251
Pronolagus, 248
Propaganda, 200
Protectionism, 181, 298
Protectorate, 67, 197, 209
Protopterus, 245
Province of Équateur, 332
Proxy war, 52
Prussia, 185
Psammobates, 246
Psammophis, 245
Pseudacraea, 244
Pseudhymenochirus, 245
Pseudobarbus, 245
Pseudopontia paradoxa, 244
Psittacus, 246
Pterocles, 247
Ptolemaic dynasty, 29
Ptolemaic Kingdom, 375
Ptychadena, 245
Public opinion, 200
Public works, 176
PubMed Identifier, 15–17
Pulmonata, 241
Punics, 37
Punic Wars, 32, 33
Purchasing power parity, 321
Pygmies, 199, 202
Pygmy, 331, 361
Pygmy music, 376
Pygmy peoples, 12, 23
Pyramid, 28
Pyramids of Giza, 27
Python (genus), 245
Pythonidae, 245
Pytilia, 247

Q10701282, 165

Qaableh, 34
Qafzeh, 5
Qenet, 370, 375
Quailfinch, 247
Quedenfeldtia, 246
Queen mothers (Africa), 79
Quelimane, 84
Quiche, 368
Quinine, 84, 181

Radama II of Madagascar, 67
Radama I of Madagascar, 67
Radical centrism, 251
Radical-Socialist Party (France), 200
Radopholus, 241
Raffia palm, 23
Raï, 370, 375
Rainforest, 23, 236
Rain shadow, 237
Rain stick, 378
Ranavalona I, 67
Ranidae, 245
Rap, 369
Raphicerus, 249
Ras ben Sakka, 215, 228
Ras Dashen, 220
Ras Deshen, 435
Ras Hafun, 216, 228
Rashidun Caliphate, 18, 56, 58
Rastafarianism, 393
Rastafari movement, 159
Rattle (percussion instrument), 377, 378
Reactionary, 251
Rebecca L. Cann, 14
Rebellion, 103
Recent African origin of modern humans, **3**, 18, 64
Reconquista, 55
Reconstruction Era of the United States, 159
Recorded history, 18, 20
Recording studio, 381
Red-billed quelea, 247
Redigobius, 245
Red river hog, 249
Red Sea, 5, 7, 18, 23, 30, 38, 102, 127, 195, 215, 217, 236, 403
Red Sea Rift, 232
Reduncinae, 249
Ref n1, 399
Reformism, 251
Reggae, 159
Regime, 85, 202
Reginald Copeland, 96
Region, 401
Regional Economic Communities, 258, 267
Regions of Africa, 373

482

Regions of the African Union, 266, 403, 404
Religion by country, 385
Religion in Africa, **385**
Religious, 359
Religious music, 376
Religious Society of Friends, 154
Remi Kabaka, 381
Rene Caille, 84
René Caillié, 121, 201
Repeating rifle, 83
Reporters Without Borders, 278
Republic of Congo, 137
Republic of the Congo, 87, 188, 197, 205, 265, 268, 275, 282, 293, 307, 318, 351, 395, 402
Republics, 51
Rer Bare, 345
Réunion, 173, 225, 259, 308, 334, 392, 396, 402, 411
Revanchism, 200
Revolt of the Mercenaries, 33
Rhabdomys, 248
Rhacophoridae, 245
Rhapta, 65
Rhebok, 249
Rhinoleptus, 245
Rhodesia, 183
Rhodesian Bush War, 303
Rhodesia (region), 406
Rhodes University, 383
Rhoptropus, 246
Rhythm and Blues, 369, 381
Rhytididae, 242
Rice, 67
Richard Francis Burton, 84, 121
Richard Pares, 152
Rifaa al-Tahtawi, 121
Rift (geology), 230
Rift Valley Lakes, 406
Right of conquest, 63
Right-wing politics, 251
Rimba language, 345
Rinderpest, 81
Rio de Janeiro, 144
Río de Oro, 88, 207
Río Muni, 88, 207
Riverine rabbit, 248
Roads, 295
Robert Adams (sailor), 121
Robert Mugabe, 269, 303
Robert Needham Cust, 356
Robin Blackburn, 163
Rock art, 23
Rockfowl, 246
Rock-jumper, 246
Rock music, 381

Rock & Roll, 369
Rod72, 422
Rodent, 248
Rodrigues (island), 228
Roger Blench, 345
Roger Casement, 190
Roger Nkodo Dang, 256, 258, 262
Roger van Boxtel, 160
Romance languages, 354
Roman Egypt, 36
Roman emperor, 35
Roman Empire, 32, 33, 37, 169
Roman Greece, 36
Roman Italy, 36
Roman mosaic, 35
Roman portraiture, 36
Rommel, 93
Ronald Robinson, 97
Ronald Segal, 119, 422
Roots (1977 miniseries), 158
Roots Homecoming Festival, 159
Roots: The Saga of an American Family, 158
Root vegetable, 369
Rovuma River, 223
Royal Africa Company, 144
Royal Navy, 155, 186
Rozwi Empire, 61
Ruanda-Urundi, 86, 204
Rubber, 188
Rudolf Hellgrewe, 203
Rudyard Kipling, 200
Rufiji River, 223
Rum, 131
Runyakitara language, 348
Russia, 204, 321
Ruvuma River, 65, 102
Ruwenzori Range, 218
Rwanda, 47, 66, 86, 88, 95, 204, 205, 258, 262, 265, 269, 271, 277, 282, 292, 308, 318, 348, 351, 352, 396, 402, 411
Rwandan Genocide, 95
Rwenzori Mountains, 220, 238

Saadi dynasty, 56, 73
Sabaeans, 33, 38
Saguia el-Hamra, 88, 203, 207
Sahara, 18, 23, 24, 26, 102, 103, 127, 203, 217, 261, 371, 403, 405, 406
Sahara Desert, 18, 219, 234, 236
Saharan languages, 355
Saharan Metacraton, 231
Sahel, 18, 23, 39, 44, 71, 75, 78, 194, 219, 234, 236, 335, 339, 342, 369, 371, 405, 407
Sahrawi Arab Democratic Republic, 264, 265, 351, 352

Saint Helena, 225, 403
Saint Helena, Ascension and Tristan da Cunha, 259
Sais, Egypt, 28
Sakalava people, 67
Sakura (mansa), 72
Saladin, 57
Salsa music, 369, 373
Salt road, 112
Samaritan, 421
Samba, 369, 373
Sami people, 201
Samir Amin, 320
Samoa, 201
Samuel White Baker, 84
Sandawe language, 344, 409
Sandawe people, 9, 12, 336
Sandgrouse, 247
Sandton, South Africa, 272
Sango language, 345
San Miguel de Gualdape, 145
San people, 9, 12, 331, 336
Santo Antão, Cape Verde, 228
Sao civilisation, 43
Sao civilization, 24, 42
São Tomé, 48
Sao Tome and Principe, 407
São Tomé and Príncipe, 265, 277, 308, 318, 352, 395, 402, 411
São Tomé e Príncipe, 88
São Tomé Island, 88, 170, 206
Saqaliba, 110
Sara languages, 354
Sarangesa, 244
Sara people, 42
Sarotherodon, 245
Sasanian Empire, 39
Saudi Arabia, 119
Savage Islands, 259
Savanna, 21, 23, 236, 261
Sayfawa Dynasty, 43, 44
Scaphiophryninae, 245
Scarabaeus, 243
Scattered islands in the Indian Ocean, 205, 259
Schilbeidae, 245
Schismaderma, 245
Schlieffen Plan, 204
Scientific racist, 202
Scramble for Africa, 18, 84–86, 167, 179, **179**
Scribe, 358
Scrub hare, 248
Sculpture, 359
Scutellonema, 241
Seaman, 31
Seamount, 232
Seasoning (slave), 143

Second Battle of Dongola, 18
Second Boer War, 83, 193, 194
Second Cataract, 24
Second Franco-Dahomean War, 77
Second Intermediate Period of Egypt, 28
Second Italo-Abyssinian War, 187
Second Italo-Ethiopian War, 205
Second Punic War, 32
Second Sino-Japanese War, 204
Second Sudanese Civil War, 110
Second World War, 18
Secretary bird, 246
Sedentism, 23
Sedimentary basin, 231
Seedcracker, 247
Semi-desert climate, 233
Semien Mountains, 220
Semitic languages, 334, 336, 342, 354
Semi-tropical, 234
Sena language, 352
Senegal, 23, 71, 87, 137, 138, 194, 202, 205, 228, 265, 277, 308, 318, 345, 351, 352, 370, 387, 397, 403, 405, 411
Senegalese Tirailleurs, 206
Senegal River, 116, 222
Senegambia (geography), 137
Senegambian languages, 355
Sennar, 59
Sennar (sultanate), 18, 59
Senufo people, 336
Sepedi, 348
Sepoys in British India, 184
Serbia, 204
Serer people, 72
Serer religion, 387
Serval, 249
Sesotho language, 348, 352
Sétif, 35
Setswana language, 348
Seventeenth Dynasty of Egypt, 30
Seventh-day Adventists, 388
Seychelles, 265, 277, 308, 318, 345, 396, 402
Seychellois Creole, 345
Shabaka, 28
Shabo language, 345
Shafi, 389
Shaka, 81
Shaker (instrument), 378
Sharia, 110
Shark Island Concentration Camp, 199
Sharm el-Sheikh, 273
Shear zone, 231
Shebelle River, 223
Sheep, 367
Sheng (linguistics), 348
Shia, 391

Shia Islam, 53
Shilluk Kingdom, 24, 45
Shilluk language, 354
Shoebill, 247
Shoghi Effendi, 391
Shona language, 348, 352, 354
Shona people, 60, 69
Shoshenq I, 28
Siad Barre, 285
Sicily, 32
Sidama, 107
Siddi, 114
Siege of Jerusalem (1187), 57
Sierra Leone, 88, 96, 137, 209, 265, 277, 308, 318, 345, 391, 397, 403, 407, 412
Sierra Leone Krio language, 345
Sign language, 339
Sign languages, 341
Sijilmasa, 70, 112
Sikhism, 393
SIL Ethnologue, 335, 339
Siluriformes, 245
Silver, 25
Silves, Portugal, 105
Simba, 381
Simon of Cyrene, 388
Sinai, 8
Sinai Peninsula, 95, 215, 257, 389
Sindh, 119
Single market, 274, 304, 316, 321
Single-origin hypothesis, 22
Sino-French War, 200
Sirenia, 248
Sirocco, 227
Sirte, 273
Sirte Declaration, 256, 260
Six-Day War, 95
Skin color, 11
Skink, 246
Slaty egret, 247
Slave Coast of West Africa, 132, 160, 406
Slave raid, 108
Slavery, 101, 123, 126, 193
Slavery Abolition Act 1833, 156
Slavery in Africa, 297
Slavery in Mauritania, 110
Slavery in Somalia, 135
Slavery in the Ottoman Empire, 104
Slave ship, 143, 144
Slave trade, 108, 161, 192
Slave Trade Act 1807, 131, 155
Slave Trade Act of 1794, 155
SLC24A5, 11
Slender-snouted crocodile, 246
Slit gong, 377
Slum, 175

Slush fund, 299
Smallpox, 190
Smart phone, 311
Smithsonian Institution, 17
SMS Panther, 196
Soba (city), 58
Sobat River, 222
Soca music, 373
Socialism, 186, 303
Society of Jesus, 52
Socotra, 116, 119, 225
Sofala, 60, 67, 119
Sokoto, 74
Sokoto Caliphate, 46, 74, 202
Solomonic dynasty, 51, 112
Somalia, 26, 88, 103, 106, 119, 185, 209, 216, 228, 259, 265, 277, 285, 308, 318, 347, 351, 352, 396, 402, 405, 407
Somali Civil War, 285
Somali cuisine, 368
Somaliland campaign (1920), 198
Somali language, 51, 335, 340, 342, 346–349, 352, 354, 407
Somali people, 33, 34, 50, 112, 135, 334
Somali Plate, 230, 231
Somalis, 106
Songbird, 247
Songhai Empire, 18, 44, 56, 72, 389
Songhai language, 355
Songhai people, 72, 333, 336
Songhay language, 342
Songhay languages, 342, 408
Soninke language, 345
Soninke people, 40, 54, 70, 71
Son (music), 382
Sonni Ali, 72
Sorbonne University, 426
Sorghum, 23, 39, 42, 71, 367
Soricomorpha, 248
Sotho–Tswana peoples, 62
Sotho language, 354
Sotho people, 62
Soukous, 370, 382
Soumaoro Kanté, 71
Souq, 111, 118
South Africa, 42, 82, 85, 88, 94, 95, 159, 173, 194, 208, 209, 215, 228, 237, 243, 257, 265, 268, 271–273, 277, 282, 291, 292, 308, 310, 329, 334, 335, 339, 343, 348, 351–353, 370, 391–393, 397, 403, 411
South African general election, 1994, 96
South African Plateau, 217
South African Republic, 82, 194
South America, 216, 225, 239
South American Plate, 230
South Arabia, 38

485

South Asia, 344
South Atlantic Islands, 225
South Cushitic languages, 345
Southeast Africa, 101, 335, 339, 346
Southeast Alaska, 146
Southeast Asia, 67, 167, 409
Southern Africa, 18, 21, 23, 59, 183, 194, 236, 325, 330, 331, 335, 339, 346, 371, 376, 378, 391, 401, 403, 407
Southern Africa Development Community, 268
Southern African Customs Union, 305, 317, 322
Southern African Development Community, 261, 305, 317, 318, 321
Southern Bantoid languages, 336
Southern Dispersal, 3, 5
Southern Europe, 18, 167
Southern Mbundu people, 138
Southern Ndebele language, 348, 352
Southern Rhodesia, 85, 88, 208, 209, 406
South Holland, 343
South Ndebele people, 62
South Sudan, 42, 45, 228, 265, 277, 285, 308, 318, 331, 346, 396, 402, 407, 411
South Sudanese independence referendum, 2011, 284
South West Africa, 185
South-West Africa, 209
South West Africa campaign, 90
Sovereign state, 257, 261
Soviet Union, 283
Space agency, 260
Spain, 104, 130, 159, 259
Spalacidae, 248
Spaniards, 143
Spanish Empire, 125, 146, 170
Spanish Guinea, 88, 207
Spanish language, 256, 343, 352, 407
Spanish Morocco, 88, 207
Spanish North Africa (disambiguation), 261
Spanish Protectorate in Morocco, 197
Spanish Sahara, 88, 203, 207
Spanish West Africa, 207
Specialised Technical Committees of the African Union, 264
Species barrier, 14
Species diversity, 244
Species richness, 244
Speckle-throated otter, 249
Spencer Wells, 17
Spices, 51, 126
Spinach, 366
Spotted hyena, 240
Springbok (antelope), 364
Springhare, 248

Sri Vijaya, 103
Stairs Expedition, 189
Standard language, 348
Stanley Engerman, 151
Starch, 369
State of emergency, 94
St Augustine of Hippo, 388
St. Domingue, 147
Stem cell factor, 11
Stenocephalemys, 248
Stenogobius, 245
Stephopaedes, 245
Steppe, 23, 236, 239
Steve Winwood, 380, 381
St. Martins Press, 179
St Maurice, 388
Stock exchange, 315
Stone age, 6
Stonehenge, 24
Stone partridge, 247
Stork, 247
Strait of Hormuz, 51
Streptaxidae, 242
String instrument, 377
Striped grass mouse, 248
Striped polecat, 249
Strongylopus, 245
Subduction, 231
Sub-Equatorial Africa, 346
Subregion, 401
Sub-Saharan, 34, 35, 303
Sub-Saharan Africa, 26, 31, 66, 85, 181, 237, 281, 290, 388, 401, 406, 407
Sub-Saharan African, 290
Sub-Saharan African music traditions, 373, 376
Sub-Saharan Africans, 11
Subtropical highland climate, 233
Subtropical ridge, 234
Subulinidae, 242
Sudan, 6, 24, 88, 89, 114, 185, 193–195, 210, 259, 265, 273, 277, 292, 308, 318, 335, 339, 343, 345–347, 351, 393, 396, 401, 405, 407, 410
Sudanese sign languages, 346
Sudanian Savanna, 405
Sudan (region), 112, 405, 406
Suez Canal, 93, 183, 184, 215
Sufis, 391
Sufism, 59
Sugar, 131
Sugar cane, 104
Suleyman (mansa), 72
Sultan, 112, 196
Sultanate of Damagaram, 43
Sultanate of Mogadishu, 51, 291

Sultanate of Oman, 66
Sultanate of Zanzibar, 102, 113
Sultanates, 51
Sunbird, 246
Sundiata Keita, 71
Sunni, 389
Sunni Ali, 389
Sunni Islam, 57
Sun squirrel, 248
Supercontinent, 231
Superpower, 28
Surat, 51, 119
Susenyos of Ethiopia, 52
Sustainability, 281
Sustainable development, 258
Susu people, 71
SUV, 314
Swahili Coast, 64, 65, 102, 119, 331, 389, 406
Swahili culture, 64
Swahili language, 65, 112, 173, 256, 261, 335, 340, 346, 348, 349, 352, 354, 371, 381, 407
Swahili people, 51, 59, 64, 65, 69, 80, 102, 127, 331
Swaziland, 81, 89, 194, 209, 265, 277, 308, 318, 348, 397, 403, 412
Swazi language, 348
Swazi lilangeni, 412
Swazi people, 62
Sylviane Diouf, 377
Syncretic politics, 251
Syncretism, 386, 393
Syncretistic, 388
Synoptic scale meteorology, 236
Syro-Palestine, 29

Table Bay, 63
Table Mountain, 238
Tadjoura, 107, 119
Taghaza, 71, 73
Taharqa, 28
Taiwan, 186
Takrur, 71, 72
Talapoin, 249
Talking drum, 378, 379
Tanakia, 245
Tana River (Kenya), 223
Tanganyika, 173, 194, 244
Tanganyika Territory, 88, 209
Tangier, 119
Tangiers, 55, 196
Tantamani, 28
Tanzania, 42, 65–67, 88, 102, 119, 205, 209, 219, 220, 228, 238, 243, 265, 268, 277, 303, 308, 318, 335, 339, 342, 344–348, 351, 352, 396, 402, 406, 407, 411

Tanzania Craton, 231
Tanzanian sign languages, 346
Taoism, 392
Taoudeni Basin, 231
Tarfaya Strip, 88
Target rat, 248
Tarikh al-Sudan, 121
Tartary, 113
Ta-Seti, 26, 29
Taukhe River, 223
Taurotragus, 249
Tax evasion and corruption in Greece, 300
Techiman, 76
Tectonic plate, 230
Tectonic plates, 231
Teff, 23, 367
Telecommunications, 295
Temperate climate, 234
Template:African Economic Community, 305, 317, 322
Template:AU evolution timeline, 261
Template:Human history, 21
Template:Life in the African Union, 257, 321
Template:New Imperialism, 180
Template:Party politics, 252
Template:Political corruption sidebar, 303
Template:Politics of the African Union, 262
Template:Religions by country sidebar, 385
Template:Slavery, 101, 123
Template:Supranational African Bodies, 267
Template talk:African Economic Community, 305, 317, 322
Template talk:AU evolution timeline, 261
Template talk:Human history, 21
Template talk:Life in the African Union, 257, 321
Template talk:New Imperialism, 180
Template talk:Party politics, 252
Template talk:Political corruption sidebar, 303
Template talk:Politics of the African Union, 262
Template talk:Religions by country sidebar, 385
Template talk:Slavery, 101, 123
Template talk:Supranational African Bodies, 267
Template talk:World economy, 289
Template:World economy, 289
Tenrec, 248
Tenth Dynasty of Egypt, 28
Teodoro Obiang Nguema Mbasogo, 269
Terceira Rift, 231
Terence Ranger, 85
Teriomima, 244
Termite, 242, 243
Termit Massif, 26

Terracotta, 40
Terranes, 231
Territorial integrity, 257
Territories and regions, 290
Terror regime, 190
Tertiary, 232, 239
Tertullian, 388
Tewfik Pasha, 192
Textile, 51, 364
Thaba Bosiu, 82
Thabana Ntlenyana, 220
Thabo Mbeki, 260, 268
Thailand, 10
The American Journal of Human Genetics, 16
The annual customs of Dahomey, 141
Thebes, Egypt, 28, 30
The British Museum, 100
The Cambridge History of Africa, 98
The Economist, 320, 434
The Expansion of England, 180
The Gambia, 88, 137, 138, 259, 265, 273, 276, 307, 369, 397, 403, 407, 412
The Great Game, 179
The Guardian, 432
The Hague, 375
The Igbo in the Atlantic slave trade, 138
The Imperialism of Free Trade, 180
The Journey of Man, 17
The Languages of Africa, 356
The Lebanese Diaspora, 335
The Lion King, 381
The Lion King II: Simbas Pride, 381
The Meadows of Gold, 120
The Narrative of Robert Adams, 121
Théophile Delcassé, 196
Théophile Obenga, 99
Theophilus Shepstone, 194
The Origins of Totalitarianism, 200, 426
The Rolling Stones, 381
The Scramble for Africa (book), 212
The Seven Daughters of Eve, 17
The Statesmans Yearbook, 296
The Washington Post, 425
The White Mans Burden, 200
The World Book Encyclopedia, 387
The World Factbook, 305, 317, 322
Thick-billed raven, 247
Thicket rat, 248
Third India-Africa Forum Summit, 271
Third Intermediate Period of Egypt, 28
Third Position, 251
Third Punic War, 32, 169
Thirteen Colonies, 161
Tho98, 422
Thomas Clarkson, 140
Thomas Huxley, 13

Thomas Jefferson, 154
Thomas Kitchin, 134
Thomas Pakenham (historian), 212
Thumb piano, 374
Tianyuan man, 8
Tiaret, 70, 112
Tibesti mountains, 220
Tichitt, 23
Tigray Region, 38
Tigray-Tigrinya people, 334
Tigrinya language, 347, 352, 354, 407
Tilapia, 245
Timbuktu, 72, 119, 120, 201
Time Life, 418
Timeline of historic inventions, 148
Timgad, 36
Timor, 185
Tin, 183
Tindouf Basin, 231
Tipasa, 36
Tippu Tip, 113
Tirpitz Plan, 186
Tit-hylia, 247
Tizita, 371, 376
Tlingit people, 146
Toba catastrophe theory, 5
Tobacco, 131
Tockus, 247
Togo, 88, 137, 138, 205, 265, 277, 282, 308, 318, 353, 387, 393, 397, 403, 411
Togoland, 185
Togoland Campaign, 90
Tomopterna, 245
Tonal language, 342, 344, 350, 379
Tonal sandhi, 350
Tone contour, 350
Tone (linguistics), 342, 350
Tony Blair, 161
Topographic isolation, 220
Topographic prominence, 220
Tortoise, 246
Torwa dynasty, 60
Total war, 89
Toubkal, 220
Toutswemogala Hill, 62
Trade, 101, 290
Trade bead, 116
Trade language, 346
Trade route, 120
Trade surplus, 181
Trade winds, 237
Traditional African religions, 386
Traditional music, 376
Traditional sub-Saharan African harmony, 379, 381
Traffic (band), 380, 381

Tragelaphus, 249
Trajan, 35, 36
Trans-African Highway network, 295
Transatlantic slave trade, 106
Trans-cultural diffusion, 121
Transitional Federal Government, 285
Trans-Saharan trade, 39, 70, 105, 119, 127
Transvaal Colony, 88, 209
Transvaal Province, 59
Treaty of Addis Ababa, 209
Treaty of Frankfurt (1871), 200
Treaty of Paris (1814), 156
Trekboer, 64
Triangular trade, 123
Tribal chief, 160
Trinidad, 147
Triple Alliance (1882), 185
Triple junction, 233
Tripoli, 44, 55, 108, 118, 119, 264
Tripolitania, 114, 186
Trogon, 247
Tropical Africa, 83
Tropical and subtropical grasslands, savannas, and shrublands, 248
Tropical climate, 234
Tropical climate zone, 233
Tropical cyclone, 236
Tropical disease, 181
Tropical diseases, 134
Tropical monsoon climate, 233
Tropical wave, 236
Tropical wet and dry climate, 233
Tropic of Cancer, 233
Tropic of Capricorn, 233
Tropics, 239
Tropiocolotes, 246
Truck, 314
Trumpet, 377
Tsetse fly, 228, 243
Tshiluba language, 354
Tshivenda, 348
Tsitambala, 67
Tsoa language, 352
Tsonga language, 354
Tswana language, 348, 353, 354
Tswana people, 62
Tuareg languages, 354
Tuareg music, 370, 375
Tuareg people, 72, 333
Tuaregs, 201
Tuberculosis, 329
Tubulidentata, 248
Tugela River, 81
Tuna, 369
Tunis, 31, 55, 108, 316

Tunisia, 54, 93, 95, 168, 184, 215, 228, 265, 277, 308, 316, 318, 319, 333, 346, 347, 351, 390, 396, 401, 405, 407, 410
Tunisia campaign, 93
Tunisian cuisine, 369
Tunisian Sign Language, 346
Tunjur people, 45
Tupi people, 144
Turkana County, 23
Turkish Abductions, 108
Turkish people, 198
Tutsi, 68, 95
Tuu languages, 344
Twenty-fifth Dynasty of Egypt, 28
Twenty-second Dynasty of Egypt, 28
Twenty-sixth Dynasty of Egypt, 28
Two-party system, 252
Type 2 diabetes, 327
Typhlopidae, 245
Typhlops, 245
Tyrannius Rufinus, 389
Tyre, Lebanon, 31

Ubangian languages, 341, 343, 344, 354
Ubangi-Shari, 205
U-Boat, 204
Ugali, 367
Uganda, 47, 66, 67, 88, 161, 176, 193, 220, 238, 259, 265, 272, 277, 282, 308, 318, 345, 348, 352, 367, 391, 396, 402, 406, 411
Uganda Protectorate, 68, 88, 209
Uli I of Mali, 72
Umar, 389
Umayyad, 103
Umayyad Caliphate, 53
Umbundu, 353
Umbundu language, 354
Umhlanga (ceremony), 281
Umuahia, 80
Umzimkulu River, 81
UNAMID, 259
Unclassified language, 335, 339
Unclassified languages, 341, 345
Underdevelopment, 297
UNESCO, 99, 159
Unguja, 102
Ungulate, 249
UNICEF, 326
Union Government of Africa, 265
Union of African States, 259
Union of South Africa, 88, 183, 209
United Arab Emirates, 5
United Kingdom, 159, 181, 196, 205
United Kingdom of Great Britain and Ireland, 79, 170

United Nations, 259, 292, 313, 433
United Nations African Union Mission in Darfur, 285
United Nations Department of Economic and Social Affairs, 292
United Nations General Assembly, 274
United Nations General Assembly observers, 274
United Nations geoscheme for Africa, 403, 404
United Nations Security Council, 263, 282
United Nations Security Council Resolution 1907, 285
United Nations Security Council Resolution 1973, 282
United States, 159, 161, 173, 204, 209, 260
United States Army Africa, 230
United States Congress, 155, 285
United States Department of Agriculture, 298
United States dollar, 289, 290, 293, 321, 411
United States House of Representatives, 162
United States of Africa, 265, 304, 317
United States Senate, 162
Unity government, 282
Universal Declaration of Human Rights, 258
Universal House of Justice, 392
University of California Press, 435
University of Cape Town, 238
University of Massachusetts Amherst, 303
University of Pretoria, 100
UN Slavery Memorial, 159
Unsupported attributions, 37, 40, 41, 146
Upper Egypt, 26, 29
Upper Guinea, 137
Upper Miocene, 13
Urabi Revolt, 192
Uraeginthus, 247
Urbanization, 35
Urewe, 41
Urn, 368
Uroplatus, 246
Usman dan Fodio, 74
USSR, 303
Uvular consonant, 350

Vaal River, 62
Vandalic, 344
Vandalic War, 37
Vandal Kingdom, 32, 37, 375
Vandals, 169, 333
Varieties of Arabic, 335, 336, 340, 349
Vasco da Gama, 51
Vegetable, 366
Venda language, 353
Venetian glass, 116
Venice, 51
Venison, 369

Vervet monkey, 249
Vichy government, 93
Vicia faba, 367
Viking Press, 164
Vipera, 245
Viperinae, 245
Virginia, 161, 425
Virginia General Assembly, 161
Virunga mountains, 220
Vizier (Ancient Egypt), 26
Voandzeia, 23
Vodun, 387
Volta–Niger, 355
Volta–Niger languages, 336
Volta River, 222
Voortrekkers, 82
Vosges mountains, 200

Wadai Empire, 24, 45
Wage, 202
Walter Rodney, 101, 129, 148, 150, 153, 162, 296, 424
War, 140
War crime, 285
Warsangali Sultanate, 18, 198
Wars of national liberation, 187
Warthog, 249, 367
Washington State University, 100
Water drum, 378
Watermelon, 23
Wat (food), 367
Wattled crane, 247
Wattle-eye, 246
W. E. B. Du Bois Institute, 424
Weltpolitik, 185
Werneria, 245
West Africa, 18, 112, 119, 123, 132, 194, 236, 325, 331, 335, 339, 366, 376, 378, 401–403, 407, 410–412
West African Craton, 231
West African Economic and Monetary Union, 305, 317, 322
West African music, 376, 377
West African Pidgin English, 345
West African Vodun, 387
West Africa Squadron, 156, 157
Westerlies, 237
Western Asia, 23, 39, 101, 167, 335, 339, 342
Western Desert campaign, 93
Western Europe, 123, 167, 376
Western green mamba, 246
Western imperialism in Asia, 179
Western Province (Kenya), 66
Western Sahara, 54, 88, 207, 277, 397, 401
Western Sudan, 112
West Indies, 144, 147

Weyto language, 345
What information to include, 108
Wheat, 23, 367
Whey, 366
White Africans, 334
White-eyelid mangabey, 249
White Mans Burden, 184
White Namibians, 344
White-necked raven, 247
White Nile, 30, 45
White rhinoceros, 249
Wikipedia, 421
Wikipedia:Avoid weasel words, 315
Wikipedia:Citation needed, 10, 23, 24, 26, 32, 35–37, 41, 42, 45, 48, 51, 52, 59, 64, 66–68, 74, 77–79, 85, 96, 97, 112, 113, 133, 134, 140, 145, 180, 186, 195, 203, 283, 284, 321, 348, 349, 359, 361, 366, 388, 389, 392, 394
Wikipedia:Citing sources, 119
Wikipedia:Please clarify, 145, 232, 256, 389
Wikipedia:Verifiability, 42
Wikt:Dark Continent, 84
Wikt:secretariat, 259
Wildebeest, 249
Wilhelm Hübbe-Schleiden, 186
Wilhelm II, German Emperor, 186
Wilhelm II of Germany, 171
William Easterly, 183
William Ewart Gladstone, 194, 200
William L. Langer, 96
William Rubinstein, 190
William Wilberforce, 154, 155
Wind instrument, 377
Wind of change, 339
Wolof Empire, 72
Wolof language, 355
Wolof people, 138, 331
Wolterstorffina, 245
Woodcarving, 359
Work song, 376
World Bank, 210, 292, 293
World Bank Institute, 320
World Christian Encyclopedia, 391
World Conference Against Racism, 159
World economy, 289
World Health Organization, 326
World Health Organization (WHO), 326
World Meteorological Organization, 428
World population estimates, 326
World War I, 90, 171, 186
World War II, 167, 204, 334
WP:NOTRS, 382
Wuchereria bancrofti, 241

Xanthosoma, 369

Xenomystus nigri, 245
Xenopus, 245
Xhosa language, 344, 348, 349, 353, 354
Xhosa people, 59, 62, 82
Xhosa Wars, 82
Xitsonga, 348
Xitsonga language, 352
Xylophone, 373, 377

Yaka people, 48
Yale University, 389
Yam (vegetable), 75, 369
Yao people, 106
Yaoundé, 264
Yaqubi, 120
Yaws, 83
Yayi Boni, 269
Year of Africa, 18, 94
Yeke Kingdom, 189
Yellow fever, 83, 228
Yemen, 106, 110, 119, 303
Yeshaq I of Ethiopia, 51
Yodel, 377
Yombe people, 360
Yom Kippur War, 95
Yoruba language, 336, 340, 342, 349, 353, 355
Yoruba music, 332, 370
Yoruba people, 12, 41, 77, 138, 331
Yoruba religion, 386, 387
Youth bulge, 323
Yoweri Museveni, 161, 282
Yuhi V of Rwanda, 68
Yu Huan, 418
Yusuf ibn Tashfin, 54

Zabīd, 119
Zaghawa language, 354
Zaghawa people, 333
Zagwe dynasty, 51
Zalama, 106
Zambezi, 42, 223
Zambezi River, 59, 69, 221
Zambia, 42, 47, 48, 85, 88, 194, 209, 265, 277, 282, 308, 318, 325, 391, 396, 402, 411
Zande language, 354
Zanj, 65, 101, 112, 113
Zanj Rebellion, 103
Zanzibar, 64–67, 88, 106, 109, 119, 209, 347, 351
Zaramo, 106
Zarma language, 355
Zarma people, 333
Zebra, 249
Zeila, 49, 119
Zenaga language, 354
Zenaga people, 54

Zenata, 54
Zheng He, 66
Zhirendong, 5
Zigua people, 106
Zigula language, 354
Zimbabwe, 42, 47, 59, 85, 88, 94, 194, 209, 265, 269, 277, 281, 282, 291, 293, 303, 308, 318, 334, 343, 348, 351–353, 393, 397, 402, 411
Zoblazo, 370
Zoroastrianism, 393
Zouk, 373
Zulu, 364
Zulu Kingdom, 62, 81
Zulu language, 344, 348, 349, 353, 354, 381
Zulu people, 62
Zygaspis, 246

www.ingramcontent.com/pod-product-compliance
Lightning Source LLC
Chambersburg PA
CBHW030514230426
43665CB00010B/609